RFID Technology Integration for Business Performance Improvement

In Lee
Western Illinois University, USA

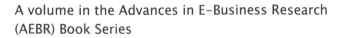

A volume in the Advances in E-Business Research (AEBR) Book Series

An Imprint of IGI Global

Managing Director:	Lindsay Johnston
Production Editor:	Jennifer Yoder
Development Editor:	Erin O'Dea
Acquisitions Editor:	Kayla Wolfe
Typesetter:	John Crodian
Cover Design:	Jason Mull

Published in the United States of America by
Business Science Reference (an imprint of IGI Global)
701 E. Chocolate Avenue
Hershey PA, USA 17033
Tel: 717-533-8845
Fax: 717-533-8661
E-mail: cust@igi-global.com
Web site: http://www.igi-global.com

Library of Congress Cataloging-in-Publication Data

RFID technology integration for business performance improvement / In Lee, editor.
     pages cm
  Includes bibliographical references and index. Summary: "This book presents emerging research surrounding the use and valueof Radio Frequency Identification (RFID) technology for cost reduction, supply chain improvement, inventory management, and partner relationship management"-- Provided by publisher. ISBN 978-1-4666-6308-4 (hardcover : alk. paper) -- ISBN 978-1-4666-6309-1 (ebook) -- ISBN 978-1-4666-6311-4 (print & perpetual access) 1. Radio frequency identification systems. 2. Management. I. Lee, In, 1958- editor of compilation.

  TK6570.I34R495 2015
  621.3841'92--dc23

                              2014018593

This book is published in the IGI Global book series Advances in E-Business Research (AEBR) (ISSN: 1935-2700; eISSN: 1935-2719)

British Cataloguing in Publication Data
A Cataloguing in Publication record for this book is available from the British Library.

All work contributed to this book is new, previously-unpublished material. The views expressed in this book are those of the authors, but not necessarily of the publisher.

For electronic access to this publication, please contact: eresources@igi-global.com.

Advances in E-Business Research (AEBR) Book Series

In Lee
Western Illinois University, USA

ISSN: 1935-2700
EISSN: 1935-2719

MISSION

Technology has played a vital role in the emergence of e-business and its applications incorporate strategies. These processes have aided in the use of electronic transactions via telecommunications networks for collaborating with business partners, buying and selling of goods and services, and customer service. Research in this field continues to develop into a wide range of topics, including marketing, psychology, information systems, accounting, economics, and computer science.

The **Advances in E-Business Research (AEBR) Book Series** provides multidisciplinary references for researchers and practitioners in this area. Instructors, researchers, and professionals interested in the most up-to-date research on the concepts, issues, applications, and trends in the e-business field will find this collection, or individual books, extremely useful. This collection contains the highest quality academic books that advance understanding of e-business and addresses the challenges faced by researchers and practitioners.

COVERAGE

- E-procurement Methods
- Outsourcing and E-business Technologies
- Collaborative commerce
- E-business Models and Architectures
- Trends in E-business Models and Technologies
- Virtual Organization
- Online Consumer Behavior
- E-Business Management
- E-CRM
- Evaluation Methodologies for E-business Systems

IGI Global is currently accepting manuscripts for publication within this series. To submit a proposal for a volume in this series, please contact our Acquisition Editors at Acquisitions@igi-global.com or visit: http://www.igi-global.com/publish/.

Titles in this Series

For a list of additional titles in this series, please visit: www.igi-global.com

RFID Technology Integration for Business Performance Improvement
In Lee (Western Illinois University, USA)
Business Science Reference • copyright 2015 • 337pp • H/C (ISBN: 9781466663084) • US $225.00 (our price)

Integrating Social Media into Business Practice, Applications, Management, and Models
In Lee (Western Illinois University, USA)
Business Science Reference • copyright 2014 • 325pp • H/C (ISBN: 9781466661820) • US $225.00 (our price)

Electronic Payment Systems for Competitive Advantage in E-Commerce
Francisco Liébana-Cabanillas (University of Granada, Spain) Francisco Muñoz-Leiva (University of Granada, Spain)
Juan Sánchez-Fernández (University of Granada, Spain) and Myriam Martínez-Fiestas (ESAN University, Perú)
Business Science Reference • copyright 2014 • 393pp • H/C (ISBN: 9781466651906) • US $215.00 (our price)

Trends in E-Business, E-Services, and E-Commerce Impact of Technology on Goods, Services, and Business Transactions
In Lee (Western Illinois University, USA)
Business Science Reference • copyright 2014 • 347pp • H/C (ISBN: 9781466645103) • US $185.00 (our price)

Interdisciplinary Perspectives on Business Convergence, Computing, and Legality
Reema Khurana (Institute of Management Technology-Ghaziabad, India) and Rashmi Aggarwal (Institute of Management Technology-Ghaziabad, India)
Business Science Reference • copyright 2013 • 354pp • H/C (ISBN: 9781466642096) • US $165.00 (our price)

Research and Development in E-Business through Service-Oriented Solutions
Katalin Tarnay (University of Pannonia, Hungary & Budapest University of Technology and Economics, Hungary)
Sandor Imre (Budapest University of Technology and Economics, Hungary) and Lai Xu (Bournemouth University, UK)
Business Science Reference • copyright 2013 • 328pp • H/C (ISBN: 9781466641815) • US $185.00 (our price)

Mobile Services Industries, Technologies, and Applications in the Global Economy
In Lee (Western Illinois University, USA)
Information Science Reference • copyright 2013 • 368pp • H/C (ISBN: 9781466619814) • US $190.00 (our price)

Strategy, Adoption, and Competitive Advantage of Mobile Services in the Global Economy
In Lee (Western Illinois University, USA)
Information Science Reference • copyright 2013 • 451pp • H/C (ISBN: 9781466619395) • US $190.00 (our price)

DISSEMINATOR of KNOWLEDGE

www.igi-global.com

701 E. Chocolate Ave., Hershey, PA 17033
Order online at www.igi-global.com or call 717-533-8845 x100
To place a standing order for titles released in this series, contact: cust@igi-global.com
Mon-Fri 8:00 am - 5:00 pm (est) or fax 24 hours a day 717-533-8661

Table of Contents

Detailed Table of Contents

Chapter 1
S. H. Choi, The University of Hong Kong, Hong Kong
H. H. Cheung, The University of Hong Kong, Hong Kong
B. Yang, The University of Hong Kong, Hong Kong
Y. X. Yang, The University of Hong Kong, Hong Kong

This chapter proposes an item-level RFID-enabled store management system to help improve retail business. The system adopts an integral design approach to exploit RFID and the e-pedigree established for anti-counterfeiting and tracking of product items in a supply chain. Various modules, such as back-store inventory, smart shelves, interactive mirrors and fitting, and self-checkout services, can be subsequently implemented for retail operations and management. Features for anti-counterfeiting and individual customer marketing can also be incorporated to enhance brand image and customer experience. Moreover, intelligent algorithms may be integrated to mine useful information, such as the sales history of products and the shopping behaviour of customers from the data captured by the RFID devices to facilitate business decision-making and proactive individual marketing. As such, the efficiency of store operations and the overall retail business can be expected to improve substantially. The chapter presents the design approach of the proposed system and discusses some implementation issues, exemplified by two basic applications: (1) track-and-trace anti-counterfeiting to prevent injection of faked products into the back-store inventory and (2) smart product collocation to promote individual customer marketing and cross selling.

Although many firms have initiated RFID projects, they often face significant difficulties in integrating RFID systems into their existing IT landscape. One such difficulty is the upfront estimation of the cost of the RFID integration project. This chapter addresses this issue by using a design science approach to provide a cost calculation for RFID integration projects. Drawing from literature in the fields of information systems and RFID, software engineering and supply chain management, the authors develop the cost calculation method that is then implemented in a prototype. The prototype is developed and evaluated in an iterative fashion using focus groups, RFID experts, and the cognitive walkthrough method. The authors contribute to theory by proposing a new cost calculation method to estimate the costs of RFID integration projects. Practical implications include a more accurate estimation of the cost of integrating RFID systems into the existing IT landscape and a risk reduction for RFID projects.

Chapter 3

The navigation ecosystem is rapidly changing. Indoor navigation has attracted attention with the introduction of mobile devices into the market. Although mobile devices are used more often for outdoor navigation, they have opened up opportunities for indoor navigation proponents. Near Field Communication in indoor navigation is still in its exploratory stage. Despite an increase in the variety of indoor navigation research, challenges remain in designing a framework that is neither complex nor expensive. NFC is a novel method of navigating in indoor environments. Providing an overview of its benefits and usefulness compared with existing indoor navigation technologies is the subject of this chapter.

Despite the proliferation of RFID (Radio Frequency Identification) applications, there are still only a limited number of open-loop inter-enterprise applications that address global supply chains. The implementation of such inter-enterprise applications hinges on standards and techniques for discovering and accessing RFID tagged objects across different repositories of RFID information residing across different administrative domains. In this chapter, the authors introduce an open and novel implementation of an ONS (Object Naming Service) solution for inter-enterprise tracking and tracing RFID applications. The solution is part of the open source AspireRFID project and provides a sound basis for integrating tracking ("google-of-things" like) applications for the RFID and the Internet-of-Things (IoT). As part of the presentation of the solution, this chapter illustrates the main challenges associated with the integration of inter-enterprise applications, along with strategies for confronting them.

Chapter 5

Nikos Kefalakis, Athens Information Technology, Greece
John Soldatos, Athens Information Technology, Greece

In recent years we have witnessed a proliferation of RFID (Radio Frequency Identification) middleware systems and projects (including several open source projects), which are extensively used to support the emerging wave of RFID applications. Some of the RFID middleware projects come with simple tools, which facilitate the application development, configuration, and deployment processes. However, these tools tend to be fragmented since they address only part of an RFID system (such as the filtering of tag streams and/or the generation of business events). In this chapter, the authors introduce an Integrated Development Environment (IDE) for RFID applications, which addresses multiple parts of an RFID application, while at the same time supporting the full application development lifecycle (i.e. design, development, deployment, and testing of RFID applications). The introduced IDE comprises a wide range of tools, which have been implemented as modular plug-ins to an Eclipse-based environment. The various tools enable application development, deployment, testing, and configurations over the middleware infrastructure established by the AspireRFID (AspireRFID Consortium, 2013), and their evaluation has proven that they can significantly ease RFID application development.

Chapter 6

Fred van Blommestein, University of Groningen, The Netherlands
Dávid Karnok, MTA Sztaki Budapest, Hungary
Zsolt Kemény, MTA Sztaki Budapest, Hungary

Many supply chains require open tracking and tracing systems. In open tracking and tracing systems, attributes of objects are not known beforehand, as the type of objects and the set of stakeholders may evolve over time. In this chapter, a method is presented that enables components of tracking and tracing systems to negotiate at run time what attributes may be stored for a particular object type. Components may include scanning equipment, data stores, and query clients. Attributes may be of any data type, including time, location, status, temperature, and ownership. Apart from simple attributes, associations between objects may be recorded and stored (e.g. when an object is packed in another object, loaded in a truck or container, or assembled to be a new object). The method was developed in two European-funded research projects: TraSer and ADVANCE.

Chapter 7

Edward T. Chen, University of Massachusetts – Lowell, USA

RFID plays a critical role in the improvement of supply chain management and consumer applications. This chapter introduces a brief history of RFID and how it works. The recent shift of incorporating RFID into consumer-oriented products has raised serious concerns of customer privacy and security. These concerns are rooted in the fact that consumers are typically unaware that their purchases are being tracked and monitored, as well as the fear of private information being hacked or stolen via insecure RFID systems. This chapter provides a theoretical debate over the privacy rights and addresses the consumer role in the RFID technology. This chapter concludes that the government must ensure legislation to maintain protections on the individual's security and privacy in the society.

Logistics is an integral part of the supply chain. Many logistics service providers have acknowledged that if they want to operate more efficiently and responsively, they must adopt technologies that help manufacturers, warehouses, and retailers to communicate with each other more efficiently. Radio Frequency Identification (RFID) technology has been identified as an important application among many logistics technologies and is increasingly gaining both practitioners' and researchers' attention. The purpose of this chapter is to explore the factors affecting logistics service providers' intentions to use RFID technology, with special emphasis on its environmentally friendly green characteristics. The theoretical perspective diffusion of innovations is used for the purpose. The data is collected using a questionnaire survey among the UK logistics companies. The analysis shows that observability of green characteristics positively influences the intention to use RFID.

Chapter 9

Radio Frequency Identification (RFID) refers to wireless technology that uses radio waves to automatically identify items within a certain proximity. It is being widely used in various applications, but there is reluctance in the deployment of RFID due to the high cost involved and the challenging problems found in the observed colossal RFID data. The obtained data is of low quality and contains anomalies like false positives, false negatives, and duplication. To enhance the quality of data, cleaning is the essential task, so that the resultant data can be applied for high-end applications. This chapter investigates the existing physical, middleware, and deferred approaches to deal with the anomalies found in the RFID data. A novel hybrid approach is developed to solve data quality issues so that the demand for RFID data will certainly grow to meet the user needs.

Chapter 10

An effective information system is essential for a business or industry to be successful in today's highly competitive market. Perhaps the most compelling case for RFID-embedded technologies in the healthcare field has been increased efficiency in supply chain performance measurements, which generally consist of financial and non-financial indicators. Many research studies have assumed that these efficiency measures are transferrable in the medical services field. Such optimism is fuelled by the expectations that such supply chain measures will result in equally impressive results in the healthcare field. Although this transfer may be somewhat flawed and imperfectly applied, research has verified certain elements of operational optimism. There are still a number of technical, ethical, and legal issues or hurdles that surround RFID applications in the healthcare industry that must be successfully overcome. However, few can successfully argue against freeing hospital staff from the routine duties associated with traditional inventory so that they may be free to serve patients. With recent governmental regulations and the concern for increased access to universal medical care and its astronomical costs, these issues need to be addressed.

Chapter 11

RFID-based solutions are essential inventory management tools, supplying more information than the standard barcode that help eliminate the potential for inventory stock-outs and reducing theft-based inventory shrinkage. A relatively detailed discussion of these techniques is included in this chapter by addressing some of the many concerns of inventory shrinkage. As is evident from the empirical section of this chapter, although RFID may be perceived as a cutting-edge business solution, RFID systems and its implementations still prove to be a difficult process to implement and achieve. Many companies have avoided the idea of introducing RFID systems, possibly due to being overwhelmed with the new technologies. However, its impacts on reducing inventory shrinkage are fairly clear and decisive.

Chapter 12

In this chapter, the authors explore the factors affecting the UK logistics service providers' intention to use RFID technology from the theoretical perspective of a Technology-Acceptance Model (TAM). The survey data analysis shows that perceived usability of RFID has a significant relationship with the levels of adoption of the technology, but perceived privacy issues and perceived security issues do not have such a significant relationship. Using further moderation analysis, the authors find that the relationship between usability and adoption becomes stronger if there is a high level of support for RFID projects within an organisation. The study points to the need to improve the appreciation and support in an organisation for RFID projects. For example, top management should be well informed so as to provide good support, while employees should be motivated to back the use of RFID in their operations. An appropriate level of the required infrastructure will also help increase the usability and hence the adoption of RFID in UK logistics.

Radio Frequency Identification (RFID) became one of the major disruptive innovations that have attracted the attention of researchers and practitioners around the world. Recognizing the business value of RFID, firms are rapidly adopting RFID technology in a wide range of industries including hospitals, logistics, manufacturing, and retailing. Since the adoption of RFID largely depends on the perceived potential benefits and the investment costs, firms need to carefully assess every intangible and tangible benefits and costs to make sure the adoption is financially, operationally, and strategically justifiable. This chapter provides a literature review on RFID applications in business and valuation methods for RFID and presents an analytical evaluation model for RFID investment for manufacturing and retail organizations. Finally, this chapter concludes with the implications of the chapter for academics and practitioners.

Preface

Radio Frequency Identification (RFID) technology is one of the major disruptive innovations in the 21st century. Recognizing the business value of RFID, firms are rapidly adopting RFID technology in a wide range of industries including hospitals, logistics, manufacturing, and retailing. In various industries, RFID technology shows great potential for cost reduction, business process redesign, supply chain improvement, and on-site customer support. The global industry for RFID technology has been growing steadily and is expected to expand quickly for some time.

The dwindling prices of RFID tags are a driver for widespread adoption of item-level tagging. Currently, the United States has the largest market worldwide, followed by Europe. Although developed markets such as US and Europe will continue to remain the largest revenue generators for RFID manufacturers and software developers, future growth in the market will be primarily driven by major Asian countries such as China and South Korea with the support extended by their governments (PRWeb, 2012).

RFID technology has been touted as the foundational enabling technologies for the realization of the Internet of Things (IoT). IoT is based on uniquely identifiable objects and Internet technologies. Devices on the IoT identify, create, collect, share, and store data in an Internet-like structure. For supply chain management, the IoT may use sensors to track RFID tags attached to objects moving through supply chains, thus improving inventory management and information flow while reducing transportation costs. The market for RFID hardware, software, and infrastructure will be strong with the growth of pervasive computing and the IoT.

RFID is projected to grow rapidly with the phenomenal advancements in wireless communication technologies. Given the growing interest in RFID investments by managers, researchers need to further develop theories and measurement models that will help managers apply knowledge gained from the research to make a judicious RFID investment decision and to enhance the value of RFID. Although a large volume of literature is already available on RFID, many new applications and technologies are constantly emerging and provide potential opportunities for further research. In this light, it is imperative for researchers to take stock of the new knowledge on RFID and stimulate further interest in this area. *RFID Technology Integration for Business Performance Improvement* provides a reference source for researchers and industry practitioners to develop their research ideas, theories, and practical experiences, and discuss challenges and opportunities in the RFID area. This book aims to publish high quality original works highlighting management issues, innovative technologies, and evaluation of RFID products and services. This book is composed of 13 chapters in a wide variety of topics such as operational strategies, cost estimation, tracking and tracing applications, data management, and adoption factors. This book will provide professors, researchers, students, and professionals with cutting-edge management strategies and technologies integrated with a solid grounding in theories and practices. A brief introduction of each chapter follows.

Chapter 1, "Item-Level RFID for Retail Business Improvement," by S. H. Choi, H. H. Cheung, B. Yang, and Y. X. Yang proposes an item-level RFID-enabled store management system to help improve retail business. The system adopts an integral design approach to exploit RFID and the e-pedigree established for anti-counterfeiting and tracking of product items in a supply chain. Various modules, such as back-store inventory, smart shelves, interactive mirrors and fitting, and self-checkout services, can be subsequently implemented for retail operations and management. Features for anti-counterfeiting and individual customer marketing can also be incorporated to enhance brand image and customer experience. Moreover, intelligent algorithms may be integrated to mine useful information, such as the sales history of products and the shopping behaviour of customers from the data captured by the RFID devices to facilitate business decision-making and proactive individual marketing. As such, the efficiency of store operations and the overall retail business can be expected to improve substantially. The chapter presents the design approach of the proposed system and discusses some implementation issues, exemplified by two basic applications: (1) track-and-trace anti-counterfeiting to prevent injection of faked products into the back-store inventory and (2) smart product collocation to promote individual customer marketing and cross selling.

Chapter 2, "CostRFID: Design and Evaluation of a Cost Estimation Method and Tool for RFID Integration Projects," by Tobias Engel, Suparna Goswami, Andreas Englschalk, and Helmut Krcmar, uses a design science approach to provide a cost calculation for RFID integration projects. Drawing from literature in the fields of information systems and RFID, software engineering, and supply chain management, the authors develop the cost-calculation method that is then implemented in a prototype. The prototype is developed and evaluated in an iterative fashion using focus groups, RFID experts, and the cognitive walkthrough method. The authors contribute to theory by proposing a new cost calculation method to estimate the costs of RFID integration projects. Practical implications include a more accurate estimation of the cost of integrating RFID systems into the existing IT landscape and a risk reduction for RFID projects.

Chapter 3, "Can Near Field Communication Solve the Limitations in Mobile Indoor Navigation?" by Wilson E. Sakpere and Michael O. Adeyeye, provides an overview of the benefits and usefulness of Near Field Communication (NFC) compared with existing indoor navigation technologies. The navigation ecosystem is rapidly changing. Indoor navigation has attracted attention with the introduction of mobile devices into the market. Although mobile devices are used more often for outdoor navigation, they have opened up opportunities for indoor navigation proponents. Near Field Communication in indoor navigation is still in its exploratory stage. Despite an increase in the variety of indoor navigation research, challenges remain in designing a framework that is neither complex nor expensive. Although NFC devices are used more often for outdoor navigation, it has opened up opportunities for indoor navigation proponents.

Chapter 4, "Open Source Object Directory Services for Inter-Enterprise Tracking and Tracing Applications," by Konstantinos Mourtzoukos, Nikos Kefalakis, and John Soldatos, introduces an open and novel implementation of an ONS (Object Naming Service) solution for inter-enterprise tracking and tracing RFID applications. Despite the proliferation of RFID (Radio Frequency Identification) applications, there are still only a limited number of open-loop inter-enterprise applications that address global supply chains. The implementation of such inter-enterprise applications hinges on standards and techniques for discovering and accessing RFID tagged objects across different repositories of RFID information residing across different administrative domains. In this chapter, the authors introduce an open and novel implementation of an ONS (Object Naming Service) solution for inter-enterprise tracking and tracing

RFID applications. The solution is part of the open source AspireRFID project and provides a sound basis for integrating tracking ("google-of-things" like) applications for the RFID and the Internet-of-Things (IoT). As part of the presentation of the solution, this chapter illustrates the main challenges associated with the integration of inter-enterprise applications, along with strategies for confronting them.

Chapter 5, "An Integrated Development Environment for RFID Applications," by Nikos Kefalakis and John Soldatos, introduces an Integrated Development Environment (IDE) for RFID applications. IDE addresses multiple parts of an RFID application, while at the same time supporting the full application development lifecycle (i.e. design, development, deployment, and testing of RFID applications). Some of the RFID middleware projects come with simple tools, which facilitate the application development, configuration, and deployment processes. However, these tools tend to be fragmented, since they address only part of an RFID system (such as the filtering of tag streams and/or the generation of business events). The introduced IDE comprises a wide range of tools, which have been implemented as modular plug-ins to an Eclipse-based environment. The evaluation has proven that IDE can significantly ease RFID application development.

Chapter 6, "Meta-Data alignment in Open Tracking and Tracing Systems," by Fred van Blommestein, Dávid Karnok, and Zsolt Kemény, presents a method that enables components of tracking and tracing systems to negotiate at run-time what attributes may be stored for a particular object type. In tracking and tracing systems, attributes of objects (such as location, time, status, and temperature) are recorded as these objects move through a supply chain. In open tracking and tracing systems, the attributes are not known beforehand, as the type of objects and the set of stakeholders may evolve over time. Components may include scanning equipment, data stores, and query clients. Apart from simple attributes, associations between objects may be recorded and stored (e.g., when an object is packed in another object, loaded in a truck or container, or assembled to be a new object).

Chapter 7, "RFID Technology and Privacy," by Edward Chen, reviews consumer privacy issues in RFID applications. RFID plays a critical role in the improvement of business automation and supply chain management and offers significant benefits to businesses in terms of logistics and cost savings, particularly labor savings. However, RFID use for consumer-oriented purposes has been met with much greater debate and resistance upon consumer privacy rights. These concerns are rooted in the fact that consumers are typically unaware that their purchases are being tracked and monitored, as well as the fear of private information being hacked or stolen via insecure RFID systems. Therefore, it is important for consumers to understand the capabilities and limitations of RFID and its implications for businesses and privacy.

Chapter 8, "Green Characteristics of RFID Technologies: An Exploration in the UK Logistics Sector from Innovation Diffusion Perspective," by Ramakrishnan Ramanathan, Lok Wan Lorraine Ko, Hsin Chen, and Usha Ramanathan, explores the factors affecting logistics service providers' intention to use RFID technology, with special emphasis on its environmentally friendly green characteristics. Logistics is an integral part of the supply chain. RFID technology has been identified as an important application among many logistics technologies and is increasingly gaining both practitioners' and researchers' attention. The theoretical perspective diffusion of innovations is used to understand the factors that affect intention to use RFID technology. The analysis shows that observability of green characteristics positively influences the intention to use RFID.

Chapter 9, "Data Management Issues in RFID Applications," by A. Anny Leema and M. Hemalatha, investigates the existing physical, middleware, and deferred approaches to deal with the anomalies found in the RFID data. A hybrid approach integrates the existing approaches to solve the issues so that the demand for RFID data will certainly grow to meet the user needs. RFID is being widely used in various applications, but there is reluctance in the deployment of RFID due to the high cost and the challenging features found in the observed colossal RFID data. The obtained data is of low quality and it contains anomalies like false positives, false negatives, and duplication. To enhance the quality of data, cleaning is the essential task, so that the resultant data can be applied for high-end applications.

Chapter 10, "Operational Strategies Associated with RFID Applications in Healthcare Systems," by Alan Smith, discusses various operational strategies associated with RFID applications in healthcare systems. While many studies have assumed that operational efficiency is transferrable in the medical services field, this transfer may be somewhat flawed and imperfectly applied. This chapter identifies a number of technical, ethical, and legal issues or hurdles that surround RFID applications in the healthcare industry that must be successfully overcome. With recent governmental regulations and the concern for increased access to universal medical care and its astronomical costs, these issues need to be addressed urgently.

Chapter 11, "Inventory Management, Shrinkage Concerns, and Related Corrective RFID Strategies," by Alan Smith, addresses concerns of inventory shrinkage. RFID-based solutions are essentially inventory management tools supplying more information than the standard barcode that help eliminate the potential for inventory stock-outs and reducing theft-based inventory shrinkage. Although RFID may be perceived as a cutting-edge business solution, RFID systems and their implementation still prove to be a difficult process to implement and achieve. However, their impact on reducing inventory shrinkage are fairly clear, and inventory managers need to learn how to deploy them strategically and in a successful manner.

Chapter 12, "An Analysis of the Diffusion of RFID in the UK Logistics Sector using a Technology-Acceptance Perspective," by Ramakrishnan Ramanathan, Usha Ramanathan, and Lok Wan Lorraine Ko, explores the factors affecting the UK logistics service providers' intention to use RFID technology from the theoretical perspective of a Technology-Acceptance Model (TAM). Their survey data analysis shows that perceived usability of RFID has a significant relationship with the levels of adoption of the technology, but perceived privacy issues and perceived security issues do not have such a significant relationship. Using further moderation analysis, the authors found that the relationship between usability and adoption becomes stronger if there is a high level of support for RFID projects within an organisation. Top management should be well informed so as to provide good support, while employees should be motivated to back the use of RFID in their operations.

Chapter 13, "RFID Technology in Business and Valuation Methods," by In Lee, provides a literature review on RFID applications in business and valuation methods for RFID, and presents an analytical evaluation model for RFID investment for manufacturing and retail organizations. RFID became one of the major disruptive innovations that have attracted the attention of researchers and practitioners around the world. Since the adoption of RFID largely depends on the perceived potential benefits and the investment costs, firms need to carefully assess every intangible and tangible benefit and costs to make sure the adoption is financially, operationally, and strategically justifiable. Finally, this chapter concludes with the implications of the chapter for academics and practitioners.

Despite the popularity of RFID technology, many challenges may lie ahead in the implementation of RFID systems, as we have already observed signs of overinvestment in RFID systems. It is easy to overinvest in IT when a company sees a strategic value of the IT and fear that they will succumb to their competition without RFID investments. It should be noted that RFID technologies affect multiple stakeholders differently, and their perceived values may be different from each other. Taking into consideration the varying degrees of benefits and costs among these stakeholders is important for the successful RFID investment.

RFID Technology Integration for Business Performance Improvement is an excellent collection of the latest research and practices associated with theories, user behaviors, and practices in RFID. While RFID is an important subject of study for academic researchers, there is still a lack of comprehensive reference sources that provide the most up-to-date research findings and future directions for contemporary enterprises. This book fills this void by covering a wide range of topics such as management issues, literature analysis, adoption and diffusion of RFID, and evaluation of RFID applications. As leading experts in the RFID area, the contributors did an outstanding job of providing the readers with extensive coverage of the most important research topics: new concepts, management strategies, application development, privacy issues, and trends. The projected audience includes managers, employees, researchers, professors, and college students in various management and engineering programs. I expect this book to expose new insights for researchers, educators, and practitioners to better understand the important issues of RFID research and technologies.

In Lee
Western Illinois University, USA

Acknowledgment

I sincerely thank Mehdi Khosrow-Pour, Jan Travers, and other members of IGI Global, whose support throughout the whole process from the inception of the initial idea to the final publication has been invaluable. I also would like to express my heartfelt gratitude to all authors and reviewers for their invaluable contributions and collaboration.

In Lee
Western Illinois University, USA

Chapter 1
Item–Level RFID for Retail Business Improvement

S. H. Choi
The University of Hong Kong, Hong Kong

H. H. Cheung
The University of Hong Kong, Hong Kong

B. Yang
The University of Hong Kong, Hong Kong

Y. X. Yang
The University of Hong Kong, Hong Kong

ABSTRACT

This chapter proposes an item-level RFID-enabled store management system to help improve retail business. The system adopts an integral design approach to exploit RFID and the e-pedigree established for anti-counterfeiting and tracking of product items in a supply chain. Various modules, such as back-store inventory, smart shelves, interactive mirrors and fitting, and self-checkout services, can be subsequently implemented for retail operations and management. Features for anti-counterfeiting and individual customer marketing can also be incorporated to enhance brand image and customer experience. Moreover, intelligent algorithms may be integrated to mine useful information, such as the sales history of products and the shopping behaviour of customers from the data captured by the RFID devices to facilitate business decision-making and proactive individual marketing. As such, the efficiency of store operations and the overall retail business can be expected to improve substantially. The chapter presents the design approach of the proposed system and discusses some implementation issues, exemplified by two basic applications: (1) track-and-trace anti-counterfeiting to prevent injection of faked products into the back-store inventory and (2) smart product collocation to promote individual customer marketing and cross selling.

DOI: 10.4018/978-1-4666-6308-4.ch001

INTRODUCTION

To survive and thrive in competitive retail business, companies need to promote omni-channel retailing to enhance customer experience and hence improve operation efficiency and profit margins. This may be achieved by innovative adoption and integration of advanced technologies, including cloud computing, mobile devices/payment, and Radio Frequency Identification (RFID) (Ganesan et al., 2009; Tajima, 2007; Violino, 2013).

RFID, as a non-line-of-sight identification technology, has great potential to improve physical process efficiency and overall supply chain visibility (Ngai and Gun 2009; Vlachos, 2013). Vlachos (2013) studied the impact of RFID practices on retail supply chain performance, and reported that RFID could improve the performance of distribution systems, including products dispatched and inventory in transit by 33.8% and stock availability by 45.6%, respectively.

Advancement of RFID and the related technologies in recent years has made real-time identification and tracking of individual product items a realistic possibility (Tajima, 2007), which is not practicable with barcodes. Using barcodes, it is not easy for retailers to achieve identification and tracking of individual product items in supply chain processes, from source to store. It is often time-consuming and impractical in item-level applications to read a barcode attached to a product item, a case, or a pallet, one by one.

Hence, a number of pilot projects have been conducted to adopt RFID to enhance source-to-store supply chain management, including production tracking, pack and ship verification for logistics services, warehouse management, product anti-counterfeiting, and retail business enhancement. Kwok and Wu (2009) proposed an RFID-based intra-supply chain system for textile industry to facilitate coordination and integration of supply chain functions and activities for enhancing the overall performance of a supply chain. It has been demonstrated that RFID offers huge potential to elevate the visibility of product items and the overall efficiency of supply chains to levels not previously practicable.

Furthermore, full visibility of product items, from source to store, facilitates omni-channel retailing and improves in-store inventory accuracy. This is because available inventory from any location, whether in stores or distribution centres, or in transit, or on order from the manufacturer, can be located and allocated in real time. Indeed, adoption of RFID for real-time identification and tracking of individual product items from source to store highlights its benefits for improving inventory accuracy, on-shelf availability, differentiated customer experience, brand image, and store operation efficiency. As such, the efficiency of retail operations and profit margins can be improved accordingly.

The success of item-level RFID application hinges greatly on generating and maintaining a trustworthy electronic pedigree (e-pedigree) that records the movement of products to uphold the integrity of the supply chain. A main implementation issue concerns formulation and real-time tag programming of a unique product identifier (PID) and the related production data of a product item at the manufacturing source, and subsequent updating and synchronization of all the transaction records of each of the product items across various nodes of the supply chain, from the manufacturer's warehouse to the logistics service providers and wholesale distributors, and finally to the retail stores and the end-customers.

We propose an item-level RFID-enabled store management system to help improve retail business. This system is primarily aimed to achieve better intra-organisational coordination within a retail enterprise through synchronisation and management of information at item-level along the whole supply chain, with a possible extension in future development to facilitate inter-organisation/cross-enterprise coordination. It is integrated with a track-and-trace anti-counterfeiting system to generate product PIDs at manufacturing and maintain a trustworthy e-pedigree for subsequent authentication and tracking of product items in the supply chain. Such an integral design approach facilitates implementation of various modules for retail operations and management, including back-store inventory, smart shelves, interactive mirrors and fitting, and self-checkout services. Features for anti-counterfeiting and individual customer marketing can also be incorporated to enhance brand image and customer experience. Moreover, intelligent algorithms may be developed to mine useful information from the large amount of data captured by the RFID devices to facilitate business decision-making and proactive individual marketing. As such, the efficiency of store operations and the overall retail business may be improved substantially.

RELATED WORK

A number of studies have recently been conducted to illustrate possible applications of item-level RFID for better inventory control and replenishment, stock-out reduction, increased operation efficiency, improved customer experience and differentiation, better prevention of product theft, better brand protection by RFID-based product anti counterfeiting, and hence improved sales in store (Marco et al., 2012; Szmerekovsky and Zhang, 2008; Vlachos, 2013).

RFID can provide item-level product visibility from source to store. Such real-time and accurate product information facilitates supply chain coordination, increases inventory accuracy, and reduces out-of-stocks. Vlachos (2013) developed a model to study the potential benefits of using RFID in retail supply chain, and found that RFID can help improve supply, inventory, distribution, plan, sales, and forecasting substantially.

Marco et al. (2012) built a structural and simulation model based on the case-project to deploy item-level RFID technology in the retail stores of Miroglio Fashion S.r.l., a leading Italian Ap-

parel and Fashion retailer, to study the value that the technology could bring about through sales growth and cost efficiency in fast fashion trades. The results revealed that adoption of item-level RFID in the retail store may not only reduce operational costs, but may also help increase revenue through sales growth.

Furthermore, some researchers have attempted to use RFID to track the flow of product items, from back-store to store-floor, to monitor product availability on the shelves and hence improve inventory control and replenishment. As a result, out-of-stocks can be minimized and hence sales volume increased.

Rekik et al. (2008) reported that RFID can be used to reduce product misplacement errors at retail stores to improve inventory accuracies. They provided an analytical expression of RFID tag cost for cost-effective deployment.

Metzder et al. (2013) developed a mathematical model for periodic review and RFID-enabled retail shelf-inventory management, and analysed the impact of false-negative reads on the performance of RFID-based shelf inventory control policies. Their results show that for low to medium demand rates and low tag cost, RFID systems may operate at lower costs than periodic review systems, cutting cost by 25.7% while increasing service levels by 2%.

Condea et al. (2012) proposed an RFID-enabled shelf-replenishment method for inventory control and replenishment in retail stores. This method adopts RFID to detect bi-directional product movements between the backroom and the sales floor of a store. They also conducted a simulation to compare the performance of the RFID-based inventory control policies to traditional schemes with periodic reviews. The simulation results show that the RFID-based policies have the potential to improve cost efficiency and service levels.

In retail stores, RFID may not be used only for inventory control and prevention of theft, but also for collecting customer shopping behaviour (CSB), in order to enhance in-store intelligence and provision of services to improve customer shopping experience (CSE) and loyalty, and hence sales volume. For this purpose, retailers are obliged to take effective measures to protect customer privacy when RFID is adopted to collect CSB data for marketing and business applications (Jones et al., 2004; Boeck et al., 2011).

Hou and Chen (2011) proposed an RFID-based shopping service system for retailers with large-spaced shop floors to generate customized shopping recommendations for individual customers. Their study illustrates that the quality of shopping services in retail can be enhanced, and the sales volume of commodities increased considerably.

Jung and Kwon (2011) used RFID to identify the shopping paths of customers in major sales areas by collecting and analysing information on the customers' main travel paths. Based on such data, retailers can better understand the customers' consumption behaviour, and hence decide whether the product display and layout should be modified to increase sales volume.

The research works above have demonstrated the potential values of RFID in supply chain management and retail business. They have established a foundation for further exploration of item-level RFID applications in retail stores to improve business operation efficiency, inventory accuracy, customer experience and satisfaction, and thereby increase sales volume.

However, these works tended to have focused mainly on studying some specific yet fragmented issues of RFID applications in supply chains or retail stores by using simulation, or case studies, or mathematical and statistical analysis.

Therefore, we instead propose an integrated item-level RFID-enabled retail store management system, which adopts RFID and related IT technologies to establish a complete e-pedigree, from manufacturing to retailing, for real-time tracking and tracing of product items in an entire supply chain. Such an integral approach greatly improves product visibility that facilitates collection and analysis of CSB to enhance retail business

operations and store inventory management, which in turn help provide better shopping services to increase customer satisfaction and loyalty, and hence sales volume.

THE PROPOSED ITEM-LEVEL RFID-ENABLED RETAIL STORE MANAGEMENT SYSTEM

An RFID-Based Track-and-Trace Anti-Counterfeiting System

As discussed above, a complete and trustworthy source-to-store product e-pedigree is crucial to the success of item-level RFID applications in retail stores. The major issues in establishing and maintaining such an e-pedigree involve formulation and real-time tag programming of PID and the related production data for each of the product items at the manufacturing source, and subsequent updating and synchronization of all the transaction records of each of the product items across various nodes of the supply chain, from the manufacturer's warehouse to the logistics service providers and wholesale distributors, and finally to the retail stores and the end-customers.

To address these issues, the authors have recently developed an RFID-based track-and-trace anti-counterfeiting system to establish and maintain a product e-pedigree for anti-counterfeiting of relatively high-end consumer products (Cheung and Choi, 2011; Choi and Poon, 2008).

Figure 1 shows the flow of this system. It consists mainly of two layers, namely a front-end RFID-enabled layer for tag programming and product data acquisition, and a back-end anti-counterfeiting layer for processing product pedigree and authentication.

The back-end layer consists of a set of computer servers that together enforce track-and-trace anti-counterfeiting. The Information Server collects company information from the supply chain partners. The information is crucial for the product

Figure 1. The flow of the RFID-based track-and-trace anti-counterfeiting system

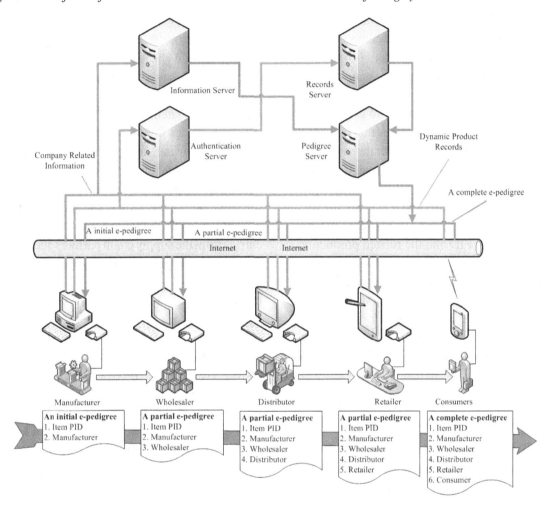

pedigrees because they form the geographical picture of the product history; it also facilitates problem tracing when suspected counterfeits emerge. As the products move along the supply chain, supply chain partners should record each transaction accordingly.

The products are identified by the embedded RFID tags, each of which is programmed with a unique PID. The PID forms the basis of a transaction record, which is sent to the Authentication Server. The Authentication Server verifies the transaction records and screens out suspicious activities. The screened records are then sent to the Record Server for storage and subsequent follow-up. The supply chain partners can verify

the partial product pedigree from the point of manufacturing to the previous owners by making requests to the Pedigree Server, which in turn retrieves transaction records from the Records Server as well as company information from the Information Server to generate the required e-pedigree. They should reject any products with a suspicious or partial pedigree. The Pedigree Server is also responsible for generating complete product e-pedigrees, through the Internet and the mobile phone network, to end-consumers for verification. When a customer is satisfied that a product is genuine and has paid for it, the retailer should generate a sale record, which is subsequently sent to the Authentication Server. Any further transactions of the same product after the sale record are deemed suspicious.

The front-end layer mainly controls RFID devices to read (program) data from (to) the tags attached to product items for processing the data together with the related product information. This layer is particularly crucial to establishing and ensuring accurate e-pedigrees that record all transactions of each of the product items moving along the supply chain, from the manufacturing source to the retail stores. To facilitate its implementation, we have proposed a scheme for PID formulation and a mechanism for real-time tag programming of PID and the related production data for each of the product items during manufacturing. As such, the initial e-pedigree data for each product item can be created and synchronized in the servers at the back-end layer for subsequent management and anti-counterfeiting across all nodes of the supply chain. The main operations are as follows.

Manufacturer

At a manufacturing or packaging line, it is essential to write in real time a unique identification number and the related product information into an RFID tag embedded in a product item being processed in an efficient and accurate manner. These data must be synchronised in a database for subsequent inventory management and uploaded to the back-end layer to initialise the product e-pedigree for subsequent authentication. The finished products are stored in a warehouse for shipment. The manufacturer is required to generate a Release Record to the Authentication Server before transferring the products to the next partner. This is the first record of the product e-pedigree. The Release Record serves the purpose of certifying the root source of the product item, which assures the following partners in the supply chain that they are receiving genuine products from the right manufacturer.

Supply Chain Partners

Upon receiving the products, the supply chain partners should check against the partial product e-pedigree which records the transactions of the items since after manufacturing. They should only receive product items with a plausible history. Any suspicious items should be rejected or returned to the previous owner, and reported to the host company. After verifying and accepting the product items, the company continues to process the items for value-adding activities and then update the e-pedigree to the Pedigree Server. The pedigree entries from the supply chain partners accumulate to form the complete product e-pedigree.

Retailers

Upon receiving the products, the retailers should verify the product e-pedigrees in the way described above. The retailers hold a stake in so doing because their goodwill and reputation would be damaged if any of their products is found a counterfeit. When a consumer has paid for a product, the sale record should be uploaded to the Authentication Server. Any further sale attempts or transactions of supposed-to-have-been-sold products are deemed suspicious.

End-Consumers

In order to protect their own stake, consumers should verify the e-pedigrees of the products they are buying before payment. They can do so by reading the PIDs with a handheld RFID device connected to the Authentication Server.

Building on the foundation of the PID and a complete e-pedigree of each product item from manufacturing to retailing, an item-level RFID-enabled retail store management system will be designed and subsequently developed to integrate with RFID-based track-and-trace anti-counterfeiting for enhancing retail business operations. With this system, retailers can take advantage of full visibility of product items for provision of innovative services and enhancement of customer experience. Moreover, retailers can achieve omni-channel retailing because available inventory from any location, whether in the store, in distribution centres, in transit, or on order from the manufacturer, can be located and allocated in real time. As such, the efficiency of retail operations and profit margins can be enhanced accordingly.

Design of the Proposed System

The proposed item-level RFID-enabled retail store management system is primarily targeted at relatively high-end apparels, although it may be conveniently adapted for other products.

For the fashion apparel and footwear industry to survive economic challenges, Liard (2009) pointed out that item-level RFID has become a potential strategy to help improve inventory visibility, services, and the overall CSE and loyalty, and hence increase sales. It was also reported that American Apparel, which is the largest clothing manufacturer in the United States, tested an item-level RFID pilot project that tracked 40,000 items in one of its New York stores in 2007 and subsequently expanded into an eight-store pilot in 2008. The results showed that the contributions of item level RFID included an increase of 14% in per-store sales, an improvement of inventory accuracy by 99% with subsequent elimination of 10% to 20% in lost stock, and monthly labour savings of nearly 190 hours per-store. The American Apparel had a plan to adopt item-level RFID systems throughout its entire organization as part of its long-term strategy (Liard, 2009).

In our proposed item-level RFID-enabled retail store management system, RFID readers are installed at appropriate locations of the store, including entrance and exit doors, shelves, fitting rooms and POS, for tracking and tracing product items as well as for collecting CSB. As shown in Figure 2, the system mainly consists of six major modules, namely: (1) Data Management;

(2) Item-level RFID-enabled Retail Store Inventory Management; (3) Smart Fitting Room; (4) Smart Mirror and Virtual Fitting; (5) RFID- and Mobile-enabled Shopping Recommendation and Marketing; and (6) RFID-enabled POS, Product Anti-theft and Anti-Counterfeiting. The design and functions of each of these modules are presented in the following sections.

Data Management Module

For item-level RFID applications in retail business, networked RFID readers are used not only for real-time reading of product item PIDs, but also for collecting CSB. Data related to CSB may include what product items have been browsed and/or tried on by customers, which zones and how long individual customers have visited to and stayed in, and what they have purchased. Such data are stored in the database and then analysed for subsequent retail store management applications. As these data would often accumulate to huge amounts, data management is of crucial importance. Hence, it is critical to design a robust database server with a set of databases and intelligent data-mining algorithms, as shown in Figure 3, for real-time management and processing of big data for various applications to facilitate omni-channel retailing.

In our previous work (Choi and Poon, 2008), the Record Server was developed to store the PID of item-level RFID tags and all transaction records, from the manufacturer to retailers, to maintain a trustworthy product e-pedigree for product anti-counterfeiting throughout the supply chain.

The Record Server contains four major databases, namely (1) the Information Database for recording the information related to supply chain partners and contact persons; (2) the Pedigree Database for storing the item-level tag PID being requested through the Pedigree Server; (3) the Records Database for recording data that are directly used to generate e-pedigree and all transaction records at each node of the supply chain; and (4)

Figure 2. Major modules of the proposed item-level RFID-enabled retail store management system

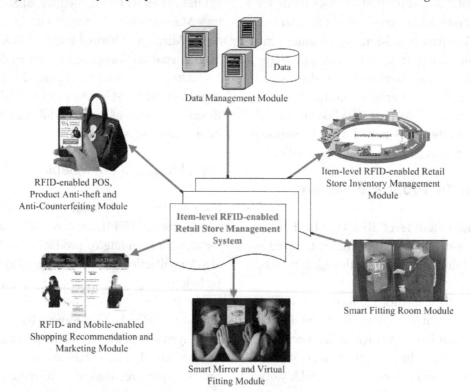

the System Database for storing the information of all users of the system and user logins.

This server architecture builds a foundation for developing item-level RFID applications in retail stores, such as authentication of product items to prevent injection of fake products into the back-store inventory. However, the existing four databases are not enough for other applications, like capturing CSB, data-mining of useful information for decision-making of business strategies and improvements.

Hence, two more databases have to be developed and integrated, namely (1) the Customer Shopping Behaviour Database for recording customer data about shopping behaviour and sales history to help improve CSE and loyalty; and (2) the Store Inventory Database for recording in-store and back-store inventory to facilitate inventory control and replenishment. Furthermore,

a set of intelligent data-mining algorithms will be developed to extract useful information to assist retail pricing and promotion strategies for individual customers.

Item-Level RFID-Enabled Retail Store Inventory Management Module

With item-level RFID, the locations, available quantities, and other information of product items in a store can be tracked and traced in real-time. Such information is useful for inventory control to minimize over-stock to reduce inventory costs, as well as for shelf replenishment to prevent out-of-stocks to increase sales. This is particularly important in complex and dynamic markets.

This module controls RFID-enabled gate door and shelf systems to capture product information at item-level for the following three main functions:

Figure 3. Major databases of the data management module and data flow of the proposed system

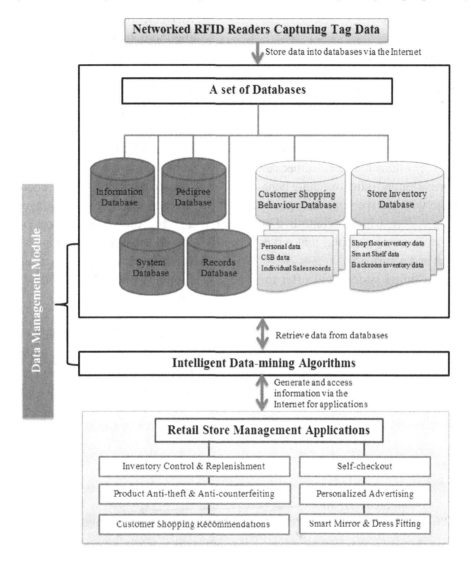

1. Back-store inventory management for processing product receipt, authentication, and recording of what, when, and how many products are moved into front shop floor when products are delivered to the store;

2. Store-floor inventory management for monitoring the types and amount of product items being displayed on shelves, and for recording product items being sold out; and

3. Processing of item-level product data captured by RFID devices to facilitate inventory control and shelf replenishment.

In comparison with the traditional processes of inventory management based on periodic reviews, the RFID-enabled approach facilitates agile responses to actual demands by maintaining products at optimal inventory levels. As such, the salespersons can be relieved from watching over the inventory; they can instead spend more time to cater to customer needs.

Smart Fitting Room Module

As shown in Figure 4, the smart fitting room (SFR) module mainly consists of a fixed RFID reader installed at the top and an interactive fitting system. The RFID reader automatically reads the product items taken in by a customer. The customer can get product information and other matching items and communicate with salespersons through the interactive fitting system, which is controlled by a computer and an interactive display that serves as a touch screen and a mirror.

The interactive fitting system will offer the following functions:

1. **Product information/search:** A customer can enquire about the availability of sizes and colours of a garment on the screen. If a preferred item is out of stock, the customer can check the available date.

2. **Call for assistance:** A customer can seek assistance from salespersons, like help bringing more items into the fitting room.

3. **Collection of CSB:** The RFID readers read what items are taken into the fitting room and what items are browsed through the interactive computer system. Such information is stored into the databases to facilitate the management team to formulate retailing strategies, such as designing new promotions to attract customers, changing product designs and store display layout.

4. **Product matching service:** Product matching information that enhances cross-selling can be provided based on what products are brought to the fitting room and the past sales history.

The SFR module helps retailers better understand customers' needs and shopping behaviour, such that appropriate shopping services can be provided accordingly to enhance CSE.

Figure 4. Design of a smart fitting room

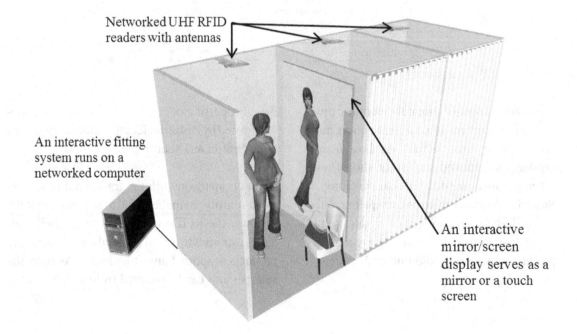

Networked UHF RFID readers with antennas

An interactive fitting system runs on a networked computer

An interactive mirror/screen display serves as a mirror or a touch screen

Smart Mirror and Virtual Fitting Module

The smart mirror and virtual fitting (SMVF) module combines RFID, video camera, 3D digitizing, computer graphics, sensing, interactive touch mirror display and virtual reality (VR) technologies, as shown in Figure 5. It is designed for customers to try on apparels in a VR environment, before going to a fitting room to physically try on the preferred items. This module helps achieve better cross-selling by product matching by providing a VR environment for customers to try on various garments. Customers do not have to queue up at traditional fitting rooms, and hence can spend more time on shopping. As a result, sales would likely increase.

The SMVF module consists of a kiosk equipped with RFID readers, video cameras, sensors for measuring the weight, height and posture of a customer, a computer with a gesture-based interface, an interactive touch mirror display, and a suite of software for avatar generation and virtual fitting based on the customer's posture captured by the video cameras and the virtual garments. The customer can virtually try on the garments by viewing the 3D avatar from various perspectives controlled by hand gestures. This interactive fitting approach provides customers with a more realistic try-on experience compared with the traditional approach of imposing a garment onto the customer's reflected image in a mirror.

The major processes of the proposed smart mirror and virtual fitting module are as follows:

Figure 5. Design of an SMVF kiosk

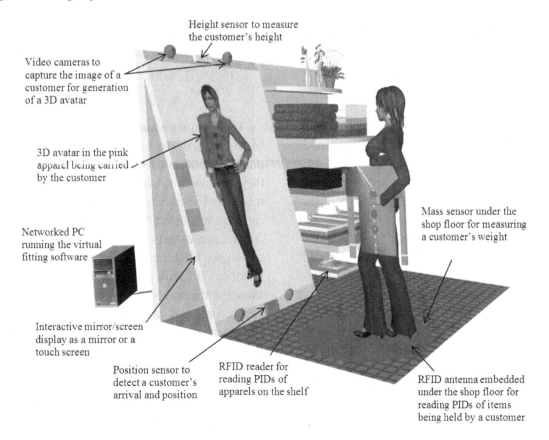

Height sensor to measure the customer's height

Video cameras to capture the image of a customer for generation of a 3D avatar

3D avatar in the pink apparel being carried by the customer

Networked PC running the virtual fitting software

Interactive mirror/screen display as a mirror or a touch screen

Position sensor to detect a customer's arrival and position

RFID reader for reading PIDs of apparels on the shelf

Mass sensor under the shop floor for measuring a customer's weight

RFID antenna embedded under the shop floor for reading PIDs of items being held by a customer

1. When a sensor detects a customer standing in front of an interactive mirror/screen display, an RFID reader is triggered to read the PIDs of product items being held by the customer. Subsequently, the display pops up a menu for the customer to set it either as a traditional reflective mirror or as a touch screen for virtual fitting to suit different requirements of individual customers;

2. In virtual fitting mode, video cameras and sensors capture the customer's posture and generate a 3D avatar, with which the customer can interact by hand gestures for virtual fitting of the selected product items in a VR environment. The customer can search for other preferred product items for further virtual fitting;

3. For some customers who may find it awkward with the 3D avatar in virtual fitting, the display can be set and used as a traditional mirror;

4. The customer can subsequently store the preferred items in a list to request for sending the physical product items to a fitting room for physical fitting.

In all cases, only the information of try-on items is stored for subsequent CSB analysis. There is not any privacy issue because no personal data or images of the customer are involved.

The proposed SMVF module needs efficient graphics algorithms to generate 3D avatars and virtual product models for virtual fitting in an immersive VR environment. Development of such software is being planned for implementation of a practical and efficient smart mirror and virtual fitting tool.

RFID and Mobile-Enabled Shopping Recommendation and Marketing Module

This module adopts RFID and smart mobile technologies to generate customized shopping recommendations for individual customers, in-cluding an item matching list and a shopping route with guidance, to help customers locate preferred product items. It consists of the following features:

1. A software for generation of customized shopping recommendations;

2. A mobile navigation application allows customers to navigate 2D and 3D layout of retail stores, view a recommended shopping item list and shopping route, and locate the items on which shelf;

3. Kiosks controlled by a computer, with touch screens and RFID readers installed at various locations near to the shelves for customers who do not have mobile devices to run the applications;

4. A mobile marketing application to be installed by customers in their mobile devices, such as a mobile phone and a tablet, to receive personalized advertisements and promotions based on the shopping behaviour and sales records of individual customers. The customers can search, browse, and order products anytime and anywhere through the Internet.

The shopping recommendation software takes advantage of the real-time data of customer shopping behaviour, such as items browsed, how long they stay in a particular product zone, and the past record and sales history, to generate customized shopping recommendations for individual customers. It can cater for both member and non-member customers. Each member customer has an RFID member card with a unique identifier (UID) to associate the real-time shopping behaviour with past records and sales history. For non-member customers, they would each be given a temporary RFID shopping card to associate only with the real-time shopping behaviour data for generation of shopping recommendations.

It should be pointed out that the real-time customer shopping behaviour is collected only for accumulation of product metadata, such as how many times an item has been browsed or tried on, rather than who has browsed or tried on it. Therefore, privacy is not an issue for non-member customers to be concerned about, while member customers may need to accept some prescribed privacy policy when they apply for membership.

Overall, this module helps customers locate their preferred products quickly. Moreover, marketing information can also be efficiently extracted to target at potential customers. As such, CSE and hence sales can be expected to increase significantly.

RFID-Enabled POS, Product Anti-Theft and Anti-Counterfeiting Module

This module integrates RFID and POS technologies for payment and product return processing, theft prevention, and verification of product authenticity, as shown in Figure 6. Besides, this module includes a self-checkout kiosk, which consists of an RFID reader, a touch-screen tablet, a POS and product authentication software for self-payment via electronic means like credit cards, PayPal, Google wallet, and mobile phones.

The module uses an RFID reader to read the PIDs of multiple product items and calculate the total amount payable by retrieving the sales prices via the data management module. Before making payment, the customer can verify the authenticity of each product item from its e-pedigree. If the customer is satisfied that the products are genuine, payment is confirmed and the transaction records are updated in the database. Furthermore, the module controls the readers installed at entrance and exit doors to read RFID tag PIDs of product items being taken out stores and verify again the transaction records. An alarm will be alerted to prevent theft if any product item has not been paid for.

This module can speed up payments considerably, because an RFID reader can read multiple tag PIDs at a time. Moreover, product authenticity can help protect brand image and increase customer loyalty, while product security can prevent loss by theft.

Figure 6. Design of a self-checkout kiosk

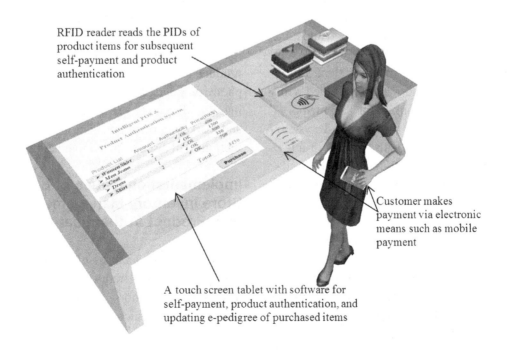

PRODUCT ITEM IDENTIFICATION AND IMPLEMENTATION ISSUES

The proposed item-level RFID-enabled retail store management system is designed to help improve retail business by achieving omni-channel retailing through provision of quality services and enhancement of CSE. For successful implementation of the proposed system in apparel retail stores, it is necessary to first formulate an appropriate data format of PIDs for product item identification and subsequent programming of the RFID tags attached to individual product items during manufacturing, and then address the implementation issues of the various modules.

PID Format for Product Item Identification

An appropriate PID format is essential for establishing a trustworthy product e-pedigree for tracking and tracing of individual product items in the supply chain. We assume that each apparel item is tagged with a Class-1 Generation-2 (C1G2) UHF RFID tag, with which the unique PID of the item is programmed during manufacturing.

As shown in Figure 7a, the memory of a C1G2 UHF RFID tag can be logically grouped into four memory banks, namely Bank 00 for Reserved memory, Bank 01 for EPC memory, Bank 10 for TID memory which is normally hardcoded with the UID of the tag, and Bank 11 for User memory.

The PID adopted in the proposed system combines 96 bits of EPC with the UID of a tag (Cheung and Choi, 2011). A customized closed-loop EPC numbering scheme for apparel products is shown in Figure 7b. It uses the 96 bits of the EPC memory in six groups.

The first group has 16 bits for four hexadecimal digits that represent the manufacturer's country code; the second group has 12 bits for three hexadecimal digits to represent the factory code; the third group has 12 bits for three hexadecimal digits to represent the manufacturing line number;

the fourth group has 20 bits for five hexadecimal digits to represent production date; the fifth group has 20 bits for five hexadecimal digits to represent product property; and the final group has 16 bits for four hexadecimal digits to represent a unique serial number for an apparel item produced on a particular line in a particular factory on a particular production date.

To facilitate subsequent collection of customer behaviour for shopping recommendation applications, the 20 bits in the fifth group is further divided into five sub-groups to identify different properties of an apparel product, as shown in Figure 7c. The first sub-group uses one bit to represent two apparel sorts, namely men and women; the second sub-group uses three bits to represent seven apparel sizes; the third sub-group uses four bits to represent 12 apparel types; the fourth sub-group has four bits to represent six different apparel textures; and the last sub-group uses eight bits to represent 20 colours.

System Implementation

The proposed system is in an initial stage of implementation. As parts of the modules for anti-counterfeiting and customer shopping recommendation, we are currently developing algorithms for (1) back-store inventory management with product authentication to prevent injection of phony products; and (2) collection and processing of CSB data to generate product collocation and marketing recommendations. The following sections will discuss such implementation issues.

Implementation Issues of Back-Store Inventory Management with Product Authentication

According to the analysis of BRIDGE projects (Bridge, 2009), the frequency of phony product injection/ importation (or illicit transactions) in retail store was much higher than that in other supply chain partners (manufacturers or distribu-

Figure 7. (a) Memory structure of a C1G2 tag hardcoded with unique identifier (UID) in the Bank 10 (b) Customized numbering scheme for the 96-bit EPC that combines with the tag UID to form the PID of a product item (c) 20 bits of EPC memory for representing product property of apparel products

a. Memory structure of a C1G2 tag hardcoded with unique identifier (UID) in the Bank 10

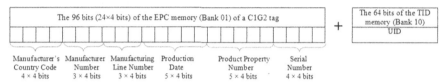

b. Customized numbering scheme for the 96-bit EPC that combines with the tag UID to form the PID of a product item

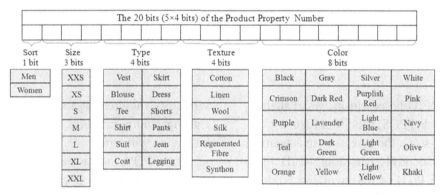

c. 20 bits of EPC memory for representing product property of apparel products

tors). As showed in Figure 8, retailers are the final supply chain nodes that directly connect end-consumers who are the ultimate targets of potential counterfeiters.

As to counterfeiters, injection of fake products at retail level can escape many authenticity checks at upstream supply chain nodes. As to retailers, they may not be all honest and determined to uphold their reputation, especially in competitive markets. Some retailers may even intentionally import illicit products from grey markets. This can be well-illustrated by the lawsuit against Carrefour that allegedly sold fake Louis Vuitton bags in Shanghai in 2006 (Dyer, 2006). As to

end-consumers, they are often not knowledgeable about product authenticity.

Therefore, a reliable and feasible anti-counterfeiting method should be integrated into the proposed item-level RFID-enabled retail management module to authenticate products being delivered, and hence prevent possible injection of fake products, into the back-store inventory.

For effective authentication of product items in a retail store, three operations, namely identification, authentication, and data synchronization, should be processed. To elaborate these operations, an RFID-enabled apparel retail store, with a layout

Figure 8. Possible injection of counterfeits

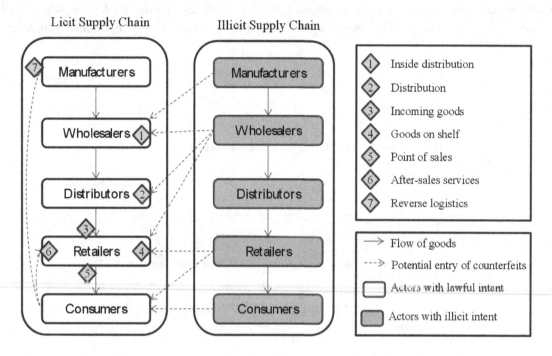

that includes RFID-based kiosks, smart shelves, and RFID-enabled POS, is built in Figure 9.

In the back-store, the inventory management module firstly controls gate-door RFID readers to read the PIDs of the incoming products from upstream supply chain partners, and then verify product authenticity by checking via the data management module against the e-pedigree stored in the back-end server. Only those product items with plausible e-pedigree are accepted, while suspicious items, if any, will be treated as fake and rejected. Upon confirming receipt of the product items, the databases of the data management module are updated to synchronize the e-pedigree throughout all nodes of the supply chain. Information of suspicious items, if any, is recorded. As such, all product items available in back-store can be expected to be genuine.

In the store, customers can conveniently verify product authenticity via a self-checkout kiosk, or an RFID-enabled mobile device, such as a mobile phone and a tablet. This product authentication

service can assure customers' confidence in purchasing genuine products, and hence enhance the retailer's reputation.

At the POS, the cashier will authenticate the product items before payment to help enhance the customer's confidence and to avoid possible future dispute. If the customer is satisfied and confirms payment, a sale record should complete the e-pedigree of these product items as sold, and update the back-end databases accordingly. Any further sale attempts of products with the same PIDs would be deemed suspicious.

Obviously, efficient and reliable authentication of product items in retail stores depends largely on the accuracy of reading the tag identification and the speed of data synchronization when product items are checked into back-store. As this safeguards genuine products and prevents injection of illicit items, the computer software and the RFID equipment should be integrated and fine-tuned for processing incoming goods and synchronizing product e-pedigree to the databases

Figure 9. An RFID-enabled apparel retail store

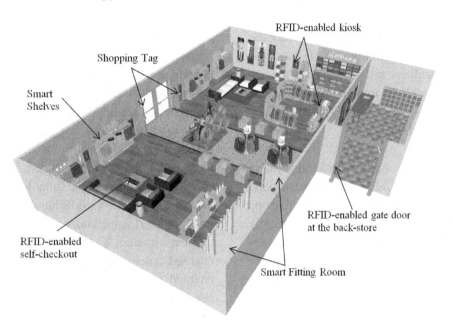

without hampering normal business operations. In this regard, the following practical issues need to be addressed.

1. There should be an effective way for PID acquisition and data synchronization to authenticate incoming products. However, misreading of tags, which often occurs due to inappropriate setup of RFID devices or software configuration, may impair the accuracy of product authentication and thus the integrity of product e-pedigree. Besides, fake or cloned products, which may be injected by malicious upstream supply chain partners, may tamper the process of authentication. Similarly, product theft, which could happen during distribution or transportation, may cause unwanted loss of items and then damage the integrity of product e-pedigree.

2. There should be a counterfeit-handling mechanism to screen out suspicious products with fake/cloned PIDs or dubious e-pedigree. This mechanism should deny circulation of such suspicious products in the supply

chain by recording them in back-end server databases.

3. Authentication rate, anti-counterfeiting rate, and anti-lost rate should be evaluated. Authentication rate refers to the success rate of confirming genuine products by the anti-counterfeiting system. Assuming there are 100 genuine products identified in a batch, but the system just only recognizes 99 items; the authentication rate is 99%. Similarly, anti-counterfeiting rate refers the system's capability of recognizing suspicious items, while anti-lost rate refers the capability of generating alerts about items that have been reported lost. Ideally, authentication rate, anti-counterfeiting rate and anti-lost rate should be 100%.

Due to the scope of this chapter, we focus only on the implementation issues of product authentication in the process of receiving and checking products into the back-store. To study these implementation issues, RFID-enabled facilities like gate doors are set up to emulate receipt of relatively high-end apparel products.

In the following sections, we first introduce the preparatory work, and then outline the design of the RFID-enabled facilities, and subsequently present methods to deal with the implementation issues.

Preparatory Work

As the track-and-trace anti-counterfeiting system relies on participation of all supply chain partners, implementation of such a system in retail shops warrants operations from the upstream supply chain nodes. Operations at upstream nodes establish and synchronize the product partial e-pedigree through the supply chain, from manufacturers to wholesalers.

The preparatory work for this case study is to generate e-pedigree for apparel product items in back-end databases and physically associate RFID tags with garments at item-level and case-level. The method to generate product e-pedigree has been presented in our previous work (Cheung and Choi, 2011), including selection of UHF tags, format of EPC data schema, and e-pedigree data model. It should be noted that these e-pedigree data are crucial to evaluation of authentication rate and anti-fake rate.

Front-End RFID-Enabled Facilities for Product Receipt in Back-Store

Traditional checking is mainly based on human operations. So product counting and defect/fake detection are inefficient and unreliable. Without hampering the normal operation of receiving products, the time between container loading and storing products into the back-store is considered a suitable period to check the authenticity using track-and-trace anti-counterfeiting system. Hence, traditional checking is replaced by the automatic operation of RFID-enabled anti-counterfeiting system.

The processes of the RFID-enabled product receipt and authentication include four main steps, namely Product Identification, Product Authentication, Counterfeiting-handling, and Product E-pedigree Synchronization.

Product Identification requires a range of RFID facilities for reading of batch items. Currently, RFID-enabled tunnels and gate doors or hand-held readers are frequently used in industry for advanced supply chain management. An RFID-enabled tunnel is fixed and suitable for identifying products in box-level, while hand-held readers are much more flexible and suitable for identifying products in item-level. Compared with RFID-enabled tunnels and hand-held readers, RFID-enabled gate doors are more advantageous for batch product receipt (pallet-level) in back-store.

In this design, RFID-enabled gate doors are selected as the main RFID equipment for product identification. Besides, hand-held readers are also prepared for subsidiary use. This is also highly recommended for practical implementation in industry. Product Authentication and E-pedigree Synchronization are conducted by the back-end anti-counterfeiting system.

Figure 10 shows the layout design of the RFID-enabled facilities for product receipt. Based on the product authentication procedures, three zones are designated for all operations, namely Identification Zone, Authentication/Screening Zone and Counterfeit-handling Buffer Zone.

In the Identification Zone, an RFID-enabled gate door is set up as the gate door to the retail back-store. The number of RFID readers mounted to the door frame and the height of the readers can be adjusted according to the application requirements in different environments.

The Authentication Zone includes an Internet-connected PC which runs the backroom inventory management application, and a display screen which shows the authentication results for the products passing through the Identification Zone. Visual and audio alerts would be given in real-time if fake or lost items are detected.

Figure 10. RFID-enabled product receipt facilities

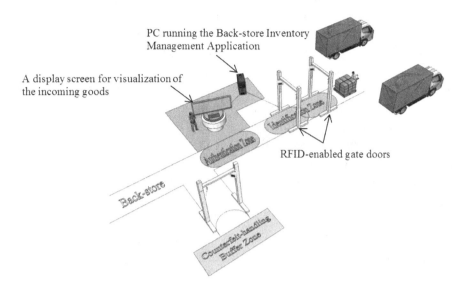

Based on the results from the Authentication Zone, products are then delivered to the back-store or Counterfeit-handling Buffer Zone, respectively. Operations in the buffer zone consist of unpacking the container or checking the item individually. However, it should be noted that the rules for handling suspicious products should follow business contacts and negotiations between the supply chain partners concerned.

Methods for Tag Identification and Product Authentication

To facilitate product item identification, the anti-counterfeiting system takes advantage of product containment relationship information which is captured / synchronized in the upstream supply chain nodes. By referring to the containment relationship data, the system will generate alerts in real time if there is misreading (including missed reading and reading error) when products pass through the gate door.

From a hardware perspective, redundant but necessary RFID-enabled gate doors can be set up. In cases of misreading, further processes, such as slowing down passing speed, spinning the pallet in the reading range, are conducted to confirm the number of product items. After confirmation, products are sent to the Authentication Zone.

The process of product authentication relies on the back-end product e-pedigree data, including release records, transaction records and sale records. The detail of the mechanism is available in our previous work (Choi and Poon, 2008).

There may be four possible authentication results, namely (AR1) the item has release record, plausible transaction records, and the e-pedigree is complete; (AR2) the item has release record but the e-pedigree is implausible/incomplete; (AR3) the item does not has release record; (AR4) invalid status of the upstream company.

Only cartons containing all product items with AR1 would be accepted and confirmed. Others found to contain any suspicious, fake, or missing items (even if only one item) would be transferred to the Counterfeit-handling Buffer Zone.

Counterfeit-Handling Mechanism

The Counterfeit-handling Buffer Zone, as showed in Figure 10, is designed for temporary storage of suspicious products for further handling.

For items with authentication result AR4, they have not been processed by any valid upstream company and hence there is no need to further identify or authenticate them. As such, there will be no updating and synchronization of e-pedigree to the back-end servers.

For items with AR2, they might have been sold before, or wrongly distributed, or illicitly cloned, while for AR3 items, they are apparently injected. The anti-counterfeiting system should marked "fake" in the e-pedigree of all AR2 and AR3 items to prevent further transactions.

Data Capturing and Processing CSB for Product Collocation

To win in highly competitive apparel retail business, it is vital for a company to enhance CSE, which refers to a total summary of a customer's interaction with the retail company beginning before he walks into the store and ending long after he leaves (Bikshorn, 2011). We consider the totality of CSE as being made up of three phases of interaction experience, namely pre-sales, in-store, and after-sales.

Before going to shop in a retail store, customers may check the company's website, or call to enquire, or rely on advertisement or even hearsay about the prospective products of their interest. Good pre-sales experience helps attract customers to visit the store in person.

When customers come to shop in the store, they often expect proactive, informative and pleasant interactions with products and/or the store staff, such that their needs are fully satisfied. Such in-store shopping experience hugely affects the purchase decisions of customers, and is particularly crucial to retail business.

After sale, customers often expect an interactive channel for them to express feedbacks or seek follow-ups on the purchased products, if necessary, in order to establish and maintain brand loyalty and long-term relationship with the company.

In our research, we focus mainly on enhancement of in-store shopping experience by proposing an RFID-based system that facilitates provision of personalized and interactive shopping service for customers.

In a traditional apparel retail store, the shopping services provided may not meet customers' needs due to a number of factors, such as difficulties in finding target products; out-of-stocks; a lack of professional assistance for selection of products; and long waiting for apparel fitting and payments. Any of such problems may aggravate CSE considerably.

Using item-level RFID, the in-store inventory of individual products can be tracked in real time. Moreover, CSB can be captured and exploited accordingly. For example, what product items have individual customers browsed and/or tried on, which zones and how long they have visited to and stayed in, and what they have purchased, can be efficiently captured and analysed. Taking advantage of such information, management team can make appropriate policies in responses to customer needs and to increase operation efficiency. As a result, better CSE can be provided to help improve sales.

We therefore propose a smart product collocation shopping recommendation (SPCSR) application for automatic generation of product collocation recommendation lists for customers. This module helps enhance CSE by providing intelligent marketing assistance for customers to select the right fashion product items.

In this module, a virtual shopping basket (VSB) is provided for each individual customer to record the product items intended to buy. As such, the customer does not need to carry a physical shopping basket / trolley around in the store for the interested items before making payment.

The VSB consists of a shopping tag driven a set of computer applications. It is an UHF RFID tag with a UID to be distributed to each individual incoming customer at the entrance of the store. Customers can take a tag at appropriate locations, often near to smart shelves in the store for easy access.

With a shopping tag, a customer can cart his / her selected product items into a temporary carted-item table of the shopping behaviour database. This can be done at a kiosk, which is equipped with a touch-screen tablet and an RFID reader, or by using an RFID-enabled mobile device, such as the customer's mobile phone, which is installed with the appropriate application.

The carted items associated with a particular customer are delivered to the customer after confirming the purchase by presenting the shopping tag at an RFID-enabled POS or a self-checkout kiosk. At the same time, the e-pedigrees of the sold items are updated, while the shopping tag is recycled for reuse by erasing all the information of the VSB associated this shopping tag stored.

In this way, customers can easily add their preferred product items into the VSB via either the kiosks in the store or their smart phones. They can be relieved from carrying a physical shopping basket around in the store, but to fully enjoy their shopping. More importantly, data of CSB can be collected conveniently for analyses and subsequent generation of product collocation recommendations, when the customer tries on a garment either in a smart mirror or a smart fitting room.

The SPCSR module contains a fuzzy screening algorithm to generate product collocation recommendations by computing and analysing the levels of product category popularity and product category fashion of a product item.

Product category popularity is defined as how popular of a product item is among customers during a period of time. The level of product category popularity is obtained by calculating and statistically analysing a number of elements (Decker et al., 2003; Kardes et al., 2011), including:

1. **The number of a product category browsed by customers:** An RFID tagged item is hanged on a smart shelf, which is installed with an RFID reader. When a

particular item is taken by a customer from the shelf to outside the reading range of the reader, it is counted as being browsed once. Subsequently, the data are stored in the database.

2. **The number of items to be carted by customers:** The number of items added by customers to the VSP via kiosks or mobile devices.

3. The number of items sold.

On the other hand, product category fashion is defined as how matching of a product category with other product categories. There are a number of product category properties, such as sort, size, colour, and length. Only those important properties to apparel collocation (Liu and Hou, 2009; Wong et al., 2009) are selected to calculate the fashion degree of a product category in this research, they are:

1. **Sort:** The sort of a product is classified as man and woman. The sort of the product determines how it is suitable for a male or a female customer.

2. **Type:** The type of a product means it belongs to which one of design patterns of apparel items, such as tee, skirt, etc.

3. **Colour:** The colour of a product.

As discussed in the proposed EPC numbering scheme, 20 bits in EPC memory is used to represent each product's sort, type, and colour for generation of product collocations.

Figure 11 shows the flow of the proposed VSB. When a customer with a shopping tag firstly starts a shopping journey, his or her shopping behaviour data, such as the number of a product category browsed and the number of items carted, are captured by the RFID readers installed at shelves and kiosks.

Such behaviour data are then stored into the CSB database of Data Management Module while product properties are on-line recorded during

Figure 11. The flow of proposed SPCSR application

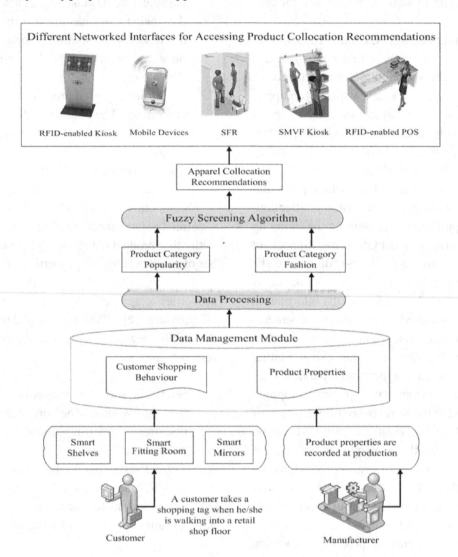

production. Within Data Processing, the behaviour data are further aggregated and calculated to obtain the popularity levels of each product category. At the same time, the fashion levels of each product category are obtained from the product properties. Subsequently, the levels of product category popularity and the levels of product category fashion are inputted to the proposed fuzzy screening algorithm for generating product collocation recommendations of either browsed or carted items. Finally, the customer can access the results of product collocation via different networked interfaces, including RFID-enabled kiosks, personalized mobile devices, SFRs, SMVF kiosks, and RFID-enabled POS.

The proposed SPCSR module can be expected to provide professional assistance to customers, who even do not have adequate apparel knowledge, to choose matching garments easily. Hence, better cross-selling can be achieved and sales volume boosted.

DISCUSSION AND FUTURE WORK

The proposed item-level RFID-enabled store management system, when fully implemented, would be a practical tool to achieve omni-channel retailing for overall business improvement. In particular, it can be expected to bring about a number of advantages:

1. **Improved Operation Efficiency and Reduced Labour Cost:** The system can be used for automatic product receipt into the back-store by reading the PIDs of multiple product items for authentication and recording into the database. Moreover, it can track and update the in-store and back-store inventory to avoid over-stock or out-of-stock, relieving store staff from having to count inventory manually for subsequent inventory replenishments and reorder. As a result, operation efficiency and manual labour can be reduced.
2. **Enhanced Customer Experience and Differentiation:** The system can collect and analyse CSB to provide individual shopping recommendations, such as product collocation and shopping journey. It can also provide interactive virtual and physical services, self checkout and product authentication services. Such services help customers locate preferred items easily, and cut queuing time for fitting and payment. As a result, sales would be enhanced substantially.
3. **Increase Sales:** The system allows salespersons to spend less time on routine manual operations, and more time on providing services to customers. As a result, sales profits can be expected to improve.

Currently, the functions and architectural design of the proposed system have been formulated, while the major implementation issues are being studied. As part of the system, we are currently implementing an RFID-enabled application receiving and authenticating products at back-store, and another for product collocation recommendation and marketing. Implementation issues, including product item-related and all transactions data synchronization in a store, reading rate at the RFID-enabled gate doors, and methods for capturing CSB data and subsequent processing the CSB data for generating product collocations, are being addressed.

For future work, the proposed databases will be enhanced and implemented. The intelligent data-mining algorithms will be integrated to process huge amounts of item-level product data and the related transactions data for subsequent retail store management applications, and provision of more differentiated customer services and individual marketing. Moreover, smart mirrors and smart fitting, self-checkout, and product anti-theft and anti-counterfeiting will be integrated.

CONCLUSION

This chapter presents an item-level RFID-enabled retail store management system for enhancing retail store operations and CSE to achieve omni-channel retailing, and hence improve business.

The proposed system is integrated with an RFID-based track-an-track anti-counterfeiting system, which establishes a trustworthy e-pedigree for tracking individual product items, from manufacturing to retailing in the supply chain. It can track and trace product items in retail stores to facilitate various applications and services, including back-store inventory management, smart shelve management, interactive smart mirrors and smart fitting, self-checkout, personalized advertising and promotion, product theft prevention and anti-counterfeiting; as a result, customer experience and differentiation, brand image, and the store operation efficiency, and hence sales, may be improved accordingly. Besides, an apparel retail store is presented to elaborate some implementation issues regarding prevention of fake product injection into a back-store. Other issues of capturing CSB and subsequent generation of product collocation recommendations for individual customers are also discussed.

As a conclusion, the proposed system is deemed a practical tool, when fully implemented, that integrates and exploit item-level RFID for retail business improvement. For further development, it may be worthwhile to extend the system to facilitate cooperative and co-opetitive processes within and across supply chains. This may require incorporating modelling techniques like multi-agent and multi-tier networking to handle issues of information asymmetry, decentralized and distributed decision-making etc.

REFERENCES

Bikshorn, M. (2011). From Customer Service to Customer Experience Enhancement. *Customer Experience Reporting*. Retrieved in March 8, 2011, from http://www.serviceexcellencegroup.com

Boeck, H., Roy, J., Durif, F., & Grégoire, M. (2011). The effect of perceived intrusion on consumers' attitude towards using an RFID-based marketing program. *Procedia Computer Science*, 5, 841–848. doi:10.1016/j.procs.2011.07.116

Bridge, (2009). *Building radio frequency identification solutions for the global environment*. Retrieved August 20, 2013, http://www.bridge-project.eu/data/File/BRIDGE_Final_report.pdf

Cheung, H. H., & Choi, S. H. (2011). Implementation issues in RFID-based anti-counterfeiting systems. *Computers in Industry*, 62(7), 708–718. doi:10.1016/j.compind.2011.04.001

Choi, S. H., & Poon, C. H. (2008). An RFID-based anti-counterfeiting system. *International Journal of Computer Science*, 35(1), 1–12.

Condea, C., Thiesse, F., & Fleisch, E. (2012). RFID-enabled shelf replenishment with backroom monitoring in retail stores. *Decision Support Systems*, 52(4), 839–849. doi:10.1016/j.dss.2011.11.018

Decker, C., Kubach, U., & Beigl, M. (2003). Revealing the Retail Black Box by Interaction Sensing. In Proceedings of the 23rd International Conference on Distributed Computing Systems (pp. 328-333). Washington, DC: IEEE Computer Society.

Dyer, G. (2006, April 20). Louis Vuitton sues Carrefour in China over 'fake' handbags. *Financial Times*.

EPCglobal Inc. (2009). *EPC™ radio-frequency identity protocols class-1 generation-2 RFID protocol for communications at 860 MHz–960 MHz v1.2.* Author.

Ganesan, S., George, M., Jap, S., Palmatier, R. W., & Weitz, B. (2009). Supply chain management and retailer performance: Emerging trends, issues, and implications for research and practice. *Journal of Retailing*, 85(1), 84–94. doi:10.1016/j.jretai.2008.12.001

Hou, J. L., & Chen, T. G. (2011). An RFID-based shopping service system for retailers. *Advanced Engineering Informatics*, 25(1), 103–115. doi:10.1016/j.aei.2010.04.003

Jones, P., Clarke-Hill, C., Comfort, D., Hillier, D., & Shears, P. (2004). Radio frequency identification in retailing and privacy and public policy issues. *Management Research News*, 27(8/9), 46–60. doi:10.1108/01409170410784563

Jung, I. C., & Kwon, Y. S. (2011). Grocery customer behavior analysis using RFID-based shopping paths data. *World Academy of Science. Engineering and Technology*, 59, 1404–1408.

Kardes, F. R., Cronley, M. L., & Cline, T. W. (2011). Consumer Behavior. Mason, OH: South-Western, Cengage Learning.

Kwok, S. K., & Wu, K. W. (2009). RFID-based intra-supply chain in textile industry. *Industrial Management & Data Systems, 109*(9), 1166–1178. doi:10.1108/02635570911002252

Liard, M. (2009). *RFID Item-level Tagging in Fashion Apparel and Footwear*. ABI Research.

Liu, L., & Hou, J. H. (2009). *Costume Aesthetics*. Beijing, China: Chemical Industry Press.

Macro, A., & D, . (2012). Using system dynamics to access the impact of RFID technology on retail operations. *International Journal of Production Economics, 135*(1), 333–344. doi:10.1016/j.ijpe.2011.08.009

Metzger, C., Thiesse, F., Gershwin, S., & Fleisch, E. (2013). The impact of false-negative reads on the performance of RFID-based shelf inventory control policies. *Computers & Operations Research, 40*(7), 1864–1873. doi:10.1016/j.cor.2013.02.001

Ngai, E., & Gunasekaran, A. (2009). RFID adoptions: Issues and challenges. *International Journal of Enterprise Information Systems, 5*(1), 1–8. doi:10.4018/jeis.2009010101

Rekik, Y., Sahin, E., & Dallery, Y. (2008). Analysis of the impact of the RFID technology on reducing product misplacement errors at retail stores. *International Journal of Production Economics, 112*(1), 264–278. doi:10.1016/j.ijpe.2006.08.024

Szmerekovsky, J. S., & Zhang, J. (2008). Coordination and adoption of item-level RFID with vendor managed inventory. *International Journal of Production Economics, 114*(1), 388–398. doi:10.1016/j.ijpe.2008.03.002

Tajima, M. (2007). Strategic value of RFID in supply chain management. *Journal of Purchasing & Supply Chain Management, 13*(4), 261–273. doi:10.1016/j.pursup.2007.11.001

Violino, B. (2013). Marks & Spencer rolls out RFID to all its stores. *RFID Journal*. Retrieved May 4, 2013, from http://www.rfidjournal.com/articles/view?10536

Vlachos, I. P. (2013). (Article in Press). A hierarchical model of the impact of RFID practices on retail supply chain performance. *Expert Systems with Applications*. doi:10.1016/j.eswa.2013.07.006

Wong, W. K., Zeng, X. H., Au, W. M. R., Mok, P. Y., & Leung, S. Y. S. (2009). A fashion mix-and-match expert system for fashion retailers using fuzzy screening approach. *Expert Systems with Applications, 36*(2), 1750–1764. doi:10.1016/j.eswa.2007.12.047

KEY TERMS AND DEFINITIONS

Customer Shopping Behaviour (CSB): A process by which a customer searches for, selects, purchases, uses, and disposes of goods and services, in satisfaction of his needs and wants.

Customer Shopping Experience (CSE): A total summary of a customer's interaction with the retail company beginning before he walks into the store and ending long after he leaves.

E-Pedigree: An electronic record of the movement of a product item.

Item-Level RFID: A C1G2 UHF RFID tag attached to a product item and programmed with a PID to facilitate tracking and tracing of the movement of the product item in the supply chain.

Omni-Channel Retailing: An innovative supply chain strategy to provide customer shopping services via all available shopping channels, such as mobile devices, computers, television, and catalogues. Item-level RFID empowers omni-channel retailing because this technology facilitates real-time tracking and tracing of product items to enhance product visibility and inventory control in the supply chain.

Product Identifier (PID): A unique number formed by combining 96 bits of EPC with a hard-coded UID in the TID memory bank of a C1G2 UHF RFID tag for identification of a product item.

Track-and-Trace: A process of determining the status, including the current and past locations, ownership and other information, of a product item in a supply chain.

Chapter 2

CostRFID:
Design and Evaluation of a Cost Estimation Method and Tool for RFID Integration Projects

Tobias Engel
Technische Universität München, Germany

Suparna Goswami
Technische Universität München, Germany

Andreas Englschalk
Technische Universität München, Germany

Helmut Krcmar
Technische Universität München, Germany

ABSTRACT

Although many firms have initiated RFID projects, they often face significant difficulties in integrating RFID systems into their existing IT landscape. One such difficulty is the upfront estimation of the cost of the RFID integration project. This chapter addresses this issue by using a design science approach to provide a cost calculation for RFID integration projects. Drawing from literature in the fields of information systems and RFID, software engineering and supply chain management, the authors develop the cost calculation method that is then implemented in a prototype. The prototype is developed and evaluated in an iterative fashion using focus groups, RFID experts, and the cognitive walkthrough method. The authors contribute to theory by proposing a new cost calculation method to estimate the costs of RFID integration projects. Practical implications include a more accurate estimation of the cost of integrating RFID systems into the existing IT landscape and a risk reduction for RFID projects.

DOI: 10.4018/978-1-4666-6308-4.ch002

INTRODUCTION

RFID offers several advantages over traditional auto-ID technologies such as higher object identification speed, higher storage capacity, and allows firms to improve processes in the fields of manufacturing, distribution, transportation and retail (Roh, Kunnathur, & Tarafdar, 2009; Roussos, 2006; Rutner, Waller, & Mentzer, 2004; Thiesse, 2005; Want, 2006; Weinstein, 2005). Furthermore, RFID-technology allows for improved data quality and information availability, and therefore enhances intra-organizational operations (Fosso Wamba & Chatfield, 2009), and increases information visibility among supply chain partners (Delen, Hardgrave, & Sharda, 2007; L. Lee, Fiedler, & Smith, 2008). Therefore, many firms are considering investments into RFID technology or have already invested in the technology (L. Lee, et al., 2008). One major aspect of RFID implementation projects is the integration of RFID systems into the existing information technology (IT) systems of the organization so that it can enhance business processes (Strueker & Gille, 2008), and allow firms to optimize information and material flow (Fosso Wamba & Chatfield, 2009). However, the integration of RFID-systems into the existing IT-systems of firms is a complex process that can result in several implementation problems. In particular, the upfront estimation of RFID system integration costs can be difficult due to the complexity and uniqueness of RFID projects, leading to a wrong estimation of the cost and effort required for executing the integration project (Angeles, 2005).

Having relatively accurate project cost estimation is an important factor in the decision making process of firms during the early stages of project planning, and is a well-known issue in the field of information systems (IS) (Boehm, Abts, & Chulani, 2000). Realistic expectations and the definition of clear objectives are necessary for IT projects in general (Hartman & Ashrafi, 2002; Reel, 1999; Smithson & Hirschheim, 1998), and for RFID software projects in particular (Dickson, 2007). Since RFID projects have to integrate hardware and software into the existing IT infrastructure, traditional software cost estimation methods are not suitable for the upfront cost estimation of RFID projects. While RFID system integration has been identified as a major cost factor in RFID-projects, the lack of an appropriate cost estimation method still represents a major drawback for the widespread adoption of the technology (Asif & Mandviwalla, 2005). Being able to calculate the cost at the project outset in advance can help organizational decision-makers to decide if and when to carry out the implementation project, and also decide on the various applications that they can design around the technology by integrating it with other existing IT systems within the organization. Therefore, this research aims to develop a cost estimation method for RFID projects specifically focusing on the integration of RFID into existing IT systems within the organization.

Considering the inter-disciplinary aspects of RFID technology, we draw from the domains of information systems, auto-identification technology and software engineering to develop a cost estimation method for RFID integration projects. The cost estimation method developed is based on established cost estimation methods that exist for software development projects, and in particular draws upon the COCOTS model that incorporates commercial-of-the-shelf (COTS) components in the cost estimation of software projects (Abts, Boehm, & Clark, 2000). Since a typical RFID system infrastructure comprises off-the-shelf components that are configurable (such as tags, readers, middleware) (Maier, 2005; Thiesse, 2005), the COCOTS model is particularly applicable in the context of RFID projects. We further adapt the COCOTS model to take RFID-specific requirements into account, and develop a new cost estimation method for RFID integration projects. The developed cost estimation method is used as a basis for designing the RFID cost calculator tool. The iterative development and evaluation of the RFID Cost Calculator is congruent with the design science paradigm and the three cycle view on information system design as proposed by Hevner (2007). The cost estimation method and the cost calculation tool can support managers and practitioners in calculating RFID-system integration costs more accurately, and can therefore help in determining the economic viability of RFID integration projects. For instance, the tool offers the possibility of simulating several RFID application scenarios and then estimating their costs in order to gain a better understanding of emerging costs in RFID integration projects beforehand, or choosing among various RFID use cases that should be implemented first. Further, the tool supports the controlling of RFID-projects.

The rest of this book chapter is structured as follows. In the next section, we provide an overview on RFID technology and the relevant RFID-infrastructure. Furthermore, existing cost estimation methods are introduced and their applicability in the context of RFID system integration is described. Concluding the theoretical background section, the design science paradigm which serves as the theoretical framework during the design exercise, is presented. In the design section, the problem relevance using a simple use case scenario is demonstrated followed by a detailed description of the design and evaluation of the RFID cost calculator tool. In the subsequent sections, we provide a discussion of our findings, research limitations and implications and a conclusion.

BACKGROUND AND RELATED WORK

In this section, we provide an overview of RFID technology and describe the basic IT infrastructure configurations which are necessary for RFID implementation and integration. Furthermore, we analyze software cost estimation methods and evaluate their applicability to RFID projects. Fi-

nally, we introduce the design science paradigm, which serves as a basis for our methodological approach.

Basics of RFID Systems

The components of a typical RFID system can be categorized into three different layers according to their level of abstraction from the underlying physical processes. An illustrative architecture of IT components that are used in RFID projects, adapted from (Dittmann & Thiesse, 2005), is depicted in Figure 1.

The *infrastructure layer* includes RFID transponders and RFID readers, referred to as components. These components are used to identify physical objects and to acquire data via electromagnetic waves. The RFID transponder, also referred to as RFID tag, is a combination of a transmitter and a responder (Roussos & Kostakos, 2009), and has to be attached to every item that needs to be identified. The RFID reader acquires the data using the built-in antennae and radio waves and forwards it to the integration layer.

The *integration layer* contains middleware and edgeware and integrates the RFID reading devices into existing IT-systems allowing data exchange between the components (Thiesse & Gross, 2006). Edgeware components are part of the middleware and preprocess data through filtering, correction or format transformation. Edgeware is also used to coordinate the communication between the RFID hardware and middleware (Hansen & Gillert, 2006).

There are two possible strategies for the integration of RFID components into existing IT-systems. The first possibility is to implement an interface directly into the IT-system or the RFID-system. This strategy faces the problem of economic feasibility especially with regards to big sized IT-backend systems and their high level of complexity. The second possibility is to use enterprise application integration (EAI) which offers a range of opportunities. The EAI compo-

Figure 1. RFID components, adapted from Dittmann and Thiesse (2005)

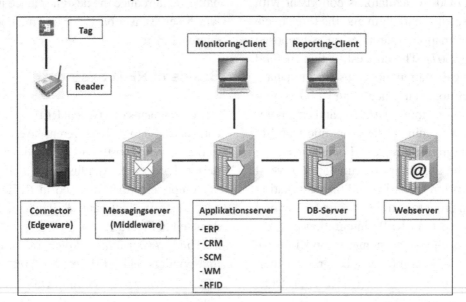

nent is located between the RFID system and the corporate IT-backend system and enables data exchange between the systems. In one direction, the EAI component forwards information to the backend system through standardized protocols such as XML messages. In the other direction, the EAI component receives commands from the backend system and delivers them to the RFID system (Fleisch & Mattern, 2005). It is possible to include any desired system into this infrastructure by the use of interfaces or data mapping (Krcmar, 2010).

The *application layer* describes the processing of RFID data using IT-backend systems. Information can be shared with internal systems or inter-organizational networks (Thiesse & Gross, 2006). The application server enables the separation of processing logic from data storage and presentation. In RFID systems, the application server hosts every component used to gather, analyze and store RFID data. Additionally, the application server can host IT infrastructure components such as enterprise resource planning, customer resource management, supply chain management or warehouse management systems.

RFID information is stored on the database server which can only be accessed in read mode by complementary systems. Moreover, monitoring clients can be used to trace the RFID system in real time, while the reporting client files reports and analyses in order to ensure the efficiency of business processes. Security is ensured by the combined usage of a firewall, a webserver and web-client ensuring data encryption and protection against internal, external and internet attacks on the system (Krcmar, 2010).

All components and systems discussed in this section were considered in the process of developing the RFID cost calculation method.

Past Research on Software Cost Estimation

The purpose of a cost estimation method is to indicate cost sources and factors influencing costs in order to enhance accuracy in the evaluation of upcoming tasks and efforts (Dowie, 2009; Schuster, 2012; Vollmann, 1990). Influencing factors can be categorized as product specific and project specific. Product specific factors include the quantity and complexity of tasks as well as the expected quality of results. Project specific factors include basic parameters of the project such as estimated length, level of know-how, programming and modeling languages, development environment and many more (Sneed, 2005). Due to the variety of parameters, each estimation method is based on an individual set of factors (Wieczorrek & Mertens, 2011). In the course of our literature review, we analyzed cost estimation methods from the domains of software engineering and information systems including function-point analysis, data-point analysis and object-point analysis (Bundschuh & Fabry, 2000; Sneed, 2005). We found that the majority of the reviewed cost estimation methods were applicable to the development of new code, whereas RFID projects are usually realized through the use of commercial-off-the-shelf (COTS) components. Commonly expected benefits of COTS components include reduced development time, lower costs and higher product quality (Abts, et al., 2000). Therefore, COCOTS - a cost estimation method based on COTS components, and derived as an extension of COCOMO I and COCOMO II can be considered as relevant to RFID-system integration projects, due to its focus on system integration and its applicability for reusable components (Abts, et al., 2000).

COCOMO is an abbreviation for the Constructive Cost Model which was developed in 1981. Cost estimation using COCOMO I is based on code instructions in the form of lines of code (LOC). With the help of predefined formulas, COCOMO allows for calculation of project costs regarding labor effort and system complexity. However, since neither product quality nor project specific parameters are taken into account as influencing factors, the use of this model is not plausible from a present-day perspective.

The COCOMO II model extends COCOMO I, and uses a three-step approach for cost estimation. In the first step, the early prototyping phase, the effort for developing a reusable prototype is estimated. The aim of this estimation is to give a first impression of the overall project effort. The second step, the early design phase, takes place after the definition of system requirements and following the design of an early draft. The draft is then translated into lines of code (LOC) and used for the cost estimation. In the third step, the post-architecture level, the effort estimation takes place in hindsight of the entire development process. This step uses LOC which are derived from the final architecture and offers more detailed insights into support and maintenance efforts (Boehm, Madachy, & Steece, 2000; Gencel, Heldal, & Lind, 2009; Zhang, 2009). While COCOMO II takes a more holistic view of the project in order to estimate development costs, it is still primarily based on lines of code and therefore cannot be used in the context of RFID integration projects, where there is little effort involved in code development (Boehm, Madachy, et al., 2000).

The COCOTS estimation method extends COCOMO II by incorporating commercial-of-the-shelf (COTS) components in the calculation of costs. COTS components offer instant availability for use with standards compliance, therefore fulfilling modern software development requirements like the implementation of various standards, protocols, toolkits and technologies (Vigder & Dean, 1997). The COCOTS model identifies four phases which depict the software development process. First, initial and detailed assessments have to be conducted to arrive at a selection of necessary components. The second step, tailoring, addresses the integration of the selected components into the existing system. The glue code development and associated test cycles complement the system with necessary functionalities and further ensure the interoperability of system components. In the final phase, system volatility, code changes and updates by the manufacturer that may result in training effort are evaluated (Abts, et al., 2000; Naunchan & Sutivong, 2007; Yang, Boehm, & Wu, 2006).

Although, none of the analyzed cost estimation methods fully satisfy the necessary criteria required for RFID system integration projects, they do provide partial solutions. RFID projects are inter-disciplinary in nature and their configuration is usually very specific to the organization. Therefore, while RFID projects make use of COTS components, there is also significant effort involved in fine tuning the project to handle the specific requirements of the organization. Therefore, based on our literature review, we believe that a cost estimation method for RFID projects could draw from COCOMO I & II and COCOTS as relevant bases for the calculation of information system integration costs for RFID-projects.

Design Science Paradigm

We chose the design science paradigm (March & Smith, 1995) as the research methodology guiding the systematic development of the RFID cost calculator tool (Hevner, 2007). Design science is technology-orientated research that includes the creation of artifacts and its assessment against criteria of value or utility (March & Smith, 1995). Constructs, models, methods or instantiations are outputs of design science and can be referred to as design artifacts (March & Smith, 1995). More specifically, drawing on three cycle view of information systems design that comprises relevance cycle, design cycle and rigor cycle (see Figure 2) as proposed by Hevner (2007), we used an iterative process to design, develop and evaluate the RFID cost calculator.

In our research, the design artifact is manifested in the form of the RFID cost calculator prototype application. Knowledge base of software engineering and existing cost calculation methods substantiate the design of the artifact (Hevner, March, Park, & Ram, 2004). Building and evaluating the artifact are the two major activities in any design science research. According to Hevner (2007) the *design cycle* process is an iterative loop, allowing the generation, evaluation and optimization of alternatives until a satisfactory status of the artifact is accomplished. Functionality, completeness, consistency, accuracy, performance, reliability and usability are the main evaluation criteria for design artifacts (Peffers et al., 2006). The necessary requirements for the design arti-

Figure 2. Design science research cycles, adapted from Hevner (2007)

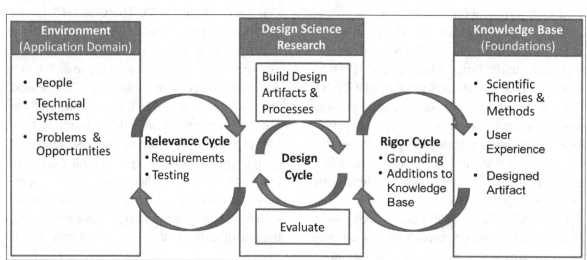

fact have to be identified in the specific context of each application to ensure a stable basis for building, optimizing and evaluating the artifact. Additionally, the results of the artifact need to be iteratively studied and evaluated in the application domain through testing. Eliciting requirements from the field testing and the application forms the relevance cycle (Hevner, 2007). The iterative process of examining the design artifact on the foundation of existing scientific knowledge and the derivation of practical and theoretical insights is referred to as the *rigor cycle*.

RFID COST CALCULATOR DESIGN ARTIFACT

The development process of the RFID cost calculator is based on the three cycle view (see Figure 2) discussed above. We first elaborate on the problem relevance, followed by a description of the design of the artifact based on existing cost calculation methods adapted to the RFID-context. Subsequently, the evaluation of the artifact is conducted through the use of expert interviews (Myers & Newman, 2007).

Problem Relevance

Let us put forward a scenario that illustrates the importance of cost estimation in anticipation of the RFID system integration process. A medium to large sized retail store includes a storage area with incoming and outgoing goods departments, a sales area and a point of sale. From the retailer's perspective, RFID can increase efficiency by improving internal product flows, and allows personalized communication with the customer (Loebbecke, 2005). Furthermore, incoming goods equipped with RFID tags can be handled in an automated manner (Rutner, et al., 2004) offering the possibility to optimize storage surface, improve inventory visibility and synchronize data with IT-

backend systems. Therefore, RFID can support the detection of wrongly located inventory (Maloni & DeWolf, 2006; Richardson, 2004), thus improving product availability (Loebbecke, 2005) and also help with theft prevention measures. Further, at the point of sale, checkout procedures can be accelerated leading to more customer satisfaction, better utilization of store area and a potential to appoint employees differently.

Notwithstanding the aforementioned benefits, short term payoff is uncertain in many cases (Laubacher, Kothari, Malone, & Subirana, 2005) and about 50 percent of all RFID projects fail (Vojdani, Spitznagel, & Resch, 2006). In our example, the retail store has to invest in hardware and software, accompanied by an integration of the RFID components into its existing IT infrastructure (Strueker & Gille, 2008). RFID-system integration costs have significant influence on the success of initial implementation (Maloni & DeWolf, 2006). The approximate percentage of RFID-system integration costs ranges from 22% (Maurno, 2005) to over 80% (Trunick, 2005). However, textbook guidelines for managers are often restricted to general illustrations of RFID technology and system integration costs are only scarcely considered (Angeles, 2005; Karkkainen, 2003).

A model to assess RFID and simulate several scenarios can offer guidance to managers during the project rollout (Asif & Mandviwalla, 2005), and can provide relatively accurate predictions of system integration costs that are essential to the project planning of RFID-projects (Dickson, 2007). While there is some research about cost-benefits of RFID-usage over time (Tsai & Huang, 2012; Uckelmann, 2012), there is little research for quantifying the IT-integration costs for RFID projects in advance. Moreover, the application of conventional cost estimation methods is complex (Boehm, Madachy, et al., 2000) and cannot be applied directly to RFID-system integration projects. Our research fills this gap by designing and evaluating a cost estimation method and tool that takes into account the specific requirements of RFID-system integration projects.

Prototype Design

The RFID cost calculator allows firms to calculate project costs upfront for the integration of a RFID-system into an existing information system environment. The RFID cost calculator considers project attributes and processes, can be adapted according to the existing information systems infrastructure in the organization, and incorporates RFID specific requirements and conditions.

As discussed in the theoretical background section, a RFID system is made up of three layers and comprises several components that contribute towards the cost of the overall project. Many of these components such as the tags, readers, edgeware are standard components that are commercially manufactured, and require very little customization. Therefore, these components can be considered as commercial-off-the-shelf

(COTS) components, thus making COCOTS a suitable choice that can serve as a basis for the development of RFID cost estimation method. Further, we drew from various aspects of CO-COMO I and COCOMO II in order to develop a comprehensive cost calculation method. Therefore, our method ensures a complete coverage of all RFID-components and systems (see also Figure 1) for an upfront cost calculation. This method was then used as a basis to develop the RFID cost estimation tool prototype.

Steps in the Design of RFID Cost Calculator

We followed the University of Southern California Center for Software Engineering (USC-CSE) multi-step modeling methodology that has been used for software cost estimation models (Abts, et al., 2000; Chulani, 1998). This modeling methodology consists of seven steps, which build on each other and iterate in case of any necessary refinement (see Figure 3).

Figure 3. Steps in the design of RFID cost calculator

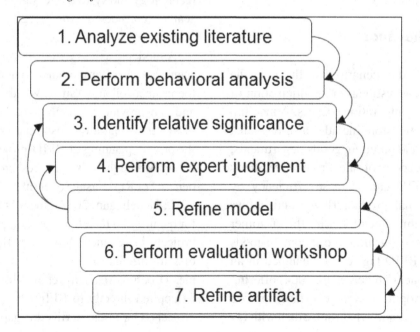

1. Analyze existing literature
2. Perform behavioral analysis
3. Identify relative significance
4. Perform expert judgment
5. Refine model
6. Perform evaluation workshop
7. Refine artifact

As a first step, we reviewed the existing literature in RFID and other auto-identification technology, and software engineering, more specifically software cost estimation. The purpose behind conducting this literature review was to gain an understanding of RFID-systems, their basic infrastructure and the various components involved, and also the different kinds of cost calculation methods that are already being used in practice. The next step involved a behavioral analysis. The purpose of the behavioral analysis was to broaden our understanding of existing processes, components, requirements and cost estimation methods. This was followed by identifying relative significance, i.e., we analyzed current calculation problems and related reasons for failures of RFID-system integration projects. Furthermore, we analyzed factors influencing RFID-system integration, and analyzed the relative significance of the various factors on the overall cost of the RFID integration project, as these would then be incorporated into the cost calculation tool and the cost calculation method.

In a fourth step, we presented our findings regarding the significance of these identified factors to a panel of RFID-experts from the industry. Our experts comprised RFID system-integrators. The experts assisted us in validating the importance of identified processes, components and methods by providing us with valuable feedback. We then incorporated experts' feedback, and refined the cost calculation model. This was then used as a basis to build the first spreadsheet-based prototype. We finally evaluated the developed prototype in focus group settings with experts, and refined the prototype based on feedback obtained during the focus group evaluations. The iterative development process allowed us to enhance the general usability and validity of the prototype, and ensure its usefulness for practitioners.

RFID-CC: A Cost Calculation Method for RFID Projects

The five steps in cost calculation are adapted from COCOTS (see Figure 4). While, the initial assessment and the detailed assessment are adapted from COCOTS, we developed the tailoring step from COCOMO I. Furthermore, we adapt the idea of re-usability of existing code including the volatility from COCOMO II. While, the assessment steps are used to select components for the planned RFID-system, the tailoring step links RFID-components with existing IT-systems such as specifying security protocols. Furthermore, the glue code development step is used to program additional code which incorporates RFID-components and the RFID-system with the existing IT-system including the testing of the code. The volatility step ensures the deployment of new version or updates from vendors. Accordingly, COCOTS allows the combination of economic, technical and strategic elements together. Therefore, we use COCOTS as base to develop a cost calculation (CC) method for RFID-projects. Figure 4 gives an overview of the adapted RFID-CC method with its phases. In the left column, the different phases of the COCOTS model are depicted, while in the right column the adapted phases of the RFID-CC method are listed. The RFID-CC method is structured along the RFID-components, except the first phase.

Checklist: The first step in the COCOTS method is the initial cost assessment phase to roughly estimate the complete cost for a project. In the case of RFID cost calculation, we propose a slight variation of this step and name it as 'Checklist'. The checklist intends to ensure a complete overview of the RFID-project. More specifically, the checklist helps to get a mutual understanding of existing material and information flows. Furthermore, it supports the definition process of the planned RFID-system with its material

Figure 4. RFID-CC method and its adaptation from the COCOTS method

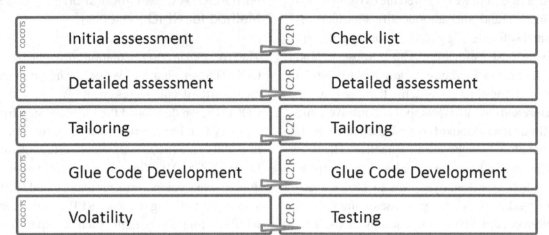

flow, information flow and specific constraints of RFID-systems. Therefore, we modified the initial assessment phase towards a checklist without any cost calculation functions, as our experts indicated the importance of an in-depth RFID-knowledge. According to the experts, this includes an understanding of needed hardware, software, processes and information systems in order to estimate costs. In consequence, practitioners can gain a better understanding of the existing systems and the expected design of the RFID-system. Therefore, the checklist enables a mutual understanding and awareness of planned changes in the material and information flow. As an addition, our analysis showed that RFID-cost calculations should be preferably lead by experienced people, who have a broad knowledge and understanding of RFID-technology and its cross-disciplines. However, our results also indicate that it is advisable to estimate the costs in a team with mutual goals. Finally, as we did not include any cost function for the initial assessment step, this phase needs to be covered from overhead costs.

Detailed Assessment: The second step in the COCOTS method is the detailed assessment phase. We adapt the detailed assessment towards an estimation of costs to improve the understanding of each RFID-component structured according to the presented RFID-architecture (see theoretical background section). The criteria are the same for all components and include aspects such as security, functionality or maturity of the component. Therefore, the costs have to be estimated according to the developed criteria for each component such as application server or database server. This detailed assessment process shall enable RFID-project members to acquire sufficient information and competencies to estimate further costs within the next steps. However, we did not include the RFID-infrastructure elements tag and reader for the detailed assessment and tailoring step, as tags and readers profit from their advantage as standard components. In consequence, tags and readers do not add costs for basic implementations, while more specific requirements might lead to costs. Therefore, tags and readers are not excluded in the glue code development step and the testing step.

The detailed assessment costs are estimated for each component based on the developed criteria. For each criterion, it is necessary to estimate the duration in days and to list the costs per day. This results in costs per criterion (see Formula 1). The costs per criterion will automatically sum up for each component (see Formula 2), and the costs for each component results in the total costs for the detailed assessment step (Formula 3). In case there are no costs, project members can leave the fields blank or insert zero days as duration to document their choice. Figure 5 depicts a screenshot of the developed prototype and illustrates the Detailed Assessment step for one of the components – the connector or edgeware.

Formula 1: Detailed assessment- Costs per criterion

$$Costs\ per\ Criterion = (Days) \times (Costs\ per\ Day)$$

Formula 2: Detailed assessment- Costs per RFID-component:

$$Costs\ per\ Component = \\ \sum (Criterion\ 1) + (Criterion\ 2) + (...) + (Criterion\ n)$$

Formula 3: Detailed assessment- Total costs

$$Total\ Costs\ Detailed\ Assessment = \\ \sum \begin{matrix}(Component\ 1) + \\ (Component\ 2) + (...) + (Component\ n)\end{matrix}$$

Tailoring: The third cost estimation step covers the integration of the RFID-system into the existing IT-infrastructure and includes the initial setup and integration steps for the RFID-system. We also structured the cost estimation process according to the presented RFID-architecture (see theoretical background section) and developed criteria for each component. The criteria are developed based on possible roles each component can play or the activities it can perform. Therefore, we have different amounts of criteria per component. The cost estimation process does not differ between the components and is similar to the introduced process in the tailoring step. However, we implemented a simple and advanced cost calculation process, as requested during the evaluation.

Within the simple cost calculation process, each criterion needs to be multiplied with the expected duration (hours) and the hourly rate resulting in costs per criterion (see Formula 4). This allows to automatically sum up the costs per

Figure 5. Screenshot for detailed assessment in the developed prototype

Components	Detailed attributes/variants	Estimation Duration in days	Costs per day	Total costs	decision/result
Connector (Edgeware) Assessment Attributes			0 €		
Correctness	Accuracy, Correctness	0	0 €	0 €	
Availability/Robustness	Availability, Fail safe, Fail soft, Fault tolerance, Reliability	0	0 €	0 €	
Security	Security	0	0 €	0 €	
Performance	Execution performance	0	0 €	0 €	
Ease of Use	Usability	0	0 €	0 €	
Version Compatibility	Downward compatibility, Upward compatibility	0	0 €	0 €	
Intercomponent Compatibility	Compatibility with other components, Interoperability	0	0 €	0 €	
Flexibility	Flexibility	0	0 €	0 €	
Installation/Upgrade Ease	Installation Ease, Upgrade/Refresh ease	0	0 €	0 €	
Portability	Portability	0	0 €	0 €	
Functionality	Functionality	0	0 €	0 €	
Price	Initial purchase costs	0	0 €	0 €	
Maturity	Product Maturity	0	0 €	0 €	
Vendor Support	Response time for critical problems, Support, Warranty	0	0 €	0 €	
Training	User training	0	0 €	0 €	
Total Costs				0 €	

component (see Formula 5). Further, the costs per component result in the total costs for the tailoring step (Formula 6). In case there are no cost, project members leave the fields blank or add zero hours as indication for their choice.

The advanced cost calculation process is the same, however, some functionalities are developed for experienced users. For example, imagine an IT-department with RFID-specialists who provide a cost calculation sheet as template for their firm: To support RFID-projects, the project members can simply use bars within the prototype to indicate the level of difficulty of processes (represented by the criteria). The bars represent five levels. The first level represents the shortest time, indicating experienced users or project teams, while the fifth group represents the opposite. By using the bars, the prototype calculates the needed hours. This is done by multiplying hours with an hourly rate. Therefore, the RFID-specialists have to pre-estimate the needed hours for each of the five levels. If the pre-estimation is done, the user calculates the costs per criterion by simply using the bars, while the duration is based on the estimation of the RFID-specialists. Accordingly, the advanced calculation process can either be used internally from RFID-specialists who implement RFID-systems more often or as support functionality within a firm. Figure 6 represents a screenshot of the Tailoring assessment step within our prototype. It illustrates the simple and advanced cost calculation processes for the connector or edgeware and messaging server or middleware.

Formula 4: Tailoring- Costs per criterion

$$Costs\ per\ Criterion = (Days) \times (Costs\ per\ Day)$$

Formula 5: Tailoring- Costs per RFID-component

$$Costs\ per\ Component = \sum \frac{(Criterion\ 1) + (Criterion\ 2) +}{(...) + (Criterion\ n)}$$

Formula 6: Tailoring- Total costs

$$Total\ Costs\ Tailoring = \sum \frac{(Component\ 1) +}{(Component\ 2) + (...) + (Component\ n)}$$

Glue code development: The fourth step estimates costs for the development of new code in case further functionalities are requested, the provided code is not sufficient or even no code is available. Therefore, the developed code can be expected to be unique for one RFID-project. Based on our evaluation, we extracted the testing of the glue code and created an own step within our RFID-CC. Therefore, our glue code development step only refers to the development of code. Glue code development might become necessary in case additional functionalities are requested and cannot be covered during the system integration phase. Further examples are the integration of RFID into supply chain networks, as different systems

Figure 6. Screenshot for Tailoring in the developed prototype

Tailoring Activities & Aids	simple	difficult	Overview Tailoring - difficult		VL	L	N	H	VH	y level: Expected working h need to be filled	Needed h	Costs / h	Total costs	Needed h	Costs / h	Total costs	Total costs chosen on variant
				1,66							365		6.600 €		Overview Tailoring - simple		
Connector (Edgeware) Tailoring Complexity			Overall rating	3		x				1	2	3	4	5	40	0 €	4.000 €	30	0 €	2.400 €	5.000 €
Install, upgrade	x			3		x				1	3	5	7	9	5	100 €	500 €	10	80 €	800 €	800 €
Specify application settings		x		4				x		1	5	15	30	45	30	100 €	3.000 €	5	90 €	400 €	3.000 €
Start the service	x			2		x				4	5	7	9	11	5	100 €	500 €	15	80 €	1.200 €	1.200 €
Messaging Server (Middleware) Tailoring Complexity			Overall rating	3,66			x			1	2	3	4	5	26	0 €	2.600 €	30	0 €	2.400 €	2.700 €
Install, upgrade	x			5				x		1	2	3	4	5	5	100 €	500 €	10	80 €	800 €	800 €
Specify standard application settings	x			2		x				6	7	8	9	10	7	100 €	700 €	5	80 €	400 €	700 €
Security /Access Protocol Initialization & Set-up	x			4				x		11	12	13	14	15	14	100 €	1.400 €	15	80 €	1.200 €	1.200 €

within the network complicate the data transfer among firms. Moreover, internal requests such as additional possibilities to analyze data influence the amount of needed glue code. In consequence, many influences have to be covered during the code development. Therefore, we created three eight by eight matrix. For each component up to nine different connections can be setup, while more connections can be added. This results in more than 1.800 possible interfaces between the components. Therefore, RFID-projects can estimate costs for many different purposes.

The first matrix gives users the possibility to indicate whether they want to develop glue code or not, and in case code needs to be developed the user has to estimate the needed lines of code (LOC). For the second matrix, the estimated duration (in minutes) per line needs to be filled out. As an addition, the hourly rate for the code developer has to be defined. As an addition, we incorporated an influence factor due to the feedback during the evaluation phase. The influence factor allows to "fine-tune" the cost estimation process. This might be necessary in situations such as firms have new developers or the developer first needs to be trained in a new programming language. Finally, the costs per interface will be automatically calculated based on the input.

Furthermore, the matrix provides the total costs for the complete code development process (see Formula 7). Figure 7 represents the Glue Code assessment step of our prototype for the connector or edgeware and messaging server or middleware components. In specific, Figure 7 illustrates the first matrix of the Glue Code development for up to nine functionalities.

Formula 7: Glue code development- Total costs

$$Total\ Costs\ Glue\ Code\ Development = \sum (\#\,LOC) * (Duration\ per\ LOC) * (Hourly\ Rate) * (Influence\ Factor)$$

Testing: The last step is testing. The testing step is used to ensure a stable RFID-system. The prototype automatically transfers all selected interfaces during the glue code development step towards the testing step. Therefore, the prototype provides an automatic indication of additional testing effort. As testing was mentioned as crucial step for RFID-projects, we organized the glue code testing process as own process in contrast to the COCOTS method. Further, we did not integrate the volatility step from COCOTS, as we learned that RFID-projects end by implementing the

Figure 7. Screenshot for glue code development in the developed prototype

# of Code Lines / Glue Code Dev. Necessary?			Connector (Edgeware)									Messaging Server (Middleware)								
			Variante 1			Variante 2			Variante 3			Variante 1			Variante 2			Testsystem		
			C11	C12	C13	C21	C22	C23	C31	C32	C33	MS11	MS12	MS13	MS21	MS22	MS23	MS31	MS32	MS33
Connector (Edgeware)	1	C11				X	X													
		C12				X														
		C13										X								
	2	C21	X	X																
		C22	X																	
		C23																		
	3	C31																		
		C32																		
		C33																		
Messaging Server (Middleware)	1	MS11			X															
		MS12																		
		MS13																		
	2	MS21																		
		MS22																		
		MS23																		
	Testsystem	MS31																		
		MS32																		
		MS33																		

RFID-infrastructure and its software. Updates and modifications are considered as new projects.

In consequence, the test costs are derived from the chosen glue code connections. Our prototype allows for filtering of the relevant connections and can calculate the test costs with up to three iterations. In a first step, the user needs to indicate whether there shall be a testing or not. If testing is required the user has to estimate the test loops (from one to three), and for the first test loop the duration and the hourly rate (Formula 8). If there is more than one test loop, it is necessary to indicate the duration and hourly rates for the other test loops. The duration in the second and third test loop has to be specified in percentage using the initial time for the first test (Formula 9). Based on the amount of test loops, the duration and the hourly rate, our prototype calculates the total test costs (see Formula 10). Figure 8 is a screenshot of the developed prototype and illustrates the Testing step for two functionalities. The first functionality depicts the need for two optimization cycles, while the second functionality only needs one optimization. As an addition, if a functionality needs an optimization cycle, the fields, which need to be filled become yellow.

Formula 8: Testing- Test costs loop 1

$$Test\ Costs\ Loop\ 1 = Duration * Hourly\ Rate$$

Formula 9: Testing- Test costs loop 2 or 3

$$Test\ Costs\ Loop\ 2\ or\ 3 =$$
$$(Duration\ Test\ Loop\ 1 *$$
$$(Duration\ Test\ Loop\ 2\ or\ 3)\ /\ 100) *$$
$$Hourly\ Rate$$

Formula 10: Testing- Total test costs

$$Total\ Test\ Costs =$$
$$\sum \left[\begin{pmatrix} Test\ Loop\ 1 \end{pmatrix} + \begin{pmatrix} Test\ Loop\ 2 \end{pmatrix} + \\ \begin{pmatrix} Test\ Loop\ 3 \end{pmatrix} \right] * Hourly\ Rate$$

Prototype Evaluation

Theory and Research Methodology

An important step in design science research is the evaluation of the designed artifact (Hevner, 2007). The RFID cost calculator was developed to increase the upfront cost estimation accuracy of RFID-system integration projects. Therefore, the goal of the prototype evaluation is to assess the extent to which the RFID cost calculator allows for a more accurate estimation of RFID system integration costs taking into account the technical and functional elements of a RFID-system and its cross-functional requirements.

We drew upon previous research to identify relevant methodologies that can be used for the evaluation of our prototype. We also tried to ensure that the evaluation methodology used, allowed us to evaluate our artifact's fit in the context of information systems, supply chain and RFID. We

Figure 8. Screenshot for testing in the developed prototype

Zelle	Test (y/n)	Duration (h)	Opt.-Cycle	OC1-Effort	OC1-Dura	OC2-Effort	OC2-Dura	Total Dura	€ / h	Total cost (€)
C21, C11	x	10 h	2	20%	2,00 h	5%	0,50 h	12,50 h	100 €	1.250 €
C22, C11	x	5 h	1	10%	0,50 h		0,00 h	5,50 h	100 €	550 €
					0,00 h		0,00 h	0,00 h		0 €
					0,00 h		0,00 h	0,00 h		0 €
					0,00 h		0,00 h	0,00 h		0 €
					0,00 h		0,00 h	0,00 h		0 €
					0,00 h		0,00 h	0,00 h		0 €
					0,00 h		0,00 h	0,00 h		0 €
					0,00 h		0,00 h	0,00 h		0 €

therefore chose the cognitive walkthrough methodology, which is recommended for practicing software developers without background in cognitive psychology and only some experience in interface evaluation. The cognitive walkthrough methodology enables practicing software developers to examine their artifact and identify subtle problems (Wharton, Rieman, Lewis, & Polson, 1994). We further decided to use the "cognitive walkthrough with users" variant (Mahatody, Sagar, & Kolski, 2010), which can be considered as helpful in the case of a complicated cross-functional domain like RFID (Granollers & Lorés, 2006). Applying this variant of cognitive walkthrough enables us to uncover mismatches between implicit and explicit expectations of users by incorporating the three phases (Granollers & Lorés, 2006; Wharton, et al., 1994). Therefore, we consider the "cognitive walkthrough with users" methodology as a well suited approach (Mahatody, et al., 2010; Wharton, et al., 1994).

The cognitive walk through process is structured in three main phases. The *first phase* defines the input for the cognitive walkthrough methodology (Wharton, et al., 1994). This includes (1) the choice of representative users (Granollers & Lorés, 2006; Wharton, et al., 1994), (2) a definition of tasks for the evaluation (Wharton, et al., 1994), (3) the planned action sequence in the prototype (Wharton, et al., 1994) and (4) a definition of the interface (Wharton, et al., 1994). In the *second phase* the users are invited to perform the tasks defined in the first phase. During the evaluation process, users are asked to express aloud their thoughts, feelings and opinions (Granollers & Lorés, 2006). In consequence, researchers can use this direct feedback as second source to improve the prototype. As primary source, researchers analyze observational data, which needs to be collected during the evaluation process (Wharton, et al., 1994). Furthermore, users are asked to comment on detected deficiencies more in detail after each sequence (Granollers & Lorés, 2006). In the *third*

phase experts review the collected data to improve the prototype (Granollers & Lorés, 2006).

In the second phase, we conducted semi-structured interviews (Myers & Newman, 2007) after each sequence to refine and strengthen the usefulness of our evaluation data, and ensure the inclusion of cross-functional aspects of RFID-projects. As semi-structured interviews are a powerful gathering technique, it is often used in the field of IS due to its flexibility, and allowed us to explore relationships in this cross-functional field (Myers & Newman, 2007).

Ensuring a proper evaluation setting, we provided a prototype, supported by a fictional case study about RFID-system integration within the retail industry (Wharton, et al., 1994). The evaluation was recorded (Lewis, Polson, & Rieman, 1991; Wharton, 1992; Wharton, Bradford, Jeffries, & Franzke, 1992) and analyzed according to the semi-structured interview guidelines from Myers and Newman (2007).

Setup of the Evaluation

The evaluation process was split into two sets. Both sets – experts and focus group – were evaluated using the cognitive walkthrough method. Further, the workshop combined the guidelines from Ericsson and Simon (1993) and Browne and Rogich (2001), allowing us to collect and to properly analyze the feedback after each cost calculation step.

The first data set consisted of two expert interviews enhancing us to get detailed insight and feedback for our prototype. Employing theoretical sampling, rather than random sampling allowed us to interview two experts in the field of RFID (Corbin & Strauss, 2008), supporting our intention to include cross-functional aspects. The identified experts were system integrators, ensuring professional and technical knowledge in all cross-functional disciplines (RFID, IS, Project Management). As RFID is not specific to an industry, we paid attention to practical experience of our experts, declaring in each expert having more than 10 years of experience with RFID, more than 23 years of industry experience and each conducted more than 36 RFID-projects.

The second part of the evaluation was conducted with a focus group, ensuring usefulness of the artifact for the cross-functional target audience. All focus group participants were classified as potential adopters (Karahanna, Straub, & Chervany, 1999), i.e., specialists who had knowledge of RFID but had not implemented RFID, and potential users. Seven individuals participated in the focus group. All participants were male and ranged in the age from 27 to 53, with an average of 42 years. 57% held a master's degree, 29% held a bachelor's degree, while 14% held a diploma for three year training on the job. Participants' average experience in the industry was 17.1 years, while their average RFID experience was 7.4 years. 71% of the participants had knowledge in information systems and already conducted some information system integration projects, 86% stated they had project management knowledge and all of them confirmed knowledge in the field of RFID. The participants are from the fields of supply chain management and information systems. While three employees are on an operational level, four employees are on the managerial level.

In case of the experts, we sat beside them, introduced them to each of the cost estimation steps in short and explained them the task such as calculation of tailoring costs. While the experts tried to achieve their given task, we noted their problems and discussed the problems with the experts after each step. One expert was interviewed in a meeting room at the university, whereas the second expert was interviewed within his company. The first interview lasted one and a half hour, whereas the second interview was held in one hour. Both interviews were conducted in the same logical order and structure, applying the cognitive walkthrough method. We handed the fictional case study to our first expert, starting with the second phase of the cognitive walkthrough, collecting

comments from the expert, noting observations and using our semi-structured interview questionnaire to clarify open issues and problems for our understanding. We supported the experts during the cognitive walkthrough in case we uncovered a mismatch between our implicit assumptions of the RFID cost calculator usage and issues experienced by our experts. Furthermore, we briefly introduced each sequence before our expert started with it. After the first expert judgment, we analyzed the transcript and our observational data, which allowed us to modify our prototype before the second expert tested the prototype. The process resulted in a more sophisticated prototype based on two iterative improvements underlying our analysis data.

With the focus group, we proceeded in a similar manner. The focus group evaluated our prototype in a workshop, which lasted for about one a half hour. The workshop was prepared and led by one of the authors. Further, one independent researcher supported the walkthrough process with the focus group. First, we introduced the general topic, the fictional case study as base for the test and briefly the cost calculation steps of the prototype. Second, the participants had twenty minutes to solve the fictional case study. We asked them to give us their feedback about the usefulness of the sequence, the cost estimation process, and their experience of the user-interface, and to comment on deficiencies after each sequence (Granollers & Lorés, 2006). In a further step, we walked with the participants through the prototype, explaining the participants our idea of the process. Fourth, we briefly discussed the differences and noted the problems the participants experienced within each cost estimation step. Fifth, we asked the focus group to redo the cost calculation before we finally had an open discussion. While there was no need to modify the elaborated RFID-CC cost calculation method (see prototype design section), we refined our prototype based on our design rationales and the collected data.

Analysis and Findings
of the Evaluation

The first prototype was based on literature, mainly derived from COCOMO I, COCOMO II and COCOTS. Therefore, the RFID cost calculator included the phases (1) initial assessment, (2) detailed assessment, (3) tailoring, (4) glue code development and (5) volatility. The final RFID cost calculator includes a (1) checklist, (2) detailed assessment, (3) tailoring, (4) glue code development and (5) testing. The development and evaluation of the tool was around nine months.

As RFID projects differ even within the same company, we modified the *initial assessment phase* towards a checklist (1) to document existing material and information flow processes, services and functions, and (2) plan the requirements for the target processes, services and functions. In consequence, the initial assessment phase has to be covered by overhead costs and contributes by supporting the completeness of aspects in the cost calculation process.

Major changes in the *detailed assessment phase* are the removal of RFID reader and RFID tag towards the checklist. This is grounded on the reason of RFID (system integration) projects itself, as it is seen as mandatory to acquire knowledge about tags and readers in advance. Furthermore, the estimation unit has been changed from hours to days, and an easier process for cost entries has been established.

The tailoring phase has been adapted closely from the COCOTS model and includes the same attributes and infrastructure classes like the detailed assessment phase. However, we adapted the tailoring phase for experienced users and repeating calculations (advanced version), and for un-experienced users and non-repeating calculations (simple version). In consequence, the easier version can also be used for scenarios in which services are bought from 3rd parties, while the more difficult version contributes, i.e., to a higher standardization such as in large enterprises with special departments dedicated to RFID projects, or RFID service providers.

The glue code development phase has undergone an extension from a simple matrix towards a matrix consisting out of more than 550 fields. Furthermore, the matrix has been cloned two times, leading to the total of 3 matrixes with more than 1.800 fields. The main drivers for the change are the extension of processes, service and functions into the calculation scheme. Further, the RFID cost calculator now allows users to adjust the calculation with an influence factor requested by the focus group. The influence factor can be used for many purposes such as adjusting the knowledge of the programming language, new project members (learning curve), or supply-chain-wide usage of RFID. Moreover, the matrix of the RFID cost calculator can be extended in case more than nine connections within one RFID-infrastructure class are needed.

The testing phase was conducted after the first expert interview. We got the understanding that RFID system integration projects are treated like normal business projects implying project termination after completion. Therefore, RFID system integration projects are finished shortly after launch. In case of further requirements, firms will setup a successive project and do not treat issues as volatility. Furthermore, we integrated a filter for better manageability of the over 1.800 fields, based on the feedback from our second expert.

Overall, based on the interview notes and the group discussion, it can be stated that the reviewers found our cost calculation tool to be helpful for estimating costs for RFID system integration projects in advance before the actual start of the project. For instance, our reviewers indicated that it was particularly helpful to be able to incorporate off the shelf components in the overall cost estimation, and could also incorporate scenarios where certain integration and implementation services are acquired from third party service providers. Therefore, the use of our prototype and formulas contribute to a more effective cost estimation process ahead of starting a RFID-project. This will also help firms to realize a faster return-on-investment.

DISCUSSION

Current research and practical developments in RFID technology reflect the potential of RFID in the field of supply chain management (Rutner, et al., 2004) and advantages of RFID over traditional auto-ID technologies (Thiesse, 2005; Want, 2006). The potential has been demonstrated in industry projects (Cocca & Schoch, 2005; Ming-Ling Chuang & Shaw, 2007) and analyzed from a research perspective (Holmqvist & Stefansson, 2006; Tzeng, Chen, & Pai, 2008). However, the introduction of RFID systems in the processes of firms is often forced by the stronger supply chain partner (Ming-Ling Chuang & Shaw, 2007). This reserved behavior of firms can be explained by skepticism to reach an early break-even point and the possibility to generate value (Ming-Ling Chuang & Shaw, 2007; Vijayaraman & Osyk, 2006). Further constraints are different risk factors such as technology maturity, availability of expertise and most importantly from an economical perspective the cost to value ratio (Fontanella, 2004).

While there is research about how to measure the benefits of RFID systems after their implementation (Tsai & Huang, 2012; Uckelmann, 2012), the challenge to estimate RFID system adaptation costs for the integration into an existing IT landscape beforehand has been scarcely addressed (Asif & Mandviwalla, 2005). The design and evaluation of the RFID cost calculator aims to fill this gap through the development of a RFID cost calculation approach and an applicable tool which covers the implementation steps and requirements of RFID systems, and therefore enhances firms to calculate costs more appropriately for RFID system integrations in advance.

Our study further contributes to IS research by showing the applicability of the cognitive walk-through method in the context of cost calculation tools. Furthermore, we developed an upfront cost calculation method for RFID-system integration projects using previous research from the fields of software cost calculation, supply chain management and RFID. Moreover, our evaluation indicated that regardless of whether participants were experts or not, they considered our RFID cost calculator as a useful tool to estimate RFID-system integration costs more accurately, resulting in a satisfaction with the tool and the intention to use it. This gives direct validation to the claim that our tool addresses the expectations of users. In addition, this also validates the applicability for small and medium sized enterprises as well as for internationally acting firms.

In the current study, we developed a RFID cost calculation tool and analyzed the usefulness, satisfaction and the intention to use the RFID cost calculator. In fact, while this study was primarily concerned with the development with a RFID system integration cost calculation approach and evaluating the prototype, future research can investigate the correctness of our formulas including the usability in a practical scenario, given that the tool is derived from three different fields.

LIMITATIONS AND IMPLICATIONS FOR FUTURE RESEARCH

The RFID cost calculator, as well as the evaluation study should be interpreted in the context of its limitations. The developed RFID cost calculator is an initial approach to calculate system integration costs more accurately beforehand. However, RFID-projects always differ and therefore new challenges might occur, which are probably not addressed in the current version of the cost calculator tool.

The RFID cost calculator was developed based on practical relevance claiming that current RFID projects miss their economic goals (Straube, 2009; Thiesse, Al-Kassab, & Fleisch,

2009; Vojdani, et al., 2006). This holds particularly true for inter-organizational supply chains, as the general project risk level increases (Fontanella, 2004) and economic and socio-political aspects occur (Kumar & van Dissel, 1996; H. Lee, Padmanabhan, & Whang, 1997), reflecting the need for incentive alignment (Barzel, 1997; Klein & Rai, 2009). Therefore, the RFID cost calculator allows firms or supply networks to calculate RFID system integration costs beforehand for internal projects and also for inter-organizational projects. In consequence, the RFID cost calculator enhances to reduce the overall RFID project risk due to a more accurate cost calculation in advance. Moreover, based on a more precise calculation supply networks can align economic aspects and further RFID-project related incentives. The increasing amount of RFID implementations (L. Lee, et al., 2008; Sarac, Absi, & Dauzère-Pérès, 2010), its analysis from a research perspective (Ngai, Moon, Riggins, & Yi, 2008; Sellitto, Burgess, & Hawking, 2007; Thiesse & Condea, 2009) and its introduction in the area of consumers (Bamasak, 2011; Dahlberg, Mallat, Ondrus, & Zmijewska, 2006; Engel et al., 2012; Köbler, Goswami, Koene, Leimeister, & Krcmar, 2011; Michael & Michael, 2010; Ondrus & Pigneur, 2005, 2007) indicate the growing importance and popularity in the society. Therefore, future research endeavors may be targeted towards the verification of the RFID cost calculator and its extension and usability in different use contexts. Further, research could investigate the use in a field study.

Using the cognitive walkthrough methodology to evaluate the cost calculator results in limitations that are inherent to this research methodology. Future studies could assess the different phases from an observational setting or post-perspective setting where users are less likely to feel constrained by conducting field experiments. In our evaluations, a fictional case study was used to evaluate the prototype. While this fictional case study might not cover all constraints of specific RFID-projects, it can be considered sufficient for the evaluation

and acceptance of the RFID cost calculator in general RFID-projects. However, future studies that allow RFID-adopters to use and evaluate the RFID cost calculator over a longer period of time could be designed to get a better gauge of missing aspects and first-hand experiences with the cost calculator and their willingness for a continuous usage of the tool. Furthermore, conducting expert interviews and run focus group evaluations to assess a prototype is appropriate in a field with limited research results (Corbin & Strauss, 2008; Yin, 2009), and therefore the use of experts and focus groups does not raise serious concerns in this study. Further, our experts and the participants of the focus group were generally reflective for RFID-projects as all subjects had experience with RFID and supply chain management.

CONCLUSION

In spite of the growing popularity of RFID-technology in the field of supply chain management, and an observed trend towards usage within the society (Bamasak, 2011; Ondrus & Pigneur, 2007), currently, there is little theoretically grounded understanding of the cost-drivers for the integration, and the integration costs of RFID-systems into an existing IT-landscape of firms. Identifying this gap, we conceptualized a cost calculation tool for a more accurate calculation of RFID-system integration costs in advance of implementing RFID-projects, and assessed the extent to which the RFID cost calculator allows estimating system integration costs more accurately; considering the technical and functional elements of a RFID-system and its cross-functional requirements.

We developed the RFID cost calculator as first approach in a research context. The prototype allows users to calculate costs in advance of the implementation of a RFID-system into an existing IT-landscape. Further, the cost calculator can be applied for internal and inter-organizational cost calculations. In this paper, we derived a new cost calculation method from literature to identify and assign RFID-system integration costs. In a successive step, we outlined the design of the RFID cost calculator, along with an evaluation of the tool using the "cognitive walkthrough method with users" in a laboratory setting, supported by interviews and open discussions. The findings suggest that prospective users perceive the prototype as useful and are satisfied with it. Further, they indicate an intention to use the prototype if it is available to them.

Our results further indicate that RFID-experts and users confronted with RFID-technology in the field of supply chain management perceive the cost calculator as useful and are satisfied with it. This indicates that there is significant need to calculate costs more accurately upfront for RFID-systems from diverse perspectives in conjunction with completeness of RFID-infrastructure attributes. For instance, being able to calculate costs in a standardized manner may be particular useful for big firms, who have the opportunity to centralize RFID-knowledge; while smaller firms need more flexibility in their calculation. Thus, the flexibility provided by the RFID cost calculator can be thought of as the opportunity to integrate service providers, who implement certain aspects of an RFID-system due to missing knowledge at the responsible contractor. Further, standardization can be useful for centralized departments, in charge and control of firm-wide RFID-implementations. Future research could therefore assess the need for further mechanism to support standardization and flexibility aspects for users in charge of RFID-implementations. Finally, more comprehensive, long-term studies should be designed and executed to assess the extent to which different user groups find the application useful and how its usage influences the accuracy of RFID-system integration calculations.

REFERENCES

Abts, C., Boehm, B. W., & Clark, E. B. (2000). *COCOTS: A COTS software integration lifecycle cost model-model overview and preliminary data collection findings.* Paper presented at the ESCOM-SCOPE Conference. Munich, Germany.

Angeles, R. (2005). RFID technologies: Supply-chain applications and implementation issues. *Information Systems Management, 22*(1), 51–65. doi:10.1201/1078/44912.22.1.20051201/85739.7

Asif, F., & Mandviwalla, M. (2005). Integrating the Supply Chain with RFID: A Technical and Business Analysis. *Communications of the Association for Information Systems, 15*(24), 393–426.

Bamasak, O. (2011). Exploring consumers acceptance of mobile payments – An empirical study. *International Journal of Information Technology, Communications and Convergence, 1*(2), 173–185.

Barzel, Y. (1997). *Economic Analysis of Property Rights.* Cambridge University Press. doi:10.1017/CBO9780511609398

Boehm, B., Abts, C., & Chulani, S. (2000). Software development cost estimation approaches — A survey. *Annals of Software Engineering, 10*(1-4), 177–205. doi:10.1023/A:1018991717352

Boehm, B., Madachy, R., & Steece, B. (2000). *Software Cost Estimation with COCOMO II.* New Jersey: Prentice Hall PTR.

Browne, G. J., & Rogich, M. B. (2001). An Empirical Investigation of User Requirements Elicitation: Comparing the Effectiveness of Prompting Techniques. *Journal of Management Information Systems, 17*(4), 223–249.

Bundschuh, M., & Fabry, A. (2000). *Aufwandschätzung von IT-Projekten.* MITP-Verlag.

Chulani, S. (1998). *Incorporating Bayesian Analysis to Improve the Accuracy of COCOMO II and its Quality Model Extension* (USC-CSE tech. report 98-506). Academic Press.

Cocca, A., & Schoch, T. (2005). RFID-Anwendungen bei der Volkswagen AG—Herausforderungen einer modernen Ersatzteillogistik. In E. Fleisch, & F. Mattern (Eds.), *Das Internet der Dinge* (pp. 197–208). Springer-Verlag. doi:10.1007/3-540-28299-8_10

Corbin, J. M., & Strauss, A. L. (2008). *Basics of qualitative research: techniques and procedures for developing grounded theory*. Los Angeles, CA: Sage Publications.

Dahlberg, T., Mallat, N., Ondrus, J., & Zmijewska, A. (2006). Mobile Payment Market and Research - Past, Present and Future. *Sprouts: Working Papers on Information Systems, 6*(48), 6-48.

Delen, D., Hardgrave, B. C., & Sharda, R. (2007). RFID for Better Supply-Chain Management through Enhanced Information Visibility. *Production and Operations Management, 16*(5), 613–624. doi:10.1111/j.1937-5956.2007.tb00284.x

Dickson, G. (2007). *Software Cost Estimation*. Faculty of Computer Science, Faculty of Engineering, University of Brunswick.

Dittmann, L., & Thiesse, F. (2005). *Integration und Interoperabilität von RFID-Softwarearchitekturen Schriftenreihe Wirtschaft & Logistik*. Hamburg, Germany: Deutscher Verkehrs-Verlag.

Dowie, U. (2009). Testaufwandsschätzung in der Softwareentwicklung: Modell der Einflussfaktoren und Methode zur organisationsspezifischen Aufwandsschätzung (Vol. 1). Lohmar - Köln: Josef Eul Verlag.

Engel, T., Lunow, S., Fischer, J., Köbler, F., Goswami, S., & Krcmar, H. (2012). *Value Creation in Pharmaceutical Supply Chains using Customer-Centric RFID Applications*. Paper presented at the European Conference on Smart Objects, Systems and Technologies (Smart SysTech). Munich, Germany.

Ericsson, K. A., & Simon, H. A. (1993). *Protocol analysis: Verbal reports as data* (Rev. Ed.). Cambridge, MA: MIT Press.

Fleisch, E., & Mattern, F. (2005). *Das Internet Der Dinge: Ubiquitous Computing Und Rfid in Der Praxis: Visionen, Technologien, Anwendungen, Handlungsanleitungen*. Springer.

Fontanella, J. (2004). Finding the ROI in RFID. *Supply Chain Management Review, 8*(1), 13–16.

Fosso Wamba, S., & Chatfield, A. T. (2009). A contingency model for creating value from RFID supply chain network projects in logistics and manufacturing environments. *European Journal of Information Systems, 18*(6), 615–636. doi:10.1057/ejis.2009.44

Gencel, C., Heldal, R., & Lind, K. (2009). *On the relationship between different size measures in the software life cycle*. Paper presented at the Asia-Pacific Software Engineering Conference (APSEC). Hong Kong, China.

Granollers, T., & Lorés, J. (2006). Incorporation of users in the Evaluation of Usability by Cognitive Walkthrough. In R. Navarro-Prieto, & J. L. Vidal (Eds.), *HCI related papers of Interacción 2004* (pp. 243–255). Springer. doi:10.1007/1-4020-4205-1_20

Hansen, W. R., & Gillert, F. (2006). *RFID für die Optimierung von Geschäftsprozessen: Prozess-Strukturen, IT-Architekturen, RFID-Infrastruktur* (Vol. 1). München: Carl Hanser Verlag.

Hartman, F., & Ashrafi, R. (2002). Project management in the information systems and information technologies. *Project Management Journal, 33*(3), 5–15.

Hevner, A. R. (2007). A Three Cycle View of Design Science Research. *Scandinavian Journal of Information Systems, 19*(2).

Hevner, A. R., March, S. T., Park, J., & Ram, S. (2004). Design Science in Information Systems Research. *Management Information Systems Quarterly, 28*(1), 75–105.

Holmqvist, M., & Stefansson, G. (2006). *Mobile RFID—A case from volvo on innovation in SCM*. Paper presented at the 39th Hawaii International Conference on System Sciences (HICSS). Wailea, HI.

Karahanna, E., Straub, D. W., & Chervany, N. L. (1999). Information Technology Adoption Across Time: A Cross-Sectional Comparison of Pre-Adoption Beliefs and Post-Adoption Beliefs. *Management Information Systems Quarterly, 23*(2), 183–213. doi:10.2307/249751

Karkkainen, M. (2003). Increasing Efficiency in the Supply Chain for Short Shelf Life Goods Using Rfid Tagging. *International Journal of Retail & Distribution Management, 31*(10), 529–536. doi:10.1108/09590550310497058

Klein, R., & Rai, A. (2009). Interfirm strategic information flows in logistics supply chain relationships. *Management Information Systems Quarterly, 33*(4), 735–762.

Köbler, F., Goswami, S., Koene, P., Leimeister, J. M., & Krcmar, H. (2011). NFriendConnector: Design and Evaluation of An Application for Integrating Offline and Online Social Networking. *AIS Transactions on Human-Computer Interaction, 4*(3), 214–235.

Krcmar, H. (2010). *Informationsmanagement* (Vol. 5). Heidelberg, Germany: Springer. doi:10.1007/978-3-642-04286-7

Kumar, K., & van Dissel, H. G. (1996). Sustainable Collaboration: Managing Conflict and Cooperation in Interorganizational Systems. *Management Information Systems Quarterly, 20*(2), 279–300. doi:10.2307/249657

Laubacher, R., Kothari, S. P., Malone, T. W., & Subirana, B. (2005). What is RFID worth to your company? - Measuring performance at the activity level. *MIT Center for eBusiness Research Brief, 7*(2), 1-6.

Lee, H., Padmanabhan, V., & Whang, S. (1997). The Bullwhip Effect In Supply Chains. *Sloan Management Review, 38*(3), 93–102.

Lee, L., Fiedler, K., & Smith, J. (2008). Radio frequency identification (RFID) implementation in the service sector: A customer-facing diffusion model. *International Journal of Production Economics, 112*(2), 587–600. doi:10.1016/j.ijpe.2007.05.008

Lewis, C., Polson, P. G., & Rieman, J. (1991). *Cognitive walkthrough forms and instructions* (Institute of Cognitive Science Technical Report, ICS 91-14). Academic Press.

Loebbecke, C. (2005). RFID Technology and Applications in the Retail Supply Chain: The Early Metro Group Pilot. In *Proceedings of 18th Bled conference on eIntegration in action*, (pp. 5-6). Bled.

Mahatody, T., Sagar, M., & Kolski, C. (2010). State of the Art on the Cognitive Walkthrough Method, Its Variants and Evolutions. *International Journal of Human-Computer Interaction, 26*(8), 741–785. doi:10.1080/10447311003781409

Maier, K. (2005). A COTS developer's point of view on Radio Frequency Identification. *CompactPCI and AdvancedTCA Systems, 9*(3), 42–47.

Maloni, M., & DeWolf, F. (2006). *Understanding radio frequency identification (RFID) and its impact on the supply chain*. Penn State Behrend–RFID Center of Excellence.

March, S. T., & Smith, G. F. (1995). Design and natural science research on information technology. *Decision Support Systems, 15*(4), 251–266. doi:10.1016/0167-9236(94)00041-2

Maurno, D. A. (2005). Going for (Not So) Broke: The True Cost of RFID. *Inbound Logistics, 25*(7).

Michael, K., & Michael, M. G. (2010, 7-9 June). *The diffusion of RFID implants for access control and epayments: A case study on Baja Beach Club in Barcelona*. Paper presented at the IEEE International Symposium on Technology and Society (ISTAS). Wollongong, Australia.

Ming-Ling Chuang, M. L., & Shaw, W. H. (2007). RFID: Integration Stages in Supply Chain Management. IEEE *Engineering Management Review, 35*(2), 80–87. doi:10.1109/EMR.2007.899757

Myers, M. D., & Newman, M. (2007). The qualitative interview in IS research: Examining the craft. *Information and Organization, 17*(1), 2–26. doi:10.1016/j.infoandorg.2006.11.001

Naunchan, P., & Sutivong, D. (2007). *Adjustable cost estimation model for COTS-based development*. Paper presented at the 18th Australian Software Engineering Conference (ASWEC). Melbourne, Australia.

Ngai, E. W. T., Moon, K. K. L., Riggins, F. J., & Yi, C. Y. (2008). RFID research: An academic literature review (1995-2005) and future research directions. *International Journal of Production Economics, 112*(2), 510–520. doi:10.1016/j.ijpe.2007.05.004

Ondrus, J., & Pigneur, Y. (2005). *A Disruption Analysis in the Mobile Payment Market*. Paper presented at the 38th Annual Hawaii International Conference on System Sciences (HICSS). Wailea, HI.

Ondrus, J., & Pigneur, Y. (2007). *An Assessment of NFC for Future Mobile Payment Systems*. Paper presented at the International Conference on the Management of Mobile Business (ICMB). Toronto, Canada.

Peffers, K., Tuunanen, T., Gengler, C. E., Rossi, M., Hui, W., Virtanen, V., et al. (2006). *The design science research process: A model for producing and presenting information systems research*. Paper presented at the 1st International Conference on Design Science Research in Information Systems and Technology (DERIST). Claremont, CA.

Reel, J. S. (1999). Critical success factors in software projects. *Software, 16*(3), 18–23. doi:10.1109/52.765782

Richardson, H. L. (2004). Bar codes are still getting the job done. *Logistics Today, 45*(12), 38–39.

Roh, J. J., Kunnathur, A., & Tarafdar, M. (2009). Classification of RFID adoption: An expected benefits approach. *Information & Management, 46*(6), 357–363. doi:10.1016/j.im.2009.07.001

Roussos, G. (2006). Enabling RFID in retail. *Computer, 39*(3), 25–30. doi:10.1109/MC.2006.88

Roussos, G., & Kostakos, V. (2009). RFID in pervasive computing: State-of-the-art and outlook. *Pervasive and Mobile Computing, 5*(1), 110–131. doi:10.1016/j.pmcj.2008.11.004

Rutner, S., Waller, M. A., & Mentzer, J. T. (2004). A Practical Look at RFID. *Supply Chain Management Review, 8*(1), 36–41.

Sarac, A., Absi, N., & Dauzère-Pérès, S. (2010). A literature review on the impact of RFID technologies on supply chain management. *International Journal of Production Economics, 128*(1), 77–95. doi:10.1016/j.ijpe.2010.07.039

Schuster, T. (2012). *Modellierung, Integration und Analyse von Ressourcen in Geschäftsprozessen* (Vol. 1). Karlsruhe: KIT Scientific Publishing.

Sellitto, C., Burgess, S., & Hawking, P. (2007). Information quality attributes associated with RFID-derived benefits in the retail supply chain. *International Journal of Retail & Distribution Management, 35*(1), 69–87. doi:10.1108/09590550710722350

Smithson, S., & Hirschheim, R. (1998). Analysing information systems evaluation: Another look at an old problem. *European Journal of Information Systems, 7*(3), 158–174. doi:10.1057/palgrave.ejis.3000304

Sneed, H. M. (2005). *Software-Projektkalkulation: Praxiserprobte Methoden der Aufwandsschätzung für verschiedene Projektarten.* Hanser.

Straube, F. (2009). *RFID in der Logistik - Empfehlungen für eine erfolgreiche Einführung.* TU Berlin, Univ.-Bibliothek.

Strueker, J., & Gille, D. (2008). *The SME Way of Adopting RFID Technology: Empirical Findings from a German Cross-Sectoral Study.* Paper presented at the 16th European Conference on Information Systems (ECIS). Galway, Ireland.

Thiesse, F. (2005). *Architektur und Integration von RFID-Systemen.* Institut für Technologiemanagement, Universität St. Gallen.

Thiesse, F., Al-Kassab, J., & Fleisch, E. (2009). Understanding the value of integrated RFID systems: A case study from apparel retail. *European Journal of Information Systems, 18*(6), 592–614. doi:10.1057/ejis.2009.33

Thiesse, F., & Condea, C. (2009). RFID data sharing in supply chains: What is the value of the EPC network? *International Journal of Electronic Business, 7*(1), 21–43. doi:10.1504/IJEB.2009.023607

Thiesse, F., & Gross, S. (2006). Integration von RFID in die betriebliche IT-Landschaft. *Wirtschaftsinformatik, 48*(3), 178–187. doi:10.1007/s11576-006-0041-y

Trunick, P. A. (2005). Where's the ROI for RFID? *Logistics Today, 46*(1), 10–11.

Tsai, F.-M., & Huang, C.-M. (2012). *Cost-Benefit Analysis of Implementing RFID System in Port of Kaohsiung.* Paper presented at the International Conference on Asia Pacific Business Innovation and Technology Management (APBITM). Pattaya, Thailand.

Tzeng, S.-F., Chen, W.-H., & Pai, F.-Y. (2008). Evaluating the business value of RFID: Evidence from five case studies. *International Journal of Production Economics, 112*(2), 601–613. doi:10.1016/j.ijpe.2007.05.009

Uckelmann, D. (2012). Performance Measurement and Cost Benefit Analysis for RFID and Internet of Things Implementations in Logistics. In D. Uckelmann (Ed.), *Quantifying the Value of RFID and the EPCglobal Architecture Framework in Logistics* (pp. 71–100). Berlin, Germany: Springer. doi:10.1007/978-3-642-27991-1_4

Vigder, M. R., & Dean, J. (1997). *An architectural approach to building systems from COTS software components.* Paper presented at the Conference of the Centre for Advanced Studies on Collaborative Research (CASCON). Toronto, Canada.

Vijayaraman, B. S., & Osyk, B. A. (2006). An empirical study of RFID implementation in the warehousing industry. *International Journal of Logistics Management, 17*(1), 6–20. doi:10.1108/09574090610663400

Vojdani, N., Spitznagel, J., & Resch, S. (2006). Konzeption einer systematischen Identifikation und Bewertung von RFID-Einsatzpotenzialen. *Zeitschrift für wirtschaftlichen Fabrikbetrieb, 3*, 102-108.

Vollmann, S. (1990). *Aufwandsschätzung im Software engineering: Neue Verfahren und Arbeitshilfen.* Vaterstetten bei München: IWT-Verl.

Want, R. (2006). An introduction to RFID technology. *Pervasive Computing, 5*(1), 25–33. doi:10.1109/MPRV.2006.2

Weinstein, R. (2005). RFID: A technical overview and its application to the enterprise. *IT Professional, 7*(3), 27–33. doi:10.1109/MITP.2005.69

Wharton, C. (1992). *Cognitive walkthroughs: Instructions, forms, and examples*. University of Colorado.

Wharton, C., Bradford, J., Jeffries, R., & Franzke, M. (1992). *Applying cognitive walkthroughs to more complex user interfaces: Experiences, issues, and recommendations*. Paper presented at the SIGCHI Conference on Human Factors in Computing Systems. Monterey, CA.

Wharton, C., Rieman, J., Lewis, C., & Polson, P. (1994). The cognitive walkthrough method: A practitioner's guide. In J. Nielsen, & R. Mack (Eds.), *Usability inspection methods* (pp. 105–140). New York: John Wiley & Sons.

Wieczorrek, H. W., & Mertens, P. (2011). *Tipps und Tricks für Leiter von IT-Projekten Management von IT-Projekten* (pp. 297–306). Berlin, Germany: Springer.

Yang, Y., Boehm, B., & Wu, D. (2006). *COCOTS risk analyzer*. Paper presented at the 5th International Conference on Commercial-off-the-Shelf (COTS)-Based Software Systems. Orlando, FL.

Yin, R. K. (2009). *Case Study Research: Design and Methods* (4th ed.). Los Angeles, CA: Sage Publications Inc.

Zhang, H. (2009). *An investigation of the relationships between lines of code and defects*. Paper presented at the 25th International Conference on Software Maintenance (ICSM). Edmonton, Canada.

KEY TERMS AND DEFINITIONS

COCOMO: Abbreviation for Constructive Cost Model, which is a software cost estimation method based on code instructions in the form of lines of code.

COCOTS: A software cost estimation method that incorporates commercial off-the-shelf components.

Cognitive Walkthrough Methodology: A methodology for information technology artifact (in particular, interfaces) evaluation which is based on cognitive psychology and allows developers to identify subtle problems with their developed interfaces.

Design Science: A research methodology or paradigm for the systematic development and evaluation of information technology artifacts.

Project Cost Calculation: Refers to estimating RFID-project costs in advance of the RFID-project. The estimated costs are summed up to Total Costs for RFID-integration projects.

Prototype Development: A prototype is an early sample, model or release of a product, service or software. Prototype Development can be described as an iterative process to verify and evaluate a concept or process to ensure a match between the final product, service of software and the customers' expectations.

RFID: Radio Frequency Identification, an auto identification technology that primarily comprises tags (or transponders) and tag readers.

Chapter 3
Can Near Field Communication Solve the Limitations in Mobile Indoor Navigation?

Wilson E. Sakpere
Cape Peninsula University of Technology, South Africa

Michael O. Adeyeye
Cape Peninsula University of Technology, South Africa

ABSTRACT

The navigation ecosystem is rapidly changing. Indoor navigation has attracted attention with the introduction of mobile devices into the market. Although mobile devices are used more often for outdoor navigation, they have opened up opportunities for indoor navigation proponents. Near Field Communication in indoor navigation is still in its exploratory stage. Despite an increase in the variety of indoor navigation research, challenges remain in designing a framework that is neither complex nor expensive. NFC is a novel method of navigating in indoor environments. Providing an overview of its benefits and usefulness compared with existing indoor navigation technologies is the subject of this chapter.

1. INTRODUCTION

With the advent of the mobile phone, computing has become increasingly mobile, ubiquitous and context-aware. The mobile phone and smartphone in extension, is the most popular and widely used mobile device today and is fast becoming an irreplaceable device. Due to the computational power of the smartphone, it can be used for a number of functions including alarm clock, calendar, email, web search, game and navigation, with navigation forming an interesting aspect of it.

Traditionally, road signs and billboards were means of navigating outdoors and locating a destination. With the advent of the Global Positioning System (GPS), navigation has metamorphosed into a simplified activity. Users have the choice of using either or both of the traditional and/or technological means of navigation. GPS has been widely adopted for outdoor navigation where it can be used to locate people or objects effectively. It is accurate and precise but has one flaw that it has not been able to support indoor navigation (Renaudin, Yalak, Tome, & Merminod, 2007).

DOI: 10.4018/978-1-4666-6308-4.ch003

This is due to buildings and walls which serve as an obstacle to the satellite's signals. Thus, navigating indoors with mobile devices became an interesting subject in the past decade.

An indoor navigation system consists of a network of devices used in locating objects or people inside a building. Upon knowing where something or someone is, a lot can be done with the information depending on one's objective, such as tracking and position determination. Mobile indoor navigation involves an individual finding his/her way around in order to arrive at a desired destination using an interactive navigation system. The major challenge in indoor navigation is determining the current location of a user. Without this information, a suitable path to the destination cannot be routed or re-routed as the case may warrant.

Navigating in indoor environments is gradually attracting wider interest (Aebi, 2012; Chandgadkar, 2013; Choo, Cheong, Lee, & Teh, 2012; Hammadi, Hebsi, Zemerly, & Ng, 2012; Huang & Gao, 2013; Kannan et al., 2013; Link, Smith, Viol, & Wehrle, 2011; Rao & Fu, 2013; Wang, 2012; Zinkiewicz, 2012). Indoor positioning and navigation have been investigated over the past decades using variety of technologies (Fallah, Apostolopoulos, Bekris, & Folmer, 2013; Gu, Lo, & Niemegeers, 2009; Lukianto & Sternberg, 2011; Mautz, 2009). Various challenges and limitations exist for indoor navigation solutions. There is minimal universal solutions that address all of these challenges as there will always be a trade-off. However, there are existing solutions that effectively address specific indoor navigation challenges implicitly and we shall provide an overview of these solutions.

Fallah et al., (2013, p. 21) noted that people navigate considering either or both of path integration and/or landmark-based navigation. Path integration simply involves the use of a reference point or landmark only to locate a destination where the use of a map is needed. Landmark-based

navigation, on the other hand, involves the use of a 'physical or cognitive map' of the environment with multiple reference points or landmarks in the navigation process. A situation where a visitor arrives at a campus for the first time and wishes to locate an office within a large building, the landmark-based approach is easily preferred. In mobile indoor navigation, the landmark-based navigation is employed since the user does not know his/her destination. Mobile indoor navigation involves three stages: (1) the current position of a user, (2) the most suitable path for the user to navigate on and, (3) the destination of the user (Huang & Gartner, 2010).

In this chapter, we will discuss the techniques and technologies used in indoor positioning systems. We will give an overview of the strength of these technologies, the problems and limitations currently inherent in them and how NFC may play a role.

2. POSITIONING TECHNIQUES

Positioning techniques are used to localize and estimate the position of sensor nodes in order to improve positioning accuracy. They are used to help users have easy access to position and navigation information. To determine the position of a user, two techniques, namely Signal Characteristics/Metrics and Positioning Algorithm, are employed.

2.1 Signal Characteristics/Metrics

Positioning systems can be classified by the measurement techniques they employ. The signal metrics has to do with the measurement of geometrical parameters (signal, angle or distance). The collection of these parameters allow estimating the object's position using calculations. In general, there are various types or methods of measurement and some popular methods are discussed below:

2.1.1 Angle of Arrival (AOA)

It is used to calculate the position of a transmitter based on the angle and distance relative to multiple reference points. But the hardware tends to be complex and expensive. AOA is used in the triangulation technique. In practice, however, few sensor localisation algorithms absolutely require AOA information, though several are capable of using it when present (Amundson & Koutsoukos, 2009; Brás, Carvalho, Pinho, Kulas, & Nyka, 2012).

2.1.2 Time of Arrival (TOA)

TOA is sometimes called time of flight (TOF). It measures the time taken by a signal to arrive at a receiver from a transmitter. It uses the absolute time of arrival at the receiver rather than the measured time difference between departing from a transmitter and arriving at the receiver. The distance between the transmitter and the receiver can be directly calculated from the time of arrival. TOA provides high accuracy but at a cost of higher hardware complexity (Nuaimi & Kamel, 2011; Xiao, Liu, Yang, Liu, & Han, 2011).

2.1.3 Time Difference of Arrival (TDOA)

TDOA is an improvement on TOA. It measures the difference in TOA at two different receivers. It determines the relative position of the transmitter based on the difference in the propagation time of signals. Thus, modification of the transmitter is eliminated. TDOA provides high accuracy. Both TOA and TDOA are used in the trilateration technique (Brás et al., 2012; Xiao et al., 2011).

2.1.4 Received Signal Strength Indication (RSSI)

It is a measure of the power level of the received signal strength (RSS) present in a radio infrastructure, and can be used to estimate the distance between mobile devices. RSSI is the relative RSS in a wireless environment. The higher the RSSI, the better the signal quality. However, in indoor environments where it is difficult to obtain line-of-sight, the RSSI and positioning are affected by multipath and shadow. RSSI is normally used in the proximity technique (Brás et al., 2012; Xiao et al., 2011).

2.2 Positioning Algorithm

Positioning algorithms translate recorded signal metrics into distances and angles, and then computes the actual position or location of a target object (Huang & Gartner, 2010). Several techniques exist for obtaining bearing, range, or proximity information based on signal measurement. The following four algorithmic techniques are discussed: triangulation, trilateration, proximity and scene analysis.

2.2.1 Triangulation

Angles are used to compute the distance between fixed points in order to locate an object. The object to be located is used as a fixed point of a triangle (Brás et al., 2012; Liu, Darabi, Banerjee, & Liu, 2007).

2.2.2 Trilateration

The position of an object is computed by using the distance between it and three other known points. Multilateration is similar to trilateration except that four or more points are used in multilateration (Nuaimi & Kamel, 2011).

2.2.3 Proximity

A grid of antennas with known positions is used. When a mobile device is detected in motion, the closest antenna is used to calculate its position. But if the mobile device is detected by more than one antenna, the antenna with the strongest signal is used to calculate its position (Brás et al., 2012; Gu et al., 2009; Liu et al., 2007).

2.2.4 Scene Analysis

Information is collected from a scene and the position of an object is estimated by matching or comparing the collected information with the one in the existing database. Fingerprinting is normally used in scene analysis (Liu et al., 2007; Nuaimi & Kamel, 2011).

3. POSITIONING TECHNOLOGIES

Trigony (2012) stated that three key problems challenge the adoption and widespread use of indoor positioning systems. The first one is non-line-of-sight signal propagation which is due to the walls, people and obstacles in indoor environment. This affects radio signal measurements and leads to significant position errors. The second one is sparsity of reference points. This results in an ambiguity in position estimation and calculation. The third one is large spatial variation in the

accuracy of location sensors. This is difficult to measure empirically, leading to inaccuracy.

Determining the current position of a user is the most important and yet challenging in indoor positioning. Without the current location, rerouting a path to the destination is difficult and navigation becomes cumbersome. Henniges (2012) classified indoor positioning using three topologies – network-based, terminal-based and terminal-assisted. However, various technologies have been used to investigate and classify positioning in indoor navigation (Gu et al., 2009; Koyuncu & Yang, 2010; Liu et al., 2007; Nuaimi & Kamel, 2011; Xiao et al., 2011). These investigations are based on the following metrics: accuracy, performance, cost, usability, privacy and complexity of the technology used. Our classification shall be based on Gu et al.'s.

Indoor positioning systems can be classified into six major groups namely: Infrared (IR), Ultrasound/Ultrasonic, Magnetic, Vision-Based/ Optical, Audible sound and Radio-Frequency (RF) (Fallah et al., 2013; Gu et al., 2009; Mautz, 2009; Xiao et al., 2011). The classification is based on the main medium used to determine location (see Figure 1).

Figure 1. Classification of indoor positioning systems

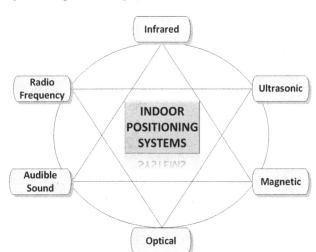

3.1 Infrared Positioning System

Infrared positioning system (Aitenbichler & Muhlhauser, 2003; Lee et al., 2004; Lee & Song, 2007) is one of the earliest indoor positioning systems. It is a method that uses infrared signals to determine the position of objects or people based on their presence. This makes real-time tracking impractical to implement. Infrared light is invisible to the human eye and does not penetrate through walls. Thus, an infrared tracking system would need several receivers in each room or space installed in order to improve accuracy. The placement of the infrared tag to the reader can cause line-of-sight problems. System architectures for positioning based on infrared signals differ significantly. Mautz (2012) noted that the three general methods of exploring infrared signals are: (1) use of active beacons (Atsuumi & Sano, 2010), (2) infrared imaging using natural (thermal) radiation (Hauschildt & Kirchhof, 2010) and, (3) artificial light sources (Lee & Song, 2007).

3.1.1 The Active Badge

The Active Badge system (Hopper, Harter, & Blackie, 1993; Want, Hopper, Falcão, & Gibbons, 1992) is an infrared system for the location of objects or people wearing a badge. These badges transmit signals with a unique code every 15 seconds. The periodic signals provide information about their location to a centralized location (server) through a network of infrared sensors. The positioning techniques used are trilateration and TOA.

3.1.2 Limitations

The accuracy of this system is moderate. More receivers will be needed to improve accuracy. This will lead to infrastructure complexity and high cost of the overall solution. Scaling the solution can also become very costly over time. Another limitation is the interference of infrared waves

with fluorescent light and sunlight, this reduces the usability of the system. Also, since there is a server computing user location, privacy issues arises (Ekahau, 2005).

3.2 Ultrasound/Ultrasonic Positioning System

Using ultrasound/ultrasonic signal (Hazas & Hopper, 2006; Hazas & Ward, 2002; Holm, 2012; Medina, Segura, & De la Torre, 2013) is another way of position measurement. Ultrasound signals are used by bats to navigate at night. This inspired researchers to design similar navigation system. The ultrasonic positioning system is based on the principle of trilateration and in some cases triangulation. Triangulation based methods do not usually produce very accurate positioning results and are very susceptible to errors due to walls, furniture and other obstacles in the building (Ekahau, 2005).

3.2.1 The Active Bat

The Active Bat (Koyuncu & Yang, 2010; Woodman & Harle, 2010) is an ultrasonic positioning system that improves accuracy over Active Badge by using radio and ultrasound signals. Users and objects are tagged with ultrasonic tags. Signal receivers, mounted across the ceiling, detect the ultrasound signal from the Active Bat tags. This signal is sent to a centralised location (server). The exact position of a user is computed by finding the distance to about three reference nodes using the time of arrival lateration technique.

3.2.2 Cricket System

Cricket system (Priyantha, 2005) is an ultrasonic positioning system that consists of cricket nodes. It improves upon the Active Bat system by using the radio signal arrival time to narrow the time window in which arriving signals are considered (Xiao et al., 2011). The ultrasound emitters (beacons) are fixed to the ceiling or wall of a building while the receivers (listeners) are attached to target objects or people for position determination. The beacons transmit messages to the listener intermittently while the listener 'listens' for transmissions and uses the information to determine its position. This approach provides user privacy by performing position triangulation calculation locally in the located object. The Cricket system uses less number of emitters fixed on the ceiling. It addresses the issue of fault tolerance by using RF signals as a second method of proximity positioning if enough emitters are not available. The system is scalable for implementation in a large building and offers efficient performance and low cost deployment. It uses TOA measuring method and triangulation location technique to locate a target (Gu et al., 2009; Priyantha, 2005).

3.2.3 Dolphin System

Dolphin – Distributed Object Locating System for Physical-space Internetworking – (Fukuju, Minami, Morikawa, & Aoyama, 2003; Minami et al., 2004) is another ultrasound positioning system based on a hop-by-hop locating mechanism. The position principle is similar to that of active bat and cricket. There are two types of nodes namely: reference node and normal node. Dolphin requires only a few pre-configured reference nodes for locating all other nodes in the system. The system consists of nodes with RF, ultrasound transmission function and one-chip Central Processing Unit (CPU). The location of a few nodes is known while the remaining nodes can determine their location based on the location of reference nodes by using RF and ultrasound transmission function. A reference node transmits RF signal while other nodes start internal pulse counter on receiving the signal. The RF signal contains predetermined position of the reference node. The reference node also transmits ultrasonic pulse to other nodes. The nodes stop internal counter and compute distances to the reference node on receiving the

ultrasonic pulse. The advantage of this system is that it requires only a few nodes to determine all position of nodes. (Fukuju et al., 2003; Gu et al., 2009; Minami et al., 2004; Xiao et al., 2011).

3.2.4 Limitations

One general problem that is still inherent in this system is low accurate positioning due to multipath effects and line of sight (Fallah et al., 2013; Gu et al., 2009; Medina et al., 2013). In some cases, privacy concerns could be an issue where a server stores users' position information.

3.3 Magnetic Positioning System

Magnetic Positioning System (Blankenbach, Norrdine, & Hellmers, 2012; Kim, Kim, Yoon, & Kim, 2012; Paperno, Sasada, & Leonovich, 2001) involves the use of magnetic signals for position determination. This is an old way of position measuring and tracking. This method of positioning is based on previous works on magnetic fields, the earth's magnetic field and the compass (Li, Gallagher, Dempster, & Rizos, 2012). The loggerhead sea turtle and pied flycatcher are two animals that use the earth's magnetic field for position determination and navigation. This has helped researchers understand how animals use magnetic signals for positioning and navigation (Storms, 2009). The magnetic system consists of fixed transmitters, and receivers mounted on the user. The receivers receive magnetic signals from the transmitter and send the position information to a centralised location for position determination. The magnetic positioning system has high accuracy and does not suffer from non-line of sight (Chung et al., 2011; Gu et al., 2009).

3.3.1 Limitations

One issue with the magnetic positioning system is that of limited coverage. This affects the efficiency and robustness of the system. In order to improve the coverage range, an increase in magnetic sensors and infrastructure may be needed to cover sufficient areas. This will likely increase the complexity of the system (Li et al., 2012).

3.4 Optical/Vision Based Positioning System

Optical/Vision based Indoor Positioning System (Klopschitz, Schall, Schmalstieg, & Reitmayr, 2010; Mautz & Tilch, 2011; Tilch & Mautz, 2011) involves the position determination of a person or object in a building with the aid of a mobile sensor or camera carried by the user. It can be done in two ways. The visual information can be gotten from the mobile phone camera (Chang & Tsai, 2007; Vazquez-Briseno et al., 2012) or via Augmented Reality (Jang, 2010; Klopschitz et al., 2010), by seamlessly overlaying a user's view with location information linked to an image database in a centralised location or server. The server performs optical marker detection, image sequence matching, and location recognition. It transmits the recognized location information to the mobile device. This enables real-time positioning and navigation. The system provides the ability to identify similar locations in the image database and display location-related information. With Quick Response (QR) code, positioning is not real-time. The position determined is the position of the marker. The markers are distributed around the navigation environment and position is determined by placing the mobile device in close proximity to the marker (Kim & Jun, 2008; Lukianto & Sternberg, 2011).

3.4.1 Limitations

In some cases, privacy concerns may be an issue since a server stores position information. The system suffers from interference from multiple effects, bright light and significant accumulative errors which could lead to poor performance. Accuracy is not impressive. With QR code, the

accuracy depends on the range of the marker position to the device; the range depends on the resolution of the device's camera. Significant amount of computing power may be required to perform image matching thereby affecting performance (Huang & Gao, 2013; Klopschitz et al., 2010).

3.5 Audible Sound Positioning System

Audible sound positioning system (Liu, Liu, & Li, 2013; Mandal et al., 2005; Rishabh, Kimber, & Adcock, 2012; Rossi, Seiter, Amft, Buchmeier, & Tröster, 2013) consists of sensor network and end user mobile device. Most mobile devices, like Smartphone and Personal Digital Assistant (PDA), are able to emit audible sound. Audible sound is omni-directional. The use of audible sound eliminates the need for additional infrastructure by the user. The audible sound system uses acoustic sound to measure distance by calculating time of flight for sound pulses. The acoustic sensors, which are mounted in the building, are connected to a central server through a wireless network. Each sensor has a processing unit and a microphone for sensing acoustic signals (Lopes, Haghighat, Mandal, Givargis, & Baldi, 2006). They receive audible sound from the user's mobile device and send these data to the central server through the wireless connection. After computing the device's position, the server then sends the position information to the mobile device. TOA and triangulation methods are used to estimate the position of the device. A relatively good accuracy is achieved (Gu et al., 2009).

3.5.1 Limitations

One concern with this system is the audio transmission issue like interference, noise, reflection and low penetration power through walls and obstacles. These have a negative effect on the system's accuracy. Privacy is also a concern (Liu et al., 2013; Lukianto & Sternberg, 2011).

3.6 Radio-Frequency Positioning System

Radio-Frequency Positioning Systems consists of Bluetooth, Ultra-wideband (UWB), Sensor networks, Wireless Local Area Network (WLAN), Radio-Frequency Identification (RFID) and Near Field Communication (NFC). These formed the bulk of research in the past decade (see Figure 2).

The advantage of this technology is that radio waves can penetrate walls and other obstacles, resulting in a larger coverage area. RF-based positioning systems can reuse existing RF infrastructure, thus reducing cost. Radio wave-based methods work in two ways: by proximity detection, in the case of RFID/NFC tags, and by measuring the received signal strength indicator (RSSI) of installed infrastructure nodes such as WLAN, UWB, Bluetooth or sensor networks (Lukianto & Sternberg, 2011). Triangulation and fingerprinting techniques are widely used in RF-based positioning systems. Gu et al. (2009, p. 22) noted that, "For complicated indoor environments, location fingerprinting is an effective position estimation method, which uses location related characteristics such as RSS and location information of the transmitters to calculate the location of a user or a device".

3.6.1 Bluetooth Based Positioning System

Bluetooth-based positioning systems (Aung, Yang, Cho, & Gerla, 2008; Diaz, Maues, Soares, Nakamura, & Figueiredo, 2010; Fernandes, 2011; Scheerens, 2012) locate and track objects and people inside a building by providing real-time location data of radio and mobile phone users using Bluetooth beacons connected to a LAN. The Bluetooth beacons are installed in strategic locations within the building such that they can track the position of any discoverable device, record and send information to a centralised server (Chawathe, 2008; Muñoz-Organero, Muñoz-Merino, & Kloos, 2012; Zafeiropoulos et al., 2010). Most mobile devices have Bluetooth embedded in them. Bluetooth provides three connection status parameters namely: Link Quality (LQ), Received Signal Strength Indicator (RSSI) and Transmitted Power Level (TPL). Devices cannot support more than a single Bluetooth connection, making triangulation difficult (Subhan, Hasbullah, Rozyyev, & Bakhsh, 2011). Also, more devices will be needed in order to provide adequate coverage. One drawback of Bluetooth-based localisation methods is that device discovery is inherently a slow process (Bekkelien, 2012; Bielawa, 2005).

Figure 2. Types of radio-frequency positioning system

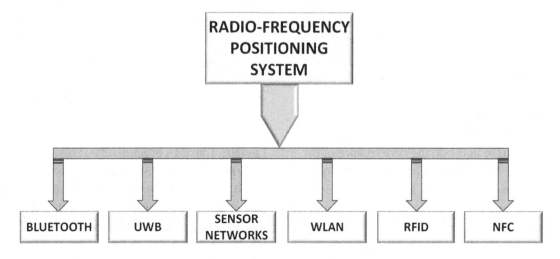

3.6.2 Ultra-Wideband Based Positioning System

UWB based positioning systems (Meissner, Leitinger, Fröhle, & Witrisal, 2013; Senger & Kaiser, 2006; Waldmann, Weigel, Ebelt, & Vossiek, 2012; Ye, 2012) send ultra-short pulses to transmit signal which has the magnitude of the bandwidth. The position estimation is based on TOA technique. UWB can be used for precise indoor positioning and can operate across a broad area of the radio spectrum. The use of more UWB readers and their strategic placement could reduce the effect of signal impairments, such as interference and multipath, which makes close proximity use with Wi-Fi networks and other RF signals possible. UWB makes use of technologies that are not in line with existing standards, hence its public use is not certain. UWB could be expensive to scale and battery use could be costly. It has high penetrating power, low power consumption and good positioning accuracy. (Canovic, 2007; Liu et al., 2007; Mautz, 2012; Xiao et al., 2011).

3.6.3 Sensor Network Based Positioning System

Sensor network based positioning system (Chen & Wang, 2009; Giorgetti, Farley, Chikkappa, Judy, & Kaleas, 2012; Lazos, Poovendran, & Čapkun, 2005) consists of a large number of sensors fixed in predefined locations. The location of a person or object can be determined by sensor signals. Sensor network positioning systems are quite challenging to implement. This is because the sensors are quite limited with respect to transmission range, computing resources and processing power. If several sensor nodes try to know their position at the same time and send the positioning information through the network, the performance of the system may be impeded. The network protocol, which determines how the nodes communicate during the positioning process, comes in handy at this point.

Positioning systems based on Received Signal Strength Indicator (RSSI) are preferred for measuring signal strength because of its low cost. The low cost of the sensors facilitate scalability and highly parallel computation. However, each node is likely to have limited power, limited reliability, and only local communication with a modest number of neighbours. The disadvantage of RSSI - based systems is that its position accuracy is quite low compared to other approaches (Bachrach & Taylor, 2005; Giorgetti et al., 2012; Robles, Munoz, De la Cuesta, & Lehnert, 2012).

Self-localisation and self-organisation are important traits in sensor networks. Sensor network positioning algorithms determine the position of sensors by using knowledge of the absolute positions of a few sensors and inter-sensor measurements. Sensor nodes can operate as coordinator, anchor nodes (static) or non-anchor nodes (mobile). The coordinator is connected to a centralised location or server which gathers position information for position estimation (with the help of the positioning algorithm) and configuration of the network. Sensors with known location information are called anchors and can be powered externally while those with unknown location information are called non-anchor nodes and can be powered with batteries. In sensor network applications, one of the essential problems is the localisation of non-anchor nodes for location based service. Thus sensor network positioning system is used to determine the position of the non-anchor nodes (Mao, Fidan, & Anderson, 2007; Robles et al., 2012; Yick, Mukherjee, & Ghosal, 2008; Yun, Lee, Chung, Kim, & Kim, 2009).

3.6.4 WLAN Based Positioning System

WLAN-based positioning system (Cypriani, Lassabe, Canalda, & Spies, 2011; Ma, Li, Tao, & Lu, 2008; Vicent, 2013; Wierenga & Komisarczuk, 2005) is mostly used where GPS is inadequate due to various causes including multipath and signal interference indoors. It uses existing WLAN infrastructure in indoor environments to determine a user's position or location. Also, WLAN is not affected by line of sight. Position determination using WLAN technology has the advantage of performing indoors and outdoors, whereas GPS can only work outdoors.

The calculation of a user's location can be done in two phases namely: offline and online phase. In the offline phase, grid points are computed at different locations in the building, each with a list of RSSI values for visible access points at that particular location. This process is also known as fingerprinting, which is a time consuming process. In the online phase, the grid points are used to compute the most feasible position of the user. The accuracy of location estimations in WLAN positioning is based on measuring the intensity of the received signal strength or on fingerprinting. The use of RSSI with WLAN can be grouped into four approaches namely: Propagation modelling, Cell of Origin (CoO), Fingerprinting (FP) and multilateration (Mautz, 2012; Retscher, Moser, Vredeveld, & Heberling, 2006; Wang & Jia, 2007). However, the positioning techniques based on Received Signal Strength (RSS) could sometimes be less accurate (Sayrafian-Pour & Perez, 2007).

More attention is given to the WLAN technology for positioning because of its better performance. Due to the complexity, inaccuracy and high cost of this technology indoors, more researchers tend to now favour the hybrid model (Galván-Tejada, Carrasco-Jiménez, & Brena, 2013; Wang & Jia, 2007) in order to compensate for the limitations of single model positioning technologies. The hybrid model is a combination of two or more positioning technologies and/or positioning techniques. It is also complex and expensive but improves accuracy. Some WLAN-based positioning systems are commercially available and include RADAR (Bahl & Padmanabhan, 2000), WIPS (Kitasuka, Nakanishi, & Fukuda, 2003), Ekahau (Ekahau, 2005) and Skyhook (Mautz, 2012). Although these are viable systems in improving distance estimation, speed and accuracy are still

issues. Also, wireless information access is not readily available in developing countries due to the high cost of equipment and deployment.

3.6.5 Radio-Frequency Identification Based Positioning Systems

Radio-Frequency Identification (RFID) is an automatic identification process of objects through radio interface. It is quite similar to the QR code or barcode in operation except that the barcode is replaced with an electronic microchip attached to an antenna, and the identification process is by radio instead of optics (Grover & Berghel, 2011; Renaudin et al., 2007). An RFID system consists of three main components namely: tag, reader and server. The tag stores data while the reader reads or writes tag data. The server is a centralised location where position computation is done. The RFID tags can be classified into two namely: active and passive tags. Active tags are battery powered transceivers and thus have a wider transmission range, hence reducing the number of tags required for an installation. The limitation with active tags is that the batteries need to be replaced from time to time. On the other hand, passive tags do not use batteries, they get their power source from the reader's signal before they can respond with information. They have a shorter transmission range. They are simply receivers. The passive tags are cheaper than the active tags (Fallah et al., 2013; Grover & Berghel, 2011; Harper, 2004) (see Table 1).

RFID positioning systems (Ni, Liu, Lau, & Patil, 2003; Saab & Nakad, 2011; Wang, Wu, & Tzeng, 2007; Wang, Huang, Chen, & Zheng, 2009) are usually used in complex indoor environments. In an 'active' positioning system, either the reader or active tags can be mounted within the building. That is, either of them can be mobile while the other is stationary. The same concept can also be used in the 'passive' positioning system with the reader and passive tags. The major limitations with the RFID positioning system are security and privacy

Table 1. Comparison of active and passive tags

	Active	Passive
Power	Battery Powered	No Battery
Signal Strength	Low	High
Transmission Range	Wide	Short
Storage	128 kb (Larger)	128 b (Smaller)
Tag Life	Long	Short
Cost	High	Low
Size	Large	Small
Operation	Transmitters	Receivers

concerns (Ahuja & Potti, 2010; Berghel, 2013; Darcy, Pupunwiwat, & Stantic, 2011; Langheinrich, 2008). Privacy has been described as the right to be left alone. Users do not want to be tracked to the point that every information about their private lives is known to others. More so, if they do not want their location to be monitored. This made Ann Cavoukian, who was once Information and Privacy Commissioner of Canada, to develop the concept known as "Privacy by Design". He postulated seven foundational principles of the concept. Privacy by Design refers to "the philosophy and approach of embedding privacy into the design specifications of various technologies" (Cavoukian, 2009). Eavesdropping, spoofing and sniffing are security concerns in RFID (Grover & Berghel, 2011; Khor, Ismail, Younis, Sulaiman, & Rahman, 2010; Sarma, Weis, & Engels, 2003).

3.6.6 Limitations

Although, each one of the RF based positioning system possess unique problems, there are however those that are common to all of them. Both the range (coverage) and signal for radio waves are limited. They are also prone to disturbance by almost anything. Certain electronics, storms, and even organic matter can disturb or distort radio signals. As an RF signal travels through the air and other mediums in an indoor environment, it exhibits certain behaviours such as absorption, reflection, scattering, refraction, interference, multipath and attenuation. These behaviours, also known as propagation effects, are signal impediments which affect a signal's transmission between two locations thereby causing significant loss and degradation of the received signal. Their effects could sometimes be unhelpful and have a negative effect on performance and accuracy (Coleman & Westcott, 2009; Ekahau, 2005; Mautz, 2012). To improve performance and accuracy, more infrastructure will be needed leading to increase in system complexity and increase in cost. Scaling the solution could also lead to high cost. Also, privacy is a concern since positions are computed with a server.

4. NEAR FIELD COMMUNICATION

There is a growing number of applications where a form of very short range wireless communication is needed. One short range technology that can meet this need is Near Field Communication (NFC). NFC is an interesting technology that has emerged in recent years and seems an ideal possibility to the development of pervasive, ubiquitous and context-aware systems. The number of mobile devices integrated with NFC is growing every year. NFC is based on the technology used for RFID. It is a short-range radio technology that operates on the 13.56 MHz frequency with data transfers of up to 424 Kbit/s at a distance of up to 10cm. NFC works in four ways namely: Phone to phone, Phone to device, Phone to tag and Phone to reader. For two devices to communicate using NFC, one device must have an NFC reader/writer while the other could be an NFC reader or tag (Agrawal & Bhuraria, 2012; Al-Ofeishat & Al Rababah, 2012).

NFC has two communication terminals namely: the initiator and the target. The initiator starts the communication process while the target receives the initiator's request and responds accordingly. Two communication modes exists in NFC, they are passive mode and active mode. In the passive communication mode, the initiator is active while the target is passive. In the active communication mode, both initiator and target are active as they communicate.

There are three main operating modes in NFC:

1. **Card Emulation Mode:** An NFC device acts as Proximity Inductive Coupling Card (PICC) (Mulliner, 2009) in this mode. In other words, an external reader reads the content of the NFC chip which is the same as that of a contactless smart card. This makes NFC a good medium for contactless transactions without changing existing infrastructure.
2. **Peer-to-Peer (p2p) Mode:** This mode enables a link-level communication between devices. Mobile devices easily interact with each other in order to share data, exchange business cards, documents, photos or other types of personal information in p2p data transfers.
3. **Reader/Writer Mode:** Mobile devices read data stored in NFC passive tags embedded in public posters, displays and products. This mode also enables mobile devices to write data to tags (Benyó, Sódor, Fördos, Kovács, & Vilmos, 2010).

NFC is useful in mobile payment, authentication and access control, data transfer between NFC enabled devices like Smartphone, digital cameras, notebooks, etc. It can be used to unlock a service (such as opening another communication link for data transfer like in Bluetooth or Wi-Fi), access digital information (read contents from smart poster to NFC phone, download maps from smart poster to NFC phone, record location e.g. a parking in NFC phone), and ticketing (Miraz, Ruiz, & Gomez-Nieto, 2009; Mulliner, 2009). One advantage of NFC technology is that mobile devices can be used both as an information storage and an NFC reader. NFC is compatible with existing RFID infrastructures, existing RFID tags and contactless smart cards. It is easy to use. The transmission range is so short that, when a user separates two devices, the communication between the devices is broken. This brings inherent security. NFC raises the bar for security, performance and convenience. Since this technology has a very short range of operation, it is hard to eavesdrop (Coskun, Ozdenizci, & Ok, 2012; Pampattiwar, 2012).

5. NFC POSITIONING SYSTEM

An NFC positioning system consists of three main components namely: tag, reader and server. The tag stores data while the reader, which is a mobile device, reads the content of the tag. The server is a centralised location where indoor map data of the building is stored. NFC positioning system (Bolz, 2011; Hammadi et al., 2012; Ozdenizci, Ok, Coskun, & Aydin, 2011) is a novel area in indoor positioning. Indoor positioning using NFC tags is gradually gaining traction. An NFC tag, also referred to as a smart tag, is a passive device which contains a small microchip with an antenna. It has a small amount of memory that can store small amount of data in the NFC Data

Exchange Format (NDEF). The NFC tag contains the position information, such as coordinates, at that point of the building. It also contains the Uniform Resource Identifier (URI) of the map data location. The Unique Identifier (UID) of the NFC tag could be associated with the position information. The tag is usually stuck to the wall.

NFC positioning involves a user tapping an NFC embedded mobile device to NFC tags spread within a building in order to determine current position. A user entering a building can tap the NFC tag at the entrance with a mobile device. The map data of the building is downloaded from the server via mobile network and displayed on the navigation system in the mobile device. The navigation system starts automatically because it communicates with the NFC Application Programming Interface (API). The position of the user is computed within the navigation system on the mobile device. Since all the tags contain the same information, a user who forgets to tap the tag at the entrance of a building can do so within the building after tapping any tag and the map data can be downloaded. Once the map data is downloaded, subsequent tapping of tags will only display the user's current location without downloading the map again. At the point where a user taps a tag, the location of the tag is the location of the user. This is a simple and effective way of accurate location determination. The position accuracy is quite high (Bolz, 2011; Hammadi et al., 2012; Ozdenizci et al., 2011).

Ozdenizci et al., (2011, p. 12) noted that the described system above can work seamlessly with GPS if a user navigates outdoors and then continues indoors. They posited that, "NFC technology is a seamless solution for indoor navigation systems when compared with all other existing solutions." Reducing cost, improving speed, accuracy and effectiveness are the goals of developing a positioning system. Indoor positioning using NFC tags is cheap, fast and accurate. However, real-time navigation is not achievable with NFC.

5.1 Benefits of NFC Positioning System

5.1.1 Cost

One of the most important benefits of NFC in indoor positioning is cost savings. The passive tags used are cheaper compared with that of other technologies, because they do not use batteries. Only the tags and the map data are set up, no other infrastructure is required. The user uses his mobile device as the reader or transmitter. For any organisation implementing this solution, it is cost effective. Also, the cost of maintenance is very minimal. There is little or no maintenance done for the tags, and minimal maintenance for the server with the map data. The cost factor is very important for developing nations. Due to the high cost implication, including maintenance costs, of other technologies, it may be expensive to implement in developing countries. Thus, NFC is a viable and pervasive alternative.

5.1.2 Accuracy and Precision

The position estimation is very accurate, more accurate than other technologies' because the tags are stationary.

5.1.3 Simplicity and Performance

The system is a very simple one consisting of NFC tags and the map database. Position estimation is done on the mobile device and not on the server. This increases speed and improves performance.

5.1.4 Usability

This is an important factor in the navigation system. NFC makes a navigation system usable by the physically challenged also. The processes involved are not cumbersome and complicated. It can also be designed in such a way that the visually impaired can also use it.

5.1.5 Scalability

Scaling the system is easily achievable. All that is needed is to install more NFC tags and nothing more. This is also friendly on cost.

5.1.6 Privacy

Privacy is guaranteed in this system because position computation is not done in the server. The server is meant to store the map data, and retrieve it when necessary.

5.2 Summary

Based on Table 2 below and the aforementioned, NFC positioning system is an ideal possibility for a pervasive and ubiquitous system. NFC can solve the limitations in other positioning technologies based on the following performance metrics: cost, accuracy and precision, simplicity and performance, usability, scalability, privacy and security.

6. FUTURE RESEARCH DIRECTIONS

In order to manage the limitations presented in this paper, it is necessary to have a thorough understanding of positioning technologies, and their strengths and weaknesses from a localisation and navigation point of view. Then, it becomes necessary to implement and improve on these technologies. This will result in simplicity, usability and great value to users. One positioning technology that seems promising is WLAN, because of its coverage and existing infrastructure. However, the presence of this infrastructure does not necessarily reduce cost especially in developing countries. Due to restriction in WLAN access, implementation of WLAN could lead to complexity and high cost. One possible area of future work is to find a way of using WLAN as a cost effective solution for indoor positioning in developing countries in order to improve robustness and usability.

In addition, we pointed out that the hybrid positioning model is becoming more popular and will improve accuracy and reduce complexity. This

Table 2. Summary and comparison of indoor positioning technologies

	Technique	Algorithm	Accuracy	Cost	Complexity	Scalability	Privacy/Security	Real-Time
Infrared	Trilateration	TOA/TDOA	Medium	High	High	Medium	Low	Yes
Magnetic	Triangulation	AOA/TOA	High	High	High	Low	Low	Yes
Optical/Vision	Scene Analysis & Proximity	RSSI	Low	Medium	Medium	Low	Low	Yes
Audible Sound	Triangulation	AOA/TOA	Medium	Medium	Medium	Medium	Low	Yes
Ultrasound/Ultrasonic								
Active Bat	Trilateration	TOA/TDOA	Medium	Medium	Medium	Medium	Low	Yes
Cricket	Triangulation	AOA/TOA	Medium	Low	Medium	Medium	Medium	Yes
Dolphin	Trilateration	TOA/TDOA	Medium	Low	Medium	Medium	Low	Yes
Radio Frequency								
Bluetooth	Scene Analysis	RSSI	Low	High	Medium	Medium	Low	Yes
UWB	Trilateration	TOA/TDOA	High	Medium	Medium	High	Low	Yes
Sensor Networks	Scene Analysis	RSSI	Low	Medium	Medium	Medium	Low	Yes
WLAN	Scene Analysis	RSSI	Low	Medium	High	Medium	Low	Yes
RFID	Scene Analysis	RSSI	Low	Medium	Medium	High	Low	Yes
NFC	Proximity	RISSU	High	Low	Low	High	High	No

model merges two or more technologies, thereby compensating for their weaknesses. Due to ongoing research work on NFC, it will be very popular in the nearest future because of its low cost and ubiquity. In order to tap into the potentials of NFC, it can be used in a hybrid make-up with WLAN or Bluetooth in order to achieve real-time mobile indoor navigation since NFC cannot work real-time. Although, there is the likelihood of system complexity, NFC will reduce system complexity thus balancing the trade-off.

In all the positioning technologies we discussed, we noted that map and position data are stored in a server, except NFC which stores only map data in the server. It is not impossible that the NFC technology would grow to a point where map data could be stored directly on the NFC tags thus bypassing the database of map data and server. However, due to the size of the NFC tags presently, map data cannot be stored on the tags. Eliminating the server completely and compressing the map significantly into the NFC tag is a consideration for future work.

7. CONCLUSION

In this chapter, we have provided a comprehensive overview of state-of-the-art positioning techniques and technologies used in indoor positioning and navigation systems. We noted that GPS has drastically influenced orientation and wayfinding in outdoor environment, helping people navigate with good accuracy and precision. However, the same cannot be said of navigating in indoor environment. Neither GPS nor current indoor positioning technologies have worked well indoors. Each positioning and navigation technologies provide different benefits to users in their unique and dynamic scenario.

The positioning technologies were discussed based on six different classifications namely: IR, Ultrasound/Ultrasonic, Magnetic, Vision-Based/Optical, Audible sound and RF. We discussed these positioning technologies based on the main medium and techniques used to determine position. The RF-based positioning system were classified into: Bluetooth, UWB, sensor networks, WLAN, RFID and NFC. We compared the different technologies and discussed their strengths and weaknesses based on the following factors: positioning technique, cost, accuracy and precision, simplicity and performance, usability, scalability, privacy and security. While some of these technologies suffer from line-of-sight or multipath effect, others suffer from inaccurate positioning. Indoor navigation systems have not been widely adopted mainly due to issues pertaining to these factors.

We focused on the limitations that these positioning technologies face specifically in their usage scenarios. These limitations tend to affect the functionality and performance of the positioning system. Thus, certain trade-offs exist. For instance, a system that will have a very good accuracy in real-time will tend to increase complexity and/or cost in order to achieve this. Therefore, a trade-off between accuracy and complexity or cost exists.

We posited that NFC is an ideal possibility to the development of pervasive and ubiquitous systems. NFC positioning system is able to take care of all the limitations that exist in other positioning technologies. NFC has the advantage and benefits of cost, accuracy and precision, simplicity and performance, usability, scalability and privacy. However, we noted that NFC cannot determine a user's location in real-time while navigating. In future research, this could be eliminated by an NFC hybrid positioning system in order to provide good user interaction.

REFERENCES

Aebi, F. (2012). *Autonomous indoor navigation: implementation of an autonomous indoor navigation system on android.* (Master's thesis). University of Fribourg, Fribourg, Switzerland. Retrieved from http://diuf.unifr.ch/drupal/sites/diuf.unifr.ch.drupal.softeng/files/teaching/studentprojects/aebi/autonomous-indoor-navigation.pdf

Agrawal, P., & Bhuraria, S. (2012). Near field communication. In P. B. Malla (Ed.), *Business Innovation through Technology: Winning with IT* (Vol. 10, pp. 67–74). Retrieved from http://www.infosys.com/infosys-labs/publications/Documents/winning-it.pdf

Ahuja, S., & Potti, P. (2010). An introduction to RFID technology. *Communications and Network, 2*(3), 183–186. doi:10.4236/cn.2010.23026

Aitenbichler, E., & Muhlhauser, M. (2003). An IR local positioning system for smart items and devices. In *Proceedings of the 23rd IEEE International Conference on Distributed Computing Systems Workshops* (pp. 334–339). IEEE. doi:10.1109/ICDCSW.2003.1203576

Al Hammadi, O., Al Hebsi, A., Zemerly, J. M., & Ng, J. W. P. (2012). Indoor localization and guidance using portable Smartphones. In *Proceedings of IEEE/WIC/ACM International Conferences on Web Intelligence and Intelligent Agent Technology* (Vol. 3, pp. 337–341). Macau: IEEE. doi:10.1109/WI-IAT.2012.262

Al Nuaimi, K., & Kamel, H. (2011). A survey of indoor positioning systems and algorithms. In *Proceedings of International Conference on Innovations in Information Technology* (pp. 185–190). Abu Dhabi: Academic Press. doi:10.1109/INNOVATIONS.2011.5893813

Al-Ofeishat, H. A., & Al Rababah, M. A. A. (2012). Near Field Communication (NFC). *International Journal of Computer Science and Network Security, 12*(2), 93–99. Retrieved from http://paper.ijcsns.org/07_book/201202/20120216.pdf

Amundson, I., & Koutsoukos, X. D. (2009). A survey on localization for mobile wireless sensor networks. In *Proceedings of the 2nd international conference on Mobile entity localization and tracking in GPS-less environments* (pp. 235–254). Orlando, FL: Springer. doi:10.1007/978-3-642-04385-7_16

Atsuumi, K., & Sano, M. (2010). Indoor IR azimuth sensor using a linear polarizer. In *Proceedings of International Conference on Indoor Positioning and Indoor Navigation* (IPIN) (pp. 1–5). Zurich: IPIN. doi:10.1109/IPIN.2010.5647328

Aung, E. D., Yang, J., Cho, D. K., & Gerla, M. (2008). *BluEyes–Bluetooth localization and tracking.* Retrieved from http://nrlweb.cs.ucla.edu/publication/download/532/BluEyes_08.pdf

Bachrach, J., & Taylor, C. (2005). Localization in sensor networks. In I. Stojmenovic (Ed.), *Handbook of Sensor Networks: Algorithms and Architectures* (pp. 277–310). John Wiley & Sons Inc. Retrieved from http://people.csail.mit.edu/jrb/Projects/poschap.pdf

Bahl, P., & Padmanabhan, V. N. (2000). RADAR: An in-building RF-based user location and tracking system. In *Proceedings of the Nineteenth Annual Joint Conference of the IEEE Computer and Communications Societies, INFOCOM 2000* (Vol. 2, pp. 775–784). Tel Aviv, Israel: IEEE. doi:10.1109/INFCOM.2000.832252

Bekkelien, A. (2012). *Bluetooth indoor positioning.* (Master's thesis). University of Geneva. Retrieved from http://cui.unige.ch/~deriazm/masters/bekkelien/Bekkelien_Master_Thesis.pdf

Benyó, B., Sódor, B., Fördos, G., Kovács, L., & Vilmos, A. (2010). A generalized approach for NFC application development. In *Proceedings of Second International Workshop on Near Field Communication* (NFC) (pp. 45–50). Monaco: NFC. doi:10.1109/NFC.2010.23

Berghel, H. (2013). RFIDiocy: It's déjà vu all over again. *Computer, 46*(1), 85–88. doi:10.1109/MC.2013.28

Bielawa, T. M. (2005). *Position location of remote Bluetooth devices*. (Master's thesis). Virginia Polytechnic Institute and State University. Retrieved from http://scholar.lib.vt.edu/theses/available/etd-07112005-222918/unrestricted/tbielawa_thesis.pdf

Blankenbach, J., Norrdine, A., & Hellmers, H. (2012). A robust and precise 3D indoor positioning system for harsh environments. In *Proceedings of International Conference on Indoor Positioning and Indoor Navigation* (IPIN) (pp. 1–8). Sydney, Australia: IPIN. doi:10.1109/IPIN.2012.6418863

Bolz, J. (2011). *Indoor positioning using NFC tags*. (Bachelor's thesis). Beuth Hochschule für Technik, Berlin, Germany. Retrieved from http://taglocate.googlecode.com/files/Thesis.pdf

Brás, L., Carvalho, N. B., Pinho, P., Kulas, L., & Nyka, K. (2012). A review of antennas for indoor positioning systems. *International Journal of Antennas and Propagation, 2012*, 1–14. doi:10.1155/2012/953269

Canovic, S. (2007). *Application of UWB technology for positioning, a feasibility study*. Retrieved August 12, 2013, from http://www.diva-portal.org/smash/get/diva2:347581/FULLTEXT01.pdf

Cavoukian, A. (2009). *Privacy by design*. Ontario, Canada: Office of the Information and Privacy Commissioner, Canada. Retrieved August 12, 2013, from http://www.ipc.on.ca/images/Resources/2009-06-23-TrustEconomics.pdf

Chandgadkar, A. (2013). *An indoor navigation system for Smartphones*. Retrieved August 15, 2013, from http://www.doc.ic.ac.uk/teaching/distinguished-projects/2013/a.chandgadkar.pdf

Chang, Y., & Tsai, S. (2007). A wayfinding system based on geo-coded QR codes and social computing for individuals with cognitive impairments. *International Journal of Advances in Information Sciences and Services, 2*, 69–74. Retrieved from http://mobile.kaywa.com/files/wayfinding-systems-with-qrcode.pdf

Chawathe, S. S. (2008). Beacon placement for indoor localization using Bluetooth. In *Proceedings of 11th International IEEE Conference on Intelligent Transportation Systems* (pp. 980–985). Beijing: IEEE. doi:10.1109/ITSC.2008.4732690

Chen, M.-X., & Wang, Y.-D. (2009). An efficient location tracking structure for wireless sensor networks. *Computer Communications, 32*(13), 1495–1504. doi:10.1016/j.comcom.2009.05.005

Choo, J. H., Cheong, S. N., Lee, Y. L., & Teh, S. H. (2012). I2Navi: An indoor interactive NFC navigation system for android smartphones. *World Academy of Science, Engineering and Technology*, (72), 735–739. Retrieved from http://www.waset.org/journals/waset/v72/v72-131.pdf

Chung, J., Donahoe, M., Schmandt, C., Kim, I.-J., Razavai, P., & Wiseman, M. (2011). Indoor location sensing using geo-magnetism. In *Proceedings of 9th international conference on Mobile systems, applications, and services* (pp. 141–154). New York, NY: Academic Press. doi:10.1145/1999995.2000010

Coleman, D. D., & Westcott, D. A. (2009). *CWNA Certified Wireless Network Administrator Official Study Guide: Exam PW0-104*. John Wiley & Sons.

Coskun, V., Ozdenizci, B., & Ok, K. (2012). A survey on near field communication (NFC) technology. *Wireless Personal Communications, 71*(3), 2259–2294. doi:10.1007/s11277-012-0935-5

Cypriani, M., Lassabe, F., Canalda, P., & Spies, F. (2011). Open wireless positioning system: a Wi-Fi-based indoor positioning system. In *Proceedings of 70th IEEE Vehicular Technology Conference Fall* (pp. 1–5). Anchorage, AK: IEEE. doi:10.1109/VETECF.2009.5378966

Darcy, P., Pupunwiwat, P., & Stantic, B. (2011). The challenges and issues facing the deployment of RFID technology. In C. Turcu (Ed.), *Deploying RFID - Challenges, Solutions, and Open Issues* (pp. 1–26). InTech. doi:10.5772/16986

Diaz, J. J. M., Maues, R. de A., Soares, R. B., Nakamura, E. F., & Figueiredo, C. M. S. (2010). Bluepass: An indoor Bluetooth-based localization system for mobile applications. In *Proceedings of IEEE Symposium on Computers and Communications* (pp. 778–783). Riccione, Italy: IEEE. doi:10.1109/ISCC.2010.5546506

Ekahau. (2005). *Comparison of wireless indoor positioning technologies*. Retrieved August 27, 2013, from http://www.productivet.com/docs-2/Wireless_Comparison.pdf

Fallah, N., Apostolopoulos, I., Bekris, K., & Folmer, E. (2013). Indoor human navigation systems: A survey. *Interacting with Computers*, 25(1), 21–33. doi:10.1093/iwc/iws010

Fernandes, T. (2011). Indoor localization using Bluetooth. In *Proceedings of 6th Doctoral Symposium in Informatics Engineering*, (pp. 1–10). Retrieved from http://paginas.fe.up.pt/~prodei/dsie11/images/pdfs/s5-4.pdf

Fukuju, Y., Minami, M., Morikawa, H., & Aoyama, T. (2003). DOLPHIN: An autonomous indoor positioning system in ubiquitous computing environment. In *Proceedings of IEEE Workshop on Software Technologies for Future Embedded Systems* (pp. 53–56). IEEE. doi:10.1109/WST-FES.2003.1201360

Galván-Tejada, C. E., Carrasco-Jiménez, J. C., & Brena, R. F. (2013). Bluetooth-WiFi based combined positioning algorithm, implementation and experimental evaluation. *Procedia Technology*, 7, 37–45. doi:10.1016/j.protcy.2013.04.005

Giorgetti, G., Farley, R., Chikkappa, K., Judy, E., & Kaleas, T. (2012). Cortina: Collaborative indoor positioning using low-power sensor networks. *Journal of Location Based Services*, 6(3), 137–160. doi:10.1080/17489725.2012.690217

Grover, A., & Berghel, H. (2011). A survey of RFID deployment and security issues. *Journal of Information Processing Systems*, 7(4), 561–580. doi:10.3745/JIPS.2011.7.4.561

Gu, Y., Lo, A., & Niemegeers, I. (2009). A survey of indoor positioning systems for wireless personal networks. *IEEE Communications Surveys and Tutorials*, 11(1), 13–32. doi:10.1109/SURV.2009.090103

Harper, J. (2004). *RFID tags and privacy: How bar-codes-on-steroids are really a 98-Lb. weakling*. Competitive Enterprise Institute. Retrieved July 15, 2013, from http://heartland.org/policy-documents/rfid-tags-and-privacy-how-bar-codes-steroids-are-really-98-lb-weakling

Hauschildt, D., & Kirchhof, N. (2010). Advances in thermal infrared localization: challenges and solutions. In *Proceedings of International Conference on Indoor Positioning and Indoor Navigation* (IPIN) (pp. 1–8). Zurich: IPIN. doi:10.1109/IPIN.2010.5647415

Hazas, M., & Hopper, A. (2006). Broadband ultrasonic location systems for improved indoor positioning. *IEEE Transactions on Mobile Computing*, 5(5), 536–547. doi:10.1109/TMC.2006.57

Hazas, M., & Ward, A. (2002). A novel broadband ultrasonic location system. In *Proceedings of the 4th International Conference on Ubiquitous Computing* (pp. 264–280). Sweden: Academic Press. doi:10.1007/3-540-45809-3_21

Henniges, R. (2012). Current approaches of Wifi positioning. In *Proceedings of IEEE Conference Publications*, (pp. 1–8). IEEE. Retrieved from http://www.snet.tu-berlin.de/fileadmin/fg220/courses/WS1112/snet-project/wifi-positioning_henniges.pdf

Holm, S. (2012). Ultrasound positioning based on time-of-flight and signal strength. In *Proceedings of International Conference on Indoor Positioning and Indoor Navigation* (IPIN) (pp. 1–6). Sydney: IPIN. doi:10.1109/IPIN.2012.6418728

Hopper, A., Harter, A., & Blackie, T. (1993). *The active badge system.* Retrieved August 27, 2013, from http://www.cl.cam.ac.uk/research/dtg/attarchive/ab.html

Huang, B., & Gao, Y. (2013). Ubiquitous indoor vision navigation using a smart device. *Geospatial. Information Science*, *16*(3), 177–185. doi:10.1080/10095020.2013.817110

Huang, H., & Gartner, G. (2010). A survey of mobile indoor navigation systems. In G. Gartner, & F. Ortag (Eds.), *Cartography in Central and Eastern Europe* (pp. 305–319). Springer.

Jang, S. H. (2010). A QR code-based indoor navigation system using augmented reality. *giscience.* Retrieved April 15, 2013, from http://www.giscience.org/proceedings/abstracts/giscience2012_paper_110.pdf

Kannan, B., Meneguzzi, F., Dias, B. M., Sycara, K., Gnegy, C., Glasgow, E., & Yordanov, P. (2013). Predictive indoor navigation using commercial smart-phones. In *Proceedings of the 28th Annual ACM Symposium on Applied Computing* (pp. 519–525). ACM. doi:10.1145/2480362.2480463

Karl, H., & Willig, A. (2006). Localization and positioning. In *Protocols and Architectures for Wireless Sensor Networks*. Chichester, UK: John Wiley & Sons Inc. doi:10.1002/0470095121.ch9

Khor, J. H., Ismail, W., Younis, M. I., Sulaiman, M. K., & Rahman, M. G. (2010). Security problems in an RFID system. *Wireless Personal Communications*, *59*(1), 17–26. doi:10.1007/s11277-010-0186-2

Kim, J., & Jun, H. (2008). Vision-based location positioning using augmented reality for indoor navigation. *IEEE Transactions on Consumer Electronics*, *54*(3), 954–962. doi:10.1109/TCE.2008.4637573

Kim, S.-E., Kim, Y., Yoon, J., & Kim, E. S. (2012). Indoor positioning system using geomagnetic anomalies for smartphones. In *Proceedings of International Conference on Indoor Positioning and Indoor Navigation* (IPIN) (pp. 1–5). Sydney: IPIN. doi:10.1109/IPIN.2012.6418947

Kitasuka, T., Nakanishi, T., & Fukuda, A. (2003). Wireless LAN based indoor positioning system WiPS and its simulation. In *Proceedings of IEEE Pacific Rim Conference on Communications, Computers and signal Processing* (Vol. 1, pp. 272–275). IEEE. doi:10.1109/PACRIM.2003.1235770

Klopschitz, M., Schall, G., Schmalstieg, D., & Reitmayr, G. (2010). Visual tracking for augmented reality. In *Proceedings of International Conference on Indoor Positioning and Indoor Navigation* (IPIN) (pp. 1–4). Zurich: IPIN. doi:10.1109/IPIN.2010.5648274

Koyuncu, H., & Yang, S. H. (2010). A survey of indoor positioning and object locating systems. *International Journal of Computer Science and Network Security*, *10*(5), 121–128. Retrieved from http://paper.ijcsns.org/07_book/201005/20100518.pdf

Langheinrich, M. (2008). A survey of RFID privacy approaches. *Personal and Ubiquitous Computing*, *13*(6), 413–421. doi:10.1007/s00779-008-0213-4

Lazos, L., Poovendran, R., & Čapkun, S. (2005). ROPE: Robust position estimation in wireless sensor networks. In *Proceedings of Fourth International Symposium on Information Processing in Sensor Networks*, (pp. 324–331). Academic Press. doi:10.1109/IPSN.2005.1440942

Lee, C., Chang, Y., Park, G., Ryu, J., Jeong, S.-G., Park, S., … Lee, M. H. (2004). Indoor positioning system based on incident angles of infrared emitters. In *Proceedings of 30th Annual Conference of IEEE Industrial Electronics Society* (Vol. 3, pp. 2218–2222). IEEE. doi:10.1109/IECON.2004.1432143

Lee, S., & Song, J. (2007). Mobile robot localization using infrared light reflecting landmarks. In *Proceedings of International Conference on Control, Automation and Systems* (pp. 674–677). Seoul: Academic Press. doi:10.1109/ICCAS.2007.4406984

Li, B., Gallagher, T., Dempster, A. G., & Rizos, C. (2012). How feasible is the use of magnetic field alone for indoor positioning? In *Proceedings of International Conference on Indoor Positioning and Indoor Navigation* (IPIN) (pp. 1–9). Sydney: IPIN. doi:10.1109/IPIN.2012.6418880

Link, J. A. B., Smith, P., Viol, N., & Wehrle, K. (2011). Footpath. Accurate map-based indoor navigation using smartphones. In *Proceedings of International Conference on Indoor Positioning and Indoor Navigation* (IPIN) (pp. 1–8). IPIN. doi:10.1109/IPIN.2011.6071934

Liu, H., Darabi, H., Banerjee, P., & Liu, J. (2007). Survey of wireless indoor positioning techniques and systems. *IEEE Transactions on Systems, Man and Cybernetics. Part C, Applications and Reviews*, *37*(6), 1067–1080. doi:10.1109/TSMCC.2007.905750

Liu, K., Liu, X., & Li, X. (2013). Guoguo: enabling fine-grained indoor localization via smartphone. In *Proceeding of the 11th annual international conference on Mobile systems, applications, and services* (pp. 235–248). Academic Press. doi:10.1145/2462456.2464450

Lopes, C. V., Haghighat, A., Mandal, A., Givargis, T., & Baldi, P. (2006). Localization of off-the-shelf mobile devices using audible sound: Architectures, protocols and performance assessment. *Mobile Computing and Communications Review*, *10*(2), 38–50. doi:10.1145/1137975.1137980

Lukianto, C., & Sternberg, H. (2011). *Overview of current indoor navigation techniques and implementation studies*. Retrieved August 15, 2013, from http://www.fig.net/pub/fig2011/papers/ts09a/ts09a_lukianto_sternberg_5102.pdf

Ma, J., Li, X., Tao, X., & Lu, J. (2008). Cluster filtered KNN: A WLAN-based indoor positioning scheme. In *Proceedings of International Symposium on a World of Wireless, Mobile and Multimedia Networks* (pp. 1–8). Academic Press. doi:10.1109/WOWMOM.2008.4594840

Mandal, A., Lopes, C. V., Givargis, T., Haghighat, A., Jurdak, R., & Baldi, P. (2005). Beep: 3D indoor positioning using audible sound. In *Proceedings of Second IEEE Consumer Communications and Networking Conference* (pp. 348–353). IEEE. doi:10.1109/CCNC.2005.1405195

Mao, G., Fidan, B., & Anderson, B. D. O. (2007). Wireless sensor network localization techniques. *Computer Networks*, *51*(10), 2529–2553. doi:10.1016/j.comnet.2006.11.018

Mautz, R. (2009). Overview of current indoor positioning systems. *Geodesy and Cartography*, *35*(1), 18–22. doi:10.3846/1392-1541.2009.35.18-22

Mautz, R. (2012). *Indoor positioning technologies.* (Habilitation thesis). ETH Zurich. Retrieved from http://e-collection.library.ethz.ch/eserv/eth:5659/eth-5659-01.pdf

Mautz, R., & Tilch, S. (2011). Survey of optical indoor positioning systems. In *Proceedings of International Conference on Indoor Positioning and Indoor Navigation* (IPIN) (pp. 1–7). IPIN. doi:10.1109/IPIN.2011.6071925

Medina, C., Segura, J. C., & De la Torre, Á. (2013). Ultrasound indoor positioning system based on a low-power wireless sensor network providing sub-centimeter accuracy. *Sensors (Basel, Switzerland)*, *13*(3), 3501–3526. doi:10.3390/s130303501 PMID:23486218

Meissner, P., Leitinger, E., Fröhle, M., & Witrisal, K. (2013). Accurate and robust indoor localization systems using ultra-wideband signals. In *Proceedings of European Conference on Navigation* (pp. 1–10). Vienna, Austria: Academic Press. Retrieved from http://arxiv.org/abs/1304.7928

Minami, M., Fukuju, Y., Hirasawa, K., Yokoyama, S., Mizumachi, M., Morikawa, H., & Aoyama, T. (2004). DOLPHIN: A practical approach for implementing a fully distributed indoor ultrasonic positioning system. In N. Davies, E. D. Mynatt, & I. Siio (Eds.), *UbiComp 2004: Ubiquitous Computing* (pp. 347–365). Springer. doi:10.1007/978-3-540-30119-6_21

Miraz, G. M., Ruiz, I. L., & Gomez-Nieto, M. A. (2009). How NFC can be used for the compliance of European higher education area guidelines in European universities. In *Proceedings of First International Workshop on Near Field Communication* (pp. 3–8). Hagenberg. doi:10.1109/NFC.2009.9

Mulliner, C. (2009). Vulnerability analysis and attacks on NFC-enabled mobile phones. In *Proceedings of International Conference on Availability, Reliability and Security* (pp. 695–700). Fukuoka: Academic Press. doi:10.1109/ARES.2009.46

Muñoz-Organero, M., Muñoz-Merino, P. J., & Kloos, C. D. (2012). Using Bluetooth to implement a pervasive indoor positioning system with minimal requirements at the application level. *Mobile Information Systems*, *8*(1), 73–82. doi:10.3233/MIS-2012-0132

Nambiar, A. N. (2009). RFID technology: A review of its applications. In *Proceedings of the World Congress on Engineering and Computer Science* (Vol. 2, pp. 1253–1259). San Francisco, CA: Academic Press. Retrieved from http://www.iaeng.org/publication/WCECS2009/WCECS2009_pp1253-1259.pdf

Ni, L. M., Liu, Y., Lau, Y. C., & Patil, A. P. (2003). LANDMARC: Indoor location sensing using active RFID. In *Proceedings of the First IEEE International Conference on Pervasive Computing and Communications* (pp. 407–415). Fort Worth, TX: IEEE. doi:10.1109/PERCOM.2003.1192765

Ozdenizci, B., Ok, K., Coskun, V., & Aydin, M. N. (2011). Development of an indoor navigation system using NFC technology. In *Proceedings of Fourth International Conference on Information and Computing* (pp. 11 – 14). Phuket Island: Academic Press. doi:10.1109/ICIC.2011.53

Pampattiwar, S. (2012). Literature survey on NFC, applications and controller. *International Journal of Scientific and Engineering Research*, *3*(2), 1–4. Retrieved from http://www.ijser.org/researchpaper/Literature-Survey-On-NFC-applications-and-controller.pdf

Paperno, E., Sasada, I., & Leonovich, E. (2001). A new method for magnetic position and orientation tracking. *IEEE Transactions on Magnetics*, *37*(4), 1938–1940. doi:10.1109/20.951014

Priyantha, N. B. (2005). *The cricket indoor location system*. (Doctoral thesis). Massachusetts Institute of Technology. Retrieved from https://nms.csail.mit.edu/papers/bodhi-thesis.pdf

Rao, H., & Fu, W.-T. (2013). A general framework for a collaborative mobile indoor navigation assistance system. In *Proceedings of the 3rd International Workshop on Location Awareness for Mixed and Dual Reality* (pp. 21–24). Retrieved from http://www.dfki.de/LAMDa/2013/accepted/LAMDa13Proceedings.pdf#page=25

Renaudin, V., Yalak, O., Tome, P., & Merminod, B. (2007). Indoor navigation of emergency agents. *European Journal of Navigation*, *5*(3), 36–45. Retrieved from http://infoscience.epfl.ch/record/109915/files/EJN July S-RenaudinLR-Reprint.pdf

Retscher, G., Moser, E., Vredeveld, D., & Heberling, D. (2006). Performance and accuracy test of the WLAN indoor positioning system "ipos". In *Proceedings of the 3rd Workshop on Positioning, Navigation and Communication* (pp. 7–16). Retrieved from http://www.wpnc.net/fileadmin/WPNC06/Proceedings/6_Performance_and_Accuracy_Test_of_the_WLAN_Indoor_Positioning_System_IPOS.pdf

Rishabh, I., Kimber, D., & Adcock, J. (2012). Indoor localization using controlled ambient sounds. In *Proceedings of International Conference on Indoor Positioning and Indoor Navigation* (IPIN) (pp. 1–10). Sydney: IPIN. doi:10.1109/IPIN.2012.6418905

Robles, J. J., Munoz, E. G., De la Cuesta, L., & Lehnert, R. (2012). Performance evaluation of an indoor localization protocol in a 802.15. 4 sensor network. In *Proceedings of International Conference on Indoor Positioning and Indoor Navigation* (IPIN) (pp. 1–10). Sydney: IPIN. doi:10.1109/IPIN.2012.6418936

Rossi, M., Seiter, J., Amft, O., Buchmeier, S., & Trster, G. (2013). RoomSense: An indoor positioning system for smartphones using active sound probing. In *Proceedings of the 4th Augmented Human International Conference* (pp. 89–95). Stuttgart, Germany: Academic Press. doi:10.1145/2459236.2459252

Saab, S. S., & Nakad, Z. S. (2011). A stand-alone RFID indoor positioning system using passive tags. *IEEE Transactions on Industrial Electronics*, *58*(5), 1961–1970. doi:10.1109/TIE.2010.2055774

Sarma, S. E., Weis, S. A., & Engels, D. W. (2003). RFID systems and security and privacy implications. In C. Paar (Ed.), *B. S. Kaliski, çetin K. Koç* (pp. 454–469). Cryptographic Hardware and Embedded Systems. doi:10.1007/3-540-36400-5_33

Sayrafian-Pour, K., & Perez, J. (2007). Robust indoor positioning based on received signal strength. In *Proceedings of 2nd International Conference on Pervasive Computing and Applications* (pp. 693–698). Birmingham, UK: Academic Press. doi:10.1109/ICPCA.2007.4365532

Scheerens, D. (2012). *Practical indoor localization using Bluetooth*. (Master's thesis). University of Twente. Retrieved from http://essay.utwente.nl/61496/

Senger, C., & Kaiser, T. (2006). Indoor positioning with UWB beamforming. In *Proceedings of the 3rd Workshop on Positioning, Navigation and Communication* (pp. 149–158). Retrieved from http://www.wpnc.net/fileadmin/WPNC06/Proceedings/26_Indoor_Positioning_with_UWB_Beamforming.pdf

Storms, W. F. (2009). *Magnetic field aided indoor navigation*. (Master's thesis). Air Force Institute of Technology, Air University. Retrieved from http://www.dtic.mil/cgi-bin/GetTRDoc?Location=U2&doc=GetTRDoc.pdf&AD=ADA497156

Subhan, F., Hasbullah, H., Rozyyev, A., & Bakhsh, S. T. (2011). Indoor positioning in bluetooth networks using fingerprinting and lateration approach. In *Proceedings of International Conference on Information Science and Applications* (pp. 1–9). Jeju Island: Academic Press. doi:10.1109/ICISA.2011.5772436

Tilch, S., & Mautz, R. (2011). CLIPS proceedings. In *Proceedings of International Conference on Indoor Positioning and Indoor Navigation* (IPIN) (pp. 1–6). IPIN. doi:10.1109/IPIN.2011.6071937

Trigony, N. (2012). *Challenges and approaches to improving the accuracy of indoor positioning systems*. Retrieved August 28, 2013, from http://talks.cam.ac.uk/talk/index/40689

Vazquez-Briseno, M., Hirata, F. I., Sanchez-Lopez, J. de D., Jimenez-Garcia, E., Navarro-Cota, C., & Nieto-Hipolito, J. I. (2012). Using RFID/NFC and QR-code in mobile phones to link the physical and the digital world. In I. Deliyannis (Ed.), *Interactive Multimedia* (pp. 219–242). InTech. doi:10.5772/37447

Vicent, J. P. A. (2013). *WiFi indoor positioning for mobile devices, an application for the UJI smart campus*. (Master's thesis). Repositorio Universidade Nova. Retrieved from http://hdl.handle.net/10362/9193

Waldmann, B., Weigel, R., Ebelt, R., & Vossiek, M. (2012). An ultra wideband local positioning system for highly complex indoor environments. In *Proceedings of International Conference on Localization and GNSS* (pp. 1–5). GNSS. doi:10.1109/ICL-GNSS.2012.6253125

Wang, C., Wu, H., & Tzeng, N.-F. (2007). RFID-based 3-D positioning schemes. In *Proceedings of 26th IEEE International Conference on Computer Communications* (pp. 1235–1243). Anchorage, AK: IEEE. doi:10.1109/INFCOM.2007.147

Wang, C.-S., Huang, C.-H., Chen, Y.-S., & Zheng, L.-J. (2009). An implementation of positioning system in indoor environment based on active RFID. In *Proceedings of 2009 Joint Conferences on Pervasive Computing* (pp. 71–76). Academic Press. doi:10.1109/JCPC.2009.5420212

Wang, H., & Jia, F. (2007). A hybrid modeling for WLAN positioning system. In *Proceedings of International Conference on Wireless Communications, Networking and Mobile Computing* (pp. 2152–2155). Shanghai: Academic Press. doi:10.1109/WICOM.2007.537

Wang, L. E. (2012). *iNavigation: An image based indoor navigation system*. (Master's thesis). Auckland University of Technology. Retrieved from http://hdl.handle.net/10292/4743

Want, R., Hopper, A., Falcão, V., & Gibbons, J. (1992). The active badge location system. *ACM Transactions on Information Systems*, *10*(1), 91–102. doi:10.1145/128756.128759

Wierenga, J., & Komisarczuk, P. (2005). SIMPLE: Developing a LBS positioning solution. In *Proceedings of the 4th International Conference on Mobile and Ubiquitous Multimedia* (pp. 48–55). Academic Press. doi:10.1145/1149488.1149497

Woodman, O. J., & Harle, R. K. (2010). Concurrent scheduling in the active bat location system. In *Proceedings of 8th IEEE International Conference on Pervasive Computing and Communications Workshops* (pp. 431–437). Mannheim, Germany: IEEE. doi:10.1109/PERCOMW.2010.5470631

Xiao, J., Liu, Z., Yang, Y., Liu, D., & Han, X. (2011). Comparison and analysis of indoor wireless positioning techniques. In *Proceedings of International Conference on Computer Science and Service System* (pp. 293–296). Nanjing: Academic Press. doi:10.1109/CSSS.2011.5972088

Ye, R. (2012). *Ultra-wideband indoor localization systems*. (Doctoral thesis). Oregon State University. Retrieved from http://scholarsarchive. library.oregonstate.edu/xmlui/handle/1957/30349

Yick, J., Mukherjee, B., & Ghosal, D. (2008). Wireless sensor network survey. *Computer Networks*, *52*(12), 2292–2330. doi:10.1016/j. comnet.2008.04.002

Yun, S., Lee, J., Chung, W., Kim, E., & Kim, S. (2009). A soft computing approach to localization in wireless sensor networks. *Expert Systems with Applications*, *36*(4), 7552–7561. doi:10.1016/j. eswa.2008.09.064

Zafeiropoulos, A., Papaioannou, I., Solidakis, E., Konstantinou, N., Stathopoulos, P., & Mitrou, N. (2010). Exploiting Bluetooth for deploying indoor LBS over a localisation infrastructure independent architecture. *International Journal of Computer Aided Engineering and Technology*, *2*(2), 145–163. doi:10.1504/IJCAET.2010.030542

Zinkiewicz, D. (2012). *Indoor navigation based on cloud computing*. Retrieved August 26, 2013, from http://ec.europa.eu/digital-agenda/events/cf/ictpd12/document.cfm?doc_id=23009

ADDITIONAL READING

Agrawal, R., & Vasalya, A. (2012). Bluetooth navigation system using Wi-Fi access points, 1–8. Retrieved from http://arxiv.org/pdf/1204.1748

Akyildiz, I. F., Su, W., Sankarasubramaniam, Y., & Cayirci, E. (2002). Wireless sensor networks: A survey. *Computer Networks*, *38*(4), 393–422. doi:10.1016/S1389-1286(01)00302-4

Attia, M., Moussa, A., Zhao, X., & El-Sheimy, N. (2011). Assisting personal positioning in indoor environments using map matching. In *Archives of Photogrammetry, Cartography and Remote Sensing* (Vol. 22, pp. 39–49). Retrieved from http://www.sgp.geodezja.org.pl/ptfit/wydawnictwa/krakow2011/APCRS vol. 22 pp. 39-49.pdf

Aye, N., Maung, M., & Kawai, M. (2012). Hybrid RSS-SOM localization scheme for wireless ad hoc and sensor networks. In *International Conference on Indoor Positioning and Indoor Navigation (IPIN)* (pp. 1–7). doi:10.1109/IPIN.2012.6418903

Baggio, A., & Langendoen, K. (2008). Monte Carlo localization for mobile wireless sensor networks. *Ad Hoc Networks*, *6*(5), 718–733. doi:10.1016/j.adhoc.2007.06.004

Balakrishnan, H., & Priyantha, N. B. (2003). The Cricket Indoor Location System: Experience and Status. In *Proceedings of the 2003 Workshop on Location-Aware Computing* (pp. 7–9). Seattle, Washington, USA. Retrieved from http://research.microsoft.com/pubs/64616/2003workshoponlocationawarecomputing.pdf

Bekkali, A., Sanson, H., & Matsumoto, M. (2007). RFID Indoor Positioning Based on Probabilistic RFID Map and Kalman Filtering. In *Third IEEE International Conference on Wireless and Mobile Computing, Networking and Communications*. White Plains, NY. doi:10.1109/WIMOB.2007.4390815

Boochs, F., Schütze, R., Simon, C., Marzani, F., Wirth, H., & Meier, J. (2010). Increasing the accuracy of untaught robot positions by means of a multi-camera system. In *International Conference on Indoor Positioning and Indoor Navigation (IPIN)* (pp. 1–9). Zurich. doi:10.1109/IPIN.2010.5646261

Brajdic, A., & Harle, R. (2012). Scalable indoor pedestrian localisation using inertial sensing and parallel particle filters. In *International Conference on Indoor Positioning and Indoor Navigation (IPIN)* (pp. 1–10). Sydney, NSW. doi:10.1109/IPIN.2012.6418879

Chang, Yao-jen, Chu, Y., Chen, C., & Wang, T. (2008). Mobile computing for indoor wayfinding based on Bluetooth sensors for individuals with cognitive impairments. In *3rd International Symposium on Wireless Pervasive Computing* (pp. 623–627). Santorini. doi:10.1109/ISWPC.2008.4556284

D'Atri, E., Medaglia, C. M., Serbanati, A., Ceipidor, U. B., Panizzi, E., & D'Atri, A. (2007). A system to aid blind people in the mobility: A usability test and its results. In *Second International Conference on Systems*. Martinique. doi:10.1109/ICONS.2007.7

Dao, T.-K., Pham, T.-T., & Castelli, E. (2013). A robust WLAN positioning system based on probabilistic propagation model. In *9th International Conference on Intelligent Environments* (pp. 24–29). Athens. doi:10.1109/IE.2013.8

Feldmann, S., Kyamakya, K., Zapater, A., & Lue, Z. (2003). An indoor Bluetooth-based positioning system: Concept, implementation and experimental evaluation. In *International Conference on Wireless Networks* (pp. 109–113). Retrieved from http://projekte.l3s.uni-hannover.de/pub/bscw.cgi/S48c2249c/d27118/An Indoor Bluetooth-based positioning system: concept, Implementation and experimental evaluation.pdf

Fischer, C., Muthukrishnan, K., Hazas, M., & Gellersen, H. (2008). Ultrasound-aided pedestrian dead reckoning for indoor navigation. In *Proceedings of the first ACM international workshop on Mobile entity localization and tracking in GPS-less environments* (pp. 31–36). New York, USA. doi:10.1145/1410012.1410020

Galvan-Tejada, C. E., Galvan-Tejada, I., Sandoval, E. I., & Brena, R. (2012). WiFi Bluetooth based combined positioning algorithm. *Procedia Engineering*, *35*, 101–108. doi:10.1016/j.proeng.2012.04.170

Gorostiza, E. M., Galilea, J. L. L., Meca, F. J. M., Monzú, D. S., Zapata, F. E., & Puerto, L. P. (2011). Infrared sensor system for mobile-robot positioning in intelligent spaces. *Sensors (Basel, Switzerland)*, *11*(5), 5416–5438. doi:10.3390/s110505416 PMID:22163907

Hu, L., & Evans, D. (2004). Localization for mobile sensor networks. In *Proceedings of the 10th annual international conference on Mobile computing and networking* (pp. 45–57). New York, USA. doi:10.1145/1023720.1023726

Huang, B., & Gao, Y. (2012). A floor plan based vision navigation system for indoor navigation with smart device. *Journal of Global Positioning Systems*, *11*(1), 71–79. doi:10.5081/jgps.11.1.71

Itagaki, Y., Suzuki, A., & Iyota, T. (2012). Indoor positioning for moving objects using a hardware device with spread spectrum ultrasonic waves. In *International Conference on Indoor Positioning and Indoor Navigation (IPIN)* (pp. 1–6). Sydney, NSW. doi:10.1109/IPIN.2012.6418850

Ji, X., & Zha, H. (2004). Sensor positioning in wireless ad-hoc sensor networks using multidimensional scaling. In *Twenty-third Annual Joint Conference of the IEEE Computer and Communications Societies* (Vol. 4, pp. 2652–2661). doi:10.1109/INFCOM.2004.1354684

Kaemarungsi, K. (2005). *Design of Indoor Positioning Systems based on Location Fingerprinting Technique.* Doctoral thesis, University of Pittsburg. Retrieved from http://d-scholarship.pitt.edu/6395/

Krishnan, S., Sharma, P., Guoping, Z., & Woon, O. H. (2007). A UWB based localization system for indoor robot navigation. In *IEEE International Conference on Ultra-Wideband* (pp. 77–82). Singapore. doi:10.1109/ICUWB.2007.4380919

Kuo, R. J., & Chang, J. W. (2013). Intelligent RFID positioning system through immune-based feed-forward neural network. *Journal of Intelligent Manufacturing.* doi:10.1007/s10845-013-0832-0

Li, B., Salter, J., Dempster, A. G., & Rizos, C. (2006). Indoor positioning techniques based on wireless LAN. In *First IEEE International Conference on Wireless Broadband and Ultra Wideband Communications* (pp. 1–7). Retrieved from http://citeseerx.ist.psu.edu/viewdoc/summary?doi=10.1.1.72.1265

Li, X., & Wang, J. (2012). Image matching techniques for vision-based indoor navigation systems: performance analysis for 3D map based approach. In *International Conference on Indoor Positioning and Indoor Navigation (IPIN)* (pp. 1–8). Sydney, NSW. doi:10.1109/IPIN.2012.6418946

Liu, C.-H., & Lo, C.-Y. (2010). The study for the WLAN with Bluetooth positioning system. In *International Conference on Advances in Energy Engineering* (pp. 154–157). Beijing. doi:10.1109/ICAEE.2010.5557591

Luo, Y., & Law, C. L. (2012). Indoor positioning using UWB-IR signals in the presence of dense multipath with path overlapping. *IEEE Transactions on Wireless Communications, 11*(10), 3734–3743. doi:10.1109/TWC.2012.081612.120045

Ma, Y.-W., Lai, C.-F., Hsu, J.-M., Chen, N.-K., & Huang, Y.-M. (2010). RFID-based positioning system for telematics location-aware applications. *Wireless Personal Communications, 59*(1), 95–108. doi:10.1007/s11277-010-0192-4

Mangas, E., & Bilas, A. (2009). FLASH: Fine-grained localization in wireless sensor networks using acoustic sound transmissions and high precision clock synchronization. In *29th IEEE International Conference on Distributed Computing Systems* (pp. 289–298). Montreal, QC. doi:10.1109/ICDCS.2009.33

Mautz, R. (2009). The challenges of indoor environments and specification on some alternative positioning systems. In *Proceedings of the 6th Workshop on Positioning, Navigation and Communication* (pp. 29–36). Hannover. doi:10.1109/WPNC.2009.4907800

Mazuelas, S., Bahillo, A., Lorenzo, R. M., Fernandez, P., Lago, F. a., Garcia, E., … Abril, E. J. (2009). Robust indoor positioning provided by real-time RSSI values in unmodified WLAN networks. *IEEE Journal of Selected Topics in Signal Processing, 3*(5), 821–831. doi:10.1109/JSTSP.2009.2029191

Möller, A., Kranz, M., Huitl, R., Diewald, S., & Roalter, L. (2012). A mobile indoor navigation system interface adapted to vision-based localization. In *Proceedings of the 11th International Conference on Mobile and Ubiquitous Multimedia* (pp. 1–10). doi:10.1145/2406367.2406372

Mulloni, A., Wagner, D., Schmalstieg, D., & Barakonyi, I. (2009). Indoor positioning and navigation with camera phones. *IEEE Pervasive Computing / IEEE Computer Society [and] IEEE Communications Society, 8*(2), 22–31. doi:10.1109/MPRV.2009.30

Nagaosa, T., & Iguchi, H. (2012). Performance evaluation of a Wireless LAN positioning system using spot information. In *12th International Conference on ITS Telecommunications* (pp. 512–516). Taipei. doi:10.1109/ITST.2012.6425232

Papliatseyeu, A., Kotilainen, N., Mayora, O., & Osmani, V. (2009). FINDR: Low-cost indoor positioning using FM radio. In J.-M. Bonnin, C. Giannelli, & T. Magedanz (Eds.), *Mobile Wireless Middleware* (pp. 15–26). Operating Systems, and Applications. doi:10.1007/978-3-642-01802-2_2

Peter, M., Fritsch, D., Schafer, B., Kleusberg, A., Link, J. A. B., & Wehrle, K. (2012). Versatile geo-referenced maps for indoor navigation of pedestrians. In *International Conference on Indoor Positioning and Indoor Navigation (IPIN)* (pp. 1–4). Retrieved from http://www.comsys.rwth-aachen.de/fileadmin/papers/2012/2012-bitsch-IPIN-vegemite.pdf

Priyantha, N. B. Chakraborty, A., & Balakrishnan, H. (2000). The Cricket location-support system. In *Proceedings of the 6th annual international conference on Mobile computing and networking* (pp. 32–43). Boston, MA, USA. doi:10.1145/345910.345917

Sichitiu, M. L., & Ramadurai, V. (2004). Localization of wireless sensor networks with a mobile beacon. In *IEEE International Conference on Mobile Ad-hoc and Sensor Systems* (pp. 174–183). doi:10.1109/MAHSS.2004.1392104

Suzuki, A., Iyota, T., & Watanabe, K. (2012). Real-time distance measurement for indoor positioning system using spread spectrum ultrasonic waves. In A. A. dos Santos Junior (Ed.), *Ultrasonic Waves* (pp. 173–188). InTech. doi:10.5772/30215

Tilch, S., & Mautz, R. (2010). Development of a new laser-based, optical indoor positioning system. In J. P. Mills, D. M. Barber, P. E. Miller, & I. Newton (Eds.), *Proceedings of the ISPRS Commission V Mid-Term Symposium "Close Range Image Measurement Techniques"* (Vol. XXXVIII, pp. 575–580). Newcastle upon Tyne, United Kingdom. Retrieved from http://www.isprs.org/proceedings/XXXVIII/part5/papers/98.pdf

Wang, J., & Katabi, D. (2013). Dude, where's my card?: RFID positioning that works with multipath and non-line of sight. *Proceedings of the ACM SIGCOMM 2013 conference on SIGCOMM, 43*(4), 51–62. doi:10.1145/2534169.2486029

Wang, X., Yuan, S., Laur, R., & Lang, W. (2011). Dynamic localization based on spatial reasoning with RSSI in wireless sensor networks for transport logistics. *Sensors and Actuators, 171*(2), 421–428. doi:10.1016/j.sna.2011.08.015

Wang, Y., Shi, S., Yang, X., & Ma, A. (2010). Bluetooth indoor positioning using RSSI and least square estimation. Retrieved July 15, 2013, from http://202.175.25.24/papers/2010/fcc2010y-apeng.pdf

Wang, Y., Yang, X., Zhao, Y., Liu, Y., & Cuthbert, L. (2013). Bluetooth positioning using RSSI and triangulation methods. In *10th IEEE Consumer Communications and Networking Conference* (pp. 837–842). Las Vegas, NV. doi:10.1109/CCNC.2013.6488558

Wirz, M., Roggen, D., & Tröster, G. (2010). A wearable, ambient sound-based approach for infrastructureless fuzzy proximity estimation. In *International Symposium on Wearable Computers* (pp. 1–4). Seoul. doi:10.1109/ISWC.2010.5665863

Xiang, Z., Song, S., Chen, J., Wang, H., Huang, J., & Gao, X. (2004). A wireless LAN-based indoor positioning technology. *IBM Journal of Research and Development*, *48*(5), 617–626. doi:10.1147/rd.485.0617

Yucel, H., Edizkan, R., Ozkir, T., & Yazici, A. (2012). Development of indoor positioning system with ultrasonic and infrared signals. In *International Symposium on Innovations in Intelligent Systems and Applications* (pp. 1–4). Trabzon. doi:10.1109/INISTA.2012.6246983

Zwirello, L., Schipper, T., Harter, M., & Zwick, T. (2012). UWB localization system for indoor applications: Concept, realization and analysis. *Journal of Electrical and Computer Engineering*, *2012*, 1–11. doi:10.1155/2012/849638

KEY TERMS AND DEFINITIONS

Global Positioning System (GPS): GPS is a satellite based system that makes use of GPS receivers, like Garmin and TomTom, for timing, positioning and navigation purposes in an outdoor environment.

Navigation: Navigation is the orientation from a point of departure and travelling through a path towards a destination without colliding with an obstacle.

Near Field Communication (NFC): NFC is a short-range wireless technology that aids contactless communication between NFC embedded mobile devices and NFC tags and contactless smart cards in close proximity of not more than 10cm.

Positioning: Positioning is the process of determining the location of a person, place or object by employing positioning techniques within a network.

Radio Frequency Identification (RFID): RFID is a wireless and contactless technology that uses radio waves to read and capture information stored in a tag for the purpose of tracking and identification within a 100m radius.

Reader: A reader is a device that reads compatible information from a tag. For example, a mobile phone.

Server: A server is a computer system that stores, processes and manages access to resources by other devices that connect to it.

Tag: A tag is an integrated circuit or microchip that stores information that is read by a reader.

Chapter 4
Open Source Object Directory Services for Inter-Enterprise Tracking and Tracing Applications

Konstantinos Mourtzoukos
Athens Information Technology, Greece

Nikos Kefalakis
Athens Information Technology, Greece

John Soldatos
Athens Information Technology, Greece

ABSTRACT

Despite the proliferation of RFID (Radio Frequency Identification) applications, there are still only a limited number of open-loop inter-enterprise applications that address global supply chains. The implementation of such inter-enterprise applications hinges on standards and techniques for discovering and accessing RFID tagged objects across different repositories of RFID information residing across different administrative domains. In this chapter, the authors introduce an open and novel implementation of an ONS (Object Naming Service) solution for inter-enterprise tracking and tracing RFID applications. The solution is part of the open source AspireRFID project and provides a sound basis for integrating tracking ("google-of-things" like) applications for the RFID and the Internet-of-Things (IoT). As part of the presentation of the solution, this chapter illustrates the main challenges associated with the integration of inter-enterprise applications, along with strategies for confronting them.

DOI: 10.4018/978-1-4666-6308-4.ch004

1. INTRODUCTION

During the last decade we are witnessing a constant increase in the use and integration of RFID (Radio Frequency Identification) technologies in more and more fields of everyday life and across various industries. Industry sectors such as livestock management, ticketing, retail billing and supply chain management take advantage of RFID technology to lower their costs, streamline processes and increase their efficiency. Indeed, RFID technology presents proven benefits for supply chain management and inventory management systems, especially when it comes to managing complex logistics processes spanning multiple enterprises and stakeholders. In particular, it is wireless and contactless, so products can be scanned en masse even while they are inside shipping containers. The namespace is huge and it can be considered virtually infinite for most applications. The tag itself is small and durable, and can be embedded inside an object or otherwise protected from physical ware and harm. And while there are proprietary of industry specific coding schemes, most of the tags are based in a few well defined and interoperable standards.

Nevertheless, RFID deployments are also associated with a host of technical and organizational challenges such as the need to filter out information that is not useful for a given application context, the need to interface to multiple heterogeneous readers, as well as the need to identify and route application events to the appropriate enterprise applications (such as Enterprise Resource Planning -ERP, Warehouse Management Systems -WMS and other corporate applications) (Kefalakis, 2009). These technical challenges are usually addressed by RFID middleware and related middleware standards. Prominent places among these standards hold those specified by EPCglobal Architecture Review Committee (2013), including:

- The EPC Tag Data Specification (EPCglobal, 2013c), which defines the overall structure of the Electronic Product Code (EPC), including mechanisms for federating between different coding schemes.
- The EPC Reader Interface (EPCglobal, 2013e), which provides a group of standards that define the means to command an RFID reader to read, write and access other features of tags, and also provide access to RFID reader management functions.
- The Filtering and Collection standards (EPCglobal, 2013a), which provide the means for client applications to request EPC data from one or more data sources. It also specifies mechanisms for filtering, grouping and counting EPC data.
- The Electronic Product Code Information Service (EPCIS) (EPCglobal, 2013b), which provides a path where EPCIS events, generated from capturing applications, can be stored with enhanced business context (Dimitropoulos 2010) to a repository. These events provide the stored data on demand, to enterprise systems through some connector application (Leontiadis, 2009).

These standards specify functionalities that are useful to applications deployed within an enterprise. However, the full potential of RFID enabled supply chains will be realized in the scope of inter-enterprise applications involving multiple stakeholders/organizations across value chains and supply chains (Vijayaraman, 2006).

At this point it worth's to mention that by inter-enterprise applications we refer to applications that involve multiple companies and are executed throughout the lifecycle of a supply chain. For instance, an inter-enterprise application refers to a supply chain whose objects of interest move from any location in the factory till a retail store shelf regardless to whether these business locations belong to the same company or no. Whereas by open-loop intra-enterprise applications we refer to applications that involve a single company and are executed throughout the lifecycle of its supply chain. For instance, an intra-enterprise application refers to a supply chain whose objects of interest move from any location in the factory till the retail store where business locations belong to the same company.

Seamless collaboration and automatic integration, which is the basic nature of such inter-enterprise applications is the key to realizing emerging concepts such as «The Internet of Things» (Sundmaeker, 2010) and «Machine-to-Machine (M2M) Communications» (Lawton, 2004) in a larger scale than before. Based on these concepts we shall witness the manifestation of novel applications such as product traceability to the initial producer level, counterfeit prevention and authenticity verification down to the consumer

level and 'Google of things' types of search engines for objects. The above concepts and applications hold a symbiotic relationship with RFID – That RFID is the key behind their existence and they are the cornerstone from which RFID can take off and deliver benefits beyond the four walls of an enterprise.

Such industry wide applications are by nature distributed, and the amount of information generated is impossible to store and manage centrally – or locally for that matter. Being distributed also implies that often there is no apriori knowledge of location or available interfaces between all partners, and such information has to be discovered (as shown in Figure 1). There rises the need for an 'Object Loop-up Service'. This is an incarnation of the directory service found in all distributed systems, this time associating object names (the unique RFID tag the object is carrying) with sources of information regarding the particular

Figure 1. Inter-enterprise applications pose the challenge of discovering additional partners

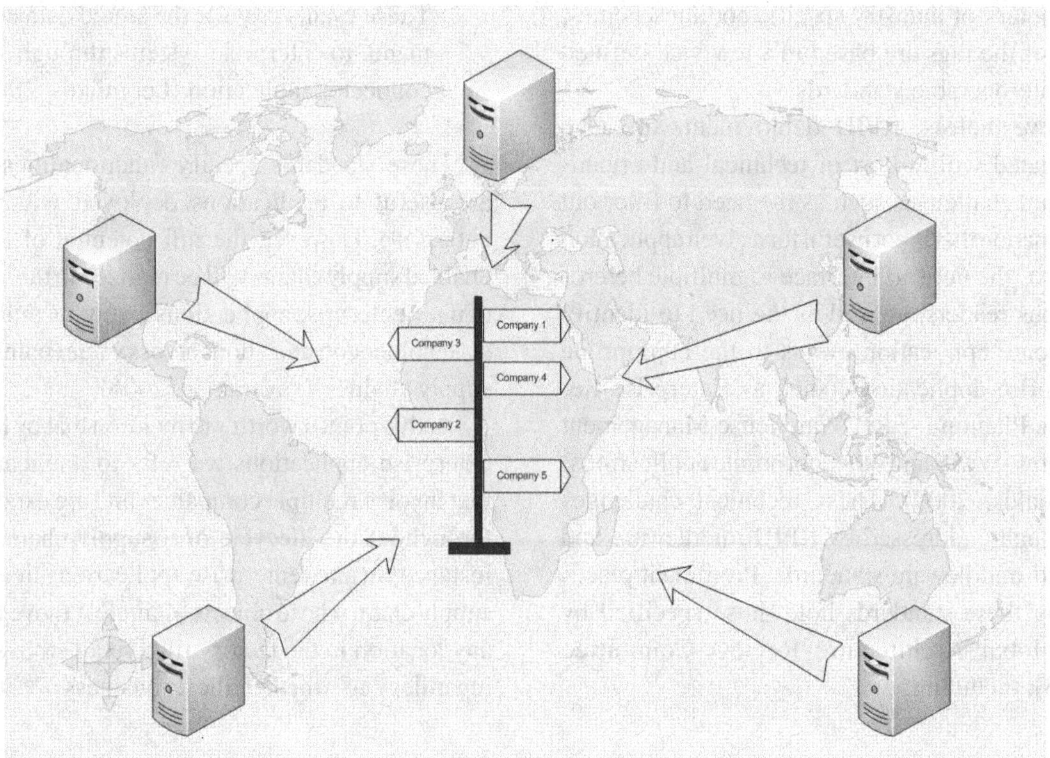

object. EPCglobal does provide the specification for such a service called Object Naming Service (ONS) (EPCglobal, 2013d), along with its position in the overall framework and the interaction with the rest of the components. At the moment there are only a few implementations of the service, and most of them are proprietary.

2. MAIN FOCUS OF THE CHAPTER

In this chapter we introduce an open source implementation of a distributed look-up / service for RFID tags. The implementation lends itself on the ONS standards and provides the core directory service for EPCIS accessing applications, as defined in the EPCglobal framework. Using the ONS server, an enterprise application can discover and retrieve data from partner applications running on foreign domains. Besides the core server we provide an API (in Java) that allows application to perform lookup for EPC tags on the ONS server. While the server, and the API (Application Programming Interface) is based on the standard proposed by EPCglobal, both can be easily adapted to serve as basis for directory services in the Internet of Things (IoT) era of applications. This adaptation involves the registration and discovery of wider classes of sensors. Along with the implementation we introduce a representative application that manifests the concept and the added-value of inter-enterprise applications. The application allows the automated tracking of company products, as they move between business partners. To this end, each partner has an already established RFID infrastructure (an EPCIS repository as defined by EPCglobal standards and outlined above) and the application works in tandem with it as an add-on. Functionality wise, for every item entering the company domain, it uses the ONS server to find an appropriate endpoint and report that information to the item

owner. Naturally it also collects data reported by other business partners for the company's own products that enter their domains. Finally an interface is provided for accessing applications to request all available data about a specific EPC tag. Data about a specific tag can be plotted on a map presenting a visual course and history of the product in question.

The contents of this chapter are as follows:

- Section 3 following the above introductory statements, presents briefly the operation of the ONS service according to the respective EPCglobal standard. The presentation will also illustrate the various relevant services that are needed for the operation of ONS, with a view to facilitating readers to understand the structure of an inter-enterprise RFID application.
- Section 4 illustrates the implementation details of the ONS core server. The ONS server implementation is effectively a DNS server implementation, which has been based on the BIND (Internet Systems Consortium, 2013) open source software. BIND has been selected on the basis of the fact that it is a de-facto reference and most widely accepted and used DNS implementation. Along with the implementation details, typical messages flows across the various servers comprising an ONS/DNS implementation are provided.
- Section 5 presents a reference application that builds upon the ONS service along with suggestions about future possible value-added applications. The application comprises an object tracking and an object tracing interface, which enables the implementation of simple tracking and tracing IoT applications, but also of RFID traceability applications. The various interfaces are illustrated on the basis of a sample

inter-enterprise deployment, which is depicted in Figure 3. Note that the (graphical) user-interface (GUI) of the application is depicted in Figure 4 and has been implemented based on the Google Web Toolkit (GWT) (Google, 2013).

- Section 6 positions the ONS implementation in the wider context of the AspireRFID (2013) middleware, with an emphasis on how it could be used in conjunction with other middleware libraries and tools of the AspireRFID platform. Note that the source code of the implementation is available as part of the AspireRFID project.

- Section 7 concludes the work and provides an outlook associated with the extension of the introduced systems towards addressing the needs of wider classes of Internet-of-Things (IoT) applications.

3. OBJECT NAMING SERVICE (ONS) OVERVIEW

The Object Naming Service (ONS) is a name lookup/directory service for EPC tags. It is a service that returns a list of network accessible service endpoints that pertain to a requested Electronic Product Code (EPC).In the software engineering context a directory is mapping between names and values. Therefore the service allows to look up the values which are usually not easy to remember and may change over time, given the name which is unique, making it easy to remember and immutable over a long period of time. It functions similar to a dictionary, and likewise a given name can have more than one value attached to it – more than one interpretation.

A high level example of the functionality provided by an ONS enabled look-up/ service is depicted in Figure 2. When the manufacturer tags the product, the EPC information related to the product (e.g. manufacture date, location, expiration date, etc.) is stored in its local EPC IS.

The product is then shipped to the retailer. Once received, the retailer record some information related to the product in its EPC IS. If the retailer wants to retrieve some manufacturer information related to a specific product, the retailer needs to use the look-up/ service implementation and send a request to the root ONS, which knows the location of the local ONS of the manufacturer (1). The retailer can then send a request to the local ONS of the manufacturer (2), which knows the location of the EPC IS related to the EPC of the specific product requested. Finally, the retailer can access the EPC IS of the manufacturer to retrieve the information related to the product (3).

Other ONS enabled look-up/ service examples, except the traceability of products described above, include but are not limited to the implementation of anti-counterfeiting systems and policies, as well as improved planning and forecasting in the supply chain.

Directory services are a core and integral part of every distributed system. Prominent examples include:

- DNS (Domain Name System) (Mockapetris, 1987; Braden, 1989; Elz, 1987): Matching domain names –www.example.com – to URI's (Universal Resource Identifiers) – 192.0.32.10
- LDAP (Lightweight Directory Access Protocol) (Zeilenga, 2006), which is an application protocol for accessing and maintaining distributed directory information services over an Internet Protocol, and the various descendants of X.500 suite of protocols, that include a series of computer networking standards covering electronic directory services: Matching resource names – usual folder names in a network – with their actual location at the network.

ONS is based on DNS and follows the same distributed nature and hierarchy of servers. Provided with a request about a specific EPC tag, the ONS server shall return service end-points where

Figure 2. ONS high level example

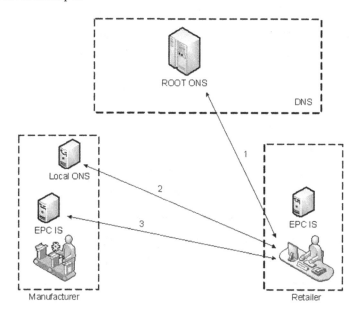

Figure 3. Hierarchy and message flow of ONS servers

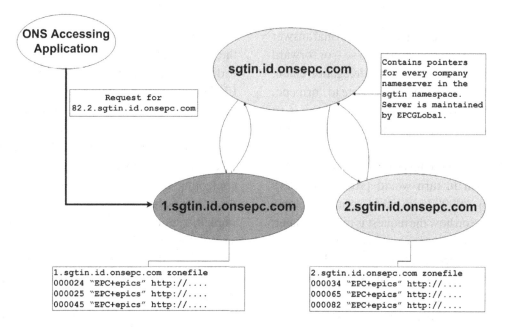

additional information can be obtained about this tag. There can be multiple end- points associated with a single tag, each one, providing potentially different information or the same information in different formats.

Each EPC translates to an alphanumeric string, which is treated like a Universal Resource Identifier (URI). The URI is separated in distinct parts by dots (.), with each dot indicating different domains and points of delegation of authority. Each entity in

Figure 4. Overview of an inter-enterprise RFID deployment based on the ONS implementation

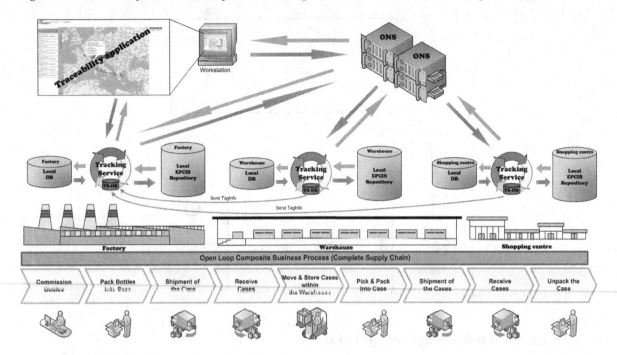

this hierarchy shall either provide the final answer to the query –if responsible to do so – or forward the query to the next point in the delegation chain. For example an EPC might translate to "urn:epc: id:sgtin:0614141.000024.400" (this format is an 96 bit sgtin pure URI tag which is consisted from the company prefix: "0614141", the item reference: "000024" and the product's serial number: "400") which in turn would produce an ONS request for "000024.0614141.sgtin.id.onsepc. com" –more on how the request is produced later. The first domain ".com" is a top level domain. "onsepc" is owned and managed by EPCglobal, Serialized Global Trade Item Number (SGTIN) by the organization responsible for SGTIN code namespace and "0614141" is owned and managed by the company that has purchased the particular namespace. Requests like that to an ONS server would yield a result like: "http://epc-is.example. com/epc-wsdl.xml", which is the web service EPCIS interface for the company example.com which owns and has issued the specific tag.

As a standard, the ONS service defines only the core functionality needed for an application to discover information end-point about a specific EPC tag. Contrary to other directory services, it does not provide any information about what kind of additional information the end-points provide or how to actually consume the new-found services. Such information has to be obtained by contacting the provider of the service outside the context of the ONS request. Given that RFID implementations are based on still emerging and sometimes open standards we believe this is an acceptable trade-off for the sake of simplicity and robustness. Also, in its current incarnation the ONS definition does not have any support of provision for security or user authentication. Future implementation can include this, as the use of DNS-SEC (Arends, 2005) (secure version of the DNS protocol upon which ONS is working) becomes more widespread. Our proposal fully implements the ONS standard version 1.0.1, yet later versions have already become available. The provided ONS server accessing API automatically does any necessary processing to go from the EPC tag format to the ONS request format as defined in the EPCglobal protocol. This is illustrated in the API that is described in following sections.

4. DIRECTORY SERVER ARCHITECTURE AND IMPLEMENTATION

According to the EPCglobal ONS standard, ONS servers are standard DNS servers containing the appropriate zone files for their domain of responsibility. Each zone file contains Name Authority Pointer (NAPTR) (Mealling, 2000) records which match specific EPC classes with one or more service end-points. The endpoints can be EPCIS repository interfaces, SAOP or XML-RCP endpoints or anything else that can accept further queries about the specific tag.

Since the ONS server is in effect a DNS server, our implementation uses the BIND (Internet Systems Consortium, 2013) open source software on a Windows platform. BIND is the de-facto reference and most widely accepted and used DNS implementation, thus the reason for our selection. For our example lets presume we have a company named ACME that has implemented the EPC architecture across it's sites and wants to track and trace their products. We set up the DNS server as an authoritative only server for all EPC tags belonging to ACME – all tags share the same company identifier – according to the BIND installation manual (Internet Software Consortium, 2001). There were no special settings used, and the server is accessible via requests at ports TCP/UDP 53 as per the default set-tings for DNS requests. A sample zone file, for ACME with identifier 1 and product classes 3 and 4 would be as shown in Table 1. As we can see ACME is using the SGTIN encoding scheme, and is currently offering two (2) classes of products, with identifiers three (3) and four (4). For each class, both an EPC-IS and a /tracking endpoint are defined.

This particular zone file defines two service endpoints for every product of classes 3 and 4 belonging to ACME. One is the EPCIS repository – of type "EPC+epcis" – and the other one is the tracking application – of type "EPC+ws". As mentioned before ACME is using the Serialized Global Trade Item Number (SGTIN) coding scheme for the issued tags.

This ONS server, which resides outside ACME and can be accessed from anywhere, has the domain name: "ns1.1.sgtin.id.onsepc.com" and is responsible for all URI's that fall under the "1. sgtin.id.onsepc.com" domain. It can and shall give an authoritative answer for any URI in that domain – if the necessary records exist. For any query regarding an URI that is outside the authoritative namespace of the server, the server is responsible for forwarding the query to the ONS server directly above it in the ONS/DNS hierarchy for resolving. The process will continue recursively until the query reached the final responsible ONS server. So if a retailer that receives an ACME's product would like to track and trace a product's EPC tag a special application would have to be

Table 1. Sample zone file

```
$TTL 6h
$ORIGIN 1.sgtin.id.onsepc.com.
@ IN SOA ns1.1.gtin.id.onsepc.com " info.1 gtin.id.onsepc.
com (
2010112107
10800
3600
604800
86400)
@ NS ns1.1. sgtin.id.onsepc.com
ns1 IN A 127.0.0.1
3 IN NAPTR 0 0 "u" "EPC+ws" "!^.*$!
http://epc-is.example.com//aspireRfidTracking/tracking.wsdl!"

.
4 IN NAPTR 0 0 "u" "EPC+ws" "!^.*$!
http://epc-is.example.com//aspireRfidTracking/tracking.wsdl!"

.
3 IN NAPTR 0 0 "u" "EPC+epcis" "!^.*$!
http://epc-is.example.com//aspireRfidEpcisRepository/query.
wsdl!" .
4 IN NAPTR 0 0 "u" "EPC+epcis" "!^.*$!
http://epc-is.example.com//aspireRfidEpcisRepository/query.
wsdl!" .
```

used (described below) to access its local ONS server and ask for the owner of that specific tag ID. Then the ONS server would check its records and if the specific SGTIN id class existed it would forward ACME's URI (sgtin.id.onsepc.com) to the retailer. If it wasn't available it would forward the message to the next ONS server following a hierarchical order. The retailer, upon receiving of ACME's URI, would be able to collect the relevant information regarding the product's trace thru the supply chain and specifications. A sample flow is illustrated Figure 3.

To allow applications to access and send requests to the ONS server, an API was specified and implemented. The API consists of several Java™ classes that accept as input the IP (Internet Protocol) address of the ONS server along with an EPC tag, and return the ONS server answer (if available). The API is based on the open source dnsjava (Dnsjava Org, 2013) library. In order to form a valid ONS request from a specific EPC tag certain processing has to occur. Quoting from the ONS standard we have that: «In order to query the DNS for the EPC, the URI form specified above must be converted to domain name form in Step 2. The procedure for this conversion is as follows:

1. Begin with an EPC represented in the pure identity URI form (as defined in Section 4.3.3 of the EPCglobal Tag Data Standards (EPCglobal, 2013c)). For example, "urn:epc:id:sgtin:0614141.000024.400".
2. Remove the "urn:epc:" prefix (in the example, leaving "id:sgtin:0614141.000024.400").
3. Remove the serial number field. In all tag formats currently defined in [EPC] (SGTIN, SSCC, SGLN, GRAI, GIAI, and GID), the serial number field is the rightmost period (.) character and all characters to the right of it. (In the example, this leaves "id:sgtin:0614141.000024")
4. Replace each colon (:) character with a period (.) character (in the example, leaving "id.sgtin.0614141.000024")

5. Invert the order of the remaining period-delimited fields (in the example, leaving "000024.0614141.sgtin.id")
6. Append .onsepc.com. In the example, the result is "000024.0614141.sgtin.id.onsepc.com".

The API does all the processing required so as to provide a clean and data agnostic interface to any application. It supports all EPC coding schemes currently defined by EPCglobal, namely: (a) SGTIN (Serialized Global Trade Item Number), (b) SSCC (Serial Shipping Container Code) (c) SGLN (Serialized Global Location Number), (d) GRAI (Global Returnable Asset Identifier), (e) GIAI (Global Individual Asset Identifier), (f) GID (General Identifier). To cater for future revisions and expansions, the API provides the capability for issuing DNS requests without the processing needed for EPC tags. As a final note maintenance of the ONS server zone files and additional administration should be done following the recommendations for DNS servers.

5. TRACKING APPLICATION AND INTERFACES

5.1 System Overview

In order to validate the ONS implementation, we have designed and implemented a novel application that uses the functionality of the ONS server infrastructure. Such an application will typically become part of already existing RFID deployment within a company. In this context deployments are associated with EPCIS repositories.

The EPCIS repository is a standard defined and regulated by EPCglobal. Its goal is to enable disparate applications to leverage EPC data via EPC-related data sharing, both within and across enterprises. More specifically it defines a standard interface through which EPC-related data can be both captured and queried by accessing applications. It defines the use of persistent databases for storing EPC-related data but also facilitates for the direct exchange of such data between applications. Since it stands as the higher layer in the EPCglobal Architectural Framework, it also serves as the natural entry point to other enterprise systems (WMS, ERP) that interface with it.

In the EPCglobal architecture the EPCIS-repository handles not only real-time observation data, but also historical data hence the use of persistent databases for storing purposes. Since EPCIS specifications does not allow the deletion of data even if an item leaves from the premises of a warehouse all its lifecycle history (see Figure 4) throughout this specific Business Location (i.e. from the time it entered the warehouse thru the receiving gate till the time it leaves from the shipping gate and all the intermediate steps) is available for future use. So EPCIS is –as the name implies – the central repository of all EPC-related data regarding a particular deployment. Moreover, the EPCIS deals not just with raw EPC observation data– e.g. 'Product carrying tag X was observed at time Y' - but also enhance these observations with business context that are related with specific business steps of the supply chain. So EPCIS stores also data that imbue those observations with meaning relative to the physical world and to specific steps in operational or analytical business processes – e.g. 'Product with RFID tag X was ob-served at time Y, and this was done at business step S of the fulfillment process for order #145. Observation was recorded by RFID gate Z which is located at the main entrance of business location L, with geographical location x.xx x.zz'.

The proposed application facilitates data exchange between repositories on different enterprises for the purpose of tracking EPC tagged products as they move from one administrative domain to the next, as part of supply chain. It is based on the 3-tiered model paradigm. Core functionality, which spans the data and the application tier, is the following:

A new '/tracking' interface is added to the EPCIS repository is the application is attached to, along with the '/query' and '/capture' interfaces. The tracking interface can be used by an external accessing application to obtain data about any EPC tag belonging to this particular company/repository. Data includes both events from the local repository and data reported from foreign domains as products move to them. The tracking interface is a Simple Object Access Protocol (SOAP) interface.

The tracking interface can also be used by foreign applications to report data about an EPC tag. Data includes at least time, date, geographical coordinates and information about the company which received the item and issued the data. Data can also include details about the particular item (name, features, price, date of production etc.) if available. All data of this kind is stored in a local database, separate from the EPCIS repository database. Finally the application polls the attached EPCIS repository periodically for any events regarding EPC tags having a company identifier different than the one designated as 'parent company'. Events are grouped together by company, a query is send to the ONS server for an EPCIS/tracking service endpoint, and an attempt is made to report the events.

A typical deployment scenario would involve several business partners – a factory that makes the products, a wholesale business with a warehouse and a retailer. Each partner has EPCIS repository installations along with the proposed traceability application. The applications on both the wholesale business and the retailer report data about incoming products to the factory, by making use of the ONS server to discover appropriate service endpoints. An application message interaction cycle is depicted in Figure 4 for the first participant in a supply chain after the producer. Namely:

1. The warehouse receives cases of products from the factory. An EPC event is generated and stored on the local EPCIS repository

2. The tracking application on the warehouse polls the attached EPCIS repository for any new EPC events. The newly generated event is fetched.

3. Having received new events about EPC tags not belonging to the company, the ONS is polled to find an appropriate /tracking interface to report the events. The interface be-longing to the factory installation is discovered.

4. The events are reported back to /tracking interface of the factory EPCIS-repository.

5.2 Data and Application Tier

The data tier of the application consists of two parts of a supply chain, as shown in Figure 4, making use of the ONS server to report tag data to the producer. One is a connection to the attached EPCIS repository via the '/query' web service interface. When a request about a specific EPC tag arrives, the local EPCIS repository is queried about all events containing that tag. While events from the EPCIS repository might contain additional data, in the current incarnation of the system only tag, date, time and geographical coordinates of the reader capturing the event are kept. The second part of the systems data tier is a local database. It stores the bulk of the application data, namely all events that are reported from foreign tracking application running on business partners.

Note that since all of the data is generated by events retrieved from EPCIS repositories, it would be possible not to use a separate database and store all the data on the attached EPCIS repository itself. Several challenges are however faced as part of this solution. While EPCIS repositories follow similar structures for storing their data, a lot of parameterization can occur. This alone can cause severe non compatibilities from system to system which cannot be solved with simple settings tweaking. Even for identical EPCIS repositories there are systemic issues when trying to capture data directly as events in the repository. Records inside

the EPCIS carry semantic meaning relevant to the company that created them. Examples include records about 'business locations' or 'business steps'. Keeping such re-cords from another company makes little sense – and raises a lot of data privacy issues. Also, since the EPCIS is the central storage for all EPC related data and accessed by all kinds of other applications (readers, WMS ERP), its database already faces a considerable load. Further increasing that load is not recommended. Finally, the goal for the application is to be a 'value adding add-on', which can be enabled when needed without affecting the operation of the EPCIS repository. Hence, keeping all data on a different database allows users to enable or disable the tracking infrastructure without affecting existing systems and without polluting their EPCIS repository with out of scope data. It also enables them to use the system even when only a fraction of their business partners choose to do so, since those who do choose to use it will enjoy the added functionality without negative results for those who don't.

Technology wise the tracking interface for the attached EPCIS repository is a SOAP web service, which exchanges structured data in XML format. The implementation for the font-end to the out-side world is done on Java using the JAX-WS technology for creating xml web services. The open source Apache CXF framework was used for the final development and deployment.

As described in the earlier paragraphs the /tracking interface supports two main functions. First is the query function. It accepts as input a fully qualified URI representing a tag - urn:epc:id:gid:1.3.128 – and returns a list of all data objects available for this EPC tag. The purpose of the query function is to serve as the main information end-point for third-party consumers and service providers, which can include entities both inside and outside the boundaries of the company.

Second is the report function. This is used by the tracking application running on remote domains to report data about company products as they move into their domain – and vice versa. The application polls the attached EPCIS repository periodically for new EPC event data, discards everything regarding epc-tags that have are 'mother' company property, contacts the ONS server to locate an appropriate endpoint and proceeds. The input to this function is a structured XML document. An example document containing two data objects is provided in Table 2.

The implementation offers a simple client for consumers of the web-service. The client uses the CXF framework which is used for the rest of the application. Naturally prospective consumers can develop their own clients using the WSDL (Web Service Description Language) (Christensen, 2001) interface definition. So let's presume again that two items produced in ACME's factory (Fig-

Table 2. XML payload to report a pair of EPC tags to the producer

```
<?xml version="1.0" encoding="UTF-8"?>
<trackerdocument xmlns:xsi="http://www.w3.org/2001/
XMLSchema-instance"
creationDate="2006-05-04T18:13:51.0Z" uri="http://www.
example.com/epcis/query.wsdl">
<companyInfo>
<name> Intermediary Warehouse LTD</name>
<description>Widgets</description>
<address>19.7 Markopoulou Ave</address>
<country>GR</country>
<region>Attica</region>
<email>info@intermediary.gr</email>
<tel>210-555-555</tel>
<fax>210-555-556</fax>
</companyInfo>
<tagIdList idCount="2">
<tag Id="urn:epc:id:gid:1.3.128">
<geoCoords>35.25:14.28</geoCoords>
<time>01:01:01.001</time>
<userData JSONEncUserData=""/>
<epcClassProperty JSONEncProList=""/>
</tag>
<tag Id="urn:epc:id:gid:1.3.129">
<geoCoords>35.25:14.28</geoCoords>
<time>01:01:01.001</time>
<userData JSONEncUserData=""/>
<epcClassProperty JSONEncProList=""/>
</tag>
</tagIdList>
</trackerdocument>
```

ure 4) with tag ids "urn:epc:id:gid:1.3.128" and "urn:epc:id:gid:1.3.129" respectively are shipped to Intermediary Warehouse LTD company. As soon as the item passes thru the first RFID point (gate) of Intermediary's Warehouse company it gets recorded to the local EPCIS repository. The time that the local Tracking Application will run it will retrieve the two new tag ids captured from the local EPCIS repository. The Tracking Application will communicate with the ONS server to find out to which company the tag ids with epc class "urn:epc:id:gid:1.3.*" belong to. As soon as it receives the ACME's URI the Tracking Application will construct the XML document presented in Table 2 which informs ACME that their items have arrived to the Intermediary Warehouse LTD (with the rest of company info) with "35.25, 14.28" geo coordinates and time "01:01:01.001". By following this pattern ACME's Tracking Application collects all the relevant track and tracing information regarding their products and is able, in any given time, to provide this information to the company's management staff or an interested third party.

5.3 Presentation Tier and Sample Applications

The directory system is designed to provide a service that is consumed by end users and so it does not have a dedicated (per-se) presentation tier. Final consumers are expected to define and implement their own presentation applications to match their needs. A sample such use-case is presented in the following paragraph. The scenario involves a traceability application with 'Google of things' like interface. The user can enter a tag in the form or a URI, and search for any data available. Data is presented on a map for visual reference. The user can click any point on the map to reveal additional information about the product that carries the tag and also the company that generated each data point Figure 5. The demo application was created using the Google Web

Figure 5. GWT based GUI of the traceability application

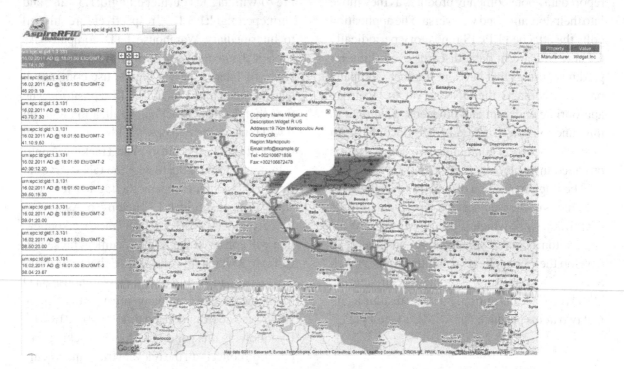

Toolkit (Google, 2013) open source framework for web application.

Component interaction for the proposed Traceability application, shown in Figure 5, follows a similar flow to the rest of the system as depicted in Figure 3. Following a user request for a specific EPC tag, the server backend contacts the ONS server to locate the appropriate '/tracking' interface and invokes the query function. The tracking application retrieves all relevant data from the EPCIS-repository and the local database and returns them to the user agent for presentation.

By extending, customizing and modifying the sample traceability application, several new applications can be implemented including:

- **Fraud Prevention:** Companies can offer their customers globally an easy way to check if the product they bought is indeed genuine.

- **Quality Control:** Companies handling food or other sensitive products can visually track where items from a potential faulty production lot have shipped and easily recall them.

- **Product Profiles:** Companies or state organizations can provide product profiles based on ori-gin of materials used, or country of production and assembly. Customers can then for example choose products that support eco-friendly production or avoid foods that contain certain genetically mutated ingredients.

- **Supply Chain Management:** Companies can involve in statistical analysis about the effectiveness of their supply chains by tracking and comparing processing times versus product or business partner.

- **Market Analysis:** Companies can track and compare product dispersion versus location, prod-uct type and time of year.

6. OPEN SOURCE IMPLEMENTATION

The Tracking Service module is part of the AspireRFID Open Source project. The AspireRFID project, which architecture is shown in Figure 6, aims at developing and promoting an open-source, lightweight, standards-compliant, scalable, privacy-friendly and integrated middleware along with several tools to ease the development, deployment and management of RFID-based applications and sensor-based applications. It implements several specifications from consortiums such as EPCglobal, NFC Forum, JCP (Java Community Process) and OSGi Alliance. Also, AspireRFID collaborates, contribute to and/or uses other open source implementations like the Fosstrak (Floerkemeier, 2007) EPCIS repository.

AspireRFID provides also a set of tools enabling RFID consultants to define, generate and deploy the specifications of RFID enabled processes without a need for tedious low-level programming. Moreover it has the ability to generate all the RFID artefacts required to deploy these solutions over the AspireRFID middleware separately with stand alone tools or all together (see APDL and PE (Kefalakis 2011)). To support the Open Source philosophy, AspireRFID has chosen LGPL V2.1 as it is one of the most open and versatile licensing schemas.

As we can see in Figure 6 the Tracking service module resides at the outer limit of the AspireRFID middleware and is connected directly, via Web Services, with the EPCIS repository. So it is the point which enables the middleware's connectivity with the outside world when an Open Loop (Kefalakis, 2011) supply chain solution is required.

There are also other Open Source RFID middleware that implement the EPCglobal specifications. Most of them, like Rifidi (Palazzi, 2009), implement only a small portion of EPC Global Specs with the module of choice being the ALE (Application Level Events) (EPCglobal, 2013a) or in other words Filtering and Collection server. One of the most complete OSS middleware implementations is the Fosstrak (Floerkemeier, 2007) project which gets up to the EPCIS level. To our knowledge there is no OSS implementation that supports ONS layer except the AspireRFID and the module described in this chapter.

Figure 6. AspireRFID architecture

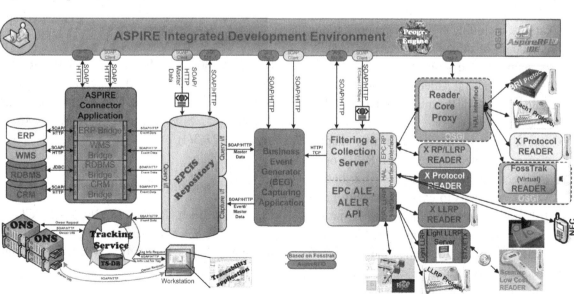

7. CONCLUSION

Inter-enterprise deployments of RFID and IoT solution can maximize the Return-on-Investment (ROI) associated with these technologies. This has been already manifested in a number of applications including logistics and supply chain management, where inter-enterprise deployments allow multiple stakeholders to benefit from fully automated traceability services. Nevertheless, the deployment of large scale applications that transcend corporate boundaries is still associated with several technical and organizational challenges. The availability of object directory services is one step towards alleviating these challenges, given that such directory services constitute essential building blocks of any non-trivial inter-enterprise deployment.

This chapter has introduced an open source implementation of an object directory service, which is based on EPCglobal's ONS standards. The implementation has been carried out in a way that respects the ONS standard, while at the same time minimizes interference with existing enterprise system. Overall, the open source implementation facilitates business partners to achieve automated and rapid tracing of assets and products, as the latter flow through the supply chain. This is a foundation for a number of applications, including high-impact applications such as "google-of-things" and green eco-friendly supply chains. In the scope of this chapter we have re-ported several added-value applications that could be based on the introduced traceability infra-structure.

Overall, the work described in this chapter has been contributed to the AspireRFID open source project. Such an open source contribution empowers researchers to experiment with large scale IoT applications, while at the same time enables business to provide customized added-value traceability infra-structure. Hence, the introduced system can be seen as a novel extensible added-value infra-structure that could boost a number of innovative applications. Additional work towards interfacing the services to other enterprise applications (such as ERP and WMS systems) could facilitate more expressive (i.e. rich in information) traceability services. At the same time, the system could be easily blended with an authentication and authorization infrastructure, which is certainly required towards the exploitation of the system in the scope of partner B2B chains and private industrial networks.

REFERENCES

Arends, R., et al. (2005, March). *RFC4033 "DNS Security Introduction and Requirements"*. Retrieved September 2013, http://tools.ietf.org/html/rfc4033

AspireRFID Project. (n.d.). *The AspireRFID project*. Retrieved September 2013, from http://forge.ow2.org/projects/aspire/

Braden, R. (1989, October). *RFC1123 Requirements for Internet Hosts -- Application and Support*. Retrieved September 2013, from http://tools.ietf.org/html/rfc1123

Christensen, E., Curbera, F., Meredith, G., & Weerawarana, S. (2001, March). *Web service description language (WSDL) 1.1*. Retrieved September 2013, from http://www.w3.org/TR/wsdl

Dimitropoulos, P. & Soldatos, J. (2010). RFID-enabled Fully Automated Warehouse Management: Adding the Business Context. *International Journal of Manufacturing Technology and Management, 21*(3/4).

Dnsjava Org. (2013). *Dns java implementation*. Retrieved from http://www.dnsjava.org/

Elz, R., & Bush, R. (1987). *RFC2181 "Clarifications to the DNS specification"*. Retrieved September 2013, from http://tools.ietf.org/html/rfc2181

EPCglobal. (2013a). *The Application Level Events (ALE) Specification (version 1.1.1), parts 1 and 2*. Retrieved September 2013, from http://www.gs1.org/gsmp/kc/epcglobal/ale

EPCglobal. (2013b). *EPC Information Services (EPCIS) Specification (version 1.0.1)*. Retrieved September 2013, from http://www.gs1.org/gsmp/kc/epcglobal/epcis

EPCglobal. (2013c). *EPC Tag Data Standard (version 1.7)*. Retrieved September 2013, from http://www.gs1.org/gsmp/kc/epcglobal/tds/

EPCglobal. (2013d). *Object Name Service (ONS) (version 2.0.1)*. Retrieved September 2013, from http://www.gs1.org/gsmp/kc/epcglobal/ons

EPCglobal. (2013e). *Low Level Reader Protocol (LLRP) (version 1.1)*. Retrieved September 2013, from http://www.gs1.org/gsmp/kc/epcglobal/llrp

EPCglobal Architecture Review Committee. (2013). *The EPCglobal Architecture Framework (version 1.5)*. Retrieved September 2013, from http://www.gs1.org/gsmp/kc/epcglobal/architecture

Floerkemeier, C., Roduner, C., & Lampe, M. (2007, December). RFID Application Development with the Accada Middleware Platform. *IEEE Systems Journal, 1*(2), 82–94. doi:10.1109/JSYST.2007.909778

Google. (2013). *Google Web Toolkit*. Retrieved September 2013, from http://code.google.com/webtoolkit/

Internet Software Consortium. (2001). *BIND 9 Administration reference manual*. Available online at: http://www.scs.stanford.edu/~reddy/links/dns/bind9arm.pdf

Internet Systems Consortium. (n.d.). *The BIND software*. Retrieved September 2013, from http://www.isc.org/software/bind

Kefalakis, N., Leontiadis, N., Soldatos, J., & Donsez, D. (2009). Middleware Building Blocks for Architecting RFID Systems. In *Proceedings of the MOBILIGHT 2009 Conference*, (pp. 325-336). MOBILIGHT.

Kefalakis, N., Soldatos, J., Konstantinou, N., & Prasad, N. (2011). APDL: A reference XML schema for process-centered definition of RFID solutions. Int Journal of Systems & Software, 84, 1244-1259. doi:10.1016/j.jss.2011.02.036

Lawton, G. (2004, September). Machine-to-Machine Technology Gears Up for Growth. *IEEE Computer, 37*(9), 12–15. doi:10.1109/MC.2004.137

Leontiadis, N., Kefalakis, N., & Soldatos, J. (2009). Bridging RFID Systems and Enterprise Applications through Virtualized Connectors. *International Journal of Automated Identification Technology, 1*(2), 2009.

Mealling, M., & Daniel, R. (2000, September). *RFC2915 "The Naming Authority Pointer (NAPTR) DNS Resource Record"*. Retrieved September 2013 from http://tools.ietf.org/html/rfc2915

Mockapetris, P. (1987, November). *RFC1035 Domain Names, Implementation and Specification", Internet Engineering Taskforce Network Working Group*. Retrieved September 2013, from http://tools.ietf.org/html/rfc1035

Palazzi, C., Ceriali, A., & Dal Monte, M. (2009, August). RFID Emulation in Rifidi Environment. In *Proc. of the International Symposium on Ubiquitous Computing* (UCS'09). Beijing, China: UCS.

Sundmaeker, H., Guillemin, P., Friess, P., & Woelffl, S. (2010, March). *Vision and Challenges for Realizing the Internet of Things*. Academic Press. doi:10.2759/26127

Vijayaraman, B. S., & Osyk, B. A. (2006). An empirical study of RFID implementation in the ware-housing industry. *The International Journal of Logistics Management, 17*(1), 6–20. doi:10.1108/09574090610663400

Zeilenga, K. (2006, June). *RFC4510 "Lightweight Directory Access Protocol (LDAP): Technical Specification Road-map"*. Retrieved September 2013, from http://tools.ietf.org/html/rfc4510

ADDITIONAL READING

Ahmed, N., & Ramachandran, U. (2010). RFID middleware systems: a comparative analysis. In *Unique Radio Innovation for the 21st Century: Building Scalable and Global RFID Networks*. Berlin: Springer.

Balakrishnan, H., Kaashoek, M., Karger, D., Morris, R., & Stoica, I. (2003). Looking up data in P2P systems. *Communications of the ACM, 46*(2), 43–48. doi:10.1145/606272.606299

Bauer, M., Chartier, P., Moessner, K., Cosmin-Septimiu, N., Pastrone, C., Parreira, J., et al. *Catalogue of IoT Naming, Addressing and Discovery Schemes in IERC Projects*, retrieved September 2013, http://www.theinternetofthings.eu/sites/default/files/%5Buser-name%5D/IERC-AC2-D1-v1.7.pdf

Bröring, A., Echterhoff, J., Jirka, S., Simonis, I., Everding, T., & Stasch, C. et al. (2011). New Generation Sensor Web Enablement. *Sensors (Basel, Switzerland), 11*(3), 2652–2699. doi:10.3390/s110302652 PMID:22163760

Calbimonte, J., Jeung, H., Corcho, O., & Aberer, K. (2011), *Semantic Sensor Data Search in a Large-Scale Federated Sensor Network* in the Proc. of The 4th International Workshop on Semantic Sensor Networks 2011 (SSN11), 23-27 October, Bonn, Germany

Cheshire, S., & Krochmal, M. (2011). *DNS-Based Service Discovery*, IETF Zeroconf Working Group, www.zeroconf.org/ and www.dns-sd.org/, draft-cheshire-dnsext-dns-sd.txt, 2011

Cheshire, S. & M. Krochmal (2011), *Multicast DNS*, draft-cheshire-dnsext-multicastdns-15 (work in progress), December 2011.

Echterhoff, J. (2010). *OGC Implementation Standard 09-001: SWE Service Model Implementation Standard*. Wayland, MA, USA: Open Geospatial Consortium.

Floerkemeier, C., & Lampe, M. (2005), *RFID middleware design – addressing application requirements and RFID constraints*, in Proceedings of SOC'2005 (Smart Objects Conference), Grenoble, France, Oct. 2005, pp. 219–224.

Heath, T., & Bizer, C. (2011), Linked Data: Evolving the Web into a Global Data Space (1st edition). Synthesis Lectures on the Semantic Web: Theory and Technology, 1:1, 1-136. Morgan & Clay-pool.

Jara A., Zamora M. & Skarmeta A. (2012), *GLoWBAL IPv6: An adaptive and transparent IPv6 integration in the Internet of Things*, Mobile Information, IOS Press, ISSN: 1574-017x, 2012.

Jirka, S. (2009). Bröring, A. & Stasch, C (2009), *Discovery Mechanisms for the Sensor Web*. *Sensors (Basel, Switzerland), 9*, 2661–2681. doi:10.3390/s90402661 PMID:22574038

Karnstedt, M., Sattler, K., & Hauswirth, M. (2012). Scalable distributed indexing and query processing over Linked Data. *Journal of Web Semantics, 10*, 3–32. doi:10.1016/j.websem.2011.11.010

Kefalakis, N., Leontiadis, N., Soldatos, J., Gama, K., & Donsez, D. (2008). Supply chain management and NFC picking demonstrations using the AspireRFID middleware platform. *Middleware (Companion), 2008*, 66–69.

Klyne, G., & Carroll, J. (2004), *Resource Description Framework (RDF): Concepts and Abstract Syntax*, http://www.w3.org/TR/rdf-concepts/

M. Mealling (Network Working Group) (2008, January), *RFC5134, A Uniform Resource Name Namespace for the EPC global Electronic Product Code (EPC) and Related Standards*, Request for Comments 5134.

Pfisterer, D. et al. (2011). SPITFIRE: toward a semantic web of things. *IEEE Communications Magazine, 49*(11), 40–48. doi:10.1109/MCOM.2011.6069708

Prud'hommeaux, E., & Seaborne, A. (2008), *SPARQL Query Language for RDF,* http://www.w3.org/TR/rdf-sparql-query/, 2008

Renz, J., & Nebel, B. (2007). Qualitative spatial reasoning using constraint calculi. In M. Aiello, I. Pratt-Hartmann, & J. van Benthem (Eds.), *Handbook of Spatial Logics* (pp. 161–215). Springer-Verlag. doi:10.1007/978-1-4020-5587-4_4

Sarma, S. (2004). Integrating RFID. *ACM Queue; Tomorrow's Computing Today, 2*(7), 50–57. doi:10.1145/1035594.1035620

Soldatos, J., Serrano, M., & Hauswirth, M. (2012). Convergence of Utility Computing with the Internet-of-Things. *IMIS, 2012,* 874–879.

Stoica I., Morris R., Karger D., Kaashoek M., Balakrishnan H. & Chord, (2001)*: A scalable peer-to-peer lookup service for internet applications*, in: Proceedings of the 2001 SIGCOMM Conference, San Diego, CA, USA, August 2001, pp. 149–160.

Taylor, K. (2011), *Semantic Sensor Networks: The W3C SSN-XG Ontology and How to Semantically Enable Real Time Sensor Feeds*, Semantic Technology Conference, June 5-9, San Francisco CA, USA

Vijayaraman, B. S., & Osyk, B. A. (2006). An empirical study of RFID implementation in the warehousing industry. *The International Journal of Logistics Management, 17*(1), 6–20. doi:10.1108/09574090610663400

Yanbo, W., Ranasinghe, D., & Sheng, Q. (2011). Zeadally S., Yu J., (2011), *RFID enabled traceability networks: a survey. Distributed and Parallel Databases, 29,* 397–443. doi:10.1007/s10619-011-7084-9

Zarokostas, N., Dimitropoulos, P., & Soldatos, J. (2007, September). RFID Middleware Design for Enhancing Traceability in the Supply Chain Management. *IEEE PIMRC, 2007,* 1–5.

KEY TERMS AND DEFINITIONS

Discovery (Discovery of "Things"): Is the process of discovering uniquely identifiable virtual objects in an Internet-like structure.

Inter-Enterprise Applications: Are the applications that involve multiple companies and are executed throughout the lifecycle of a supply chain.

IoT (Internet of Things): Is a computing concept that describes uniquely identifiable objects and their virtual representations in an Internet-like structure.

ONS (Object Naming Service): Is the mechanism that leverages Domain Name System (DNS) to discover information about a product and related services from the Electronic Product Code (EPC).

RFID (Radio Frequency Identification): The wireless non-contact use of radio-frequency electromagnetic fields to transfer data, for the purposes of automatically identifying and tracking tags attached to objects.

Traceability: The ability to verify the history, location, or application of an item by means of documented recorded identification.

Tracking and Tracing: The process of observing of objects (item or property) on the move, in a supply chain, and supplying a timely ordered sequence of respective location data for determining their current and past locations.

Chapter 5
An Integrated Development Environment for RFID Applications

Nikos Kefalakis
Athens Information Technology, Greece

John Soldatos
Athens Information Technology, Greece

ABSTRACT

In recent years we have witnessed a proliferation of RFID (Radio Frequency Identification) middleware systems and projects (including several open source projects), which are extensively used to support the emerging wave of RFID applications. Some of the RFID middleware projects come with simple tools, which facilitate the application development, configuration, and deployment processes. However, these tools tend to be fragmented since they address only part of an RFID system (such as the filtering of tag streams and/or the generation of business events). In this chapter, the authors introduce an Integrated Development Environment (IDE) for RFID applications, which addresses multiple parts of an RFID application, while at the same time supporting the full application development lifecycle (i.e. design, development, deployment, and testing of RFID applications). The introduced IDE comprises a wide range of tools, which have been implemented as modular plug-ins to an Eclipse-based environment. The various tools enable application development, deployment, testing, and configurations over the middleware infrastructure established by the AspireRFID (AspireRFID Consortium, 2013), and their evaluation has proven that they can significantly ease RFID application development.

1. INTRODUCTION

During recent years we are witnessing a proliferation of successful RFID deployments in areas such as manufacturing, logistics, trade and industry. Several of these deployments deal with numerous tags/objects, RFID readers, reading cycles and RFID generated events, which route to a wide range of enterprise applications such as ERP (Enterprise Resource Planning), MRP (Manufacturing Resource Planning) and WMS (Warehouse Management Systems) (Kefalakis,

DOI: 10.4018/978-1-4666-6308-4.ch005

2009). RFID middleware is the cornerstone of most of the above non-trivial deployments of RFID technology. RFID middleware undertakes crucial tasks in the scope of RFID applications, which typically include (Dimitropoulos, 2010):

- Collecting RFID data from a variety of heterogeneous physical readers, through reading the tagged items. At this level middleware implementations insulate higher layers from knowing what reader / models have been chosen. Moreover, they achieve virtualization of tags, which allows RFID applications to support different tag formats.
- Filtering the RFID sensor streams according to application needs and accordingly emits events pertaining to the application at hand. At this level middleware implementations insulate the higher layers from the physical design choices on how tags are sensed and accumulated and how the time boundaries of events are triggered.
- Mapping the filtered readings to business semantics as required by the target applications and business processes. The respective business semantics are consolidated into business events, which are routed (by the RFID middleware) to one or more enterprise applications that use them. At this level middleware implementations insulate enterprise applications from understanding the details of how individual steps are carried out in a business process.

Note that most of these middleware tasks are defined in the scope of the EPC Global Architecture (EPCGlobal Architecture Review Committee, 2013), which is supported by a wide range of relevant standards. The importance of RFID middleware, has given rise to the development of several RFID middleware frameworks, which are nowadays providing functionality for RFID data collection, filtering, event generation, as well as translation of tag streams into business semantics. These frameworks have been developed as part of both research initiatives (Prabhu, 2006) and vendor products. Furthermore, several research initiatives have produced numerous open-source RFID frameworks, such as Mobitec (Mobitec, 2013) and the Fosstrak project (Floerkemeier, 2007), which provide royalty-free implementations of RFID middleware stacks. In addition to providing middleware libraries for RFID applications, most of these projects provide simple tools for configuring and managing the underlying RFID infrastructures. These tools facilitate application development and monitoring, yet they do not obviate the (still needed) tedious low-level tasks.

Apart from RFID middleware projects, RFID initiatives have also emerged, focusing on application development tools (e.g., LogicAlloy (2013), Rifidi (Palazzi, 2009) and its successor projects). In several cases, these initiatives also offer RFID middleware libraries (e.g., the LogicAlloy (2013) Server), while in other cases they are mostly focused in visual RFID application development. Despite the emergence of these efforts, there are no integrated environments for RFID deployment. As a matter of fact, most of the above tools are focused on parts of the RFID middleware development effort (e.g., the configuration of filtering mechanisms, the management of metadata and the management of reader devices) rather than on a holistic approach to RFID solution deployment. As a result, most of RFID middleware solutions are implemented on a per-case basis, rather than based on a more convenient and cost-effective integrated paradigm.

2. MAIN FOCUS OF THE CHAPTER

In this book chapter the efforts of the AspireRFID (AspireRFID, 2013) project are presented in order to offer a suite of Visual Tools for easing the development and deployment of RFID solutions. To this end, AspireRFID has developed a large number of open source tools for visual RFID development, along with a programmability model that enables their combination for developing end-to-end RFID solutions. The AspireRFID programmability model specifies a set of RFID-solutions related metadata, which are managed by the combination of the above-mentioned visual tools. This programmability model has enabled the modular integration of the various tools in a first of a kind Integrated Development Environment (IDE) for building and deploying RFID solutions. This IDE (called AspireRFID IDE), is available online as an open source software within the AspireRFID project. The AspireRFID IDE complements the AspireRFID middleware and programmability developments, which have been described in earlier publications of the authors (such as (Kefalakis, 2009, 2011a, 2011b; Dimitropoulos, 2010; Leontiadis, 2009)), since it enables the configuration of the various middleware components described in these publications, as well as, their combination towards the development of complete integrated end-to-end solutions. From a functional viewpoint the visual tools of the AspireRFID project include:

- A standalone set of IDE plug-ins that enables the configuration and management of specific modules of the AspireRFID middleware. These plug-ins offer interfaces for the configuration of the low level capabilities of the middleware.
- The Business Process Workflow Management Editor (BPWME) plug-in, an integrated environment for configuring and deploying end-to-end (Open Loop Composite Business Processes) RFID solutions based on high level semantics, rather than low level middleware configuration (Lampe, 2007). This tool hides from RFID consultants and integrators, the required detailed knowledge of an RFID middleware and its specifications for describing a complex RFID solution. BPWME uses the services and functionality as a combined

version of the above mentioned standalone tools, based on the APDL (ASPIRE business Process Description Language) schema described in (Kefalakis, 2011b).

The most important stand-alone tools of AspireRFID IDE, which are provided as plug-ins in an Eclipse OSGi (Open Source Gateway Interface) infrastructure, include:

- The ECSpec Editor Plug-in, used to edit the ECSpec (Event Cycle Specification) XML document which controls the behavior of the filtering & collection layer of an RFID solution, based on the EPC-ALE (Application Level Events) specification of the (EPCGlobal, 2013a).
- The LRSpec Editor Plug-in, used to edit logical readers specifications (LRSpecs) according to the definition of a logical reader in the EPCGlobal architecture.
- The ALE Server Configurator Plug-in, which is used to manage the ECSpecs and LRSpecs at the Filtering and collection layer.
- The Business Event Generator Plug-in, which is used to manage the Business Event Generation (BEG) module that is responsible for the conversion of low-level EPC-ALE events to business events (i.e. events with business semantics) and forward them to the EPCIS (Electronic Product Code Information Sharing) repository (EPCGlobal, 2013b).
- The Physical Reader Configuration & Management Plug-in, used to manage the Reader Core Proxy layer of the Fosstrak project.
- The Master Data Editor Plug-in, a tool which enables the user to edit and save Master Data to an EPCIS-enabled Repository (EPCGlobal, 2013b).
- The RFID Business Location GMF Editor, a tool that provides a graphical inter-

face for the user to edit retrieve and store Master Data Business Locations to an EPCIS (EPCglobal, 2013b) repository (as the latter is specified in the EPCGlobal architecture).

- The BPWME tool, which enables an IDE-like integration of multiple of the above tools and supports the APDL specifications (Kefalakis, 2011b). BPWME guides users in the generation of the APDL (Kefalakis, 2011b) and in the configuration of complex supply chain scenarios. The integration of the above tools on the basis of the BPWME leads to a multiplicative benefit comparing to the use of each one of the tools alone (i.e. in isolation from the others).

The AspireRFID IDE is based on Eclipse platform which is modularly extensible based on the Open Source Gateway Interface (OSGI) standards, hence, different AspireRFID related components (ALE, BEG, EPCIS, etc.) are configured by using an integrated tool that allows users to have a centralized view for the configuration of the architecture. The IDE facilitates the development of fully fledged RFID solutions based on the programmable composition of filters, events, workflows etc. These components are reusable and are usually derived from distributed libraries of reusable RFID components.

Overall, the work presented in this chapter, stems from a joint effort of twelve (open source) contributors, who produced over 130 thousand lines of code. Some of the ASPIRE tools have received a very positive feedback from the RFID Open Source community, featuring hundreds of downloads during their short lifetime. Some users and/or developers have already used these tools in order to facilitate realistic RFID pilot deployments, including the pilot use cases of the FP7 ASPIRE project. According to the feedback from adopters, the AspireRFID IDE platform and related standalone tools significantly facilitate the development of RFID applications and bring

benefits to practical RFID implementations for SMEs, as well as, a radical change in the current paradigm of RFID deployments. The rest of this book chapter follows the below structure:

- Section 3 following this introduction presents the baseline middleware infrastructure of the AspireRFID project, which is the foundation for solution deployment based on the AspireRFID IDE. The aim will be to familiarize the reader with the various middleware building blocks that will be configured on the basis of the IDE.
- Section 4 provides an overview of the functionality for each one of the stand-alone tools that comprise the IDE, along with their role as Eclipse plug-ins to the IDE.
- Section 5 is devoted to the description of the implementation of the Business Process Workflow Management Editor (BPWME) tool, which uses all the rest in order to deliver the end-to-end integrated development experience.
- Section 6 illustrates the evaluation feedback and the comments received by the AspireRFID community in terms of the use of the various tools. Furthermore, it provides an assessment of the potential contribution of the IDE in the cost-effectiveness of the RFID development process.
- Section 7 concludes the chapter and outlines the advantages and limitations of the IDE approach of the AspireRFID project along with its potential to be used in the wider class of Internet-of-Things applications.

3. ASPIRERFID MIDDLEWARE ARCHITECTURE

AspireRFID IDE is an integrated development environment which allows the visual, model-driven development of an RFID solution. It offers a graphical, user-friendly interface to trigger the services of the following eight (8) principal middleware modules/components, which comprise the AspireRFID architecture:

- **Hardware Abstraction Layer (HAL):** The role of this layer is to unify the way the ASPIRE middleware interacts with the RFID readers, which can be diverse in protocols. This relies on a hardware abstraction layer (HAL) and a fixed instruction set for upstream middleware layers that receive RFID readings.
- **Reader Core Proxy (RCP):** The role of RCP is to transform non-EPC (Electronic Product Code) Reader Protocol (RP) readers into compliant readers. By deploying the appropriate HAL (Hardware Abstraction Layer) module at the Reader Core, we can ensure its compliance to the RP. Every reader with an implementation of the Hardware Abstraction interface can be controlled over the Reader Protocol (RP).
- **Filtering & Collection Server (F&C Server, EPC-ALE compliant):** This layer provides several operations like accumulation, filtering, according to the requests by end users and is implemented according to the EPC-ALE specification of the EPC Global. AspireRFID uses the EPC-ALE implementation of the Fosstrak project.
- **Business Event Generator (BEG):** The role of the BEG is to automate the mapping between reports stemming from F&C and IS events. Instead of requiring developers to implement the mapping logic, the BEG enables application builders to configure the mapping based on the semantics of the RFID application.
- **Information Sharing Repository (EPCIS compliant):** This module is responsible for receiving application-agnostic RFID data

from the filtering & collection (F&C) middleware server through the Business Event Generation (BEG) application. The resulting RFID data constitute EPCIS compliant business events and are stored in an EPCIS repository. AspireRFID uses the EPCIS implementation of the Fosstrak project.
- **Connector Application (Connector):** The purpose of connector components is to abstract the interface between the Information Sharing repository and Enterprise Information Systems (EIS), such as EPR and WMS systems. Connectors offer APIs that enable proprietary EIS systems to exchange business information with the AspireRFID middleware system.
- **Management:** JMX (Java Management Extensions) (Oracle, 2014) wrappers allow the implementation of sophisticated RFID management applications. Management applications can also be used to both interface and control actuators. Moreover, based on JMX, commands for the control of actuators can be issued upon the occurrence of certain events at any middleware layer.
- **Actuators:** Based on sensor events, the actuator control framework defines interfaces and connectors for third party applications to successfully interact with analogue or digital devices. These sensors may either be RFID or other ASPIRE-supported physical sensors. Using this framework, the application is, for example, able to register event handler that interacts with a flashlight when a specific group of tags passes through a RFID aggregation gate.

Figure 1 illustrates the role of AspireRFID's IDE in the AspireRFID Architecture. It offers standard interfaces to interact with the several services issued by the AspireRFID architecture and therefore allows to:

Figure 1. AspireRFID middleware architecture and the role of AspireRFID IDE

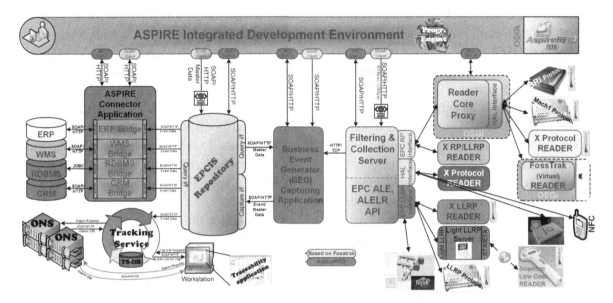

- Configure physical readers and their operational parameters and environments via Reader Core Proxy (through The Physical Reader Configuration Editor).

- Support the definition of logical readers (LLRP (EPCglobal, 2013c), RP, HAL and Simulator readers) by means of the Logical Reader Configuration Editor.

- Edit, as well as management, of F&C server Filtering Specifications (through the Reading Specifications Editor).

- Provide a control client to execute Application Level Event specification (ALE) commands on a reader or component that implements the ALE specification (through the F&C Commands Execution).

- Interact with the Connector application to reveal all its functionalities and configurations, enabling the configuration of connectors to different systems and databases (through the Connector Configurator).

- Enable users and/or consultants to edit enterprise data including information about the company's location, its business locations, read-points, as well as its business

processes (through the Master Data Editor tools).

- Offer business users and RFID consultants a graphical user interface for manipulating complex business processes, which are composed as workflows of elementary business processes (through the Business Process Workflow Management Editor).

The workflow management tool leverages the functionality of the above tools to support RFID deployments in accordance to specific business processes. In short, Aspire IDE allows end users to configure all the modules of AspireRFID architecture (which include several EPC Global compliant modules) in a simple and friendly way.

4. OVERVIEW OF THE TOOLS OF THE ASPIRE IDE

The AspireRFID IDE components provide means of configuring the underlying ASPIRE infrastructure. In practice, the user supplies the requirements to the IDE, which in turn translates them into configuration messages for the appropriate modules of the AspireRFID middleware infrastructures. The AspireRFID IDE has been designed as an Eclipse RCP (Rich Client Platform) application that runs over Equinox OSGI server. It uses the command API to define menus, pop-up menu items and toolbars so as to support plug-ins and provide more control. Every tool is an eclipse plug-in/bundle that can be installed or removed on demand. In this way, many editions of the AspireRFID IDE can be released depending on the functionality required by different RFID users/applications. In the sequel we illustrate the tools that comprise the AspireRFID IDE and their role in the application development, deployment and configuration process. As already discussed, most of the tools are implemented as Eclipse plug-ins which facilitates their modular combination and use.

4.1 ALE Server Configurator Plug-In

The ALE Server Configurator tool, depicted in Figure 2, enables the execution of Application Level Event specification (ALE) commands on an

RFID reader or other component that implements the ALE specification. In particular, the tool allows the configuration of the F&C middleware server (Dimitropoulos, 2010) according to a valid specification of ALE commands (ECSpec) in XML format. As specified in the EPC-ALE standard, an ECSpec details the way RFID tag streams will be filtered and grouped based on specific application requirements. The tool enables the loading, deletion and execution of XML files that correspond to valid ECSpec. Based on the tool one can also:

- Associate the ECSpec (under execution) with a notification URI of a remote capturing application. This association indicates the application that will receive the results (i.e. tag streams) of the filtering and collection functionalities specified in the ECSpec.
- Define/create a specification of Logical Readers that will contribute data to the F&C process. Therefore, the tool enables the definition of LRSpec (Logical Readers

Figure 2. ALE server configurator interfaces (ECSpec and LRSpec config.)

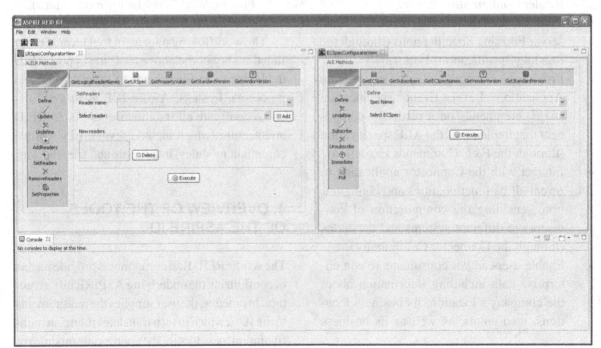

Specifications) XML files, which specify such Logical Readers. Following the definition of LRSpecs the tool enables their association with the specific instance of the F&C Server, which will undertake the processing of data supplied by the logical reader(s).

4.2 Business Event Generator (BEG) Plug-In

The main objective of the Business Event Generator (BEG) plug-in tool, depicted in Figure 3, is to provide the means to configure the Business Event Generator (BEG) of the AspireRFID middleware,

in order to translate the outcome of the F&C server (i.e. ECReports according to EPC-ALE terminology) to specific business events (compliant to the EPCIS specification) according to the set of Master Data that have been defined within the EPCIS repository; hence, the operation of the tool hinges on the (earlier) appropriate configuration of the EPCIS repository in terms of the definition of the master data required for the RFID system/ application at hand.

The tool provides also a dedicated view, which can depict the processed readings for each event in real-time. The subsequent functionality is extremely useful for testing and debugging applications that generate complex business events.

Figure 3. Business event generator plug-in

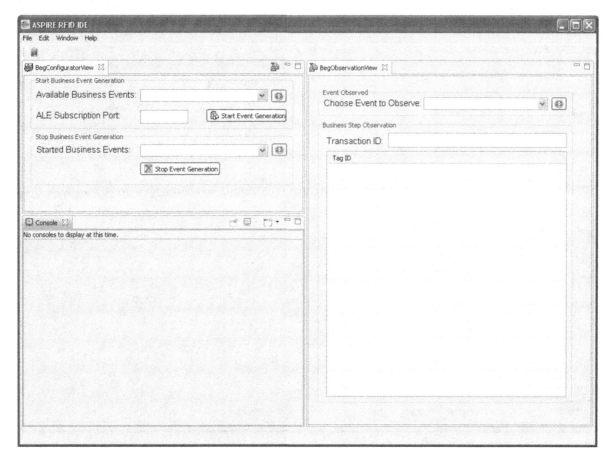

4.3 Physical Reader Configuration and Management Plug-In

Physical Reader Configuration & Management plug-in, depicted in Figure 4, provides a management front-end for the Reader Core proxy of the AspireRFID middleware infrastructure. It enables end users to edit the runtime parameters of the proxy and to manage its status. The respective management interfaces are accessible through any JMX capable console. In practice, the tool is used to manage RFID readers through the proxy module of the architecture.

4.4 ECSpec Editor Plug-In

The ECSpec editor is the tool that enables the user to produce and edit ECSpec documents (according to the EPC ALE V1.1 specification). As already outlined, these documents specify the behavior of the Filtering & Collection's module/server, in terms of the format of the reports that it will produce, but also in terms of the logical readers it will use to produce the reports. A snapshot of the ECSpec editor is depicted in Figure 5. Note that the ECSpec editor provides an interface to generate and/or edit (valid) ECSpec files. The ECSpecs define how the Filtering and Collection

Figure 4. Reader management console preferences window

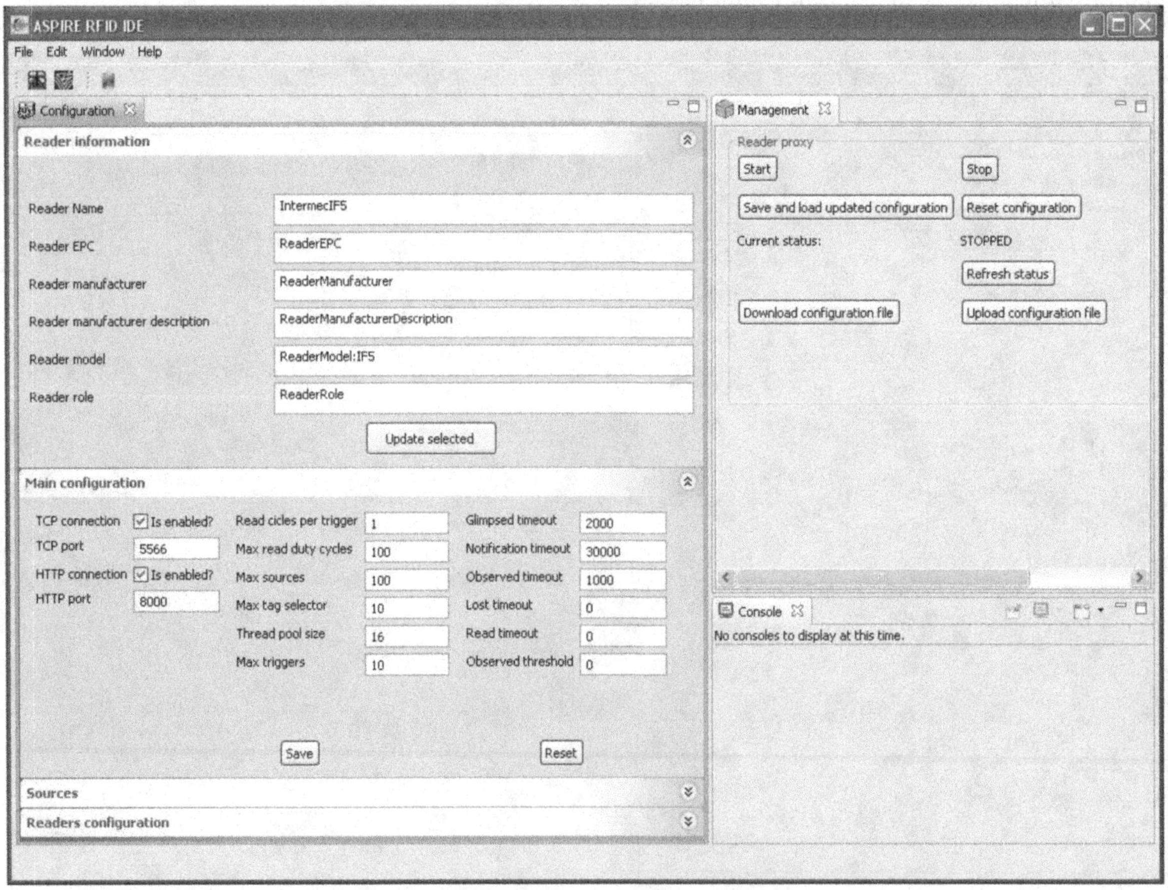

Figure 5. ECSpec & LRSpec editors view

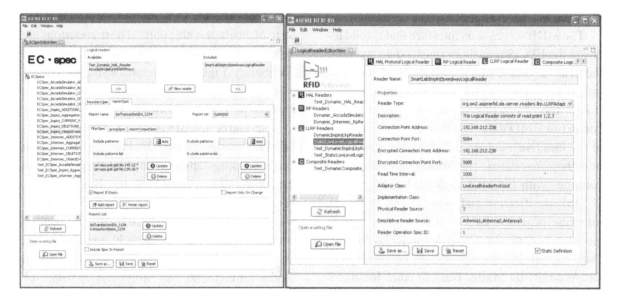

(EPC-ALE compliant) server will generate reports. Depending on the defined ECSpec, the F&C will report either the tags that have been read/detected in a given event cycle or report the tags that have been added (seen for the first time) or deleted (removed i.e. from a shelf that was monitored) with respect to the previous event cycle.

4.5 LRSpec Editor Plug-In

As evident from the description of earlier tools, several functionalities rely on the specification of appropriate logical reader (LR) instead of physical readers. Indeed, the execution of processing functions (e.g., filtering) on the basis of logical readers, alleviates the dependencies of those functions from the low-level details of the physical readers configurations. Due to the extensive use of the logical reader concept in the scope of RFID application development, the AspireRFID IDE provides a dedicated tool for defining and managing logical readers, through editing and managing LRSpec files i.e. XML files that define logical reader compositions. A snapshot of this tool is provided in Figure 5. It should be noted

that the tools support the definition of logical readers based on combinations of different types of physical readers including: (a) Reader compliant to the EPC Reader Protocol (RP), (b) Readers compliant to the EPC Low Level Reader Protocol (LLRP) (EPCglobal, 2013c), (c) Non-EPC compliant readers, which implement the HAL (Hardware Abstraction Layer) layer specified in the AspireRFID middleware architecture.

4.6 Master Data Editor Plug-In

The Master Data Editor (MDE) tool/plug-in enables providers of RFID solutions to edit enterprise data (i.e. Master Data) including information about the company's location, its business locations, read points, as well as, its business processes. In practice, the MDE can be used for populating and managing vocabularies in the Master Data. Therefore, organizations can use this tool for the proper population of the Master Data without the need to know the associations and low-level details of the Master Data vocabularies (Database Schema). The reason is that all the relations among the RFID data and the restrictions are delegated to be the MDE's responsibility.

The MDE serves as an interface that is used to create the EPCIS repository master data and edit them, as needed. Using the MDE RFID solution providers can populate the EPCIS vocabularies and store all the information needed to provide business context to RFID data. The data are manipulated in an intuitive manner and the user can view how they are related. The MDE implementation complies with EPC EPCIS V1.0.1 (EPCglobal, 2013b) specification and uses the EPCIS query interface provided by Fosstrak project, which has been enhanced with the AspireRFID Master Data capture interface. It should be noted that the AspireRFID Master Data Capture Interface extends the Fosstrak's project implementation, in a way that allows editing of the vocabularies of the EPCIS repository. This enables users (i.e. solution developers) to modify already existing master data.

Using the MDE the user is able to define a process, assign attributes that are descriptive to it and convey useful information about it. Additionally, the user can define all of the events that compose the process. The events are treated as transactions and their EPC is stored in the business transaction vocabulary. In the attributes' vocabulary for

the transactions, all of the related information for the events and the transactions are stored in the form of attribute-value pairs. The transactions are associated with the events through the attributes' vocabulary. Figure 6 illustrates a snapshot of the transaction tab of the tool, which is used to define a whole process as a series of EPCIS events.

It should be noted that MDE users can populate different master data vocabularies using a set of corresponding tabs, i.e. tabs corresponding to the Disposition vocabulary, the Business Step vocabulary, the Readers vocabulary, the Transaction Type vocabulary and the Business Location vocabulary. MDE users can add a new element, associate attributes with it, edit existing element, search for elements etc. Moreover, by using the business location tag, an organization can accurately describe all of the locations it owns in a hierarchical manner. For example, the fact that an organization has two warehouses and two sections within the first warehouse, can be reflected in the database and represented visually to the user who can add a location either as a single entity or as part of another location and associate attributes to it. Furthermore, the MDE allows its end-users to manage the locations (e.g., warehouses) of different organizations, including capabilities for defining «inactive» or «depreciated» locations,

Figure 6. Master data editor (transactions and business location tabs) within the MDE plug-in

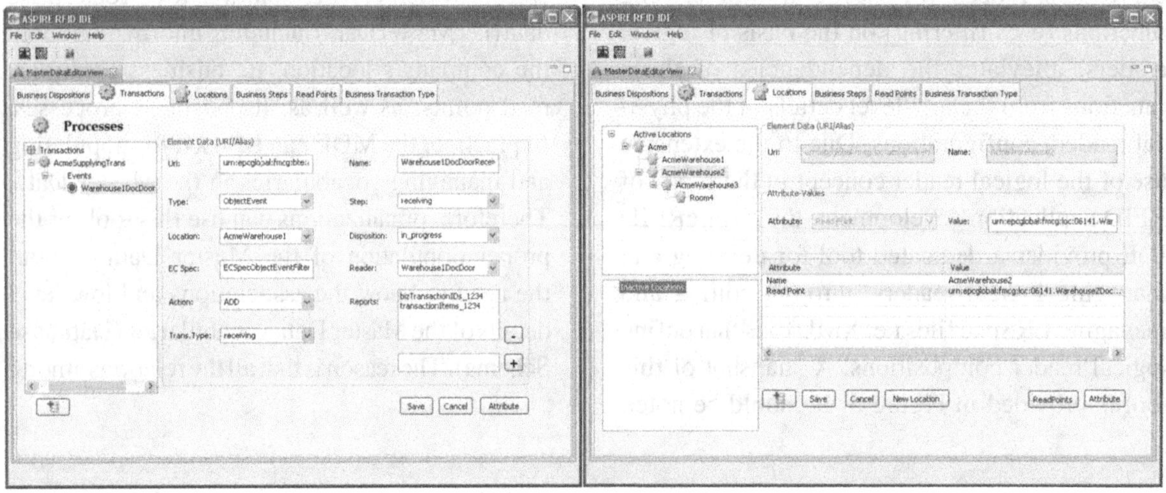

which renders them out-of-scope. A snapshot of the Locations tab that demonstrates the above mentioned management of locations, is depicted in Figure 6.

4.7 RFID Business Location GMF (Graphical Modeling Framework) Editor

The RFID Business Location Editor is a valuable add-one tool to the Master Data Editor, which allows the definition/specification of the elements (e.g., Rooms, Conveyors, Read Points, Containers, Handheld Readers) that comprise an RFID business location (e.g., warehouse, factory, plant) in a visual manner. A snapshot of the tool is illustrated in Figure 7. It should be noted that the RFID Business Location Editor is based on the Eclipse Graphical Modeling Framework (GMF) and therefore, behaves as an Eclipse Rich Client Platform Application. Therefore, it is a multi-threading application, which enables multiple Business Locations diagrams to be open and under process at the same time.

Similar to the MDE, the RFID Business Location Editor communicates with the EPCIS repository through web services and more specifically the above-mentioned EPCIS interfaces provided by the Fosstrak and AspireRFID projects. It should be noted that upon launching a new instance of the tool, it collects business locations information (from the EPCIS repository) and visualizes it. In this way, the tool synchronizes its status with the information contained in the EPCIS repository.

5. BUSINESS PROCESS WORKFLOW MANAGEMENT EDITOR PLUG-IN

In addition to the tools that have been presented in the previous section, the AspireRFID IDE includes a more integrated tool, which is conveniently called Business Process Workflow Management Editor

(BPWME) and is also a plug-in of the IDE. This tool supports an integrated programming model, which emphasizes the integrated configuration of all of the underlying modules on the basis of the Aspire business Process Description Language (APDL), and is described in Kefalakis, 2011b. Instead of configuring the modules comprising an RFID solution one-by-one (i.e. using the tools outlined above), this integrated programming models leverages the APDL language in order to provide an integrated description of the RFID solution. The BPWME tool enables end-users (e.g., RFID solution providers) to visually design an RFID solution and to encode it into an appropriate APDL file accordingly. Accordingly, the tool can parse the APDL file in order to activate the configuration of the various middleware modules of the AspireRFID architecture.

The use of BPWME (in conjunction with APDL) boosts the visual development of RFID solutions, which obviate the need for tedious low-level RFID programming. In particular, the BPWME enables RFID solution developers to describe a complex RFID solution as a workflow diagram, while guiding them in order to provide the required information in a valid manner. In Figure 8 a snapshot of the BPWME depicts the workflow design process It should be noted that a workflow process design is a more straightforward procedure compared to detailed configurations of distributed software and hardware components by using various configuration interfaces (such as the individual plug-in tools outlined in the previous section). As such, the use of the workflow editor reduces significantly the time and effort required for the configuration of an RFID solution. Additionally, it provides the ability to register and store complete RFID solutions in a single configuration file. This can significantly facilitate reusability across classes of similar RFID solutions, since it allows the adoption of existing solutions rather than their original development. Furthermore, the BPWME reduces the knowledge overhead

Figure 7. RFID business location editor

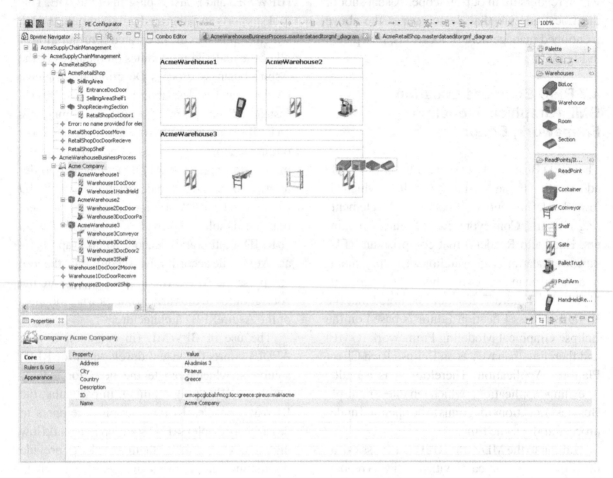

imposed by the need to use various tools, while easing debugging and maintenance efforts.

The BPWME supports multiple views of the solution, including the Workflow View (illustrated in Figure 8), the Business Location Editor View (illustrated in Figure 7) and the XML Editor View which depicts the APDL document that is generated from the last two views. The tool provides access to the MDE, the ECSpec and LRSpec editor tools, in order to facilitate the solution provider to access the master data and the configuration of the F&C solution respectively. Furthermore, it provides a pallet with the main elements of the APDL language, along with a drag and drop interface that enables the visual development of

workflows diagrams. BPWME users can also drill down to the properties of each APDL element, based on appropriate forms and dialog boxes.

6. EVALUTION OF THE ASPIRERFID TOOLS

6.1 Practical Validation Scenarios

The AspireRFID IDE has been used to facilitate the configuration and deployment of the AspireRFID platform in various supply chain management scenarios, two of which involve the apparel and packaging industry and are described as follows:.

Figure 8. BPWME combo editor (workflow view)

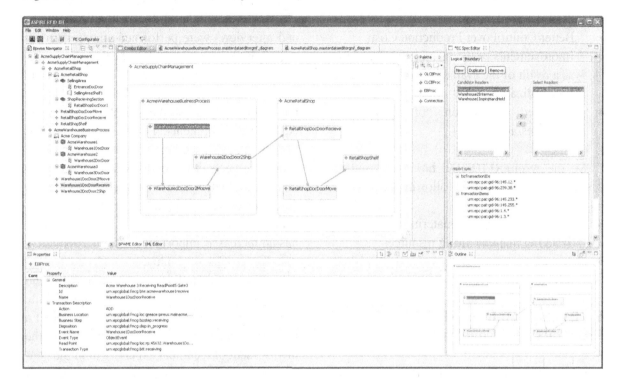

6.2 Apparel Industry

One of the leading apparel manufacturer companies (Rhea, 2010) in the Greek market specialized in denim apparel, required to automate their warehouse processes. In this scenario the RFID technology is used in order to facilitate the following processes, necessary the company's operations:

- Automatically count the apparels during Receiving, Shipping and Inventory;
- Automatically verify the Picking and Packing of apparel;
- Perform rapid inventory of clothes in the warehouse shelves or in the shelves of retail shops.

So the AspireRFID IDE has been used to describe and configure the following RFID processes:

- Receiving apparel goods;
- Collecting and packaging of products;
- Shipment of Sales orders;
- Inventory of products.

6.3 Packaging Industry

One of the leading companies in the Greek market in packaging (Toffaletti, 2014) required a system for improving specific issues after the application of RFID related technologies and the AspireRFID platform. These issues included the:

- Improvement of the estimation/forecast of the cost of finished products;
- Achievement of more accurate inventory for source materials;
- Achievement of more accurate inventory for second materials;
- Achievement of more accurate inventory for semi-finished products;

- Improvements of Quality Control processes of the production;
- Better Control over Production Cost;
- Improvements of the managerial decisions as a result of the availability of nearly real-time utilization data;
- Improved utilization of production resources/assets.

So the AspireRFID IDE has been used to describe and configure the following processes:

- Tracking and tracing materials;
- Tracking manufacturing resources;
- Tracking semi-finished and finished products.

6.4 Evaluation from RFID Solution Providers and Developers

In order to evaluate the above-listed tools and their integration within the AspireRFID IDE we collected feedback from the RFID Solution Providers and RFID Developers, including contributors to the ASPIRE technical developments and uses of the AspireRFID middleware and tools. Different modalities were employed in order to collect and analyze this feedback including: (a) direct contacts (i.e. interview and discussions) with contributors to the ASPIRE technical developments, (b) questionnaires, filled-in by all developers and users of the AspireRFID middleware and tools, (c) testing of several aspects of the ASPIRE middleware and tools by technical experts, useful in assessing functionality and performance aspects. Several of the modalities outlined above are closely linked to the evaluation of the technical aspects of the ASPIRE middleware. The evaluation of such aspects required a good knowledge of the technical characteristics of ASPIRE, along with a wider understanding of the functionalities offered and expected by an RFID middleware and tool suite. Thus, the technical evaluation relied on the involvement of evaluators with experience in

RFID middleware, tools and the specific AspireRFID developments. In particular, discussions and interviews were performed among five key contributors to AspireRFID. At the same time, questionnaires were filled-in by contributors and users. It should be noted that very few of the evaluators possessed a global view of all the ASPIRE developments. The reason is that most of them had focused on using or contributing to specific aspects of the middleware and tools. To this end, evaluators have been asked to specify with which module(s) they had practical experience. Likewise, their opinion for the respective modules has an increased importance. Another remark is that the groups of evaluators included technical experts from both consortium members and third-party community users or developers. While the involvement of third-party users provided a level of objectivity to the assessment process, the involvement of technical experts within the consortium was also deemed necessary due to their deep knowledge of the AspireRFID developments (including strengths and weaknesses).

The most important issues documented and raised during the evaluation included:

- **Performance Issues:** It was stated that the performance of the underlying middleware should be improved. This concerned (mainly) the response of the software in certain reading and filtering operations, notably read cycles that involve multiple items.
- **Effort Allocation towards Increased Robustness and Functionality:** Some of the participants noticed that more effort should be allocated on developing further the project towards increasing both its robustness and its functionality. Indeed, integrating the AspireRFID middleware and tools requires significant efforts from the end-users or integrators. These efforts are devoted not only to writing integration code, but also testing and (sometimes)

fixing functionalities. Thus, there is still a lot of room for improving AspireRFID in terms of technical maturity.

- **Improvement of the Documentation:** Several of the participants required from the AspireRFID founders and core community members to provide more detailed documentation (e.g., in terms of users and developers' manual), along with more screenshots illustrating the usage of the tools. Documentation is indeed very important for the wide adoption of the ASPIRE open source developments.
- **Documentation for Non-Experts:** There was an explicit comment requesting more documentation especially for non-experts. According to this comment, the documentation for technically knowledgeable members (e.g., developers) is much more extensive comparing to the documentation available for non-experts (e.g., users).
- **Modularity Associated with Practical Applications:** One participant mentioned that AspireRFID modules should be more flexibly inserted in practical applications. This comment implied a need for creating certain AspireRFID configurations for using AspireRFID within practical applications. These configurations could take the form of certain instances of APDL files, as well as, pre-configured demonstrations targeting specific use cases and applications.

The above-listed issues have been taken into account in order to improve the AspireRFID middleware and IDE presented in this chapter.

6.5 Techno-Economic Evaluation

The techno-economic evaluation of the AspireRFID IDE, aimed at evaluating the benefits of an AspireRFID based solution comparing to alternative (conventional) options for implementing, configuring and deploying RFID middleware. To this end, the costs associated with RFID software licensing, integration and maintenance in the scope of one of the practical deployments of the AspireRFID middleware in the apparel sector (and more specifically its deployment for warehouse management in the scope of a jeans/denim company (Rhea, 2010) were examined and analyzed. As already outlined, the analysis emphasized on the assessment of RFID software/middleware as an element of the Total Cost of Ownership (TCO) of the solution, given that the rest of the cost (e.g., hardware, consumable/tags) remained the same, regardless of the programming model and tools used.

For the purposes of the evaluation process, the following assumptions were made:

- The adoption/selection of a middleware suite solution instead of a custom RFID middleware development. It should be noted that, nowadays, several integrators choose to develop a custom proprietary solution from scratch, instead of integrating, customizing and deploying an RFID middleware stack. While custom development solutions might be more cost effective for an initial deployment associated with few processes, they are not scalable to multiple processes and requirements as in the case of the apparel deployment at hand. Since the apparel company agreed to deploy a middleware suite rather than resort to a custom development of the solution, a custom development approach was not considered in the analysis.
- That software integration and deployment costs are part of the overall consulting and integration costs. The fact, however, that consulting and integration costs comprise other cost components as well, such as the effort required in deploying, testing and fine-tuning the hardware for increased performance and reliability, should be taken into consideration.

- The costs of infrastructure software are not taken into account in the analysis. Infrastructure software refers to databases, application servers, directory servers and other software used to support the RFID deployment. It is assumed that royalty free software is used to this end, in order to decouple the RFID related analysis from investments in other type of software. We therefore assume that any additional investments of the apparel company in infrastructure software were not related (or correlated) to its selection of infrastructure software. It should be noted that the cost of infrastructure software (e.g., enterprise class application servers or databases) may be a significant contributing factor to the total cost of ownership of the solution; however, it is not directly associated with the option selected for RFID software/middleware. There is practically a sole exception, which refers to infrastructure software associated with the enterprise class commercial middleware, given that the operation/execution of this middleware presupposes the deployment of certain application/middleware servers.

With the above assumptions in mind, the following RFID middleware options and associated programming models were evaluated:

- **Enterprise Scale RFID Middleware Solution:** This option refers to the selection and deployment of an enterprise-level middleware solution from large reputable vendors. A ballpark estimation of the price has been made, taking also into account the minimum infrastructure software costs incurred by the solution. Enterprise scale solutions come usually as part of wide middleware solutions (e.g., application-servers, sensor-edge servers) of the (usually large software) vendor.

- **Commercial Middleware Solution:** This option refers to the selection and deployment of a commercial/proprietary RFID middleware solution, notably out of the solutions focused on RFID. Contrary to the enterprise solutions, these are less scalable solutions, which can however be appropriate for RFID deployments within an SME. A gross estimation of the respective licensing cost has been made for the purposes of the analysis.

- **Open-Source (AspireRFID) Middleware Solution (with Integration Based on Software Development):** This option refers to the selection and deployment of an open source solution (such as AspireRFID), based on a respective programming effort for integrating the middleware libraries. In this case the solution cost has been estimated on the basis of a zero cost software license and the real-pilot cost (in terms of person months) incurred for the software integration and deployment.

- **Open-Source (AspireRFID) Middleware Solution (with Integration Based on AspireRFID Tools):** This option refers to the selection and deployment of an open source solution (such as AspireRFID), based on the AspireRFID tools and RFID IDE (Integrated Development Environment). The use of the AspireRFID IDE was estimated to have reduced the solution development effort associated with the deployment by 20%. Hence, the solution costs have been estimated on the basis of zero licensing costs and the 20% reduced cost for the development, integration and deployment effort.

- **Open-Source (AspireRFID) Middleware Solution (with Integration Based on AspireRFID Programmability and APDL):** This option refers to the selection and deployment of an open source solution (such as AspireRFID), based on the AspireRFID programmability features such as the ASPIRE business Process Description Language (APDL) and the Business Process Workflow Management Editor (BPWME). This option has been tested on the deployment on the production/authoring of the proper APDL files comprising the RFID-enabled processes of the apparel company. The deployment effort was minimal, thanks however to the fact that the analysis of the company's processes and the required RFID artifacts had already been performed. Therefore, towards estimating the respective effort (based on the APDL programming and deployment model), we added efforts associated with business process analysis, population of master data and identification of the required RFID data collection, filtering and business eventing mechanisms. Overall, we concluded that APDL based programming could reduce the software development and deployment costs up to 50%.

A realistic maintenance cost was also added to each of the above options when estimated their contribution to the TCO of the solution. For the commercial solutions, maintenance costs were estimated as a percentage (20%) of the licensing costs. Likewise, for the open source solutions, maintenance costs, taking into account the peculiar needs of the RFID deployment. Based on the above considerations the overall software, integration and maintenance costs for the target solutions are depicted in Table 1. According to the comparison of different options, as seen in Figure 9, AspireRFID based solutions are preferred over commercial solution, due to their lower software licensing costs. The fact that the AspireRFID programmability model can indeed lead to further cost savings, is also proven.

Figure 9 also illustrates the contribution of each option to the TCO of the solution, based on the analysis of the total costs associated with the solution (including hardware and consumable costs). AspireRFID can lead to an approx. 5% reduction in the overall TCO of the solution. Overall, the software components correspond to a small percentage of the overall TCO. This is due to the fact that the apparel deployment required item-level tagging within a large warehouse, which resulted in extremely high consumables and personnel costs. It is expected that in the scope of deployments with less consumables (e.g., palette-level RFID tagging deployments), the software component within the TCO will be much more significant. Likewise, AspireRFID contribution to lowering the TCO could be much more significant (e.g., AspireRFID could reduce the TCO at the levels of 15%-20%).

At this point, however, it should also be recalled that there is uncertainty associated with cost estimations, while intangible and qualitative benefits cannot always be quantified. For example, one may argue that a commercial solu-

Table 1. Overview of the costs associated with the various RFID options for the real-life apparel deployment

Solution/Costs	Software Licensing	Software Integration	Software Maintenance	Total Software/ Middleware
Open Source (AspireRFID) with conventional Integration	0,00€	50.000,00€	5.000,00€	55.000,00€
Open Source (AspireRFID)	0,00€	40.000,00€	5.000,00€	45.000,00€
Open Source (AspireRFID)	0,00€	25.000,00€	5.000,00€	30.000,00€
Commercial Solution	10.000,00€	50.000,00€	7.000,00€	67.000,00€
Enterprise Scale Commercial Solution	20.000,00€	50.000,00€	9.000,00€	79.000,00€

Figure 9. Comparison to cost and contribution to TCO of the various solutions in the scope of the apparel deployment

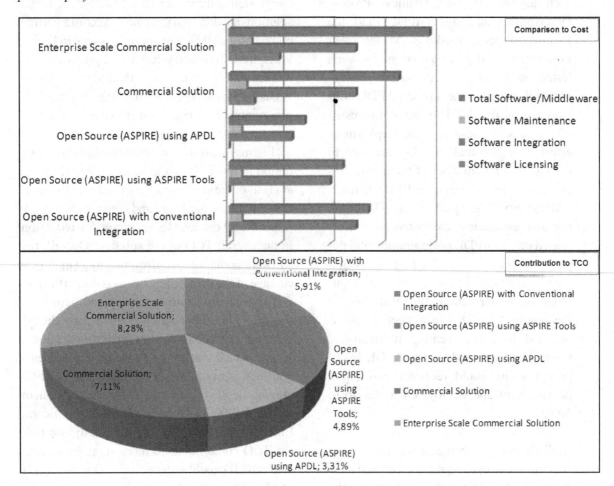

tion might be more robust and sustainable than the AspireRFID open source solution. Moreover, the quality of maintenance and support cannot be taken into account in this quantification. Despite these considerations, it is shown that AspireRFID could lead to economic benefits and represents an added-value proposition at least for companies committed to the adoption, deployment and use of open-source software.

Another important remark relates to the scope of the applicability of the AspireRFID programmability options, which yields the highest economic benefit. Currently, APDL supports a class of

supply chain management and logistics oriented solutions, notably solutions that adopt parts of the EPCGlobal architecture framework. For these solutions, solution providers could come up with deployable APDL files that could accelerate the RFID deployment. At the same time, there is a broad range of RFID deployments that cannot be covered based on the current version of APDL. As a remedy, AspireRFID provides the set of stand-alone tools / plug-ins that could facilitate parts of the RFID deployment, even in the scope of solutions that are not supported by APDL.

7. CONCLUSION

Nowadays, most of proposed RFID middleware solutions are implemented on a per-case basis and do not offer an integrated development environment supporting third-party developments. In this chapter, we introduced the AspireRFID integrated development environment (AspireRFID IDE), which encompasses a set of tools for visual development of programmable RFID solutions based on the AspireRFID middleware Architecture. These integrated tools facilitate the development of fully fledged RFID solutions based on the programmable composition of filters, events, workflows etc. The AspireRFID IDE is based on the Eclipse platform which is modularly extensible. Therefore, different AspireRFID related components (ALE, BEG, EPCIS, etc.) are configured by using an integrated tool that allows users to have a centralized view of the configuration of the architecture. In the scope of this chapter, a comprehensive overview of the main features and functionalities of several tools / plug-ins has been given. All these tools / plug-ins are reusable and are usually derived from distributed libraries of reusable RFID components. Furthermore, they are available on-line as open source components from the AspireRFID (2013) project based on the business friendly LGPL license.

Feedback from early adopters certifies that the AspireRFID IDE platform and its related stand-alone tools can significantly facilitate the development of RFID applications, while at the same time introducing a radical change in the current paradigm for RFID solution development and deployment. Furthermore, the techno-economic evaluation of the tools in the scope of a specific solution deployment has demonstrated their potential to contribute to the cost-effectiveness of an RFID development.

On the other side the AspireRFID integrated development environment and the AspireRFID platform is constrained by some limitations. The main of which is that it is a solution mostly suitable for logistics and supply chain management applications, it has limited support for real-time applications and it lacks support for standards other than EPC Global. These limitations could be surpassed in the future along with the potential of enhancing the system in order to support additional applications in other areas (e.g., document management, security).

ACKNOWLEDGMENT

Part of this work has been carried out in the scope of the ASPIRE project (FP7-215417) (http://www.fp7-aspire.eu). The authors acknowledge help and contributions from all partners of the project. Furthermore, the authors acknowledge the work of AIT students (Vassiliki Koletti, Yongming Luo, Karageorgiou Eleftherios and Mertikas Efstathios) that contributed in the implementation of the presented tools which are also listed in the AspireRFID contributor page (http://wiki.aspire.ow2.org/xwiki/bin/view/Main/Contributors).

REFERENCES

RFID Aspire. (2013). *The AspireRFID project*. Retrieved from http://forge.ow2.org/projects/aspire/

Dimitropoulos, P., & Soldatos, J. (2010). RFID-enabled Fully Automated Warehouse Management: Adding the Business Context. *International Journal of Manufacturing Technology and Management*, *21*(3/4), 2010. doi:10.1504/IJMTM.2010.035436

EPCglobal. (2013a). *The Application Level Events (ALE) Specification (version 1.1.1), parts 1 and 2*. Retrieved from http://www.gs1.org/gsmp/kc/epcglobal/ale

EPCglobal. (2013b). *EPC Information Services (EPCIS) Specification (version 1.0.1)*. Retrieved from http://www.gs1.org/gsmp/kc/epcglobal/epcis

EPCglobal. (2013c). *Low Level Reader Protocol (LLRP) (version 1.1)*. Retrieved from http://www.gs1.org/gsmp/kc/epcglobal/llrp

EPCGlobal Architecture Review Committee. (2013). *The EPCglobal Architecture Framework (version 1.5) EPCglobal*. Retrieved from http://www.gs1.org/gsmp/kc/epcglobal/architecture

Floerkemeier, C., Roduner, C., & Lampe, M. (2007). RFID Application Development with the Accada Middleware Platform. *IEEE Systems Journal*, *1*(2), 82–94. doi:10.1109/JSYST.2007.909778

Kefalakis, N., Leontiadis, N., Soldatos, J., & Donsez, D. (2009). *Middleware Building Blocks for Architecting RFID Systems*. Paper presented at the MOBILIGHT 2009 Conference. New York, NY.

Kefalakis, N., Soldatos, J., Konstantinou, N., & Prasad, N. R. (2011b). APDL: A reference XML schema for process-centered definition of RFID solutions. *Journal of Systems and Software*, *84*(7), 1244–1259. doi:10.1016/j.jss.2011.02.036

Kefalakis, N., Soldatos, J., Mertikas, E., & Prasad, N. (2011a). *Generating Business Events in an RFID network*. Paper presented at RFID-TA. New York, NY.

Lampe, M., & Floerkemeier, C. (2007). High-Level System Support for Automatic-Identification Applications. In *Proceedings of Workshop on Design of Smart Products*, (pp. 55-64). Furtwangen, Germany: Academic Press.

Leontiadis, N., Kefalakis, N., & Soldatos, J. (2009). Bridging RFID Systems and Enterprise Applications through Virtualized Connectors. *International Journal of Automated Identification Technology*, *1*(2), 2009.

LogicAlloy. (2013). *LogicAlloy RFID System*. Retrieved from http://www.logicalloy.com/index.cfm

Mobitec. (2013). *Cuhk epcglobal RFID middleware*. Retrieved from http://mobitec.ie.cuhk.edu.hk/rfid/middleware/

Oracle. (2014). *Java Management Extensions (JMX) Technology*. Retrieved from http://www.oracle.com/technetwork/java/javase/tech/java-management-140525.html

Palazzi, C., Ceriali, A., & Dal Monte, M. (2009, August). RFID Emulation in Rifidi Environment. In *Proc. of the International Symposium on Ubiquitous Computing* (UCS'09). Beijing, China: UCS.

Prabhu, S., Su, X., Ramamurthy, H., Chu, C., & Gadh, R. (2006). *WinRFID –A Middleware for the enablement of Radio Frequency Identification (RFID) based Applications. In Mobile, Wireless and Sensor Networks: Technology, Applications and Future Directions*. John Wiley.

Rhea Wessel. (2010). *Staff Jeans to Introduce RFID-Enabled Customer Services*. Retrieved September, 2013 from http://www.rfidjournal.com/articles/view?7899

Toffaletti, S., & Soldatos, J. (2014). *RFID-ROI-SME Project Promises Big Help for Small Business*. Retrieved February, 2014 from http://www.rfidjournal.com/articles/view?7661

ADDITIONAL READING

Anagnostopoulos, A., Soldatos, J., & Michalakos, S. (2009). REFiLL: A Lightweight Programmable Middleware Platform for Cost Effective RFID Application Development. *Journal of Pervasive and Mobile Computing (Elsevier)*, *5*(1Issue 1), 49–63. doi:10.1016/j.pmcj.2008.08.004

Brusey, J., Floerkemeier, C., Harrison, M., & Fletcher, M. (2003), *Reasoning about Uncertainty in Location Identification with RFID,* in Workshop on Reasoning with Uncertainty in Robotics at IJCAI-2003, Acapulco, Mexico.

Chawathe, S., Krishnamurthyy, V., Ramachandrany, S., & Sarma, S. (2004), *Managing RFID Data,* in Proceedings of the 30st international conference on very large data bases (VLDB). Toronto, Canada: VLDB Endowment, pp. 1189–1195.

Dimakis, N., Soldatos, J., Polymenakos, L., Fleury, P., Curín, J., & Kleindienst, J. (2008). Integrated Development of Context-Aware Applications in Smart Spaces. *IEEE Pervasive Computing / IEEE Computer Society [and] IEEE Communications Society,* 7(4), 71–79. doi:10.1109/MPRV.2008.75

Floerkemeier, C., & Lampe, M. (2005, October). *RFID middleware design – addressing application requirements and RFID constraints.* In Proceedings of SOC'2005 (Smart Objects Conference), pages 219–224, Grenoble, France.

Garfinkel, S., & Rosenberg, B. (2005). *RFID: Applications, Security, and Privacy.* Addison-Wesley.

Kefalakis N., Leontiadis N., Soldatos J., Gama K., & Donsez D. (2008 December), *Supply Chain Management and NFC Picking Demonstrations using the AspireRFID Middleware Platform,* Demonstration in the scope of the ACM Middleware 2008 conference, Leuwen, Belgium.

Legner, C., & Thiesse, F. (2006). RFID-based maintenance at Frankfurt airport. *IEEE Pervasive Computing / IEEE Computer Society [and] IEEE Communications Society,* 5(1), 34–39. doi:10.1109/MPRV.2006.14

Martinelli, L., Kefalakis, N., & Soldatos, J. (2011, October), *Automatic Document Tracing Using the RFID Technology,* In the Proc. of the eChallenges 2011 conference, Florence, Italy.

Nath B., Reynolds F., & Want, R. (2006, March), *RFID Technology and Applications,* IEEE Pervasive Computing, Vol. 5, No. 1, Jan.-March 2006, pp. 22- 24.

Opasjumruskit, K., Thanthipwan, T., Sathusen, O., Sirinamarattana, P., Gadmanee, P., & Pootarapan, E. et al. (2006). Self-powered wireless temperature sensors exploit RFID technology. *IEEE Pervasive Computing / IEEE Computer Society [and] IEEE Communications Society,* 5(1), 54–61. doi:10.1109/MPRV.2006.15

Riekki, J., Salminen, T., & Alakarppa, I. (2006). Requesting Pervasive Services by Touching RFID Tags. *IEEE Pervasive Computing / IEEE Computer Society [and] IEEE Communications Society,* 5(1), 40–46. doi:10.1109/MPRV.2006.12

Romer, K., Schoch, T., Mattern, F., & Dubendorfer, T. (2004). Smart Identification Frameworks for Ubiquitous Computing Applications. *Wireless Networks,* 10(6), 689–700. doi:10.1023/B:WINE.0000044028.20424.85

Sarma, S. (2004). Integrating RFID. *ACM Queue; Tomorrow's Computing Today,* 2(7), 50–57. doi:10.1145/1035594.1035620

Soldatos J. (2009, March, 16), *AspireRfid Can Lower Deployment Costs,* RFID Journal.

Soldatos J. (2009, March, 16), *The AspireRfid Project: Is Open Source RFID Middleware still an option?,* RFID World.

Soldatos, J., Dimakis, N., Stamatis, K., & Polymenakos, L. (2007, March). *A Breadboard Architecture for Pervasive Context-Aware Services in Smart Spaces: Middleware Components and Prototype Applications,* Personal and Ubiquitous Computing Journal (Springer London), ISSN 1617-4909 (Print), Issue Volume 11, Number 3, Pages 193-212.

Soldatos, J., Serrano, M., & Hauswirth, M. (2012). Convergence of Utility Computing with the Internet-of-Things. *IMIS*, *2012*, 874–879.

Staake, T., Thiesse, F., & Fleisch, E. (2005, March), *Extending the EPC network: the potential of RFID in anti-counterfeiting,* in SAC '05: Proceedings of the 2005 ACM symposium on Applied computing. Santa Fe, NM, USA: ACM Press, pp. 1607–1612.

Stanford, V. (2002). Pervasive Computing Goes to Work: Interfacing to the Enterprise. *IEEE Pervasive Computing / IEEE Computer Society [and] IEEE Communications Society*, *1*(3), 6–12. doi:10.1109/MPRV.2002.1037716

Stanford, V. (2003). *Pervasive computing goes the last hundred feet with RFID systems, Pervasive Computing* (pp. 9–14). IEEE Computer Science.

Thiesse, F., Fleisch, E., & Dierkes, M. (2006). LotTrack: RFID-based process control in the semiconductor industry. *IEEE Pervasive Computing / IEEE Computer Society [and] IEEE Communications Society*, *5*(1), 47–53. doi:10.1109/MPRV.2006.9

Toffaletti S., & Soldatos J. (2010, June, 14), *RFID-ROI-SME Project Promises Big Help for Small Business*, RFID Journal.

Tuán A., Quoc H., Serrano M., Hauswirth M., Soldatos J., Papaioannou T., & Aberer K. (2012), *Global Sensor Modeling and Constrained Application Methods Enabling Cloud-Based Open Space Smart Services,* UIC/ATC 2012: 196-203.

Want, R. (2004). Enabling Ubiquitous Sensing with RFID. *Computer*, *37*(4), 84–86. doi:10.1109/MC.2004.1297315

KEY TERMS AND DEFINITIONS

APDL (AspireRFID Process Description Language): Is an XML based specification for describing and configuring RFID solutions based on the EPC global architecture specifications.

Eclipse Plug-In: Is a software component that adds a specific feature to Eclipse integrated development environment.

EPC: Is a universal identifier that provides a unique identity for every physical object anywhere in the world, for all time. Its structure is defined from the EPCglobal and it is a 'pure-identity URI' representation that is intended for use when referring to a specific physical object.

EPC-ALE: A standard created by EPCglobal, part of the EPC architecture, which defines a layer that provides several operations like accumulation and filtering over RFID data streams.

EPCIS (EPC Information Services): Is an EPCglobal standard designed to enable EPC-related data sharing within and across enterprises.

RFID Middleware: Is a middleware platform that conforms and supports the RFID technology.

RFID Tools: Software that facilitates the RFID application development, configuration and deployment processes.

Chapter 6
Meta–Data Alignment in Open Tracking and Tracing Systems

Fred van Blommestein
University of Groningen, The Netherlands

Dávid Karnok
MTA Sztaki Budapest, Hungary

Zsolt Kemény
MTA Sztaki Budapest, Hungary

ABSTRACT

Many supply chains require open tracking and tracing systems. In open tracking and tracing systems, attributes of objects are not known beforehand, as the type of objects and the set of stakeholders may evolve over time. In this chapter, a method is presented that enables components of tracking and tracing systems to negotiate at run time what attributes may be stored for a particular object type. Components may include scanning equipment, data stores, and query clients. Attributes may be of any data type, including time, location, status, temperature, and ownership. Apart from simple attributes, associations between objects may be recorded and stored (e.g. when an object is packed in another object, loaded in a truck or container, or assembled to be a new object). The method was developed in two European-funded research projects: TraSer and ADVANCE.

1. OPEN TRACKING AND TRACING

In the present business landscape, companies should not be considered to be independent entities, but parts of supply chains that are interwoven to multi-echelon networks. Material flow transparency, specifically the visibility to inventories and deliveries in the whole supply network, is considered an imperative requirement for suc-cessful supply-chain management, and has been associated with significant efficiency and quality improvements (Ala-Risku and Kärkkäinen, 2004; Ballard, 1996; Clarke, 1998; Främling et al., 2004; Kärkkäinen et al., 2004).

Apart from logistics, transparency of the origin of goods and their manufacturing conditions is increasingly required by consumers and regulators. Food safety and food composition are hot topics.

DOI: 10.4018/978-1-4666-6308-4.ch006

Consumers wish to be informed under what conditions products were produced and packed, and use criteria such as sustainability, animal well-being, fair trade and worker's conditions to guide their purchasing (Hiscox and Smyth, 2011).

Manufacturers, on the other hand, need to know where their products are ultimately sold and consumed. They are increasingly held responsible for maintenance, spare parts supply and reverse logistics (Kosk, 2014). In case of defects or quality issues, consumers may need to be warned and products may need to be recalled. Without a system that keeps track of product destinations, too many products must be called back and too many consumers are alarmed unnecessary.

Tracking products and electronic product representations across enterprise boundaries currently requires substantial manual work, or extensive system-to-system integration work. From an application point of view, tracking functionality is tightly coupled to the systems and practices of the individual supply chain participants, resulting in network level operational processes being rare and expensive. Few companies, regardless of their desire for supply-chain efficiency, have implemented supply-chain transparency solutions (Kaplan, 1998; Gunasekaran and Ngai, 2004). Even fewer have developed solutions for transparent product customisation, delivery or the networks involved in maintenance and repair.

An example in the food industry may illustrate the problem area. Initially, a tracking and tracing system is used to track pallets through the supply chain, from distribution centres to outlets. Each pallet is identified, and is by means of scanning linked to a purchase order, a picking event, a loading event and a receiving event. Supply chain partners upload the scan data to a (centralised or distributed) database that is accessible to all of them. A few years later, the temperature of the pallets is to be controlled by the same tracking and tracing system. The data to be processed after each event is extended with the temperature at the time of scanning. Yet later, the system is to track

the products that are stacked on the pallets, their source and their best before date. So an event is added: the stack event. Then at the time of receiving in the outlets, the outlet inventory system is to be updated after scanning the pallet. Again an extension of the data to be processed, both by uploading and by querying systems, is needed. Note that the roll-out of the extra functions may be stretched over a lengthy period, one outlet at the time. During roll-out, systems may need to support multiple versions.

Most present tracking and tracing (T&T) systems are closed. Their use is limited to the supply chain partners of one product brand or function (e.g., transport). Companies that serve multiple brands need to install multiple systems. Systems, dedicated for some function (e.g., transport, anti-theft or product quality) are seldom interconnected.

EPC Global (2014) is a relative open system. Every company may join if they adhere to the conditions and pay a fee. The types of events that may be recorded in the system and the types of data that is stored are extensible. However, extensions should be approved by the EPC Global standardisation committees. Private extensions are allowed, but no mechanism exists to inform supply chain partners of such extensions. In any case, implementation of extensions requires reprogramming of all systems in the affected supply chain.

Note that not only products need to be tracked, but also the equipment that is used to produce and transport the products and the people that are responsible for that (Ilie-Zudor et al., 2011). Events may cause very complex transactions in T&T systems.

As supply chains are interwoven, solutions that are tailored for a specific product or brand are not viable. The same type of product may be sold to factories as components for other products, to wholesalers and directly to ultimate consumers via a web shop. Transport companies may carry goods of various industry sectors.

Trading relationships are not cast in concrete, they are volatile. Smaller companies, such as retailers, may not be expected to modify their IT system to accommodate the tracking and tracing solution of each new supplier.

The only feasible system that may support the above mentioned challenges is an open tracking and tracing system. In the next section requirements of such a system are listed. In the remainder of this chapter, the main requirement: the ability for the system to extend the information model of product types with new attributes and associations is elaborated.

2. REQUIREMENTS FOR OPEN T&T

From the observations in section 1 we can formulate the following requirements for an open Tracking & Tracing system:

1. **Any party must be able to use it: An** Open T&T system should be open. The system components and the services that maintain them should allow interconnection with components of any other user. Of course security should be guaranteed.
2. **It must be possible to track any product type:** It cannot be foreseen what T&T requirements will develop in the future and how supply chains will interconnect. So any product type or better, any object type should be traceable with the system.
3. **The types of information, stored for a product type must be extensible:** As it cannot be foreseen what products will be tracked, it certainly cannot be foreseen what information of the products or objects should be traced. So the object information model must be extensible 'on the fly', while the system is being used.
4. **Owners must be able to disclose information to selected receivers:** Supply chain information may be sensitive and is sometimes even strategic for companies. They must be able to shield this information from, e.g., competitors.
5. **Scalability: the system must be distributed:** The value of an open T&T system increases with its size and scope. It may need to track billions of objects. On that scale it is not feasible to organise it around a central component. So the system should be truly distributed.

3. OPEN T&T ARCHITECTURE

An open T&T system consists of the following components:

*   Objects that carry a unique identification number
*   Reading devices that can read Object Identifications
*   Upload Clients that allow users to register Object related observations with or without reading devices
*   Servers that store Object related observations
*   Query Clients that may query or subscribe to Object related information

Objects may be tangible (a box) or intangible (a purchase order). Objects are of a certain type. Objects have properties. The Object type prescribes the kind of properties (Property Types) an object may have. Properties are directed, tagged associations with other objects or with data types. For example Objects that are of Object Type "Box" may have dimensions and weight as attributes and may have a "stacked on" association with an object that is of Object Type "Pallet".

Objects have a world-wide unique identification number as a special property. The identification of an Item consists of a URI and a number, unique within the scope of that URI (Främling, 2002). Identifications may be affixed to the object in the form of a machine readable label: a bar code, an RFID tag or otherwise. For many (most) objects however, the ID-URI combination is virtual. It only exists in information systems. Only the objects that have to be tracked have an automatic readable tag or label. Objects, such as locations, companies, persons, production equipment and orders, that need to be associated with the objects-to-be-tracked are known to the information system that uploads tracking information to the open T&T system.

The function of the URI is twofold. Through the Internet Domain Name Service it guarantees uniqueness of the identification number, provided that the owner of the URI does not assign duplicate numbers. It also defines the Internet address where information on the Object can be obtained and where information may be uploaded.

Note that many existing T&T systems do not provide a URI as part of the Object identification. These systems (e.g., GS1 EPC Global, 2014) use other methods to guarantee uniqueness of the identification numbers. Such systems still can be part of an open T&T system if they provide the Internet addresses where information may be uploaded and obtained in some other way. The URI is then implicitly known, if the Object identification can be identified as being part of the specific existing system.

In open T&T systems, all objects carry an ID (and a URI), also locations, companies and production lines that are needed as part of the tracking information on products. The owner of the information on these non-product objects may be different from the product owner. The information may be retrievable from different URI's than the URI that is part of the product identification.

For the open T&T system to function, the (explicit or implicit) URI must be resolvable and must support defined protocols to store and retrieve Object information. Specification of these technical (Web Service) protocols is beyond the scope of this chapter. Here we focus on the content of the messages to be exchanged between nodes and servers (Figure 2).

Reading devices read the identification of labels or tags of Items. They may also read or add other information and transmit that to the Client that is to upload the recorded information as an observation. For instance, the RFID chip that is affixed to the object may in addition to the ID and URI contain temperature information. The reading device or the upload client may add a timestamp and location information, plus the information that the object was unpacked from a box (with another ID and URI). The observation that is recorded and will be uploaded to the Server node then contains {ID, URI, temperature, timestamp, location, {unpacked from: ID, URI}}.

The upload client agrees with the server node which information to upload for an object type. The upload client needs to know of which type an object is. The upload client therefore first queries the server client. If it is the first time the upload client handles an object of this type, it then queries the server node what information the server node expects for the specific event. The upload client then uploads the information by means of an observation message (see Figure 3).

The server node then stores the uploaded information. That information may be retrieved by Query clients, or it may actively be distributed to Clients that have subscribed to the information. Events may affect other Items as well. Based on rules to be stored on the Server, events may be created and uploaded to the applicable servers. In the above example, for instance, the observation may be forwarded to the server node that services information on the pallet ("pallet.com").

Query Clients may retrieve Item related information from Servers by querying them or by subscribing on periodic or event triggered reports. Server nodes should always provide information that has an ID@URI as key to query clients that are entitled to receive the information. Free queries and selection of items by other properties can optionally be serviced.

4. META-DATA ALIGNMENT

In requirement 3 in section 2 is stated that the object information model must be extensible 'on the fly', while the system is being used. This is not the case in present T&T systems. In the EPC Global (2014) system, for example, data sets to be processed are extensible, but when they are extended, message schemas and application interfaces change. So systems must be reprogrammed or at least reconfigured. This is undesirable in many situations. E.g., in the example in section 1, some outlets may be less advanced than other outlets. An update of the T&T system should not force outlets to change simultaneously.

In open T&T systems, extensions should not be managed centrally (and certainly not by standardisation committees), but bilaterally, peer to peer.

For extension and alignment of meta-data in an open T&T system, we therefore use the method, described in Blommestein (2014). The method is based on ontology engineering (Sowa, 2000). In ontology engineering, both individual objects (instances) and types or classes are treated in a similar way and may be mixed in reasoning. They are both organised in triples: Object (type) - Property (type) - Object (type). This way of organising knowledge is derived from the structure of natural languages, in which a subject and an object (both objects or object types) are glued together by a verb and possible adverbs (together constituting the property or property type).

The meta-data in the open T&T system consists of:

- Data types of object properties
- Object property types
- Object types
- Event types

Both query and upload clients may interrogate server nodes which property-, object- and event types the server node supports. If some type is not supported, but required, the server node may be requested to add the type to its meta data scheme.

As meta-data is to be manipulated, it is stored as normal data. E.g. names of object and event types are ordinary properties (see Figure 1).

Open T&T clients and server nodes may, apart from observations, queries and responses, exchange the following messages to align meta data:

- *Definitions* of new object types and of new data types. Definition of new object types is elaborated in section 5, definition of new data types is described in section 6.
- *Extensions* of object types with new properties (attributes and associations). Extensions are described in section 6.
- *Observation types*, the structure of the information to be uploaded, depending on object type and event type. Definition of new observation types is described in section 7.

5. DEFINITION OF NEW OBJECT TYPES

New object types may be defined by genus and difference. An object type inherits its definition from a more general object type (the genus) and adds a set of constraints to the properties of the general object type to differentiate itself from other specializations or subtypes of the more general object type. Objects that are instances of the newly defined object type are also instances of the more general object type. The 'differences' are defined by constraining the properties. Properties can only be constrained if they have been defined. In order to define a specialisation therefore the properties that are to be constrained must have been defined on the level of the more general object type.

New object types are defined based on existing object types, so the basic semantics of object types and properties are already known. Those semantics are refined by further constraining the

Figure 1. Data model

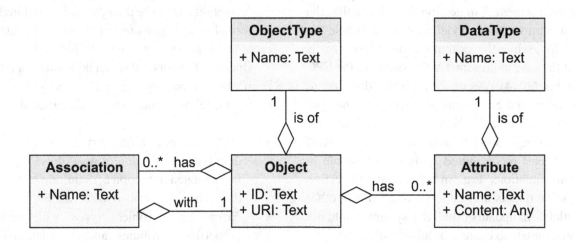

Figure 2. Open T&T configuration

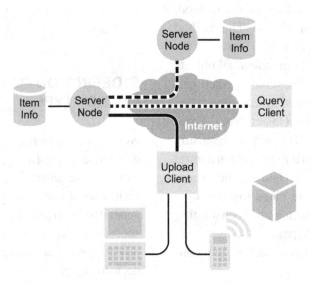

properties of the object type members, in other words, the 'membership' criteria are made stricter (Figure 4).

As an illustration, we take the example of a pallet. A pallet is defined as "Transport Equipment, consisting of a portable platform on which goods can be moved, stacked, and stored, with the aid of a forklift". Inspection of this definition reveals that the genus of a pallet is "Transport Equipment". The difference consists of three elements:

- Shape (a portable platform)
- Function (on which goods can be moved, stacked, and stored)
- Usage (with the aid of a forklift).

Figure 3. Conversation between upload clients and server nodes

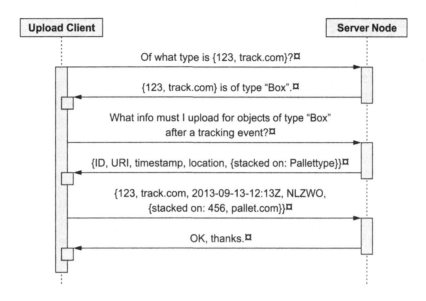

Figure 4. Object type

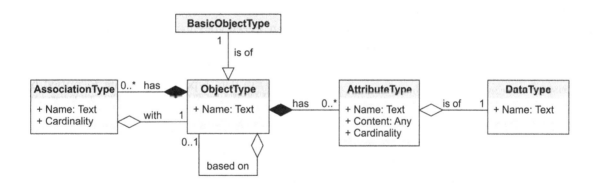

This means that generic Transport Equipment must also have a shape, function and usage. The elements are narrowed to define a pallet as transport equipment. E.g., where generic transport equipment may also be shaped as a box (e.g. a container), a pallet is shaped as a platform.

The Definition pattern is illustrated by means of the XML snippet in Box 1.

The definition by means of genus and difference, structured in properties, is not strictly needed for Server nodes to be able to store the observations uploaded by client nodes. The data model in figure 1 allows storing observations on objects of

Box 1.

```
<Definition>
<ObjectType Name="Pallet">
<BasedOnObjectType Name="Transport Equipment"/>
<Attribute Name="Shape" Datatype="ShapeCode" Value="Platform"/>
<Association Name="Move" ObjectType="Goods"/>
<Association Name="Stack" ObjectType="Goods"/>
<Association Name="Store" ObjectType="Goods"/>
<Association Name="Use" ObjectType="Forklift">
</ObjectType>
</Definition>
```

arbitrary object types and with arbitrary properties. The information is however ultimately to be used by business information systems, such as ERP systems. Such systems usually are less tolerant with regard to the data model. The definition of object types as specialisation of existing object types allows such a system to store the information on a pallet as information on transport equipment.

The definition does not specify all properties, only the properties that are needed to recognise a pallet among all transport equipment. The additional properties that may be used in observations are specified by means of Extensions. The XML snippet in Box 2 illustrates an Extension:

Definitions and extensions, accepted or amended by a server node need to be propagated to other server nodes, to prevent differently defined object types with the same name.

The properties, defined in Definitions and Extensions are available for Observations that are uploaded by Upload clients.

6. DEFINITION OF ATTRIBUTES

An object type can be referred to by a name and is represented by a set of properties. Properties are directed, tagged associations with other objects or with data types. Objects are identified by a

Box 2.

```
<Extension>
<ObjectType Name="Pallet">
<BasedOnObjectType Name="Transport Equipment"/>
<Attribute Name="Length" DataType="LengthMeasure"/>
<Attribute Name="Width" DataType="LengthMeasure"/>
<Attribute Name="MaxLoad" DataType="WeightMeasure"/>
<Attribute Name="Location" DataType="UNLoCode"/>
<Association name="Load" ObjectType="Vehicle"/>
<Association name="Unload" ObjectType="Vehicle"/>
<Association name="Place" ObjectType="Warehouse_Location"/>
</ObjectType>
</Extension>
```

unique identifier. Data type instances, however, are identified by their values.

For example, a numeric data type has a number as the value of an instance. A number represents a point on the mathematical numeric scale. A textual data type has as instance values strings of characters of some alphabet. Usually such text has some meaning in a natural language.

In this section the structure and representation of data types and data type values are inspected.

The scales on which data type values are projected may be abstract mathematical scales (such as the numeric scale) but may also be physical scales, such as the scale of geographical locations or the time scale. Data type scales need not to be one-dimensional and the different dimensions of a scale may have very different semantics. For example a 'measurement' may consist of a (one-dimensional) value and a measure unit that is defined on the 'measure unit scale' (e.g. the SI system).

It is possible to define subsets on scales. This is done by means of 'facets'. Facets may limit the length of the scale, the precision or may define specific value patterns.

Data typing includes the mapping of semantic units or ontological constructs to sign systems. To enable the processing of signs by computers, signs and sign constructs are encoded in binary systems. In fact binary systems are a special kind of sign systems, using bits as signs. Other sign systems include printed text, icons, sounds, etc.

Names and values might be directly represented in bit patterns. However, different computer languages, operating systems and storage technologies use different bit representations for the same functional content. In order to be technology-independent and to be able to specify T&T communication between computers that use different languages and operating systems, the data type system to use for T&T should be layered. In the higher layers of the stack, semantic structures can be specified, while in the lower layers, mappings can be realized to character and bit representation. For open T&T we propose to use the XML language for this representation.

Figure 5. Encoding of information

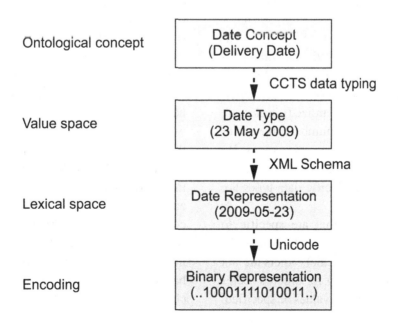

The Core Component Technical Specification (CCTS) (UN/ECE, 2003) offers a language to describe data models and messages in a technology- and syntax-neutral way. CCTS 3.0 makes a distinction between Core Data Types (CDTs) and Business Data Types (BDTs). BDTs specialise CDTs: the domain value of a CDT is restricted for a BDT. CDTs (and therefore also BDTs) have a not-too-complex internal structure, but they are not scalars. In the sequel of this section the CCTS data type system is taken as the basis for open T&T communication (Figure 5).

A more generic data type system is described in the XML Schema specification (W3C, 2004). The XML schema specification makes a distinction between the value space of a data type and the lexical space of a data type. The value space denotes the semantic scale of the represented information, such as Date Time, Numeric, or Text. The lexical space defines the way in which values in that dimension are represented in Unicode (for XML messaging).

CCTS data types are not one-dimensional scalars. CCTS defines data types consisting of a Content Components and one or more Supplementary Components that further specify the semantics of the content. E.g. an Amount has a number as content and a currency code as Supplementary Component to specify the currency. This mechanism resembles closely the "Semantic Values" as proposed by Sciore (1994) and Lee (2000).

Data types are defined bottom-up. At the bottom a number of (pre-standardized) scales are defined, such as the set of numbers, the set of texts and the set of date-time combinations. By constraining these scales by means of facets and by combining them, the specific data types are being defined.

Facets are constraints that are specific to the scale. Some scales are ordered (such as the numeric and the date-time scale); others are not (such as the text scale). Only for ordered scales can minimum and maximum values be specified.

Precision may be specified for numerics in a straightforward way, for dates and times precision is fairly complex (Figure 6).

The basic scales that are needed for the CCTS v.2.01 data types are the textual scale, numeric scale and the date-time scale. These scales map (not coincidental) neatly to the data type system of XML Schema. From this system, only date-Time, string and decimal are used for open T&T systems (Figure 7).

The basic scales are called "Primitive types" in CCTS (Table 1).

Based on the three Primitive Types ten Core Data Types are defined in CCTS (Table 2).

In fact many more scales (Core Data Types or even Primitive Data Types) could be defined, such as a colour scale, a location scale, a taste scale, etc. For e.g. locations, many different representations exist (postal, geographical, official, etc.). Each of them has a different structure (number-pairs, codes, text blocks). It seems therefore more feasible for an open T&T system to build forward on the three mentioned Primitive Types, by defining Core Data Types and specialise those in Business Data Types.

Transmitting XML data between nodes poses an important challenge. Similarly typed message-parts might not represent the same data on both sides of an XML exchange. If XML is chosen as a basis for a type system with subtyping, methods are required that can tell the relation between two schemas. To match XML-parts, similarity measures have been proposed, such as Jeong et al. (2008) which use supervised learning. Another example is the Cupid generic schema matching tool (Madhavan et al., 2001), which employs linguistics-based matching, element- and structure-based matching and key and reference constraints. Unfortunately, common tools and methods such as Cupid or the XML reduction algorithm mentioned above do not provide the required information. By always basing new types on previously agreed types, the challenge is avoided.

Figure 6. Data-type meta-model

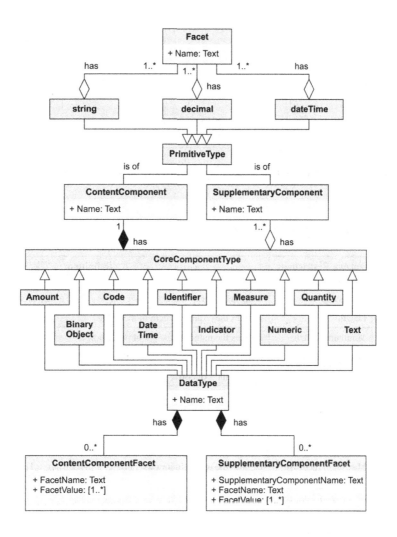

The "Based On" relationship is grounded in type theory, as elaborated in Milner (1978). The challenge is to construct a type system, for information systems to be tolerant with regard to new types, for instance when information flows are extended with new event types or specialised attributes.

How to process specialised or generalised types is defined by a (meta)property named "Variance". In modern type theory; the following three variance types are defined (Karnok and Kemény, 2012)

- **Covariance:** Where you expect a type T, you may pass in a U, where U extends T
  - **Example:** You want to print a comma separated list of objects, you can pass in a list of strings safely, because strings extend object and are allowed to be treated as simple objects ('String' is based on 'Object').
  - Function input types are considered covariant

Figure 7. XML data type system

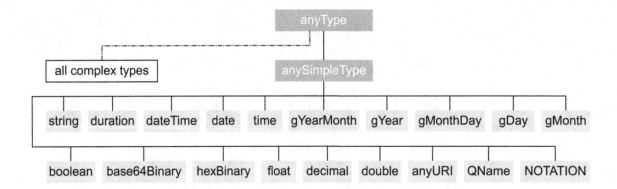

Table 1. Primitive types (from UN/ECE, 2003)

Primitive Type	Format Restrictions or Facets	Definition
String	Expression	Defines the set of characters that can be used at a particular position in a string.
	Length	Defines the required length of the string.
	Minimum Length	Defines the minimum length of the string.
	Maximum Length	Defines the maximum length of the string.
	Enumeration	Defines the exhaustive list of allowed values.
Decimal	Total Digits	Defines the maximum number of digits to be used.
	Fractional Digits	Defines the maximum number of fractional digits to be used.
	Minimum Inclusive	Defines the lower limit of the range of allowed values. The lower limit is also an allowed value.
	Maximum Inclusive	Defines the upper limit of the range of allowed values. The upper limit is also an allowed value.
	Minimum Exclusive	Defines the lower limit of the range of allowed values. The lower limit is no allowed value.
	Maximum Exclusive	Defines the upper limit of the range of allowed values. The upper limit is no allowed value.
Date-Time	Minimum Inclusive	Defines the lower limit of the range of allowed dates. The lower limit is also an allowed date.
	Maximum Inclusive	Defines the upper limit of the range of allowed dates. The upper limit is also an allowed date.
	Minimum Exclusive	Defines the lower limit of the range of allowed dates. The lower limit is no allowed date.
	Maximum Exclusive	Defines the upper limit of the range of allowed dates. The upper limit is no allowed date.

- **Contra Variance:** Where you expect a type T, you may pass in an U where T extends U
  - **Example:** I return an apple to my client but he treats it only as fruit ('Apple is based on 'Fruit').

Table 2. Core data types (from UN/ECE, 2003)

CCT Dictionary Entry Name	Definition	Content and Supplementary Components
Amount. Type	A number of monetary units specified in a currency where the unit of currency is explicit or implied.	Amount. Content (Decimal) Amount Currency. Identifier (String) Amount Currency. Code List Version. Identifier (String)
Binary Object. Type	A set of finite-length sequences of binary octets.	Binary Object. Content (String) Binary Object. Format. Text (String) Binary Object. Mime. Code (String) Binary Object. Encoding. Code (String) Binary Object. Character Set. Code (String) Binary Object. Uniform Resource. Identifier (String) Binary Object. Filename. Text (String)
Code. Type	A character string (letters, figures or symbols) that for brevity and/or language independence may be used to represent or replace a definitive value or text of an *Attribute* together with relevant supplementary information.	Code. Content (String) Code List. Identifier (String) Code List. Agency. Identifier (String) Code List. Agency Name. Text (String) Code List. Name. Text (String) Code List. Version. Identifier (String) Code. Name. Text (String) Language. Identifier (String) Code List. Uniform Resource. Identifier (String) Code List Scheme. Uniform Resource. Identifier (String)
Date Time. Type	A particular point in the progression of time together with relevant supplementary information.	Date Time. Content (Date-Time) Date Time. Format. Text (String)
Identifier. Type	A character string to identify and distinguish uniquely, one instance of an object in an identification scheme from all other objects in the same scheme together with relevant supplementary information.	Identifier. Content (String) Identification Scheme. Identifier (String) Identification Scheme. Name. Text (String) Identification Scheme Agency. Identifier (String) Identification Scheme. Agency Name. Text (String) Identification Scheme. Version. Identifier (String) Identification Scheme Data. Uniform Resource. Identifier (String) Identification Scheme. Uniform Resource. Identifier (String)
Indicator. Type	A list of two mutually exclusive Boolean values that express the only possible states of a *Property*.	Indicator. Content (String) Indicator. Format. Text (String)
Measure. Type	A numeric value determined by measuring an object along with the specified unit of measure.	Measure. Content (Decimal) Measure Unit. Code (String) Measure Unit. Code List Version. Identifier (String)
Numeric. Type	Numeric information that is assigned or is determined by calculation, counting, or sequencing. It does not require a unit of quantity or unit of measure.	Numeric. Content (Decimal) Numeric. Format. Text (String)
Quantity. Type	A counted number of non-monetary units possibly including fractions.	Quantity. Content (Decimal) Quantity. Unit. Code (String) Quantity Unit. Code List. Identifier (String) Quantity Unit. Code List Agency. Identifier (String) Quantity Unit. Code List Agency Name. Text (String)
Text. Type	A character string (i.e. a finite set of characters) generally in the form of words of a language.	Text. Content (String) Language. Identifier (String) Language. Locale. Identifier (String)

- ○ Function return types are considered contra variant
- **No Variance:** You expect a T and you get a T, not any subtype or super type
  - ○ **Example:** I give you an apple, you take a bite and give it back to me as Apple
  - ○ Functions doing side-effects on its parameter (modifies it in place)

In terms of an open T&T type system the variance cases can be described via the "Based On" or "Specialise" operator. The operator is not XML specific; it is independent from syntactical representation of the types. As newly defined associations, attributes and data types are always "Based on" existing types, they are covariant to the existing types. This means that a system that supports the existing type also will support the new type.

The covariancy is defined on the lexical representation of data types, not on the semantics. Semantically information may be lost. If one receives the height of a pallet load, but stores it as a Pallet Measurement, syntactically this information will fit. Semantically, though, we are not sure any more which pallet measurement has been stored: it could be the pallet length or width instead of the height. In these cases a type code or qualifier is needed to retain the semantics.

A definition of a new data type is illustrated by the XML snippet in Box 3.

7. DEFINITION OF NEW MESSAGES

The information that is uploaded by Upload clients to Server Nodes is assembled in observation messages (Figure 8).

The combination of an Event Type and an Object Type determines the Observation Type. The structure of an Observation Type is communicated by the Server Node to the Upload Client. That structure follows the data model of Figure 1.

In fact the information to be uploaded is a sub set of the information model of the Object Type. Not all Attributes and Associations in the information model need to be present in the Observation Type, but all Attributes and Associations in the Observation Type must exist in the information model.

An Observation Type definition is illustrated by the XML snippet in Box 4.

Definitions of Observation Types are propagated by Server Nodes to the other Server Nodes.

An actual Observation as an instance of this Observation Type may look as it does in Box 5.

8. IMPLEMENTATION CONSIDERATIONS

As stated previously, the technical protocols to be used for uploading and querying in an open T&T system are outside the scope of this chapter. A simple web service protocol, as specified in WS-i (2006) suffices. The XML messages to be used have a very simple structure, as was illustrated in the various XML snippets. A few

Box 3.

```
<Definition>
<DataType="LengthMeasure">
<BasedOn DataType="Measure">
<SupplementaryComponentFacet>
<MeasureUnit>MTR</MeasureUnit>
</SupplementaryComponentFacet>
</DataType>
<DataType="ShapeCode">
<BasedOn type="Code">
<ContentComponentFacet>
<Enumeration>Box</Enumeration>
<Enumeration>Platform</Enumeration>
<Enumeration>Pipe</Enumeration>
</ContentComponentFacet>
</DataType>
</Definition>
```

Figure 8. Observation type

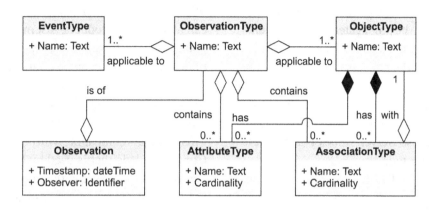

Box 4.

```
<Definition>
<ObservationType Name="UnloadPallet">
<Object ObjectType="Pallet"/>
<Event EventType="Unload"/>
<Attribute Name="Location"
Datatype="UNLoCode"/>
<Association Name="Use"
ObjectType="Forklift">
</ObservationType>
</Definition>
```

XML schemas may be defined and referenced to in WSDL files that support dialogues such as illustrated in Figure 3.

The ID-URI combination offers a simple but powerful mechanism for identification. It can be integrated in transport labels, such as described by ISO 15394 (ISO, 2009) and ISO 22742 (ISO, 2010). The identification may also be programmed into RFID transponders or be printed as part of consumer labels with product information, optionally together with usage instructions and freshness information (Kemény.et al., 2011b). For consumers, applications (or 'apps') may be developed, that immediately present relevant information upon scanning the identification with a mobile phone or tablet.

As the information upload protocol is not very complex, the upload function may be performed by an 'app' in a mobile phone as well. That would allow any party in a supply chain to scan product

Box 5.

```
<Observation Timestamp="2013-09-14-15:38:00Z" Observer="8734567">
<ObservationType Name="UnloadPallet"/>
<Event EventType="Unload"/>
<Object ObjectType="Pallet" ID="123" URI="pallet.com">
<Attribute Name="Location" Value="NLZWO"/>
<Association Name="Use" ObjectType="Forklift" ID="567" URI="truck.com"/>
</Object>
</Observation>
```

identifications and upload information, without previous agreements or arrangements.

Prerequisite for an open T&T system is that the Server Nodes are interconnected, as (at least) definitions need to be propagated. Upload Clients need to connect to the Server Nodes that administer the URI's of the Objects the Upload Client handles. Query clients in fact need to connect to only one Server Node. As Server Nodes are interconnected, Queries and Query-parts may be propagated to those Server Nodes that hold the information requested.

Although the T&T system is open, it does not mean that all data contained in the system is available to everyone. Tracking and Tracing information is often sensitive. Information owners need to control who is entitled to which information. Server Nodes are under the control of the Object information owner (the one that assigned the URI to the Object). Therefore the information owner can control who has access to the information (what queries will be responded to). The authentication mechanism and the authorisation scheme to use is outside the scope of this chapter.

When the ownership of an Object is transferred, the new owner should take over the ability to control information access. As the URI may be affixed to the Object in an unalterable way (programmed in an RFID chip, printed as a barcode or otherwise), this poses a challenge. One of the solutions is to use Server Node services that are trusted by all participants in the supply chain. Another solution may be some technical redirect mechanism. To specify such mechanism also is outside the scope of this chapter.

9. DISCUSSION AND FUTURE WORK

In this chapter an open Tracking and Tracing system is described that allows to track and trace any object through any supply chain. Because the data model of the objects is extensible the system is truly ubiquitous. It can be used for tracking logistical units through a transport chain, for determining the source of products and ingredients, for controlling maintenance and reverse logistics etc. The system can handle food products, fast moving consumer goods, high tech equipment, apparel, in fact any type of objects that can be identified.

The open T&T system can work with any identification scheme, for instance the "License plate" scheme that is standardized by ISO (ISO, 2006). This scheme is compatible with the Serial Shipping Container Code that is used by the Fast Moving Consumer Goods sector, the Logistics sector and the Automotive sector. It is also compatible with the EPC Global system. The only extra element is the inclusion of a URI where messages can be sent to and where information on the objects can be retrieved.

The description in this chapter is not complete. The architecture and protocols are only sketched. Data structures and message structures are only illustrated, not exactly specified. In implementation projects the details must be elaborated. That may (and should) lead to standardisation of the protocols.

REFERENCES

ADVANCE Project Consortium. (2010). *ADVANCE official project website*. Retrieved from http://advance-logistics.eu/

Ala-Risku, T., & Kärkkäinen, M. (2004). *A Solution for the Material Delivery Problems in Construction Projects*. Paper presented at the Thirteenth International Working Seminar on Production Economics. Innsbruck, Austria.

Ballard, R. (1996). Methods of inventory monitoring and measurement. *Logistics Information Management*, 9(3), 11–28. doi:10.1108/09576059610116653

Clarke, M. (1998). Virtual logistics. *International Journal of Physical Distribution & Logistics Management, 28*(7), 486–507. doi:10.1108/09600039810247461

Främling, K. (2002). *Tracking of material flow by an Internet-based product data management system. Tieke EDISTY Magazine, 1.*

Främling, K., Kärkkäinen, M., Ala-Risku, T., & Holmström, J. (2004). *Managing Product Information in Supplier Networks by Object-oriented Programming Concepts.* Paper presented at the International IMS Forum. Lake Como, Italy.

EPC Global. (2014). Retrieved from http://www.epcglobalinc.org/index.html

Gunasekaran, A., & Ngai, E. W. T. (2004). Information systems in supply-chain integration and management. *European Journal of Operational Research, 159*(2), 269–295. doi:10.1016/j.ejor.2003.08.016

Hiscox, M.J., & Smyth, N.F.B. (2011, April). *Is There Consumer Demand for Improved Labor Standards? Evidence from Field Experiments in Social Product Labeling.* Social Science Research Network.

Ilie-Zudor, E., Kemény, Z., van Blommestein, F., Monostori, L., & van der Meulen, A. (2011, January). A survey of applications and requirements of unique identification systems and RFID techniques. *Computers in Industry.*

International Organization for Standardization (ISO). (2006). *ISO/IEC 15459-1:2006 Information technology -- Unique identifiers -- Part 1: Unique identifiers for transport units.* Author.

International Organization for Standardization (ISO). (2009). Packaging -- Bar code and two-dimensional symbols for shipping, transport and receiving labels. *ISO, 15394,* 2009.

International Organization for Standardization (ISO). (2010). Packaging -- Linear bar code and two-dimensional symbols for product packaging. *ISO, 22742,* 2010.

Jeong, B., Lee, D., Cho, H., & Lee, J. (2008). A novel method for measuring semantic similarity for XML schema matching. *Expert Syst. Appl., 34*(3), 1651–1658. DOI: 10.1016/j.eswa.2007.01.025

Kaplan, R. S. (1998). Innovation Action research: Creating New Management Theory and Practice. *Journal of Management Accounting Research, 10,* 89–118.

Kärkkäinen, M., Ala-Risku, T., & Främling, K. (2004). Efficient tracking in short-term multi-company networks. *International Journal of Physical Distribution & Logistics Management, 34*(7), 545–564. doi:10.1108/09600030410552249

Karnok, D, & Kemény, Z. (2012). Definition and handling of data types in a dataflow-oriented modelling and processing environment. In *Proceedings of MITIP 2012.* MITIP.

Kemény, Z., Ilie-Zudor, E., Fülöp, J., Ekárt, A., Buckingham, C., & Welch, P. G. (2011a). Multiple-participant hub-and-spoke logistics networks: challenges, solutions and limits. In *Proc. of the 13th International Conference on Modern Information Technology in the Innovation Processes of Industrial Enterprises* (MITIP 2011) (pp. 20-29). Trondheim, Norway: MITIP.

Kemény, Z., Szathmári, M., Kemény, L., Bozóki, S., & Ilie-Zudor, E. (2011b). Quality indication and supply management of perishable products with optical labels for low-end demands. In *Proc. of the 13th Int. Conf. on Modern Information Technology in the Innovation Processes of Industrial Enterprises* (MITIP 2011) (pp. 202-211). Trondheim, Norway: MITIP.

Kosk, N. (2014). *The Reverse Logistics Cycle, Supply & Demand-Chain Executive*. Retrieved from http://www.sdcexec.com/

Lee. (2000). Context-dependent Semantic Values for E-negotiation. In *Proceedings of WECWIS*. WECWIS.

Madhavan, J., Bernstein, P. A., & Rahm, E. (2001). Generic Schema Matching with Cupid. In *Proceedings of the 27th International Conference on Very Large Data Bases* (VLDB '01) (pp. 49–58). Morgan Kaufmann Publishers Inc. Retrieved from http://dl.acm.org/citation.cfm?id=645927.672191

Milner, R. (1978). A theory of type polymorphism in programming. *Journal of Computer and System Sciences*, *17*(3), 348–375. doi:10.1016/0022-0000(78)90014-4

Monostori, L., Kemény, Z., Ilie-Zudor, E., Szathmári, M., & Karnok, D. (2009). Increased transparency within and beyond organizational borders by novel identifier-based services for enterprises of different size. *CIRP Annals – Manufacturing Technology*, *58*(1), 417–420. DOI: 10.1016/j.cirp.2009.03.086

Sciore. (1994). Using Semantic Values to Facilitate Interoperability Among Heterogeneous Information Systems. *ACM Transactions on Database Systems*, *19*(2).

Sowa, J. (2000). *Knowledge representation*. Pacific Grove, CA: Brooks Cole Publishing Co.

TraSer Project Consortium. (2006). *TraSer official project website*. Retrieved from http://www.traser-project.eu/

UN/ECE. (2003). *Core Component Technical Specification*. Retrieved from http://www.unece.org/fileadmin/DAM/cefact/codesfortrade/CCTS/CCTS_V2-01_Final.pdf, retrieved 2013-09-14

van Blommestein, F. B. E. (2014). *Structured Communication for Dynamic Business*. (PhD thesis). University of Groningen. Retrieved from http://www.flowcanto.com/thesis.pdf

W3C. (2004). *XML Schema Part 2: Datatypes Second Edition, 2004*. Retrieved from http://www.w3.org/TR/xmlschema-2/

WS-i. (2006). *Webservice Interoperability Organisation Basic Profile Version 1.1 Final Material 2006-04-10*. Retrieved from http://www.ws-i.org/profiles/basicprofile-1.1.html

KEY TERMS AND DEFINITIONS

Client: Computer program or device that uses services, offered by a Server.

Data Type: A classification identifying the set of possible values for a data element, the operations that can be done on values of that type, the meaning of the data and the way values of that type can be stored.

Identification Tag: Label or device, affixed to a physical object, with an automatic readable identification number of that object (and possible additional information).

Meta-Data: Data about data, such as the name, the definition and the data type of a data element.

RFID: Radio Frequency IDentification, technology to read identification numbers from a distance, using electromagnetic frequencies in the radio spectrum.

Server: Computer program or device that offers services over a network connection to one or more Clients.

Supply Chain: A system of organizations, people, activities, information, and resources involved in moving products or services from (original) suppliers to (ultimate) customers.

Tracking and Tracing System: An information system that allows to determine the current and past locations and other information of unique physical objects during their lifecycle.

URI: Universal Resource Identifier: A string of characters used to uniquely identify a web resource.

WSDL: Web Service Description Language is a W3C recommendation. It specifies an XML-based interface description language that is used for describing the functionality offered by a web service.

Chapter 7
RFID Technology and Privacy

Edward T. Chen
University of Massachusetts – Lowell, USA

ABSTRACT

RFID plays a critical role in the improvement of supply chain management and consumer applications. This chapter introduces a brief history of RFID and how it works. The recent shift of incorporating RFID into consumer-oriented products has raised serious concerns of customer privacy and security. These concerns are rooted in the fact that consumers are typically unaware that their purchases are being tracked and monitored, as well as the fear of private information being hacked or stolen via insecure RFID systems. This chapter provides a theoretical debate over the privacy rights and addresses the consumer role in the RFID technology. This chapter concludes that the government must ensure legislation to maintain protections on the individual's security and privacy in the society.

INTRODUCTION

Radio Frequency Identification is a form of technology that tracks objects via radio wave transmission. While the technology itself is not groundbreaking, the RFID market has recently experienced significant innovation and growth. The technology is increasingly used for a multitude of purposes, across a wide range of industries. This increased usage signifies that companies find strong value in RFID technology (Heim, Wentworth, & Peng, 2009; May, 2007; Thiesse, Al-kassab, & Fleisch, 2009). Businesses are attracted to RFID technology because it enables them to create a more efficient supply chain, effectively track and manage inventory levels, monitor consumer behavior and demand, and bet-

ter forecast future sales (Beitelspacher, Hansen, Johnston & Dietz, 2012).

Many large retailers, such as Wal-Mart and Target, as well as the Department of Defense, now require the use of RFID within all aspects of their supply chain because of the cost-savings associated with the technology, mainly in reduced labor costs (Asif & Mandviwalla, 2005; Roberti, 2010; Smart, Bunduchi, & Gerst, 2010). This mandate caused the economy of scale for RFIDs to decrease prices, and also led to an industry technology standard to use EPCglobal's Electronic Product Code standard (EPCglobal Inc., 2005). Previously, the technology was stifled by a lack of uniformity between different RFID manufacturers' software platform causing customers to need different receivers to detect and use different RFIDs. These advances are expected to continue the growth of the use of

DOI: 10.4018/978-1-4666-6308-4.ch007

RFIDs across industries. Businesses are demanding that their suppliers use RFIDs to track incoming shipments as it allows the organizations to make real time decisions for inventory management and control. When businesses can project the time their supplies will arrive, they can coordinate to make business decisions based on projected inventory. This practice helps things such as manufacturing scheduling, floor layouts, and even sales (May, 2007; Zhou & Piramuthu, 2013).

RFIDs are also commonly used in tracking individual objects that are high value enough to warrant the additional expense of a tag (Kapoor, Zhou, & Piramuthu, 2009). In the case of one Tennessee hospital, instead of relying on nurses to scan barcodes high value implantable surgical devices or catheter bags prior to using them in a patient, the use of RFIDs on the products has helped save over $500,000 annually in wasted items, preventing theft, and preventing incorrect billing due to incorrectly tracked items that patients did not receive (Swedberg, 2009). It is very common now that expensive, pilferage-able, or items with a high theft rate in a store such expensive liquors, condoms, pharmaceuticals, and jewelry have RFIDs included in the packaging to prevent theft and retain profits.

Instead of tracking shipments and products, another application of RFID is tracking animals. Cows are high value items to ranchers that are commonly stolen or escape when they are allowed to graze over large pasture land. In the US, Canada, and Australia, the beef industries are actively encouraging the use of RFID to track cows (Dobkin, 2013). This tracking allows for individual tracking of large herds of animals to be able to keep an accurate count of moving animals, their locations, and ages which allows farmers to identify specific cows at the optimum time for slaughter and ensure no loss of accountability. Additionally, researchers have been tagging various wild animals so that they can further their studies of things such as migration patterns, lifespan, and even establish protection zones for the animals or even people. In the case of whales, knowing their locations by RFID allows protection groups to set up boundaries so that ships do not get too close and harm the animals. In the case of sharks that have been tagged, RFIDs allow protection groups to keep out swimmers when they are in the area to protect humans (Wang & Loui, 2009).

RFIDs can even be used for tracking humans. They are commonly used in prisoner bracelets as a way of maintaining accountability of the prisoners. Even some resorts and theme parks sell RFID tracking brackets that can be worn by children so that their parents can always track their whereabouts (Dobkin, 2013). RFIDs are becoming commonplace for use to get quickly through toll booths to debit a user's account when they pass through a toll area. The US Government uses RFID chips in their passports so that Customs and Border Protection inspectors will be able to access photographs and other biographical information stored in secure government databases as the traveler approaches an inspection station. With RFIDs located in smart phones, it is also possible to track the location of almost any smart phone user (Martinez-Balleste, Perez-Martinez, & Solanas, 2013).

Understandably, with this advanced technology come concerns over the privacy and security of the information being transmitted (Good & Benaissa, 2013; Kamruzzaman, Azad, Karmakar, Karmakar, & Srinivasan, 2013; Li, Deng, & Bertino, 2013). This is particularly true for RFID technology that has become introduced to the public and consumer goods market (Dean, 2013; Golding & Tennant, 2010). For instance, a product that has an RFID tag can continue to be monitored once the product has been purchased. The technology that makes up an RFID tag or chip does not automatically shut down upon consumer purchase (Chen, Fung, Mohammed, Desai, & Wang, 2013; Grover & Berghel, 2011; Song, 2013).

Theoretically, there is concern that an individual can be tracked via an object or their clothing's RFID tag, raising concern of a "big brother" spyware situation (Albrecht & McIntyre, 2004). Studies show that consumers are uneasy not knowing when or if the tracking tag or chip officially stops working, particularly when the RFID in question is transmitting or tracking personal information. The consumer advocacy group Consumers Against Supermarket Privacy Invasion and Numbering (CASPIAN) has cited situations where RFID chips were secretly embedded in company customer loyalty cards to track purchasing behavior, without the consumer's knowledge (CASPIAN, 2003; Dean, 2013). RFID chips are sometimes even referred to as "spychips" because of this concern over privacy and the fact that they are virtually unnoticeable to consumers (Albrecht & McIntyre, 2005; Chen, et al., 2013). This issue of consumer privacy rights is one that has become heavily debated and highly controversial (Aggarwal, Ashish, & Sheth, 2013; Grover & Berghel, 2011; Song, 2013).

The chapter will highlight the various and wide-ranging uses of RFID technology. The benefits that RFID can provide to organizations include reduced labor costs as a result of remote inventory tracking. This chapter will also examine the mechanical application of RFID to understand how the technology works in order to best address the concerns raised over the privacy and security of information that is tracked via RFID. This chapter will then focus on the impact to the consumer, considering both benefits and risks of the technology. Additionally, this chapter will suggest courses of action for businesses to consider regarding the security and privacy of data transmitted via RFID technology.

HISTORY OF RFID

Interestingly, RFID technology has been in use for well over a decade. In its primitive form, it was first used to distinguish between ally and enemy aircraft during World War II (Slettemeås, 2009). However, it was Mario Cardullo's patented RFID design in 1969 that brought RFID technology closer to what we know today. His invention of a passive radio transponder with stored memory has become the central design component for tollbooth tracking devices such as the EZ-Pass system that are commonly used today (Cardullo, 2003; Good & Benaissa, 2013).

In the 1980's, RFID tags were introduced to the agricultural industry as a way to track and monitor livestock. Both agricultural and domestic animal tracking are currently a popular use for the technology. In 1984, the technology was first used in the automotive industry, as a method of inventory control for monitoring the pieces of equipment that were assembled on the frames (Atkinson, 2004; Zare Mehrjerdi, 2008; Slettemeås, 2009).

RFID technology became more widely used for back-end supply chain and distribution channel management purposes in the 1990's. In 2003, Wal-Mart and the U.S. Department of Defense highlighted the benefits of RFID use within supply chain management. They mandated that all suppliers working with them, respectively, would be required to implement RDIF technology into their products and shipments. This mandate set a huge precedent in the supply chain management world, as the scale of suppliers affected was rather large, due to the large sizes of both organizations. Within recent years, the technology spread into the retail and consumer goods market. Now, RFID can be found on virtually anything, from U.S. soldiers' boots in Afghanistan to racing bibs on athletes to even underwear (Grewal, Ailawadi, Gauri, Hall, & Kopalle, 2011; Kapoor, Zhou, & Piramuthu, 2009; Pramatari & Theotokis, 2009).

The technology can be used as a payment system, common forms being the EZ-Pass and other toll-tracking devices as well as Mobile's Speedpass payment system, where customers can purchase gas on their credit card by simply flashing their card to the gas pump. RFID has become a globally used technology that is gaining popularity across the world. For example, the RFID market in the Asia-Pacific region, considered one of the most rapidly growing RFID markets, has already exceeded $150 million, which is a 150% increase from 2004. By 2014, the Asia-Pacific RFID market is expected to reach $850 million. Globally, the RFID market is expected to reach $24.5 billion in 2015 (Park et al., 2010). At present time, it is safe to say that the technology has become a central method of information tracking in virtually every industry and its uses appear limitless. Some researchers assert that RFID usage is limited by only our human imaginations (Cazier, Jensen, & Dave, 2008; Hossain & Prybutok, 2008; Juban & Wyld, 2004; Pramatari & Theotokis, 2009).

HOW THE RFID TECHNOLOGY WORKS

RFID technology is, at its core, a rather basic technology that has been in use for over 80 years. It was first patented in 1926. However, as with any technological advancement, the RFID technology has continued to be developed, expanded, and improved. RFID has been utilized in highly complex supply chain distribution and channel management operations. The technology has recently been introduced to the public sector (Golding & Tennant, 2010; Martinez-Balleste, et al., 2013). As the technology has advanced, the fundamental aspect of how the technology works has remained the same. All forms of RFID technology are based upon the interaction between three key components: RFID tags, RFID readers, and back-ends (Atkinson, 2004).

RFID Tags

RFID tags are the components that are placed on the inventory or object to be tracked. Consumers have become increasingly familiar with these tags in the retail industry. They have begun to reduce the use of traditional tags with a printed barcode on them. The RFID tags come in a variety of sizes

and forms but they all contain two main pieces: a microchip and a metal coil. The microchip stores and processes data. Different types of chips have different processing and storing capabilities. The second piece of an RFID tag is the metal coil, which transmits information from the reader to the tag and vice versa. Essentially, the metal coil is the antenna of the RFID tag and links the tag with the rest of the RFID system (Glasser, Goodman, & Einspruch, 2007; Trujillo-Rasua, Solanas, Perez-Martinez & Domingo-Ferrer, 2012).

Categorically, there are three different types of RFID tags: active, semi-active, and passive. Passive RFID tags are by far the most commonly used types in the consumer industry (Wong, Hui, & Chan, 2006). They are small, low-cost, long-lasting and low-maintenance. These tags can only be read within very close proximity to a reader, and rely on the power source from the reader to transmit information. Because the passive tags rely on a reader for power, they can be produced at a large scale and low cost (Hsu, Chao, & Park, 2011). These passive RFID tags are the types that are typically found in clothing and have begun to compete with the use of the UPC barcode in the retail industry. Conversely, active RFID tags are able to emit and transmit information to a reader based upon their own power source. This means that active RFID tags are generally very large and costly. They have the ability to transmit information over a greater distance (Grewal, et al., 2011).

Typically, passive tags cost approximately $0.05 per unit, while an active tag costs closer to $50.00 per unit (Trujillo-Rasua, et al., 2012). Due to the massive cost difference, it is easy to understand why passive tags are the preferred method in the retail industry. A tag placed on a good to be sold cannot easily be replaced. Semi-passive tags are hybrid of passive and active tags. They have their own power source, but still rely on a signal from the reader to transmit information (Hsu, Chao, & Park, 2011; Slettemeås, 2009).

RFID Readers

The second component of RFID technology is the RFID reader. The RFID reader is similar to the traditional barcode scanner in some ways: it triggers the RFID tag to send information stored in the tag back to the reader. A traditional scanner requires a line of sight connection to transmit data, while RFID readers simply need to be within frequency range to transmit radio waves. Hence, the name of the technology is called *radio frequency identification* (Atkinson, 2004). The metal coil "antennas" in the tags pick up the radio waves emitted from the readers to send the information. Then, the readers in turn send the information to the back end computer within the system. Essentially, the RFID readers are the middlemen in the transmittal process for tracking and computing information (Trujillo-Rasua, et al., 2012).

Back-Ends

The back-ends are the larger, behind-the-scenes databases within computer powerhouses that actually identify, track, monitor, manage, and process all of the information transmitted by the RFID tags via the readers. The back-ends provide the brainpower for creating quantifiable data based upon the information received (Kapoor, et al., 2009; Trujillo-Rasua, et al., 2012).

RFID VS. UPC

RFID technology is an expansion of the traditional inventory tracking system known as the barcode system, or Universal Product Code (UPC). RFID can be thought of as a technologically advanced version of a barcode. RFID also allows for the identification and tracking of inventory and consumer goods as well as personal documentation. RFID tags are considered to be much more effective and efficient in transmitting information than the traditional barcode. RFID tags can pro-

vide significantly more information from greater distances, with less need for human intervention. While the UPC barcode is unique for each product type, RDIF technology is centered on an Electronic Product Code (EPC) that tracks each individual product unit (EPCglobal Inc., 2005; Sarma, 2005).

Traditionally, UPC barcode needs to be manually scanned one at a time. The barcode has to be readily visible and intact to be properly scanned. With RFID tags, you can quickly process multiple tags with one reader. Most RFID tags can be read through materials and do not need to be openly visible to be scanned. UPC scans only track the 13-digit information that is unique to that product barcode. RFID tags, on the other hand, are able to hold immensely more information and store information. RFID tags have the ability to be "killed" or "put to sleep" to stop them from reading and transmitting information, while UPCs need to physically be dismantled. The major caveat is that while RFID tags have the ability and capability of being electronically de-activated, it does not mean they always are. For example, RFID tags are not automatically "killed" upon purchase, which is a very important point of contention for many consumer advocacy groups (EPCglobal Inc., 2005; Sarma, 2005).

While there are many benefits to using RFIDs, the UPC still maintains some advantages over an RFID, mainly in lower costs for initial implementation and potential for unlimited lifetime use, pending the UPC tag remains intact (Bellian, 2012). One major drawback for companies to utilize RFID technology is the high cost of initial implementation. For example, Wal-Mart's requirement that all suppliers utilize RFID technology came at an extremely high cost for their suppliers who did not already apply the technology. For companies who shipped around 50 million cases per year, which is rather standard for a large supplier, the estimated costs for implementing RFID tagging alone ranged between $13 - $23 million cases per year, plus an additional $8-$13 million in system implementation costs. This up-front

RFID implementation costs may be difficult for smaller companies to afford, but the long-term SCM benefits typically outweigh these upfront costs of implementation (Juban & Wyld, 2004; Smart, Bunduchi, & Gerst, 2010; Roberti, 2010).

Consumer-Oriented RFID Use

Previously, RFIDs have been considered most beneficial to companies for use within their production and supply chain management systems (Asif & Mandviwalla, 2005). Within the past few years, there has been an increasing shift to incorporate RFIDs into consumer-oriented products within the retail industry (Grewal, et al., 2011; Roberti, 2010). When being used within this public and consumer goods industry, the technology can be geared towards both SCM purposes and to perform varying levels of market research on consumers. According to Park, et al. (2010), the most common uses of RFID typically involve identification, authentication, location, and automatic data acquisition (ADA).

RFID technology can be used in the public and consumer goods industry in a variety of ways (Martinez-Balleste, et al., 2013). One specific example of RFID use is fashion-retailer Prada's decision to place RFID readers in dressing rooms to read RFID tags embedded in the clothes that are brought into the room. Information identified from the clothing is then transmitted via an RFID system and linked with a TV monitor in the dressing room that streams footage of Prada fashion shows. The styles of clothes that are brought into the dressing room dictate what Prada fashion shows are played on the TV monitor. The RFID technology helps Prada to feature fashion shows representative of a particular consumers style and clothing interest (Moon & Ngai, 2008; Wasieleski & Gal-Or, 2008).

In South Korea, McDonalds has utilized RFID technology to create an ordering system where customers are able to place their food orders from their cell phones. They will receive a notification once their food is ready. Other common RFID usages in the consumer goods industry are to track consumer purchases and purchasing trends via a customer's loyalty card or store credit card. Companies can utilize that knowledge to further appeal to the consumer, such as by sending coupons and other promotional information targeted at a consumer's frequently purchased products. Overall, RFID usage trends within the public and consumer goods industry echo RFID usage in general - the technological uses are limitless (Golding & Tennant, 2010; Hossain & Prybutok, 2008; Martinez-Balleste, et al., 2013; Park, et al, 2010).

Consumer Role in RFID Technology

One very important variable in the implementation of RFID technology, particularly within the public goods sector, is the consumer. It is critical to address the impact that RFID technology has on consumers. Consumer perspectives are essential to account for because consumer who naturally becomes the end-user of the RFID technology. RFID usage in the retail and public goods industry is increasingly aimed towards tracking consumer behaviors. Once implemented, RFID tracking technology is typically permanent. Therefore, consumers are impacted by this technology whether it is intended for their use or not (Cazier, Jensen, & Dave, 2008; Hossain & Prybutok, 2008).

It is also interesting to note that the cost-savings and benefits of RFID technology may be clear to businesses. Consumers seem to be much less aware of the benefits they gain by having access to RFID technology. Studies have shown that many times the end consumer is entirely unaware of the RFID technology they are carrying around. Many consumers are not familiar with RFID technology. Therefore, they are uninformed of the security and privacy issues it presents. A 2004 study by Cap Gemini Ernest and Young found that only 23% of consumers had even heard of RFID technology (Juban & Wyld, 2004). Thus, those consumers who are unfamiliar with RFID technology cannot be aware of the potential security and privacy issues that are associated with it. Out of those who have heard of the technology, less than half had a favorable view of it. Privacy was a major concern for consumers, with 45% of surveyed consumers stating that they would not willingly purchase a product with RFID if it meant their purchase information would be stored (Pramatari & Theotokis, 2009; Zare Mehrjerdi, 2011).

SECURITY VS. PRIVACY CONCERNS

For the purpose of this chapter, security concerns are separate from privacy concerns. They can be considered as two different arenas of public issues. In this chapter, security concerns refer to the *unintentional* risks that occur when using RFID technology such as hackers who steal sensitive information via RFID transmittal. Privacy concerns are *intentional* breaches of consumer information that are initiated by businesses such as tracking customer purchasing behavior via an RFID chip embedded in a store loyalty card without the customer's knowledge. However, either type of breaches - intentional or unintentional - can have a significant impact on the consumer. Businesses should be held accountable for both forms. Businesses must take both concerns into careful consideration when they are deciding if and how to implement RFID technology. Beitelspacher, et al. (2012) suggest that businesses that do decide to implement RFID technology bear the responsibility of addressing these consumer privacy concerns as well as possible security issues before they occur.

Security Concerns

Security concerns are prevalent in relation to RFID technology usage (Good & Benaissa, 2013; Kamruzzaman, et al., 2013; Li, et al., 2013). The key core competency of RFID technology compared to UPC scanning is the ability to transmit very specific product information via radio waves, instead of less unique product information via direct, visual contact with a barcode. Ironically, this competitive advantage also poses a significant security threat in using this technology. The tags' metal coils will transmit information to any reader within the necessary proximity, whether the information is intended for that reader or not. Readers that gain access to tag information even though they are not the intended recipients are called adversaries (Piramuthu, 2012). One major area of concern is with credit cards or other forms of payment cards that contain RFIDs. A hacker simply needs to come up next to a person using an adversary. They can quickly gain access to personal information linked to the RFID within the card. Businesses cannot be guaranteed that information contained in RFID tags will be kept secure and private away from adversaries. This creates an obvious security concern from both the business and consumer perspectives (Cazier, Jensen, & Dave, 2008; Grover & Berghel, 2011).

Security concerns of RFID usage are greatly exacerbated with the introduction of RFIDs into the public sector. When RFIDs are used in a business, supply chain, or distribution channel, the environment is generally a controlled environment, with limited potential for adversaries or hackers to enter into the environment. However, once RFIDs are exposed to use within the public sector, the environment becomes much less controllable. It offers much greater potential for information stored in the RFID tags to be stolen, corrupted, or blocked from being read. One way this exposure has occurred is actually through use in the private supply chain management. The tags can remain activated even once the good is passed on to the consumer (Piramuthu, 2010). Many times, a product item will be embedded with an RFID tag or chip to help track the item through the supply chain. The tag or chip still remains on the item after the point of sale. The item has the potential to continually be tracked and generally without the knowledge of the consumer. Also, because the passive tags used on public and commercial goods are cheap and rather basic, they do not have the ability to contain security features necessary to maintain information privacy (Doss, Zhou, Sundaresan, Yu, & Gao, 2012).

As RFIDs are becoming increasingly popular in the public sector, a significant amount of research is being conducted to look for ways to make RFIDs more secure. According to Piramuthu (2012), and Doss, et al., (2012), there is still considerable work to be done. We cannot be fully confident that RFID technology is entirely secure and private. Studies are continuously being conducted that dispel previous studies touting security breakthroughs. These studies focus on highlighting security concerns by citing errors or gaps in other studies. Piramuthu (2012) stresses that the general public will not embrace RFID technology until these security concerns are resolved or significant advancements are made.

Privacy Concerns

There is an entirely different level of privacy concerns relating to information that is collected by retailers. These concerns fall to what retailers do with the information that is collected and raising awareness about the prevalence of RFID usage in general. This concern over privacy in RFID use has long been an issue (Albrecht & McIntyre, 2004; CASPIAN, 2003). In fact, Mario Cardullo (2003) cites privacy concerns as a major hesitancy in utilizing his early-stage RFID technology within toll collection systems. Consumer advocacy groups feel that consumers deserve the right to know if the products they are purchasing such as clothes or using such as a Mobile Speedpass contain a RFID. CASPIAN cites a multitude of examples where retailers utilize RFID technology to track and monitor unsuspecting consumers. For example, Texas Instruments recently unveiled a new RFID loyalty card that is able to monitor all purchases made by the consumer, as well as

track their movement throughout the store. The consumer advocacy group calls-out retailers such as Calvin Klein, Abercrombie & Fitch and Champion for secretly sewing "invisible" RFID tags into their clothing. CASPIAN also cites Gillette's consumer privacy invasion plan to embed RFID chips onto razor packaging, and then take close-up pictures of potential customers' faces (Albrecht & McIntyre, 2004; Beitelspacher, et al., 2012; Cazier, et al., 2008).

Because RFID tags are increasingly used in the public sector to manage consumer information and purchasing behavior, the information being transmitted is oftentimes much more sensitive than what is tracked for distribution and supply chain management purposes. RFID tags can be found in a multitude of products used by consumers on a daily basis such as credit cards, store loyalty cards, and clothing. RFIDs found on credit cards and store loyalty cares often contain highly sensitive consumer information such as name, address, phone number, social security number, and even back account information. Problematically, many consumers are entirely unaware that these items they carry with them have the ability to track them. Consumer privacy has the potential to be violated on a multitude of levels from the lack of awareness of embedded RFID tags on products to the potential for adversaries to gain access to this sensitive information (Bailey & Caidi, 2005; Belanger, Hiller, & Smith, 2002; Culnan & Armstrong, 1999).

Theoretical Debate over Privacy Rights

At the core of this debate over the ethical, privacy, and security aspects of RFIDs, the term privacy is always a hot topic (Song, 2013; Zhou & Piramuthu, 2013). Different people have different opinions as to what exactly constitutes privacy and the boundaries of consumer rights. Therefore, privacy laws based on RFID usage are all the more difficult to enact. Wasieleski and Gal-Or (2008) suggest that privacy, when taken in its most literal meaning, assume completely withdrawing from society. A more liberal usage is to determine for oneself what and how much personal information is shared with others. The purpose of their argument is to highlight that privacy itself is not a term that is generally agree upon. There are widely varying beliefs over the level of privacy. We as members of society have rights to. Park, et al. (2010) states that some of the aversion to RFID technology can be contributed to cultural norms. They suggest that society is slow to accept the technology because it is still relatively new and unknown to them (Chowdhury & Ray, 2013; Good & Benaissa, 2013).

Ethical Debate

In addition to privacy and security concerns of RFID use, there is a growing concern as to whether RFIDs can even be used ethically and legally within the public consumer goods sector. This concern is based upon security and privacy fears of the consumer and takes into account of consumers' rights. This ethical concern questions the value and need for RFIDs in the public and consumer goods industry. Adding to the ethical concern is the fact that most consumers are entirely unaware that their products purchased contain these hidden RFIDs. Even if the consumer is somehow aware that their product contains an RFID, they cannot be sure what information the RDIF is storing and transmitting; who is receiving the information or how it is being used (Heim, et al., 2009; Wasieleski & Gal-Or, 2008; Song, 2013; Zhou & Piramuthu, 2013).

Understandably, this has caused consumer advocate groups to loudly protest against RFIDs and question the legality of their usage. Many states have begun to take legislative action in an attempt to balance business needs with consumer rights. Businesses chose to use RFIDs on consumer products are held accountable for ensuring the information is transmitted securely and privately.

As we discussed above, RFID technology is not immune to security breaches. Therefore, companies are walking a thin line in utilizing this technology, particularly without consumer consent (Beitelspacher, et al., 2012; Cochran, Tatikonda, & Magid, 2007; Glasser, et al., 2007; Wasieleski & Gal-Or, 2008).

Response to Privacy Concerns

Businesses within the consumer goods industry are well aware of the uneasiness surrounding RFID use. Organizations such as CASPIAN have fought hard to highlight the consumer privacy concerns over RFID use. One response to these consumer privacy concerns is to create the ability for "tag killing", where the RDIF tag can be disabled, or killed. Typically, the tag killing occurs at the point of sale and the consumer has no way to ensure that the retailer successfully deactivated the tag. This is especially true given that retailers seek to benefit from continuously monitoring consumers for repeat purchasing patterns. Therefore, this method is not embraced as entirely reliable or impactful (Kumar, Anselmo, & Berndt, 2009; Wasieleski & Gal-Or, 2008).

State and government legislatures have begun to react to these security and privacy concerns. Back in 2004, Senator Patrick Leahy of Vermont gave a speech at Georgetown University Law Center that highlighted RFID consumer privacy laws and emphasized "...the RFID train is beginning to leave the station, and now is the right now to begin a national discussion about where, if at all, any lines will be drawn to protect privacy rights" (Albrecht & McIntyre, 2004). California State Senator Debra Bowen has also been an outspoken critic of RFID tracking, and famously called out Wal-Mart for deciding to place RFID tags on underwear. The privacy impact of letting manufacturers and stores put RFID chips in the clothes, groceries, and everything else you buy is enormous. Since then, multiple laws have been presented that aim to protect consumers from RFID privacy infringement. In Europe, there has been more success in legally addressing the consumer impact of new technologies such as RFID, including the Data Protection Directive, The Electronic Commerce Directive, and the Privacy and Electronic Communications Directive. Globally, the EPC Global Class-1 Generation-2 Standard Act was passed, in an effort to maintain a level of RFID security standards that requires RFID systems to conform to certain technological standards (Albrecht & McIntyre, 2004; Slettemeås, 2009; Wang, Wong & Ye, 2008).

Consumer Benefits

While the focus of this chapter is privacy and security concerns relating to RFID use for consumers. It is important to highlight the benefit that consumers gain as well. RFID technology offers significant consumer benefits, which are oftentimes ignored by opponents of the technology. For example, consumers benefit from lower product costs that result from lower distribution costs when RFID is used in SCM. Another favorable use of RFID technology is chip implantation in pets. Cap Gemini Ernest & Young that cites the top five consumer benefits of RFID use are: (1) faster recovery of stolen items, (2) improved anti car theft capabilities, (3) consumer savings due to decreases in manufacturing and retail costs, (4) improved security of prescription drugs, and (5) faster, more reliable recalls and improved food safety quality (Juban and Wyld, 2004; Zare Mehrjerdi, 2011).

BUSINESS IMPLICATIONS

The bottom line in the use of RFIDs in the marketplace is to MOVE – TRACK – And EXCHANGE Goods FASTER and CHEAPER. RFIDs are becoming more accepted and common that we have discussed previously such as rapidly declining prices, industry demands on suppliers, increased range, and standardized software and signaling. Many organizations do not have a choice and must adapt to this change such as suppliers of the Department of Defense or Wal-Mart. Many organizations in industries that depend on faster response time and cost as their competitive advantage will need to adopt RFID to eliminate the cost and time involved in manual tracking and inventorying of goods.

RFIDs overall are another use of technology that reduces the hours of human interaction and labor costs. As the technology is adapted to more and more applications, organizations have less need to do manual tracking and accounting, and rely more on computer reports and automation. This will lead to organizations moving away from many of the unskilled labor positions of cashiers and inventory laborers, but will create more software and IT/IS managers and specialists that will need to analyze the computer data and make decisions. Cost and Return on Investment (ROI) will be major managerial decisions for managers in the adoption of RFID hardware and software with the trade-off of labor hours. There are also intangible benefits that are not easy to calculate in the ROI decision of RFIDs for the increased speed of processing and inventory accuracy over manual tracking. With the various sizes and costs for RFIDs depending on the transmission range and lifespan, organizations must also choose the best tradeoff of which RFID band to use that will suit their needs at the lowest cost.

The implication of RFID technology has the potential to change the way the organizations conduct their current logic tracking to include all manpower. This will require changes both in the way employees operate, reduce inventory times, and possibly decrease inventory levels through more accurate inventory management. The future for this RFID technology is almost unlimited. It is generally thought that RFIDs will replace all bar codes in the future. Without bar codes, there is also no need for cashiers, as consumers can be charged when they leave a store building. This could have the implication of reshaping the look and setup of traditional stores. Imagine if perimeter scanners were set up across multiple exits in a big fair ground. Consumers could walk into the premises, pick up whatever items they wanted, and exit in any direction and be charged automatically. The purchases would all be tied to the individual, so that recommended purchases were automatically configured. A screen on a smart cart could automatically make your shopping list when you enter into a store and generate sales enticing you to buy certain items based on your profile.

The largest implication is that of a cashless society. Massachusetts recently announced that it would be eliminating all toll booth workers in the near future and replacing all toll lanes with the E-Z Pass RFID Transponders to automate toll collection. Even for users out of state, their license plate would be photographed if they did not have a transponder and they would be mailed a bill (Gellerman, 2013). Automated financial transactions make it easier and faster to move people, objects, and money.

In addition to being able to track every financial transaction that every individual makes, this would enable the government oversight of all transactions for greater national security and taxation. With a move to recorded financial transactions, businesses would not be able to have inaccurate accounting of their profits or hide cash sales. All business earnings and spending would be automatically recorded. This would also enable an accurate way to move to a consumption tax on purchases rather than an income tax since financial transactions could not easily be hidden in anonymous cash transactions. There are many additional applications for this technology such as key cards or access control devices to open doors that are not explored in this discussion as they have a more minor role in current organizational and marketplace change. However, as this RFID technology expands, there could be more new applications for RFID that have a much

more profound impact on the marketplace than just logistics tracking and financial transaction automation.

Through researching privacy and security concerns in utilizing RFID technology in consumer-oriented goods, it is quite evident that businesses are aware of these questions and issues. Extensive studies are needed to be conducted in regards to RFID securitization. Currently, the technology cannot be considered secure. CASPIAN and other consumer advocacy groups along with government officials have been outspoken critics of the technology. Particularly, as it pertains to consumer use and privacy rights. Industries and organizations are responsible for taking these concerns into account when creating and implementing their business initiatives. Businesses need to take responsibility for ensuring they are using RFID technology is as private and secure a manner as possible. This does not imply that businesses should entirely abandon the technology. Rather, there are multiple benefits that can be derived from RFID use both to businesses and consumers. However, businesses cannot continue to deceive and manipulate consumers through unethical and secretive RFID use. Saito (2011) introduces three steps to a more data-secure world when considering business implications. These three steps include: (1) inform the public of data products' vulnerabilities, (2) make security a design data priority, and (3) set high standards and enforce them.

New technology needs to be used in an honest and open manner. Theoretically, this honest presentation on the part of retailers may work to their benefit if they can highlight the consumer benefits of using RFID technology. Given the secretive implications of RFID in the consumer world, a candid demonstration from retailers may become a welcome relief to consumers. After all, at the core of most business intentions for tracking consumer behavior, openly or not, is to provide the consumer with a product that is appealing to them. That in itself is not necessarily negative.

The method for going about the data gathering, on the other hand, is typically the root of concern (Aggarwal, et al., 2013; Kumar, Anselmo, & Berndt, 2009).

CONCLUSION

The purpose of this chapter paper is to explore the validity of privacy and security concerns that have been raised in regards to the application of RFID technology for identification and tracking use for consumer goods. As mentioned above, RFID is a continuously advancing technology. Increased privacy and security are some of the few areas of growth and opportunity for RFID. It should be a significant area of focus as this information sharing technology continues to develop. Companies risk huge public relations nightmares, financial loss, and severe legal ramifications if their RFID systems do not prove to be secure. While RFID technology can help increase the efficiency and effectiveness in which information is transferred within a company, these companies must not lose sight of the vulnerability that comes with this form of remote information sharing. In the end, it is important to note that RFID technology itself is not negative, rather, it is how the technology can be utilized that has a negative impact (Chowdhury & Ray, 2013).

RFIDs are changing the marketplace by replacing jobs that were normally done using humans for manual tracking, input and transactions with automated processes. Everything from inventory management and location tracking to financial transactions can be greatly accomplished using RFIDs and computers. Organizations are adopting this technology because it allows for easier, faster, and cheaper ways to move people, merchandises, and money. Many positions from inventory personnel, clerks, cashiers, and toll booth workers will become obsolete with this technology. However, new positions will be created with an increased demand for secure networks and Information Technology and Information System with IT technicians and managers that can analyze the data. As with any new technology, organizations must adapt to survive. The government must ensure legislation to maintain protections on the individual's security and privacy in society (Wang & Loui, 2009).

REFERENCES

Aggarwal, C. C., Ashish, N., & Sheth, A. P. (2013). The internet of things: a survey from the data-centric perspective. In C. C. Aggarwal (Ed.), *Managing and Mining Sensor Data* (pp. 383–428). New York: Springer. doi:10.1007/978-1-4614-6309-2_12

Albrecht, K., & McIntyre, L. (2004). CASPIAN consumer privacy, RFID: the big brother bar code. *ALEC Policy Forum, 6*(3), 49-54.

Albrecht, K., & McIntyre, L. (2005). *Spychips: how major corporations and government plan to track your every move with RFID*. Nashville, TN: Nelson Current.

Asif, Z., & Mandviwalla, M. (2005). Integrating the supply chain with RFID: An in-depth technical and business analysis. *Communications of the Association for Information Systems, 15*(1), 393–427.

Atkinson, W. (2004). Tagged: the risks and rewards of RFID technology. *Risk Management Journal, 51*(7), 12–19.

Bailey, S. G. M., & Caidi, N. (2005). How much is too little? Privacy and smart cards in Hong Kong and Ontario. *Journal of Information Science, 31*(5), 354–364. doi:10.1177/0165551505055400

Beitelspacher, L. S., Hansen, J. D., Johnston, A. C., & Dietz, G. D. (2012). Exploring consumer privacy concerns and RFID technology: The impact of fear appeals on consumer behaviors. *Journal of Marketing Theory and Practice, 20*(2), 147–159. doi:10.2753/MTP1069-6679200202

Belanger, F., Hiller, J., & Smith, W. (2002). Trustworthiness in electronic commerce: The role of privacy, security, and site attributes. *The Journal of Strategic Information Systems, 11*(3/4), 245–270. doi:10.1016/S0963-8687(02)00018-5

Bellian, C. (2012). Bar codes or RFID tags: Key factors to consider in choosing the correct data collection technology for your customer. *The Mheda Journal.* Retrieved September 10, 2013 from: http://www.themhedajournal.org/index.php/2010/07/bar-codes-or-rfid-tags/

Cardullo, M. (2003). Genesis of the Versatile RFID Tag. *RFID Journal.* Retrieved September 1, 2013 from http://www.rfidjournal.com/articles/view?392

CASPIAN. (2003). Scandal: Wal-Mart, P&G involved in secret RFID testing. *Consumers Against Supermarket Privacy Invasion and Numbering (CASPIAN).* Retrieved September 1, 2013 from http://www.spychips.com/press-releases/broken-arrow.html

Cazier, J. A., Jensen, A. S., & Dave, D. S. (2008). The impact of consumer perceptions of information privacy and security risks on the adoption of residual RFID technologies. *Communications of the AIS, 23*(14), 235–256.

Chen, R., Fung, B. C. M., Mohammed, N., Desai, B. C., & Wang, K. (2013). Privacy-preserving trajectory data publishing by local suppression. *Information Sciences, 231,* 83–97. doi:10.1016/j.ins.2011.07.035

Chowdhury, M. U., & Ray, B. R. (2013). Security risks/vulnerability in a RFID system and possible defenses. In N. Karmakar (Ed.), *Advanced RFID Systems, Security, and Applications* (pp. 1–15). Hershey, PA: Information Science Reference. doi:10.4018/978-1-4666-4707-7.ch084

Cochran, P. L., Tatikonda, M. V., & Magid, J. M. (2007). Radio frequency identification and the ethics of privacy. *Organizational Dynamics, 36*(2), 217–229. doi:10.1016/j.orgdyn.2007.03.008

Culnan, M. J., & Armstrong, P. K. (1999). Information privacy concerns, procedural fairness, and impersonal trust: An empirical investigation. *Organization Science, 10*(1), 104–116. doi:10.1287/orsc.10.1.104

Dean, D. H. (2013). Anticipating consumer reaction to RFID-enabled grocery checkout. *Services Marketing Quarterly, 34*(1), 86–101. doi:10.1080/15332969.2013.739945

Dobkin, D. M. (2013). *The RF in RFID: UHF RFID In Practice.* Oxford, UK: Newnes Publications.

Doss, R., Zhou, W., Sundaresan, S., Yu, S., & Gao, L. (2012). A Minimum disclosure approach to authentication and privacy in RFID systems. *Computer Networks, 56*(15), 3401–3416. doi:10.1016/j.comnet.2012.06.018

EPCglobal Inc. (2005). *Guidelines on EPC for consumer products.* Lawrenceville.

Gellerman, B. (2013). *Mass. seeks to eliminate tollbooths for cashless system.* WBUR, National Public Radio. Retrieved March 2, 2013 from http://www.wbur.org/2013/03/27/mass-tollbooths-cashless

Glasser, D. J., Goodman, K. W., & Einspruch, N. G. (2007). Chips, tags and scanners: Ethical challenges for radio frequency identification. *Ethics and Information Technology, 9*(2), 101–109. doi:10.1007/s10676-006-9124-0

Golding, P., & Tennant, V. (2010). Using RFID Inventory Reader at the Item-Level in a Library Environment: Performance Benchmark. *Electronic Journal of Information Systems Evaluation, 13*(2), 107–120.

Good, T., & Benaissa, M. (2013). A holistic approach examining RFID design for security and privacy. *The Journal of Supercomputing, 64*(3), 664–684. doi:10.1007/s11227-010-0497-9

Grewal, D., Ailawadi, K. L., Gauri, D., Hall, K., Kopalle, P., & Robertson, J. R. (2011). Innovations in retail pricing and promotions. *Journal of Retailing, 87*, 43–52. doi:10.1016/j.jretai.2011.04.008

Grover, A., & Berghel, H. (2011). A survey of RFID deployment and security issues. *Journal of Information Processing Systems, 7*(4), 561–580. doi:10.3745/JIPS.2011.7.4.561

Heim, G. R., Wentworth, W. R. Jr, & Peng, X. (2009). The value to the customer of RFID in service applications. *Decision Sciences, 40*(3), 477–512. doi:10.1111/j.1540-5915.2009.00237.x

Hossain, M. M., & Prybutok, V. R. (2008). Consumer acceptance of RFID technology: An exploratory study. *IEEE Transactions on Engineering Management, 55*(2), 316–328. doi:10.1109/TEM.2008.919728

Hsu, C. H., Chao, H. C., & Park, J. H. (2011). Threshold jumping and wrap-around scan techniques toward efficient tag identification in high density RFID systems. *Information Systems Frontiers, 13*(4), 471–480. doi:10.1007/s10796-009-9209-5

Juban, R. L., & Wyld, D. C. (2004). Would you like chips with that? Consumer perspective of RFID. *Management Research News, 27*(11/12), 29–44. doi:10.1108/01409170410784653

Kamruzzaman, J., Azad, A. K., Karmakar, N. C., Karmakar, G., & Srinivasan, B. (2013). Security and privacy in RFID systems. In N. Karmakar (Ed.), *Advanced RFID Systems, Security, and Applications* (pp. 16–40). Hershey, PA: Information Science Reference.

Kapoor, G., Zhou, W., & Piramuthu, S. (2009). Challenges associated with RFID tag implementations in supply chain. *European Journal of Information Systems, 18*(6), 526–533. doi:10.1057/ejis.2009.41

Kumar, S., Anselmo, M. J., & Berndt, K. J. (2009). Transforming the retail industry: potential and challenges with RFID technology. *Transportation Journal, 48*(4), 61–71.

Lee, H., & Ozer, O. (2007). Unlocking the value of RFID. *Production and Operations Management, 16*(1), 40–64. doi:10.1111/j.1937-5956.2007.tb00165.x

Li, Y., Deng, R. H., & Bertino, E. (2013). RFID security and privacy. *Synthesis Lectures on Information Security, Privacy, and Trust, 4*(3), 1–157. doi:10.2200/S00550ED1V01Y201311SPT007

Liu, A., Chang, H. K., Lo, Y. S., & Wang, S. Y. (2012). The increase of RFID privacy and security with mutual authentication mechanism in supply chain management. *International Journal of Electronic Business Management, 10*(1), 1–7.

Martinez-Balleste, A., Perez-Martinez, P. A., & Solanas, A. (2013). The pursuit of citizens' privacy: A privacy-aware smart city is possible. *IEEE Communications Magazine, 51*(6), 136–141. doi:10.1109/MCOM.2013.6525606

May, T. (2007). Strategic value of RFID in supply chain management. *Journal of Purchasing and Supply Management, 13*(4), 261–273. doi:10.1016/j.pursup.2007.11.001

Moon, K. L., & Ngai, E. W. T. (2008). The adoption of RFID in fashion retailing: a business value-added framework. *Industrial Management + Data Systems, 108*(5), 596-612.

Piramuthu, S. (2012). Vulnerabilities of RFID protocols proposed in ISF. *Information Systems Frontiers, 14*(3), 647–651. doi:10.1007/s10796-010-9291-8

Pramatari, K., & Theotokis, A. (2009). Consumer acceptance of RFID-enabled services: A model of multiple attitudes, perceived system characteristics and individual traits. *European Journal of Information Systems, 18*(6), 541–552. doi:10.1057/ejis.2009.40

Roberti, M. (2010). Wal-Mart relaunches EPC RFID effort, starting with men's jeans and basics. *RFID Journal.* Retrieved September 1, 2013 from http://www.rfidjournal.com/articles/view?7753/

Saito, W. H. (2011). Our naked data. *The Futurist, 45*(4), 42–25.

Sarma, S. (2005). A history of the EPC. In S. Garfinkel, & B. Rosenberg (Eds.), *RFID* (pp. 37–55). Upper Saddle River, NJ: Addison-Wesley.

Slettemeås, D. (2009). RFID - the 'next step' in consumer-product relations or Orwellian nightmare? Challenges for research and policy. *Journal of Consumer Policy, 32*(3), 219–244. doi:10.1007/s10603-009-9103-z

Smart, A. U., Bunduchi, R., & Gerst, M. (2010). The costs of adoption of RFID technologies in supply networks. *International Journal of Operations & Production Management, 30*(4), 423–447. doi:10.1108/01443571011029994

Song, B. (2013). Privacy issues in RFID. In A. Miri (Ed.), *Advanced Security and Privacy for RFID Technologies* (pp. 126–138). Hershey, PA: Information Science Reference. doi:10.4018/978-1-4666-3685-9.ch008

Swedberg, C. (2009). Tennessee hospital tracks high-value items. *RFID Journal.* Retrieved February 20, 2014 from http://www.rfidjournal.com/articles/view?5106

Thiesse, F., Al-kassab, J., & Fleisch, E. (2009). Understanding the value of integrated RFID systems: A case study from apparel retail. *European Journal of Information Systems, 18*(6), 592–614. doi:10.1057/ejis.2009.33

Wang, J. L., & Loui, M. C. (2009). Privacy and ethical issues in location-based tracking systems. In *Proceedings of the 2009 IEEE International Symposium on Technology and Society*. IEEE.

Wong, K. H. M., Hui, P. C. L., & Chan, A. C. K. (2006). Cryptography and authentication on RFID passive tags for apparel products. *Computers in Industry, 57*(4), 342–349. doi:10.1016/j.compind.2005.09.002

Zare Mehrjerdi, Y. (2008). RFID-enabled systems: A brief review. *Assembly Automation, 28*(3), 235–245. doi:10.1108/01445150810889493

Zare Mehrjerdi, Y. (2011). RFID adoption: A systems thinking perspective through profitability engagement. *Assembly Automation, 31*(2), 182–187. doi:10.1108/01445151111117773

Zhou, W., & Piramuthu, S. (2013). Technology regulation policy for business ethics: An example of RFID in supply chain management. *Journal of Business Ethics, 116*(2), 327–340. doi:10.1007/s10551-012-1474-4

Zuo, Y. (2012). Survivability experiment and attack characterization of RFID. *IEEE Transactions on Dependable and Secure Computing, 9*(2), 289–302. doi:10.1109/TDSC.2011.30

KEY TERMS AND DEFINITIONS

Automatic Data Acquisition: The automatic collection of source data from sensors and readers in a factory, shopping store, or public environment for data entry into the computer.

Privacy: The state of an individual's ability to personally control information about themselves and the condition of free from being observed or disturbed by other people.

Radio Frequency Identification (RFID): Technologies that use a wireless system comprised of two components, tags and readers, to identify people or objects carrying encoded microchips.

Return on Investment (ROI): Is the most common profitability ratio, which calculates the percentage rate that measures the relationship between the amount the business gets from an investment and the amount invested.

RFID Reader: A device used to communicate with RFID tags. The reader is a device that has one or more antennas that emit radio waves and receive signals back from the RFID tag. The reader is also sometimes called an interrogator because it interrogates the tag.

RFID Tags: An RFID tag, also called an RFID transponder, consists of a microchip, some memory and an antenna. RFID tags that contain their own power source are known as *active* tags. Those without a power source are known as *passive* tags.

Supply Chain Management (SCM): Is the management of the integrated flow of goods. Processes are linked across companies to track the movement and storage of raw materials, work-in-process inventory, and finished goods from point of origin to point of consumption.

Chapter 8
Green Characteristics of RFID Technologies:
An Exploration in the UK Logistics Sector from Innovation Diffusion Perspective

Ramakrishnan Ramanathan
University of Bedfordshire, UK

Lok Wan Lorraine Ko
Nottingham University, UK

Hsin Chen
University of Bedfordshire, UK

Usha Ramanathan
University of Bedfordshire, UK

ABSTRACT

Logistics is an integral part of the supply chain. Many logistics service providers have acknowledged that if they want to operate more efficiently and responsively, they must adopt technologies that help manufacturers, warehouses, and retailers to communicate with each other more efficiently. Radio Frequency Identification (RFID) technology has been identified as an important application among many logistics technologies and is increasingly gaining both practitioners' and researchers' attention. The purpose of this chapter is to explore the factors affecting logistics service providers' intentions to use RFID technology, with special emphasis on its environmentally friendly green characteristics. The theoretical perspective diffusion of innovations is used for the purpose. The data is collected using a questionnaire survey among the UK logistics companies. The analysis shows that observability of green characteristics positively influences the intention to use RFID.

DOI: 10.4018/978-1-4666-6308-4.ch008

INTRODUCTION

Radio frequency identification (RFID) is one type of auto-identification technology that uses radio frequency (RF) waves to identify, track and locate individual physical items. This technology has been used in many applications including manufacturing and distribution of products (Lin & Ho, 2009a,b). While RFID is useful in improving several functions within a firm, we focus on the logistics function in this study. Applying RFID can help improve logistics in several ways. Lin (2009) points out that the capabilities of RFID to closely monitor and track positions of vehicles can assist companies to successfully manage their warehouses and supply chains. Additionally, cost savings, supply chain visibility, and new process creation have been identified as three key benefits of RFID adoption (Roh et al., 2009). Wamba (2012) claims that RFID can be useful in integrating supply chains by improving shipping and receiving processes, automatically trigger specific processes, foster higher level of information sharing among supply chain partners and finally promote the use of new business processes.

In worldwide academic research on RFID technology, the majority of papers have focused either on the general overview of RFID, or the applications of RFID in various industries, such as in fashion (Luyskens & Loebbecke, 2007; Moon & Ngai, 2008), service (Lee, et al., 2008), retail (Jones, et al., 2005), manufacturing (Wang et al., 2010), electronics (Muller-Seitz et al., 2009), library (Rong, 2004), and automotive industry (Schmitt, et al., 2007). However to date, there has been a limited amount of published knowledge on the discussion of the drivers or influencing factors that lead logistics industry to consider RFID. Further, prior research has not applied Innovation Diffusion Theory to study RFID adoption, especially in the logistics industry. Moreover, none of the previous studies considered green characteristics of RFID. Given the increasing importance of green issues, there is a need to understand how the perceived positive green characteristics are affecting the level of adoption of the RFID technology.

The aim of this paper is therefore to explore the factors affecting logistics service providers' intention to use RFID, with special emphasis on its environmental friendly green characteristics. We draw upon the theory of diffusion of innovations (Rogers, 1995) to develop a conceptual model of factors influencing RFID adoption. This theory suggests five attributes influence technology adoption: relative advantage, compatibility, complexity, trialability, and observability. The research question is to explore whether the innovation characteristics of RFID influence its adoption in the UK logistics industry. We have extended the theory in this research by including a new attribute that is increasingly becoming more relevant in the current business environment: environmental friendly (also called green) characteristics of RFID.

The remainder of the paper is structured as follows. In the next section, we provide a literature review on RFID adoption. We then develop our conceptual framework and research hypothesis building on the literature survey and innovation diffusion theory. This leads us to the fourth section of our paper, in which we present our research methodology including analysis methods and measure purification. In Section 5, we present our data analysis. Section 6 discusses our results. Finally, conclusions and future research directions are drawn in the last section.

LITERATURE REVIEW

Background of RFID Technology

An RFID system consists of three primary components: the tag or transponder; the readers; and the middleware. It is always connected to an enterprise application system for data processing in support of business activities (Wang, et al., 2010). RFID uses tags with embedded chips within a product, pallet, or case. These chips help to store and transmit information about the specific unit to RFID readers (which are radio frequency transmitters) (Attaran, 2007). According to Wang, et al. (2010), the middleware is an intermediate layer between the RFID readers and the enterprise application systems. It is used for reader and device management to provide a common interface to configure, monitor, deploy, and issue commands directly to readers; data management to filter raw data and pass on only useful information to the appropriate applications; application integration to provide integrated RFID data and connect disparate applications within the enterprise; and partner integration to provide collaborative solutions like business to-business integration between trading partners.

The Literature on RFID

In recent years, there has been a growing interest and attention among consultants, academics and researchers worldwide on RFID. This is indicated by the increasing volume of articles on the subject in trade publications and scholarly journals. A steadily increasing number of logistics companies adopt RFID for efficient identification of physical items, and hence several recent studies suggested that the interest of researchers in RFID should continue (Riedel, et al., 2008; Li, et al., 2010; Pedroso, et al., 2009). Li et al. (2010) classified the literature of RFID into three areas: RFID general overview, analytical studies, and empirical studies. We provide a brief literature survey following a similar classification. Table 1 summarises the literature.

We first focus on studies that provided a survey of RFID adoption. These survey papers have mainly focused on the commitment to adopt RFID, and the benefits and challenges of RFID implementation in different countries (Li et al., 2010). The adoption of RFID technology by large Brazilian companies was examined by Pedroso et al. (2009). They analyzed issues related to

implementation of RFID in Brazilian companies, including RFID applications, benefits, motiviations, barriers and organizational aspects. In the UK, Riedel et al. (2008) conducted a survey with 52 Logistics companies in 2005 in order to assess the readiness of companies to adopt RFID, and to determine whether and when it would be adopted in large scale. Key issues explored in the study include the degree of awareness, level of diffusion of RFID, barriers to adoption, priority of adoption, level of interest in features of RFID, benefits achievable through RFID addoption, and concerns about privacy issue. Vijayaraman & Osyk (2006) carried out an empirical study to determine the status of RFID implementation among companies in the US warehousing industry. A few years later, an exploratory study was carried out to investigate the status of RFID implementation in the US (Li et al., 2010).

Many of these studies have attempted to study the degree of awareness of RFID and/or stages of RFID adoption. A survey in Chinese context (Min et al., 2003) revealed that 31% of companies never heard of the technology in China, 40% heard of the technology, but had no further understanding of its application, only 9% of the participants had a deeper understanding of RFID and 20% had already used RFID in their companies. In contrast, the Brazilian survey (Pedroso et al., 2009) found out that 50% of companies had no RFID initiative underway or planned, and 50% had such initiative underway or planned. The findings indicated there was a lack of knowledge about RFID within their companies, and thus a significant need for greater education around RFID (Min et al., 2003).

To identify which stage companies are at regarding RFID adoption, the survey in the UK logistics industry (Riedel et al., 2008) showed that half of the respondents were not adopting the technology or had never investigated its applicability, 21% of respondents were carrying out an investigation, and only 17% were using RFID. Moreover, the US survey (Li et al., 2010) showed that 61% of responding firms were not considering

Table 1. A survey of the RFID literature

General Overview	
Spekman & Sweeney (2006)	RFID technology and its applications in supply chain
McFarlane & Sheffi (2003)	Benefits of RFID
Riemenschneider, Hardgrave, & Armstrong (2007)	Business values of RFID
Angeles (2005)	Managerial guidelines of RFID
Li & Visich (2006)	Implementation challenges and strategies of RFID
Tajima (2007)	The impact of RFID on competitive advantage
Visich, Li, & Khumawala (2007)	RFID in closed-loop supply chains
Twist (2005)	The impact of RFID on supply chain facilities
Acharyulu (2007); Wicks, Visich & Li (2006); Glabman (2004); Hosaka (2004)	The evaluation of RFID's managerial benefits and implementation challenges.
Analytical Studies	
Financial Studies	
Hou & Huang (2006)	Cost and benefits analysis of item-level tagging
Ozelkan & Galambose (2008)	Cash flow and risk analysis
Bottani & Rizzi (2008); Ustundag & Tanyas (2009)	The expected costs and benefits analysis in three-echelon supply chains
Inventory Studies	
Chande, Dhekane, Hemachandra, & Rangaraj (2005)	Inventory models are presented for time-sensitive products
Heese (2007); Uckun, Karaesmen, & Savas (2008)	Inventory record inaccuracy
Gaukler, Seifert, & Hausman (2007)	Item-level tagging
Karaer & Lee (2007)	Information visibility and inventory decisions in the reverse channel
Bi & Lin (2009)	The use of RFID tagged inventory to map supply networks
Manufacturing Studies	
Gaukler & Hausman (2008)	The use of RFID for mixed-model automotive assembly
Hozak & Collier (2008)	The use of RFID for data collection, shop floor control, and lot splitting
Empirical Studies	
Case Studies	
Karkkainen (2003)	Sainsbury's
Hardgrave, Aloysius, Goyal, & Spencer (2008); Hardgrave, Langford, Waller, & Miller (2008)	Wal-Mart
Loebbecke (2007)	Metro Group
Chow, Choy, Lee, & Lau (2006); Langer, Forman, Kekre, & Scheller-Wolf (2007)	GENCO
Holmqvist & Stefansson (2006a); Holmqvist & Stefansson (2006b)	Volvo's supply chain flow
Ngai, Cheng, Lai, Chai, Choi, & Sin (2007)	An RFID-based traceability system at a Hong Kong aircraft engineering company
Choy, So, Liu, Lau, & Kwok (2007)	An RFID system to improve supply chain visibility for a medium-sized third-party logistics company
Kim, Yang, & Kim (2008)	The use of a RFID-based logistics system by Korean third-party logistics provider CJ-Global Logistics Service
Pa°lsson (2008)	A container tracking study of a large packaging company and its logistics service providers

continued on following page

Table 1. Continued

Survey Papers	
Lin & Ho (2009a & 2009b)	Factors influencing the adoption of RFID technology and the relation between RFID technology adoption and supply chain performance for logistics companies in China.
Pedroso, Zwicker, & de Souza (2009)	The adoption of RFID technology by large Brazilian companies
Min, Zhou, Jui, Wang, & Chen (2003)	The adoption of RFID technology in China
Riedel, Pawar, Torroni, & Ferrari (2008)	The readiness of companies to adopt RFID technology in the UK Logistics industry
Hossain & Prybutok (2008); Muller-Seitz, Dautzenberg, Creusen, & Stromereder (2009)	Factors affecting consumer acceptance of RFID technology by developing and testing a theoretical model that contextualizes the technology acceptance model (TAM) within the context of RFID technology
Vijayaraman & Osyk (2006)	An empirical study to determine the status of RFID implementation among companies in the US warehousing industry
Li, Godon, & Visich (2010)	The status of RFID implementation in US companies' supply chain

RFID adoption within the next two years, 27% were considering adoption within the next two year period, and only 12% were adopting RFID technology in their companies. Hence, it seems that RFID adoption was not very significant in the logistics industry.

Many studies have attempted to identify reasons and motivations for adopting RFID. For example, Li et al. (2010) classified firms into two groups: considering group, and pilot / implementing/ completed (PIC) group. For firms in the considering group, inventory management (i.e. increased inventory visibility; better inventory tracking and tracing; and inventory reduction), competitive decision (i.e. strategic initiative; and competitive advantage), and cost reduction (i.e. reduced labour cost, overall internal operation costs and overall supply chain costs; and improved return on supply chain assets and return on internal assets) were the most important motiviation for RFID adoption. Firms in the PIC group had the same important motivations as for the considering group, but in different order; inventory management was the most important motivation for considering group, but competitive decision was the most important motivation for PIC group. Likewise, Vijayaraman & Osyk (2006) observed the top reason for adopting RFID was the compliance requirement

from Wal-Mart followed by better inventory and supply chain visibility.

On the other hand, Riedel et al. (2008) disclosed that the major motivations were to increase the cargo security, reduce the amount of lost/stolen/ wasted items, speed up operations and reduce the errors and costs due to human labour. Furthermore, the findings by Pedroso et al. (2009) showed that the main motivation was to reduce cost and improve service levels to clients.

These studies have found that RFID has been used in a wide variety of area and processes. For example, Li et al. (2010) found that shipping, order put-away, order picking, receiving and logistics were the most cited responses. According to Chow et al. (2007), RFID is utilized in more areas of logistics activities including broken case picking, material handling, sortation and accumulation, cross docking, unitising and shipping.

Some of the studies attempted identify how strategic a priority companies consider RFID adoption. For example, Riedel et al. (2008) found that over half of the respondents considered RFID adoption as a priority in the UK logistics industry. In opposition, 39% answered that RFID adoption was not a priority.

More studies have looked into the barriers to adoption and associated reasons for not implementing RFID (Riedel, et al., 2008; Pedroso, et al., 2009; Li, et al., 2010; Speckman and Sweeney, 2006). These studies suggested that the main reason for not having RFID initiative was lack of financial resources, and the main concern/ barrier in RFID implementation is usually cost. Riedel et al. (2008) justified the reasons of this result by arguing on the high initial investment (tags, readers, printers, middleware, software, consultancy support, employee training, system tuning, trials, redefining and developing new internal processes, and, labour to manage the change). On the other hand, Li et al. (2010) found that the major reasons for not considering RFID were lack of a business case and a lack of understanding. They realized that financial issues had a moderate impact on the adoption of RFID. However, their results also revealed that financial issues (i.e. deployment costs too high; return on investment too low; payback period too long; costs of maintaining the system too high; costs to deploy incorrect; and funding not adequate) were the main issues in RFID implementation.

Most of the above studies have attempted to understand the practical issues related to the adoption of RFID. However, in spite of very interesting findings on RFID in previous studies, we have found that there is relatively less number of studies that attempted to take theoretical perspectives on the adoption of RFID. We consider this as a serious gap in the literature and hence provide one such theoretical perspective using the theory of diffusion of innovations. We provide a brief description of this theory and develop our hypotheses based on tenets of this theory in the next section.

INNOVATION DIFFUSION THEORY AND THE RESEARCH HYPOTHESES

The theory of innovation diffusion (Rogers, 1995) is one of the most widely applied theories in the prediction of organizational level technology adoption (Wang et al., 2010). It provides the basic model of how perceived innovation characteristics affect the rate of adoption of innovation (Zhang et al., 2010).

Five Characteristics of Innovation

Rogers (1995) proposed five attributes that are key influencers on the acceptance of an innovation. These characteristics are relative advantage, compatibility, complexity, trialability and observability.

Relative Advantage

Relative advantage is the extent to which people believe that the innovation is better than the traditional one. This is ususally measured in terms that matter to users, like economic advantage, social prestige, convenience, or satisfaction. Potential adopters need to see an advantage for adopting the innovation, which may include meeting customer requirement (Foster, et al., 2005); decreasing costs (Foster, et al., 2005; Wang, et al., 2010; Luo, et al., 2007); gaining competitive advantage (Foster, et al., 2005); improving efficiency (Foster, et al., 2005); quick data capture and analysis (Wang, et al., 2010); improving security of cargos (Riedel, et al., 2008); saving time and effort (Luo, et al., 2007); improving tracking of containers (Riedel, et al., 2008); improving the accuracy of stock records (Riedel, et al., 2008); improving safety (Luo, et al., 2007); immediacy of reward (Luo, et al., 2007); improving Return On Investment (ROI) (Li, et al., 2010); and reducing paperwork (Wang, et al., 2010).

Robinson (2009) highlighted that the greater the perceived relative advantage of an innovation, the more rapid its rate of adoption is likely to be. In this study, we use intention to use RFID as the dependent variable and the following hypothesis is proposed to link relative advantage of using RFID with the intention to use:

H1: Relative advantage will have a positive effect on intention to use RFID.

Complexity

Complexity is the extent to which an innovation is perceived as relatively difficult to understand and use (Wang, et al., 2010). New innovations that are difficult to understand and that require the adopter to develop new skills and understandings may be adopted less rapidly than other innovations, and it may take users a long time to understand and implement the technology (Robinson, 2009; Wang, et al., 2010). Hence, people may not have confidence in the RFID technology if it is complex to understand (Wang, et al., 2010). The following hypothesis is proposed:

H2: Complexity will have a negative effect on intention to use RFID

Compatibility

Compatibility is the degree to which an innovation is perceived as consistent with the existing values, past values, and needs of potential adopters (Luo, et al., 2007). In the context of logistics processes, we primarily consider RFID compatibility in the following aspects:

- Compatibility between the RFID system and the existing information infrastructure (Wang, et al., 2010);
- Compatibility with the existing regulation in the logistics industry (Luo, et al., 2007);
- Compatibility between the RFID system and the firm's existing experiences/practices with similar systems (e.g. barcode) (Wang, et al., 2010);
- Compatibility with a firm's existing beliefs/values (Wang, et al., 2010).

New innovations that is incompatible with their values, norms or practices will not be adopted as rapidly as an innovation that is compatible (Robinson, 2009). Thus, high compatibility has been identified as a facilitator for innovation adoption (Wang, et al., 2010). The following hypothesis is proposed:

H3: Compatibility will have a positive effect on intention to use RFID

Trialability

Trialability is the extent to which people believe that there are chances for the innovation to be experienced before deciding whether to adopt it or not (Zhang, et al., 2010). Potential adopters want the availability of testing before actual adoption (Foster, et al., 2005). However, Wang et al. (2010) excluded the trialability in their research model. This is because they observed that trialability was not consistently related to innovation adoption. We faced similar findings during our pilot phase of our questionnaire survey. Hence, we have not included this attribute for further analysis in this study.

Observability of Benefits

Observability is the degree to which the results of an innovation are visible to others (Luo, et al., 2007). Potential adopters want to see observable results from an innovation (Foster, et al., 2005). RFID can save time (Luo, et al., 2007); reduce cost (Li, et al., 2010); reduce inventory (Luo, et al., 2007; Li, et al., 2010); increase ROI (Li, et al., 2010); improve customer service level (Luo, et al., 2007); better item tracking and tracing (Li, et al., 2010); improve accuracy (Li, et al., 2010); improve item security (Li, et al., 2010); improve information sharing (Li, et al., 2010); and improve inventory visibility (Li, et al., 2010). The easier it is for individuals to observe the benefits of RFID, the more likely they are to adopt it (Robinson, 2009). This leads to our next hypothesis.

H4: Observability of benefits (excluding green benefits) will have a positive effect on intention to use RFID

Observability of Green Benefits

Given the growing interests in environmentally friendly technologies, green issues have gained great attention by the practitioners of operations and supply chain management in the last decade (Dukovska-Popovska, et al., 2010; Krigslund et al., 2010). Hence it will be worthwhile to specifically examine the influence of green characteristics on the company's intention to use RFID. Accordingly, *observability of green benefits* of RFID includes supplier selection and sustainability improvement; tracking and tracing emission rates and wastes; tracking and tracing of energy, materials and virgin materials consumption; transportation and distribution planning; and disassembly of returned goods and distribution of parts/materials (Dukovska-Popovska et al., 2010).

Though there are no further research studies on environmental issues of RFID technology, there are several studies that look at environmental issues of technology in general. For example, Yi and Thomas (2007) have reviewed the literature on environmental impacts of Internet and Communication Technologies, and have emphasized issues related to energy consumption, transport, pollution, waste, material efficiency, etc. A similar view has been shared by Tsoulfas and Pappis (2006) on environmental issues in the design of supply chains. Thus we see that the environmental issues raised by (Dukovska-Popovska et al., 2010) in the context of RFID have been shared by researchers in the wider context of adoption of technologies in general.

Hence, our final hypothesis links observability of green benefits of RFID with intention to use the technology.

H5: Observability of green benefits will have a positive effect on intention to use RFID.

As highlighted earlier, though our review of RFID in Section 2.2 has highlighted several interesting studies, there is a paucity of studies that used the theoretical perspective of diffusion of innovations to understand the adoption of RFID. To our knowledge, very few studies have used this innovation diffusion theory to understand RFID diffusion, especially in the logistics industry. We fill this gap and this is one of the contributions of our study. In fact, we extend the innovation diffusion theory by including the important environmental sustainability (i.e., green) context. To our knowledge, there is no study that has integrated environmental benefits of RFID in the context of innovation diffusion. This is our second contribution in this paper.

The research model used in this study is presented in Figure 1.

RESEARCH METHODOLOGY

This study has used a questionnaire survey to validate the research model shown in Figure 1 and to verify the hypotheses. Details of our research methodology are provided in this section.

Construct Measures

An intensive literature study was undertaken to identify the principal construct measures. Though innovation diffusion theory has been used in the past to understand the influence of various characteristics of technologies, none of them used Innovation Diffusion theory to develop their instruments in the specific context of the use of RFID for the logistics industry. Hence measurement items were modified to fit the RFID context specialized in the logistics industry. Moreover, measurement items for green benefits have not been tested in existing literature studies, and are newly added in this study. Appendix 1 shows the full references of the measurement items.

The questionnaire consisted of two parts: one for RFID adoption, and the other one for assessing the measurement items relating to Innovation Diffusion theory. A 7-point Likert Scale has been used for all items in this study, with the responses rated as follows: 1 as strongly disagree, 2 as disagree, 3 as somewhat disagree, 4 as neither agree nor disagree, 5 as somewhat agree, 6 as agree, and 7 as strongly agree.

In contrast to most of previous studies, we explored our dependent variable, i.e. intention to use RFID, in more detail. Rather than merely measuring whether a company was an adopter or non-adopter of RFID, we also measured whether a company was an adopter or non-adopter of barcode system, the stage of RFID adoption at which the company positioned itself during the questionnaire survey (whether a company is widely adopting RFID, limitedly adopting RFID, piloting/testing RFID, already planned to invest RFID, carrying out investigation, not applying at the moment, or never investigated RFID applicability), how strategic a priority the company considered RFID adoption (whether a company considers RFID adoption as low priority, high priority, not a priority, or neutral), whether the company planned to maintain, decrease, or increase the use of RFID in future, and, how would the company predict the future trend of RFID adoption in the logistics industry (whether a company predicts the future trend of adoption in the Logistics industry as maintaining, decreasing, or increasing). All questions regarding adoption are multiple-choice questions.

Prior to sending the questionnaire to respondents, we pilot tested the questionnaire with selected academic experts and a few practitioners. The pilot survey was useful to refine the questions to add more clarity. Another major benefit of the pilot survey was the feedback that the innovation characteristic of trialability was not much relevant. Since this observation was also supported by Wang et al. (2010), we removed trialability from the questionnaire and from further analysis.

Sample Selection and Data Collection

During June – August 2011, data for this study were collected using a questionnaire survey administered in the UK. Contact details of UK Logistics companies, whose main activity code is included in the standard industrial classification

Figure 1. The research model

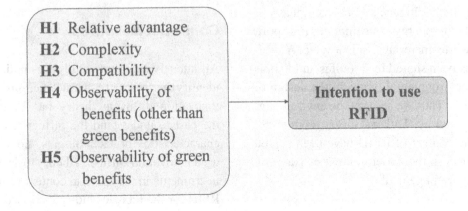

(SIC) as shown in Table 2, were obtained from the Chartered Institute of Logistics and Transport in the UK (CILT(UK)).

Companies involved in the above SIC codes were selected as the sample population of this study following suggestions from an important previous study that conducted surveys on the UK Logistics industry (Riedel et al., 2008). The CILT (UK) is a pre-eminent independent professional body for individuals associated with logistics, supply chains and all transport throughout their careers. The CILT (UK) was chosen to be the major source of companies' contact information because its Knowledge Centre has the most comprehensive, accurate and up-to-date database of Logistics companies in the UK. According to their database, there are 71905 companies engaged in the UK Logistics industry shown by the above SIC codes. Of those 71905 companies, 3533 companies were randomly selected. Cover letters with links to the online questionnaires were emailed to the owners/managers/directors of those 3533 companies. Since the response rate was too low, another 200 companies from the 71905 companies in the UK Logistics industry were randomly selected. Questionnaires with cover letters and stamped addressed envelopes were mailed to managers/directors of

those 200 companies. As an attempt to maximize the response rate, reminders were sent once per fortnight to companies via email during the survey period (i.e. June - August 2011). Consequently, a total of 174 questionnaires (consisting of 11 returned by post and 163 collected online) were received. Eliminating the incompletely filled-in questionnaires, the remaining number of valid questionnaires is a total of 107 (consisting of 4 completed questionnaires returned by post and 103 collected online).

Measure Purification and Data Analysis

The Statistical Package for the Social Sciences (SPSS), a computer program for statistical analysis, has been used to run factor analysis, reliability analysis, correlation analysis and regression analysis in this study.

Factor Analysis and Reliability Analysis

In this study, factor analysis has been first used to identify the relevant factors. In order to assess the fit between the items and their constructs, all of the primary factor loadings should be greater

Table 2. UK standard industry classification: SIC (2003)

Code	Trade Description
6010	Transport via railways
6024	Freight transport by road
6100	Water transport
6220	Non-scheduled air transport
6311	Cargo handling
6312	Storage and warehousing
6321	Other supporting land transport activities
6322	Other supporting water transport activities
6323	Other supporting air transport activities
6340	Activities of other transport agencies
6411	National post activities
6412	Courier activities other than national post activities

Source: Based on Riedel et al. (2008)

than 0.5 and have no cross-loadings (Wang et al., 2010). The appropriateness of the results of factor analysis are checked using a variety of measures. The reliability of factors is measured by the Cronbach's alpha. A Cronbach's alpha value of 0.65 or higher is used as an acceptable value for internal consistency of the measures (Hair et al., 2006). The average variance extracted (AVE) by a factor should be more than 0.50 (Hair et al., 2006). In addition, the Kaiser-Meyer-Olkin Measure of Sampling Adequacy (KMO) value of 0.50 or above with significant Bartlett's Test of Sphericity value (i.e. Sig. value is 0.05 or smaller) justify the use of factor analysis (Hair et al., 2006).

Correlation Analysis

To analyze the relationship between the dependent variable (i.e. intention to use RFID) and the independent variables, Pearson product-moment correlation coefficients are used to measure the related index between variables (Hair et al., 2006). According to Pallant (2010), the correlation coefficient value indicates the strength of the relationship between two variables. A correlation of 0 indicates no relationship, a correlation of 1 indicates a perfect positive correlation, and correlation of -1 indicates a perfect negative correlation (Pallant, 2010).

Regression Analysis

Regression analysis is used to evaluate the relationship between the dependent variable and one or more independent variables and to test the hypotheses of this study.

DATA ANALYSIS AND FINDINGS

Profile of Respondents

The survey was conducted across the UK Logistics industry. Almost 74% of the responding companies were classified as small to medium size companies, with less than 250 employees. The largest number (40%) of respondents operated in the logistics business, followed by freight forwarding (20%), warehousing and distribution (26%) businesses. A majority of respondents were managers (50%), followed by directors/board members (38%) and other positions (13%), including company owner, sales assistant, technical assistant, operation supervisor and logistics coordinator. Over 50% of respondents had more than 6 years of working experience in their current position.

Data Analysis

In the context of RFID, most of the questionnaire items loaded into factors as expected based on theory except for 8 items: T1S; T1CR; T5OBT_A; T5OBI; T5OBA; T5OBS; T5OBIS; and T5OBIV (please see Table 3 for full description of the items). These items loaded on to more than once factor and hence they were eliminated. Table 3 shows that the factor analysis resulted in five factors that measure the independent variables.

The Cronbach's alphas for independent variables ranged from 0.217 to 0.933. These values support the contention that all the factors, except for Complexity (T3U and T3D), had adequate reliability. As the Cronbach's alpha value of Complexity is below the threshold level of 0.65, items of Complexity were considered unacceptable and thus were removed. In addition, the AVE values of all variables exceed the minimum acceptable threshold level of 50%, suggesting a good fit of the internal structure of the model.

As shown in Table 3, the KMO values of all variables are 0.50 or above, and the Bartlett's test is significant as all Significance (Sig.) values are smaller than 0.05 except for Complexity that had been removed. Therefore factor analysis for the independent variables is appropriate.

The results of the factor analysis and reliability analysis for the dependent variable (Intention to Use) are shown in Table 4. It shows that the factor analysis resulted in one factor for the dependent variable, i.e. Intention to Use. The Cronbach's alpha of the dependent variable (intention to use) is 0.669, which is exceeding the acceptable coefficient alpha of 0.65, and thus this value support the view that the independent variable had adequate reliability. In addition, the AVE value is well above 50%, suggesting a good fit of the internal structure of the model. As shown in Table 4, the KMO value of dependent variable is 0.50 or above, and the Bartlett's test is significant as the Sig. value is 0.000. Therefore factor analysis for the dependent variables is also appropriate.

Table 3. Confirmatory factor analysis and Cronbach's alpha for independent variables

Items		Component				
		1	**2**	**3**	**4**	**5**
1. Relative advantage						
T1D	My company expects RFID to help quick data capture and analysis.	.866				
T1R	My company expects RFID to help immediate reward.	.890				
T1RoI	My company expects RFID to help increase return on investment.	.907				
T1CA	My company expects RFID to help gain competitive advantage.	.910				
T1G	My company expects RFID to help improve company's green image.	.768				
T1S	My company expects RFID to help improve safety.	Eliminated, due to cross-loadings				
T1CR	My company expects RFID to help meet customer requirements.					
2. Compatibility						
T2I	RFID is compatible with existing information infrastructure.		.975			
T2R	RFID is compatible with the existing regulation in the Logistics industry.		.977			
T2E	RFID development is compatible with my firm's existing experiences/practices with similar systems.		.973			
T2B	The changes introduced by RFID are consistent with my firm's existing beliefs/values.		.737			
3. Complexity						
T3U	My company believes that RFID is complex to use.			.759		
T3D	My company believes that RFID development (i.e. procedures for facilitating wider adoptions) is a complex process.			.759		
4. Observability of Benefits						
T5OBRoI	My company observed return on investment is increased from RFID adoption.				.865	
T5OBCS	My company observed customer service level is improved from RFID adoption.				.845	
T5OBC	My company observed cost is saved from RFID adoption.				.910	
T5OBT	My company observed item tracking and tracking is improved from RFID adoption.				.830	

continued on following page

Table 3. Continued

Items		Component				
		1	2	3	4	5
T5OBT_A	My company observed time is saved from RFID adoption.					
T5OBI	My company observed inventory is reduced from RFID adoption.					
T5OBA	My company observed data accuracy is improved from RFID adoption.	Eliminated, due to cross-loadings Eliminated, due to cross-loadings				
T5OBS	My company observed item security is improved from RFID adoption.					
T5OBIS	My company observed information sharing is improved from RFID adoption.					
T5OBIV	My company observed inventory visibility is improved from RFID adoption.					
5. Observability of Green Characteristics						
T5OGTC	My company observed reduced emission of toxic components from RFID adoption.					.854
T5OGR	My company observed reduced resource consumption from RFID adoption.					.917
T5OGW	My company observed reduced wastes from RFID adoption.					.866
T5OGEC	My company observed reduced energy consumption from RFID adoption.					.825
T5OGP	My company observed reduced paperwork from RFID adoption.					.745
Cronbach's Aplha		0.914	0.933	0.217	0.882	0.890
Kaiser-Meyer-Olkin (KOM) Measure of Sampling Adequacy		0.840	0.787	0.500	0.766	0.621
Average Variance Extracted (AVE)		75.659	84.869	57.618	74.487	71.097
Sig.		0.000	0.000	0.413[a]	0.000	0.000

[a] The factor complexity has been removed from further analysis because of unacceptable Cronbach's alpha, KMO statistics and significance value.

Correlation Analysis

To analyze the relationship between the intention to use RFID and independent variables (including relative advantages; compatibility; observability of benefits; and observability of green characteristics), Pearson product-moment correlation coefficients are used to measure the related index between variables. As shown in Table 5, there were weak positive correlations between the intention to use and relative advantage, compatibility, observability of benefits and observability of green characteristics. In addition, the correlation between intention to use and observability of green characteristics is significant at the 0.05 level. However the correlations between intention to use and relative advantages; compatibility; and observability of benefits are not significant as they are above the acceptable significance level of 0.1.

Regression Analysis

Regression analysis was run for the variables of Innovation Diffusion theory. Results are shown in Table 6. The regression does not suffer from multi-collinearity issues since all variable inflation factors are well below the recommended threshold of 10 (Hair et al., 2006). However the results show insufficient evidence for support of three hypotheses (H1, H3, H4), suggesting that the

Table 4. Confirmatory factor analysis and Cronbach's alpha results for dependent variable

Items		Component
		1
Intention to Use		
FutureUiC	Company's future plan in RFID adoption	.895
FutureTiLI	Future trend of RFID adoption in the UK Logistics industry	.799
Stage	Stages regarding RFID adoption	.860
Cronbach's Aplha		0.669
Kaiser-Meyer-Olkin (KOM) Measure of Sampling Adequacy		0.682
Average Variance Extracted (AVE)		72.626
Sig. value		.000

Table 5. Correlation analysis

Predictors	Relative Advantages	Compatibility	Observability of Benefits	Observability of Green Characteristics	Intention to Use
Relative Advantages	1				
Compatibility	.815**	1			
Observability of Benefits	.669**	.762**	1		
Observability of Green Characteristics	.620**	.627**	.662**	1	
Intention to Use	.249	.245	.299	.438*	1

*. Correlation is significant at the 0.05 level (2-tailed)

**. Correlation is significant at the 0.01 level (2-tailed).

Table 6. Regression analysis predicting intention to use RFID

Predictors	Std Beta Coefficient	Hypotheses	Hypothesized Effect	Hypotheses Supported?
Relative advantages	-.011	H1	No effect	No
Compatibility	-.081	H3	No effect	No
Observability of benefits	.071	H4	No effect	No
Observability of green characteristics	.449*	H5	Significant	Yes

* Regression is significant at the level of $p < 0.1$

relative advantage, compatibility and observability of benefits of RFID are insignificant in predicting intention to use the technology. The results also show that the observability of green characteristics is significant predictor of intention to use RFID. These findings only support one hypothesis (H5).

Thus our results show that, except for the observability of green benefits, all other independent variables of Innovation Diffusion theory do not seem to have significant effect on the prediction of the intention to use RFID.

DISCUSSION

Our study has both theoretical and practical implications. In terms of theory, it not only applied the established diffusion of innovation theory to understand the diffusion of RFID but also extended the theory to include green issues. In terms of pratice, we have obtained a somewhat counterintuitive finding that only green characteristics of RFID influence its diffusion in UK logistics while we found no evidence for the signficance of other innovation characteristics.

This study has demonstrated the value of using the Innovation Diffusion theory to understand RFID technology and to explore the factors that affect company's intentions to use RFID technology. Our findings suggested that observability of green characteristics is significant in predicting the intention to use RFID technology. However, the results also showed that relative advantage of RFID, its compatibility wth existing systems in a firm and observability of its benefits may not have significant influence on the firm's intention to use RFID in the UK Logistics industry. We could not verify our second hypothesis on the influence of complexity because the variable did not have the required statistical properties for use in subsequent analysis.

Relative Advantage

Our study has found that relative advantage did not have a significant influence on RFID adoption in the UK Logistics industry. The finding is consistent with those of Wang et al. (2010) in the context of RFID adoption in Taiwanese manufacturing industry and is somewhat similar to the findings of Lee and Kim (2007) on Internet-based Information Systems implementation in Korea. Wang et al. (2010) found that, while relative advantage is not a significant discriminator, this does not mean that the firms perceive RFID technology has a low level of relative advantage. The average

perceived relative advantage levels of this study is 5.61, which is above the neutral assessment of 3.5. Thus this implied that companies believe adopting RFID is beneficial for their competitive edge. Therefore the reason for making relative advantage an insignificant discriminator of RFID adoption could be because firms still have no confidence in the RFID system, as it is still in its infancy and relatively new to them. As long as firms think that they do not have sufficient technical capabilities to adopt new technology, they would rather maintain their current systems (Wang et al., 2010).

Compatibility

Compatability was found to have no significant effect on company decisions to adopt RFID technology. The finding of this study is contrary to that of Wang et al. (2010) and Lee and Kim (2007). Wang et al. (2010) observed that compatibility is positively related to RFID adoption in the Taiwanese manufacturing industry. Lee and Kim (2007) explained that the implementation of new technology is encouraged when the system is compatibile with the existing work procedures and value systems because firms want to be less hampered by unstructured task characteristics and to have a greater opportunity to make the tasks compatible with processes. However, in this case, compatibility is not relevant to predicting the intention to use RFID. The average percieved relative advantage levels of this study is 5.64, which is above the neutral assessment of 3.5. Thus this indicated that most respondents felt that RFID technology is compatible with their organizational infrastructure, practices and needs. However, as most adoption decision (71%) is still at the dicussion stage with no firm commitment to pilot studies, there is a lack of perceived compatibility of RFID with the existing infrastructure and the uncertainties as to its compatiblity with organizational practices and thus this makes compatability an insignificant discriminator of RFID adoption.

Observability of Benefits

Our results show that observability of benefits did not have significant effect on company decisions to adopt RFID technology. In the prior literature, Zhang et al. (2010) studied the people's perceptions and attitudes toward adoping E-learning and explored key factors affecting E-learning adoption behavior in China. They observed that the perception on observability had the minimum weight in comparison with other factors. This implied that fewer companies believed that the benefits of RFID technology are visible compared to other factors. Moreover, Tornatzky & Klein (1982) found that of those five factors in Innovation Diffusion theory, only compatiblity, relative advantage and complexity are consistently related to innovation adoption. Hence many prior studies (e.g., Lee and Kim, 2007; Tornatzky & Klein, 1982; Wang et al., 2010) directly excluded the trialability and observability constructs in their research models. Tornatzky & Klein (1982) also reasoned that there may be a signficant relationship between observability and adoption of new technology because their findings were often hampered by the small number of studies reporting first-order correlational data.

Observability of Green Characteristics

As highlighted earlier, the inclusion of observability of green characteristics as an innovation attribute of RFID is a primary contribution of this research. Though this attribute was not included in prior studies on innovation diffusion, a very limited number of studies (e.g. Dukovska-Popovska et al., 2010) observed that the applications of RFID in supply chain operations could support a firm's green initiatives. Our finding reveal that observability of green characteristics is a significant predictor of RFID adoption and have positive effect

on company's intention to use RFID technology. It indicates that companies are progressively aware about the green-related practices or benefits in RFID adoption, which might be due to the raising attention of the escalating deterioration of the environment, such as increasing level of all types of pollutions, diminishing natural resources and overflowing waste sites, and also due to increasing enviromental pressures on companies by different stakeholders (Kassinis and Vafeas, 2006). Moreover, in comparison with other factors in the Innovation Diffusion theory, it is found that green-related benefits of RFID technology were more visible to companies. This may be due to the fact that the governments/authority bodies have been playing an important role by imposing climate policies to protect the environment in the EU bv For instance, under the EU Emission Trading Scheme (ETS), large companies within the EU are requested to monitor their carbon dioxide emissions and provide a report annually, which is to ensure the company has not exceeded their annual emission allowance (Dukovska-Popovska et al., 2010). Therefore, green issues in the logistics industry has gained progressive attention by companies and thus the observability of green characteristics has slightly positive effect on the company's intention to use RFID.

In summary, our finding that only green characteristics seem to have significant relationship with intention to adopt RFID is somewhat counter-intuitive but there have been several previous studies (Lee and Kim, 2007; Tornatzky & Klein, 1982; Wang et al., 2010) in which one or more characteristics of innovation have been found to be insignificant. Since the measurement scales for measuing innovation characteristics are drawn from existing literature, we do not think that the startling result is due to issues related to measurement. The main contribution from our study is the fact that green characteristics of RFID seem to be a rather predominantly important driver of its adoption in the UK logistics industry. Our study points to the need for expanding innovation characteristics to include environmental friendliness of technologies. It may be possible to expand measurement scales of innovation characteristics to include environmental benefits of new technologies. For example, relative advantage, complexity or trialability can also include some elements of environmental friendliness gained by using a technology. In this sense, this study suggests extention of the theory of diffusion of innovations from an environmental perspective.

CONCLUSION

Since RFID technology has been regarded an important technology that can provide strategic and operational advantages, it is necessary to understand what determines RFID adoption in the logistics industry. This study is to explore the level of current adoption and future trends of RFID technology, and to examine the influencing factors on RFID adoption in the UK logistics industry. Based on Innovation Diffusion theory (Rogers, 1995), this study developed and validated a research model to examine the influence of contextual factors on RFID adoption.

Our study has provided valuable insight into the determinants of RFID adoption in the UK logistics industry. We found that observability of green characteristics to be facilitators of RFID adoption. Contrary to prior literature and hypotheses of this study, the relative advantage, compatibility and observability of benefits are observed to have no effect on the companies' intention to use RFID. This might be due to the fact that, as RFID technology is still in its infancy and a significant number of implementation questions remain unanswered, firms may have doubts about whether RFID meets their benefits effectively. Furthermore, RFID tech-

nology may be in its early stages of development, where firms are influenced by mainstream fashions and tend to be cost sensitive and risk averse. Hence, companies may still prefer to wait and see how well and in what direction RFID technology develops. They will not apply RFID technology without solid proof of guaranteed performance and benefits. This study found one significant facilitator of RFID adoption (i.e. observability of green characteristics), which was not explored in the prior RFID adoption research. This may be due to the fact that the governments/authority bodies have been playing an important role by imposing climate policies to protect the environment in the EU (Dukovska-Popovska et al., 2010).

This study can be extended further. This study only explores the influences of factors on the adoption of RFID technology in UK logistics industry. While there are differences between the UK and other countries in political structures, cultural background, historical perspective, social value, and so on, logistics service providers in different countries may have different views on the influences of these influential factors on the adoption of RFID technology (Lin and Ho, 2009a). Hence it will be worthwhile to advance a cross-national comparative study on the adoption of RFID technology among logistics industries in the UK and in other countries (Lin and Ho, 2009a). This study explores the influences of factors on the adoption of RFID technology in UK logistics industry based on the Innovation Diffusion theory. It will be worthwhile to apply other technology adoption theories to take other possible influential factors on the adoption of RFID technology into considerations in further studies. Finally, more items to measure environmental friendliness of new technologies in terms the five innovation characteristics – relative advantage, compatibility, complexity, trialability and observability – can be included in future RFID studies.

REFERENCES

Acharyulu, G. (2007). RFID in the healthcare supply chain: improving performance through greater visibility. *The ICFAI Journal of Management Research, 6*(11), 32–45.

Angeles, R. (2005). RFID technologies: Supply-chain applications and implementation issues. *Information Systems Management, 22*(1), 51–65. doi:10.1201/1078/44912.22.1.20051201/85739.7

Attaran, M. (2007). RFID: An enabler of supply chain operations. *Supply Chain Management: An International Journal, 12*(4), 249–257. doi:10.1108/13598540710759763

Bi, H. H., & Lin, D. K. J. (2009). RFID-enabled discovery of supply networks. *IEEE Transactions on Engineering Management, 56*(1), 129–141. doi:10.1109/TEM.2008.922636

Bottani, E., & Rizzi, A. (2008). Economical assessment of the impact of RFID technology and EPC system on the fast-moving consumer goods supply chain. *International Journal of Production Economics, 112*(2), 548–569. doi:10.1016/j.ijpe.2007.05.007

Chande, A., Dhekane, S., Hemachandra, N., & Rangaraj, N. (2005). Perishable inventory management and dynamic pricing using RFID technology. *Sadhana, 30*(2/3), 445–462. doi:10.1007/BF02706255

Chow, H. K. H., Choy, K. L., & Lee, W. B. (2007). A dynamic logistics process knowledge-based system – An RFID multi-agent approach. *Knowledge-Based Systems, 20*(4), 357–372. doi:10.1016/j.knosys.2006.08.004

Chow, H. K. H., Choy, K. L., Lee, W. B., & Lau, K. C. (2006). Design of a RFID case-based resource management system for warehouse operations. *Expert Systems with Applications, 30*(4), 561–576. doi:10.1016/j.eswa.2005.07.023

Choy, K. L., So, S. C. K., Liu, J. J., Lau, H., & Kwok, S. K. (2007). Improving logistics visibility in a supply chain: An integrated approach with radio frequency technology. *International Journal of Integrated Supply Management, 3*(2), 135–155. doi:10.1504/IJISM.2007.011973

Dukovska-Popovska, I., Lim, M. K., Steger-Jensen, K., & Hvolby, H. H. (2010). RFID Technology to Support Environmentally Sustainable Supply Chain Management. In *Proceedings of for the IEEE International Conference on RFID-Technology and Applications*, (pp. 291-295). IEEE.

Foster, S., Scheepers, H., & Rahmati, N. (2005). RFIDs: From Invention to Innovation. *Communications of the IIMA, 5*(4), 1–10.

Gaukler, G. M., & Hausman, W. H. (2008). RFID in mixed-model automotive assembly operations: Process and quality cost savings. *IIE Transactions, 40*(11), 1083–1096. doi:10.1080/07408170802167654

Gaukler, G. M., Seifert, R. W., & Hausman, W. H. (2007). Item-Level RFID in the Retail Supply Chain. *Production and Operations Management, 16*(1), 65–76. doi:10.1111/j.1937-5956.2007.tb00166.x

Glabman, M. (2004). Room for tracking: RFID technology finds the way. *Materials Management in Health Care*, 26–38. PMID:15202205

Hair, F. J., Black, W. C., Babin, B. J., Anderson, R. E., & Tatham, R. L. (2006). *Multivariate Data Analysis* (6th ed.). Upper Saddle River, NJ: Pearson Prentice Hall.

Hardgrave, B., Aloysius, J., Goyal, S., & Spencer, J. (2008a). *Does RFID improve inventory accuracy? A preliminary analysis.* Fayetteville, AR: Information Technology Research Institute, Sam M. Walton College of Business, University of Arkansas.

Hardgrave, B., Langford, S., Waller, M., & Miller, R. (2008b). Measuring the impact of RFID on out of stocks at Wal-Mart. *MIS Quarterly Executive*, *7*(4), 181–192.

Heese, H. S. (2007). Inventory Record Inaccuracy, Double Marginalization, and RFID Adoption. *Production and Operations Management*, *16*(5), 542–553. doi:10.1111/j.1937-5956.2007.tb00279.x

Holmqvist, M., & Stefansson, G. (2006a). Mobile RFID: A Case from Volvo on Innovation in SCM. In *Proceedings of the 39th Hawaii International Conference on System Sciences*. IEEE.

Holmqvist, M., & Stefansson, G. (2006b). 'Smart goods' and mobile RFID: A case with innovation from Volvo. *Journal of Business Logistics*, *27*(2), 251–272. doi:10.1002/j.2158-1592.2006.tb00225.x

Hosaka, R. (2004). Feasibility study of convenient automatic identification system of medical articles using LF-Band RFID in hospital. *Systems and Computers in Japan*, *35*(10), 571–578. doi:10.1002/scj.10581

Hou, J. L., & Huang, C. H. (2006). Quantitative performance evaluation of RFID applications in the supply chain of the printing industry. *Industrial Management & Data Systems*, *106*(1/2), 96–120. doi:10.1108/02635570610641013

Hozak, K., & Collier, D. A. (2008). RFID as an enabler of improved manufacturing performance. *Decision Sciences Journal*, *39*(4), 859–881. doi:10.1111/j.1540-5915.2008.00214.x

Jones, M. A., Wyld, D. C., & Totten, J. W. (2005). The adoption of RFID technology in the retail supply chain. *The Coastal Business Journal*, *4*(1), 29–42.

Karaer, O., & Lee, H. L. (2007). Managing the Reverse Channel with RFID-Enabled Negative Demand Information. *Production and Operations Management*, *16*(5), 625–645. doi:10.1111/j.1937-5956.2007.tb00285.x

Karkkainen, M. (2003). Increasing efficiency in the supply chain for short shelf life goods using RFID tagging. *International Journal of Retail & Distribution Management*, *31*(10), 529–536. doi:10.1108/09590550310497058

Kassinis, G., & Vafeas, N. (2006). Stakeholder pressures and Environmental performance. *Academy of Management Journal*, *49*(15), 145–159. doi:10.5465/AMJ.2006.20785799

Kim, C., Yang, K., & Kim, J. (2008). A strategy for third-party logistics systems: A case analysis using the blue ocean strategy. *Omega*, *36*(4), 522–534. doi:10.1016/j.omega.2006.11.011

Krigslund, R., Popovski, P., Dukovska-Popovska, I., Pedersen, G. F., & Manev, B. (2010). Using ICT in Greening: The Role of RFID. In *Towards Green ICT* (pp. 97–116). Denmark: River Publishers.

Langer, N., Forman, C., Kekre, S., & Scheller-Wolf, A. (2007). Assessing the impact of RFID on return center logistics. *Interfaces*, *37*(6), 501–514. doi:10.1287/inte.1070.0308

Lee, L. S., Fiedler, K. D., & Smith, J. S. (2008). Radio frequency identification (RFID) implementation in the service sector: A customer-facing diffusion model. *International Journal of Production Economics*, *112*(2), 587–600. doi:10.1016/j.ijpe.2007.05.008

Lee, S., & Kim, K. (2007). Factors affecting the implementation success of Internet-based information systems. *Computers in Human Behavior*, *23*(4), 1853–1880. doi:10.1016/j.chb.2005.12.001

Li, S., Godon, D., & Visich, J. K. (2010). An exploratory study of RFID implementation in the supply chain. *Management Research Review, 33*(10), 1005–1015. doi:10.1108/01409171011084003

Li, S., & Visich, J. K. (2006). Radio frequency identification: Supply chain impact and implementation challenges. *International Journal of Integrated Supply Management, 2*(4), 407–424. doi:10.1504/IJISM.2006.009643

Lin, C. Y. & Ho, Y. H. (2009a). RFID technology adoption and supply chain performance: an empirical study in China's logistics industry. *Supply Chain Management: An International Journal*, 369-378.

Lin, C. Y., & Ho, Y. H. (2009b). An Empirical Study on the Adoption of RFID Technology for Logistics Service Providers in China. *International Business Research, 2*(1), 23–36. doi:10.5539/ibr.v2n1p23

Lin, L. C. (2009). An integrated framework for the development of radio frequency identification technology in the logistics and supply chain management. *Computers & Industrial Engineering, 57*(3), 832–842. doi:10.1016/j.cie.2009.02.010

Loebbecke, C. (2007). Piloting RFID along the supply chain: A case analysis. *Electronic Markets, 17*(1), 29–37. doi:10.1080/10196780601136773

Luo, Z., Tan, Z., Ni, Z., & Yen, B. (2007). Analysis of RFID Adoption in China. In *Proceedings of IEEE International Conference on e-Business Engineering*, (pp. 315-318). IEEE.

Luyskens, C., & Loebbecke, C. (2007). RFID Adoption: Theoretical Concepts and Their Practical Application in Fashion. In *Organizational Dynamics of Technology-based Innovation: Diversifying the Research Agenda* (pp. 345–361). Boston: Springer.

McFarlane, D., & Sheffi, Y. (2003). The impact of automatic identification on supply chain operations. *International Journal of Logistics Management, 14*(1), 1–17. doi:10.1108/09574090310806503

Min, H., Zhou, F., Jui, S. L., Wang, T. Y., & Chen, X. J. (2003). *RFID in China*. Shanghai: Auto-ID Center.

Moon, K. L., & Ngai, E. W. T. (2008). The adoption of RFID in fashion retailing: A business value-added framework. *Industrial Management & Data Systems, 108*(5), 596–612. doi:10.1108/02635570810876732

Muller-Seitz, G., Dautzenberg, K., Creusen, U., & Stromereder, C. (2009). Customer acceptance of RFID technology: Evidence from the German electronic retail sector. *Journal of Retailing and Consumer Services, 16*(1), 31–39. doi:10.1016/j.jretconser.2008.08.002

Ngai, E., Cheng, T., Lai, K. H., Chai, P., Choi, Y., & Sin, R. (2007). Development of an RFID-based traceability system: Experiences and lessons learned from an aircraft engineering company. *Production and Operations Management, 16*(5), 554–568. doi:10.1111/j.1937-5956.2007.tb00280.x

Ozelkan, E., & Galambose, A. (2008). When does RFID make business sense for managing supply chains? *International Journal of Information Systems and Supply Chain Management, 1*(1), 15–47. doi:10.4018/jisscm.2008010102

Pallant, J. (2010). *SPSS Survival Manual*. Open University Press, McGraw-Hill Education.

Palsson, H. (2008). *Using RFID technology captured data to control material flows*. La Jolla, CA: Academic Press.

Pedroso, M. C., Zwicker, R., & de Souza, C. A. (2009). RFID adoption: Framework and survey in large Brazilian companies. *Industrial Management & Data Systems, 109*(7), 877–897. doi:10.1108/02635570910982256

Riedel, J., Pawar, K. S., Torroni, S., & Ferrari, E. (2008). A survey of Rfid awareness and use in the UK logistics industry. In *Dynamics in Logistics* (pp. 105–115). Springer Berlin Heidelberg. doi:10.1007/978-3-540-76862-3_9

Riemenschneider, C., Hardgrave, B., & Armstrong, D. (2007). *Is there a business case for RFID*. Fayetteville, AR: Information Technology Research Institute, Sam M. Walton College of Business, University of Arkansas

Robinson, L. (2009). *A summary of Diffusion of Innovations*. Available at: htpp://www.enablingchange.com.au/Summary_Diffusion_Theory.pdf

Rogers, E. M. (1995). *Diffusion of innovations*. New York: Free Press.

Roh, J. J., Kunnathur, A., & Tarafdar, M. (2009). Classification of RFID adoption: An expected benefits approach. *Information & Management, 46*(6), 357–363. doi:10.1016/j.im.2009.07.001

Rong, S. (2004). *Radio Frequency Identification (RFID) and Its Application in the Library*. Hangzhou: The Library of Hangzhou Teacher's College.

Schmitt, P., Thiesse, F., & Fleisch, E. (2007). *Adoption and diffusion of RFID technology in the automotive industry*. St. Gallen, Switzerland: 15th European Conference on Information Systems.

Spekman, R., & Sweeney, P. (2006). RFID: From concept to implementation. *International Journal of Physical Distribution & Logistics Management, 36*(10), 736–754. doi:10.1108/09600030610714571

Tajima, M. (2007). Strategic value of RFID in supply chain management. *Journal of Purchasing and Supply Management, 13*(4), 261–273. doi:10.1016/j.pursup.2007.11.001

Tornatzky, L. G., & Klein, K. J. (1982). Innovation Characteristics and Innovation Adoption Implementation: A Meta-Analysis of Findings. *IEEE Transactions on Engineering Management, EM-29*(1), 28–45. doi:10.1109/TEM.1982.6447463

Tsoulfas, G. T., & Pappis, C. P. (2006). Environmental principles applicable to supply chains design and operation. *Journal of Cleaner Production, 14*(18), 1593–1602. doi:10.1016/j.jclepro.2005.05.021

Twist, D. C. (2005). The impact of radio frequency identification on supply chain facilities. *Journal of Facilities Management, 3*(3), 226–239. doi:10.1108/14725960510808491

Uckun, C., Karaesmen, F., & Savas, S. (2008). Investment in improved inventory accuracy in a decentralized supply chain. *International Journal of Production Economics, 113*(2), 546–566. doi:10.1016/j.ijpe.2007.10.012

Ustundag, A., & Tanyas, M. (2009). The impacts of radio frequency identification (RFID) technology on supply chain costs. *Transportation Research Part E, Logistics and Transportation Review, 45*(1), 29–38. doi:10.1016/j.tre.2008.09.001

Vijayaraman, B. S., & Osyk, B. A. (2006). An empirical study of RFID implementation in the warehousing industry. *International Journal of Logistics Management, 17*(1), 6–20. doi:10.1108/09574090610663400

Visich, J. K., Li, S., & Khumawala, B. M. (2007). Enhancing product recovery value in closed-loop supply chains with RFID. *Journal of Managerial Issues, 19*(3), 436–452.

Wamba, S. F. (2012). Achieving supply chain integration using RFID technology: The case of emerging intelligent B-to-B e-commerce processes in a living laboratory. *Business Process Management Journal, 18*(1), 58–81. doi:10.1108/14637151211215019

Wang, Y. M., Wang, Y. S., & Yang, Y. F. (2010). Understanding the determinants of RFID adoption in the manufacturing industry. *Technological Forecasting and Social Change, 77*(5), 803–815. doi:10.1016/j.techfore.2010.03.006

Wicks, A. M., Visich, J. K., & Li, S. H. (2006). Radio frequency identification applications in hospital environments. *Hospital Topics: Research and Perspectives on Healthcare, 84*(3), 3–8. doi:10.3200/HTPS.84.3.3-9 PMID:16913301

Yi, L., & Thomas, H. R. (2007). A review of research on the environmental impact of e-business and ICT. *Environment International, 33*(6), 841–849. doi:10.1016/j.envint.2007.03.015 PMID:17490745

Zhang, L., Wen, H., Li, D., Fu, Z., & Cui, S. (2010). E-learning adoption intention and its key influence factors based on innovation adoption theory. *Mathematical and Computer Modelling, 51*(11-12), 1428–1432. doi:10.1016/j.mcm.2009.11.013

KEY TERMS AND DEFINITIONS

Compatibility: It is the degree to which an innovation is perceived as consistent with the existing values, past values, and needs of potential adopters.

Complexity: It is the extent to which an innovation is perceived as relatively difficult to understand and use.

Diffusion of Innovations: It is a theory to help understand how new innovations get accepted at an organizational level.

Green Characteristics: The characteristics of a technology that helps in improving environmental sustainability of an organization that embraces the technology.

Observability: It is the degree to which the results of an innovation are visible to others.

Relative Advantage: It is the extent to which people believe that an innovation is better than the traditional one.

RFID: Radio frequency identification (RFID) is one type of auto-identification technology that uses radio frequency (RF) waves to identify, track and locate individual physical items.

Trialability: It is the extent to which people believe that there are chances for the innovation to be experienced before deciding whether to adopt it or not.

APPENDIX

Table 7. Measurement items of independent variables

Variables	Measurement Items
Relative advantage (Wang et al., 2010; Foster et al., 2005; Luo et al., 2007)	My company expects RFID to help quick data capture and analysis.
	My company expects RFID to help immediate reward.
	My company expects RFID to help increase return on investment.
	My company expects RFID to help improve safety.
	My company expects RFID to help meet customer requirements.
	My company expects RFID to help gain competitive advantage.
	My company expects RFID to help improve company's green image.
Complexity (Wang et al., 2010)	My company believes that RFID is complex to use.
	My company believes that RFID development (i.e. procedures for facilitating wider adoptions) is a complex process.
Compatibility (Wang et al., 2010; Luo et al., 2007)	RFID is compatible with existing information infrastructure.
	RFID is compatible with the existing regulation in the Logistics industry.
	RFID development is compatible with my firm's existing experiences/practices with similar systems.
	The changes introduced by RFID are consistent with my firm's existing beliefs/values.
Observability of benefits (Li et al., 2010; Luo et al., 2007)	My company observed time is saved from RFID adoption.
	My company observed inventory is reduced from RFID adoption.
	My company observed return on investment is increased from RFID adoption.
	My company observed customer service level is improved from RFID adoption.
	My company observed cost is saved from RFID adoption.
	My company observed item tracking and tracking is improved from RFID adoption.
	My company observed data accuracy is improved from RFID adoption.
	My company observed item security is improved from RFID adoption.
	My company observed information sharing is improved from RFID adoption.
	My company observed inventory visibility is improved from RFID adoption.
Observability of Green characteristics (Krigslund et al, 2010; Dukovska-Popovska et al., 2010)	My company observed reduced emission of toxic components from RFID adoption.
	My company observed reduced resource consumption from RFID adoption.
	My company observed reduced wastes from RFID adoption.
	My company observed reduced energy consumption from RFID adoption.
	My company observed reduced paperwork from RFID adoption.

Chapter 9
Data Management Issues in RFID Applications

A. Anny Leema
B. S. Abdur Rahman University, India

M. Hemalatha
Karpagam University, India

ABSTRACT

Radio Frequency Identification (RFID) refers to wireless technology that uses radio waves to automatically identify items within a certain proximity. It is being widely used in various applications, but there is reluctance in the deployment of RFID due to the high cost involved and the challenging problems found in the observed colossal RFID data. The obtained data is of low quality and contains anomalies like false positives, false negatives, and duplication. To enhance the quality of data, cleaning is the essential task, so that the resultant data can be applied for high-end applications. This chapter investigates the existing physical, middleware, and deferred approaches to deal with the anomalies found in the RFID data. A novel hybrid approach is developed to solve data quality issues so that the demand for RFID data will certainly grow to meet the user needs.

INTRODUCTION

RFID is a wireless identification technology that allows data to be transmitted from an RFID tag to the compatible reader. It is used to describe a system that transmits the identity (in the form of a unique serial number) of an object or person using radio waves. This process involves tagging items with a transmitter which will emit bursts of information, including, and is not limited to the range, the identification of the tag. However, this technique is grouped under the broad category of automatic identification technologies. This technology is said to be an ADC (Automatic data capturing technology) that facilitates object tracking and identification using radio frequency waves which can work in very harsh environment. It has achieved significant growth in various fields like military, airline, library, security, manufacturing companies, healthcare, agriculture and education. The collected data about the objects is entered directly into computer systems without human participation. Bar code is another data collection technology compared to RFID but each has unique

DOI: 10.4018/978-1-4666-6308-4.ch009

characteristics valuable under varying conditions. The cost of printing a barcode is cheaper than creating an RFID tag, but the RFID based Electronic Product Code (EPC) are much in use because in Barcode technology an optical reader is required to read the data manually while in RFID, data is read through the radio signals from the RFID tag. The immense attractiveness of RFID technology is no line of sight is required between the tag and the reader. It supports a larger set of unique IDs than bar codes, and can incorporate additional data such as product type, manufacturer and even measure environmental factors such as temperature. RFID systems consist of three component's tag, reader and antenna. Tag is a small, low cost device used to uniquely identify an object. There are readers that can read more than 100 tags simultaneously, which is not possible in the barcode. It is widely used in various applications and the data collected from the RFID reader is colossal and complex that cannot be processed using existing database systems. It is an improvement over bar codes because the tags have read and write capabilities and the data stored on RFID tags can be changed, updated and locked.

RADIO FREQUENCY IDENTIFICATION

Radio frequency identification technology (RFID) has moved from obscurity into mainstream applications that help speed the handling of manufactured goods and materials. RFID tags are broadly classified as active and passive tags. The comparison between Active tag and passive tag is depicted in Table 1. Active tag has internal power source and the written data on the tag can be modified or rewritten. It is of high cost and less life duration when compared to the passive tag. Passive tag has its own demand because of its long life duration and less cost. It doesn't have an internal power source and it depends upon the reader to get energized. It is smaller and lighter than active tags but has a shorter communication range and requires a high powered reader. Tag with passive type is composed of three parts: comprises an antenna, part of semiconductor chip attached to the antenna, and also has some form of encapsulation. The tag comes in a variety of capabilities which includes read-only and read-write. (Chatterjee & Timande, 2012) says the tag reader is responsible for powering and communicating with a tag. The RFID Reader is used to interrogate the zone to discover tags within proximity of the reader range (Chen, 2006). Once the tag is discovered, captures its identification along with the reader's ID and the timestamp of the observation are also recorded. All this information is then passed through the Middleware where initial filtration is done to avoid data anomalies being recorded. Then finally, collected information will then be processed and stored within a database ready to be queried for future analysis.

RFID DESIGN APPROACH

The design approach of RFID exists for transferring power from the reader to the tag based on magnetic induction and electromagnetic (EM) wave capture follows two different design approaches: These two designs take advantage of the EM properties associated with an RF antenna the *near field* and the *far field*. The two fields can transfer enough power to a remote tag to sustain its operation typically between $10\,\mu W$ and $1\,MW$, on the basis of the tag type.

The near-field coupling is the most straightforward approach for implementing a passive RFID system. This Near field coupling technique is generally applied to RFID systems operating in the LF and HF bands with relatively short reading distances well within the radian sphere defined by $\lambda/2\pi$. The frequency operated in the near field (125 kHz, 13.56 MHz) is more reliable in many applications where read distance is not the major factor, and the properties of materials present near

Table 1. Comparisons between active and passive tag

	Comparison of Active RFID with Passive RFID	
	Active RFID	Passive RFID
Power	Battery Powered	No Internal Power
Communication Range	Long range (100 m +)	Short range (3m to 6m)
Per tag Cost	$15 - $100	$0.15-$5.00
Fixed infrastructure cost	Lower cheaper interrogators	Higher – fixed readers
Required signal strength	Low	High
Data Storage	Store up to 128 Kilobytes of data	Store up to 1 Kilobytes of data
Tag Size	Varies depending on application	Sticker to credit card size
Industries /Applications	Auto dealerships, IT asset management, auto manufacturing, remote monitoring, hospitals, asset tracking, laboratories, construction and mining	Supply chain, Item level tracking, High volume manufacturing, Electronic tolls, libraries, big stores, passports, pharmaceuticals

the surrounding of an RFID system are affected less by the degradation of RF signal as near field works on the principle of magnetic coupling.

In far field coupling, the RFID tags are based on far-field emissions that capture EM waves propagating from a dipole antenna attached to the reader. This technique is used for commercial far-field RFID tags to back scatter its id. In the far field, the radiated signal gradually decreases the read distance depending upon the condition of the environment and properties of materials/metals.

RFID APPLICATIONS

Two different applications of RFID have been discovered, and they are RFID integrated applications and RFID specific applications. Fortunately, system specifications allow a technologist to choose a frequency range that best fits a system application needs. Anyone with basic knowledge of RFID technology can randomly design a system, but technologists understand what works best in practice situations. This distinction in design and implementation is often the difference between a satisfactory system and a superb system. RFID frequency ranges are depicted in Table 2.

RFID Integrated Applications

The existing system is enhanced and made more effective and efficient using RFID technology is called as RFID integrated applications. The most common use of this is the generic supply-chain where RFID integration commonly employed by commercial stores such as Wal-Mart (Yüksel & Yüksel, 2011). There are several other applications which have integrated RFID technology into their business models such as:

- **Defense and Military:** Military department is looking forward to deploy RFID to track inventory and human being. US Department of Defense is investigating a new active tag which has the ability to access and communicate via satellites called as "Third Generation Radio Frequency Identification with Satellite Communications (3G RFID w/SATCOM)" with the hope that it will increase the visibility of the DOD's supply chain as well as increase the confidence of shipments to various war-torn regions.
- **Postal Package Tracking:** Focus the primary goal of increasing the effectiveness of tracking packages and parcels, the postal

Table 2. RFID frequency ranges

Frequency Band Name	Frequency Range	Read Range	Applications	Advantages	Disadvantages
Low Frequency	125 KHZ-134 KHZ	<5m	Animal tracking	• Operates well around water and metals ; • better able to penetrate thin metallic substances	Short read range; slow read rates
High Frequency	13.56 MHZ	<1m	Item tracking Airline baggage Smart cards Libraries Patient flow tracking	Low cost of tags Accuracy Quick read rates	Require a high power
Ultrahigh Frequency	860 MHZ-930 MHZ	3 m	Supply chain and logistics Automated toll collections Parking Access control	Transfer data faster (read many more tags per second)	Does not operate well near water or metals
Microwave Frequency	2.4 GHZ	1m	Supply chain and logistics Automated toll collections Airline Baggage	Fastest read range	Does not operate well near water or metals

service has been found to integrate RFID world-wide with thereby increasing customer's property security.

- **Aviation Industry:** Contributing two major aircraft manufacturers, like Boeing and Airbus, they have started ensuring that the supplying factory parts for the aircraft, use RFID tags for identifications resulting in an easier process to locate and identify needed parts (Collins, 2004)

- **Health Care:** One of the Taiwanese Chang-Gung Memorial Hospitals has been monitoring surgical patients provided with RFID wristbands to ensure whether maximum care is given where it is required. The informative features available in the wristbands include the ability to decrypt data, thus obtain read-only, static fields (such as blood-types) and read/write dynamic fields which may be updated and modified by medical staff.

- **Transportation:** The transportation industry is one of the leading users of RFID technology and they have identified and implemented numerous applications. Application of RFID in transportation include railroad car management, tolls and fees, traffic management, fare collec-

tion, fleet management, equipment identification, solid waste hauling, also fuel dispensing. The RFID tag alerts the tag reader when a hometown commuter passes through an express toll lane, that someone has passed through the toll and the reader then identifies the commuter and communicates the charge to an account setup in a networked computer system. It is possible to manage tractor-trailer traffic in much the same way through weigh stations. Through RFID technologies, once a semi tagged enters an interstate highway it stops at the first weigh station along its journey on the interstate to be identified and approved, moving throughout the rest of its passage along that same stretch of highway it is not required to stop at any other weigh stations. Possible way is to use RFID technology to track the truck along the highway. While making travel smart and efficient the transportation industry and related businesses are dedicated to speeding-up traffic flow and decreasing delay time.

- **Baggage/Passenger Tracing:** For Airport Terminal Systems (SEATS), the Boston Logan International Airport and the Boston Engineering Inkode Corporation have integrated RFID technology within the Secure Environment by which passengers and their baggage with passive RFID tags to track all movements from their arrival at the airport to boarding the flight. However, this technology ensures not only that passengers will be able to make their flight easier, but that their baggage location will always be known.

Specific RFID Applications

RFID is a killer technology that elegantly provides a solution for a wide range of business needs (Shepard, 2005). Some of the major examples which have been developed in the recent years include the Magic Medicine Cabinet, the Augmentation of Desktop Items, the Multipurpose Smart Box, and the Smart Shelves.

DATASET OF RFID

The format of the data recorded in the database after a tag has been read consists of three primary pieces of information depicted in Figure1 - the Electronic Product Code, the Reader Identifier and the Timestamp which contains the reading time. The Electronic Product Code (EPC) is a unique identification number introduced by the Auto-ID Center and given to each RFID Tag which is made up of a 96 bit, 25 character-long code containing numbers and letters. It is made up of a Header for

8 bits, Object Class for 24 bits, EPC Manager for 28 bits and Serial Number for 36 bits (Saxena & Doctor, 2008). Data quality has become increasingly important to many firms as they build data warehouses and focus more on customer relationship management. The term location represents the place where the RFID reader scanned the item. The attribute time denotes the time when the reading in RFID took place. RFID reader provides these tuples at fixed time intervals. At the same time, there is a possibility of generating multiple tuples when the object stays at the same location for the period of time.

CHARACTERISTICS OF RFID DATA

As we are focusing towards the data management issues of RFID technology, it is necessary to know the characteristics of RFID data. By varying diversity of RFID applications, the generated colossal RFID data share some common fundamental characteristics listed as follows

Simplicity of Data

The data observed in the RFID application is of the form (*tag_id, reader_id, timestamp*), here *tag_id* refers to EPCs (Electronic product code's) which uniquely identify the tagged item and the reader_id is RFID reader location and the timestamp is the time when the reading is occurring.

Figure 1. Dataset of RFID

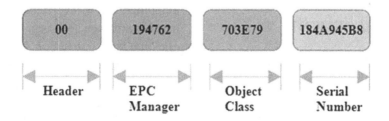

Large Volume of Data

This is one of the biggest concerns of RFID able to deal with a huge amount of information. The volume and velocity of RFID data exceed the capacity of existing technology infrastructure. Consider an example, Wal-Mart is expected to generate 7 terabytes of RFID data per day. However, each tag is tagged periodically and the data about tag EPC, reading time and location will be continuously produced in the system, even though modest RFID deployments will generate gigabytes of rapidly changing data a day. Gonzalez et al. (2006 & 2007) presented a rule engine to handle the mass data generated by the RFID reader.

Temporal and Dynamic

The observations through RFID are dynamically generated and the data carry state changes. All RFID observations are associated with the time-stamps, objects locations and the containment relationships change along the time. These attributes are very essential in RFID data management to model all such data in an expressive data suitable for application level interactions, which include tracking and monitoring (Wang & Liu., 2005).

Implicit Semantics and Inaccuracy of Data

The observed read rate accuracy in real RFID deployments remains still, on average, in the 60-70% range, which is one of the major factors limiting the widespread adoption of RFID technology (Fritz, 2010).

RFID DATA MANAGEMENT

RFID data are usually regarded as an example of streaming data, this possesses a result, by deriving the redundancy on the data level has always been handled in the general way of dealing with data streams. In particular, RFID data has its own peculiarities which have been largely ignored. The size and different characteristics of RFID data pose many challenges. It is possible to compare RFID data and general data streams to illustrate some special features of RFID data. Firstly, the data volume for RFID is usually larger (some readers can perform over 100 readings each second). Second comparison, the RFID data on average is less useful than other data streams.

The general architecture for deploying RFID system in business process consists of three layers.

- RFID tag
- Business process
- Enterprise application

The RFID system design in the business process is depicted in Figure 2.

The layered architecture for managing RFID data in business process comprises three layers. The lowest layer consists of RFID tags, which is located on objects such as individual items and pallets. Second layer consists of tag readers. Also said to be this layer as Data capture, which deals with the stream of tuples of the form of *(EPC, time, location)*. Because of the volume and the inaccuracy of RFID data, method of using a low level data process before sending the data to the next layer is inevitable. Hence, this low-level data processing would consist of data cleaning and aggregation. Moreover, one primary role of this layer is to process a stream of simple events which are generated during the interaction between readers and tagged objects.

The second layer of the architecture is the business process. This layer is responsible for mapping the low-level data streams from readers to a more manageable form that is suitable for application level interaction. The most challenging and interesting tasks in this layer are those that combine business logic with the stream of data emerging from the reader layer. Another major

Figure 2. RFID system design in business process

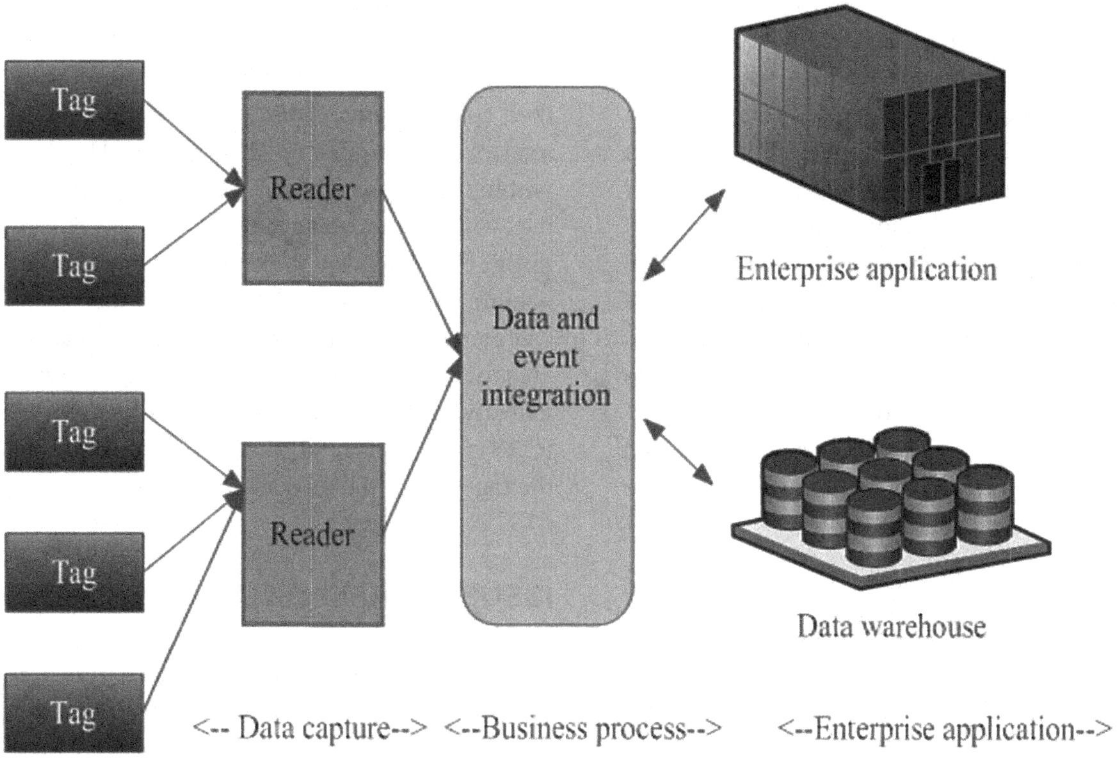

<-- Data capture--> <--Business process-->   <--Enterprise application-->

responsibility of business process is detecting more complex events.

The third level of the architecture is the Enterprise Application that supports the business process of enterprise applications such as Supply Chain Management (SCM), Asset Management runs on SAP or Customer Relationship Management (CRM) or non-SAP back-end systems.

The data capture layer is responsible for coordinating multiple tagged objects and cleaning incoming data before sending to the next layer, in addition to that detecting some simple events and reporting them to the management systems.

One of the primary factors limiting the widespread adoption of RFID technology is the inaccuracy of the data stream produced by RFID readers. This leads to the big load of unreliable data which is useless for the purpose of higher level processing. It is necessary to clean this

unreliable data which we call dirty data. RFID data cleaning is a common and challenging task found in RFID data management systems. There are many research efforts have been proposed and investigate a more comprehensive, uniform treatment of data cleaning covering several transformation phases, their specific operators and their implementation. Cleaning of large RFID data sets can be an expensive problem. More existing work on RFID cleaning has mainly focused on improving the accuracy of a stand-alone technique and largely ignored costs.

Cost-conscious approach proposed by (Gonzalez et al., 2007) is to determine the context under which inexpensive methods work better and the situation where more expensive techniques are absolutely necessary. The architecture is framed to have a set of labeled data that contain instances of tag readings annotated with features that describe the context in which the reading took place. The data set is labeled with the cleaning methods that classify each case correctly. There exists also a repository of available methods with cost information. Author proposed a cleaning plan induction method based on the idea of top-down induction of decision trees and the novel concept of cleaning cost reduction. Furthermore, DBN (Dynamic Bayesian Networks) based cleaning method takes tag readings as noisy observations of a hidden state and performs data cleaning. This work increases the speed of clean, but introduces some other anomalies. Considering all these factors this necessitates developing effective and novel technique to clean the data before they are streamed to applications.

RFID DATA WAREHOUSING

Data warehousing shown in Figure 3 is the only viable solution for providing strategic information. Since, it integrates the data collected from operational databases of various enterprise sectors and forms a large repository useful for decision analysis. It is implemented like databases and they are not designed for online transaction processing. Cross-system data integration is a relevant characteristic of data warehousing. Dynamic changes, time-dependent, huge quantities and large number of implicit semantics are some of the characteristics of the RFID data. Then data loading in a data warehouse is often a complex process involving data cleaning and transformation because the quality of data in the warehouse is a primary goal in order to respond efficiently and accurately to unforeseeable queries at any moment of time.

Efficient RFID data warehouse management considers the load and capacity of all the RFID readers in collecting all the RFID tag readings for the effective warehousing of supply chain management activities. The available RFID readers are categorized into two types. The first category is comprised of RFID readers which are having more tags in their coverage area. Second category consists of readers with very few tags in their coverage area. Subsequently the load of the readers is the number of RFID tags read by them within their coverage area. While the number of tags within the coverage area is more for readers in the first category, the chance of overloading is high. Consequently, the readers in the second category move towards the first category reader's area to avoid the chance of missing tag readings. Effectively the Centralized Repository Server (CRS) will manage all the RFID readers. Then the tag read by the readers are sent to CRS.

ISSUES IN RFID DATA

Probabilities of errors and redundancies are high in the RFID data which results in the limited deployment of RFID technology. There are three types of errors in RFID data reading. They are unexpected readings, misread, and duplicate readings depicted in Table 3.

- An RFID reader periodically sends out RF signals to its range. When an RF tag that moves within the range of the reader receives the signals, it will send a response signal along with its unique identifier code, timestamp and location ID. The reader receives the response signal and registers the data stream as one entry. There would be some RF tags which are not supposed to be detected by the reader and may be read due to the spatial divergence of RF signals sent by the reader. Such readings are termed as false positive readings.
- A significant number of tags which are within the reader's read range are not consistently read by the reader either due to their orientation with respect to the reader,

Figure 3. Data warehouse

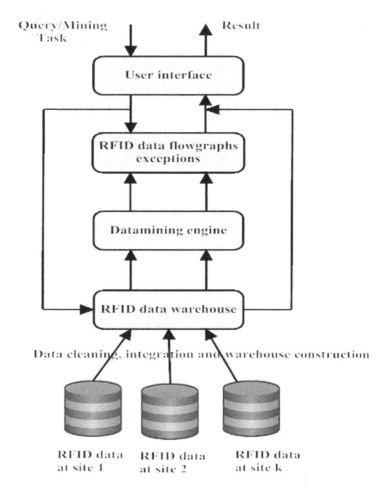

distance from the reader, presence of metal, dielectric or water material close to the tag and other factors. Practically, few of the tags might not be read in every cycle though present in the effective detection range called as false negative or missed readings.

- Duplicate readings are classified into reader duplicates and data duplicates. The former occurs when a tag is present in the vicinity of more than one reader, which is simultaneously sending signals to it; the latter occurs when a reader reads a large amount of non-difference information at a time interval.

EXISTING APPROACHES TO DEAL WITH ANOMALIES

To deal with the anomalies found in the RFID data this chapter investigated the three approaches, namely physical approach, middleware approach and deferred approach. Physical approach is doing modification in the environment to enhance the readability rate and to avoid missing readings. The success of an RFID implementation depends largely on the extensive preparedness made on all environmental factors at the time of planning. This includes determining area surveys, Feasible Reader positions, RF signal coverage and Obstructions to enhance the entire RFID environment. The

Table 3. Types of anomalies and its reasons

S.No	Types of Anomalies		Reason
1	Wrong readings/ false positive		i)When tags outside the normal Reader range ii) Due to environmental setup
2	Duplicate readings/ redundant	Reader level	i) Tag happens to pass within the overlapped region ii) When there is more than one reader deployed to cover a specific area.
		Data level	i) Scanned item stays in the reader range for a long period of time
3	Missing readings / false negatives		i) Tagged objects not being scanned ii) Object outside the scanning range. iii) Not proper orientation with respect to the reader

focus needs to be on flawless hardware installation and seamless connectivity. The common solution suggested to deal with RFID anomalies is to either install multiple readers in a specific location or to attach multiple tags with same EPC code.

Multiple readers are installed in the specific location in an attempt to enhance the reader rate and compensate for reader anomalies that may occur. There is no guarantee that every reader would identify and register the presence of each of the tags present in that location. Consider that reader R1 has a coverage area of radius r1 and has 7 tags within the location. As an ideal case, It is expected that reader R1 reads all the tags T1, T2, T3, T4, T5, T6 and T7 at all the reading cycle. This does not happen in live environments and there is the chance that few tags may be missed out at certain time stamps. This occurs due to reader error factor, and overriding tags. To avoid these missing values two readers R1 and R2 can be placed in the same location. The aggregated values will be considered as the entire data stream. Unfortunately, this method increases data redundancy and applying the business rules duplication can be eliminated.

Consider that the reader R1 is placed in a location of radius r1 and there are 3 objects that need to be tagged within the vicinity. Each object is tagged with two RFID Tags. Consider the Tags T11, T12 are attached to object A1. Tags T21, T22 is attached to object A2. Tags T21, T22 is attached to object A3 Another method of dealing with the enhancement of the read rate is to attach multiple tags housing identical EPC numbers to the same object in an effort for at least one of these tags to be read by the reader. This method again provokes redundant data and tag collisions. This data also needs to be filtered and cleaned before it could be loaded on to the database. The RFID middleware is the layer which ensures that raw data is treated to some extent before entering the master tables of the database. Some of the techniques proposed by the author based on the physical approach are depicted in Table 4.

The middleware becomes a very hot topic and it refers to employing an algorithm to eliminate anomalies found in systems to correct the data before storing it. It is a software layer residing between the RFID hardware and the existing back-end system or application software. This approach is to deal with low complex anomalies found in the RFID data. Before the data is getting stored in the database, the observed RFID data is treated to some extent by applying algorithms. More specifically, readers of RFID suffer from low read rates, thus frequently failing to read tags that are present. To correct reading errors, and allow data streams to meet the high level information requirements, the RFID middleware system is deployed. The concept behind this middleware is using a non-overlapping static window or an overlapping sliding window. RFID approach interpolates dropped readings for every tag within the time window on the collected data stream. It extracts data from the

Table 4. Pros and cons in physical approach

Author	Methodology	Representative Works	Drawbacks
Bai, Y.,Wang, F. & Liu, P. [2006]	Multiple Tags/Multiple readers	• Multiple readers are installed in the environment to enhance the reader rate • To attach multiple tags with identical EPC number to the same object	Duplicate readings, the reader and tag collision occurs The cost is increased
Rahhmati, Zhong, Hiltunen and Jana[2007]	Tag Orientation	The Reader may scan the tags on an object most effectively when the Tag is positioned at the front.	False positive rises if orientation is not proper
Potdar, Hayati and Chang [2007]	Weighing	It requires all tagged items to be weighed at the start of the transportation route and at the end of the trip to determine any difference in the cargo weight.	Cycles increased

RFID interrogators (readers), filters it, aggregates it and routes it to enterprise applications. Various techniques proposed by the authors using this approach deals with low complex anomalies and there is the risk of introducing artificially generated anomalies. If all anomalies are cleaned at the edge, then no adequate information will be provided to the cleaning algorithm to deal with high complex anomalies. Transforming the raw observations into high-level events is also not possible to middleware approach. Some of the techniques proposed by the author based on the middleware approach are depicted in Table 5.

The conventional data cleansing approach is to remove all anomalies upfront and to store only the cleaned data in a database. For example, many device controllers at the edge of an RFID network provide de-duping and primitive filtering capabilities and errors such as duplicate reads are often correctable at the edge. Such eager cleansing methods can potentially reduce the amount of data that have to be managed by

Table 5. Pros and cons in middleware approach

Author	Methodology	Representative Works	Drawbacks
Jeffery, Garofalakis and Franklin [2008]	Statistical sMoothing for Unreliable RFid data	declarative and adaptive smoothing window	Doesn't work when tag moves rapidly in and out of readers communication range. Increases the complexity of the application
Baoyan Song Pengfei Qin Hao Wang Weihong Xuan [2009]	A new "smoothing filtering" approach Based on virtual spatial granularity	Bayesian estimation Algorithm to fill up false negatives, and uses the rules to solve false positives	It doesn't provide a solution for duplication anomaly.
LingyongMeng, Fengqi Yu [2010]	Improved algorithm based on adaptive window to determine the size of the sliding window for moving a tag.	RFID data cleaning based on Adaptive window	Better than SMURF but corrects only false negative
Libe Valentine Massawe, Johnson D. M. Kinyua, Herman Vermaak [2012]	Window based smoothing method	Efficient transition detection mechanism Adapt its window size to cope with fluctuations of the tag-reader performance	It is not very efficient in an extremely noisy environment.
Hua Fan, Quanyuan Wu and Yisong Lin [2012]	Reverse order filling mechanism	Behavior-Based Smoothing for unreliable RFID data (BBS)	An error rate of BBS is lower than that of sliding window's methods but used to fill only the missing data

applications down-stream in the business process and help avoid repeated cleansing of the data at query time. However, it is not always possible to remove all anomalies beforehand. One reason is that the rules and the business context required for cleansing may not be available at the data loading time. In deferred approach cleaning is limited after storing the data into the database and anomalies are not cleaned properly. It deals with high complex anomalies and it is not possible to handle the data in real time. Each application has its own anomalies by framing cleansing rules. The content of the database is not changed directly by the rules, but are evaluated when an application issues a query. In this approach, although an application pays some cleansing overhead at query time, it gains the flexibility of being able to evolve its anomaly specifications over time. Each application specifies the detection and the correction of relevant anomalies using declarative sequence-based rules. An application query is then automatically rewritten based on the cleansing rules that the application has specified, to provide answers over cleaned data. Since the deferred approach is dependent on the user-specified rules or probabilistic algorithms, it results in additional artificial anomalies like false positive and false negative. Some of the techniques proposed by the author based on the deferred approach are depicted in Table 6.

PROPOSED APPROACH

The anomalies are not completely removed using the three existing approaches. Hence the existing approaches can be integrated to clean the anomalies completely and the resultant data obtained is completely the cleaned version. The proposed algorithms using hybrid approach are developed and to prove its accuracy and precision compared to the existing algorithms it should be tested in the dataset. In order to test our algorithm the chosen dataset is healthcare.

RFID BASED HOSPITAL MANAGEMENT SYSTEM

RFID is widely used in all applications but the role of RFID in healthcare is of more importance because minute error results in heavy financial and personal losses. The contribution of RFID system plays an effective role in hospital management. In hospital settings, considering patient safety is critically important. At the same time, all the hospitals are pressured to reduce costs. When developing strategic objectives and technologies that reduce operating expenses while providing increased patient safety must be thoroughly tested and evaluated. Radio frequency identification is one technology that holds great promise. More-

Table 6. Pros and cons in deferred approach

Author	Methodology	Representative Works	Drawbacks
Gonzalez, H., Han, J. &Shen, X. [2007].	Cost-Conscious Cleaning of Massive RFID Data Sets	Among different cleaning algorithms the least cost algorithm is chosen which would offer the highest precision in correcting the raw data	Increase the speed of clean but introduces anomalies
Peng, Ji, Luo, Wong and Tan, [2008]	Peer-to-Peer	(P2P) networks within the RFID data set to detect and remove inaccurate readings	Cleaning is limited after data stored into the database
Khoussainova, N., Balazinska, M. &Suciu, D. [2008]	Probabilistic inference to correct incoming data	The process of observing the raw partial events of RFID data and transforming these into high level probable events.	It corrects only missing readings but introduces wrong anomalies

over, RFID has a great potential to revolutionize business processes across a wide range of industries including health care. RFID technology can be used to manage hospital patient medications, outpatient compliance with medication treatment plans after hospital discharge, medical processes and medical supply usage. RFID technology can also be used to improve the security of a hospital or treatment center by controlling facility access. Both the employee and patient tags could indicate when a restricted area is entered. If such an event occurs, security alarm would be triggered to alert security personnel. Other RFID uses are also available, which includes tracking, identifying, and locating patients, equipment, supplies, clinicians, and controlled drugs in hospital facilities. Tags could be used to determine whether supplies and instruments had been sterilized. It is also suggested that using RFID tags to track residents in long-term care facilities, provide monitor access to restricted areas, also identify implantable medical devices, and scan information from implanting equipment. It is a fact that RFID would also eliminate tens of thousands of deaths and injuries caused by medical mistakes every year.

Other hospitals have begun to adopt active RFIDs for patient and personnel identification. For example RFID system is embedded in patient bracelets so that medical staff can electronically identify patients before surgery as well as before administering medications and blood transfusions. In addition to that, these systems have been implemented in order to locate where patients are and to passively collect data on patient's movements through hospital services. Simultaneously, medical staff has also been given active RFID tags on badges in order to collect data on workflow to find inefficiencies in current hospital operations. However, these latter types of systems have primarily been implemented in emergency departments and surgical centers such as places where there are large volumes of patients and heightened risks of medical error.

During the last decades, when a doctor needs to observe the drug treatment for the patients, it is necessary for the doctor must spend the whole day aside the patient and record the patient's behavior. All the collected information is then used by the doctor to determine the patient's physical and mental condition evaluation. Furthermore, this traditional technique needs a lot of human effort for collecting the patients' behavior information. But the modernized world use RFID Readers and Tags to record the patient behaviors without the help of the humans to save the human resources. After the completion of collecting the patient behaviors for a period of time, it is mandatory to establish the regular model for the patients by utilizing data mining techniques. Processing in this way, is must for the doctor to know the behavioral changes of certain patient after the drug treatment by comparing the behavior differences between the patient current behavior and the regular model. Additionally, the patient's behavior can also be monitored to automatically warn the doctor in real-time if the behavior of the patient is abnormal. Determining this kind of systems will be very helpful for patient health care and human resource saving. For the application based on drug treatment monitoring, the doctors pay their attention to the pattern changes after the treatment. Hence it is mandatory to propose a set of data mining methods for discovering the information of pattern changes.

It is well-known that hospitals own a great number of expensive medical equipments. Sometimes the equipment is stolen and it is less known to us. Unnecessarily the hospital employee would have been searching the piece of equipment for longer hours without been identified as stolen. The missing material has to be re-ordered by some employees, diverting them from patient care or management tasks. Wasted money is not the only effect of these thefts. The stolen equipment may lead to severe consequences. Radio Frequency Identification can help towards finding the solution to this sort of serious problem. The equipments can be easily tracked by embedding the RFID tags into the medical equipment. This fact reduces risk of the thefts as the hospital's technical staff is always aware of the material's whereabouts within the buildings. Furthermore, as for anti-counterfeiting, electronic tagging has a preventative effect and can help identifying stolen material. RFID gates at the hospital's exits can help notifying the security services that medical equipment is taken out of the building. The role of RFID in avoiding equipment theft is depicted in the Figure 4.

Facility-wide monitoring with automatic real-time rule-based alerts, monitor tagged high-risk patients, such as psychiatric or geriatric patients, neonates and infants. The unique identification number that is applied to the infant's RFID bracelet is generated automatically from the mother's master health record. The infant's information, including such details as bath times and medical

vital statistics, is recorded in an SQL database. The server is attached to short-read range and middle-read range RFID readers, which are responsible for programming and detecting the tags with the unique serial numbers. The server is linked to the neonatal care unit readers via Ethernet network. The medical staff has access to the RFID application user interface that is connected to RFID reader hubs. When a baby is born, two identical tags are generated based on the mother's unique hospital identification number by an RFID reader/programmer. One tag is inserted into the mother's wrist bracelet; the other is inserted into the infant's ankle bracelet. The bracelet is applied to the baby's ankle before the baby is placed in its bed in neonatal care. The RFID encoded wristband data can be read through bed linens, while patients are sleeping without disturbing them. Though RFID technology provides a method to transmit and receive data from a patient to health service provider/medical professionals without human

Figure 4. Avoid equipment theft, using RFID technology

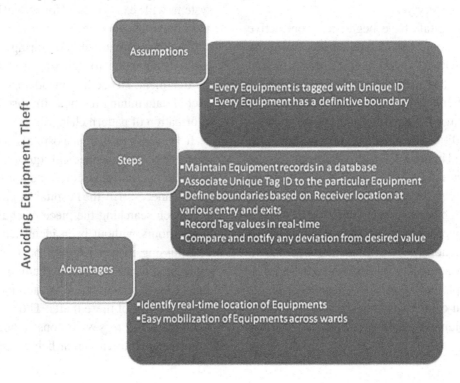

intervention (like wireless communication). This is an automated data-capture technology that can be used to track, identify and store patient information electronically contained on RFID wristband. The Nurses use a PDA device to record the baby's vital details. All of the baby's care activities, such as bathing and breastfeeding, are recorded. For the mother-baby mix-up prevention system, the RFID application verifies all mother-baby transactions. At discharge, the RFID reader verifies that mother and baby is a correct match in a final check before the discharge can proceed. Stanley healthcare released a new version Infant Protection System helps to track and locate babies as well as to identify the tags that cross the authorized area. If the infant tag crosses the authorized area audible alert arises and message sent to the server through RFID transmission. Earlier versions of the system employed proprietary active radio frequency identification tags and required the installation of a network of proprietary readers, which often made covering areas beyond the obstetrics department prohibitively expensive. The latest generation leverages a hospital's existing Wi-Fi network, thereby allowing a customer to expand a system

to an entire health-care facility or campus. The role of RFID in preventing infant theft is depicted in the Figure 5. The components of RFID based healthcare system is given in Figure 6.

This technology also helps to monitor the patient waiting time in real time. It is also used to track and locate critical files such as patient charts and records. It is a killer technology that elegantly provides a solution for a wide range of business needs including healthcare sector. The University of Maryland Medical Center (UMMC) and CaroMont Regional Medical Center improved product recalls and virtually eliminated the human errors by deploying RFID. Bahrain's King Hamad University Hospital (KHUH) has increased inventory visibility and decreased theft through RFID integration. Hospital based management system was signed by (Chowdhury et al, 2007). This system offers the tremendous benefits of healthcare management environments. Apollo Hospital in Chennai is using an Icegein Real-time locating system (RTLS/RFID) called "Patient Mantra" to move 250 patients a day through a series of up to 26 diagnostic procedures. It helps in tracking the patient, to reduce the waiting time of the patient,

Figure 5. Avoid infant theft, using RFID technology

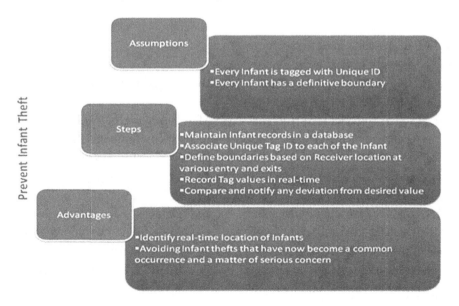

Figure 6. Components of RFID based healthcare system

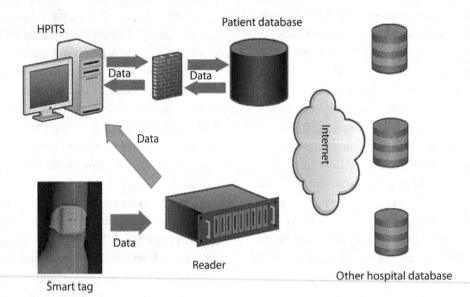

to trace the high sugar level patient and to pass the alert message to the security at the gates if the patient leaves the hospital with the tag.

Motivation Behind this Work

RFID plays an essential role in all the sub-domains of the applications in health care applications. Among them, RFID technology dominates in tracking the patients under treatment. But, there may be errors and redundancies in the obtained RFID data from all the readers. The effectiveness in cleaning the RFID data in healthcare sectors remains a concern, even though a number of literary works are available. The literary works that have been worked so far, consider the errors that are occurring only because of the missing readings. The probability of occurrence of the error due to the wrong consideration about the presence of the tags is high. This happens because of the electronic devices that are operating in the same RF range. The RFID readers may read an unavailable tag because of the interference generated by the malicious electronic device. This gives rise to erroneous reading by the corresponding RFID

reader. To a maximum, the dirty data that are read because of these errors may even leads to patients' death. Hence, in general, occurrences of errors in RFID readings that are applied in health sectors are considered as very crucial. The errors need to be cleansed in an effective manner before they are subjected to warehousing. Hence, the necessity to a have an effective data cleaning to clean these kind of dirty data peaks. The lack of such techniques in the literature has motivated to the research work in this area.

DETAILED DESIGN

After deploying the RFID in healthcare an elegant hospital environment is built and the project can be viewed as follows phases:

- Admin User Interface Module
- Database Management Module
- Code Logic Development Module to clean the anomalies
- Report Generation Module

The *Admin User Interface Module* is mainly designed for the patient registration, doctor's information and visitor's information. In *Database Management Module* the Data warehousing is the only viable solution for providing strategic information. In fact, they are very large repositories that integrate data coming from operational databases of several enterprise sectors for decisional analysis. Data loading in a data warehouse is often a complex process involving data cleaning and transformation, because quality of data in the warehouse is a primary goal in order to respond efficiently and accurately to unforeseeable queries at any moment of time. The accuracy of current RFID is improving, but there is still erroneous reading error, such as duplicate readings or missing readings. The major challenge of data warehousing is data cleaning and our work focus towards it. The *Code Logic Development Module* is mainly designed for the code analysis to implement the data cleaning technique to deal with the colossal raw RFID data. Our proposed work develops three algorithms to predict and clean the anomalies present in the huge observed RFID data. Since the real time RFID deployment deals with huge investment, the healthcare environment is simulated and the chosen premise for our work is Cellular Approach for detecting out of the range readings. The RFID readers have Omni-directional antenna and hence there are possibilities for the adjacent regions to overlap with each other. The chosen premise is a complex model and there is the high chance of all three types of errors mentioned.

Algorithm 1: Duplication Removal

Step 1: Data insertion for source (RFID Readings)
Step 2: Compare Input data stream with allowed data/character types. (Null, Alpha, Numeric, symbols)
Step 3: Check occurrence of similar incoming data streams for each set of streams using a for loop to identify data duplication

Step 4: Display set of all duplicate data streams.
Step 5: Ability for the system to identify and delete redundant records with option for manual deletion.

Algorithm 2: Algorithm for Outlier Detection [False Positive]

Step1: Initialize the location for all tag-ids in the original set.
Step 2: Repeat the steps 3 to 5 until the tag is detected.
Step 3: Find the adjacent set for the related loc_id.
Step 4: Check whether that tag_id is in the adjacent set.
Step 5: Mutate the original and the adjacent set.
Step 6: Finally obtain the tag_id which seems to appear in the locations where they are not supposed to be.

Algorithm 3: Algorithm to Detect Missing Readings [False Negative]

Step 1: All tags are initialized with time and boundary limit
Step 2: Reading is being captured periodically for every specific time frame. (say 5minutes)
Step 3: Check whether the specified tag_id appear at the allotted location in the assigned time then there is no missing readings.
Step 4: If the specific tag_id seems to be missing in any of the time frame which is being continuously observed then report the missing readings.

Case Study

For an example, assume a patient Steve assigned with tag_id P10008 is supposed to be in General ward (102) from 6.00 p.m. to 6.20 p.m. and the time reading is captured every 5 minutes. The sample readings observed by the reader are given in Table 7.

Table 7. Sample RFID readings

Case	Patient Id	Name	Ward	Reader Id	Date	Timestamp	Type
1	P10008	Steve	General Ward	102	10/4/2014	6:00:00	Normal
2	P10008	Steve	General Ward	102	10/4/2014	6:10:00	Normal
3	P10008	Steve	General Ward	102	10/4/2014	6:15:00	Normal
4	P10008	Steve	General Ward	102	10/4/2014	6:20:00	Normal
5	P10008	Steve	Infant Ward	105	10/4/2014	6:20:00	Adjacent Parallel
6	P10008	Steve	Pharmacy	110	10/4/2014	7:00:00	Crossover

In the above said cases 1, 2, 3, 4 Reading for P10008 is from the Allotted Location at the Allotted Time and Date. So this is treated as normal readings and in the fifth case he found to appear in the infant ward which is the adjacent cell of general ward and the readings shows he is simultaneously present in the location 105 and in the allotted location. And for the remaining time frame he was continuously observed in the assigned location every 5 minutes. Hence case 5 is treated as adjacent parallel and this redundant data is found using our proposed algorithm and with manual intervention it can be deleted. The reading is captured every 5 minutes and the reading at time 6.05 is not read by the allotted location implies missing reading and it predicted using our proposed algorithm. The case 6 is an example of crossover readings because the person assigned time is 6 to 6.20 p.m. and the specified location is General ward. But he appear in the pharmacy (not adjacent to general ward), the non-specified location in the non-assigned time.

SOLUTIONS AND RECOMMENDATIONS

The widespread adoption of RFID technology is a challengeable task because of the inaccuracy found in the produced data by RFID readers. This is termed as dirty data. For efficient data management, proper steps are needed to clean this dirty data appears in RFID. The most common problem in data management system is the Data Cleaning. The existing approaches to deal with anomalies have been discussed and it is understood that eliminating all problems found within RFID systems is difficult. Only specific problems are removed in each of the techniques based upon the existing approaches which may additionally introduce the artificial anomalies. RFID technology and its uses in various applications have been examined and the case study, role of RFID in healthcare is also performed. The observed RFID reading in healthcare is huge and it comprises of various anomalies. The algorithms are proposed based on the integrated approach to predict and clean the anomalies found in the RFID data set. The effectiveness of the algorithm should be proved using performance metrics precisions, recall, e-measure and accuracy.

FUTURE RESEARCH DIRECTIONS

In future, proposed algorithms can be applied to different applications not limited to, healthcare database to discover the behaviors of the database and their relationships. It is decided to record all the values associated with each tag event for future reference otherwise too much valid data will be lost. Finally the management can analyze the data and filter the information by applying business rules based on the requirement. This chapter does not provide the suggestions and solutions for tag cloning, which leads to big damage. RFID tag cloning is one of the common attacks found in the RFID system. To improve access security and privacy and to prevent the tag from cloning additionally a new authentication protocol should be introduced to avoid the leakage of sensitive information of the patients.

CONCLUSION

The main objective of this chapter is to discuss the various applications of RFID and issues like false positive, false negative and duplication found in the huge RFID data. Existing approaches have been investigated and the drawbacks have been analyzed. This work provides suggestions for the effective way of dealing with those problems by integrating the existing approaches so that the accuracy of the proposed method should be increased and error rate reduced. The effectiveness in cleaning the RFID data remains a concern made us to develop the algorithms based on integrated approach and to prove the proposed work is suitable for any kind of data sets.

REFERENCES

Chatterjee, S., & Timande, B. (2012). Public Transport System Ticketing system using RFID and ARM processor Perspective Mumbai bus facility B.E.S.T. *International Journal of Electronics and Computer Science Engineering.*

Chen, W. T., & Lin, G.-H. (2006). An efficient anti-collision method for tag identification in an RFID system. *IEICE Transactions*, 89-B(12), 3386–3392. doi:10.1093/ietcom/e89-b.12.3386

Chowdhury, B., & Khosla, R. (2007). RFID-based hospital real-time patient management system. In *Proceedings of 6th IEEE/ACIS International Conference on Computer and Information Science (ICIS)*, (pp. 363-368). IEEE.

Collins, J. (2004). Boeing outlines tagging timetable. *RFID Journal*. Available from http://www.rfidjournal.com/article/view/985/1/1

Fritz, G. (2010). Read-Error-Rate evaluation for RFID system on-line testing. In *Proceedings of Mixed-Signals, Sensors and Systems Test Workshop* (IMS3TW). IEEE.

Gonzalez, H., Han, J., Li, X., & Klabjan, D. (2006). Warehousing and analyzing massive RFID data sets. In *Proceedings of the 22nd International Conference on Data Engineering*. Academic Press.

Gonzalez, H., Han, J., & Shen, X. (2007). Cost-conscious cleaning of massive RFID data sets. In *Proceedings of International Conference on Data Engineering*, (pp. 1268-1272). Academic Press.

Saxena, M., & Doctor, G. (2008). Radio Frequency Identification (RFID): Applications and Indian Scenario. *The IUP Journal of Information Technology*, 4(3), 72–78.

Shepard, S. (2005). *RFID Radio Frequency Identification*. McGraw-Hall, Inc.

Wang, F., & Liu, P. (2005). Temporal management of RFID data. In *Proceeding of the Very Large Data Bases Conferences* (VLDB05), (pp. 1128-1139). VLDB.

Yüksel, M. E., & Yüksel, A. S. (2011). RFID Technology in business systems and supply chain management. *Journal of Economic and Social Studies*, 1(1), 53–71. doi:10.14706/JECOSS11115

KEY TERMS AND DEFINITIONS

Automatic Data Capturing Technology: A way to identify and collect information about a particular object automatically without human intervention.

Customer Relationship Management: RFID is integrated with CRM to describe business customer relationship.

Electronic Product Code (EPC): It is encoded on *RFID tags* used to track all kinds of objects including trade items, fixed assets, documents, human beings etc.

Reader: It is an interrogator used to read the RFID readings from the tag.

RFID: Radio Frequency Identification is a wireless identification technology used to uniquely identify an object.

Supply Chain Management: SCM is considered as a complex and knowledge intensive process, management of supply chain can benefit significantly from the implementation of RFID technology.

Tag: It is a small, low cost device used to uniquely identify an object. It is of two types: Active and Passive tags.

Chapter 10
Operational Strategies Associated with RFID Applications in Healthcare Systems

Alan D. Smith
Robert Morris University, USA

ABSTRACT

An effective information system is essential for a business or industry to be successful in today's highly competitive market. Perhaps the most compelling case for RFID-embedded technologies in the healthcare field has been increased efficiency in supply chain performance measurements, which generally consist of financial and non-financial indicators. Many research studies have assumed that these efficiency measures are transferrable in the medical services field. Such optimism is fuelled by the expectations that such supply chain measures will result in equally impressive results in the healthcare field. Although this transfer may be somewhat flawed and imperfectly applied, research has verified certain elements of operational optimism. There are still a number of technical, ethical, and legal issues or hurdles that surround RFID applications in the healthcare industry that must be successfully overcome. However, few can successfully argue against freeing hospital staff from the routine duties associated with traditional inventory so that they may be free to serve patients. With recent governmental regulations and the concern for increased access to universal medical care and its astronomical costs, these issues need to be addressed.

DOI: 10.4018/978-1-4666-6308-4.ch010

POTENTIAL BENEFITS USING RFID-RELATED TECHNOLOGIES

Supply Chain Management and Implementation Costs/Savings

Management at many businesses and, in the present case, hospitals are looking for ways to reduce their costs via effective supply chain management (SCM) principles and techniques. Supply related costs can run as high as 30% of total expenditure and many entities are moving toward vendor-managed inventory systems (VMI) (Bhakoo, Singh, & Sohal, 2012). In very basic terms, several key criteria which must be taken into account when choosing vendors (i.e. quality, price, agreement terms, delivery, and service). Healthcare service strategies and its associated supply chain systems in hospitals are different from for-profit businesses in many respects. For example, one the main drivers of automating prescriptions may be that many healthcare providers, who may have little to no experience in operations management and quality assurance techniques, may be prone to making substantial errors. While such human errors may have little consequences in the retail environment, they may lead to patient harm and litigation in the healthcare environment. To further complicate matters, the prescription industry is highly regulated and such mistakes due to human errors can be costly in both lives and financial resources. It takes great investments in time to bring any drug to market, and with so much money invested; pharmaceutical companies rely heavily on their marketing professionals, their contacts with the doctors and building long-term relationships with in their SCM systems. Supply chain activities can include but are not limited to evaluating inventory needs, placing orders, verifying deliveries, restocking shelves, counting inventory, identification and disposal of expired goods, and dealing with stock-outs. These activities may have no apparent value from a patient-care perspective and only serve to drive up operational costs, but are essential to an effectively management healthcare system.

In general, many hospitals operate on a different scheme than most businesses in that they never really can expect what their patient load will be, what their illness will entail, or what supplies might be needed for which surgeries, especially when it comes to emergency situations. Hospitals carry an extra amount of safety stock, since any problem resulting in a stock-out situation could be life-threatening, leading to catastrophic financial losses. Many innovations in healthcare supply chains and its management have been linked to applications of RFID-related technologies. Such innovations include self-replenishment systems, automated reordering, quality assurance improvements, and enhanced security of prescription medications. Passive RFID-enabled systems have the potential provide many applications within a single infrastructure at significantly less expense than active RFID-based technology. Passive systems are typically employed in very standardized supply chain functions as inventory and secure tracking capabilities that allow management and its customers to enhance security using same fixed readers for door-level access control/tags. These security measures can alert management when inventory are removed from devices typically through auto-notification techniques when tagged assets passes through designated areas.

Active RFID tags, which have an energy source and allow for read/write capabilities, have a number of important applications beyond inventory management in the healthcare industry. For example, perhaps the most advertised application for active tags are designed for providing additional level of security for hospital patients (i.e. neonatal, assisted living residents, and their staff personnel who needed more safety protocols in order to better manage high-value medical assets). Other applications include real-time location systems, assisted living monitoring, neonatal protection, staff duress call, resident wandering, wireless nurse calls, room and patient temperature monitoring, traditional and virtual asset tracking, guard protection, location-based tracking, emergency call systems, hand hygiene compliance, and general healthcare security applications (Smith, 2009).

There are a number of significant potential benefits using RFID-related technologies on the healthcare system, costs and infrastructure considerations. Much of the academic and practitioner-based research on the effects of automated technology and its developments in RFID-related systems have focused on improved supply chain efficiency in manufacturing and retail sectors (i.e. as the listing of related readings located at the back of this chapter has illustrated in terms of topics of research in RFID). RFID, security enhancements, are utilized in a number of areas today, including airline luggage tracking, marathon races, and electronic security keys. Organizational success depends on strategies that provide and maintain a firm's competitive advantage through is operational efficiencies (Scanlon, Swaminathan, Lee, & Chernew, 2008; Scherrer-Rathje, Boyle, & Deflorin, 2009; Smith, 2005a-b). Acquiring strategies that achieve cost reduction, increased quality satisfaction, continual quality improvement, and on-time delivery performance are crucial to the successful operations of a firm (Chen & Dubinsky, 2003; Chiou, 2004; Collier & Bienstock, 2006). Some researchers have suggested that RFID-enabled technologies are considered the next revolution in supply chain management (SCM) (Kumar, Livermont, & Mckewan, 2010; Smith & Offodile, 2007, 2008). SCM activities have traditionally been perceived as an essential strategic decision of operations management (Gaukler, Özer, & Hausman, 2008; Hu, Wang, Fetch, & Bidanda, 2008; Smith & Offodile, 2007, 2008).

In terms of the basic design and cost elements, an RFID tag often resembles a flexible computer chip on a sticker and can be affixed to any moving item. The tag allows the wireless transmission of data about the item into a computer system that may be tracking millions of individual RFID tags and painting a picture of their movement. There are at least two different types of RFID tags, passive and active. Passive tags can only be read when in close proximity to a scanner or reader; whereas active tags are powered by an on-board battery and can transmit signals to the readers from more than three meters away. The cost of RFID technology continues to fall, and individual passive RFID tags can be purchased for as little as US$0.10 to 0.50. Active tags may cost between US$0.50 and 50, but some hold up to two kilobytes of data and can be reprogrammed (Smith, 2008; Smith & Offodile, 2009). There are significant evidence that there is movement by hospital management to move toward full adoption of RFID tags on moving pieces of equipment, instruments, drugs, and patients as passive tags approach a penny each (Smith & Offodile, 2009; Swaminathan, Chernew, & Scanlon, 2008; Ustundag, 2010).

Traditionally, several studies have illustrated that RFID-related technology in hospitals has been shown to speed patient care and improve its quality, reduce inventory costs through loss recovery, and optimize the supply chain process of purchasing and restocking supplies (Seidman, Brockman, & Lewis, 2010). In some instances, RFID technology has helped hospital managers make decisions on staffing levels by seeing exactly how much time nurses were spending at the bedside versus doing administrative tasks at the nurse's station (Condea, Thiessse, & Fleisch, 2012).

RFID-enabled technology can also trigger responses in the environment, such as automatic hospital lockdowns if an infant's RFID anklet exits the birth center or an adult patient wearing an RFID necklace leaves his or her unit. In the instance of time-sensitive processes, such as patient admission and bedding, RFID tags can also increase patient satisfaction by helping staff identify time lags and tighten the process. This is true in life-saving situations as well such as heart attack care and emergency C-sections. Essentially, in addition to improving the quality of care, RFID technology has the potential to help hospitals reduce their operating costs and increased the quality of their services.

Benefits of RFID Technology over Barcoding Technology: Should Hospitals/Pharmacies Switch?

It should be emphasized that RFID technology is not really designed to replace barcoding, but to augment the operational efficiencies associated with automatic identification. Such systems should be operationally robust, or in other terms, designed to still work without much concern due to relatively small or minor variations within the working environment. Although robustness is not only a matter of operating environment, it does carry a very specific meaning in terms of operational efficiency. The widespread accessibility and almost universal acceptance of barcoding technologies essentially means that such technologies will remain in the main stream e-commerce and operational efficiency picture in the global economy for the foreseeable future.

There is a general confusion that many automatic identification and data capture (AIDC) technologies are the basically the same, as they essentially perform similar functions (Smith & Rupp, 2013a-b; Ustundag, 2010; Wamba, 2012). This confusion is apparent with bar codes and RFID, since both technologies use label-type tags. However, RFID is definitely a more powerful and efficient technology and do not have the line-of-sight and single read disadvantages associated with bar code technologies. Essentially, RFID technology and its applications allows for simultaneous reading of multiple tags that do not require line-of-sight alignments. AIDC technologies has evolved at such a pace that asset tracking has made taking inventory faster, more efficient, less costly, and more transparent to users. This transparency has recently provided for the development of Virtual Asset Trackers (VAT), which allows hosted users to automatically received

updates on inventories on their RFID handhelds and Web Asset Managers. For example, Yao and Carlson (1999) summarized nine areas where barcoding technology helps companies:

1. Communication systems can provide very detailed and accurate up-to-the-minute logistical information
2. Up-to-date screen reporting replaces batch printout reporting
3. RF (Radio Frequency) terminals can be mounted on equipment and are highly portable
4. Information can be integrated for quality information service leading to increased profits
5. Standardized procedures make inventory operations easier to be managed, adjusted, and upgraded
6. Inspection data and quality control data can be added to the barcode labels for processing, analyzing, and distributing in a matter of seconds
7. Management can collaborate with both suppliers and customers to make processes more efficient
8. Systems engineers and designers can assign grades to all tasks that involve people to make better relationships between management and labor
9. The pipeline of information can be continuously studied, evaluated, and improved to effect continuous improvement in operations management.

The direct advantages of bar-coding technologies are that its initial costs are extremely small, easy to implement and maintain, and its system management is relatively simple. Therefore, they will be for widespread use for the long foreseeable future. It is important to note that many healthcare professionals are accustomed to barcoding technology are resistance to abandon it. RFID probably will not replace barcoding, but will enhance its applications to the healthcare field. Essentially all of the above advantages of barcoding can be duplicated and enhanced by FRID-embedded systems. Although the listing the benefits of barcodes when it is the aim of this chapter to make a case for RFID seems out of place, it makes sense when the two systems are used in conjunction to enhance these advantages.

In general, RFID-related technologies have great advantages for healthcare applications, especially for drug dose and self-replenishment, patient identification and tracking. Some of the advantages of an RFID enabled replenishment program include an elimination of excess inventory, improve efficiencies, and lower operational costs. These lower costs may take various forms. Labor costs are reduced by eliminated the need for visual or manual inventory checks by sales staff. Efficiency may be increased through inventory accuracy and freeing sales staff to work on value-added projects. Ultimately, inventory is better managed through increased accuracy and capabilities of better data collection in analysis and forecasting. While much research has been done into the possible benefits of RFID implementation, empirical data on benefits of implementation of RFID enable shelf replenishment is relatively lacking. Condea, Thiessse, and Fleisch (2012) established a mathematical model for a single product in a retail store with random demand and lost sales to evaluate the effects on quality of service and costs. The assumptions for their study included unlimited backroom capacity, 100% of stock-outs caused by in stock items but not on shelf, retailer collects all data on incoming/outgoing products via barcode or other device with receipt/sale detection rates at 100%, and that RFID tags do not have a 100% read rate. By using a Poisson process, λ, represents demand and shrinkage is accounted for as γ, which is a fraction of total demand. The model was then run through a series of simulations and compared with a traditional replenishment scenario where store employees perform periodic review to determine stock levels and outcomes are used to calculate

two performance metrics: total cost, and service level. The results from multiple simulations with changing parameters of correct read rates for RFID tags indicate an advantage when correct reads can be achieved at >80%. This assumption held true even as the costs of goods are increased by adding RFID tags on a case basis, accounting for roughly 1% of case cost. These results were dependent on other factors that were estimated, such as shrinkage at 2%, special treatment of RFID feedback loops from malfunctioning tags or readers, and data quality, as well as on processes that could not be accounted for in the study like forecasting accuracy, actual demand, case size, and shelf space.

Hence, RFID-enabled replenishment holds potential for substantial reduction in stock-outs and the costs associated with restocking which could provide a substantial short-term strategic advantage to early adopters of the technology but does have its potential drawbacks. Cost can be somewhat prohibitive which is why the model is designed with only one reader located at the doorway between the backroom and the sales floor. Additional considerations are required to ensure negative feedback loops, where a misread tag indicates restocking in continuously or never necessary and shrinkage do not impede or disable the process.

In general, a number of studies have applied efficiencies research is other areas and techniques used for manufacturing application, and then creates models for use in healthcare situations. Most of these studies focus on the ideas of lean six sigma, line balancing, and reengineering processes. Such authors create mathematical models and suggest that healthcare and project managers be trained in such applications. Interestingly, de Mast, Kemper, Doe, Mandjes, and van der Bijl (2011) suggested that healthcare services can be improved, not by focusing on scientific advances, but through the efficiency of processes typically found in the hospital environment. They created models to be used with contexts and terminology to increase efficiency in healthcare delivery improvements. Their study developed models that can be used by healthcare providers to figure out what variables to measure, how these variables relate to the efficiency of their processes, and identify areas where resources are wasted or identifying and optimizing bottlenecks in processes. The models created in this study can be beneficial in process and capacity design as well as layout strategy, in reference to the actual layout of departments in a hospital even doctor offices. Scheduling can also be affected with this study, hospitals and healthcare systems can have a more accurate prediction of scheduling staff and resources to certain processes. Their approach can be associated with a response strategy, in regards to operations management, in that with these models healthcare providers can respond to customer (patient) demands more efficiently. It can also be used in a cost strategy as well, these models are suppose to identify non-value adding activities that can be eliminated reducing costs in medical processes.

de Mast, Kemper, Doe, Mandjes, and van der Bijl (2011) found that that the three elements of a healthcare delivery improvements included defining a system of metrics for quantifying capacities, utilizations, and overall resource efficiency. Develop an organizational model which breaks down healthcare processes into macro- and micro-processes, and the latter into tasks and resources. This is followed by an axiological model, which relates general business objectives of hospitals to process flow metrics. Although the authors did not develop their model on automatic identification and capture technologies, it was implied. RFID could plan a major role in defining such healthcare delivery improvements. Such approaches to analytically deal with the spiraling healthcare costs in the U.S., for example, could be adapted into the nation's healthcare system to approve efficiency of hospitals, potentially cutting costs for hospitals trickling down to cutting costs for patients.

With the well-publicized recent shutdown of the U.S. government over the high initial costs

associated with governmental subsidized health insurance, now may be the critical time to compare processes to different hospitals by potentially creating standards throughout the industry. Standardization in medical processes can lead to greater transparency for patients, hospital suppliers, and safety regulators. Since many aspects of modern healthcare systems have activities in their processes that do not add value to their service. By analytically and operationally using models to pinpoint specific activities that cause delay in processes and find ways to optimize bottlenecking procedures, healthcare costs can be significantly managed and reduced. Such an approach can be extremely beneficial in such large-scale and complicated systems as healthcare. Such models help to simplify processes, similar to that of work breakdown structures in project management, into smaller and smaller activities to identify which ones are truly needed to complete processes. RFID-enabled technologies have the potential to allow the information gather from such modelling activities to be turned into practical solutions. Of course, they may be exceptions, as some limitations may arise for these models in trying to apply them to processes that seem more random such as emergency rooms, where patients/day can vary greatly. Patients/day may also be altered by outside sources as well such as natural disasters or even hospital/organizational policies that limit patients to being seen in specific hospital.

While much research has been done into the possible benefits of RFID implementation, empirical data on benefits of implementation of RFID enable shelf replenishment is relatively lacking according to Condea, Thiessse, and Fleisch (2012). Prior data shows that inventory stock-outs, when a product is in the faculty but not on the shelf, are caused in the "last 50 yards" of the supply chain are major results of lost sales as customers tend to either favor the cheaper substitute or go to another retailer to purchase the item. It has been estimated that 25% of these stock-outs are caused by inefficiencies in the replenishment process leading to product availability of 91.7% in retail stores as opposed to 98 to 99% at the manufacturer or distributer. With space at a premium and costs a major concern in the competitive market place it has become a necessity to eliminate the reasons for keeping a backroom inventory: additional compact storage, buffer for inaccuracies, and back stock of large or high velocity items.

Previous authors (Acharyulu, 2007; Al-Sakran, 2013; Chao, Yang, & Jen, 2007; Chen, Wu, Su, & Yang, 2008) have sought to evaluate the effects of an RFID-enabled replenishment program to eliminate excess inventory, improve efficiencies, and lower costs, there are few empirically based studies to support these effects. In general, labor costs are reduced by eliminated the need for visual or manual inventory checks by sales staff. Operational efficiency is increased through inventory accuracy and freeing sales staff to work on value-added projects. Inventory is better managed through increased accuracy and capabilities of better data collection in analysis and forecasting.

Condea, Thiessse, and Fleisch (2012) established a mathematical model for a single product in a retail store with random demand and lost sales to evaluate the effects on quality of service and costs. The based assumption are: unlimited backroom capacity, 100% of stock-outs caused by "in stock but not on shelf", retailer collects all data on incoming/outgoing products via bar code or other device with receipt/sale detection rates at 100%, and that RFID tags do not have a 100% read rate. Using a Poisson process, λ, represents demand and shrinkage is accounted for as γ, which is a fraction of total demand. The model was then executed through a series of simulations and compared with a more traditional replenishment scenario, where store employees perform periodic review to determine stock levels and outcomes are used to calculate two performance metrics: total cost, and service level.

Results from multiple simulations with changing parameters of correct read rates for RFID tags indicated an advantage when correct reads

can be achieved at >80%. This assumption holds true even as the costs of goods are increased by adding RFID tags on a case basis (i.e. accounting for roughly 1% of case cost). These results are dependent on other factors that were estimated, such as shrinkage at 2%, special treatment of RFID feedback loops from malfunctioning tags or readers, and data quality, as well as on processes that could not be accounted for in the study like forecasting accuracy, actual demand, case size, and shelf space.

Ultimately, RFID-enabled replenishment holds potential for substantial reduction in stock-outs and the costs associated with restocking. Such operational efficiency and cost saving which could provide substantial short-term strategic advantages to early adopters of RFID technologies; however, such technologies do have its potential drawbacks as well. Initially costs may be somewhat prohibitive which is why the model is designed with only one reader located at the doorway between the backroom and the sales floor. Considerations are required to ensure negative feedback loops, where a misread tag indicates restocking in continuously or never necessary and shrinkage do not impede or disable the process. The results from retail applications of self-replenishment certainly have the same potential for dispersing medical supplies to the healthcare setting as well.

IMPLEMENTATION CONSIDERATION ASSOCIATED WITH RFID

Basic Concerns and Avoidance Strategies Associated with RFID Technology

RFID-enabled replenishment and identification hold potential for substantial reduction in stock-outs and the costs associated with restocking. These potential savings could provide a substantial operational advantage on the short term to early adopters of the technology (Cowles, Kiecker, &

Little, 2002; Hu, Wang, Fetch, & Bidanda, 2008; Jain, Benyoucef, & Deshmukh, 2008; Kamhawi, 2008; Kennedy & Widener, 2008), it does have its potential drawbacks. Probably the most important initial concern is the start-up costs and the need to update current facilities and train employees in how to operate and integrate these systems in their routine decision-making tasks. Routinely, the costs of goods are increased by adding RFID tags on a case or per item basis, accounting for roughly at least 1% of case/item costs. Other factors associated with costs are dependent on other factors, such as in the costs of goods are increased by adding RFID tags on a case basis, accounting for roughly 1% of case cost, RFID feedback loops from malfunctioning tags or readers, and data quality issues.

RFID technology provides many benefits to companies such as better inventory control, less cost and shrinkage, but the system is costly and at what level does the cost of the system outweigh the benefits. Based on previous studies already cited, a RFID system used to identify a pallet of products for a company can provide a savings for that level of goods, but on an individual item the cost of the RFID system could outweigh the benefits. Additional research needs to focus if the members of the supply chain share the cost of RFID will this increase the benefit to the each member of the supply chain and who would benefit more. Other non-technology factors include accounting on operational processes, inventory forecasting accuracy, actual demand, case size, and shelf space. Good operational management techniques, plus the ability to develop a consensus support from all potential stakeholders using this technology, as well as patient acceptance, will usually moderate these initial concerns.

For example, previous research studies that have traditionally analyzed supply chain dynamics and the benefit of RFID-tagging cost-sharing point to this moderation. Since each part of the supply chain has similar supply chain operations such as determining customer demand, maintaining

inventory and ordering. Ustundag (2010) used of a simulation model to evaluate the cost benefit of RFID tagging to evaluate the impact of a shared cost-tagging RFID system for each user in the supply chain. In an integrated supply chain by using an RFID-tagging system companies can keep control of the inventory and where items are in the supply chain, from manufacturer to distributer to retailer. By controlling inventory a company can differentiate itself from the competition in addition to keeping costs lower by limiting inventory.

Since RFID microchips on a sticker can be attached to almost any item that the company desires to be tracked, it has many applications. The RFID is small enough that it can fit on most items whether a single item, a case, a pallet or an entire truck load. The RFID is read by scanners or readers when it comes in close proximity to the item. RFID systems are a very useful tool for the supply chain to keep track of products in real time. There are several benefits of RFID that make it a better option than a barcode system. In a RFID system the product or merchandise does not have to be in the direct line of sight for the item to be scanned, whereas a barcode needs to be seen by the laser light that reads it. The RFID just needs to be in proximity to the reader. Some RFID devices can give off signals that can be read from longer distances instead of a few feet. The supply chain can scan the RFID many times, such as when it arrives in a vendor's building, while it is being stored and when it leaves the vendor's building.

One of the drawbacks of a RFID system is the initial cost. In addition to the scanners and computer system that maintains and process the information, each RFID has a small cost to it. From a cost/benefit stand point, it would be unrealistic to install a RFID on an individual notebook that may only have a value of US$0.50, for example. But it would be practical and cost effective to install an RFID on a pallet of 5,000 notebooks. If the retail customer such as Wal-Mart wants RFID installed on products that come to their store they would have to bear the cost or the majority of the cost themselves or negotiate with their distributor to share the cost. But if all the members of the supply chain sees the value in the use of RFID and installs them on the product at the beginning of the supply chain, each member of the supply chain could share the cost thus reducing the cost of the RFID system. This scenario can easily be applied to a healthcare supplier, where such implementation costs can be shared based on who would benefit more from the use of RFID in a shared cost-tagging system. Such suppliers can create a long-term relationship with vendors by sharing the tagging costs with them.

Examples of Successful Implementation to Overcome Challenges of RFID Technologies

Kumar, Livermont, and McKewan (2010) cited several examples that illustrate the challenges of implementing an RFID-based system. An example was Florida Hospital in Orlando where the electrophysiology department used RFID tags to track its inventory of expensive pacemakers, defibrillators, and heart catheters. By more accurately accounting for its supply, the hospital was able to save US$150,000 through reduced on-hand inventory and bulk purchasing justified by the RFID system. Vanderbilt Children's Hospital in Nashville used RFID technology in its pediatric critical care unit (CCU) to track equipment. Hospital administrators were plagued by the fact that roughly 50% of the floor's assets were missing at any given moment. After tagging all portable equipment, the nurses were able to find exactly what they needed at any given moment and tell what equipment was in use. The hospital believes that the RFID project has saved them $50,000 per month in unnecessary rental costs because all rental equipment is accounted for. RFID tags can also store data about when Vanderbilt's pediatric CCU equipment is due for maintenance. A similar study was underway at The University of Wisconsin - Madison RFID Lab is attempting to use RFID technology to improve

transfusion safety, efficiency, and accuracy in the U.S. blood products supply chain.

Some hospitals took their RFID technology to the next level by using it to track patients, which are the healthcare industry's number one product. Christiana Hospital in Newark, Delaware, used RFID tags on patients, nurses, and equipment in its 76-bed emergency department. The technology allowed the hospital to speed the treatment process and reduce inpatient length of stay, a widely accepted metric of treatment quality. (Better care means a shorter length of stay.) Even more critical, Christiana was able to provide treatment to the 4 to 5% of emergency patients who had been lost in the shuffle and were leaving without care. A survey of industry, healthcare and academic partners at the University of Amsterdam found that RFID technology used on patients themselves can also speed patient admission, discharge and transfer by 85%. In a similar move, surgical patients and then wheel chairs and portable medical instruments were affixed with RFID tags at Harrisburg Hospital in Pennsylvania for tracking and accountability purposes.

Evident in each of the cases documented by Kumar, Livermont, and McKewan (2010) are several key points about the potential of RFID tags in hospitals. However, most researchers emphasize patient safety first and foremost, operational gains in efficiency second (de Mast, Kemper, Doe, Mandjes, & van der Bijl, 2011; Gaukler, Özer, & Hausman, 2008). Such researchers generally state that RFID-enabled technology has the potential to reduce medication error, eliminate surgical errors and eliminate any problems in the pharmaceutical supply chain. This has the potential to reduce costs via lower malpractice and negligence claims. RFID tags placed on physicians and nurses can help the team quickly find each other in emergency situations and monitor performance. Patient satisfaction, which is increasingly being tied to insurance reimbursement, can also be improved with proper use of RFID technology. In general, such tags, readers, and computer system can help staff recognize and eliminate unnecessarily long wait times, communicate more effectively with patients' families, streamline patient handoffs, and allow more time at the bedside (Collier & Bienstock, 2006; Condea, Thiessse, & Fleisch, 2012; Cowles, Kiecker, & Little, 2002; Scanlon, Swaminathan, Lee, & Chernew, 2008; Scherrer-Rathje, Boyle, & Deflorin, 2009).

RFID tags on major hospital assets can help the medical staff ensure that necessary equipment is available in the right place at the right time. From the supply chain perspective, the tags also help prevent equipment over-ordering and underutilization of what the hospital already owns. The tags can also store information about when the piece of equipment needs maintenance. As hospitals begin to tag the supplies and equipment on-hand, this opens the door for tighter supply chain integration with vendors who can replenish a hospital's supply as soon as the item is scanned as having been used on a patient. Wal-Mart and its suppliers have been doing this for years in the retail setting as items leave the shelf or pass through checkout.

Through the above case studies and the general benefits of RFID in hospitals, Koong & Lin (2007) and Kumar, Livermont, and Mckewan (2010) have suggested a three-stage implementation process that should be adopted by hospitals that are rolling out RFID technology. Despite the buildup, the stages are not that profound or insightful beyond what a hospital supply chain executive would already know. Stage 1 involves tagging expensive portable equipment with RFID technology. Kumar, Livermont, and Mckewan (2010) cited a hospital in Richmond, Virginia, that saved a net US$200,000 in operating costs in the first year after RFID rollout. Another study showed that physicians spent 20% less time looking for equipment and auditors spent 50% less time looking for equipment after RFID tags were affixed to major items. Stage 2 of RFID implementation involves tagging all remaining equipment (including surgical instruments) with RFID and using it

on patients, physicians, nurses, technicians, and other personnel. All supplies in inventory are RFID tagged in Stage 3 of implementation, and they are automatically checked in and out when they move to and from hospital storage virtually eliminating the need to count them.

ACCOUNTABILITY ISSUES ASSOCIATED WITH RFID TECHNOLOGIES

Technology and Accountability for Physicians, Nurses, and/ or Other Healthcare Workers

RFID-enabled technologies can be used to tag movable equipment, surgical equipment, patients, staff, and supplies to fix a variety of problems from delays to missing equipment and team members. RFID can keep track of user identification, inventory replenishment replacement; contain safeguards for proper drug dosage and patient identification with double checking against other databases, to name a few highlights as previously documented. With the costs of insurance liability, increased safeguards and accountability should have the potential to lower such costs for all healthcare providers, as well as simultaneously add to the hospital's quality assurance – which helps out for all types of accrediting agencies. There are so many win-win scenarios; it is difficult to discuss them all. For example, a friend of the author who works for a regional health system 1,000 licensed beds, so based on a number of studies, could save $4,000 per bed or $4,000,000 per year by rolling out system-wide RFID technology. Currently, RFID systems only exist in the emergency department of the tertiary center, the obstetrics units, and in the single inpatient psychiatry unit. Such potential certainly has the management, and it will be interesting to see where this technology goes in coming years.

The pitfalls may include being too enthusiastic on all the potentials of RFID technology. Yes, RFID tags could significantly reduce or completely eliminate medication errors, but such technological applications will mean that medication errors will ever be completely eliminated by RFID applications. The action of programming the data into the RFID system is still a human process, and there is plenty of room for error. Unfortunately, all it takes is one drug being programmed in as something it is not, and the error will multiply and multiply throughout the system with disastrous effects. In such a scenario, the impact of a single error can be damaging to not just one patient as it would be ordinarily, but to millions. Undoubtedly, RFID technology could significantly reduce or eliminate malpractice, but human skill is still a determining factor in much of medicine. One surgeon's dexterity, or slipup, can cost a person his or her life whether or not RFID technology checked in the scalpel. Likewise, staff hand-washing compliance can do wonders for reducing hospital acquired infection rates, but RFID cannot yet track germs to verify compliance.

RFID Systems Eliminate Waste in Hospital's Inventory Management System

Perhaps the greatest benefit and least ethically complicated is that RFID tags essentially add visibility to many healthcare's' invisible processes. In general, adding transparency and accountability to any supply chain has risks, but largely removes subjectivity and sources of ethical violations. The essential problem is that hospitals are dynamic environments where equipment, drugs, patients, and staff move around, and the loss of any of them result in unnecessary added expense and danger to both patients and staff. Many hospitals have successfully used RFID technology in the tracking of equipment and devices. An RFID service company, for example, asserts that U.S. hospitals spend as much as US$4,000 per bed on lost and stolen equipment each year, a problem that could be almost entirely solved through RFID adoption (de Mast, Kemper, Doe, Mandjes, & van der Bijl, 2011). A secondary problem in its management of such susyems is how hospitals can best implement RFID technology to combat these problems. Although most RFID-based research has centered on manufacturing or retail, and healthcare has been largely ignored despite being an area ripe for widespread RFID adoption.

FUTURE RESEARCH DIRECTIONS

Potential Ethical Dilemmas

Many researchers gloss over the ethical dilemma of using RFID tags to trace the locations of physicians, nurses, and other personnel. Doing so is a major invasion of privacy, in the opinion of many healthcare providers as well as patients of such service. These individuals have advanced degrees, leadership roles in life and death situations and, oftentimes, big egos. For example, a number of interviewed healthcare providers for the present study have indicated that patients do not generally respond well to being tagged like tracked "pets." Also, some hospitals have unionized nursing departments, which could resist the issuance of RFID tags to nurses. One of the few instances when the author of the present study could see medical and nursing staffs embracing RFID is when it helps them prove a point to hospital administration. Examples would be to illustrate the need for increased staffing because of too little time at the bedtime or to lobby for shorter shifts because of too many waking hours on-call.

Under-Served Areas for RFID Technologies

Researchers need to address or perhaps could explore in the future is the use of RFID in healthcare outside of the hospital walls. Many touch briefly on how RFID is impacting homecare by allowing patients to transmit blood sugar levels and blood pressure back to the hospital with very inexpensive RFID tags and at-home readers. This technology may be even cheaper than the computers that some patients are being outfitted with for homecare now. Care in place is truly the future of healthcare and it is being strongly encouraged by healthcare reform, which is also looking at affordability. Companies perfecting at-home medical RFID technology may have a competitive advantage in this new landscape.

SUMMARY AND CONCLUSION

The acceptability of RFID-enabled technologies still lags behind more traditional automatic identification and data capture technologies, such as magnetic strips and barcoding applications. However, there is little doubt that the rise in popularity of RFID technologies with manufacturers, suppliers, and practitioners within the healthcare provides significant evidence that such applications do generate real potential for cost savings. This trend should continue as more studies in exposing the inefficiencies in traditional retail as well as applied areas, such as healthcare, inventory management systems are generated and become better known. There are a number of definable benefits to the organization by employing RFID-enabled systems. It will provide real-time data which will give management the most up-to-date status of all products and its use. These systems will serve as great monitors if consumer and patient behaviors which will help increase better utilization and patient satisfaction rates. RFID systems should provide more efficient and effective inventory management processes that will inform management know when the inventory of products is getting low and needs restocked. The cost of operations will be reduced, which is directly related to more efficient inventory management and a faster throughput process.

In terms of specific applications, such as shelf-replenishment applications could be compared between similar hospitals with some running the period review method of manual inventory and others running the RFID-enabled replenishment. If the forecasting was centralized, demand and shrinkage similar, and as many other variations as possible kept constant the results could be very useful in determining the actual threshold level of cost savings from implementation as well as actual real world data RFID read-rate efficiency. Much of the current evidence for RFID-related cost savings are still based on idealized mathematical modeling, but more detailed case studies on the widespread implementation of newer technologies would be more useful. A number of previous research studies cited in this chapter used simulations to determine the benefits of RFID-tagging cost-sharing for each member in the supply chain. Such simulations and research concluded that RFID tagging cost sharing initially benefits the retailer or hospital if applied to the healthcare industry, but as demand increases the benefits become more even with the other members of the supply chain. The benefits of RFID-embedded technologies are evident in each part of the supply chain from the manufacturer to the distributor to the patient/customer. The cost sharing should be spread amongst each part of the supply chain and factored into the cost based on demand and volume. Hospital management could require that the manufacturer and distributor pay for the cost of the RFID implementations, but this would not be an effective strategy to partner with distributors and manufacturers to build a close long-term relationship with them. Such a situation brings up an interesting question as to who benefits more in a RFID program where the supply chain uses RFID-tagging cost-sharing. The short answer is all members of the supply chain would benefit due to increased visibility as to where the inventory is at any given time. Each would be able to control their inventory to help eliminate shrinkage whether to theft, loss or obsolescence. But as the demand increases for an application, benefits become more balanced and the distributor and manufacturer start to see a greater benefit cost savings in using RFID-tagging cost sharing factor.

It seems that an industry's acceptance of newer technologies is still based on a wait and see attitude by its management. The appears to be a lag time until either adoption is a necessity to remain competition or the literature that supports it is widespread and provides compelling and conclusive evidence of its costs savings. The idea of decreasing the amount of inventory on hand at hospitals and lowering overall costs has widespread appeal in light of the high cost of healthcare in today's world (Smith & Rupp, 2013a,b; Wamba, 2012; Wyld; Yao, Chu, & Li, 2012). Perhaps a major challenge in some of these options is that it may reduce inventory but increases workload, at least in the minds of some healthcare professionals. As with any new technology or its application, there will always be the need for a re-adjustment period, as retraining will undoubtedly remain a major issue for users of RFID systems. The challenges of fully implementing successful VMI or stock-less supply chain systems are significant, and RFID-embedded technologies are the forefront of that fundamental change in SCM.

In terms of future research, much of the current statistics for support of RFID-embedded systems implementation has been based on retail findings. Parallel research studies in healthcare systems needs to be explored and executed. For example, such related research in self-replenishment could be expanded into a trial situation where shelf replenishment could be compared between similar stores and/or hospitals with some running the period- review method of manual inventory while others applying RFID-enabled replenishment techniques. If inventory forecasting was centralized, demand and shrinkage similar, and as many other variations as possible kept constant in a partially controlled study, costs and performance metrics could be very useful in determining the actual

threshold level of cost savings from implementation as well as actual real world data RFID read rate efficiency. Presently, a significant amount of support for RFID in the healthcare setting is based on stimulation studies. Although such mathematical modeling provides a useful baseline, more substantial empirically based studies are needed in order to justify widespread implementation of newer technologies. New applications generally lag until either adoption is a necessity to remain competition or the literature that supports it is widespread and conclusive. There is a significant body of RFID research that warrants its adoption in the healthcare field.

REFERENCES

Bhakoo, V., Singh, P., & Sohal, A. (2012). Collaborative management of inventory in Australian hospital supply chains: Practices and issues. *Supply Chain Management*, *17*(2), 217–230. doi:10.1108/13598541211212933

Chen, Z., & Dubinsky, A. J. (2003). A conceptual model of perceived customer value in e-commerce: A preliminary investigation. *Psychology and Marketing*, *20*(4), 323–347. doi:10.1002/mar.10076

Chiou, J. S. (2004). The antecedents of customer loyalty toward Internet service providers. *Information & Management*, *41*(6), 685–695. doi:10.1016/j.im.2003.08.006

Collier, J. E., & Bienstock, C. C. (2006). Measuring service quality in e-retailing. *Journal of Service Research*, *8*(3), 260–275. doi:10.1177/1094670505278867

Condea, C., Thiessse, F., & Fleisch, E. (2012). RFID-enabled shelf replenishment with backroom monitoring in retail stores. *Decision Support Systems*, *52*(4), 839–849. doi:10.1016/j.dss.2011.11.018

Cowles, D. L., Kiecker, P., & Little, M. W. (2002). Using key informant insights as a foundation for e-retailing theory development. *Journal of Business Research*, *55*(8), 629–636. doi:10.1016/S0148-2963(00)00203-4

de Mast, J., Kemper, B., Doe, R. J., Mandjes, M., & van der Bijl, Y. (2011). Process improvement in healthcare: Overall resource efficiency. *Quality and Reliability Engineering International*, *27*(8), 1095–1106. doi:10.1002/qre.1198

Gaukler, G. M., Özer, O., & Hausman, W. H. (2008). Order progress information: Improved dynamic emergency ordering policies. *Production and Operations Management*, *17*(6), 599–614. doi:10.3401/poms.1080.0066

Hu, G., Wang, L., Fetch, S., & Bidanda, B. (2008). A multi-objective model for project portfolio selection to implement lean and Six Sigma concepts. *International Journal of Production Research*, *46*(23), 6611–6648. doi:10.1080/00207540802230363

Jain, V., Benyoucef, L., & Deshmukh, S. G. (2008). What's the buzz about moving from 'lean' to 'agile' integrated supply chains? A fuzzy intelligent agent-based approach. *International Journal of Production Research*, *46*(23), 6649–6678. doi:10.1080/00207540802230462

Kamhawi, E. M. (2008). System characteristics, perceived benefits, individual differences and use intentions: A survey of decision support tools of ERP systems. *Information Resources Management Journal*, *21*(4), 66–83. doi:10.4018/irmj.2008100104

Kennedy, F. A., & Widener, S. K. (2008). A control framework: Insights from evidence on lean accounting. *Management Accounting Research*, *19*(4), 301–319. doi:10.1016/j.mar.2008.01.001

Koong, L., & Lin, C. (2007). Evaluating the decision to adopt RFID systems using Analytic Hierarchy Process. *Journal of American Academy of Business*, *11*(1), 72–77.

Kumar, S., Livermont, G., & Mckewan, G. (2010). Stage implementation of RFID hospitals. *Technology and Health Care*, *18*(1), 31–46. PMID:20231801

Scanlon, D. P., Swaminathan, S., Lee, W., & Chernew, M. (2008). Does competition improve health care quality? *Health Services Research*, *43*(6), 1931–1944. doi:10.1111/j.1475-6773.2008.00899.x PMID:18793214

Scherrer-Rathje, M., Boyle, T. A., & Deflorin, P. (2009). Lean, take two! Reflections from the second attempt at lean implementation. *Business Horizons*, *52*(1), 79–85. doi:10.1016/j.bushor.2008.08.004

Seidman, S. J., Brockman, R., Lewis, B. M., Guag, J., Shein, M. J., & Clement, W. J. et al. (2010). In vitro tests reveal sample radio frequency identification readers inducing clinically significant electromagnetic interference to implantable pacemakers and implantable cardioverter-defibrillators. *Heart Rhythm: The Official Journal of the Heart Rhythm Society*, *7*(1), 99–107. doi:10.1016/j.hrthm.2009.09.071 PMID:20129290

Smith, A. D. (2005a). Reverse logistics and their affects on CRM and online behavior. *VINE: The Journal of Information and Knowledge Management*, *35*(3), 166–181. doi:10.1108/03055720510634216

Smith, A. D. (2005b). Exploring the inherent benefits of RFID and automated self-serve Checkouts in a B2C environment. *International Journal of Business Information Systems*, *1*(1-2), 149–183. doi:10.1504/IJBIS.2005.007405

Smith, A. D. (2008). Evolution and acceptability of medical applications of RFID implants among early users of technology. *Health Marketing Quarterly*, *24*(1-2), 121–155. doi:10.1080/07359680802125980 PMID:19042524

Smith, A. D. (2009). Marketing and reputation aspects of neonatal safeguards and hospital-security systems. *Health Marketing Quarterly*, *26*(2), 117–144. doi:10.1080/07359680802619818 PMID:19408180

Smith, A. D., & Offodile, O. F. (2007). Exploring forecasting and project management characteristics of supply chain management. *International Journal of Logistics and Supply Management*, *3*(2), 174–214.

Smith, A. D., & Offodile, O. F. (2008). Gauging web portals impact on supply chain management concepts. *International Journal of Logistics and Management*, *4*(2), 184–206.

Smith, A. D., & Offodile, O. F. (2009). The perceived importance of major RFID-related technology initiatives among retail store managers. *International Journal of Services and Operations Management*, *5*(4), 520–547. doi:10.1504/IJSOM.2009.024583

Smith, A. D., & Rupp, W. T. (2013a). Supply supplier integration, procurement, and outsourcing: Case study of SCM social capital benefits. *International Journal of Logistics Systems and Management*, *14*(2), 221–241. doi:10.1504/IJLSM.2013.051340

Smith, A. D., & Rupp, W. T. (2013b). Data quality and knowledge/information management in service operations management: Regional supermarket case study. *International Journal of Knowledge-Based Organizations*, *3*(3), 35–52. doi:10.4018/ijkbo.2013070103

Swaminathan, S., Chernew, M., & Scanlon, D. P. (2008). Persistence of HMO performance measures. *Health Services Research*, *43*(6), 2033–2051. doi:10.1111/j.1475-6773.2008.00890.x PMID:18783460

Ustundag, A. (2010). Evaluating RFID investment on a supply chain using tagging cost sharing factor. *International Journal of Production Research*, *48*(9), 2549–2562. doi:10.1080/00207540903564926

Wamba, S. F. (2012). RFID-enabled healthcare applications, issues and benefits: An archival analysis (1997-2011). *Journal of Medical Systems*, *36*(6), 3393–3398. doi:10.1007/s10916-011-9807-x PMID:22109670

Wyld, D. C. (2006). RFID 101: The next big thing for management. *Management Research News*, *29*(4), 154–173. doi:10.1108/01409170610665022

Yao, A., & Carlson, J. (1999). The impact of real-time data communication on inventory management. *International Journal of Production Economics*, *59*(1), 213–219. doi:10.1016/S0925-5273(98)00234-5

Yao, W., Chu, C.-H., & Li, Z. (2012). The adoption and implementation of RFID Technologies in healthcare: A literature review. *Journal of Medical Systems*, *36*(6), 3507–3525. doi:10.1007/s10916-011-9789-8 PMID:22009254

ADDITIONAL READING

Acharyulu, G. (2007). RFID in the healthcare supply chain: Improving performance through greater visibility. *ICFAI Journal of Management Research*, *6*(11), 32–45.

Al-Sakran, H. (2013). Agent and radio frequency identification based architecture for supermarket information system. *Journal of Computer Science*, 9(6), 699–707. doi:10.3844/jcssp.2013.699.707

Chao, C., Yang, J. M., & Jen, W. (2007). Determining technology trends and forecasts of RFID by a historical review and bibliometric analysis from 1991 to 2005. *Technovation*, 27(5), 268–279. doi:10.1016/j.technovation.2006.09.003

Chen, C. C., Wu, J., Su, Y. S., & Yang, S. C. (2008). Key drivers for the continued use of RFID technology in the emergency room. *Management Research News*, 31(4), 273–288. doi:10.1108/01409170810851348

Chen, C. I., Liu, C. Y., Li, Y. C., Chao, C.-C., Liu, C.-T., Chen, C.-F., & Kuan, C.-F. (2005). Pervasive observation medicine: The application of RFID to improve patient safety in observation unit of hospital emergency department. *Studies in Heath Technology Information*, 311-315. [Online]. Retrieved December 20, 2013 from http://www.ncbi.nlm.nih.gov/pubmed/16160277

Chen, C.-L., & Wu, C.-Y. (2012). Using RFID yoking proof protocol to enhance inpatient medication safety. *Journal of Medical Systems*, 36(5), 2849–2864. doi:10.1007/s10916-011-9763-5 PMID:21811800

Chien, H.-Y., Yang, C.-C., Wu, T.-C., & Lee, C.-F. (2011). Two RFID based solutions to enhance inpatient medication safety. *Journal of Medical Systems*, 35(3), 369–375. doi:10.1007/s10916-009-9373-7 PMID:20703553

Condea, C., Thiessse, F., & Fleisch, E. (2012). RFID-enabled shelf replenishment with backroom monitoring in retail stores. *Decision Support Systems*, 52(4), 839–849. doi:10.1016/j.dss.2011.11.018

Devaraj, S., Fan, M., & Kohli, R. (2002). Antecedents of B2C channel satisfaction and preference: Validating e-commerce metrics. *Information Systems Research*, 13(3), 316–333. doi:10.1287/isre.13.3.316.77

Dutta, A., Lee, H. L., & Whang, S. (2007). RFID and operations management: Technology, value and incentives. *Production and Operations Management*, 16(5), 646–655. doi:10.1111/j.1937-5956.2007.tb00286.x

Erdem, E., Zeng, H., Zhou, J., Shi, J., & Wells, D. L. (2009). Investigation of RFID tag readability for pharmaceutical products at item level. *Drug Development and Industrial Pharmaceuticals*, 35(11), 1312–1324. doi:10.3109/03639040902902393 PMID:19832631

Ferguson, R. B. (2006). RFID loses reception: high tag costs are still putting the kibosh on returns on investment. *e-Week, 23*(10), 11-12.

Fisher, J. A., & Monahan, T. (2008). Tracking the social dimensions of RFID systems in hospitals. *International Journal of Medical Informatics*, 77(3), 176–183. doi:10.1016/j.ijmedinf.2007.04.010 PMID:17544841

Green, H., & Khermouch, G. (2005). Barcodes better watch their backs. *Business Week*. Retrieved December 8, 2012, from http://www.business-week.com/magazine/content/03_28/b3841063.htm

Huang, H.-H., & Ku, C.-Y. (2009). A RFID grouping proof protocol for medication safety of inpatient. *Journal of Medical Systems*, 33(6), 467–474. doi:10.1007/s10916-008-9207-z PMID:20052898

Kamhawi, E. M. (2008). System characteristics, perceived benefits, individual differences and use intentions: A survey of decision support tools of ERP systems. *Information Resources Management Journal*, 21(4), 66–83. doi:10.4018/irmj.2008100104

Mehrjerdi, Y. Z. (2010). RFID-enabled healthcare systems: Risk-benefit analysis. *International Journal of Pharmaceutical and Healthcare Marketing*, *4*(3), 282–300. doi:10.1108/17506121011076192

Min, D., & Yih, Y. (2011). Fuzzy logic-based approach to detecting a passive RFID tag in an outpatient clinic. *Journal of Medical Systems*, *35*(3), 423–432. doi:10.1007/s10916-009-9377-3 PMID:20703549

Ohashi, K., Ota, S., Ohno-Machado, L., & Tanaka, H. (2008). Comparison of RFID systems for tracking clinical interventions at the bedside. In: *AMIA Annual Symposium Proceedings*, pp 525-529.

Ranji, U., Lundy, J., & Salganicoff, A. (2010). US healthcare costs: A background brief. Retrieved October 27, 2013, from http://www.kaiseredu.org/topics_im.asp?imID=1&parentID=61&id=358

Smith, A. A., Smith, A. D., & Baker, D. J. (2011). Inventory management shrinkage and employee anti-theft approaches. *International Journal of Electronic Finance*, *5*(3), 209–234. doi:10.1504/IJEF.2011.041337

Smith, A. D. (2010). Corporate social responsibility in the healthcare insurance industry: A cause-branding approach. *International Journal of Electronic Healthcare*, *5*(3), 284–302. doi:10.1504/IJEH.2010.034177 PMID:20643642

Smith, A. D. (2011). Operational effectiveness and quality assurance mechanisms with stochastic demand of blood supply: Blood bank case study. *International Journal of Electronic Healthcare*, *6*(2-4), 174–191. PMID:22189177

Smith, A. D. (2012). Case studies of RFID-related applications in the healthcare and voice-recognition industries. *International Journal of Knowledge-Based Organizations*, *2*(3), 48–63. doi:10.4018/ijkbo.2012070103

Smith, A. D. (2012). Operational efficiencies and ethical issues associated with microchip implants. *International Journal of Mobile Communications*, *10*(3), 281–302. doi:10.1504/IJMC.2012.048113

Smith, A. D. (2013). Quality and technology-based management initiatives within a hospital environment: Benchmarking case study. *International Journal of Procurement Management*, *6*(6), 621–648. doi:10.1504/IJPM.2013.056746

Smith, A. D. (2013). Competitive uses of information and knowledge management tools: Case study of supplier-side management. *International Journal of Knowledge-Based Organizations*, *3*(1), 71–87. doi:10.4018/ijkbo.2013010105

Smith, A. D. (2013). Perceived value and strategic importance of supply chain options: Multi-firm case study. *International Journal of Logistics Systems and Supply Management*, *13*(2), 244–267. doi:10.1504/IJLSM.2012.048938

Ting, S. L., Kwok, S. K., Tsang, A. H. C., & Lee, W. B. (2009). Critical elements and lessons learnt from the implementation of an RFID-enabled healthcare management system in a medical organization. *Journal of Medical Systems*, *35*(4), 657–669. doi:10.1007/s10916-009-9403-5 PMID:20703523

van der Togt, R., Jan van Lieshout, E., Hensbroek, R., Beinat, E., Binnekade, J. M., & Bakker, P. J. M. (2008). Electromagnetic interference from radio frequency identification inducing potentially hazardous incidents in critical care medical equipment. *Journal of the American Medical Association*, *299*(24), 2884–2890. doi:10.1001/jama.299.24.2884 PMID:18577733

Wickboldt, A.-K., & Piramuthu, S. (2012). Patient safety through RFID: Vulnerabilities in recently proposed grouping protocols. *Journal of Medical Systems*, *36*(2), 431–435. doi:10.1007/s10916-010-9487-y PMID:20703708

Zang, C., & Fan, Y. (2007). Complex event processing in enterprise information systems based on RFID. *Enterprise Information Systems*, *1*(1), 3–23. doi:10.1080/17517570601092127

KEY TERMS AND DEFINITIONS

Automatic Identification and Data Capture Technologies (AIDC): Types of AIDC-related technologies to leave the human element out of the data collection and storage functions of information derived from manufacturing, integrated through the manufacturing process, types of authentication concerns and/or e-security strategies, and relationship links to customer profiles. Typical types of AIDC include, bar-coding, RFID, magnetic strips, touch memory, and smart cards.

Barcoding Technology: A long-term and very reliable type of AIDC technology, it is known for its very accurate and economical approaches to identity products and machine readable information from a variety of manufactured goods and services. Most barcodes use a type of standardized bars and spacing coding or symbology that is certified by an international standards body (GS1 System). This system provides for the universal global acceptance of many types of barcodes designed for a variety of shipping and identification applications. Example barcode formats that are in common use today include EAN/UPC, GS1 DataBar, GS1-128, ITF-14, GS1 DataMatrix, GS1 QR Code and Composite Components.

Ethical Dilemmas: There are a number of ethical theories that are appropriate for dealing with healthcare issues concerning automatic identification. These theories involve both individual and group behavior that are grounded in moral philosophy, especially in the concepts of consequentialism or deontology ethical philosophy. Perhaps over the last few decades, there has been a revival of virtue-theoretical work in ethical

research, especially applied to ethics of healthcare information collection and retrieval.

Healthcare Service Strategies: When it comes to the healthcare industry, an overall strategic goal is to provide affordable coverage and quality service to all citizens that need such services at affordable costs. In healthcare, creating a competitive advantage can be done through providing a service that is highly prized by its customers, or even more importantly, offering the best price for the service.

Operations Efficiency: Improving efficiency and reducing waste is a major challenge for hospitals and other patient care facilities looking to lower the cost of providing healthcare services. Far and away the largest contributor to operational costs in this industry is patient care activities. Since most clinical decisions involve managing products and medical supplies, finding ways to more efficiently manage supply chain activities can have a big impact on overall operational performance.

RFID-Embedded Technologies: RFID technologies are types of automatic data capture techniques that use a combination of active and passive senders and receivers to collect and store codified information for further uses. The implementation of such technologies should lead to improved managerial and/or supply chain performance. On the surface, there appears to be few drawbacks to implementing such technology into a production process, assuming it enhances performance and improves output of the product. The main issues surrounding the RFID applications are whether the initial costs and labor required to utilize this technology are worth it, and will result in a positive outcome of revenues.

Supply Chain Management/Performance: In basic terms, supply chain is the system of organizations, people, activities, information and resources involved in moving a product or service from supplier to customer. The configuration and management of supply chain operations is a key way companies obtain and maintain a competitive advantage. The typical manufacturing supply chain begins with raw material suppliers, or inputs. The next link in the chain is the manufacturing, or transformation step; followed the distribution, or localization step. Finally, the finished product or service is purchased by customers as outputs. Service and Manufacturing managers need to know the impact of supply on their organization's purchasing and logistics processes. However, supply chain performance and its metrics are difficult to develop and actually measure.

Vendor-Managed Inventory Systems (VMI): VMI-based systems are designed to transfer the control of inventory and its planning activities to a manufacturer or distributor in order to provide a beneficial relationship to promote a more transparent and seamless flow of goods and services at lower costs. As in many recent retailer applications, the supplier/vendor assumes responsible for replenishing and stocking inventory at appropriate levels to minimize inconvenience to the ultimate customer.

Virtual Asset Trackers (VAT): Increased transparency in supply chains and the need to track personal as well as physical assets has led to the development of Virtual Asset Trackers (VAT). VAT-based technologies allow for hosted users to automatically received updates on inventories on their RFID handhelds and Web Asset Managers. VAT is a type of application of active RFID tagging that allows healthcare practitioners to enhance security to patients, residents, and hospital staff while providing better patient and resident-care services. Ideally, proper leveraging of VAT-based technologies allow management within the healthcare setting to simultaneously improve regulatory compliance, preventing or reducing inventory shrinkage, reduce labor intensive staff assignments, and lessen spoilage of perishables. These are mainly operational advantages that are commonly associated with active RFID applications.

Chapter 11
Inventory Management, Shrinkage Concerns, and Related Corrective RFID Strategies

Alan D. Smith
Robert Morris University, USA

ABSTRACT

RFID-based solutions are essential inventory management tools, supplying more information than the standard barcode that help eliminate the potential for inventory stock-outs and reducing theft-based inventory shrinkage. A relatively detailed discussion of these techniques is included in this chapter by addressing some of the many concerns of inventory shrinkage. As is evident from the empirical section of this chapter, although RFID may be perceived as a cutting-edge business solution, RFID systems and its implementations still prove to be a difficult process to implement and achieve. Many companies have avoided the idea of introducing RFID systems, possibly due to being overwhelmed with the new technologies. However, its impacts on reducing inventory shrinkage are fairly clear and decisive.

RFID-RELATED TECHNOLOGIES IN OPERATIONS AND INVENTORY MANAGEMENT

Exploring the Growth of RFID-Related Technologies

There have been numerous investigations to investigate the benefits of radio frequency identification (RFID), especially in retail and operational situations. A number of more traditional studies have focused on the effects that RFID has on supply chain performance, especially inventory management. This chapter inspects some of this literature and empirically tests perceptions of inventory management on its effectiveness, especially in regardless to inventory shrinkage controls. In general, a plethora of literature has been written on the general overview of automatic identification and data capture technologies (AIDC), especially RFID-based solutions, and how such technologies can be applied within supply chains,

DOI: 10.4018/978-1-4666-6308-4.ch011

the benefits that it brings to firms, managerial guidelines around using it, and how to implement them (Devaraj, Fan, & Kohli, 2002; Dutta, Lee, & Whang, 2007; Zang & Fan, 2007). There have been recent writings made on its effects in the area of finance, inventory, and manufacturing (Aldaihani & Darwish, 2013; Azadeh, Gholizadeh, & Jeihoonian, 2013; Bhamu, Khandelwal, & Sangwan, 2013; Fumi, Scarabotti, & Schiraldi, 2013; Ketikidis, Hayes, Lazuras, Gunasekaran, & Koh, 2013; Mateen & More, 2013; Park & Min, 2013). In particular, Visich et al. (2009) focused on the review and classification of existing quantitative empirical evidence that has was gathered for RFID on supply chain performance. The evidence was separated out into two sections, which included processes and effects. The processes were further broken out into operational and managerial, while the effects were broken out into automation-related, informational, and transformational. The focus of the study was to identify which process and effect RFID impacts and which it does not.

Operational processes, as it relates to the RFID applications generally include labor cost reductions, improved reliability and efficiency, and reduced throughput and inventory costs. Management processes typically include administrative decisions, process control, reporting, and routine. Automation-related effects are related to the value that comes from making a process more efficient. Informational effects are those that are due to the ability of the technology to gather, store, process, and distribute information. Transformational effects are those that create innovation or transformation through technology.

Visich et al. (2009) only focused on metrics that were based on actual results that were reported from a pilot study or through actual implementation (i.e. empirically tested). To make the study more focused, they omitted cases where multiple metrics were employed. These omitted metrics included estimated benefits or benefits that were masked to protect confidentiality, results from unidentified companies (unless the results were

significant), results that were difficult to separate due to phased implementations of information management systems and RFID, and aggregated evidence from multi-year implementations across all of a company's facilities. By inspecting the data via a process-oriented framework (i.e. immediate and on-going operational benefits from enterprise resource planning implementations), they found that the empirical evidence reflected that the major effects from implementing RFID within supply chain management were automation-related effects. These effects were on operational processes via inventory control and efficiency improvements. This is followed by informational effects on managerial processes via improved decision quality, production control, and effectiveness of retails sales. The evidence for informational and transformational effects on operational processes was very limited. Similarly, the evidence showed that there were no automation-related or transformational effects for managerial processes. The empirical evidence showed that the major effects of RFID on supply chain performance are automation-related effects on operational processes and informational effects on managerial processes.

Supply Chain and Inventory Management Applications

There are many case studies of the benefits to SCM and inventory control brought forth through the implementation of RFID tags across a variety of industries, in order to identify the key benefits of implementing the program in highly differentiated industries. Such research generally has its major goal to develop a working model that may be useful to the process of identifying key benefits of RFID implementation across industries. RFID-related technology domestic sales exceeded US$7 billion in 2008 and are expected to continue increasing for the foreseeable future (Mehrjerdi, 2011). As such, many firms are looking to implement the technology to their advantage by reducing inventory or supply chain costs, increasing efficiency in delivering products or services, increasing antitheft or other security precautions, and/or to allow them the tools necessary to offer distribution through large retailers, such as Wal-Mart, or to become suppliers of large purchasers, such as the U.S. Department of Defense.

RFID tags have been used for several decades, are comprised of a silicon chip and separate antenna, and consist of four types: passive, semi-passive, semi-active, and active. Passive tags require an external power source from the tag reader while active tags are powered internally via a battery with semi-passive and semi-active using a battery to power either the antenna or the chip, respectively. The major improvements offered by RFID from the barcode are the capability of holding much more data, 96 bits or more versus 16 bits, the capability to read multiple tags simultaneously, and the ability to utilize dynamic data that can be rewritten as deemed necessary (Ustundag, 2010; Wyld, 2006; Yao & Carlson, 1999).

The implementation of RFID provides many benefits to SCM, inventory, and scheduling through its greater capacity to store dynamic information allowing this data to reflect where the item is located in both a physical location and a as a function of its completeness. RFID allows companies to better regulate procurement in a JIT manner so that inventories may be kept low and process management can become more efficient. By permitting data to be transferred relating to the quality aspects of a product such as expiration dates and holding temperature for food products. When RFID techniques are applied to a retail sector, data quality aspects may be transferred to functions of time, as styles fluctuate with the seasons (Smith & Rupp, 2013), or to functions of multiple other aspects allowing for fast and easy identification of products requiring removal from inventory to avoid obsolescence or shrinkage (Smith, Smith, & Baker, 2011). Benefits can be found through stop-loss accountability and anti-theft as the RFID tags are typically easy to

embed and simple to monitor past endpoints such as exits or trash disposals, eliminating waste from accidental disposal or theft.

Indirect benefits of RFID implementation typically include those informed in part on information gathered from implementation. It is hoped by management that by monitoring workflows and throughputs, it will be possible to redesign and better integrate manufacturing or services processes to eliminate waste from excess time in non-value added tasks such as storage or queuing. It is also possible to re-evaluate human capital and assign duties to better contribute to individual development and satisfaction in the process, decreasing labor costs by reducing the number of positions required, increasing labor's efficiency, and reducing inventory shrinkage.

Mehrjerdi (2011) analyzed pertinent literature to determine what benefits RFID implementation can have to various industries, the possibility of further adaptation, the causes of slower adaptation than expected, and areas in which future research may prove most useful. Due to the difficulty nature of analyzing different industries and their various implications and industries, a brief summary of some of the major benefits will be presented instead. Case 1 evaluated the consumer perspective towards RFID in retail, finding consumers to be most receptive of its use in self-checkout, traceability information, trolley reader, shelf tags, dynamic promotion, and dynamic pricing. Another case compared the various benefits of implementation between U.S. and Korean retailers. The researchers developed a model to investigate the relationships between RFID benefits, technological infrastructure and strategic performance. The results indicate the technologic infrastructure is a necessity in improving inventory management, store operation, and demand management. Korean firms were found to utilize RFID more for store operation and demand management while U.S. firms utilized the technology for inventory management. Each technique lead to better strategic performance but magnitude was dependent on specific benefit factors.

Other cases showcased RFID adaption to improve inventory control, food safety, and service quality. One case emphasized the dynamic nature of RFID with the restaurant considering implanting temperature sensors in order to monitor food safety. It also highlighted the benefits of reading tags outside of a line of sight, reading multiple tags at once, utilizing the data to quickly replenish supplies, and of providing real-time nutritional information to diners as the menu items passed in front of them. Some cases emphasized the potential implications in IT, focusing on the exploitation-exploration perspective. Exploitation was found to increase a firm's competitive advantage through increased SC efficiencies, while exploration increased it through increased innovation abilities. The long-term implementation of RFID then affects short and long term competitive advantages leading to a short-term advantage through "learning to adjust" and a long-term advantage through "learning to transform."

Manufacturing cases emphasis rapid reading, permissible paths for material flows, container visibility, and transparency. All of these benefits further indicate the superiority of RFID over existing static identification systems: reading multiple tags at once, input/output capabilities, readability from longer distances out of a line of sight, and traceability. Most successful cases illustrate RFID benefits and identify them as current trends leading to more widespread adaptation of the technology, such as decreasing costs of the infrastructure and the emergence of standards for use such as ISO, IEEE, and EPC as additional contributors to RFID adaptation.

There are numerous cases in the service industries that reiterate the advantages of RFID over barcodes, especially in healthcare settings. Such benefits are usually tangible and mainly in tracking equipment and supplies, but serious privacy concerns arise from use in tracking patients and their medical records (Chen, Wu, Su, & Yang,

2008; Fisher & Monahan, 2008). Service sector uses of RFID must deal with people's perception of security and privacy challenges. The wide array of previous research in RFID-related implementations is often difficult and confusing to interpret the applicability of the findings to general benefits and costs. Costs can be well established, but actual benefits and their economic worth can be somewhat subjective and arbitrary in nature, varying greatly from industry type and actual application.

As the previous studies on operational and supply chain benefits of RFID implementation, the potential benefits of remaining competitive and of adaption to evolving best practices are required of all long-term planning objectives. However, the industry specific benefits vary greatly and as such, careful consideration of cost implications, desired outcomes, and competitors' ambitions should be a necessity before pursuing a course of action. In general, case studies are usually a great method for interpreting many aspects of business process, but multiple case studies work best when confined to a specific set of characteristics that are both of interest and closely related. However, potential benefits of implementation must be weight against cost considerations in order to make a proper decision in ultimate adaption.

INVENTORY CONTROL CONSIDERATIONS

General Goals of Inventory Management

There are various inventory management techniques, but, the underling goal in most techniques is a focus on cost minimization or profit maximization while satisfying the customers demand (Drejer & Riis, 2000; Grewal, 2008; Hu, Wang, Fetch, & Bidanda, 2008; Jain, Benyoucef, & Deshmukh, 2008). Typically, companies either have too much inventory or too little inventory. Too much inventory often results in loss of space, creates a financial burden, and increases the risk of damage, shrinkage, or spoilage depending on the type of inventory. Too little inventory can lead to a risk of not having enough product on hand to fulfil customer orders in a timely manner and disrupts operations. These factors frequently lead researchers to apply advanced statistical models to determine if there is a relationship between cost minimization with inventory and financial performance. However, the choice of technology may not just reduce operational costs, but improve financial performance through reduction of inventory shrinkage. Proper inventory management is getting more attention in today's highly competitive environment to increase financial performance. This trend has resulted in management trends such as material planning systems (MRP), Just-in-time (JIT) inventory and enterprise research planning (ERP) techniques.

Inventory management has been a major focus for companies as it is the biggest cost to manufacturing companies. Inventory management has many different techniques and there have been many conflicting reports in whether lean or JIT inventory techniques result in increased performance. In both lean and JIT management, one of the major focuses is to reduce the levels of inventory that a company has on hand with a goal to increase the number of times inventory is turned-over during the year. As there have been conflicting studies on inventory management techniques, the author determined that advanced statistical analysis needs performed over a broad range of industries (chemicals, textiles and food) to determine if there is a relationship between reduced inventories and increased financial performance. Financial performance in this research paper is measured by gross profit margins and net profit margins. The results in the analysis will support whether or not inventory management techniques lead to increased financial performance.

Inventory management is a key operations management initiative. Inventory can account for a large percentage of a company's costs, when not managed correctly. Inventory that becomes obsolete, in turn becomes invaluable. On-the-other-hand, when the correct amount of inventory is not on hand, this can lead to lost revenues. Then there is the inventory that is either kept too long and becomes obsolete or is not used, however we no longer have the stock. Where do these items go? The answer, in many cases, is that the inventory may become a victim to inventory shrinkage. RFID implementation has advantages that can effectively deal with this important issue as well, which will be the major theme to be discussed in the empirical section of this chapter.

As previously developed, RFID is a developing technology that allows automatic identification of tags that are applied to items. Since an antenna reads these tags and relays a signal back to the receiver, scanning is typically faster due to there is not physical contact to scan the items. According to Koumanakos (2008), a major problem with RFID-related technologies and its implementation is that there not much research performed to determine the true financial benefits of the automated system, although such systems typically serve to reduce inventory shrinkage. Basically, does RFID technology generally return a positive return on investment (ROI)?

Pacciarelli, D'Ariano, and Scotto (2011) analyzed a company's warehouse and related activities and performed tests to determine the best layout of shelves/product to minimize costs. Their study compared the current package management process with a new process based on RFID-based technology and to develop an error-free item scanning configuration within the warehouse. Once the current configuration of the warehouse is imputed, the authors are able to tweak the layout to different scenarios depending on which layouts yields the best results. Pacciarelli et al (2011) noticed that the original layout had additional selves that were located towards the middle back portion of the warehouse. Tests showed that the RFID signals could not completely penetrate through the shelves and rolls that were made of metal. Since RFID signals could not access the tags behind these storage units, a new layout design was necessary that had selves located around the outside perimeter of the warehouse. This enables that no signals will be blocked. Once the layout problems were solved, it was important to determine the optimal number of antennas and receivers to send and retrieve these RFID signals. Through mathematical modeling, Pacciarelli, D'Ariano, and Scotto determined the optimal distance and power needed by the antennas and receivers.

There are many mathematically based optimization programs that can be custom tailored to determine the correct inventory layout design for improved RFID system performance. Koumanakos (2008) measured the financial performance of three Greek industries by calculating the gross profit margins, net profit margins, and the number of days in inventories for the food, textile, and chemical industries and compared these data with inventory performance characteristics. In general, the number of days in inventories ratio measures how many days of inventory is on-hand, meaning that management should prefer to have a low ratio that would indicate that inventory is turning over faster. Reducing inventory levels promote operating on a more JIT-type pull system. From an analysis standpoint, if the number of days in inventories decreases, then it would be expected that the gross and net profit margins increase or if the number of days in inventories increases, then it would be expected that gross and net profit margins decrease. The results varied for each industry and the only industry that resulted in regression analysis with robust linear relationships was the chemicals industry. The results were highly variable, ultimately suggesting that RFID-based solutions associated with inventory and financial relationships were not conclusive and highly dependent on the industrial sector studied.

Efficient inventory management techniques should lead to an increase in financial performance, but a more long-term strategic approach and using case studies would be a more appropri-

ate way to judge performance as each company has unique operating characteristics. There as so many variables that could cause operational and financial data to be misinterpreted when analyzing operating margins to the number of days in inventory (i.e. macroeconomic issues impacting results should be included, but rarely are analyzed). Perhaps financial performance measures, such as gross operating margins, should be compared to inventory variables as selling, general, and administrative costs should have little impact on how inventory management impacts the financial bottom-line. Financial analysis perhaps should focus on cost-of-goods-sold related items, which, in-turn makes the gross profit margin a better ratio to use when comparing inventory variables to financial performance.

Causes of Inventory Shrinkage

Employee-Based Theft

Employee theft has been proven to be one of the largest sources of retail shrinkage. It has been conservatively estimated that over 90% of all retail environments experience some time of employee theft. It has been found that employees not only steal merchandise, but cash, supplies, and company time as well. According to the U.S. Chamber of Commerce, an estimated US$40 billion is stolen annually from domestic firms, almost 10 times the lost due to domestic street crimes (Snyder, Broome, Kehoe, McIntyre, & Blair, 1991). These data has increased by almost US$10 billion over the last decade ("Challenges in the retail industry," 2008).

Retail-based loss prevention has been a very old issue, suggesting that the US$0.99 ending to most retail prices is not to induce customers into thinking that prices are lower, but to force employees to have to make change to reduce theft ("Ernst and Young's study of retail loss prevention," 2003). Traditionally, employees have found many different methods of stealing from their retail stores' place of employment. Product and cash are the two most prevalent. However, employees may steal time by having false punches on the time clock, padding their paychecks, providing deals to family and friends, by discounting product or not ringing them up at all, pocketing change or shortchanging customers, and stealing customers' credit card numbers from imprints. Such employees may have been known to void transactions and take the cash back out of the register, which then proves problematic for inventory counts and if the customers choose to return the product that was never officially sold.

The registers and customer service counters are not the only places of theft, as back doors and loading docks can present a serious opportunity or problem for inventory shrinkage. Managers that leave warehouse doors open and unattended are asking for theft. Loading docks are infamous places for missing product or boxes of product that are never officially received. Employee theft may been the cause of more than 30% of business failures, causing bankruptcy and even closures (Snyder et al., 1991).

Employees steal for many reasons, with unsatisfactory working conditions, poor pay, hardships in their personal lives, or easily susceptible to acts of dishonesty (Bolin & Heatherly, 2001). These suggested reasons may be only a few causes of inventory shrinkage. Many employers are working to change environments to create happier employees through more productive workplace environments, which should reduce employee theft-related inventory shrinkage.

There are obvious warning signals and signs that can lead a retail manager to detect dishonest or disgruntled employees (Greenberg, 1990; Kulas, McInnerney, DeMuth, & Jadwinski, 2007). Finding consistent transactional errors from one particular employee would usually tend to indicate to management of either poor training or theft. Unpleasant, rude, withdrawn, and/or angry employees are likely candidates for inventory shrinkage. Known personal issues, such as gambling problems, substance abuse problems,

or other interrelationship issues may result in employees trying to enhance their financial returns outside the traditional firm's paycheck. Employees' personal hardships, coupled with an opportunity to steal from inventories. RFID systems may reduce perceived opportunities for inventory shrinkage, even if such systems are poorly designed and implemented. Employees who are related to other employees or relationships between employees that develop may be areas of concern for retail managers. The statistics around employee theft, as previously cited, are significant and the financial impact that employee theft can have on an individual company can be devastating. Implementation costs of any RFID-based deterrent system should be greatly discounted when management considers the entire costs of such a system, particularly in light of employee-based inventory shrinkage.

Improper Cycle Counting

An equally important source of inventory shrinkage that RFID systems may effectively address is improper cycle counting. Cycle counting will continue to play an important role in attaining and measuring inventory record accuracy (Smith, 2011; Summers & Scherpereel, 2008; Tari & Sabater, 2004; Tiwari, Turner, & Sackett, 2007). Probably the two most common types of cycle counting are the ranking method and/or the control group methods. When a company counts inventory, management normally has their employees stay extended period of time and have them count the entire inventory. This method is may not the most accurate and can be directly influenced by behavioral attitudes of the firms' employees. Cycle counting methods, especially if at least partially automated, are typically superior and more accurate approaches of keeping track of inventory rather than annual counting of the entire inventory.

There are a few problems that arise when cycle counting, even if partially automated. Since certain inventory is very fluid or constantly moving, especially in retail settings, many instances occur where computerized records have not been updated. This may be especially true in the cases of significant customer returns have not been currently or properly processed (Smith, 2011). If some stock receipts are not in the correct location, sales orders and transfer stock materials have not been properly filed, and/or if customer orders are moved during counting may all lead to poor cycle counting results. Management must be diligent when deciding on which counting method to use.

The ranking method usually places greater significance on items with a large dollar-volume amounts flowing through inventory. Items are traditionally ranked in four categories from highest to lowest value in A, B, C, and D categories. As a general rule, A-categorized items that are responsible for 80% of the proposed inventory value, B items the next 15%, C items the nest 4%, while D items consist of the last 1%. Typically, such ranked items should be counted 6, 3, 2, and once a year respectively (Schreibfeder, 2008).

Control group cycle counting general has a number of well-established steps to follow. The steps include selecting the control group, counting the control group, comparing the count records, reconciling and identify causes of error, developing a corrective action, and publishing the results (Tari & Sabater, 2004, Tiwari, et al., 2007). The control group should consist of a cross section of the inventory, including high and low cost, high and low usage, and stockroom and floor stock. When recording the data be sure to keep track according to the responsibility area. The records should be compared to the computer data. Areas that have large discrepancies should be recounted. Since the counts were recorded by individuals that hold responsibility for the inventory control, it should be easier to identify the problem areas and develop a corrective action.

Once the major inventory data collection problems have been addressed, there additional steps to ensure an accurate count. Schreibfeder (2008) suggested that most basic step is to ensure that

those who are counting are appropriately knowledgeable and experienced warehouse employees. This employee selection process will help ensure that the proper items are being counted and are able to locate all items throughout the store and warehouse. It is important to develop a schedule and have operational procedure and standards that must be adhered to for the various cycle counts until the entire inventory has been counted throughout the year. If using the control group method, it is important to count the exact items each day, with different groups each time. These processes are relatively easy and automatically tracked by a properly installed RFID system.

Financial Impacts

Financial impacts of inventory shrinkage within the service sector are quite alarming in scope and notable trends have been seen through national studies over the past decade (Smith, Smith, & Baker, 2011; Smith & Rupp, 2013). Many retailers need to evaluate whether or not improved technology can assist them on eliminating shrink or if there are other scenarios to pursue such as increased customer service or salary increases to trusted employees to reduce employee turnover (Snyder, et al., 1991). Furthermore, appropriate research may be examined and then utilized in order to assist companies in measuring the effect of retail shrinkage so that top executives can make timely decisions about to handle this growing problem in an effort to keep profits on track.

A survey conducted in 2002 by the National Retail Security Group reported that retailers lost on average about 1.7% of total sales to shrinkage in a single year (Vargas, 2002). Ernst and Young, a top auditing firm, completed a study of shrinkage which backed the results of the National Retail Security Group. The study revealed that shrinkage affects all types of retailers from grocery stores to electronic retailers such as Best Buy ("Ernst and Young's study of retail loss prevention," 2003). The research examined other specialty retailers that did not fall into any main groupings in order to capture a vast variety of retail companies. Unfortunately, the figures translated into total losses for retailers at 31.3 billion U.S. dollars per year. The survey grouped shrinkage into 4 main categories. The category that causes retailers the most amount of financial loss is due to employee theft. This type of theft accounts for almost 50% of all inventory shrinkage and continues to show a rising trend. In 2000, a similar study was performed in which employee theft only accounted for about 45% of total shrink (Vargas, 2000). Thus, over a two-year period this expense has risen by nearly 5%.

Another important category of inventory shrinkage deals with shoplifting. This category is following the same trend as employee theft and continues to rise (Bolin & Heatherly, 2001; Chapman & Templar, 2004). Shoplifting activities are usually considered the major source of property crime committed in the U.S. (Vargas, 2002). Other categories that make up inventory shrinkage are administrative errors and vendor fraud, which account for about 20% of total loss inventory loss (Vargas, 2002). It is the basic premise of this chapter that such sources of inventory shrinkage are on the decline as retailers aim to maintain tighter control over inventories using better management and technologies, such as RFID, in order to enhance better security over inventories. Ultimately, if management cannot reduce the amount of employee theft and shoplifting via effective counter measures, then total inventory shrink will continue to rise in the future, driving up significant costs–of–goods–sold and reduced profit margins.

Ideally, managers would prefer that inventory shrinkage is at or near zero percent; a very commendable if not impossible goal. A company may choose to spend significant amounts on surveillance technology, but in many cases, the cost-benefit analysis does not prove to be worthwhile. This may be the case for retailers that do not sell extremely valuable items. Just as many countries outside the U.S. have invested heavily into smart cards (microchips) to enhance credit card security and reduce identity and credit fraud, domestic credit card providers are still reluctant to make such heavily investments to standardize such a process in the U.S.

For example, a case study was performed at the University of Nebraska. A major portion of this study was to identify a cost-benefit analysis on the implementation of a RFID-embedded system for a company that was noticing increased shrinkage among some of their maintenance and repair inventories (Jones, Riley, Franca, & Reigle, 2007). This study revealed essentially all of the relevant costs associated with an RFID system, which included tag identifiers, readers and antennas, software, and other technical labor. The ending result, which was verified through mathematical modeling and related financial metrics (i.e. net present value calculations), suggested that the company analyzed needed to reduce current costs by nearly 4% in order to cover the costs of the implementation of this security system (i.e. reach the break-even point). Unfortunately, many SMEs as well as retailers do not have the funding to implement such proven systems. In many instances, such as the retailer Best Buy, which has a wide variety and number of products with a quick turnover, such technologies may significantly impact unit or item profit margins, resulting in reduced competeness if prices must keep pace with implementation costs. Hence, products typically have a wide range of value and more advanced technological systems will not have a cost-benefit advantage in many of these cases.

Instead of spending large amounts of resources on technological solutions, management may need to examine economic statistical models to reduce theft at their workplaces. For example, most companies realize that they are most vulnerable during the holiday season to both employee theft as well as shoplifting. This may be due to increased crowds and the hiring of temporary workers to assist with this yearly rush. However, a research study illustrated that other factors relating to economics have an effect on these types of theft as well. The study was performed by a research and consulting firm and used historical data from 1970 until 2001 ("Retailers should brace for sharp increase ..," 2001). There were three major variables that they believe assisted in explaining shoplifting. One variable examined was domestic unemployment claims. As one might expect, when unemployment is on the rise, so is the rate of shoplifting. This result may be most likely be attributed to stores not having enough staff and/or some customers are not able to afford items and feel that they are forced to shoplift in order to survive or that a lucrative black-market exists for these stolen items.

Another important variable that is traditionally examined was the savings rate. As the economy was prosperous as it was in the early 1990s, shoplifting loses significantly declined. Retail prices are another important factor. When inflation is increasing, retailers need to adjust their prices upward to combat higher operating costs (i.e. a positive correlation between inflation and shoplifting). When a significant change in the inflation rate occurred, this was accompanied by an increase in shoplifting. By examining current situations within the economy, retailers can make better forecasts on the total amount of loss due to inventory shrinkage and make strategic efforts to fight this problem during related economic downturns.

In order for a company to make strategic decisions with respect to inventory shrinkage, they need to be able to measure its implications on the financial statements. One troubling statistic reported in Great Britain revealed that firms may lose US$11 to 15 in profits for every dollar that is attributed to inventory shrinkage (Chapman & Templar, 2004). If one defines shrinkage as any discrepancy between book stock and physical stock, there are several useful metrics that can be used to measure inventory shrinkage. Book stock can be defined as results from the last inventory count plus any net movements where these are

defined as the sum of purchases and incoming transfers minus the sum of sales and outgoing transfers. In order to properly account for inventory shrinkage, management usually follows simplified methods. Perhaps, the easiest valuation method is by adding up the sales price of all goods that have been lost due to inventory shrinkage. This presents a more dramatic number that assists in getting the attention of management, but fails to realize the ending margin implications.

A common technique for inventory shrinkage measurement is the purchase price method. This is the method used for compiling the balance sheet and tax calculations, but has a flaw in which it fails to properly apportion overhead accounting to Chapman and Templar (2004). The transfer cost method takes into account the purchase price plus apportioned costs to valuate total shrink. Once the total shrinkage has been valued, management can then look at various financial ratios to show the total effect on the company. Useful financial ratios include the percentage of inventory turnovers and total shrinkage as a percentage of profit.

The percentage of inventory turnovers ratio, which takes the total value of shrinkage divided by the value of inventory turnover, can be calculated at a gross or net level. The net calculation is more difficult because sales tax is excluded from the calculation, but can be more effective when comparing areas that have different tax rates. This statistic helps management benchmark their performance to other competitors within the industry as well as the measure of performance over time. The total shrinkage as a percentage of profit is useful for management since it stresses how underlying profits can be affected with swings in total shrinkage. It is hoped that once management understands the implications of shrinkage within their business units, they have the ability to generate strategic plans for how to handle these losses moving forward. For example, Chapman and Templar (2004) revealed that a company can either increase the number of operating stores by 30% or aim to reduce total shrinkage by half to result in a figure that would result in identical profits. Many companies may find it more advantageous and less risky to clean up total shrinkage problems under current locations and operations then raising money for additional operations, which will surely increase overall debt.

Theories and Technical Solutions to Reduce Employee Theft

Technologically Based Solutions

There are several theoretical frameworks in previous research studies designed to reduce employee theft and to control inventory shrinkage (Koong & Lin, 2007; Kulas, et al., 2007; Smith, Smith, & Baker, 2011; Smith & Rupp, 2013). Several techniques have been empirically tested to be effective, while others were found to be impractical and financially impossible, while some can be routinely utilized and effective with most retailers. To reduce retail shrinkage cause by employee theft, the causes must all be addressed, whether technologically or physically based. Using point-of-sale software that allows for real-time data collection helps managers to validate and track employee sales and all transactions including voids, returns, price matches, and no sales (Rosenblum, 2008). Unfortunately, this type of approach and the sophisticated technology can be used to enhance inventory shrinkage and identity theft, as indicated by the recent Target stores and other retailers hit with massive credit fraud and identity theft for the Christmas-related shopping season of 2013 resulting in data breach involving millions of customers' credit and debit card records ("Sources: Target investigating data breach," 2013). Other areas of technology that can be addressed or added to retail stores are RFID tagging, computerized time clock and scheduling systems, and closed circuit surveillance systems. Controlling security of employee and customer information is imperative in maintaining a good

loss prevention culture, keeping credit card information and passwords safe from potential thieves.

Technologically based solutions help to reduce shrinkage, but needs to be coupled with physical security measures. Having some kind of security or loss prevention staff is beneficial for all retailers as reluctant security systems would in parallel to discourage, if not prevent employee-based inventory shrinkage. Many of these security systems are commonsense approaches and economically feasible (i.e. keeping buildings secure, locking unused exits, arming alarm systems, and monitoring employee behavior). These proactive approaches are techniques that if employed properly can help reduce employee and customer theft. Inspecting garbage and waste removal on a regular basis can be an effective method to deter employees from attempting to steal via dumpsters and compactors. Managers need to be very knowledgeable about cycle counting and monitor shipping and receiving as well as keeping track of any and all inventory adjustments made by warehouse employees (Tari & Sabater, 2004; Tiwari, et al., 2007; Ustundag, 2010). For example, loading docks and warehouses as where 65% of management agrees is a critical area for shrink reduction (Rosenblum, 2008).

Employment Policy Solutions

Employers have also been focusing on employees' viewpoint and trying to reduce turnover to decrease the potential for theft. Improving screening and interviewing techniques are also helpful in abating this problem. While background checks, reference checks and drug tests are used by the majority of large retailers, these are not always positive indicators of a potentially dishonest employee.

Keeping employees happy and productive and providing opportunities for ownership are techniques that management commonly use. Creating groups that involve employees in activities outside of the business, giving employees stock options and bonus potential, and having a mentoring program for new employees or underperforming employees also helps to reduce turnover thus keeping loss under control. Eliminating employee theft totally may be is unfeasible. While reducing it is an ever-challenging battle, using proven techniques and the advancements in security technology help companies to control their loss and maintain profitability on their bottom line.

Theory Behind Cycle-Counting Solutions

Wilson (1995) discussed in some detail about cycle counting and the formulas to estimate the amount that needs counted. A number of research studies have suggested that process control charts are very useful and help monitor the record-keeping activities (Helo, Anussornnitisarn, & Phusavat, 2008; Ifinedo & Nahar, 2009; Johansson & Sudzina, 2008; Kamhawi, (2008). Cycle counting has several objectives, but it is extremely important to motivate employees to minimize record errors simply by increasing their awareness of the importance of record accuracy. An equally important operational objective is to remove errors so that a targeted level of record accuracy and system performance can be maintained.

It is necessary to determine the targeted level of accuracy for many reasons outside of inventory shrinkage; it is a fundamental requirement for inventory control and profitability. In cycle counting, it is started by typically determining the number of records to inspect, then, the desired level of accuracy, whether it would be 97%, 95%, or 6-sigma. Unfortunately, it is possible to ignore the errors that have more than one effect of cycle counting. Deviations from estimation errors will be made visible by looking at the expected patterns of behavior. Cycle counting has an effect of the size of the inventory depending on the level of stock. If the stock level is low, then the error rate may appear to management to be worse than if the stock was more numerous. Cycle counting allows for estimates of record accuracy that are statistically valid. It also allows for comparisons between

cycle counts from past counts. The main focus of cycle counting is the record keeping practices. If the records are not entered into the computer system in a timely manner then the amounts that were counted will become inaccurate and thus a waste of time. RFID-embedded systems are ideal work inventory control in maintaining an accurate inventory count.

METHODOLOGY

Procedure and Hypotheses

To explore the concepts of management's choices in dealing with the pressing problems of inventory shrinkage, especially employee-based theft, a basic survey instrument was developed for hypothesis-testing and statistical analysis purposes. For this particular research project, a 12-question survey was developed asking inventory managers to provide information regarding their degree of IT and RFID-based sophistication, importance of RFID implementation, degree that RFID technologies would be more cost efficient, current organization implemented infrastructure to support RFID, organization's IT infrastructure can accommodate RFID volumes, organization's RFID infrastructure promotes standards and interoperability, benefits suppliers/partners RFID capabilities, types of challenge to effective RFID implementation, timetable launching RFID, timely and substantial ROI launching RFID, track Items via RFID significantly affect pricing and delivery B2C, if not compelled to use RFID, but still would implement, and it is ultimately the inventory managers responsible to implement RFID.

The majority of the survey was comprised of primarily scale and a few selected nominal questions that simplified the use of the statistical software input and sequent analysis. The survey results were properly recorded and designed to be used to formulate graphs, Chi-square, and multiple linear regression techniques. The two specific hypotheses derived from the review of the literature based on perceived value from a RFID-related technology solution for a multitude of inventory problems.

H1: There are timely and substantial ROI (return-on-investment) associated with the launching RFID-based technologies and it should be positively related to the perceived inventory managers' operational and strategic values associated with the implementation of such systems.

H2: There are significant types of challenges to effective RFID-based technologies implementation and that it should vary as a function of the proposed timetable associated with the launching of RFID.

It is the basic premise the current research effort that an understanding of some of the important real-world problems face by inventory managers shred a different light on the many proposed advantages associated with the implementation of newer technologies designed to enhance operational effectiveness and reduce the impacts of employee-based inventory shrinkage.

The survey instrument was pretested for minimum execution time and confusion and maximum accuracy of the concepts developed from the review of the literature on sources of inventory shrinkage and the challenges associated with the implementation of RFID-embedded systems. A series of questionnaires using a standardized instrument were made available to three relatively large global retailers located in the metropolitan area of Pittsburgh, PA. Proper permission from upper management was obtained and the inventory managers were free to fill out the questionnaire at their convenience. Confidentially of both respondents and management of the two companies were assured through the data collection and analysis phases. This procedure resulted in 33 useable questionnaires from an initial sampling frame of roughly 60+ potential respondents within the organization. It was felt that a sample size of 33 resulted in a stable predictive relationship to perform the analysis, although potential problems with sufficient statistical power to generate meaningful results.

Statistical Techniques

Using a variety of graphical and hypothesis-testing techniques were utilized, although elaborate multivariate statistical techniques were not deemed appropriate with the relatively small sample size found in the present study. The Chi-square, t-test and F-test were used to test the statistical significance of the relationships determined from the hypothesis-testing process. The 0.05 level of statistical significance for a 2-tailed test was used throughout the analyses.

RESULTS

Descriptive Analysis

As displayed in Tables 1-3, the descriptive statistics and frequencies of the major variables included in the present study frame the basic personal preferences or choices, both technological and convenience, for RFID-embedded systems by inventory managers. Majority of the respondents generally agreed with the proposed RFID-based technologies in terms of its benefits as evident from an inspection of means out of 4 from Table 1 (1 = least importance, 4 = most importance). Specifically, these variables with relatively high degree of importance included RFID technologies would be more cost efficient (2.45), Benefit suppliers/partners RFID capabilities (2.39), Timely and substantial ROI launching RFID (2.76), Track Items via RFID significantly affect pricing and delivery B2C (3.00), and If not compelled RFID, still would implement (2.24).

Table 1. Descriptive statistics of scale variables collected for the present study

Variable Description	Minimum	Maximum	Mean	Std. Deviation
Importance of RFID implementation (1 = disagree, 4 = highly agree)	1	4	1.85	0.972
RFID technologies would be more cost efficient (1 = disagree, 4 = highly agree)	1	4	2.45	0.833
Current organization implemented infrastructure to support RFID (1 = disagree, 4 = highly agree)	1	4	1.76	1.032
Organization's IT infrastructure can accommodate RFID volumes	1	3	1.85	0.795
Organization's RFID infrastructure promotes standards and interoperability	1	3	1.91	0.805
Benefit suppliers/partners RFID capabilities (1 = disagree, 4 = highly agree)	1	4	2.39	0.966
Timetable launching RFID (1 = more than a year, 2 = 6-12 months, 3 = 3-6 months, 4 = immediately)	1	4	1.36	0.929
Timely and substantial ROI launching RFID (1 = disagree, 4 = highly agree)	1	4	2.76	1.200
Track Items via RFID significantly affect pricing and delivery B2C (1 = disagree, 4 = highly agree)	1	4	3.00	0.829
If not compelled RFID, still would implement (1 = disagree, 4 = highly agree)	1	4	2.24	0.902
Individuals are ultimately responsible to implement RFID (1 = disagree, 4 = highly agree)	1	4	1.58	0.902

Table 2. Related frequency statistics for types of challenges to effective RFID implementation

Coding Scheme	Frequency	Percent	Valid Percent	Cumulative Percent
Insufficient funding	12	36.4	36.4	36.4
Lack of buy in from top management	5	15.2	15.2	51.5
lack of knowledge about RFID impact on existing processes	15	45.5	45.5	97.0
Uncertainty about RFID mandates and standards	1	3.0	3.0	100.0
Total	33	100.0	100.0	

Table 3. Related frequency statistics for timetable launching RFID

	Frequency	Percent	Valid Percent	Cumulative Percent
More than a year	28	84.8	84.8	84.8
6-12 months	1	3.0	3.0	87.9
3-6 months	1	3.0	3.0	90.9
Immediately	3	9.1	9.1	100.0
Total	33	100.0	100.0	

The remaining variables with more neural or less acceptance of importance included importance of RFID implementation (1.85), current organization implemented infrastructure to support RFID (1.76), organization's IT infrastructure can accommodate RFID volumes (1.85), organization's RFID infrastructure promotes standards and interoperability (1.91) and individuals (managers) are ultimately responsible for implementation (1.58). Interestingly, these variables are more related to the organization's capability to implement RFID and inherent disadvantages associated with the technologies.

Specific-Hypothesis Testing (H1) Results

In general, the first hypothesis, H1, tests the assumption that there is a significant timely and substantial ROI associated with the launching RFID-based technologies and it should be positively related to the perceived inventory managers' operational and strategic values associated with the implementation of such systems. Table 4 displays the hypothesis-testing results associated with H1, with the dependent variable, Timely and substantial ROI launching RFID, regressed over the various scale-based operational characteristics independent variables. As shown in part A of Table 4, it was found that a relatively small 16.8% of the adjusted total variance in the dependent variable was explained by these independent variables. The relationship was found to be not be statistically significant, as expected ($F = 1.647$, $p = 0.158$). This statistical result indicates that the timely and substantial ROI associated with launching RFID-based solutions was not a major predicted factor by its various operational characteristics, perhaps due some deficiencies of the current organizational infrastructure to best make use of its benefits. Ultimately, H2 was not accepted.

Specific-Hypothesis Testing (H2) Results

The second hypothesis (H2), tested the assumption that there is a significant types of challenges to effective RFID-based technologies implementation and that it should vary as a function of the proposed timetable associated with the launching of RFID. To test this hypothesis, basic Chi-square techniques were used. Table 5 displays the statistics associated with the Chi-square test, with the cross-tabulation statistics associated with types of challenges to effective RFID implementation with timetable launching RFID. Willingness to adopt RFID technologies and its timetable its launching was not found significantly related with accessibility with various challenges associated with such adoption (Chi-square $= 7.955$, $p = 0.539$). The most common timetable associated with the adoption of RFID-based technologies was more than a year, as illustrated in Figure 1. The most common challenge of adoption was lack of knowledge about RFID impact on existing processes, followed by insufficient funding, and lack of buy-in from top management. Interesting, only one inventory management felt that uncertainty about RFID mandates and standards was a major challenge.

Evidently, newer technologies, such as RFID, to promote better inventory management practices, operations, and reduce employee-based shrinkage are still not perceived as easy-to-implement operational strategies. Ultimately, H2 was formally rejected, suggesting that proposed timetable associated with the launching of RFID are not statistically related to the several of perceived challenges to effective RFID-based technologies implementation by the sampled inventory managers. RFID appears to be a difficult sell to many managers, despite its well-documented advantages.

Table 4. Relevant statistics associated with specific hypothesis-testing results (H2). Part A displays the model summary, Part B the overall results, and Part C inspects specific contributions of each component in the hypothesis (Dependent variable: Timely and substantial ROI launching RFID).

Part A. Model Summary					
R	**R Square**		**Adjusted R Square**		**Std. Error of the Estimate**
0.654	0.428		0.168		1.094

Part B. ANOVA Results					
Sources of Variation	**Sum of Squares**	**df**	**Mean Square**	**F-ratio**	**Sig.**
Regression	19.718	10	1.972	1.647	0.158 (NS)
Residual	26.343	22	1.197		
Total	46.061	32			

Dependent Variable: Timely and substantial ROI launching RFID.

Predictors: (Constant), individuals responsible implement RFID, importance of RFID implementation, organization's IT infrastructure can accommodate RFID volumes, timetable launching RFID, track Items via RFID significantly affect pricing and delivery B2C, if not compelled RFID, still would implement, RFID technologies would be more cost efficient, organization's RFID infrastructure promotes standards and interoperability, benefit suppliers/partners RFID capabilities, and current organization implemented infrastructure to support RFID. NS denotes not statistically significant at the 0.05 level for a two-tailed test.

Part C. Coefficients-Testing Results					
Independent Variables	**Unstandardized Coefficients**		**Standardized Coefficients**	**t-test**	**Significance**
	B	**Std. Error**	**Beta**		
(Constant)	0.349	0.882		0.396	0.696
Importance of RFID implementation	-0.147	0.314	-0.119	-0.469	0.644 (NS)
RFID technologies would be more cost efficient	0.623	0.391	0.432	1.591	0.126 (NS)
Current organization implemented infrastructure to support RFID	0.393	0.408	0.338	0.963	0.346 (NS)
Organization's IT infrastructure can accommodate RFID volumes	0.126	0.419	0.084	0.301	0.766 (NS)
Organization's RFID infrastructure promotes standards and interoperability	-0.475	0.455	-0.318	1.043	0.300 (NS)
Benefit suppliers/partners RFID capabilities	-0.017	0.392	-0.014	-0.044	0.966 (NS)
Timetable launching RFID	-0.166	0.385	-0.129	-0.431	0.671 (NS)
Track Items via RFID significantly affect pricing and delivery B2C	0.196	0.312	0.135	0.626	0.538 (NS)
If not compelled RFID, still would implement	0.043	0.404	0.032	0.105	0.917 (NS)
Individuals responsible to implement RFID	0.457	0.243	0.343	1.877	0.074 (NS)

Dependent Variable, Timely and substantial ROI launching RFID. NS denotes not statistically significant at the 0.05 level for a two-tailed test.

Table 5. Cross-tabulation statistics associated with types of challenges to effective RFID implementation with timetable launching RFID (H2).

Part A. Actual Counts.						
Dependent Variable and Coding Schemes		**Timetable launching RFID**				**Total**
		More Than a Year	**6-12 Months**	**3-6 Months**	**Immediately**	
Types of challenges to effective RFID implementation	Insufficient Funding	9	0	0	3	12
	Lack of Buy-in from Top Management	5	0	0	0	5
	Lack of Knowledge about RFID Impact on Existing Processes	13	1	1	0	15
	Uncertainty about RFID Mandates and Standards	1	0	0	0	1
Total		28	1	1	3	33

Part B. Chi-Square Tests Results			
Statistics	**Value**	**df**	**Asymptotic Sig. (2-sided)**
Pearson Chi Square	7.955	9	0.539 (NS)
Likelihood Ratio	9.526	9	0.390 (NS)
Linear-by-Linear Association	2.340	1	0.126 (NS)
N of Valid Cases	33		

Note: 14 cells (87.5%) have expected count less than 5. The minimum expected count is 0.03. NS denotes not statistically significant at the 0.05 level for a two-tailed test.

Part C. Symmetric Measures			
Statistics		**Value**	**Approx. Sig.**
Nominal by Nominal	Contingency Coefficient	0.441	0.539 (NS)

NS denotes not statistically significant at the 0.05 level for a two-tailed test.

DISCUSSION

Organizational Roles and Responsibilities Associated with RFID

Each year, as suggested by O'Connor (2004), billions of dollars are lost due to fraudulent merchandise returns and exchanges to retailers. Much of this inventory shrinkage are a direct result of employee theft, shoplifting, administrative/clerical errors, and sequent vendor fraud. It was a basic premise of the current chapter and research efforts that RFID-based solutions can be a significant force in dealing with such causes if inventory shrinkage. As evident from the empirical portion of this chapter, few inventory managers will openly disagree with that assumption. However, RFID systems implementations are usually plagued with IT and other organizational infrastructure architectural problems that are not always easy to overcome. Although one of the major goals of RFID is to reduce counterfeiting and theft, managers are constantly revisiting the problems of implementation and apparently in some cases are slow to widespread invest in such inventory control systems.

The employer of one of the respondents of the present study utilized a companywide shrink plan to deter employee theft. This company uses a plan called GBOT, which stands for General Manager Third Interviews, Barometer Management, Over

Figure 1. Cross-tabulation types of challenges to effective RFID implementation with timetable launching RFID

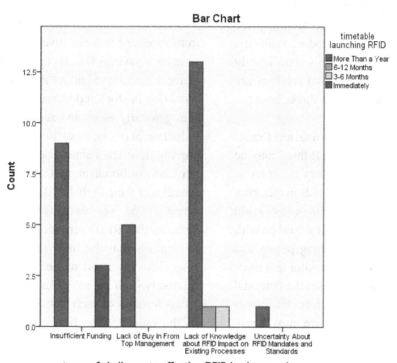

Budget Meetings and "Talking Shrink." This plan focused on the employee interaction and engagement around reducing shrinkage and in turn employee theft. The general manager does all final interviews in order to best determine character and honesty of all applicants. Barometer management consists of viewing, validating and management of each department's loss and budget maintenance. Over budget meetings are traditionally used as a performance management technique, giving ownership to leaders under management. Talking shrink is an attempt by management at the company to create a culture and giving ownership around loss prevention.

Another interesting policy put in place by this company is a fraternization rule. This policy does not allow relationships to occur within the store among employees of different level of authority. If a manger has access to the building and all

systems and is in a relationship with a part time employee, this can create an opportunity for theft, by working in pairs. This policy also applies to siblings or other family members working in the same department. By instituting these precautionary measures, this company is proactive about reducing employee theft through ownership and the creation of a culture around loss prevention.

Within the supply chain, a main concern is protection of merchandise and store property. For the past 30 years, barcodes and Universal Product Codes (UPCs), have been supplying retailers with the necessary information for product recognition, yet theft is still a major issue. RFID-embedded technologies can aid in product security, since its tags contain more detailed, unique information, which is connected to the item that is being represented. Such technologies present manufacturers and retailers with the power to determine the total of time the item was in transit, its actual location of the distribution center holding the item, names of the last persons to handle items, and important details concerning quantities and selling price that ultimately increases total product visibility. The opportunity for a loss of sale is significantly decreased, since manufactures and retailers are aware of the products at all times throughout the supply chain.

These tags are used on an individual level, case, and/or pallet load, and at times all three may be utilized. In sectors where inventory accuracy is suspect, tagging on an item level aids in reducing shrinkage. An instance where retailers would find individual coding most beneficial would be with high-valued products, such as clothing, purses, and high-end shoes. The ability to monitor and track movement of these goods decreases the potential for item theft and misplacement. It is also important to consider those items that are most at risk within a particular store. Product and package size, item availability and store visibility are common factors considered when deciding which items to steal. Not only will RFID technologies bring benefit to retailers, consumers experience some of the rewards as well. When consumers' return previously purchased goods, the return process is extensive. Many stores require consumers to provide verification that the items have been purchased, mainly through paper receipt. RFID eliminates this stage because the tag links and supplies date of purchase along with other pertinent information to the retailer computer program.

A few advantages of implementing RFID in retail stores at the item level is that tagging every item allows the stock employees to know when shelf replenishment is necessary. Knowing when to refill the shelves, product is always available for the customer to purchase thus eliminating stock-outs. An important advantage of RFID-system implementation is that inventory storage is more organized, lessening clutter; due to stores requiring fewer inventories on site. RFID tags are read at the receiving docks and also during transit to the store shelves, during which a computer software program records the decrease in inventory and alerts the supplier to send additional product.

In theory, management should notice benefits in the areas of reduced inventory through a one-time cash savings (i.e. typically estimated at 5% of total inventory) and an annual benefit from a reduction in store and warehouse labor expenses (i.e. generally estimated at 7.5%). Eventually, a reduction of out-of-stock items may result in a recurring significant annual benefit of US$700,000 per US$1 billion in annual sales for retailers who reengineer their shelf-fulfillment processes (Kearney, 2005). The ability to quantify the actual benefits that RFID provides will help reinforce to retailers that the innovative technology will save them time and money, as reflected in the relatively high means of associated operational characteristics of such technological innovations in the empirical section of the present study. Informing companies of the potential return on investment encourages suppliers to begin RFID implementation at store level, warehouses and distribution centers. Besides the savings that RFID potentially offers retailers, tags make the products easily traceable.

When inventory is delivered to the store through the shipping dock, the antenna can scan the RFID tags to know what exactly is on a pallet. Electronic data entry eliminates the potential for human error from inventory discrepancies. Since RFID tags collect real-time data, time is saved allowing stockers to unload the pallet and replenish store shelves. Reading tags on the cases from back storage rooms although management to see what items have actually been replenished, thus reducing employee theft and related shrinkage that may from systems that rely on employees to record on a handheld device (Roberti, 2005a-c, 2007). Relying on a handheld computer to scan incoming deliveries may cause a threat to the inventory, should the worker miss a read or over-scan. Placing antennae throughout the line-of-transit eliminates the human error element, increasing accuracy and efficiency.

RFID-based data let management significant impacts the amount of time that a product moves through the supply chain. This feature allows management to track how long a case or pallet is at one particular location reduces the chance for item stock outs. Retailers can view when pallets or cases were shipped from the manufacturer and delivered to the store, when product is placed on the shelves and up to point of purchase. Tracking product at each stage during transit decreases the possibility for empty store shelves, resulting in a loss of sale but also reducing money wasted from too much unaccounted for store inventory.

To reduce shopping time, many consumers create lists stating what items they intend to purchase; though during shopping, impulse buying is likely to occur. During instances when a particular item is not on store shelves, a transaction does not occur, which results in a loss of sale. Customers may decide to leave the store; consequently, other purchases the consumer may have bought would be lost. Customer dissatisfaction may cause a broken bond between the consumer and retailer, ending future visits. On the contrary, when the consumer can quickly locate the desired items, it benefits both the retail store and the consumer. Hence, reducing out-of-stocks or improving product availability may be one of the greatest areas of potential consumer benefit from the use of RFID-based technologies (Collins, 2005, 2006). It is important to having a constant supply of product available for shoppers, which enhances their shopping experience and increases the chance for reoccurring purchases.

RFID IMPLEMENTATION CONCERNS

It may a common school of thought in the RFID community that item-level RFID will move only as far as retailers choose to take it. Some of this reluctance in the implementations of RFID-based systems was reflected by some inventory managers sampled in the empirical section. A number of management may still need to see actual tangible results at smaller scales before they implement large-scale RFID systems. Many inventory managers want to view such potential benefits of RFID firsthand before they are willing to experiment with it. In order to fully prepare for an implementation as large and detailed as this, a cross-functional team should be assembled well in advance to actively investigate a particular retail area. An important focus should be on item-level deployments, since this is where the payoff will be quickest and largest. The sooner a retailer can see the direct results of the implementation, the more trust they will instill in the process going forward.

RFID has been referred to as not a science, but an art by Neco Can, who spearheaded item-level RFID trials at U.S. clothing retailers Gap, and Abercrombie & Fitch (Collins, 2006). In 2001, Can was the director of Gap's project management office, leading an RFID project that provided an inventory accuracy of up to 99.6%. Despite the success of the pilot in both improving in-store inventory and increasing sales, numerous factors caused the company to choose not to invest immediately in RFID tagging. This experience led lower management to believe that any RFID project must be supported at the highest levels of management. RFID is believed to have a slow start, which is inherent in the newness of the technology and ideas surrounding it. However, many proponents of RFID may believe that in a few years this will become an industry standard. Through Gap, and Abercrombie & Fitch's experience in RFID-based retail implementation, he maintained that tags don't have to be much cheaper than they are now to deliver a return on investment (i.e. for Gap, it was 17 cents and at A&F, it was 24 cents per tag). Despite the proven benefits of this new technology, many retailers are still cautious about deploying the project. This is partially due to the many variables that must be managed to ensure adequate tag read rates.

Besides, the cost of the RFID tag, the readers can be costly as well. For example, when the company is selling purses or shoes that are over US$800, the retail industry would not have a problem placing at US$2-priced tag on such merchandise. However, if that retailer would want to read this tag at a certain distance in order to have even less of a chance of theft, they would also need to purchase a stronger reader or active tags versus passive tags. As the distances the reader is supposed to cover increase, the more costly this technology can become.

With the use of RFID technology, there are some business and technical problems and issues that can arise. Some of these problems include: data sharing, data quality, costs and benefits, security and privacy, and RFID standards. Divergent factors can affect the perceptions of the internal and external stakeholders within an organization in the process of adopting RFID. Before attempting to share and use RFID data, an organization should consider potential costs in mastering collaborative planning and implementation with its partners.

RFID researchers and practitioners were asked to provide their viewpoints on the application of RFID technologies in the study by Koong and Lin (2007). The major managerial factor for the adaptation of RFID was the cost consideration, particularly cost of RFID tags and hardware. Industry evaluators were extremely concerned about integrating their existing hardware and new RFID systems. Most organizations would prefer to retain their current system to avoid compatibility problems. Other criteria that fell under the cost consideration category were the software, system integration, operations, and human resources. The second most important concern was the system applicability factor. Was the product simplistic in nature? Did any interference occur with existing product materials? Security and privacy issues were also placed under the category of system applicability. Finally, data quality ranked third. In RFID, data sharing is the use of a standardized data format to communicate between RFID supply chain suppliers. When considering the application of RFID technologies, companies must be assured that the data is collected in a format that both the organizations and suppliers can interpret. Koong and Lin (2007) suggested that the obstacles of RFID can be minimized by reducing the total costs of RFID; resolving the interference problems; improving the identification accuracy; protecting intellectual property rights; establishing international standards; and developing better software supports.

GENERAL CONCLUSIONS AND IMPLICATIONS

Considerations of RFID System Implementations

Analysis of multiple industries and various benefits of RFID-based system implementation allows managers and researchers to view the generalities relatively well, but the intricacies still remain obscured. From the review of the literature and the case studies discussed in this chapter, it can be safety assumed that the innovation of technology through implementation of RFID would directly correlate to creating efficiencies within operational processes. This lack of full acceptances of RFID-based solutions may be evidence that many managers need to personally see direct results before actual large-scale implementation. However, most inventory managers did feel that such systems certainty reduced inventory shrinkage, especially from employees.

There are some limitations that were found with the empirical study of this chapter. The limitations include that empirical evidence presentation are generally limited with regards to information on RFID implementation at a large scale. Without understanding the implementation of RFID itself among inventory managers, it is difficult to determine whether or not efficiencies were developed and were cost effective on the long term. Another limitation with the study was that such empirical results showing how RFID implementation impacted other processes are frequently complex and difficult to isolate. There is little doubt that proper inventory management has the potential to be a great impact on a manufacturing firm's financial bottom-line, especially in reducing loses due to inventory shrinkage. Operational techniques that are critical to inventory management include popular management techniques such as lean management, JIT inventory, MRP systems and ERP methods; these techniques are difficult to separate their impacts on inventory shrinkage from the benefits of RFID applications.

A number of cited past studies have resulted in contradictory information on RFID-based solutions in inventory management and may not have a major impact on inventory shrinkage, especially in the application of more advanced statistical models (Azadeh et al., 2013; Bhamu et al., 2013; Summers et al., 2008; Tari et al., 2004; Tiwari et al., 2007). Interestingly, Boute et al. (2006) concluded that companies with high-inventory ratios have more possibilities to be poor financial performers, rather than increased inventory management leads to increased financial results. RFID applications certainly may the situation more complex in evaluation costs and benefits in inventory shrinkage initiatives.

Aspects of Inventory Shrinkage and RFID-Based Solutions

By fully understanding the causes and effects of inventory shrinkage, only then can a company take appropriate actions to eliminate this costly problem. The causes and solutions to inventory shrink are both economic and people-related. The effects, regardless of the causes, can be equally devastating. It is apparent that product communication is important to both retailers and consumers, but it may be difficult to introduce new technologies, since consumers, manufacturers and retailers may be unaware of its benefits. By

fusing information with technology, newer and more innovative solutions to inventory shrinkage may be presented. RFID is certainly an innovation that has great potential to be financially rewarding to various industries that have begun quantifying its abilities. Information transference, reduction in employee-based theft, and eliminating stock-outs are some of main attributes that RFID provides to both manufacturing and retail industries.

Such technological innovations mandate that management needs to tweak the original layouts in order to optimize the beneficial aspects. For example, some RFID-tagging systems need adjustments due to large metal shelves frequently found in warehouses. By adjusting the layout to shift these metal shelves to the perimeter of the warehouse enabled the RFID tags to be better recognized by the antenna. By drafting layouts in order to determine the optimal distance between rows and the shelving units allows management to better suggest a better warehouse configuration that takes advantage of a more fully automated RFID-tagging system. By determining the probabilities of the antennas receiving signals would help management access whether RFID-based technology is truly a beneficial move or not. This is a critical decision area, since high powered antennas cost more hence driving down the benefits of using RFID-tagging systems.

Customer Satisfaction Considerations

In a few instances, some management may have been so excited about the benefits of new technological solutions to the many inventory management problems that they may not have evaluated the financial risks or its inherent disadvantages to using the RFID technology properly. However, many industries are pushing for this implementation, other management in other industries need to become aware of its potential benefits and risk in order to properly leverage such technologies to their advantage. When used properly, RFID utilization can increase customer satisfaction. Since such inventory data can be used to ensure that a constant shelf supply is readily accessible. Once tags are scanned during transit from the backroom to the store floor, the data are obtained, which notifies retailers when product reorders and restock are necessary.

Unfortunately, RFID-based solutions can decrease some customer satisfaction if customers feel that his/her privacy are being invaded and compromised. The recent Target Corporation's identity theft and credit card fraud previously cited are classic examples of such customers' invasion of privacy. Ultimately, it is important to remember, as suggested by Roberti (2005a-c, 2007), RFID-embedded technology is a journey that will take time for retailers and suppliers to learn how to deploy it strategically and in a successful manner before RFID vendors can improve a company's products and service. Whether or not RFID is the most appropriate or reliable solution is still open for exploration, but its impacts on reducing employee-based inventory shrinkage are fairly clear and decisive.

REFERENCES

Aldaihani, M. M., & Darwish, M. A. (2013). Optimal production and inventory decisions for supply chains with one producer and multiple newsvendors. *International Journal of Services and Operations Management*, 15(4), 430–448. doi:10.1504/IJSOM.2013.054884

Azadeh, A., Gholizadeh, H., & Jeihoonian, M. (2013). A multi-objective optimisation model for university course timetabling problem using a mixed integer dynamic non-linear programming. *International Journal of Services and Operations Management*, 15(4), 467–481. doi:10.1504/IJSOM.2013.054886

Bhamu, J., Khandelwal, A., & Sangwan, K. S. (2013). Lean manufacturing implementation in an automated production line: A case study. *International Journal of Services and Operations Management*, 15(4), 411–429. doi:10.1504/IJSOM.2013.054883

Bolin, A., & Heatherly, L. (2001). Predictors of employee deviance: The relationship between bad attitudes and bad behavior. *Journal of Business and Psychology*, 15(3), 405–418. doi:10.1023/A:1007818616389

Challenges in the Retail Industry. (2008). *Columbus IT*. Retrieved January 23, 2014 from http://www.columbusit.com/Default.aspx?ID=16095

Chapman, P., & Templar, S. (2004) *Measuring retail shrinkage: Towards shrinkage KPI*. Retrieved January 23, 2014 from http://www.losspreventionmagazine.com/customers/104120817472470/filemanager/Measuring_Shrinkage_White_Paper.pdf

Chen, C. C., Wu, J., Su, Y. S., & Yang, S. C. (2008). Key drivers for the continued use of RFID technology in the emergency room. *Management Research News*, 31(4), 273–288. doi:10.1108/01409170810851348

Collins, J. (2005). School studies RFID's effect on Wal-Mart. *RFID Journal*. Retrieved January 27, 2014 from http://www.rfidjournal.com/article/articleview/1514/1/9/

Collins, J. (2006). RFID implementation is an art. *RFID Journal*. Retrieved January 27, 2014 from http://www.rfidjournal.com/article/articleview/2427/1/1/

Drejer, A., & Riis, J.O. (2000). New dimensions of competence development in industrial enterprises. *International Journal of Manufacturing Technology and Management*, 2(1/7), 660-882.

Dutta, A., Lee, H. L., & Whang, S. (2007). RFID and operations management: technology, value and incentives. *Production and Operations Management*, *16*(5), 646–655. doi:10.1111/j.1937-5956.2007.tb00286.x

Ernst and Young's Study of Retail Loss Prevention. (2003). *Ernst and Young*. Retrieved January 23, 2014 from http://retailindustry.about.com/cs/lp_retailstore/a/bl_ey051303.htm

Fisher, J. A., & Monahan, T. (2008). Tracking the social dimensions of RFID systems in hospitals. *International Journal of Medical Informatics*, *77*(3), 176–183. doi:10.1016/j.ijmedinf.2007.04.010 PMID:17544841

Fumi, A., Scarabotti, L., & Schiraldi, M. M. (2013). The effect of slot-code optimisation on travel times in common unit-load warehouses. *International Journal of Services and Operations Management.*, *15*(4), 507–527. doi:10.1504/IJSOM.2013.054925

Greenberg, J. (1990). Employee theft as a reaction to underpayment inequity: The hidden cost of pay cuts. *Journal of Applied Psychology*, *75*(5), 561-572.

Grewal, C. (2008). An initiative to implement lean manufacturing using value stream mapping in a small company. *International Journal of Manufacturing Technology and Management*, *15*(3-4), 404–421. doi:10.1504/IJMTM.2008.020176

Helo, P., Anussornnitisarn, P., & Phusavat, K. (2008). Expectation and reality in ERP implementation: Consultant and solution provider perspective. *Industrial Management & Data Systems*, *108*(8), 1045–1158. doi:10.1108/02635570810904604

Hollinger, R. C., Lee, G., Kane, J. L., & Hayes, R. (1998). *1998 National Retail Security Survey: Executive Summary*. Gainesville, FL: University of Florida Security Research Project.

Hu, G., Wang, L., Fetch, S., & Bidanda, B. (2008). A multi-objective model for project portfolio selection to implement lean and Six Sigma concepts. *International Journal of Production Research*, *46*(23), 6611–6648. doi:10.1080/00207540802230363

Ifinedo, P., & Nahar, N. (2009). Interactions between contingency, organizational IT factors, and ERP success. *Industrial Management & Data Systems*, *109*(1), 118–126. doi:10.1108/02635570910926627

Jain, V., Benyoucef, L., & Deshmukh, S. G. (2008). What's the buzz about moving from 'lean' to 'agile' integrated supply chains? A fuzzy intelligent agent-based approach. *International Journal of Production Research*, *46*(23), 6649–6678. doi:10.1080/00207540802230462

Johansson, B., & Sudzina, F. (2008). ERP systems and open source: An initial review and some implications for SMEs. *Journal of Enterprise Information Management*, *21*(6), 649–659. doi:10.1108/17410390810911230

Jones, E., Riley, M., Franca, R., & Reigle, S. (2007). Case study: The engineering economics of RFID in specialized manufacturing. *The Engineering Economist*, *52*(3), 285–303. doi:10.1080/00137910701503951

Kamhawi, E. M. (2008). System characteristics, perceived benefits, individual differences and use intentions: A survey of decision support tools of ERP systems. *Information Resources Management Journal*, *21*(4), 66–83. doi:10.4018/irmj.2008100104

Kearney, A. T. (2005). RFID will bring great benefits for retailers. [Online]. Retrieved January 27, 2014 from http://retailindustry.about.com/cs/it_rfid/a/bl_atk111003.htm

Ketikidis, P. H., Hayes, O. P., Lazuras, L., Gunasekaran, A., & Koh, S. C. L. (2013). Environmental practices and performance and their relationships among Kosovo construction companies: A framework for analysis in transition economies. *International Journal of Services and Operations Management*, *15*(1), 115–130. doi:10.1504/IJSOM.2013.050565

Koong, L., & Lin, C. (2007). Evaluating the decision to adopt RFID systems using analytic hierarchy process. *Journal of American Academy of Business*, *11*(1), 72–77.

Kulas, J. T., McInnerney, J. E., DeMuth, R. F., & Jadwinski, V. (2007). Employee satisfaction and theft: Testing climate perceptions as a mediatorfalse. *The Journal of Psychology*, *141*(4), 389–402. doi:10.3200/JRLP.141.4.389-402 PMID:17725072

Mateen, A., & More, D. (2013). Applying TOC thinking process tools in managing challenges of supply chain finance: A case study. *International Journal of Services and Operations Management.*, *15*(4), 389–410. doi:10.1504/IJSOM.2013.054882

Mehrjerdi, Y. Z. S. (2011). RFID and its benefits: A multiple case analysis. *Assembly Automation*, *31*(3), 251–262. doi:10.1108/01445151111150596

O'Connor, M. C. (2004). Ending retail scams with RFID. *RFID Journal*. Retrieved January 27, 2014 from http://www.rfidjournal.com/article/articleview/1260/1/20/

Pacciarelli, D., D'Ariano, A., & Scotto, M. (2011). Applying RFID in warehouse operations of an Italian courier express company. *NETNOMICS: Economic Research and Electronic Networking*, *12*(3), 209–222. doi:10.1007/s11066-011-9059-4

Park, B.-N., & Min, H. (2013). Global supply chain barriers of foreign subsidiaries: The case of Korean expatriate manufacturers in China. *International Journal of Services and Operations Management.*, *15*(1), 67–78. doi:10.1504/IJSOM.2013.050562

Retailers should brace for sharp increase in shoplifting. (2001). *Checkpoint Systems*. [Online]. Retrieved January 23, 2014 from http://retailindustry.about.com/library/bl/q4/bl_rf120401.htm

Roberti, M. (2005a). Retailers say RFID will take time. *RFID Journal*. Retrieved February 3, 2014 from http://www.rfidjournal.com/article/articleview/1344

Roberti, M. (2005b). Wal-Mart begins RFID process changes. *RFID Journal*. Retrieved February 3, 2014 from http://www.rfidjournal.com/article/articleview/1385/1/20)

Roberti, M. (2005c). Wal-Mart to expand RFID tagging requirement. *RFID Journal*. Retrieved February 3, 2014 from http://rfidjournal.com/article/articleview/1930/1/9/

Roberti, M. (2007). Greater security for RFID tags. *RFID Journal*. Retrieved February 3, 2014 from http://www.rfidjournal.com/blog/entry/2939

Rosenblum, P. (2008). Managing shrink. *Chain Store Age*, *84*(1), 72–78.

Schreibfeder, J. (2008). *Cycle counting can eliminate your annual physical inventory*. Retrieved January 27, 2014 from http://www.effectiveinventory.com/article 9.html

Smith, A. A., Smith, A. D., & Baker, D. J. (2011). Inventory management shrinkage and employee anti-theft approaches. *International Journal of Electronic Finance*, *5*(3), 209–234. doi:10.1504/IJEF.2011.041337

Smith, A. D. (2011). Component part quality assurance concerns and standards: Comparison of world-class manufacturers. *Benchmarking: An International Journal, 18*(1), 128–148. doi:10.1108/14635771111109850

Smith, A. D., & Rupp, W. T. (2013). Data quality and knowledge/information management in service operations management: Regional supermarket case study. *International Journal of Knowledge-Based Organizations, 3*(3), 35–52. doi:10.4018/ijkbo.2013070103

Snyder, N. H., Broome, O. W., Kehoe, W. J., McIntyre, J. T., & Blair, K. E. (1991). *Reducing Employee Theft*. New York, NY: Quorum Books.

Sources: Target investigating data breach. (2013). *Krebs on Security*. Retrieved January 29, 2014 from http://krebsonsecurity.com/2013/12/sources-target-investigating-data-breach/

Summers, G. J., & Scherpereel, C. M. (2008). Decision making in product development: Are you outside-in or inside-out? *Management Decision, 46*(9), 1299–1314. doi:10.1108/00251740810911957

Tari, J. J., & Sabater, V. (2004). Quality tools and techniques: Are they necessary for quality management? *International Journal of Production Economics, 92*(3), 267–280. doi:10.1016/j.ijpe.2003.10.018

Tiwari, A., Turner, C., & Sackett, P. (2007). A framework for implementing cost and quality practices within manufacturing. *Journal of Manufacturing Technology Management, 18*(6), 731–760. doi:10.1108/17410380710763886

Ustundag, A. (2010). Evaluating RFID investment on a supply chain using tagging cost sharing factor. *International Journal of Production Research, 48*(9), 2549–2562. doi:10.1080/00207540903564926

Vargas, M. (2000). *Theft: Retail's real Grinch*. Retrieved January 23, 2014 from http://retailindustry.about.com/od/statistics_loss_prevention/l/aa001122a.htm

Vargas, M. (2002). *Retail theft and inventory shrinkage*. Retrieved January 23, 2014 from http://retailindustry.about.com/od/statistics_loss_prevention/l/aa021126a.htm

Visich, J. K., Li, S., Khumawala, B. M., & Reyes, P. M. (2009). Empirical evidence of RFID impacts on supply chain performance. *International Journal of Operations & Production Management, 29*(12), 1290–1315. doi:10.1108/01443570911006009

Wilson, J. M. (1995). Quality control methods in cycle counting for record accuracy management. *International Journal of Operations & Production Management, 15*(7), 27–38. doi:10.1108/01443579510090390

Wyld, D. C. (2006). RFID 101: The next big thing for management. *Management Research News, 29*(4), 154–173. doi:10.1108/01409170610665022

Yao, A., & Carlson, J. (1999). The impact of real-time data communication on inventory management. *International Journal of Production Economics, 59*(1), 213–219. doi:10.1016/S0925-5273(98)00234-5

Zang, C., & Fan, Y. (2007). Complex event processing in enterprise information systems based on RFID. *Enterprise Information Systems, 1*(1), 3–23. doi:10.1080/17517570601092127

ADDITIONAL READING

Al-Sakran, H. (2013). Agent and radio frequency identification based architecture for supermarket information system. *Journal of Computer Science, 9*(6), 699–707. doi:10.3844/jcssp.2013.699.707

Basu, P., & Nair, S. K. (2012). Supply chain finance enabled early pay: Unlocking trapped value in B2B logistics. *International Journal of Logistics Systems and Management, 12*(3), 334–353. doi:10.1504/IJLSM.2012.047605

Baxter, L. F., & Hirschhauser, C. (2004). Reification and representation in the implementation of quality improvement programmes. *International Journal of Operations & Production Management, 24*(2), 207–224. doi:10.1108/01443570410514894

Bhat, S. (2008). The effect of ordering policies for a manufacturing cell changing to lean production. *Proceedings - Institution of Mechanical Engineers, 222*(B11), 1551–1560. doi:10.1243/09544054JEM1216

Biswas, P., & Sarker, B. R. (2008). Optimal batch quantity models for a lean production system with in-cycle rework and scrap. *International Journal of Production Research, 46*(23), 6585–6610. doi:10.1080/00207540802230330

Brito, T. B., & Botter, R. C. (2012). Feasibility analysis of a global logistics hub in Panama. *International Journal of Logistics Systems and Management, 12*(3), 247–266. doi:10.1504/IJLSM.2012.047601

Browning, T. R., & Heath, R. D. (2009). Reconceptualizing the effects of lean on production costs with evidence from the F-22 program. *Journal of Operations Management, 27*(1), 23–35. doi:10.1016/j.jom.2008.03.009

Bulcsu, S. (2011). The process of liberalising the rail freight transport markets in the EU: The case of Hungary. *International Journal of Logistics Systems and Management, 9*(1), 89–107. doi:10.1504/IJLSM.2011.040061

Carvalho, H., Cruz-Machado, V., & Tavares, J. G. (2012). A mapping framework for assessing supply chain resilience. *International Journal of Logistics Systems and Management, 12*(3), 354–373. doi:10.1504/IJLSM.2012.047606

Chao, C., Yang, J. M., & Jen, W. (2007). Determining technology trends and forecasts of RFID by a historical review and bibliometric analysis from 1991 to 2005. *Technovation, 27*(5), 268–279. doi:10.1016/j.technovation.2006.09.003

Condea, C., Thiessse, F., & Fleisch, E. (2012). RFID-enabled shelf replenishment with backroom monitoring in retail stores. *Decision Support Systems, 52*(4), 839–849. doi:10.1016/j.dss.2011.11.018

Devaraj, S., Fan, M., & Kohli, R. (2002). Antecedents of B2C channel satisfaction and preference: Validating e-commerce metrics. *Information Systems Research, 13*(3), 316–333. doi:10.1287/isre.13.3.316.77

Dutta, A., Lee, H. L., & Whang, S. (2007). RFID and operations management: technology, value and incentives. *Production and Operations Management, 16*(5), 646–655. doi:10.1111/j.1937-5956.2007.tb00286.x

Hamidi, M., Farahmand, K., Sajjadi, S. R., & Nygard, K. E. (2012). A hybrid GRASP-tabu search metaheuristic for a four-layer location-routing problem. *International Journal of Logistics Systems and Management, 12*(3), 267–287. doi:10.1504/IJLSM.2012.047602

Kumar, P., Shankar, R., & Yadav, S. S. (2011). Global supplier selection and order allocation using FQFD and MOLP. *International Journal of Logistics Systems and Management, 9*(1), 43–68. doi:10.1504/IJLSM.2011.040059

Mathirajan, M., Manoj, K., & Ramachandran, V. (2011). A design of distribution network and development of efficient distribution policy. *International Journal of Logistics Systems and Supply Management, 9*(1), 108–137. doi:10.1504/IJLSM.2011.040062

More, D., & Babu, A. S. (2012). Benchmarking supply chain flexibility using data envelopment analysis. *International Journal of Logistics Systems and Management*, *12*(3), 288–317. doi:10.1504/IJLSM.2012.047603

Paksoy, T., & Cavlak, E. B. (2011). Development and optimisation of a new linear programming model for production/distribution network of an edible vegetable oils manufacturer. *International Journal of Logistics Systems and Management*, *9*(1), 1–21. doi:10.1504/IJLSM.2011.040057

Pettersson, A. I., & Segerstedt, A. (2011). Performance measurements in supply chains within Swedish industry. *International Journal of Logistics Systems and Management*, *9*(1), 69–88. doi:10.1504/IJLSM.2011.040060

Pradhananga, R., Hanaoka, S., & Sattayaprasert, W. (2011). Optimisation model for hazardous material transport routing in Thailand. *International Journal of Logistics Systems and Management*, *9*(1), 22–42. doi:10.1504/IJLSM.2011.040058

Smith, A. D. (2012). Case studies of RFID-related applications in the healthcare and voice-recognition industries. *International Journal of Knowledge-Based Organizations*, *2*(3), 48–63. doi:10.4018/ijkbo.2012070103

Smith, A. D. (2012). Operational efficiencies and ethical issues associated with microchip implants. *International Journal of Mobile Communications*, *10*(3), 281–302. doi:10.1504/IJMC.2012.048113

Smith, A. D. (2013). Online social networking and office environmental factors that affect worker productivity. *International Journal of Procurement Management*, *6*(5), 578–608. doi:10.1504/IJPM.2013.056173

Von Haartman, R. (2012). Beyond Fisher's product-supply chain matrix: Illustrating the actual impact of technological maturity on supply chain design. *International Journal of Logistics Systems and Management*, *12*(3), 318–333. doi:10.1504/IJLSM.2012.047604

Zang, C., & Fan, Y. (2007). Complex event processing in enterprise information systems based on RFID. *Enterprise Information Systems*, *1*(1), 3–23. doi:10.1080/17517570601092127

KEY TERMS AND DEFINITIONS

Automatic Identification and Data Capture Technologies (AIDC): Types of AIDC-related technologies to leave the human element out of the data collection and storage functions of information derived from manufacturing, integrated through the manufacturing process, types of authentication concerns and/or e-security strategies, and relationship links to customer profiles. Typical types of AIDC include, bar-coding, RFID, magnetic strips, touch memory, and smart cards.

Barcoding Technology: A long-term and very reliable type of AIDC technology, it is known for its very accurate and economical approaches to identity products and machine readable information from a variety of manufactured goods and services. Most barcodes use a type of standardized bars and spacing coding or symbology that is certified by an international standards body (GS1 System). This system provides for the universal global acceptance of many types of barcodes designed for a variety of shipping and identification applications. Example barcode formats that are in common use today include EAN/UPC, GS1 DataBar, GS1-128, ITF-14, GS1 DataMatrix, GS1 QR Code and Composite Components.

Inventory Management Problems and its Solutions: There are a number of inventory management problems that are not due to shrinkage. Most of these problems are based on inaccuracies that arise from poor management and record-keeping activities. Typically too much inventory can erode working capital and profits. It is important that management spends attention to supply projections, using past demand are a basis to improve upon and adjusting for identifying and quantifying less obvious patterns. Inaccurate inventory tracking can be addressed through proper use of EDI, bar-code scanning, and RFID-based solutions to reduce data entry errors. Priories of inventory needs to be established by management using an ABC analysis and proper data analysis tools Back-up and safety stock plans through contingency planning scenarios to remove uncertainties in inventory are extremely helpful tools.

Inventory Shrinkage: The term inventory shrinkage is a very generic term that is commonly used to describe almost any unintentional loss of inventory. It is usually detected by performing an actual physical count to verify that the amount of items on hand are less than manufactured or ordered stock. There are several common sources of inventory depending on retail and/or manufacturing viewpoints. From a retailer's viewpoint, inventory shrinkage might be due a direct cause of poor recordkeeping, customer/vendor shoplifting, employee theft, damage, obsolescence, and/or misplaced items. From a manufacturing viewpoint, inventory shrinkage may be due to loss of raw materials during a production process (i.e. goods in process, finished goods, and related inventories of raw materials). In many instances, shrinkage may be due to natural as well as illegal causes, such as spoilage or waste. Many sources must be classified as either normal or abnormal and must be dealt with accordingly.

RFID-Embedded Technologies: RFID technologies are types of automatic data capture techniques that use a combination of active and passive senders and receivers to collect and store codified information for further uses. The implementation of such technologies should lead to improved managerial and/or supply chain performance. On the surface, there appears to be few drawbacks to implementing such technology into a production process, assuming it enhances performance and improves output of the product. The main issues surrounding the RFID applications are whether the initial costs and labor required to utilize this technology are worth it, and will result in a positive outcome of revenues.

Supply Chain Management/Performance: In basic terms, supply chain is the system of organizations, people, activities, information and resources involved in moving a product or service from supplier to customer. The configuration and management of supply chain operations is a key way companies obtain and maintain a competitive advantage. The typical manufacturing supply chain begins with raw material suppliers, or inputs. The next link in the chain is the manufacturing, or transformation step; followed the distribution, or localization step. Finally, the finished product or service is purchased by customers as outputs. Service and Manufacturing managers need to know the impact of supply on their organization's purchasing and logistics processes. However, supply chain performance and its metrics are difficult to develop and actually measure.

Chapter 12
An Analysis of the Diffusion of RFID in the UK Logistics Sector Using a Technology–Acceptance Perspective

Ramakrishnan Ramanathan
University of Bedfordshire, UK

Usha Ramanathan
University of Bedfordshire, UK

Lok Wan Lorraine Ko
Nottingham University, UK

ABSTRACT

In this chapter, the authors explore the factors affecting the UK logistics service providers' intention to use RFID technology from the theoretical perspective of a Technology-Acceptance Model (TAM). The survey data analysis shows that perceived usability of RFID has a significant relationship with the levels of adoption of the technology, but perceived privacy issues and perceived security issues do not have such a significant relationship. Using further moderation analysis, the authors find that the relationship between usability and adoption becomes stronger if there is a high level of support for RFID projects within an organisation. The study points to the need to improve the appreciation and support in an organisation for RFID projects. For example, top management should be well informed so as to provide good support, while employees should be motivated to back the use of RFID in their operations. An appropriate level of the required infrastructure will also help increase the usability and hence the adoption of RFID in UK logistics.

DOI: 10.4018/978-1-4666-6308-4.ch012

INTRODUCTION

We live in an era in which businesses collaborate with supply chain partners located in different parts of the world. To achieve competitive advantage companies are adopting new technologies in every operation, such as production, logistics and distribution. As all chapters in this volume highlight, radio frequency identification (RFID) is an important technology available to modern businesses to streamline their operations (Roberts, 2006). This new technology provides business solutions for business-to-business supply chain partners (Curti et al., 2007; Sweeney, 2005). Although the literature is abound with a list of several advantages of RFID, this technology has not penetrated enough in the logistics sector in the UK (Ramanathan et al., 2012). Hence, the main purpose of this study is to explore factors affecting logistics service providers' intention to use RFID technology. We have used the basic tenets of Technology Acceptance Model (TAM) as our theoretical underpinning for this purpose. Specifically, we have explored how the underlying concepts of TAM, namely perceived usefulness, perceived ease of use, perceived privacy issues and perceived security issues, are related to the intention by UK logistics companies to adopt RFID. In addition, we have explored the roles of internal support environment in affecting this relationship. To our knowledge, very few studies have explored the use of TAM for the case of UK logistics, and there are no studies that extended TAM to include the influences of internal support environment, with the exception of Ramanathan et al. (2013) who explored the role of external (government) support. Finally, we use a relatively less used tool in operations management literature, namely the partial least squares structural equation modelling, for our analysis. These are the three contributions of our study.

Rest of this chapter is organised as follows. The next section provides a brief literature survey. Since much of RFID literature has been reviewed in a related chapter (Ramanathan et al., 2014) in this book, we do not repeat RFID literature but focus on TAM studies. Section 3 develops our conceptual framework and the hypotheses. Our data collection, which is closely related to those reported in Ramanathan et al. (2014), and analysis are briefly discussed in Section 4. Our results are discussed in detail in Section 5. Conclusions are presented in the last section of this chapter.

LITERATURE SURVEY

Since a detailed exposition of the RFID literature has been presented in another chapter (Ramanathan et al., 2014) in this book, we do not repeat this literature here. Instead, we focus on the theoretical framework used in this chapter, namely the Technology Assessment Model (TAM).

TAM was originally proposed by Davis (1989). The basic assumption of the TAM is that actual use of an innovation depends on the intention to make use of the technology, and that intention depends on individual attitudes toward using the technology and its perceived usefulness (Muller-Seitz et al., 2009). The attitude toward using the technology arises from the perceived usefulness and the perceived ease of use. Many researchers have utilized and validated TAM for use with numerous technological environments. According to Hossain & Prybutok (2008), some studies suggested that TAM successfully predicts an individual's acceptance of various corporate information technologies. Furthermore, TAM may hold across technologies, people, settings and times. Recently, it has been applied to the introduction of healthcare information systems (Pai & Huang, 2011), RFID technology acceptance at US universities (Hossain & Prybutok, 2008), and RFID technology acceptance in the German electronic retail sector (Muller-Seitz et al., 2009). The research model of these studies were based on TAM and have used the revised TAM proposed by Davis et al. (1989), which include perceived usefulness, perceived ease of use and the intention to use. Hossain and Prybutok (2008) extended TAM by adding perceived cultural influence, perceived privacy, perceived regulations' influence, and perceived security to the model. Table 1 presents the definitions of some common TAM constructs and related literature.

CONCEPTUAL FRAMEWORK AND HYPOTHESIS DEVELOPMENT

There is a general agreement in the TAM literature that perceived usefulness and perceived ease of use have similar impacts on adoption of innovative technologies. For example, Pai & Huang (2011) found that a positive relationship between preceived usefulness and users' intention to use, and also a positive relationship between perceived ease of use and intention to use healthcare information systems. Muller-Seitz et al. (2009) found a similar result in the context of German electronic retail sector. Hence, similar to Ramanathan et al. (2013), we have combined the constructs of perceived usefulness and perceived

ease of use into a single construct called perceived usability. Since the basic tenets of TAM leads to a positive relationships between perceived usefulness/perceived ease of use and intention to use, we propose that perceived usability of RFID is posively related to the intention to adopt RFID. This is our first hypothesis.

H1: Perceived usability is positively related to intention to adopt RFID.

In general, users will be less willing to adopt a technology if they feel they will be more vulnerable to disclose their private information to third parties when they use the technology. Thiesse (2007) has provided a number of recent examples when firms had to withdraw their RFID-based products due to customers' privacy concerns. Hossain & Prybutok (2008) assumed in their hypotheses that people with high privacy concerns and less willingness to sacrifice personal privacy has a low intention to use RFID technology. However in their results, they found that people often do not realize their privacy is threatened after RFID has been implemented. Another explanation claimed

Table 1. Definitions of common TAM constructs predictors

Acceptance Predictors	Definition	Sources
Perceived usefulness	The extent to which an individual believes that their job performance is enhanced by using a particular technology.	Deveoped by Davis et al. (1989). Applied in Hossain & Prybutok (2008); Muller-Seitz et al. (2009); Pai & Huang (2011).
Perceived ease of use	The extent to which an individual believes that using a particular system is free of effort.	Deveoped by Davis et al. (1989). Applied in Hossain & Prybutok (2008); Muller-Seitz et al. (2009); Pai & Huang (2011).
Perceived privacy	The degree to which an individual believes that he/she has the right to control the collection and use of his/her personal information, even after he/she has disclosed it to others.	Developed by Hossain & Prybutok (2008).
Perceived security	The degree to which an individual feels protected against security threats resulting from the use of RFID technology.	Developed and applied by Hossain & Prybutok (2008). Applied in Muller-Seitz et al. (2009).
Intention to use	The likelihood to use in the future.	Deveoped by Davis et al. (1989). Applied in Hossain & Prybutok (2008); Muller-Seitz et al. (2009); Pai & Huang (2011).

by Hossain & Prybutok (2008) is that consumers are aware of the potential privacy threats that RFID technology presents but they may not be paying enough attention to such issues, as they believe that the benefits of using RFID technology are greater than the potential privacy threat. In this case, it is assumed that the higher the willingness of companies to share information with internal & external parties, the higher is the intention to use RFID. Hence based on the previous studies, hypothesis 2 (H2) is formulated as follows:

H2: Perceived privacy in information sharing is positively related to intention to adopt RFID.

Perceived security issues reflect the attitude of users feel protected against security threats when they use a new technology (Hossain and Prybutok, 2008) and RFID tags, when fradulently obtained by third parties, can cause security concerns because of the information stored in them. Muller-Seitz et al. (2009) explored the customer acceptance of RFID technology at a German electronic retail corporation with regard to TAM. Their results showed that the lower the security concerns regarding RFID technology in retailing, the higher the customer acceptance of RFID. The same was found in the study of Hossain & Prybutok (2008). Their results present that the higher the perceived importance of personal information security and the less willing consumers are to sacrifice their personal information security, the lower the intention to use RFID technology. If the companies feel that their confidential data will not be captured and stored securely, the less likely they will adopt RFID and it results in lower intention to use RFID. In this line, we posit our hypothesis 3 (H3) as follows:

H3: Perceived data security is negatively related to intention to adopt RFID.

Hypotheses H1 – H3 represent direct impacts of TAM constructs on intention to adopt a technology. However, as highlighted in Section 1, RFID has not penetrated UK logistics sector sufficient enough, and this research aims to check factors responsible for this low penetration. Hence, this research aims to extend the understanding gained by validating H1-H3 by exploring additional factors that could strengthen or weaken these direct relationships. Specifically, we focus on how variables representing the level of support within a company impact the direct relationships hypothesised in H1-H3. The resulting moderating hypothesis (H4) extends the theory of TAM and is an important contribution of this chapter.

Organisations experience varying levels of support internally for implementing innovations such as RFID. It has been highlighted that a high level of commitment from the top management is a requirement for success of any innovation (Chatterjee et al., 2002). This will ensure sufficient financial and other infrastructure for the entire project, especially for large firms (Sharma et al., 2007; Sharma & Citurs, 2005; Tang & Tsai, 2009; Wang et al., 2010). Similarly, adoption is facilitated if employees are supportive (Wang et al., 2010). Thus, we posit that the direct relationships in H1-H3 will be stronger if there is a high level of internal support in a firm for implementing RFID. This leads to Hypothesis H4a,b,c.

H4a,b,c: The direct relationships in H1-H3 will be positively moderated by the level of internal support in an organisation.

Our research model incorporating the four hypotheses is presented in Figure 1.

RESEARCH METHODOLOGY AND DATA ANALYSIS

The research reported in this chapter is based on the same survey described in a related chapter (Ramanathan et al., 2014) in this book. Hence, we do not repeat the details of our questionnaire survey here. Similarly, our dependant variable, Intention to adopt RFID, is also described in de-

Figure 1. Research model for user acceptance of RFID

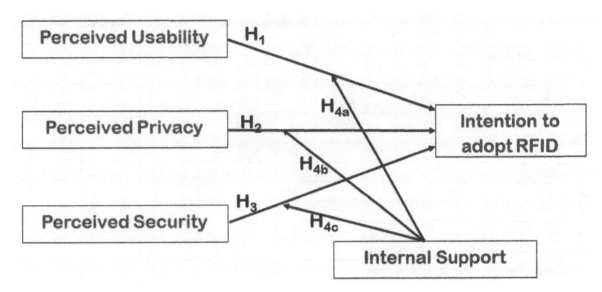

tail in Ramanathan et al. (2014) and will not be repeated here. Please see Ramanathan et al. (2014) for the details of our survey and the measures for Intention to adopt RFID.

In this research, we have used partial least squares (PLS) structural equation modelling (SEM) to verify our hypotheses. PLS has been used well in the field of marketing (Henseler et al., 2009) but is not so popular in the operations management and information systems literature. PLS has been explained in detail in Hair et al. (2013). This chapter provides one of the few applications of PLS in operations management. PLS is an extension of traditional least squares based regression to include more complex constructs. It is often recommended for use in an early stage of theoretical development in order to test and validate exploratory models, which is appropriate for the present study.

Prior to applying PLS path model, we first conducted confirmatory factor analysis to ensure that the constructs used in our model, namely usability, privacy, security and internal support, have the required statistical properties. We present the details of confirmatory factor analysis and the PLS path models in the next few sub-sections.

Confirmatory Factor Analysis

Table 2 lists measures for our constructs and their loadings obtained using confirmatory factor analysis. All the measures had high loadings (above 0.95) on constructs (well above the minimum threshold of 0.5). Reliability of the constructs was measured by Cronbach's alpha. A Cronbach's alpha of 0.65 or higher was used as an acceptable value for internal consistency of the measures (Hair et al., 2006). The Cronbach's alpha of the dependent variable (adoption) is 0.67. The Cronbach's alpha for independent variables are much higher, above 0.9. Average variance extracted is also high, well above the recommended minimum value of 0.5. These values support the contention that all the factors have adequate reliability. Thus the values shown in Table 2 validate construct validity of all our constructs.

Table 3 reports correlations among the constructs. All correlations are significant at $p < 0.01$. The values on diagonals represent composite

Table 2. Confirmatory factor analysis

	Usability	Privacy	Security	Adoption	Internal Support
Accuracy of stock records	0.983				
Less cost	0.982				
Easy to use	0.986				
Easier than convention	0.983				
Easy to integrate	0.985				
Improve tracking	0.977				
Less stress	0.974				
Improve safety	0.982				
Improve efficiency	0.987				
Save time	0.974				
Willingness to share confidential data with stakeholders		0.971			
Willingness to share confidential data with Suppliers/ Manufacturers		0.981			
Willingness to share confidential data with Clients		0.990			
Willingness to share confidential data with Logistics contractors		0.971			
Confidence in safe capture and storage of data			0.968		
RFID technology is secure			0.968		
Stages regarding RFID adoption				0.859	
Future trend of RFID adoption in the UK Logistics industry				0.801	
Company's future plan in RFID adoption				0.893	
Top management support					0.976
Employee support and knowledge of RFID					0.977
Capital investment support					0.944
Technology infrastructure support					0.979
Average Variance Extracted (AVE)	0.963	0.957	0.937	0.726	0.939
Cronbach's Alpha	0.996	0.985	0.933	0.669	0.978

Table 3. Construct correlations

	Usability	Privacy	Security	Adoption	Internal support
Usability	*0.996*				
Privacy	0.774	*0.989*			
Security	0.927	0.748	*0.967*		
Adoption	0.785	0.658	0.740	*0.888*	
Internal support	0.938	0.808	0.900	0.766	*0.984*
All correlations are significant at p<0.01. Diagonal elements represent composite reliability.					

reliability values of the constructs.. Since the composite reliability of a construct is larger than the correlations in the corresponding row/column, discriminant validity of our constructs has been established (Hair et al., 2006).

PLS Path Models

We have used Partial Least-Squares (PLS) method in two stages to test our research hypotheses. In the first stage, a simple model with three independent variables (usability, privacy and security) and one dependent variable 'adoption' is used. This stage is used to test our first three hypotheses (H1-H3) on direct links with adoption. The moderating nature of internal support is tested in Stage 2. We have used PLS version 2.0 (Ringle et al., 2005).

Results of Stage 1 of PLS model are shown in Figure 2. This model has shown good significant loadings of measures on to their constructs. The significance is indicated by asterisks next to these loadings. The relationships among the four constructs (Usability, Privacy, Security and Adoption in Figure 2) is captured in the form of structural model (also called the inner model in PLS). Figure 2 shows significant positive relationship between 'usability' and 'adoption', while the relationships between privacy and adoption, and, security and adoption are not significant. In PLS, *t*-statistics is used to check the significance of path coefficients. R^2 value of the model shows how much of the variance in the dependent variable is explained by the model. The value of R^2 for this model is high at 0.624, meaning that the model explains 62.4% of the variance in the intention to use RFID.

Thus the results of Figure 2 support our first hypothesis (H1) that the perceived usability will have a positive effect on intention to adopt RFID. But our results do not support the other two hypotheses H2 and H3. In other words, privacy and security do not have significant impact on the adoption of RFID. Hence, we reject these hypotheses H2 and H3.

In the second stage of model development, we have introduced a moderator variable 'internal support' to the PLS model of Stage 1. Results are shown in Figure 3 and more details are available in Table 4. Two of the moderating effects are significant as shown by the asterisks in Figure 3. As shown in Table 4, the product term of 'internal support' and usability has a significant positive path coefficient (0.281) in the moderation model of Figure 3. Similarly the product term of 'internal support' and privacy has a significant but lower path coefficient (0.041). Thus, there is evidence that the level of internal support to RFID implementation helps to improve the links between usability and adoption, and the link between privacy and adoption. However, the product term of security and 'internal support' is not significant, indicating that there is no evidence of the moderating role of internal support on the link between security and adoption of RFID. This result partially confirms our research hypothesis H4a,b,c; internal support positively moderates the link between usability and adoption (H4a supported) and the link between privacy and adoption (H4b supported) but does not moderate the link between security and adoption (H4c not supported).

DISCUSSION

Our study has produced interesting results in the context of factors affecting the adoption of RFID in the UK logistics sector. We have found that perceived usability of RFID is strongly related to the intention to adopt the technology. Perceived privacy issues and perceived security issues do not significantly affect the intention to adopt RFID. The most important result being that the strong positive relationship between usability and adoption of RFID is positively moderated by the level of internal support in an organisation. Further, though perceived privacy issues are not strongly related to the intention to adopt RFID, there seems to be a positive moderating impact

Figure 2. Results of the Stage 1 of the PLS model

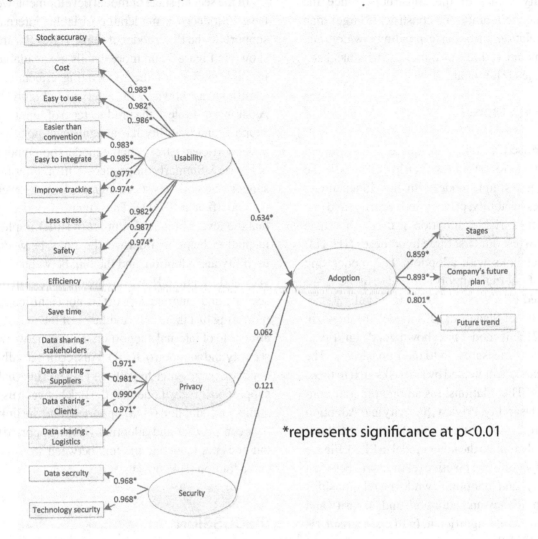

*represents significance at p<0.01

of internal support on this relationship. Finally, we have found that internal support do not have a significant moderating impact on the relationship between security issues and adoption.

Our study suggests that perceived usefulness of RFID is the single most important factor in facilitating UK logistics firms to start using the technology. This suggests that the producers of RFID technology should find ways of utilising RFID for multiple purposes in an organisation. For example, being a technology not requiring the line of sight (unlike bar codes that RFID was originally thought to substitute), RFID can go

beyond the conventional uses of bar codes. For example, RFID can be used to facilitate stock taking in a firm more frequently and accurately (Jones et al., 2005; Moon and Ngai, 2008).

In spite of some concerns that RFID could expose private information (Thiesse, 2007), our study has found that privacy issues are not significantly related to adoption. This result may be compared to the conflicting results presented in previous studies. On the one hand, several studies have highlighted serious privacy concerns with RFID tags (e.g., Ayoade, 2007; Gao et al., 2008; Thiesse, 2007). Specifically, Gao et al. (2008)

Figure 3. Moderating effect of internal support

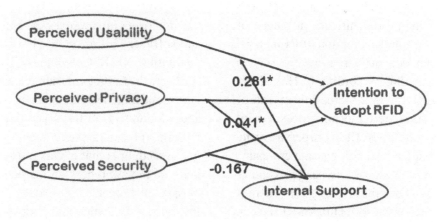

*represents significance at p <0.01

Table 4. Moderation effect of internal support ($R^2 = 0.687$)

Variable	Coefficient	t-statistic
Usability	0.592*	3.647
Privacy	0.088	1.029
Security	0.102	0.724
Internal support	0.226	1.196
Usability * Internal support	0.281*	2.424
Privacy * Internal support	0.041*	2.690
Security * Internal support	-0.167	0.715

*represents significance at p <0.01

have highlighted that the possibility of disclosing inventory data to competitors via RFID tags could be a very important privacy issue. According to them, one of the privacy issues is that a store's inventory labeled with unprotected tags may be monitored by competitors' unauthorized readers, thereby disclosing inventory data and corresponding financial information to competitors. Some companies may view this as a threat to their competitive advantage. On the other hand, other studies have found a positive link between privacy and adoption (e.g, Hossain and Prybutok, 2008). The argument here is that, though protecting their own private information is important to companies, they find it more valuable to be able to obtain private information about their competitors with the help of RFID tags. For example, companies

might desire to obtain their competitors' inventory data and significant financial value through the risks to privacy in RFID usage. Therefore, as companies' awareness about the importance of their privacy control in RFID usage increases, they may also recognize the potential benefits of gaining competitors' confidential data through the privacy issues that RFID technology presents. Our finding that privacy issues are not significant in influencing adoption may have arisen because the two conflicting nature of privacy issues – protection of own private information and benefit of obtaining private information of competitors – tend to cancel out the negative and positive impacts of privacy on adoption, leading to neutral or insignificant impact.

Unlike some previous studies (Hossain and Prybutok, 2008; Muller-Seitz et al., 2009), our study has not found a significant influence of security concerns on the adoption of RFID tags. There could be two main reasons for such a contradictory finding. According to Hossain & Prybutok (2008), the ever-increasing growth of technology such as the Internet influences perceptions about security issues. The more pervasive the positive influence of technology on a company, the less the issue of security issues (Hossain & Prybutok, 2008). Over the last few years, there is improvement in the security features in RFID such as more advanced encryption options and other privacy-enhancing technologies (Thiesse, 2007). Moreover, although companies are aware of the potential security issues that RFID technology presents, they may believe that the benefits of using RFID technology cancel out the potential security threat (Hossain & Prybutok, 2008).

Our study is the first to explore whether the level of internal support to the implementation of RFID moderates the direct relationships discussed above. We have found very strong evidence that the significant positive link between usability and adoption is moderated positively by the level of internal support. In other words, if there is stronger commitment internally in the form of top management support, financial commitment and employee support, then there will be larger level of adoption of RFID if users perceived improved usability from RFID. This can be sketched as shown in Figure 4.

Figure 4 shows that the RFID technology gets adopted by UK logistics firms faster as they perceive a given level of perception of usability, when the level of internal support (from management, employees and infrastructure) is higher. With lower levels of or no internal support, adoption rate of RFID is low as a function of usability perception. This finding could actually help understanding the mechanisms to improve the diffusion of RFID

in the UK logistics industry: ensure that the top management is committed to the RFID project, the employees are aware of the benefits of RFID and sufficient infrastructure exists in a firm for facilitating RFID technlogies. This finding is similar to the findings of Ramanathan et al. (2013) who found that the relationship between usability and adoption of RFID is positively moderated by support from the government. An implication of our finding is that efforts must be directed to increase the awareness on the benefits of RFID by specialist organisations such as the Chartered Institute of Logistics and Transport (CILT) in the UK.

Our study also found that the link between privacy issues and adoption is moderated positively by the level of internal support. Though perceived privacy issues do not influence adoption significantly, there is evidence that this relationship will be stronger if there is positive commitment for RFID from within the organisation. Following the discussion of Hossain and Prybutok (2008), we feel that this result would highlight that internal support to a RFID project is crucial especially to overcome privacy concerns of this technology.

CONCLUSION

RFID is becoming important technology in different manufacturing and retail sector but its adoption in the UK logistics sector is limited (Ramanathan et al., 2012). In this context, this study has explored the determinants of widespread adoption of RFID using the theoretical lens of technology acceptance model. In the context of UK, this is the first time the use of RFID in logistics has been studied using technology acceptance perspective. Our results have shown that perceived usability of RFID has a significant impact on the decision of firms to adopt the technology. Perceived privacy issues and perceived security issues do not affect

Figure 4. An illustration of the moderating impacts of internal support on the relationship between Usability and Adoption of RFID

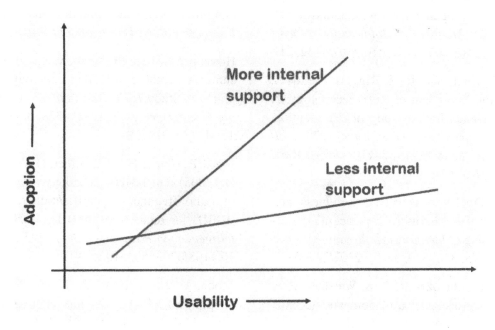

RFID adoption significantly. The most important finding of our study is that the relationship between perceived usability and adoption becomes stronger in the presence of high levels of internal support (from top management, employees and in the form of provision of adequate infrastructure) in the firm. An understanding of this moderating effect is important to help improve adoption of RFID in the UK logistics. For example, the adoption rate of RFID in UK logistics can be improved if efforts are directed towards increasing the awareness of RFID among the top management and employees of logistics firms.

This study has some limitations that also represent opportunities for future research. In general, logistics companies cover a wide range of service types. In this study, the influence of service types (such as receiving, cross-docking and putaway) of logistics companies on the adoption of RFID technology was not taken into account. Thus it is worthwhile to carry out further studies on the moderating effect of logistics service types on the adoption of RFID technology. In this research the sample population was randomly selected small or medium sized firms from CILT (UK)'s database, which might have less resources and capabilities to be able to afford RFID investments and risks. For this reason, the RFID adoption rate in the sample may be lower than the RFID adoption rate in UK businesses. Samples from different nations or industries could be collected to validate or refine the model.

REFERENCES

Ayoade, J. (2007). Roadmap to solving security and privacy concerns in RFID systems. *Computer Law & Security Report*, *23*, 555–661. doi:10.1016/j.clsr.2007.09.005

Chatterjee, D., Grewal, R., & Sambamurthy, V. (2002). Shaping up for e-commerce: Institutional enablers of the organizational assimilation of Web technologies. *Management Information Systems Quarterly, 26*(2), 65–89. doi:10.2307/4132321

Curtin, J., Kauffman, R., & Riggins, F. (2007). Making the 'most' out of RFID technology: A research agenda for the study of the adoption, usage and impact of RFID. *Information Technology Management, 8*(2), 87–110. doi:10.1007/s10799-007-0010-1

Davis, F. D. (1989). Perceived usefulness, perceived ease of use, and user acceptance of information technology. *Management Information Systems Quarterly, 13*, 318–339. doi:10.2307/249008

Davis, F. D., Bagozzi, R. P., & Warshaw, P. R. (1989). User acceptance of computer technology: A comparison of two theoretical models. *Management Science, 35*, 982–1003. doi:10.1287/mnsc.35.8.982

Gao, X., Xiang, Z., Wang, H., Shen, J., Huang, J., & Song, S. (2008). An approach to security and privacy of RFID system for supply chain. In *Proceedings of IEEE International Conference on E-Commerce Technology for Dynamic E-Business*. IEEE.

Hair, J. F. Jr, Black, W. C., Babin, B. J., Anderson, R. E., & Tatham, R. L. (2006). *Multivariate data analysis* (6th ed.). Upper Saddle River, NJ: Pearson-Prentice Hall.

Hair, J. F., Tomas, G., Hult, M., Ringle, C. M., & Sarstedt, M. (2013). *A Primer on Partial Least Squares Structural Equation Modeling (PLS-SEM)*. Thousand Oaks, CA: Sage.

Henseler, J., Ringle, C. M., & Sinkovics, R. R. (2009). The use of partial least squares path modeling in international marketing. In *Advances in International Marketing* (pp. 277–319). Emerald.

Hossain, M. M., & Prybutok, V. R. (2008). Consumer Acceptance of RFID technology: An Exploratory Study. *IEEE Transactions on Engineering Management, 55*(2), 316–328. doi:10.1109/TEM.2008.919728

Jones, P., Clarke-Hill, C., Hillier, D., & Comfort, D. (2005). The benefits, challenges and impacts of radio frequency identification technology (RFID) for retailers in the UK. *Marketing Intelligence & Planning, 23*(4), 395–402. doi:10.1108/02634500510603492

Moon, K. L., & Ngai, E. W. T. (2008). The adoption of RFID in fashion retailing: A business value-added framework. *Industrial Management & Data Systems, 108*(5), 596–612. doi:10.1108/02635570810876732

Muller-Seitz, G., Dautzenberg, K., Creusen, U., & Stromereder, C. (2009). Customer acceptance of RFID technology: Evidence from the German electronic retail sector. *Journal of Retailing and Consumer Services, 16*, 31–39. doi:10.1016/j.jretconser.2008.08.002

Pai, F. Y., & Huang, K. I. (2011). Applying the Technology Acceptance Model to the introduction of healthcare information systems. *Technological Forecasting and Social Change, 78*, 650–660. doi:10.1016/j.techfore.2010.11.007

Ramanathan, R., Bentley, Y., & Ko, L. (2012). Investigation of the status of RFID applications in the UK logistics sector. *Logistics & Transport Focus, 14*(11), 45–49.

Ramanathan, R., Ko, L., Chen, H., & Ramanathan, U. (2014). Green characteristics of RFID technologies: An exploration in the UK logistics sector from innovation diffusion perspective. In I. Lee (Ed.), *RFID Technology Integration for Business Performance Improvement*. Academic Press.

Ramanathan, R., Ramanathan, U., & Ko, L. (2013). Adoption of RFID technologies in UK logistics: Moderating roles of size, barcode experience and government support. *Expert Systems with Applications*, *41*(1), 230–236.

Ringle, C. M., Sven, W., & Alexander, W. (2005). *SmartPLS 2.0*. Retrieved from http://www.smart-pls.de

Roberts, C. M. (2006). Radio frequency identification (RFID). *Computers & Security*, *25*, 18–26. doi:10.1016/j.cose.2005.12.003

Sharma, A., & Citurs, A. (2005). Radio Frequency Identification (RFID) Adoption Drivers: A Radical Innovation Adoption Perspective. In *Proceedings of Americas Conference on Information Systems (AMCIS)*, (pp. 1213-1218). AMCIS.

Sharma, A., Citurs, A., & Konsynski, B. (2007). Strategic and Institutional Perspectives in the Adoption and Early Integration of Radio Frequency Identification (RFID). In *Proceedings of 40th Annual Hawaii International Conference on System Sciences*. IEEE.

Sweeney, P. J. (2005). *RFID for dummies*. Indianapolis, IN: Wiley Publishing.

Tang, L. L., & Tsai, W. C. (2009). *RFID adoption model for Taiwan's logistics service providers*. Taiwan: Graduate School of Management, Yuan Ze University.

Thiesse, F. (2007). RFID, privacy and the perception of risk: A strategic framework. *The Journal of Strategic Information Systems*, *16*, 214–232. doi:10.1016/j.jsis.2007.05.006

Wang, Y. M., Wang, Y. S., & Yang, Y. F. (2010). Understanding the determinants of RFID adoption in the manufacturing industry. *Technological Forecasting and Social Change*, *77*, 803–815. doi:10.1016/j.techfore.2010.03.006

KEY TERMS AND DEFINITIONS

Intention to Use: The likelihood to use a new technology in the future.

Perceived Ease of Use: The extent to which an individual believes that using a particular system is free of effort.

Perceived Privacy: The degree to which an individual believes that he/she has the right to control the collection and use of his/her personal information, even after he/she has disclosed it to others.

Perceived Security: The degree to which an individual feels protected against security threats resulting from the use of RFID technology.

Perceived Usefulness: The extent to which an individual believes that their job performance is enhanced by using a particular technology.

RFID: Radio frequency identification (RFID) is one type of auto-identification technology that uses radio frequency (RF) waves to identify, track and locate individual physical items.

Technology Acceptance Model: It is a theory to help understand how a new technology gets accepted in organisations. The basic assumption is that actual use of an innovation depends on the intention to make use of the technology, and that intention depends on individual attitudes toward using the technology and its perceived usefulness.

Chapter 13
RFID Technology in Business and Valuation Methods

In Lee
Western Illinois University, USA

ABSTRACT

Radio Frequency Identification (RFID) became one of the major disruptive innovations that have attracted the attention of researchers and practitioners around the world. Recognizing the business value of RFID, firms are rapidly adopting RFID technology in a wide range of industries including hospitals, logistics, manufacturing, and retailing. Since the adoption of RFID largely depends on the perceived potential benefits and the investment costs, firms need to carefully assess every intangible and tangible benefits and costs to make sure the adoption is financially, operationally, and strategically justifiable. This chapter provides a literature review on RFID applications in business and valuation methods for RFID and presents an analytical evaluation model for RFID investment for manufacturing and retail organizations. Finally, this chapter concludes with the implications of the chapter for academics and practitioners.

INTRODUCTION

Radio Frequency Identification (RFID) technology is one of the major disruptive innovations in the twenty-first century and continues to evolve and grow over time. In various industries, RFID technology shows great potentials for cost reduction, business process redesign, supply chain improvement, and on-site customer support. Recently, RFID technology has been touted as the foundational enabling technologies for the realization of the Internet of Things (IoT). IoT is based on uniquely identifiable objects and the

Internet technologies. Devices on the IoT have identifiable and create, collect, share store data in an Internet-like structure. For supply chain management, the IoT may use sensors to track RFID tags attached to objects moving through supply chains, thus improving inventory management and information flow while reducing transportation costs. The market for RFID hardware, software, and infrastructure has been strong and will remain strong with the growth of pervasive computing and the IoT.

Due to the ability to track movements of goods in a supply chain, RFID has given unprecedented visibility to the supply chain and has been able to

DOI: 10.4018/978-1-4666-6308-4.ch013

save labor cost, improve supply chain coordination, reduce inventory and increase product availability (Lee & Özer, 2007). RFID promises to transform supply chain management by providing detailed information on the flow of products throughout the value chain (Whitaker et al., 2007). Furthermore, RFID is considered as a strategic value information technology which brings new value propositions, creates new markets, and builds competitiveness in various industries (Christensen et al, 2004; Krotov & Junglas, 2008; Tajima, 2007). Therefore, understanding the value of the RFID will be critical to the timely adoption of RFID, as the technology advances at a stupendous speed.

RFID technology management is the process of evaluating RFID technology, developing RFID systems, and managing RFID infrastructure to achieve business goals. In the evaluation stage of RFID technology, managers identify potential business process redesign opportunities or business improvement opportunities, explore different RFID technology options, assess their cost-benefit, and choose the best technology. To assess their cost-benefit, certain metrics need to be developed including quantifiable and unquantifiable benefits and costs of each RFID technology option. Despite the popularity of RFID technology and a large body of research on RFID benefits, there is still a lack of comprehensive approach to the evaluation process which combines identification, forecasting, and assessment of RFIT technology (Baars et al., 2009).

As RFID projects often compete with other IT projects for scarce resources, the fundamental questions for the RFID adoption are whether RFID technology can create a value, how its value can be measured, and how the RFID technology will be implemented. Evidence indicates that electronic integration with RFID without business process redesign is not sufficient to deliver promised logistics services (Lai et al., 2008). Wal-Mart has implemented RFID aggressively, but faced its own implementation issues including technical problems and suppliers' pushback. It would be very challenging for a company to measure the benefits when there is no previous experience in similar technology investments.

Despite the need for a useful evaluation method in the industries, RFID valuation methods have not been fully operationalized, and developing a strong business case has been challenging for managers. Traditionally, accounting and financial project evaluation methods have been widely used to assess the value of projects. Return on investment, net present value, and payback period methods are classic in project evaluations. However, these traditional accounting and financial methods have played a limited role in justifying the RFID investment opportunities, because many benefits are hard to quantify and usually realized in the future.

In light of the ongoing debate on the valuation of RFID investment in the academia and industries, this chapter provides an overview of RFID applications in different industries and previous evaluation studies, presents an RFID investment evaluation model, and discusses a future direction for researchers and practitioners. Our chapter proceeds with literature review in Section 2, the evaluation model in Section 3, and the conclusion in Section 4.

LITERATURE REVIEW

The global industry for RFID technology has been growing steadily and is expected to expand fast for some time in the future. The dwindling prices of RFID tags are a driver for widespread adoption of item level tagging. Currently, the United States has the largest market worldwide, followed by Europe. Although developed markets such as US and Europe continue to remain the largest revenue generators for RFID manufacturers and software developers for some time, future growth in the market will be primarily driven by major Asian countries such as China and South Korea with the support extended by their governments (PRWeb, 2012).

RFID in Healthcare

RFID has been applied in the healthcare industries for the purpose of tracking medical equipment, monitoring patients, administering right medication to patient, and identifying counterfeit medicine (Ting et al., 2011). RFID technology not only offers tracking capability to locate equipment, supplies and people in real time, but also provides efficient and accurate medical data access for healthcare professionals (Yao et al., 2012). However, RFID adoption in the healthcare industry is far behind the earlier prediction. Major barriers to RFID adoption include technological limitations, interference concerns, prohibitive costs, lack of global standards and privacy concerns (Yao et al., 2012).

Bendavid et al. (2010) analyze a hospital nursing unit that has evaluated and approved a two-bin "e-kanban" replenishment system based on passive RFID tags. Results show that implementing the e-kanban RFID solution with the redesign of the ward floor and of the roles and functions can significantly improve business and operational performance. The most important benefits for the hospital include the time saved from non-value-added activities that can be transferred to patient care activities and the significant reduction of on-hand inventory at distributed storage locations.

A 2007 national survey of 1,404 Americans reveals varying degrees of sentiments regarding mobile healthcare services (Katz & Rice, 2009). The survey shows that high levels of interest in emergency intervention services, but much less interest in health information and monitoring services. The interest in RFID-based personal medical technology was positively associated with high level of trust in others and social support. Personalized RFID tags raise privacy concerns even when not directly carrying private information, as the unique tag data can be read and aggregated to identify individuals, analyze their preferences, and track their location (Park, 2011). There is a need for strong security measures for safe use of personalized RFID tags in conjunction with RFID services.

According to participant observation and interviews with hospital staff members and industry consultants in the United States, hospital staff, especially nurses, have concerns about the surveillance issues of these tracking technologies (Fisher & Monahan, 2008). Nursing staff frequently experience an intensification of labor as a result of the deployment of RFID systems, because the task of keeping the systems operational often is assigned to them. Privacy concerns and work intensification for nursing and other hospital staff should be taken into consideration in the design and implementation of the RFID technology.

RFID in Construction

RFID technology brings about cost savings for various construction projects via increased speed and accuracy of data entry. Wang (2008) proposes an RFID-based quality management system, which functions as a platform for gathering, filtering, managing, monitoring and sharing quality data, and demonstrates its effective concrete specimen inspection along with automated data collection and information management in a quality test lab. The construction industry faces unique challenges in material planning, ordering, receiving and storing, and site usage and monitoring. Poor materials management has been identified as a major source of low construction productivity, cost overrun and delays (Ren et al, 2011). RFID facilitates the flow of information in the materials management process and helps project teams to collect material storage and usage information in an active and accurate way.

RFID-based real-time locating system (RTLS) has been used for safety management at construction sites. RTLS provides accurate and robust localization performance in construction sites where it is otherwise very difficult to maintain signal availability due to many moving obstacles. RFID for the RTLS shows benefits in data storage, transfer capability, and relatively inexpensive installation cost (Lee et al., 2012).

To integrate the lifecycle management for construction material control, Lee et al. (2013) develop a framework for Information Lifecycle Management (ILM) for material control and demonstrate the management process for complex construction materials. The ILM framework includes key RFID checkpoints and material types to facilitate on-site material control. On-site trials show that the ILM framework has the benefit potential in the building industry.

RFID in Supply Chain

Like many other information technologies, the business value of the RFID technology includes lead time reduction, productivity improvement, cost reduction, increased revenue, customer satisfaction, competitive advantage, and inventory reduction (Michael & McCathie, 2005; Angeles, 2007; Veeramani et al., 2008). Supply chain RFID technology is an emerging application that has attracted a lot of attention from researchers and practitioners in the U.S., Europe, and Asia (Soon & Gutiérrez, 2008). RFID plays an important role in managing supply chain activities because of their ability to identify, track and share information throughout the supply chain (Min & Mentzer, 2004; Morton et al, 2006; Krause et al., 2007). RFID technology enables supply chains to easily and inexpensively collect and share information, thus enhancing supply chain visibility. The enhanced supply chain visibility leads to reduced stock-out, lower labor costs, reduced transaction costs, and improved inventory management in their supply chains (Twist, 2005). For example, supply chain visibility mitigates the bullwhip effect, and thus reduces excess inventory. Inaccurate inventory counts can lead to decreased profit due to overstock in a supply chain. Items-level RFID

inventory records reduce overstocking, shrinkage, etc. Although RFID cannot eliminate all errors, the errors can be detected quickly and can be dealt with effectively (Sarac, 2010).

One of the factors influencing RFID adoption in the supply chain is an adoption mandate to upstream suppliers by major retailers such as Wal-Mart and Walgreens. These mega-retailers use their purchasing power over suppliers in the supply chain RFID adoption decision. Bertolini et al. (2010) suggest that the adoption of RFID has economic advantages in the fast moving consumer goods (FMCG) supply chain. They attempted to quantify the potential benefits of RFID technology and EPC Network for the FMCG supply chain. The results of the study show that the largest part of the RFID benefits comes from collaboration between multiple supply chain partners. RFID benefits include not only operational improvements and cost reduction, but also new business opportunities and strategies.

In general, RFID benefits in supply chain are found at three levels (Attaran, 2012): (1) Immediate: on-site RFID readers can read multiple tags simultaneously, thereby can improve checkout, inventory control, and loss prevention. (2) Short-Term: RFID can improve supply chain visibility and performance through asset tracking, product origin tracing, and product recall, and (3) Long-Term: Collaborative use of RFID technologies can help supply chain partners put the right item in the right place at the right time and for the right price.

While the economic value of the RFID is one of the most important considerations for the corporate adoption, organizational and environmental factors are also known to affect the intention to adopt RFID. Kim and Garrison (2010) investigate South Korean retailers to identify key organizational characteristics that affect the evaluation of RFID. The analysis of the 278 adopting organizations show that organizational needs (Ubiquity and Performance Gaps), perceived factors (Benefits and Cost Savings), and organizational readiness (Financial Resources and Technological Knowledge) have a significant effect on RFID evaluation; and evaluation impacts its adoption and integration. Another survey of a group of early standards adopters suggests that top management support, perceived technology costs, and forces within the supply chain exert a significant influence on the adoption process (Thiesse et al., 2011).

Many organizations take a "wait and see" approach to RFID investment and hope to learn more from the early adopters, since the promised benefits of RFID are still unclear while requiring significant up-front investment (Reyes & Jaska, 2007). More recently, Visich et al. (2010) present an extensive literature review of practitioner-focused articles and research articles about supply chain performance. They find that significant quantitative benefits of RFID have been reported for a variety of supply chain entities, processes and performance measures.

RFID Valuation Methods

As RFID is entering the mainstream information technology arena, the evaluation methodologies of RFID have been a focus of a number of studies. A number of approaches have been taken to assess the value of RFID investment including field studies, frameworks, return on investment (ROI), net present value (NPV), normative models, real option approaches, and simulation studies. As RFID is one type of IT, traditional IT investment justifications are of relevance for the valuation of RFID investments. However, RFID investment evaluation needs to address specific RFID related challenges. For example, measuring potential strategic benefits and risks would be a challenge to tackle.

To assess the impact of RFID technology on tier-one suppliers, Veeramani at al. (2008) present a framework and models which measure five areas of benefit: lower operating costs, increase in revenue, lower overhead costs, reduced inventory capital cost, and lead time reduction. In order to address the discrepancy between expected and realized benefits of RFID investment, potential benefits and risks are also explored (Michael & McCathie, 2005).

As in many other IT projects, one of the barriers to the adoption of RFID by organizations is difficulty in assessing the potential ROI (Veeramani et al, 2008). In many cases, the return on investment is realized a while after the initial investment is made. While the formula for calculating ROI is relatively straightforward, the ROI method is only suitable when both the benefits and the costs of an investment are easily quantifiable and the causal relationships between benefits and costs are clear. While some cost savings such as labor costs may be easy to estimate, inventory savings, shrinkage reduction, and order cost savings are difficult to quantify. For RFID, it is not always easy to match the expected returns with the expected costs, and the estimates on ROI would not be convincing. Much of the ROI research has focused on the benefits to retailers (Rekik et al., 2008).

The NPV method is a widely used capital budgeting method for assessing cash flow-based financial performance of projects. In evaluating the investment of well-known mature technologies, experts or practitioners may subjectively give their reasonable estimates of the discount rate and cash flows. On the other hand, for new disruptive technologies like RFID, it is more difficult to estimate the risk-adjusted discount rate and cash flow. High discount rate oftentimes unfavorably penalizes IT investments. Another issue with relying on NPV is that it does not provide an overall picture of the gain or loss of executing a certain project.

For an RFID investment, it is very questionable whether we can get meaningful results from NPV and ROI analyses. To illustrate the limitations of NPV and ROI, let's take a look at an example of the decreased ordering cost due to an RFID investment. RFID is supposed to provide better order process management and therefore reduce ordering costs. Suppose the ordering cost used to be $1,000. Now, the RFID-based ordering cost is $100 with an RFID investment of $100,000. How can we calculate the inventory management cost saved by the RFID-enabled ordering cost? The ROI and NPV methods alone cannot measure the effect of reduced ordering cost on the total inventory management cost. An inventory cost model is needed to estimate the effect of the reduced ordering cost on the total inventory management cost.

Kasiri et al. (2012) adapt the balanced scorecard (BSC) model as a decision-making framework to measure the effects of RFID-enabled changes on retail store operations. They conducted a Delphi study in which 10 consultants and senior managers from leading U.S. retailers were interviewed. Their study indicates that benefits in the areas of merchandising and marketing may not be realized as directly as those in the supply chain, but their effects should not be undervalued. The modified BSC model indicates that there exist potential opportunities for item-level RFID use in retailing.

Simulation has been extensively used in RFID valuation. Simulation was exploited as a tool to investigate reengineering of RFID logistics processes and profitability (Bottani, 2008; Özelkan & Galambosi, 2008, Ustundag, 2010). Doerr et al. (2006) report on an analysis of the costs and benefits of Radio Frequency Identification/MicroElectroMechanical System (RFID/MEMS) technology for the ordnance inventory management. They combine a multi-criteria tool for the valuation of qualitative factors with a Monte-Carlo simulation. Ustundag (2010) uses a simulation model to calculate the NPV of an RFID investment on a three-echelon supply chain and to examine the effects of sharing the tagging cost between supply chain members on the NPV at the echelon level. Wang et al. (2008) focus on the analysis of simulated impact of the RFID system on the inventory replenishment of the thin film transistor liquid crystal display in Taiwan. An automatic inventory replenishment function adopting the (s, S) policy is enabled with RFID and without RFID. The result of the experiment shows that the RFID-enabled pull-based supply chain can achieve a reduction in inventory cost and an increase in turnover rate.

Simulations of a leading Italian apparel retailer show that RFID implementations are beneficial due to the increased sales, especially when a fashion retailer is focused on clerk-assisted sales strategies. Sales growth results from the impacts of RFID technology on better inventory control, faster inventory turnover, and longer time available for store personnel to assist consumers (De Marco et al., 2012). A discrete-event simulation model was used to analyze how RFID creates value within the remanufacturing operation (Ferrer et al., 2011). The study finds that the simulated gains from using RFID are quite modest, and proposes alternative justifications for the major benefits seen in practice. The study then provides a framework for deciding on the adoption of different types of RFID technology for different remanufacturing needs.

Business Process Reengineering (BPR) has been investigated in conjunction with the use of RFID technology. Business value of RFID technology can be derived through refining business processes and expanding the business model (Bose & Lam, 2008; Tzeng et al., 2008). A field study conducted in the utility industry shows how process optimization can be achieved when integrating RFID technology into information systems applications (Bendavid et al., 2006). A case study in the retail industry indicates that RFID technology can cancel, automate, or automatically trigger some business processes (Wamba et al., 2008).

The analytical approach helps us understand how new technology can affect the operational activities of a company, see how the changes in the operating activities can give rise to enhanced decisions, and generate the final performance (Lee & Ozer, 2007). de Kok et al. (2008) assess inventory policies, considering both the shrinkage fraction and the impact of RFID technology. To compare the situation with RFID and the one without RFID in terms of costs, an exact analytical expression was derived for the break-even prices of an RFID tag. Uçkun et al. (2008) consider a supply chain consisting of a retailer (distributor) and a supplier and find the optimal investment level that maximizes profit by decreasing inventory inaccuracy. They derive the optimal level of investment both for the centralized and the decentralized systems under two scenarios: inventory sharing between the warehouses is allowed and not allowed. Lee (2008) develops cost/benefit models to measure the impact of RFID-integrated quality improvement programs and to predict the ROI. Using these models, the decision makers decide whether and how much to invest in quality improvement projects based on the tangible costs such as manufacturing cost, inventory cost, setup cost, holding cost, and warranty cost. Fan et al. (2014) apply the newsvendor model to analyze the reduction of inventory shrinkage with the use of RFID. Inventory shrinkage problems are solved by optimizing order quantities and expected profits in consideration with the effect of the available rate of ordering quantity, RFID read rate improvement, and the tag cost, respectively.

Pointing that the value of investment in new IT becomes very difficult to quantify due to its wide scope of applications coupled with embedded options in its adoption, Lee and Lee (2011) employ a real option analysis to evaluate RFID adoption in the supply chain and considers the real option rule to estimate the present values of expected cash flows and expected costs in trapezoidal fuzzy numbers. Analytic Hierarchy Process (AHP) methodology is also employed as a decision analysis mechanism to analyze the RFID adoption decision processes of both RFID expert and industry evaluators and to assist organizations to judge if they are ready to adopt the RFID systems (Lin & Lin, 2007).

Our literature review shows that RFID is projected to grow rapidly with the phenomenal advancements in wireless communication technologies. As RFID technology drives the changes of business practices, researchers and practitioners need to understand the implications of these tech-

nological and organizational changes. Given the growing interest in RFID investments by managers, researchers need to further develop theories and measurement models that will help managers apply knowledge gained from the research to make a judicious RFID investment decision and to enhance the value of RFID.

The next section provides a normative RFID investment evaluation model for manufacturing and supply chain and investigates the relationships between model input parameters (e.g., demand level and RFID cost functions), decision variables (e.g., RFID investment level), and result variables (e.g., total cost savings and benefits).

THE RFID INVESTMENT EVALUATION MODEL FOR MANUFACTURING AND RETAIL ORGANIZATIONS

This section presents the base model for RFID investment and examines the relationships between model parameters and the value of RFID investment. The evaluation of the investment in RFID in manufacturing and supply chain has been a popular topic and structuring the investment problem into an analytical model has been a challenge in the research community. The proposed model is not only useful in its own right, but it also underscores the feasibility of using analytical models in the field of RFID investment (Lee & Lee, 2010). Given the slower than expected RFID adoption and importance of the investment justification, it is not enough to argue for the qualitative benefits of the technology. A real-world model and empirical evidence would be more important to measure the value of RFID. In the following subsections, we present the base model of the RFID investment decision. This base model utilizes the traditional inventory management practices of manufacturing and retail organizations. RFID is known to have real-time inventory tracking capability, resulting in reduced inventory management time and counting errors. A number of studies on RFID observe the impact of RFID on the inventory costs (de Kok et al., 2008; Hardgrave et al., 2009; Lee & Ozer, 2007; Wang et al., 2008).

The base model of the RFID investment decision is based on the classic economic order quantity (EOQ) model that is widely used in the manufacturing and retailing area. Since differences exist in the cost structure between the EOQ model and the supply chain RFID investment, our model takes into consideration a cost function and cost components that are unique to RFID investment. At the same time, the unique properties of the EOQ model are utilized by taking into account the essential cost variables of the EOQ cost function such as the unit holding cost and ordering cost. For the actual model parameters, an accounting department may provide useful information on the unit holding and ordering costs. The annual inventory holding cost typically includes the cost of the warehouse space, rent, utility, and warehouse maintenance cost. We demonstrate that RFID investment can reduce the total inventory management cost by reducing the total inventory holding cost and ordering cost. Our model shows that RFID typically reduces EOQ and therefore lowers the average inventory level. The model allows us to determine the optimal investment level in supply chain RFID technology that will minimize the total cost.

The classic EOQ model identifies the optimal order quantity that minimizes the total inventory management cost. While the EOQ model consists of ordering cost and inventory holding costs, our model adds three unique RFID investment variables: ordering efficiency, Just-In-Time (JIT) efficiency, and operational efficiency. Ordering efficiency is realized by minimizing any inefficiency related to ordering activities, and is typically dependent on the intensity of RFID technology. For example, item-level RFID tagging is generally more efficient than pallet-level or batch-level RFID tagging. While the EOQ model assumes that an instantaneous delivery of the entire batch

of order quantity takes place at the beginning of the periodic order cycle, JIT efficiency narrows the timing gap between delivery of goods/parts and actual consumption/production. JIT efficiency reflects more accurately the advantages of RFID of better inventory management, and it can be improved with such technologies as real-time merchandise tracking and locating systems. Operating efficiency is achieved by managing the individual goods/parts efficiently. For example, operating efficiency is improved by the RFID merchandise status monitoring.

Next we introduce the nomenclature we use throughout this section and discuss a model formulation.

Nomenclature

O: Fixed order cost per order cycle.
H: Annual inventory holding cost per unit.
D: Annual demand.
C: Operating cost per unit.
R: Ordering efficiency.
I: JIT efficiency.
J: Operating efficiency.
K: Investment level for ordering efficiency.
V: Investment level for JIT efficiency.
X: Investment level for operating efficiency.
d: Daily delivery rate.
c: Daily consumption/production rate.

The optimal order quantity, Q^*, and the optimal total cost (TC) of the EOQ model are given by

$$Q^* = \sqrt{\frac{2OD}{H}} \tag{1}$$

$$TC^* = O\frac{D}{Q^*} + H\frac{Q^*}{2} = \sqrt{2HOD} \tag{2}$$

The first term, $O\dfrac{D}{Q^*}$, represents the total order cost during a planning period (i.e., the fixed order cost per order cycle times the number of orders during a planning period). The second term, $H\dfrac{Q^*}{2}$, represents the total inventory holding cost during a planning period (i.e., the annual inventory cost per unit times the average inventory level). Equation (1) shows that a higher fixed order cost results in a larger optimal order quantity, and a higher inventory holding cost results in a smaller optimal order quantity. For the derivation of the optimal solution, refer to Roach (2005).

The RFID investment evaluation model extends the EOQ model by incorporating the ordering efficiency of R, JIT efficiency of I, operating efficiency of J, and investments of K, V, and X for these factors. Our model is based on a number of assumptions. It is assumed that the initiation of each periodic order cycle incurs a certain fixed order cost.

The proposed model also assumes that the total demand level is known and constant. It is common practice to use an approximate solution that is obtained by replacing stochastic demand with its mean, and using the deterministic EOQ model (Axsäter, 1996).

The mathematical formula for our model is given by:

$$TC = O\frac{RD}{Q} + IH\frac{Q}{2} + JCD + K + V + X \tag{3}$$

$$Q^* = \sqrt{\frac{2ORD}{HI}} \tag{4}$$

where

$$I = \left(\frac{d-c}{d}\right) = 1 - \frac{c}{d}, \quad 0 \leq I \leq 1 \tag{5}$$

In this model, the total cost, TC, include six cost components: ordering cost, inventory holding cost, operating cost, investment cost for ordering efficiency (K), investment cost for JIT efficiency (V), and investment cost for operating efficiency (X). Equation (4) shows the optimal order quantity which minimizes the total cost. Equation (5) indicates that JIT efficiency (I) improves as the daily delivery rate (d) approaches the daily consumption rate (c)

In the following subsections, we examine (1) investment in the ordering efficiency, (2) investment in the JIT efficiency, and (3) investment in the operating efficiency.

RFID INVESTMENT IN ORDERING EFFICIENCY

Ordering efficiency is defined as the degree to which the fixed order cost per order cycle is reduced by the investment, K. The reduced ordering cost and the reduced inventory level have been considered in a number of RFID studies. RFID improves ordering efficiency in various ways. For example, receiving accuracy reduces the count/recount in the delivery and speeds up the order fulfillment. Companies no longer need to open the box and spend long and tedious hours counting and recounting products. The loss of incoming materials is minimized. The movement of ordered products to the warehouse and production floor is smooth.

A grocery case study conducted by Kärkkäinen (2003) identifies various savings in inventory, store receiving, stock/code check, ordering productivity, and stock loss. Ordering through RFID is also three times faster than through traditional bar code. Therefore, the integration of the RFID system into supply chains has become a promising approach to the reduction of bullwhip effect and the enhancement of order management (Wang et al., 2008). Another study shows that Wal-Mart and Sara Lee achieved an 18 percent reduction in inventory level and up to a 20 percent reduction in order cycle (Attaran & Attaran, 2004).

We assume that the ordering efficiency, *R,* is an exponential function with a base *e* where the RFID investment cost, *K,* improves the ordering efficiency. Billington (1987) suggested a similar exponential function with base *e* to determine the optimal investment cost to reduce setup costs in the classic EOQ model. Researchers and practitioners have found it useful for cost estimation and productivity evaluation purposes to think of information systems development as an economic production process, whereby inputs, such as time, effort, and money for systems development, are converted into outputs such as the size and functionality of the delivered system (Banker et al., 1994). Local economies of scale are present when average productivity is increasing, and scale diseconomies prevail when average productivity is decreasing.

Our model assumes that there exist the diseconomies of RFID investment as the investment size increases due to the rapidly increasing amount of rework related to architecture, risk resolution, team compatibility, and system integration. As RFID technology improves ordering efficiency, but incurs RFID investment cost, the following cost minimization model is suggested.

$$\text{Min } TC = O\frac{RD}{Q} + IH\frac{Q}{2} + K \tag{6}$$

Mathematically, the ordering efficiency function is defined as follows:

$$R = N + (M - N)e^{-\beta K}, \\ 0 \leq N \leq M \leq 1, \text{ and } 0 \leq R \leq 1 \tag{7}$$

where *M* is the lowest ordering efficiency achieved when there is no investment in RFID technology, *N* is the highest ordering efficiency achievable by the investment of *K,* and *β* is the investment

elasticity of ordering efficiency. Note that a lower value of the ordering efficiency equates to a higher efficiency.

The first derivative of Equation (6) is taken with regard to *K* and set to zero, and solved. The results are given by

$$\frac{\partial TC}{\partial K} = \frac{R'OD}{Q} + 1 \tag{8}$$

$$\frac{\partial R}{\partial K} = -\frac{Q}{OD} \tag{9}$$

The first derivative of Equation (7) is taken with regard to *K*. The result is given by

$$\frac{\partial R}{\partial K} = -\beta(M - N)e^{-\beta K} = -\beta(R - N) < 0 \tag{10}$$

Setting Equation (9) equal to Equation (10) and substituting Equation (4) for *Q* in Equation (11) yield Equation (12). Then, by solving Equation (12), we derive the optimal ordering efficiency, *R*,* and the optimal order quantity, *Q*,* from Equation (13) and Equation (15), respectively.

$$-\frac{Q}{OD} = -\beta(R - N) \tag{11}$$

$$\beta(R - N)OD = \sqrt{\frac{2ORD}{HI}} \tag{12}$$

$$R^* = \sigma + \sqrt{\sigma^2 - N^2} \tag{13}$$

where

$$\sigma = N + \frac{1}{H\beta^2 ODI} \tag{14}$$

$$Q^* = \beta(R^* - N)OD \qquad (15)$$

Given the optimal ordering efficiency, R^*, the optimal investment, K^*, is derived from Equation (16).

$$K^* = \frac{\left(\ln \dfrac{(R^* - N)}{(M - N)} \right)}{-\beta} \qquad (16)$$

The Minimum Demand Level for RFID Investment in Ordering Efficiency

To identify the minimum demand level for the optimal investment during a planning period, Equation (13) is set less than or equal to M and solved, resulting in Equation (17). Note that the minimum demand level can be derived from Equation (17) without the optimal solution. Therefore,

$$\frac{2M}{(M - N)^2 H \beta^2 OI}$$

can serve as a threshold value for RFID investment.

$$D \geq \frac{2M}{(M - N)^2 H \beta^2 OI} \qquad (17)$$

RFID INVESTMENT IN JIT EFFICIENCY

JIT efficiency is defined as the degree to which the time gap between the point of delivery and the time of consumption/production is reduced by the investment, V. The rationale of JIT efficiency is that among others, RFID enhances the visibility of the inventory information, resulting in a better control of shrinkage and misplacement of products. RFID is not only a data collection technology, but also a technology to help businesses further streamline their production flow. Studies discuss the employment of RFID technology in regards to implementing JIT manufacturing to reduce the shop-floor work-in-progress (WIP) inventories and streamlining their flows (Huang et al., 2007; Zhang et al., 2008). Through RFID-enabled asset tracking, manufacturing activities are more visible and real time scheduling is achievable. Inventory accuracy achieved by the use of RFID technology also contributes to the JIT implementation.

The improvement of JIT efficiency decreases the inventory management costs by narrowing the time gap between the point of delivery and the time of the consumption/production. While the inventory holding cost is related to rent for the required space, labor to operate the space, interest on money invested in the inventory and space, and other direct expenses, JIT efficiency is a technology-enabled improvement. Improving JIT efficiency is achieved by investment in a particular RFID technology.

Several characteristics of RFID technology make the improvement of JIT efficiency possible. RFID has been instrumental in generating a constant flow of delivery information around-the-clock. RFID can also help transport items more efficiently by cross-docking, tracking, and just-in-time delivery. Let V represent the investment in the improvement of JIT efficiency. The cost minimization model is defined in Equation (18).

$$\text{Min } TC = O \frac{RD}{Q} + IH \frac{Q}{2} + V \qquad (18)$$

An exponential investment function for the improvement of JIT efficiency, I, is defined in Equation (19).

$$I = L + (U - L)e^{-\lambda V},$$
$$0 \leq L \leq U \leq 1, \text{ and } 0 \leq V \leq 1 \qquad (19)$$

When there is no RFID investment in JIT efficiency, the lowest efficiency, U, is incurred. L is the highest efficiency possible. α is the investment elasticity of JIT efficiency. When I is equal to 1, all ordered goods are assumed to be delivered at the beginning of each order cycle. When I is equal to 0, zero inventory costs are incurred (i.e., just-in-time inventory). An I equal to 0 implies that all ordered goods are consumed immediately as soon as the delivery is made.

The first derivative of Equation (18) is taken with regard to V and set to zero, and solved. The results are given by

$$\frac{\partial TC}{\partial V} = \frac{HI'Q}{2} + 1 \tag{20}$$

$$\frac{\partial I}{\partial V} = -\frac{2}{HQ} \tag{21}$$

The first derivative of Equation (19) is taken with regard to V. The result is given by

$$\frac{\partial I}{\partial V} = -\lambda(U - L)e^{-\lambda V} = -\lambda(I - L) < 0 \tag{22}$$

Setting Equation (21) equal to Equation (22) and substituting Equation (4) for Q in Equation (23) yield Equation (24). Then, by solving Equation (24), we derive the optimal JIT efficiency, $I*$, and the optimal order quantity, $Q*$, from Equation (25) and Equation (27), respectively.

$$-\frac{2}{HQ} = -\lambda(I - L) \tag{23}$$

$$\frac{2}{H\lambda(I - L)} = \sqrt{\frac{2ORD}{HI}} \tag{24}$$

$$I^* = w + \sqrt{w^2 - L^2} \tag{25}$$

where

$$w = L + \frac{1}{H\lambda^2 ORD} \tag{26}$$

$$Q^* = \frac{2}{H\lambda(I^* - L)} \tag{27}$$

Given the optimal JIT efficiency, $I*$, the optimal investment, $V,*$ is derived from Equation (28).

$$V^* = \frac{\left[\ln\frac{(I^* - L)}{(U - L)}\right]}{-\lambda} \tag{28}$$

The Minimum Demand Level for RFID Investment in JIT Efficiency

To identify the minimum demand level during a planning period for the optimal investment in JIT efficiency, Equation (25) is set less than or equal to U and solved, resulting in Equation (29).

$$D \geq \frac{2U}{(U - L)^2 H\lambda^2 OR} \tag{29}$$

RFID INVESTMENT IN THE OPERATING EFFICIENCY

Several characteristics of RFID technology make the reduction of operating/maintenance cost of each item possible. Reducing inaccurate inventory counts, preventing misplacement of goods, identifying defective items, and monitoring the condition of stored goods are among the benefits from the operating efficiency. For example, holding conditions for certain goods are automatically monitored and alerted to warehouse managers when the conditions are not met, thereby minimizing the spoilage costs. As RFID technology improves the operating efficiency, but incurs the RFID investment cost, the following cost minimization model is suggested.

$$\text{Min } TC = O\frac{RD}{Q} + IH\frac{Q}{2} + JCD + X \tag{30}$$

Let's assume that the operating efficiency, J, is an exponential function with base e.

$$J = E + (A - E)e^{-\chi X}, \tag{31}$$
$$0 \leq E \leq A \leq 1, \text{ and } 0 \leq J \leq 1$$

where A is the lowest operating efficiency achieved when there is no investment in RFID technology and E is the highest operating efficiency achievable by the investment, X. If the first derivative of TC is taken with regard to the investment, X and set to zero, and solved, then the results are:

$$\frac{\partial TC}{\partial X} = J'CD + 1 \tag{32}$$

$$\frac{\partial J}{\partial X} = -\frac{1}{CD} \tag{33}$$

The first derivative of Equation (31) is taken with regard to X. The result is given by

$$\frac{\partial J}{\partial X} = -\chi(A - E)e^{-\chi X} = -\chi(J - E) < 0 \tag{34}$$

Setting Equation (33) equal to Equation (34), we derive the optimal operating efficiency, J^*, from Equation (35).

$$J^* = \frac{1}{CD\chi} + E \tag{35}$$

Given the optimal operating efficiency, J^*, then the optimal investment, $X,^*$ is derived from Equation (36).

$$X^* = \frac{\ln\dfrac{1}{CD\chi(A - E)}}{-\chi} \tag{36}$$

The Minimum Demand Level for RFID Investment in the Operating Efficiency

To identify the minimum demand level during a planning period for the optimal investment, Equation (35) is set less than or equal to A and solved, resulting in Equation (37). If the demand level is equal to or greater than

$$\frac{1}{C\chi(A - E)},$$

there is an optimal investment level.

$$D \geq \frac{1}{C\chi(A - E)} \tag{37}$$

Estimation of Parameter Values

In our model, the estimation of parameter values is a very important but challenging process, since little or no past RFID investment data are usually available (Lee & Lee, 2012). The Delphi method is very useful in estimating parameter values when historical values are not readily available. The typical Delphi method requires the experts to answer questionnaires in two or more rounds. After each round, a facilitator provides an anonymous summary of the experts' parameter estimates from the previous round as well as the reasons for their judgments. Then, experts are asked again to revise their earlier estimates in light of the estimates of other members in the group. During this repetitive process, the range of the parameter values will decrease and the group will converge towards the best estimate. Sensitivity analyses of the investment model may further our understanding of the impact of the technology investment by varying the parameter values of the estimates (Talluri et al., 2006).

CONCLUSION

Despite the popularity of RFID technology, many challenges may lie ahead in the implementation of RFID systems, as we have already observed signs of overinvestment in RFID systems. It is easy to overinvest in IT when a company sees a strategic value of the IT. RFID technologies in supply chain affect multiple stakeholders differently and their perceived values may be different from each other. In the supply chain, a dominant player typically leads the RFID investment and requires other minor partners to adopt the technology. Taking into consideration the varying degrees of benefits and costs among these stakeholders is important for the success of RFID investment. In 2003, Wal-Mart announced that by January, 2005 its top 100 retailers will be required to implement RFID at the pallet and case level for all of their products, thus streamlining the supply chain processes. Since then, only about 600 of Wal-Mart's over 60,000 nationwide suppliers have engaged in the project. Despite support from major suppliers such as Procter & Gamble, Kimberly-Clark, and Unilever, Wal-Mart is reshaping its RFID strategy.

To complement the body of studies, we reviewed the literature on RFID in various industries and valuation methods, and presented the RFID investment evaluation model. The model considers RFID investment opportunities to improve the ordering efficiency, JIT efficiency, and operating efficiency, and derives optimal investment levels for these efficiency improvements. The solution structure of the model gives managers insights into

why individual companies should make idiosyncratic investment decisions on RFID technology. We derived the minimum level of sales for the RFID investment for each RFID-based efficiency improvement. The existence of the minimum sales level explains why small-sized suppliers could not meet Wal-Mart's RFID mandate. One way to facilitate the RFID investment in the supply chain would be that the dominant partner like Wal-Mart provides small-size partners with investment cost sharing especially in the early stage of the technology when the investment cost is high.

Managerial Implications

This chapter has three managerial implications. First, as is expected in technology management in general, a higher demand level will result in a larger optimal investment but with greater cost savings. For example, companies with a growth strategy are likely to enjoy greater investment benefits. An investment cost function becomes similar among companies due to standardization of RFID technologies. However, individual companies' ordering, operational, and inventory cost structures are likely to create different investment opportunities for each company. Second, the RFID investments may warrant the development of a comprehensive investment plan. To develop a comprehensive investment plan, managers need to make efforts to identify where and how RFID affects business operations and collect data on technology cost, production cost, and sales level. Finally, a firm considering RFID must ensure that it has the appropriate business process redesign. The new business process redesign should reflect the newly acquired technological capabilities to maximize the potential benefits. Business process redesign is enabled by the RFID capability to process, store, and integrate data.

REFERENCES

Angeles, R. (2007). An empirical study of the anticipated consumer response to RFID product item tagging. *Industrial Management & Data Systems*, *107*(4), 461–483. doi:10.1108/02635570710740643

Attaran, M. (2012). Critical success factors and challenges of implementing RFID in supply chain management. *Journal of Supply Chain and Operations Management*, *10*(1), 144–167.

Attaran, M., & Attaran, S. (2004). The rebirth of reengineering: x-engineering. *Business Process Management Journal*, *10*(4), 415–429. doi:10.1108/14637150410548083

Axsäter, S. (1996). Using the deterministic EOQ formula in stochastic inventory control. *Management Science*, *42*(6), 830–834. doi:10.1287/mnsc.42.6.830

Baars, H., Gille, D., & Strüker, J. (2009). Evaluation of RFID applications for logistics: a framework for identifying, forecasting and assessing benefits. *European Journal of Information Systems*, *18*, 578–591. doi:10.1057/ejis.2009.32

Banker, R. D., Chang, H., & Kemerer, C. F. (1994). Evidence on economies of scale in software development. *Information and Software Technology*, *36*(5), 275–282. doi:10.1016/0950-5849(94)90083-3

Bendavid, Y., Boeck, H., & Richard Philippe, R. (2010). Redesigning the replenishment process of medical supplies in hospitals with RFID. *Business Process Management Journal*, *16*(6), 991–1013. doi:10.1108/14637151011093035

Bendavid, Y., Wamba, S. F., & Lefebvre, L. A. (2006). Proof of concept of an RFID-enabled supply chain in a B2B e-commerce environment. In *Proceedings of the 8th international conference on Electronic commerce*. Fredericton, Canada: Academic Press.

Bertolini, M., Bottani, E., Rizzi, A., & Volpi, A. (2010). The benefits of RFID and EPC in the supply chain: Lessons from an Italian pilot study. In *Proceedings of the Internet of Things 20th Tyrrhenian Workshop on Digital Communications* (pp. 293-302). Academic Press.

Billington, P. J. (1987). The classic economic production quantity model with setup cost as a function of capital expenditure. *Decision Sciences*, *18*, 25–42. doi:10.1111/j.1540-5915.1987.tb01501.x

Bose, I., & Lam, C. Y. (2008). Facing the challenges of RFID data management. *International Journal of Information Systems and Supply Chain Management*, *1*(4), 1–19. doi:10.4018/jisscm.2008100101

Bottani, E. (2008). Reengineering, Simulation and data analysis of an RFID system. *The Journal of Theoretical and Applied Electronic Commerce Research*, *3*(1), 13–28.

Christensen, C. M., Anthony, A. D., & Roth, E. A. (2004). *Seeing What's Next*. Boston: Harvard Business School Press.

de Kok, A. G., van Donselaar, K. H., & van Woensel, T. (2008). A break-even analysis of RFID technology for inventory sensitive to shrinkage. *International Journal of Production Economics*, *112*(2), 521–531. doi:10.1016/j.ijpe.2007.05.005

De Marco, A., Cagliano, A. C., Nervo, M. L., & Rafele, C. (2012). Using System Dynamics to assess the impact of RFID technology on retail operations. *International Journal of Production Economics*, *135*(1), 333–344. doi:10.1016/j.ijpe.2011.08.009

Doerr, K. H., Gates, W. R., & Mutty, J. E. (2006). A hybrid approach to the valuation of RFID/MEMS technology applied to ordnance inventory. *International Journal of Production Economics*, *103*(2), 726–741. doi:10.1016/j.ijpe.2006.03.007

Fan, T.J., Chang, X.Y., Gu, C.H., Yi, J.J., & Deng, S. (2014). Benefits of RFID technology for reducing inventory shrinkage. *International Journal of Production Economics, 147*(Part C), 659–665.

Ferrer, G., Heath, S. K., & Dew, N. (2011). An RFID application in large job shop remanufacturing operations. *International Journal of Production Economics,* 612–621. 133(2 doi:10.1016/j.ijpe.2011.05.006

Fisher, J. A., & Monahan, T. (2008). Tracking the social dimensions of RFID systems in hospitals. *International Journal of Medical Informatics, 77*(3), 176–183. doi:10.1016/j.ijmedinf.2007.04.010 PMID:17544841

Hardgrave, B. C., Aloysius, J., & Goyal, S. (2009). Does RFID improve inventory accuracy? A preliminary analysis. *International Journal of RF Technologies: Research and Applications, 1*(1), 44–56. doi:10.1080/17545730802338333

Huang, G. Q., Zhang, Y. F., & Jiang, P. Y. (2007). RFID-based wireless manufacturing for walking-worker assembly islands with fixed-position layout. *Robotics and Computer-integrated Manufacturing, 23*(4), 469–477. doi:10.1016/j.rcim.2006.05.006

Kärkkäinen, M. (2003). Increasing efficiency in the supply chain for short shelf life goods using RFID tagging. *International Journal of Retail & Distribution Management, 31*(10), 529–536. doi:10.1108/09590550310497058

Kasiri, N., Sharda, R., & Hardgrave, B. (2012). A balanced scorecard for item-level RFID in the retail sector: a Delphi study. *European Journal of Information Systems, 21*(3), 255–267. doi:10.1057/ejis.2011.33

Katz, J.E., & Rice, R.E. (2009). Public views of mobile medical devices and services: A US national survey of consumer sentiments towards RFID healthcare technology. *International Journal of Medical Informatics, 78*(2), 104–114.

Kim, S., & Garrison, G. (2010). Understanding users' behaviors regarding supply chain technology: Determinants impacting the adoption and implementation of RFID technology in South Korea. *International Journal of Information Management, 30*(5), 388–398.

Krause, D. R., Handfield, R. B., & Tyler, B. B. (2007). The relationships between supplier development, commitment, social capital accumulation and performance improvement. *Journal of Operations Management, 25*(2), 528–545. doi:10.1016/j.jom.2006.05.007

Krotov, V., & Junglas, I. (2008). RFID as a Disruptive Innovation. *Journal of Theoretical and Applied Electronic Commerce Research., 3*(2), 44–59. doi:10.4067/S0718-18762008000100005

Lai, K., Wong, C., & Cheng, T. (2008). A coordination-theoretic investigation of the impact of electronic integration on logistics performance. *Information & Management, 45*(1), 10–20. doi:10.1016/j.im.2007.05.007

Lee, H., Lee, K., Park, M., Baek, Y., and Lee, S. (2012). RFID-based real-time locating system for construction safety management. *Journal of Computing in Civil Engineering, 26*(3), 366–377.

Lee, H., & Özer, Ö. (2007). Unlocking the value of RFID. *Production and Operations Management, 16*(1), 40–64. doi:10.1111/j.1937-5956.2007.tb00165.x

Lee, H.-H. (2008). The investment model in preventive maintenance in multi-level production systems. *International Journal of Production Economics, 112*(2), 816–828.

Lee, I. (2004). Evaluating business-process integrated information technology investment. *Business Process Management Journal, 10*(2), 214–233. doi:10.1108/14637150410530271

Lee, I., & Lee, B.-C. (2010). An investment evaluation of supply chain RFID technologies: A normative modeling approach. *International Journal of Production Economics*, *125*, 313–323. doi:10.1016/j.ijpe.2010.02.006

Lee, I., & Lee, B.-C. (2012). Measuring the value of RFID investment: Focusing on RFID budget allocation. *IEEE Transactions on Engineering Management*, *59*(4), 551–559. doi:10.1109/TEM.2011.2163072

Lee, J. H., Song, J. H., Oh, K. S., & Gu, N. (2013). Information lifecycle management with RFID for material control on construction sites. *Advanced Engineering Informatics*, *27*(1), 108–119. doi:10.1016/j.aei.2012.11.004

Lee, Y.C., &, Lee, S.S. (2011). The valuation of RFID investment using fuzzy real option. *Expert Systems with Applications*, *38*(10), 12195–12201.

Lin, K., & Lin, C. (2007). Evaluating the decision to adopt RFID systems using analytic hierarchy process. *The Journal of American Academy of Business, Cambridge*, *11*(1), 72–78.

Michael, K., & McCathie, L. (2005). The pros and cons of RFID in supply chain management. In *Proceedings of the International Conference on Mobile Business*, (pp. 623-629). Academic Press.

Min, S., & Mentzer, J. T. (2004). Developing and measuring supply chain management concepts. *Journal of Business Logistics*, *25*(1), 63–99. doi:10.1002/j.2158-1592.2004.tb00170.x

Morton, S. C., Dainty, A. R. J., Burns, N. D., Brookes, N. J., & Backhouse, C. J. (2006). Managing relationships to improve performance: a case study in the global aerospace industry. *International Journal of Production Research*, *44*(16), 3227–3241. doi:10.1080/00207540600577809

Özelkan, E. C., & Galambosi, A. (2008). When does RFID make business sense for managing supply chains? *International Journal of Information Systems and Supply Chain Management*, *1*(1), 15–47. doi:10.4018/jisscm.2008010102

Park, N. (2011). Customized healthcare infrastructure using privacy weight level based on smart device. *Convergence and Hybrid Information Technology: Communications in Computer and Information Science*, *206*, 467–474. doi:10.1007/978-3-642-24106-2_60

PRWeb. (2012). Retrieved on April 2014 from http://www.prweb.com/releases/RFID_radio_frequency/identification_technology/prweb9264497.htm

Rekik, Y., Sahin, E., & Dallery, Y. (2008). Analysis of the impact of the RFID technology on reducing product misplacement errors at retail stores. *International Journal of Production Economics*, *112*(1), 264–278. doi:10.1016/j.ijpe.2006.08.024

Ren, Z., Anumba, C. J., & Tah, J. (2011). RFID-facilitated construction materials management (RFID-CMM) – A case study of water-supply project. *Advanced Engineering Informatics*, *25*(2), 198–207. doi:10.1016/j.aei.2010.02.002

Reyes, P. M., & Jaska, P. (2007). Is RFID right for your organization or application? *Management Research News*, *30*(8), 570–580. doi:10.1108/01409170710773706

Roach, B. (2005). Origin of the economic order quantity formula: Transcription or transformation? *Management Decision*, *43*(9), 1262–1268. doi:10.1108/00251740510626317

Sarac, A., Absi, N., & Dauzère-Pérès, S. (2010). A literature review on the impact of RFID technologies on supply chain management. *International Journal of Production Economics*, *128*(1), 77–95.

Soon, C.-B., & Gutiérrez, J. A. (2008). Effects of the RFID mandate on supply chain management. *The Journal of Theoretical and Applied Electronic Commerce Research*, *3*(1), 81–91.

Tajima, M. (2007). Strategic value of RFID in supply chain management. *Journal of Purchasing and Supply Management*, *13*(4), 261–273.

Talluri, S., Chung, W., & Narasimhan, R. (2006). An optimization model for phased supplier integration into e-procurement systems. *IIE Transactions*, *38*(5), 389–399. doi:10.1080/07408170500306554

Thiesse, F., Staake, T., Schmitt, P., & Fleisch, E. (2011). The rise of the "next-generation bar code": an international RFID adoption study, *Supply Chain Management. International Journal (Toronto, Ont.)*, *16*(5), 328–345.

Ting, S. L., Kwok, S. K., Tsang, A. H. C., & Lee, W. B. (2011). Critical elements and lessons learnt from the implementation of an RFID-enabled healthcare management system in a medical organization. *Journal of Medical Systems*, *35*(4), 657–669. doi:10.1007/s10916-009-9403-5 PMID:20703523

Twist, D. C. (2005). The impact of radio frequency identification on supply chain facilities. *Journal of Facilities Management*, *3*(3), 226–239. doi:10.1108/14725960510808491

Tzeng, S.-F., Chen, W.-H., & Pai, F.-Y. (2008). Evaluating the business value of RFID: Evidence from five case studies. *International Journal of Production Economics*, *112*(2), 601–613. doi:10.1016/j.ijpe.2007.05.009

Uçkun, c., Karaesmen, f., & Savaş, S. (2008). Investment in improved inventory accuracy in a decentralized supply chain. *International Journal of Production Economics*, *113*(2), 546–566. doi:10.1016/j.ijpe.2007.10.012

Ustundag, A. (2010). Evaluating RFID investment on a supply chain using tagging cost sharing factor. *International Journal of Production Research*, *48*(9), 2549–2562. doi:10.1080/00207540903564926

Veeramani, D., Tang, J., & Alfonso Gutierrez, A. (2008). A framework for assessing the value of RFID implementation by tier-one suppliers to major retailers. *The* Journal of Theoretical and Applied Electronic Commerce Research, *3*(1), 55–70.

Visich, J., Li, S., Khumawala, B., & Reyes, P. M. (2010). Empirical evidence of RFID impacts on supply chain performance. *International Journal of Operations & Production Management*, *29*(12), 1290–1315. doi:10.1108/01443570911006009

Wamba, S.F., Lefebvre, L.A., & Bendavid, Y., & Lefebvre, Él. (2008). Exploring the impact of RFID technology and the EPC network on mobile B2B eCommerce: A case study in the retail industry. *International Journal of Production Economics*, *112*(2), 614–629. doi:10.1016/j.ijpe.2007.05.010

Wang, L.C. (2008). Enhancing construction quality inspection and management using RFID technology. *Automation in Construction*, *17*(4), 467–479.

Wang, S., Liu, S., & Wang, W. (2008). The simulated impact of RFID-enabled supply chain on pull-based inventory replenishment in TFT-LCD industry. *International Journal of Production Economics*, *112*(2), 570–586. doi:10.1016/j.ijpe.2007.05.002

Whitaker, J., Mithas, S., & Krishnan, M. S. (2007). A field study of RFID deployment and return expectations. *Production and Operations Management*, *16*(5), 599–612. doi:10.1111/j.1937-5956.2007.tb00283.x

Yao, W., Chu, C. H., & Li, Z. (2012). The adoption and implementation of RFID technologies in healthcare: A literature review. *Journal of Medical Systems*, *36*(6), 3507–3525. doi:10.1007/s10916-011-9789-8 PMID:22009254

ADDITIONAL READING

Choi, S. H., & Poon, C. H. (2008). An RFID-based anti-counterfeiting system. *International Journal of Computer Science*, *35*(1), 1–12.

Ramanathan, R, Ramanathan, U and Ko, L., (2013), Adoption of RFID technologies in UK logistics: Moderating roles of size, barcode experience and government support, *Expert Systems with Applications* (Special issue 21st Century Logistics and Supply Chain Management), *41*(1), 230-236.

Smith, A. D. (2012). Operational efficiencies and ethical issues associated with microchip implants. *International Journal of Mobile Communications*, *10*(3), 281–302. doi:10.1504/IJMC.2012.048113

Smith, A. D. (2013). Perceived value and strategic importance of supply chain options: Multi-firm case study. *International Journal of Logistics Systems and Supply Management*, *13*(2), 244–267. doi:10.1504/IJLSM.2012.048938

Soldatos, J., Serrano, M., & Hauswirth, M. (2012). Convergence of Utility Computing with the Internet-of-Things. *IMIS*, *2012*, 874–879.

KEY TERMS AND DEFINITIONS

JIT Efficiency: The degree to which the time gap between the point of delivery and the time of consumption/production is reduced by the investment for the inventory cost reduction.

Operating Efficiency: The degree to which the operating cost is reduced by the investment for the operating cost reduction technology such as RFID merchandise monitoring systems.

Ordering Efficiency: The degree to which the fixed order cost per order cycle is reduced by the investment for the ordering cost reduction.

RFID Technology Management: The process of evaluating RFID technology, developing RFID systems, and managing RFID infrastructure to achieve business objectives.

Compilation of References

Abts, C., Boehm, B. W., & Clark, E. B. (2000). *COCOTS: A COTS software integration lifecycle cost model-model overview and preliminary data collection findings*. Paper presented at the ESCOM-SCOPE Conference. Munich, Germany.

Acharyulu, G. (2007). RFID in the healthcare supply chain: improving performance through greater visibility. *The ICFAI Journal of Management Research*, 6(11), 32–45.

ADVANCE Project Consortium. (2010). *ADVANCE official project website*. Retrieved from http://advance-logistics.eu/

Aebi, F. (2012). *Autonomous indoor navigation: implementation of an autonomous indoor navigation system on android*. (Master's thesis). University of Fribourg, Fribourg, Switzerland. Retrieved from http://diuf.unifr.ch/drupal/sites/diuf.unifr.ch.drupal.softeng/files/teaching/studentprojects/aebi/autonomous-indoor-navigation.pdf

Aggarwal, C. C., Ashish, N., & Sheth, A. P. (2013). The internet of things: a survey from the data-centric perspective. In C. C. Aggarwal (Ed.), *Managing and Mining Sensor Data* (pp. 383–428). New York: Springer. doi:10.1007/978-1-4614-6309-2_12

Agrawal, P., & Bhuraria, S. (2012). Near field communication. In P. B. Malla (Ed.), *Business Innovation through Technology: Winning with IT* (Vol. 10, pp. 67–74). Retrieved from http://www.infosys.com/infosys-labs/publications/Documents/winning-it.pdf

Ahuja, S., & Potti, P. (2010). An introduction to RFID technology. *Communications and Network*, 2(3), 183–186. doi:10.4236/cn.2010.23026

Aitenbichler, E., & Muhlhauser, M. (2003). An IR local positioning system for smart items and devices. In *Proceedings of the 23rd IEEE International Conference on Distributed Computing Systems Workshops* (pp. 334–339). IEEE. doi:10.1109/ICDCSW.2003.1203576

Al Hammadi, O., Al Hebsi, A., Zemerly, J. M., & Ng, J. W. P. (2012). Indoor localization and guidance using portable Smartphones. In *Proceedings of IEEE/WIC/ACM International Conferences on Web Intelligence and Intelligent Agent Technology* (Vol. 3, pp. 337–341). Macau: IEEE. doi:10.1109/WI-IAT.2012.262

Al Nuaimi, K., & Kamel, H. (2011). A survey of indoor positioning systems and algorithms. In *Proceedings of International Conference on Innovations in Information Technology* (pp. 185–190). Abu Dhabi: Academic Press. doi:10.1109/INNOVATIONS.2011.5893813

Ala-Risku, T., & Kärkkäinen, M. (2004). *A Solution for the Material Delivery Problems in Construction Projects*. Paper presented at the Thirteenth International Working Seminar on Production Economics. Innsbruck, Austria.

Albrecht, K., & McIntyre, L. (2004). CASPIAN consumer privacy, RFID: the big brother bar code. *ALEC Policy Forum*, 6(3), 49-54.

Albrecht, K., & McIntyre, L. (2005). *Spychips: how major corporations and government plan to track your every move with RFID*. Nashville, TN: Nelson Current.

Aldaihani, M. M., & Darwish, M. A. (2013). Optimal production and inventory decisions for supply chains with one producer and multiple newsvendors. *International Journal of Services and Operations Management*, 15(4), 430–448. doi:10.1504/IJSOM.2013.054884

Al-Ofeishat, H. A., & Al Rababah, M. A. A. (2012). Near Field Communication (NFC). *International Journal of Computer Science and Network Security*, *12*(2), 93–99. Retrieved from http://paper.ijcsns.org/07_book/201202/20120216.pdf

Amundson, I., & Koutsoukos, X. D. (2009). A survey on localization for mobile wireless sensor networks. In *Proceedings of the 2nd international conference on Mobile entity localization and tracking in GPS-less environments* (pp. 235–254). Orlando, FL: Springer. doi:10.1007/978-3-642-04385-7_16

Angeles, R. (2005). RFID technologies: Supply-chain applications and implementation issues. *Information Systems Management*, *22*(1), 51–65. doi:10.1201/1078/44912.22.1.20051201/85739.7

Angeles, R. (2007). An empirical study of the anticipated consumer response to RFID product item tagging. *Industrial Management & Data Systems*, *107*(4), 461–483. doi:10.1108/02635570710740643

Arends, R., et al. (2005, March). *RFC4033 "DNS Security Introduction and Requirements"*. Retrieved September 2013, http://tools.ietf.org/html/rfc4033

Asif, F., & Mandviwalla, M. (2005). Integrating the Supply Chain with RFID: A Technical and Business Analysis. *Communications of the Association for Information Systems*, *15*(24), 393–426.

Asif, Z., & Mandviwalla, M. (2005). Integrating the supply chain with RFID: An in-depth technical and business analysis. *Communications of the Association for Information Systems*, *15*(1), 393–427.

AspireRFID Project. (n.d.). *The AspireRFID project*. Retrieved September 2013, from http://forge.ow2.org/projects/aspire/

Atkinson, W. (2004). Tagged: the risks and rewards of RFID technology. *Risk Management Journal*, *51*(7), 12–19.

Atsuumi, K., & Sano, M. (2010). Indoor IR azimuth sensor using a linear polarizer. In *Proceedings of International Conference on Indoor Positioning and Indoor Navigation* (IPIN) (pp. 1–5). Zurich: IPIN. doi:10.1109/IPIN.2010.5647328

Attaran, M. (2007). RFID: An enabler of supply chain operations. *Supply Chain Management: An International Journal*, *12*(4), 249–257. doi:10.1108/13598540710759763

Attaran, M. (2012). Critical success factors and challenges of implementing RFID in supply chain management. *Journal of Supply Chain and Operations Management*, *10*(1), 144–167.

Attaran, M., & Attaran, S. (2004). The rebirth of reengineering: x-engineering. *Business Process Management Journal*, *10*(4), 415–429. doi:10.1108/14637150410548083

Aung, E. D., Yang, J., Cho, D. K., & Gerla, M. (2008). *BluEyes–Bluetooth localization and tracking*. Retrieved from http://nrlweb.cs.ucla.edu/publication/download/532/BluEyes_08.pdf

Axsäter, S. (1996). Using the deterministic EOQ formula in stochastic inventory control. *Management Science*, *42*(6), 830–834. doi:10.1287/mnsc.42.6.830

Ayoade, J. (2007). Roadmap to solving security and privacy concerns in RFID systems. *Computer Law & Security Report*, *23*, 555–661. doi:10.1016/j.clsr.2007.09.005

Azadeh, A., Gholizadeh, H., & Jeihoonian, M. (2013). A multi-objective optimisation model for university course timetabling problem using a mixed integer dynamic non-linear programming. *International Journal of Services and Operations Management*, *15*(4), 467–481. doi:10.1504/IJSOM.2013.054886

Baars, H., Gille, D., & Strüker, J. (2009). Evaluation of RFID applications for logistics: a framework for identifying, forecasting and assessing benefits. *European Journal of Information Systems*, *18*, 578–591. doi:10.1057/ejis.2009.32

Bachrach, J., & Taylor, C. (2005). Localization in sensor networks. In I. Stojmenovic (Ed.), *Handbook of Sensor Networks: Algorithms and Architectures* (pp. 277–310). John Wiley & Sons Inc. Retrieved from http://people.csail.mit.edu/jrb/Projects/poschap.pdf

Bahl, P., & Padmanabhan, V. N. (2000). RADAR: An in-building RF-based user location and tracking system. In *Proceedings of the Nineteenth Annual Joint Conference of the IEEE Computer and Communications Societies, INFOCOM 2000* (Vol. 2, pp. 775–784). Tel Aviv, Israel: IEEE. doi:10.1109/INFCOM.2000.832252

Bailey, S. G. M., & Caidi, N. (2005). How much is too little? Privacy and smart cards in Hong Kong and Ontario. *Journal of Information Science, 31*(5), 354–364. doi:10.1177/0165551505055400

Ballard, R. (1996). Methods of inventory monitoring and measurement. *Logistics Information Management, 9*(3), 11–28. doi:10.1108/09576059610116653

Bamasak, O. (2011). Exploring consumers acceptance of mobile payments – An empirical study. *International Journal of Information Technology, Communications and Convergence, 1*(2), 173–185.

Banker, R. D., Chang, H., & Kemerer, C. F. (1994). Evidence on economies of scale in software development. *Information and Software Technology, 36*(5), 275–282. doi:10.1016/0950-5849(94)90083-3

Barzel, Y. (1997). *Economic Analysis of Property Rights*. Cambridge University Press. doi:10.1017/CBO9780511609398

Beitelspacher, L. S., Hansen, J. D., Johnston, A. C., & Dietz, G. D. (2012). Exploring consumer privacy concerns and RFID technology: The impact of fear appeals on consumer behaviors. *Journal of Marketing Theory and Practice, 20*(2), 147–159. doi:10.2753/MTP1069-6679200202

Bekkelien, A. (2012). *Bluetooth indoor positioning*. (Master's thesis). University of Geneva. Retrieved from http://cui.unige.ch/~deriazm/masters/bekkelien/Bekkelien_Master_Thesis.pdf

Belanger, F., Hiller, J., & Smith, W. (2002). Trustworthiness in electronic commerce: The role of privacy, security, and site attributes. *The Journal of Strategic Information Systems, 11*(3/4), 245–270. doi:10.1016/S0963-8687(02)00018-5

Bellian, C. (2012). Bar codes or RFID tags: Key factors to consider in choosing the correct data collection technology for your customer. *The Mheda Journal*. Retrieved September 10, 2013 from: http://www.themhedajournal.org/index.php/2010/07/bar-codes-or-rfid-tags/

Bendavid, Y., Wamba, S. F., & Lefebvre, L. A. (2006). Proof of concept of an RFID-enabled supply chain in a B2B e-commerce environment. In *Proceedings of the 8th international conference on Electronic commerce.* Fredericton, Canada: Academic Press.

Bendavid, Y., Boeck, H., & Richard Philippe, R. (2010). Redesigning the replenishment process of medical supplies in hospitals with RFID. *Business Process Management Journal, 16*(6), 991–1013. doi:10.1108/14637151011093035

Benyó, B., Sódor, B., Fördos, G., Kovács, L., & Vilmos, A. (2010). A generalized approach for NFC application development. In *Proceedings of Second International Workshop on Near Field Communication* (NFC) (pp. 45–50). Monaco: NFC. doi:10.1109/NFC.2010.23

Berghel, H. (2013). RFIDiocy: It's déjà vu all over again. *Computer, 46*(1), 85–88. doi:10.1109/MC.2013.28

Bertolini, M., Bottani, E., Rizzi, A., & Volpi, A. (2010). The benefits of RFID and EPC in the supply chain: Lessons from an Italian pilot study. In *Proceedings of the Internet of Things 20th Tyrrhenian Workshop on Digital Communications* (pp. 293-302). Academic Press.

Bhakoo, V., Singh, P., & Sohal, A. (2012). Collaborative management of inventory in Australian hospital supply chains: Practices and issues. *Supply Chain Management, 17*(2), 217–230. doi:10.1108/13598541211212933

Bhamu, J., Khandelwal, A., & Sangwan, K. S. (2013). Lean manufacturing implementation in an automated production line: A case study. *International Journal of Services and Operations Management, 15*(4), 411–429. doi:10.1504/IJSOM.2013.054883

Bielawa, T. M. (2005). *Position location of remote Bluetooth devices*. (Master's thesis). Virginia Polytechnic Institute and State University. Retrieved from http://scholar.lib.vt.edu/theses/available/etd-07112005-222918/unrestricted/tbielawa_thesis.pdf

Bi, H. H., & Lin, D. K. J. (2009). RFID-enabled discovery of supply networks. *IEEE Transactions on Engineering Management, 56*(1), 129–141. doi:10.1109/TEM.2008.922636

Bikshorn, M. (2011). From Customer Service to Customer Experience Enhancement. *Customer Experience Reporting*. Retrieved in March 8, 2011, from http://www.serviceexcellencegroup.com

Billington, P. J. (1987). The classic economic production quantity model with setup cost as a function of capital expenditure. *Decision Sciences*, *18*, 25–42. doi:10.1111/j.1540-5915.1987.tb01501.x

Blankenbach, J., Norrdine, A., & Hellmers, H. (2012). A robust and precise 3D indoor positioning system for harsh environments. In *Proceedings of International Conference on Indoor Positioning and Indoor Navigation* (IPIN) (pp. 1–8). Sydney, Australia: IPIN. doi:10.1109/IPIN.2012.6418863

Boeck, H., Roy, J., Durif, F., & Grégoire, M. (2011). The effect of perceived intrusion on consumers' attitude towards using an RFID-based marketing program. *Procedia Computer Science*, *5*, 841–848. doi:10.1016/j.procs.2011.07.116

Boehm, B., Abts, C., & Chulani, S. (2000). Software development cost estimation approaches — A survey. *Annals of Software Engineering*, *10*(1-4), 177–205. doi:10.1023/A:1018991717352

Boehm, B., Madachy, R., & Steece, B. (2000). *Software Cost Estimation with COCOMO II*. New Jersey: Prentice Hall PTR.

Bolin, A., & Heatherly, L. (2001). Predictors of employee deviance: The relationship between bad attitudes and bad behavior. *Journal of Business and Psychology*, *15*(3), 405–418. doi:10.1023/A:1007818616389

Bolz, J. (2011). *Indoor positioning using NFC tags*. (Bachelor's thesis). Beuth Hochschule für Technik, Berlin, Germany. Retrieved from http://taglocate.googlecode.com/files/Thesis.pdf

Bose, I., & Lam, C. Y. (2008). Facing the challenges of RFID data management. *International Journal of Information Systems and Supply Chain Management*, *1*(4), 1–19. doi:10.4018/jisscm.2008100101

Bottani, E. (2008). Reengineering, Simulation and data analysis of an RFID system. *The Journal of Theoretical and Applied Electronic Commerce Research*, *3*(1), 13–28.

Bottani, E., & Rizzi, A. (2008). Economical assessment of the impact of RFID technology and EPC system on the fast-moving consumer goods supply chain. *International Journal of Production Economics*, *112*(2), 548–569. doi:10.1016/j.ijpe.2007.05.007

Braden, R. (1989, October). *RFC1123 Requirements for Internet Hosts -- Application and Support*. Retrieved September 2013, from http://tools.ietf.org/html/rfc1123

Brás, L., Carvalho, N. B., Pinho, P., Kulas, L., & Nyka, K. (2012). A review of antennas for indoor positioning systems. *International Journal of Antennas and Propagation*, *2012*, 1–14. doi:10.1155/2012/953269

Bridge, (2009). *Building radio frequency identification solutions for the global environment*. Retrieved August 20, 2013, http://www.bridgeproject.eu/data/File/BRIDGE_Final_report.pdf

Browne, G. J., & Rogich, M. B. (2001). An Empirical Investigation of User Requirements Elicitation: Comparing the Effectiveness of Prompting Techniques. *Journal of Management Information Systems*, *17*(4), 223–249.

Bundschuh, M., & Fabry, A. (2000). *Aufwandschätzung von IT-Projekten*. MITP-Verlag.

Canovic, S. (2007). *Application of UWB technology for positioning, a feasibility study*. Retrieved August 12, 2013, from http://www.diva-portal.org/smash/get/diva2:347581/FULLTEXT01.pdf

Cardullo, M. (2003). Genesis of the Versatile RFID Tag. *RFID Journal*. Retrieved September 1, 2013 from http://www.rfidjournal.com/articles/view?392

CASPIAN. (2003). Scandal: Wal-Mart, P&G involved in secret RFID testing. *Consumers Against Supermarket Privacy Invasion and Numbering (CASPIAN)*. Retrieved September 1, 2013 from http://www.spychips.com/press-releases/broken-arrow.html

Cavoukian, A. (2009). *Privacy by design*. Ontario, Canada: Office of the Information and Privacy Commissioner, Canada. Retrieved August 12, 2013, from http://www.ipc.on.ca/images/Resources/2009-06-23-TrustEconomics.pdf

Cazier, J. A., Jensen, A. S., & Dave, D. S. (2008). The impact of consumer perceptions of information privacy and security risks on the adoption of residual RFID technologies. *Communications of the AIS*, *23*(14), 235–256.

Challenges in the Retail Industry. (2008). *Columbus IT.* Retrieved January 23, 2014 from http://www.columbusit.com/Default.aspx?ID=16095

Chande, A., Dhekane, S., Hemachandra, N., & Rangaraj, N. (2005). Perishable inventory management and dynamic pricing using RFID technology. *Sadhana, 30*(2/3), 445–462. doi:10.1007/BF02706255

Chandgadkar, A. (2013). *An indoor navigation system for Smartphones.* Retrieved August 15, 2013, from http://www.doc.ic.ac.uk/teaching/distinguished-projects/2013/a.chandgadkar.pdf

Chang, Y., & Tsai, S. (2007). A wayfinding system based on geo-coded QR codes and social computing for individuals with cognitive impairments. *International Journal of Advances in Information Sciences and Services, 2,* 69–74. Retrieved from http://mobile.kaywa.com/files/wayfinding-systems-with-qrcode.pdf

Chapman, P., & Templar, S. (2004). *Measuring retail shrinkage: Towards shrinkage KPI.* Retrieved January 23, 2014 from http://www.losspreventionmagazine.com/customers/104120817472470/filemanager/Measuring_Shrinkage_White_Paper.pdf

Chatterjee, S., & Timande, B. (2012). Public Transport System Ticketing system using RFID and ARM processor Perspective Mumbai bus facility B.E.S.T. *International Journal of Electronics and Computer Science Engineering.*

Chatterjee, D., Grewal, R., & Sambamurthy, V. (2002). Shaping up for e-commerce: Institutional enablers of the organizational assimilation of Web technologies. *Management Information Systems Quarterly, 26*(2), 65–89. doi:10.2307/4132321

Chawathe, S. S. (2008). Beacon placement for indoor localization using Bluetooth. In *Proceedings of 11th International IEEE Conference on Intelligent Transportation Systems* (pp. 980–985). Beijing: IEEE. doi:10.1109/ITSC.2008.4732690

Chen, C. C., Wu, J., Su, Y. S., & Yang, S. C. (2008). Key drivers for the continued use of RFID technology in the emergency room. *Management Research News, 31*(4), 273–288. doi:10.1108/01409170810851348

Chen, M.-X., & Wang, Y.-D. (2009). An efficient location tracking structure for wireless sensor networks. *Computer Communications, 32*(13), 1495–1504. doi:10.1016/j.comcom.2009.05.005

Chen, R., Fung, B. C. M., Mohammed, N., Desai, B. C., & Wang, K. (2013). Privacy-preserving trajectory data publishing by local suppression. *Information Sciences, 231,* 83–97. doi:10.1016/j.ins.2011.07.035

Chen, W. T., & Lin, G.-H. (2006). An efficient anti-collision method for tag identification in an RFID system. *IEICE Transactions, 89-B*(12), 3386–3392. doi:10.1093/ietcom/e89-b.12.3386

Chen, Z., & Dubinsky, A. J. (2003). A conceptual model of perceived customer value in e-commerce: A preliminary investigation. *Psychology and Marketing, 20*(4), 323–347. doi:10.1002/mar.10076

Cheung, H. H., & Choi, S. H. (2011). Implementation issues in RFID-based anti-counterfeiting systems. *Computers in Industry, 62*(7), 708–718. doi:10.1016/j.compind.2011.04.001

Chiou, J. S. (2004). The antecedents of customer loyalty toward Internet service providers. *Information & Management, 41*(6), 685–695. doi:10.1016/j.im.2003.08.006

Choi, S. H., & Poon, C. H. (2008). An RFID-based anti-counterfeiting system. *International Journal of Computer Science, 35*(1), 1–12.

Choo, J. H., Cheung, S. N., Lee, Y. L., & Teh, S. H. (2012). I2Navi: An indoor interactive NFC navigation system for android smartphones. *World Academy of Science, Engineering and Technology,* (72), 735–739. Retrieved from http://www.waset.org/journals/waset/v72/v72-131.pdf

Chowdhury, B., & Khosla, R. (2007). RFID-based hospital real-time patient management system. In *Proceedings of 6th IEEE/ACIS International Conference on Computer and Information Science (ICIS),* (pp. 363-368). IEEE.

Chowdhury, M. U., & Ray, B. R. (2013). Security risks/vulnerability in a RFID system and possible defenses. In N. Karmakar (Ed.), *Advanced RFID Systems, Security, and Applications* (pp. 1–15). Hershey, PA: Information Science Reference. doi:10.4018/978-1-4666-4707-7.ch084

Chow, H. K. H., Choy, K. L., & Lee, W. B. (2007). A dynamic logistics process knowledge-based system – An RFID multi-agent approach. *Knowledge-Based Systems*, *20*(4), 357–372. doi:10.1016/j.knosys.2006.08.004

Chow, H. K. H., Choy, K. L., Lee, W. B., & Lau, K. C. (2006). Design of a RFID case-based resource management system for warehouse operations. *Expert Systems with Applications*, *30*(4), 561–576. doi:10.1016/j.eswa.2005.07.023

Choy, K. L., So, S. C. K., Liu, J. J., Lau, H., & Kwok, S. K. (2007). Improving logistics visibility in a supply chain: An integrated approach with radio frequency technology. *International Journal of Integrated Supply Management*, *3*(2), 135–155. doi:10.1504/IJISM.2007.011973

Christensen, E., Curbera, F., Meredith, G., & Weerawarana, S. (2001, March). *Web service description language (WSDL) 1.1*. Retrieved September 2013, from http://www.w3.org/TR/wsdl

Christensen, C. M., Anthony, A. D., & Roth, E. A. (2004). *Seeing What's Next*. Boston: Harvard Business School Press.

Chulani, S. (1998). *Incorporating Bayesian Analysis to Improve the Accuracy of COCOMO II and its Quality Model Extension* (USC-CSE tech. report 98-506). Academic Press.

Chung, J., Donahoe, M., Schmandt, C., Kim, I.-J., Razavai, P., & Wiseman, M. (2011). Indoor location sensing using geo-magnetism. In *Proceedings of 9th international conference on Mobile systems, applications, and services* (pp. 141–154). New York, NY: Academic Press. doi:10.1145/1999995.2000010

Clarke, M. (1998). Virtual logistics. *International Journal of Physical Distribution & Logistics Management*, *28*(7), 486–507. doi:10.1108/09600039810247461

Cocca, A., & Schoch, T. (2005). RFID-Anwendungen bei der Volkswagen AG — Herausforderungen einer modernen Ersatzteillogistik. In E. Fleisch, & F. Mattern (Eds.), *Das Internet der Dinge* (pp. 197–208). Springer-Verlag. doi:10.1007/3-540-28299-8_10

Cochran, P. L., Tatikonda, M. V., & Magid, J. M. (2007). Radio frequency identification and the ethics of privacy. *Organizational Dynamics*, *36*(2), 217–229. doi:10.1016/j.orgdyn.2007.03.008

Coleman, D. D., & Westcott, D. A. (2009). *CWNA Certified Wireless Network Administrator Official Study Guide: Exam PW0-104*. John Wiley & Sons.

Collier, J. E., & Bienstock, C. C. (2006). Measuring service quality in e-retailing. *Journal of Service Research*, *8*(3), 260–275. doi:10.1177/1094670505278867

Collins, J. (2004). Boeing outlines tagging timetable. *RFID Journal*. Available from http://www.rfidjournal.com/article/view/985/1/1

Collins, J. (2005). School studies RFID's effect on Wal-Mart. *RFID Journal*. Retrieved January 27, 2014 from http://www.rfidjournal.com/article/articleview/1514/1/9/

Collins, J. (2006). RFID implementation is an art. *RFID Journal*. Retrieved January 27, 2014 from http://www.rfidjournal.com/article/articleview/2427/1/1/

Condea, C., Thiesse, F., & Fleisch, E. (2012). RFID-enabled shelf replenishment with backroom monitoring in retail stores. *Decision Support Systems*, *52*(4), 839–849. doi:10.1016/j.dss.2011.11.018

Corbin, J. M., & Strauss, A. L. (2008). *Basics of qualitative research: techniques and procedures for developing grounded theory*. Los Angeles, CA: Sage Publications.

Coskun, V., Ozdenizci, B., & Ok, K. (2012). A survey on near field communication (NFC) technology. *Wireless Personal Communications*, *71*(3), 2259–2294. doi:10.1007/s11277-012-0935-5

Cowles, D. L., Kiecker, P., & Little, M. W. (2002). Using key informant insights as a foundation for e-retailing theory development. *Journal of Business Research*, *55*(8), 629–636. doi:10.1016/S0148-2963(00)00203-4

Culnan, M. J., & Armstrong, P. K. (1999). Information privacy concerns, procedural fairness, and impersonal trust: An empirical investigation. *Organization Science*, *10*(1), 104–116. doi:10.1287/orsc.10.1.104

Curtin, J., Kauffman, R., & Riggins, F. (2007). Making the 'most' out of RFID technology: A research agenda for the study of the adoption, usage and impact of RFID. *Information Technology Management, 8*(2), 87–110. doi:10.1007/s10799-007-0010-1

Cypriani, M., Lassabe, F., Canalda, P., & Spies, F. (2011). Open wireless positioning system: a Wi-Fi-based indoor positioning system. In *Proceedings of 70th IEEE Vehicular Technology Conference Fall* (pp. 1–5). Anchorage, AK: IEEE. doi:10.1109/VETECF.2009.5378966

Dahlberg, T., Mallat, N., Ondrus, J., & Zmijewska, A. (2006). Mobile Payment Market and Research - Past, Present and Future. *Sprouts: Working Papers on Information Systems, 6*(48), 6-48.

Darcy, P., Pupunwiwat, P., & Stantic, B. (2011). The challenges and issues facing the deployment of RFID technology. In C. Turcu (Ed.), *Deploying RFID - Challenges, Solutions, and Open Issues* (pp. 1–26). InTech. doi:10.5772/16986

Davis, F. D. (1989). Perceived usefulness, perceived ease of use, and user acceptance of information technology. *Management Information Systems Quarterly, 13*, 318–339. doi:10.2307/249008

Davis, F. D., Bagozzi, R. P., & Warshaw, P. R. (1989). User acceptance of computer technology: A comparison of two theoretical models. *Management Science, 35*, 982–1003. doi:10.1287/mnsc.35.8.982

de Kok, A. G., van Donselaar, K. H., & van Woensel, T. (2008). A break-even analysis of RFID technology for inventory sensitive to shrinkage. *International Journal of Production Economics, 112*(2), 521–531. doi:10.1016/j.ijpe.2007.05.005

de Mast, J., Kemper, B., Doe, R. J., Mandjes, M., & van der Bijl, Y. (2011). Process improvement in healthcare: Overall resource efficiency. *Quality and Reliability Engineering International, 27*(8), 1095–1106. doi:10.1002/qre.1198

Dean, D. H. (2013). Anticipating consumer reaction to RFID-enabled grocery checkout. *Services Marketing Quarterly, 34*(1), 86–101. doi:10.1080/15332969.2013.739945

Decker, C., Kubach, U., & Beigl, M. (2003). Revealing the Retail Black Box by Interaction Sensing. In *Proceedings of the 23rd International Conference on Distributed Computing Systems* (pp. 328-333). Washington, DC: IEEE Computer Society.

Delen, D., Hardgrave, B. C., & Sharda, R. (2007). RFID for Better Supply-Chain Management through Enhanced Information Visibility. *Production and Operations Management, 16*(5), 613–624. doi:10.1111/j.1937-5956.2007.tb00284.x

Diaz, J. J. M., Maues, R. de A., Soares, R. B., Nakamura, E. F., & Figueiredo, C. M. S. (2010). Bluepass: An indoor Bluetooth-based localization system for mobile applications. In *Proceedings of IEEE Symposium on Computers and Communications* (pp. 778–783). Riccione, Italy: IEEE. doi:10.1109/ISCC.2010.5546506

Dickson, G. (2007). *Software Cost Estimation*. Faculty of Computer Science, Faculty of Engineering, University of Brunswick.

Dimitropoulos, P. & Soldatos, J. (2010). RFID-enabled Fully Automated Warehouse Management: Adding the Business Context. *International Journal of Manufacturing Technology and Management, 21*(3/4).

Dittmann, L., & Thiesse, F. (2005). *Integration und Interoperabilität von RFID-Softwarearchitekturen Schriftenreihe Wirtschaft & Logistik*. Hamburg, Germany: Deutscher Verkehrs-Verlag.

Dnsjava Org. (2013). *Dnsjava implementation*. Retrieved from http://www.dnsjava.org/

Dobkin, D. M. (2013). *The RF in RFID: UHF RFID in Practice*. Oxford, UK: Newnes Publications.

Doerr, K. H., Gates, W. R., & Mutty, J. E. (2006). A hybrid approach to the valuation of RFID/MEMS technology applied to ordnance inventory. *International Journal of Production Economics, 103*(2), 726–741. doi:10.1016/j.ijpe.2006.03.007

Doss, R., Zhou, W., Sundaresan, S., Yu, S., & Gao, L. (2012). A Minimum disclosure approach to authentication and privacy in RFID systems. *Computer Networks, 56*(15), 3401–3416. doi:10.1016/j.comnet.2012.06.018

Dowie, U. (2009). Testaufwandsschätzung in der Softwareentwicklung: Modell der Einflussfaktoren und Methode zur organisationsspezifischen Aufwandsschätzung (Vol. 1). Lohmar - Köln: Josef Eul Verlag.

Drejer, A., & Riis, J.O. (2000). New dimensions of competence development in industrial enterprises. *International Journal of Manufacturing Technology and Management, 2*(1/7), 660-882.

Dukovska-Popovska, I., Lim, M. K., Steger-Jensen, K., & Hvolby, H. H. (2010). RFID Technology to Support Environmentally Sustainable Supply Chain Management. In *Proceedings of for the IEEE International Conference on RFID-Technology and Applications*, (pp. 291-295). IEEE.

Dutta, A., Lee, H. L., & Whang, S. (2007). RFID and operations management: technology, value and incentives. *Production and Operations Management, 16*(5), 646–655. doi:10.1111/j.1937-5956.2007.tb00286.x

Dyer, G. (2006, April 20). Louis Vuitton sues Carrefour in China over 'fake' handbags. *Financial Times*.

Ekahau. (2005). *Comparison of wireless indoor positioning technologies*. Retrieved August 27, 2013, from http://www.productivet.com/docs-2/Wireless_Comparison.pdf

Elz, R., & Bush, R. (1987). *RFC2181 "Clarifications to the DNS specification"*. Retrieved September 2013, from http://tools.ietf.org/html/rfc2181

Engel, T., Lunow, S., Fischer, J., Köbler, F., Goswami, S., & Krcmar, H. (2012). *Value Creation in Pharmaceutical Supply Chains using Customer-Centric RFID Applications*. Paper presented at the European Conference on Smart Objects, Systems and Technologies (Smart SysTech). Munich, Germany.

EPCGlobal Architecture Review Committee. (2013). *The EPCglobal Architecture Framework (version 1.5) EPCglobal*. Retrieved from http://www.gs1.org/gsmp/kc/epcglobal/architecture

EPCglobal Inc. (2005). *Guidelines on EPC for consumer products*. Lawrenceville.

EPCglobal Inc. (2009). *EPC™ radio-frequency identity protocols class-1 generation-2 RFID protocol for communications at 860 MHz–960 MHz v1.2*. Author.

EPCglobal. (2013a). *The Application Level Events (ALE) Specification (version 1.1.1), parts 1 and 2*. Retrieved from http://www.gs1.org/gsmp/kc/epcglobal/ale

EPCglobal. (2013b). *EPC Information Services (EPCIS) Specification (version 1.0.1)*. Retrieved September 2013, from http://www.gs1.org/gsmp/kc/epcglobal/epcis

EPCglobal. (2013c). *EPC Tag Data Standard (version 1.7)*. Retrieved September 2013, from http://www.gs1.org/gsmp/kc/epcglobal/tds/

EPCglobal. (2013c). *Low Level Reader Protocol (LLRP) (version 1.1)*. Retrieved from http://www.gs1.org/gsmp/kc/epcglobal/llrp

EPCglobal. (2013d). *Object Name Service (ONS) (version 2.0.1)*. Retrieved September 2013, from http://www.gs1.org/gsmp/kc/epcglobal/ons

EPCglobal. (2013e). *Low Level Reader Protocol (LLRP) (version 1.1)*. Retrieved September 2013, from http://www.gs1.org/gsmp/kc/epcglobal/llrp

EPC Global. (2014). Retrieved from http://www.epcglobalinc.org/index.html

Ericsson, K. A., & Simon, H. A. (1993). *Protocol analysis: Verbal reports as data* (Rev. Ed.). Cambridge, MA: MIT Press.

Ernst and Young's Study of Retail Loss Prevention. (2003). *Ernst and Young*. Retrieved January 23, 2014 from http://retailindustry.about.com/cs/lp_retailstore/a/bl_ey051303.htm

Fallah, N., Apostolopoulos, I., Bekris, K., & Folmer, E. (2013). Indoor human navigation systems: A survey. *Interacting with Computers, 25*(1), 21–33. doi:10.1093/iwc/iws010

Fan, T.J., Chang, X.Y., Gu, C.H., Yi, J.J., & Deng, S. (2014). Benefits of RFID technology for reducing inventory shrinkage. *International Journal of Production Economics, 147*(Part C), 659–665.

Fernandes, T. (2011). Indoor localization using Bluetooth. In *Proceedings of 6th Doctoral Symposium in Informatics Engineering*, (pp. 1–10). Retrieved from http://paginas.fe.up.pt/~prodei/dsie11/images/pdfs/s5-4.pdf

Ferrer, G., Heath, S. K., & Dew, N. (2011). An RFID application in large job shop remanufacturing operations. *International Journal of Production Economics*, 612–621.133(2 doi:10.1016/j.ijpe.2011.05.006

Fisher, J. A., & Monahan, T. (2008). Tracking the social dimensions of RFID systems in hospitals. *International Journal of Medical Informatics*, 77(3), 176–183. doi:10.1016/j.ijmedinf.2007.04.010 PMID:17544841

Fleisch, E., & Mattern, F. (2005). *Das Internet Der Dinge: Ubiquitous Computing Und Rfid in Der Praxis: Visionen, Technologien, Anwendungen, Handlungsanleitungen.* Springer.

Floerkemeier, C., Roduner, C., & Lampe, M. (2007, December). RFID Application Development with the Accada Middleware Platform. *IEEE Systems Journal*, 1(2), 82–94. doi:10.1109/JSYST.2007.909778

Fontanella, J. (2004). Finding the ROI in RFID. *Supply Chain Management Review*, 8(1), 13–16.

Fosso Wamba, S., & Chatfield, A. T. (2009). A contingency model for creating value from RFID supply chain network projects in logistics and manufacturing environments. *European Journal of Information Systems*, 18(6), 615–636. doi:10.1057/ejis.2009.44

Foster, S., Scheepers, H., & Rahmati, N. (2005). RFIDs: From Invention to Innovation. *Communications of the IIMA*, 5(4), 1–10.

Främling, K., Kärkkäinen, M., Ala-Risku, T., & Holmström, J. (2004). *Managing Product Information in Supplier Networks by Object-oriented Programming Concepts.* Paper presented at the International IMS Forum. Lake Como, Italy.

Främling, K. (2002). *Tracking of material flow by an Internet-based product data management system. Tieke EDISTY Magazine, 1.*

Fritz, G. (2010). Read-Error-Rate evaluation for RFID system on-line testing. In *Proceedings of Mixed-Signals, Sensors and Systems Test Workshop* (IMS3TW). IEEE.

Fukuju, Y., Minami, M., Morikawa, H., & Aoyama, T. (2003). DOLPHIN: An autonomous indoor positioning system in ubiquitous computing environment. In *Proceedings of IEEE Workshop on Software Technologies for Future Embedded Systems* (pp. 53–56). IEEE. doi:10.1109/WSTFES.2003.1201360

Fumi, A., Scarabotti, L., & Schiraldi, M. M. (2013). The effect of slot-code optimisation on travel times in common unit-load warehouses. *International Journal of Services and Operations Management.*, 15(4), 507–527. doi:10.1504/IJSOM.2013.054925

Galván-Tejada, C. E., Carrasco-Jiménez, J. C., & Brena, R. F. (2013). Bluetooth-WiFi based combined positioning algorithm, implementation and experimental evaluation. *Procedia Technology*, 7, 37–45. doi:10.1016/j.protcy.2013.04.005

Ganesan, S., George, M., Jap, S., Palmatier, R. W., & Weitz, B. (2009). Supply chain management and retailer performance: Emerging trends, issues, and implications for research and practice. *Journal of Retailing*, 85(1), 84–94. doi:10.1016/j.jretai.2008.12.001

Gao, X., Xiang, Z., Wang, H., Shen, J., Huang, J., & Song, S. (2008). An approach to security and privacy of RFID system for supply chain. In *Proceedings of IEEE International Conference on E-Commerce Technology for Dynamic E-Business*. IEEE.

Gaukler, G. M., & Hausman, W. H. (2008). RFID in mixed-model automotive assembly operations: Process and quality cost savings. *IIE Transactions*, 40(11), 1083–1096. doi:10.1080/07408170802167654

Gaukler, G. M., Özer, O., & Hausman, W. H. (2008). Order progress information: Improved dynamic emergency ordering policies. *Production and Operations Management*, 17(6), 599–614. doi:10.3401/poms.1080.0066

Gaukler, G. M., Seifert, R. W., & Hausman, W. H. (2007). Item-Level RFID in the Retail Supply Chain. *Production and Operations Management*, 16(1), 65–76. doi:10.1111/j.1937-5956.2007.tb00166.x

Gellerman, B. (2013). *Mass. seeks to eliminate tollbooths for cashless system.* WBUR, National Public Radio. Retrieved March 2, 2013 from http://www.wbur.org/2013/03/27/mass-tollbooths-cashless

Gencel, C., Heldal, R., & Lind, K. (2009). *On the relationship between different size measures in the software life cycle.* Paper presented at the Asia-Pacific Software Engineering Conference (APSEC). Hong Kong, China.

Giorgetti, G., Farley, R., Chikkappa, K., Judy, E., & Kaleas, T. (2012). Cortina: Collaborative indoor positioning using low-power sensor networks. *Journal of Location Based Services*, 6(3), 137–160. doi:10.1080/17489725.2012.690217

Glabman, M. (2004). Room for tracking: RFID technology finds the way. *Materials Management in Health Care*, 26–38. PMID:15202205

Glasser, D. J., Goodman, K. W., & Einspruch, N. G. (2007). Chips, tags and scanners: Ethical challenges for radio frequency identification. *Ethics and Information Technology*, 9(2), 101–109. doi:10.1007/s10676-006-9124-0

Golding, P., & Tennant, V. (2010). Using RFID Inventory Reader at the Item-Level in a Library Environment: Performance Benchmark. *Electronic Journal of Information Systems Evaluation*, 13(2), 107–120.

Gonzalez, H., Han, J., & Shen, X. (2007). Cost-conscious cleaning of massive RFID data sets. In *Proceedings of International Conference on Data Engineering*, (pp. 1268-1272). Academic Press.

Gonzalez, H., Han, J., Li, X., & Klabjan, D. (2006). Warehousing and analyzing massive RFID data sets. In *Proceedings of the 22nd International Conference on Data Engineering*. Academic Press.

Good, T., & Benaissa, M. (2013). A holistic approach examining RFID design for security and privacy. *The Journal of Supercomputing*, 64(3), 664–684. doi:10.1007/s11227-010-0497-9

Google. (2013). *Google Web Toolkit*. Retrieved September 2013, from http://code.google.com/webtoolkit/

Granollers, T., & Lorés, J. (2006). Incorporation of users in the Evaluation of Usability by Cognitive Walkthrough. In R. Navarro-Prieto, & J. L. Vidal (Eds.), *HCI related papers of Interacción 2004* (pp. 243–255). Springer. doi:10.1007/1-4020-4205-1_20

Greenberg, J. (1990). Employee theft as a reaction to underpayment inequity: The hidden cost of pay cuts. *Journal of Applied Psychology*, 75(5), 561-572.

Grewal, C. (2008). An initiative to implement lean manufacturing using value stream mapping in a small company. *International Journal of Manufacturing Technology and Management*, 15(3-4), 404–421. doi:10.1504/IJMTM.2008.020176

Grewal, D., Ailawadi, K. L., Gauri, D., Hall, K., Kopalle, P., & Robertson, J. R. (2011). Innovations in retail pricing and promotions. *Journal of Retailing*, 87, 43–52. doi:10.1016/j.jretai.2011.04.008

Grover, A., & Berghel, H. (2011). A survey of RFID deployment and security issues. *Journal of Information Processing Systems*, 7(4), 561–580. doi:10.3745/JIPS.2011.7.4.561

Gunasekaran, A., & Ngai, E. W. T. (2004). Information systems in supply-chain integration and management. *European Journal of Operational Research*, 159(2), 269–295. doi:10.1016/j.ejor.2003.08.016

Gu, Y., Lo, A., & Niemegeers, I. (2009). A survey of indoor positioning systems for wireless personal networks. *IEEE Communications Surveys and Tutorials*, 11(1), 13–32. doi:10.1109/SURV.2009.090103

Hair, F. J., Black, W. C., Babin, B. J., Anderson, R. E., & Tatham, R. L. (2006). *Multivariate Data Analysis* (6th ed.). Upper Saddle River, NJ: Pearson Prentice Hall.

Hair, J. F., Tomas, G., Hult, M., Ringle, C. M., & Sarstedt, M. (2013). *A Primer on Partial Least Squares Structural Equation Modeling (PLS-SEM)*. Thousand Oaks, CA: Sage.

Hansen, W. R., & Gillert, F. (2006). *RFID für die Optimierung von Geschäftsprozessen: Prozess-Strukturen, IT-Architekturen, RFID-Infrastruktur* (Vol. 1). München: Carl Hanser Verlag.

Hardgrave, B., Aloysius, J., Goyal, S., & Spencer, J. (2008a). *Does RFID improve inventory accuracy? A preliminary analysis*. Fayetteville, AR: Information Technology Research Institute, Sam M. Walton College of Business, University of Arkansas.

Hardgrave, B., Langford, S., Waller, M., & Miller, R. (2008b). Measuring the impact of RFID on out of stocks at Wal-Mart. *MIS Quarterly Executive*, 7(4), 181–192.

Harper, J. (2004). *RFID tags and privacy: How bar-codes-on-steroids are really a 98-Lb. weakling.* Competitive Enterprise Institute. Retrieved July 15, 2013, from http://heartland.org/policy-documents/rfid-tags-and-privacy-how-bar-codes-steroids-are-really-98-lb-weakling

Hartman, F., & Ashrafi, R. (2002). Project management in the information systems and information technologies. *Project Management Journal, 33*(3), 5–15.

Hauschildt, D., & Kirchhof, N. (2010). Advances in thermal infrared localization: challenges and solutions. In *Proceedings of International Conference on Indoor Positioning and Indoor Navigation* (IPIN) (pp. 1–8). Zurich: IPIN. doi:10.1109/IPIN.2010.5647415

Hazas, M., & Ward, A. (2002). A novel broadband ultrasonic location system. In *Proceedings of the 4th International Conference on Ubiquitous Computing* (pp. 264–280). Sweden: Academic Press. doi:10.1007/3-540-45809-3_21

Hazas, M., & Hopper, A. (2006). Broadband ultrasonic location systems for improved indoor positioning. *IEEE Transactions on Mobile Computing, 5*(5), 536–547. doi:10.1109/TMC.2006.57

Heese, H. S. (2007). Inventory Record Inaccuracy, Double Marginalization, and RFID Adoption. *Production and Operations Management, 16*(5), 542–553. doi:10.1111/j.1937-5956.2007.tb00279.x

Heim, G. R., Wentworth, W. R. Jr, & Peng, X. (2009). The value to the customer of RFID in service applications. *Decision Sciences, 40*(3), 477–512. doi:10.1111/j.1540-5915.2009.00237.x

Helo, P., Anussornnitisarn, P., & Phusavat, K. (2008). Expectation and reality in ERP implementation: Consultant and solution provider perspective. *Industrial Management & Data Systems, 108*(8), 1045–1158. doi:10.1108/02635570810904604

Henniges, R. (2012). Current approaches of Wifi positioning. In *Proceedings of IEEE Conference Publications,* (pp. 1–8). IEEE. Retrieved from http://www.snet.tu-berlin.de/fileadmin/fg220/courses/WS1112/snet-project/wifi-positioning_henniges.pdf

Henseler, J., Ringle, C. M., & Sinkovics, R. R. (2009). The use of partial least squares path modeling in international marketing. In *Advances in International Marketing* (pp. 277–319). Emerald.

Hevner, A. R. (2007). A Three Cycle View of Design Science Research. *Scandinavian Journal of Information Systems, 19*(2).

Hevner, A. R., March, S. T., Park, J., & Ram, S. (2004). Design Science in Information Systems Research. *Management Information Systems Quarterly, 28*(1), 75–105.

Hiscox, M.J., & Smyth, N.F.B. (2011, April). *Is There Consumer Demand for Improved Labor Standards? Evidence from Field Experiments in Social Product Labeling.* Social Science Research Network.

Hollinger, R. C., Lee, G., Kane, J. L., & Hayes, R. (1998). *1998 National Retail Security Survey: Executive Summary.* Gainesville, FL: University of Florida Security Research Project.

Holm, S. (2012). Ultrasound positioning based on time-of-flight and signal strength. In *Proceedings of International Conference on Indoor Positioning and Indoor Navigation* (IPIN) (pp. 1–6). Sydney: IPIN. doi:10.1109/IPIN.2012.6418728

Holmqvist, M., & Stefansson, G. (2006a). Mobile RFID: A Case from Volvo on Innovation in SCM. In *Proceedings of the 39th Hawaii International Conference on System Sciences.* IEEE.

Holmqvist, M., & Stefansson, G. (2006b). 'Smart goods' and mobile RFID: A case with innovation from Volvo. *Journal of Business Logistics, 27*(2), 251–272. doi:10.1002/j.2158-1592.2006.tb00225.x

Hopper, A., Harter, A., & Blackie, T. (1993). *The active badge system.* Retrieved August 27, 2013, from http://www.cl.cam.ac.uk/research/dtg/attarchive/ab.html

Hosaka, R. (2004). Feasibility study of convenient automatic identification system of medical articles using LF-Band RFID in hospital. *Systems and Computers in Japan, 35*(10), 571–578. doi:10.1002/scj.10581

Hossain, M. M., & Prybutok, V. R. (2008). Consumer acceptance of RFID technology: An exploratory study. *IEEE Transactions on Engineering Management, 55*(2), 316–328. doi:10.1109/TEM.2008.919728

Hou, J. L., & Chen, T. G. (2011). An RFID-based shopping service system for retailers. *Advanced Engineering Informatics, 25*(1), 103–115. doi:10.1016/j.aei.2010.04.003

Hou, J. L., & Huang, C. H. (2006). Quantitative performance evaluation of RFID applications in the supply chain of the printing industry. *Industrial Management & Data Systems, 106*(1/2), 96–120. doi:10.1108/02635570610641013

Hozak, K., & Collier, D. A. (2008). RFID as an enabler of improved manufacturing performance. *Decision Sciences Journal, 39*(4), 859–881. doi:10.1111/j.1540-5915.2008.00214.x

Hsu, C. H., Chao, H. C., & Park, J. H. (2011). Threshold jumping and wrap-around scan techniques toward efficient tag identification in high density RFID systems. *Information Systems Frontiers, 13*(4), 471–480. doi:10.1007/s10796-009-9209-5

Huang, B., & Gao, Y. (2013). Ubiquitous indoor vision navigation using a smart device. *Geo-spatial. Information Science, 16*(3), 177–185. doi:10.1080/10095020.2013.817110

Huang, G. Q., Zhang, Y. F., & Jiang, P. Y. (2007). RFID-based wireless manufacturing for walking-worker assembly islands with fixed-position layout. *Robotics and Computer-integrated Manufacturing, 23*(4), 469–477. doi:10.1016/j.rcim.2006.05.006

Huang, H., & Gartner, G. (2010). A survey of mobile indoor navigation systems. In G. Gartner, & F. Ortag (Eds.), *Cartography in Central and Eastern Europe* (pp. 305–319). Springer.

Hu, G., Wang, L., Fetch, S., & Bidanda, B. (2008). A multi-objective model for project portfolio selection to implement lean and Six Sigma concepts. *International Journal of Production Research, 46*(23), 6611–6648. doi:10.1080/00207540802230363

Ifinedo, P., & Nahar, N. (2009). Interactions between contingency, organizational IT factors, and ERP success. *Industrial Management & Data Systems, 109*(1), 118–126. doi:10.1108/02635570910926627

Ilie-Zudor, E., Kemény, Z., van Blommestein, F., Monostori, L., & van der Meulen, A. (2011, January). A survey of applications and requirements of unique identification systems and RFID techniques. *Computers in Industry.*

International Organization for Standardization (ISO). (2006). *ISO/IEC 15459-1:2006 Information technology -- Unique identifiers -- Part 1: Unique identifiers for transport units.* Author.

International Organization for Standardization (ISO). (2009). Packaging -- Bar code and two-dimensional symbols for shipping, transport and receiving labels. *ISO, 15394,* 2009.

Internet Software Consortium. (2001). *BIND 9 Administration reference manual.* Available online at: http://www.scs.stanford.edu/~reddy/links/dns/bind9arm.pdf

Internet Systems Consortium. (n.d.). *The BIND software.* Retrieved September 2013, from http://www.isc.org/software/bind

Jain, V., Benyoucef, L., & Deshmukh, S. G. (2008). What's the buzz about moving from 'lean' to 'agile' integrated supply chains? A fuzzy intelligent agent-based approach. *International Journal of Production Research, 46*(23), 6649–6678. doi:10.1080/00207540802230462

Jang, S. H. (2010). A QR code-based indoor navigation system using augmented reality. *giscience.* Retrieved April 15, 2013, from http://www.giscience.org/proceedings/abstracts/giscience2012_paper_110.pdf

Jeong, B., Lee, D., Cho, H., & Lee, J. (2008). A novel method for measuring semantic similarity for XML schema matching. *Expert Syst. Appl., 34*(3), 1651–1658. DOI: 10.1016/j.eswa.2007.01.025

Johansson, B., & Sudzina, F. (2008). ERP systems and open source: An initial review and some implications for SMEs. *Journal of Enterprise Information Management, 21*(6), 649–659. doi:10.1108/17410390810911230

Jones, E., Riley, M., Franca, R., & Reigle, S. (2007). Case study: The engineering economics of RFID in specialized manufacturing. *The Engineering Economist, 52*(3), 285–303. doi:10.1080/00137910701503951

Jones, M. A., Wyld, D. C., & Totten, J. W. (2005). The adoption of RFID technology in the retail supply chain. *The Coastal Business Journal, 4*(1), 29–42.

Jones, P., Clarke-Hill, C., Comfort, D., Hillier, D., & Shears, P. (2004). Radio frequency identification in retailing and privacy and public policy issues. *Management Research News, 27*(8/9), 46–60. doi:10.1108/01409170410784563

Jones, P., Clarke-Hill, C., Hillier, D., & Comfort, D. (2005). The benefits, challenges and impacts of radio frequency identification technology (RFID) for retailers in the UK. *Marketing Intelligence & Planning, 23*(4), 395–402. doi:10.1108/02634500510603492

Juban, R. L., & Wyld, D. C. (2004). Would you like chips with that? Consumer perspective of RFID. *Management Research News, 27*(11/12), 29–44. doi:10.1108/01409170410784653

Jung, I. C., & Kwon, Y. S. (2011). Grocery customer behavior analysis using RFID-based shopping paths data. *World Academy of Science. Engineering and Technology, 59*, 1404–1408.

Kamhawi, E. M. (2008). System characteristics, perceived benefits, individual differences and use intentions: A survey of decision support tools of ERP systems. *Information Resources Management Journal, 21*(4), 66–83. doi:10.4018/irmj.2008100104

Kamruzzaman, J., Azad, A. K., Karmakar, N. C., Karmakar, G., & Srinivasan, B. (2013). Security and privacy in RFID systems. In N. Karmakar (Ed.), *Advanced RFID Systems, Security, and Applications* (pp. 16–40). Hershey, PA: Information Science Reference.

Kannan, B., Meneguzzi, F., Dias, B. M., Sycara, K., Gnegy, C., Glasgow, E., & Yordanov, P. (2013). Predictive indoor navigation using commercial smartphones. In *Proceedings of the 28th Annual ACM Symposium on Applied Computing* (pp. 519–525). ACM. doi:10.1145/2480362.2480463

Kaplan, R. S. (1998). Innovation Action research: Creating New Management Theory and Practice. *Journal of Management Accounting Research, 10*, 89–118.

Kapoor, G., Zhou, W., & Piramuthu, S. (2009). Challenges associated with RFID tag implementations in supply chain. *European Journal of Information Systems, 18*(6), 526–533. doi:10.1057/ejis.2009.41

Karaer, O., & Lee, H. L. (2007). Managing the Reverse Channel with RFID-Enabled Negative Demand Information. *Production and Operations Management, 16*(5), 625–645. doi:10.1111/j.1937-5956.2007.tb00285.x

Karahanna, E., Straub, D. W., & Chervany, N. L. (1999). Information Technology Adoption Across Time: A Cross-Sectional Comparison of Pre-Adoption Beliefs and Post-Adoption Beliefs. *Management Information Systems Quarterly, 23*(2), 183–213. doi:10.2307/249751

Kardes, F. R., Cronley, M. L., & Cline, T. W. (2011). Consumer Behavior. Mason, OH: South-Western, Cengage Learning.

Karkkainen, M. (2003). Increasing Efficiency in the Supply Chain for Short Shelf Life Goods Using Rfid Tagging. *International Journal of Retail & Distribution Management, 31*(10), 529–536. doi:10.1108/09590550310497058

Kärkkäinen, M., Ala-Risku, T., & Främling, K. (2004). Efficient tracking in short-term multi-company networks. *International Journal of Physical Distribution & Logistics Management, 34*(7), 545–564. doi:10.1108/09600030410552249

Karl, H., & Willig, A. (2006). Localization and positioning. In *Protocols and Architectures for Wireless Sensor Networks*. Chichester, UK: John Wiley & Sons Inc. doi:10.1002/0470095121.ch9

Karnok, D, & Kemény, Z. (2012). Definition and handling of data types in a dataflow-oriented modelling and processing environment. In *Proceedings of MITIP 2012*. MITIP.

Kasiri, N., Sharda, R., & Hardgrave, B. (2012). A balanced scorecard for item-level RFID in the retail sector: a Delphi study. *European Journal of Information Systems, 21*(3), 255–267. doi:10.1057/ejis.2011.33

Kassinis, G., & Vafeas, N. (2006). Stakeholder pressures and Environmental performance. *Academy of Management Journal, 49*(15), 145–159. doi:10.5465/AMJ.2006.20785799

Katz, J.E., & Rice, R.E. (2009). Public views of mobile medical devices and services: A US national survey of consumer sentiments towards RFID healthcare technology. *International Journal of Medical Informatics, 78*(2), 104–114.

Kearney, A. T. (2005). RFID will bring great benefits for retailers. [Online]. Retrieved January 27, 2014 from http://retailindustry.about.com/cs/it_rfid/a/bl_atk111003.htm

Kefalakis, N., Leontiadis, N., Soldatos, J., & Donsez, D. (2009). Middleware Building Blocks for Architecting RFID Systems. In *Proceedings of the MOBILIGHT 2009 Conference*, (pp. 325-336). MOBILIGHT.

Kefalakis, N., Soldatos, J., Konstantinou, N., & Prasad, N. (2011). APDL: A reference XML schema for process-centered definition of RFID solutions. Int Journal of Systems & Software, 84, 1244-1259. doi:10.1016/j.jss.2011.02.036

Kefalakis, N., Soldatos, J., Mertikas, E., & Prasad, N. (2011a). *Generating Business Events in an RFID network*. Paper presented at RFID-TA. New York, NY.

Kemény, Z., Ilie-Zudor, E., Fülöp, J., Ekárt, A., Buckingham, C., & Welch, P. G. (2011a). Multiple-participant hub-and-spoke logistics networks: challenges, solutions and limits. In *Proc. of the 13th International Conference on Modern Information Technology in the Innovation Processes of Industrial Enterprises* (MITIP 2011) (pp. 20-29). Trondheim, Norway: MITIP.

Kemény, Z., Szathmári, M., Kemény, L., Bozóki, S., & Ilie-Zudor, E. (2011b). Quality indication and supply management of perishable products with optical labels for low-end demands. In *Proc. of the 13th Int. Conf. on Modern Information Technology in the Innovation Processes of Industrial Enterprises* (MITIP 2011) (pp. 202-211). Trondheim, Norway: MITIP.

Kennedy, F. A., & Widener, S. K. (2008). A control framework: Insights from evidence on lean accounting. *Management Accounting Research*, *19*(4), 301–319. doi:10.1016/j.mar.2008.01.001

Ketikidis, P. H., Hayes, O. P., Lazuras, L., Gunasekaran, A., & Koh, S. C. L. (2013). Environmental practices and performance and their relationships among Kosovo construction companies: A framework for analysis in transition economies. *International Journal of Services and Operations Management*, *15*(1), 115–130. doi:10.1504/IJSOM.2013.050565

Khor, J. H., Ismail, W., Younis, M. I., Sulaiman, M. K., & Rahman, M. G. (2010). Security problems in an RFID system. *Wireless Personal Communications*, *59*(1), 17–26. doi:10.1007/s11277-010-0186-2

Kim, S., & Garrison, G. (2010). Understanding users' behaviors regarding supply chain technology: Determinants impacting the adoption and implementation of RFID technology in South Korea. *International Journal of Information Management*, *30*(5), 388–398.

Kim, S.-E., Kim, Y., Yoon, J., & Kim, E. S. (2012). Indoor positioning system using geomagnetic anomalies for smartphones. In *Proceedings of International Conference on Indoor Positioning and Indoor Navigation* (IPIN) (pp. 1–5). Sydney: IPIN. doi:10.1109/IPIN.2012.6418947

Kim, C., Yang, K., & Kim, J. (2008). A strategy for third-party logistics systems. A case analysis using the blue ocean strategy. *Omega*, *36*(4), 522–534. doi:10.1016/j.omega.2006.11.011

Kim, J., & Jun, H. (2008). Vision-based location positioning using augmented reality for indoor navigation. *IEEE Transactions on Consumer Electronics*, *54*(3), 954–962. doi:10.1109/TCE.2008.4637573

Kitasuka, T., Nakanishi, T., & Fukuda, A. (2003). Wireless LAN based indoor positioning system WiPS and its simulation. In *Proceedings of IEEE Pacific Rim Conference on Communications, Computers and signal Processing* (Vol. 1, pp. 272–275). IEEE. doi:10.1109/PACRIM.2003.1235770

Klein, R., & Rai, A. (2009). Interfirm strategic information flows in logistics supply chain relationships. *Management Information Systems Quarterly*, *33*(4), 735–762.

Klopschitz, M., Schall, G., Schmalstieg, D., & Reitmayr, G. (2010). Visual tracking for augmented reality. In *Proceedings of International Conference on Indoor Positioning and Indoor Navigation* (IPIN) (pp. 1–4). Zurich: IPIN. doi:10.1109/IPIN.2010.5648274

Köbler, F., Goswami, S., Koene, P., Leimeister, J. M., & Krcmar, H. (2011). NFriendConnector: Design and Evaluation of An Application for Integrating Offline and Online Social Networking. *AIS Transactions on Human-Computer Interaction*, *4*(3), 214–235.

Koong, L., & Lin, C. (2007). Evaluating the decision to adopt RFID systems using analytic hierarchy process. *Journal of American Academy of Business, 11*(1), 72–77.

Kosk, N. (2014). *The Reverse Logistics Cycle, Supply & Demand-Chain Executive.* Retrieved from http://www.sdcexec.com/

Koyuncu, H., & Yang, S. H. (2010). A survey of indoor positioning and object locating systems. *International Journal of Computer Science and Network Security, 10*(5), 121–128. Retrieved from http://paper.ijcsns.org/07_book/201005/20100518.pdf

Krause, D. R., Handfield, R. B., & Tyler, B. B. (2007). The relationships between supplier development, commitment, social capital accumulation and performance improvement. *Journal of Operations Management, 25*(2), 528–545. doi:10.1016/j.jom.2006.05.007

Krcmar, H. (2010). *Informationsmanagement* (Vol. 5). Heidelberg, Germany: Springer. doi:10.1007/978-3-642-04286-7

Krigslund, R., Popovski, P., Dukovska-Popovska, I., Pedersen, G. F., & Manev, B. (2010). Using ICT in Greening: The Role of RFID. In *Towards Green ICT* (pp. 97–116). Denmark: River Publishers.

Krotov, V., & Junglas, I. (2008). RFID as a Disruptive Innovation. *Journal of Theoretical and Applied Electronic Commerce Research., 3*(2), 44–59. doi:10.4067/S0718-18762008000100005

Kulas, J. T., McInnerney, J. E., DeMuth, R. F., & Jadwinski, V. (2007). Employee satisfaction and theft: Testing climate perceptions as a mediatorfalse. *The Journal of Psychology, 141*(4), 389–402. doi:10.3200/JRLP.141.4.389-402 PMID:17725072

Kumar, K., & van Dissel, H. G. (1996). Sustainable Collaboration: Managing Conflict and Cooperation in Interorganizational Systems. *Management Information Systems Quarterly, 20*(2), 279–300. doi:10.2307/249657

Kumar, S., Anselmo, M. J., & Berndt, K. J. (2009). Transforming the retail industry: potential and challenges with RFID technology. *Transportation Journal, 48*(4), 61–71.

Kumar, S., Livermont, G., & Mckewan, G. (2010). Stage implementation of RFID hospitals. *Technology and Health Care, 18*(1), 31–46. PMID:20231801

Kwok, S. K., & Wu, K. W. (2009). RFID-based intra-supply chain in textile industry. *Industrial Management & Data Systems, 109*(9), 1166–1178. doi:10.1108/02635570911002252

Lai, K., Wong, C., & Cheng, T. (2008). A coordination-theoretic investigation of the impact of electronic integration on logistics performance. *Information & Management, 45*(1), 10–20. doi:10.1016/j.im.2007.05.007

Lampe, M., & Floerkemeier, C. (2007). High-Level System Support for Automatic-Identification Applications. In *Proceedings of Workshop on Design of Smart Products,* (pp. 55-64). Furtwangen, Germany: Academic Press.

Langer, N., Forman, C., Kekre, S., & Scheller-Wolf, A. (2007). Assessing the impact of RFID on return center logistics. *Interfaces, 37*(6), 501–514. doi:10.1287/inte.1070.0308

Langheinrich, M. (2008). A survey of RFID privacy approaches. *Personal and Ubiquitous Computing, 13*(6), 413–421. doi:10.1007/s00779-008-0213-4

Laubacher, R., Kothari, S. P., Malone, T. W., & Subirana, B. (2005). What is RFID worth to your company? - Measuring performance at the activity level. *MIT Center for eBusiness Research Brief, 7*(2), 1-6.

Lawton, G. (2004, September). Machine-to-Machine Technology Gears Up for Growth. *IEEE Computer, 37*(9), 12–15. doi:10.1109/MC.2004.137

Lazos, L., Poovendran, R., & Čapkun, S. (2005). ROPE: Robust position estimation in wireless sensor networks. In *Proceedings of Fourth International Symposium on Information Processing in Sensor Networks,* (pp. 324–331). Academic Press. doi:10.1109/IPSN.2005.1440942

Lee, C., Chang, Y., Park, G., Ryu, J., Jeong, S.-G., Park, S., ... Lee, M. H. (2004). Indoor positioning system based on incident angles of infrared emitters. In *Proceedings of 30th Annual Conference of IEEE Industrial Electronics Society* (Vol. 3, pp. 2218–2222). IEEE. doi:10.1109/IECON.2004.1432143

Lee, H., Lee, K., Park, M., Baek, Y., and Lee, S. (2012). RFID-based real-time locating system for construction safety management. *Journal of Computing in Civil Engineering, 26*(3), 366–377.

Lee, H.-H. (2008). The investment model in preventive maintenance in multi-level production systems. *International Journal of Production Economics, 112*(2), 816–828.

Lee, S., & Song, J. (2007). Mobile robot localization using infrared light reflecting landmarks. In *Proceedings of International Conference on Control, Automation and Systems* (pp. 674–677). Seoul: Academic Press. doi:10.1109/ICCAS.2007.4406984

Lee, Y.C., &, Lee, S.S. (2011). The valuation of RFID investment using fuzzy real option. *Expert Systems with Applications, 38*(10), 12195–12201.

Lee. (2000). Context-dependent Semantic Values for E-negotiation. In *Proceedings of WECWIS*. WECWIS.

Lee, H., & Ozer, O. (2007). Unlocking the value of RFID. *Production and Operations Management, 16*(1), 40–64. doi:10.1111/j.1937-5956.2007.tb00165.x

Lee, H., Padmanabhan, V., & Whang, S. (1997). The Bullwhip Effect In Supply Chains. *Sloan Management Review, 38*(3), 93–102.

Lee, I. (2004). Evaluating business-process integrated information technology investment. *Business Process Management Journal, 10*(2), 214–233. doi:10.1108/14637150410530271

Lee, I., & Lee, B.-C. (2010). An investment evaluation of supply chain RFID technologies: A normative modeling approach. *International Journal of Production Economics, 125*, 313–323. doi:10.1016/j.ijpe.2010.02.006

Lee, I., & Lee, B.-C. (2012). Measuring the value of RFID investment: Focusing on RFID budget allocation. *IEEE Transactions on Engineering Management, 59*(4), 551–559. doi:10.1109/TEM.2011.2163072

Lee, J. H., Song, J. H., Oh, K. S., & Gu, N. (2013). Information lifecycle management with RFID for material control on construction sites. *Advanced Engineering Informatics, 27*(1), 108–119. doi:10.1016/j.aei.2012.11.004

Lee, L., Fiedler, K., & Smith, J. (2008). Radio frequency identification (RFID) implementation in the service sector: A customer-facing diffusion model. *International Journal of Production Economics, 112*(2), 587–600. doi:10.1016/j.ijpe.2007.05.008

Lee, S., & Kim, K. (2007). Factors affecting the implementation success of Internet-based information systems. *Computers in Human Behavior, 23*(4), 1853–1880. doi:10.1016/j.chb.2005.12.001

Leontiadis, N., Kefalakis, N., & Soldatos, J. (2009). Bridging RFID Systems and Enterprise Applications through Virtualized Connectors. *International Journal of Automated Identification Technology, 1*(2), 2009.

Lewis, C., Polson, P. G., & Rieman, J. (1991). *Cognitive walkthrough forms and instructions* (Institute of Cognitive Science Technical Report, ICS 91-14). Academic Press.

Li, B., Gallagher, T., Dempster, A. G., & Rizos, C. (2012). How feasible is the use of magnetic field alone for indoor positioning? In *Proceedings of International Conference on Indoor Positioning and Indoor Navigation* (IPIN) (pp. 1–9). Sydney: IPIN. doi:10.1109/IPIN.2012.6418880

Liard, M. (2009). *RFID Item-level Tagging in Fashion Apparel and Footwear*. ABI Research.

Lin, C. Y. & Ho, Y. H. (2009a). RFID technology adoption and supply chain performance: an empirical study in China's logistics industry. *Supply Chain Management: An International Journal*, 369-378.

Lin, C. Y., & Ho, Y. H. (2009b). An Empirical Study on the Adoption of RFID Technology for Logistics Service Providers in China. *International Business Research, 2*(1), 23–36. doi:10.5539/ibr.v2n1p23

Link, J. A. B., Smith, P., Viol, N., & Wehrle, K. (2011). Footpath: Accurate map-based indoor navigation using smartphones. In *Proceedings of International Conference on Indoor Positioning and Indoor Navigation* (IPIN) (pp. 1–8). IPIN. doi:10.1109/IPIN.2011.6071934

Lin, K., & Lin, C. (2007). Evaluating the decision to adopt RFID systems using analytic hierarchy process. *The Journal of American Academy of Business, Cambridge, 11*(1), 72–78.

Lin, L. C. (2009). An integrated framework for the development of radio frequency identification technology in the logistics and supply chain management. *Computers & Industrial Engineering, 57*(3), 832–842. doi:10.1016/j.cie.2009.02.010

Li, S., Godon, D., & Visich, J. K. (2010). An exploratory study of RFID implementation in the supply chain. *Management Research Review*, *33*(10), 1005–1015. doi:10.1108/01409171011084003

Li, S., & Visich, J. K. (2006). Radio frequency identification: Supply chain impact and implementation challenges. *International Journal of Integrated Supply Management*, *2*(4), 407–424. doi:10.1504/IJISM.2006.009643

Liu, K., Liu, X., & Li, X. (2013). Guoguo: enabling fine-grained indoor localization via smartphone. In *Proceeding of the 11th annual international conference on Mobile systems, applications, and services* (pp. 235–248). Academic Press. doi:10.1145/2462456.2464450

Liu, A., Chang, H. K., Lo, Y. S., & Wang, S. Y. (2012). The increase of RFID privacy and security with mutual authentication mechanism in supply chain management. *International Journal of Electronic Business Management*, *10*(1), 1–7.

Liu, H., Darabi, H., Banerjee, P., & Liu, J. (2007). Survey of wireless indoor positioning techniques and systems. *IEEE Transactions on Systems, Man and Cybernetics. Part C, Applications and Reviews*, *37*(6), 1067–1080. doi:10.1109/TSMCC.2007.905750

Liu, L., & Hou, J. H. (2009). *Costume Aesthetics*. Beijing, China: Chemical Industry Press.

Li, Y., Deng, R. H., & Bertino, E. (2013). RFID security and privacy. *Synthesis Lectures on Information Security, Privacy, and Trust*, *4*(3), 1–157. doi:10.2200/S00550ED-1V01Y201311SPT007

Loebbecke, C. (2005). RFID Technology and Applications in the Retail Supply Chain: The Early Metro Group Pilot. In *Proceedings of 18th Bled conference on eIntegration in action*, (pp. 5-6). Bled.

Loebbecke, C. (2007). Piloting RFID along the supply chain: A case analysis. *Electronic Markets*, *17*(1), 29–37. doi:10.1080/10196780601136773

LogicAlloy. (2013). *LogicAlloy RFID System*. Retrieved from http://www.logicalloy.com/index.cfm

Lopes, C. V., Haghighat, A., Mandal, A., Givargis, T., & Baldi, P. (2006). Localization of off-the-shelf mobile devices using audible sound: Architectures, protocols and performance assessment. *Mobile Computing and Communications Review*, *10*(2), 38–50. doi:10.1145/1137975.1137980

Lukianto, C., & Sternberg, H. (2011). *Overview of current indoor navigation techniques and implementation studies*. Retrieved August 15, 2013, from http://www.fig.net/pub/fig2011/papers/ts09a/ts09a_lukianto_sternberg_5102.pdf

Luo, Z., Tan, Z., Ni, Z., & Yen, B. (2007). Analysis of RFID Adoption in China. In *Proceedings of IEEE International Conference on e-Business Engineering*, (pp. 315-318). IEEE.

Luyskens, C., & Loebbecke, C. (2007). RFID Adoption: Theoretical Concepts and Their Practical Application in Fashion. In *Organizational Dynamics of Technology-based Innovation: Diversifying the Research Agenda* (pp. 345–361). Boston: Springer.

Ma, J., Li, X., Tao, X., & Lu, J. (2008). Cluster filtered KNN: A WLAN-based indoor positioning scheme. In *Proceedings of International Symposium on a World of Wireless, Mobile and Multimedia Networks* (pp. 1–8). Academic Press. doi:10.1109/WOWMOM.2008.4594840

Macro, A., & D, . (2012). Using system dynamics to access the impact of RFID technology on retail operations. *International Journal of Production Economics*, *135*(1), 333–344. doi:10.1016/j.ijpe.2011.08.009

Madhavan, J., Bernstein, P. A., & Rahm, E. (2001). Generic Schema Matching with Cupid. In *Proceedings of the 27th International Conference on Very Large Data Bases* (VLDB '01) (pp. 49–58). Morgan Kaufmann Publishers Inc. Retrieved from http://dl.acm.org/citation.cfm?id=645927.672191

Mahatody, T., Sagar, M., & Kolski, C. (2010). State of the Art on the Cognitive Walkthrough Method, Its Variants and Evolutions. *International Journal of Human-Computer Interaction*, *26*(8), 741–785. doi:10.1080/10447311003781409

Maier, K. (2005). A COTS developer's point of view on Radio Frequency Identification. *CompactPCI and AdvancedTCA Systems*, *9*(3), 42–47.

Maloni, M., & DeWolf, F. (2006). *Understanding radio frequency identification (RFID) and its impact on the supply chain*. Penn State Behrend–RFID Center of Excellence.

Mandal, A., Lopes, C. V., Givargis, T., Haghighat, A., Jurdak, R., & Baldi, P. (2005). Beep: 3D indoor positioning using audible sound. In *Proceedings of Second IEEE Consumer Communications and Networking Conference* (pp. 348–353). IEEE. doi:10.1109/CCNC.2005.1405195

Mao, G., Fidan, B., & Anderson, B. D. O. (2007). Wireless sensor network localization techniques. *Computer Networks*, *51*(10), 2529–2553. doi:10.1016/j.comnet.2006.11.018

March, S. T., & Smith, G. F. (1995). Design and natural science research on information technology. *Decision Support Systems*, *15*(4), 251–266. doi:10.1016/0167-9236(94)00041-2

Martinez-Balleste, A., Perez-Martinez, P. A., & Solanas, A. (2013). The pursuit of citizens' privacy: A privacy-aware smart city is possible. *IEEE Communications Magazine*, *51*(6), 136–141. doi:10.1109/MCOM.2013.6525606

Mateen, A., & More, D. (2013). Applying TOC thinking process tools in managing challenges of supply chain finance: A case study. *International Journal of Services and Operations Management.*, *15*(4), 389–410. doi:10.1504/IJSOM.2013.054882

Maurno, D. A. (2005). Going for (Not So) Broke: The True Cost of RFID. *Inbound Logistics, 25*(7).

Mautz, R. (2012). *Indoor positioning technologies*. (Habilitation thesis). ETH Zurich. Retrieved from http://e-collection.library.ethz.ch/eserv/eth:5659/eth-5659-01.pdf

Mautz, R., & Tilch, S. (2011). Survey of optical indoor positioning systems. In *Proceedings of International Conference on Indoor Positioning and Indoor Navigation* (IPIN) (pp. 1–7). IPIN. doi:10.1109/IPIN.2011.6071925

Mautz, R. (2009). Overview of current indoor positioning systems. *Geodesy and Cartography*, *35*(1), 18–22. doi:10.3846/1392-1541.2009.35.18-22

McFarlane, D., & Sheffi, Y. (2003). The impact of automatic identification on supply chain operations. *International Journal of Logistics Management*, *14*(1), 1–17. doi:10.1108/09574090310806503

Mealling, M., & Daniel, R. (2000, September). *RFC2915 "The Naming Authority Pointer (NAPTR) DNS Resource Record"*. Retrieved September 2013 from http://tools.ietf.org/html/rfc2915

Medina, C., Segura, J. C., & De la Torre, Á. (2013). Ultrasound indoor positioning system based on a low-power wireless sensor network providing sub-centimeter accuracy. *Sensors (Basel, Switzerland)*, *13*(3), 3501–3526. doi:10.3390/s130303501 PMID:23486218

Mehrjerdi, Y. Z. S. (2011). RFID and its benefits: A multiple case analysis. *Assembly Automation*, *31*(3), 251–262. doi:10.1108/01445151111150596

Meissner, P., Leitinger, E., Fröhle, M., & Witrisal, K. (2013). Accurate and robust indoor localization systems using ultra-wideband signals. In *Proceedings of European Conference on Navigation* (pp. 1–10). Vienna, Austria: Academic Press. Retrieved from http://arxiv.org/abs/1304.7928

Metzger, C., Thiesse, F., Gershwin, S., & Fleisch, E. (2013). The impact of false-negative reads on the performance of RFID-based shelf inventory control policies. *Computers & Operations Research*, *40*(7), 1864–1873. doi:10.1016/j.cor.2013.02.001

Michael, K., & McCathie, L. (2005). The pros and cons of RFID in supply chain management. In *Proceedings of the International Conference on Mobile Business*, (pp. 623-629). Academic Press.

Michael, K., & Michael, M. G. (2010, 7-9 June). *The diffusion of RFID implants for access control and epayments: A case study on Baja Beach Club in Barcelona*. Paper presented at the IEEE International Symposium on Technology and Society (ISTAS). Wollongong, Australia.

Milner, R. (1978). A theory of type polymorphism in programming. *Journal of Computer and System Sciences*, *17*(3), 348–375. doi:10.1016/0022-0000(78)90014-4

Min, H., Zhou, F., Jui, S. L., Wang, T. Y., & Chen, X. J. (2003). *RFID in China*. Shanghai: Auto-ID Center.

Minami, M., Fukuju, Y., Hirasawa, K., Yokoyama, S., Mizumachi, M., Morikawa, H., & Aoyama, T. (2004). DOLPHIN: A practical approach for implementing a fully distributed indoor ultrasonic positioning system. In N. Davies, E. D. Mynatt, & I. Siio (Eds.), *UbiComp 2004: Ubiquitous Computing* (pp. 347–365). Springer. doi:10.1007/978-3-540-30119-6_21

Ming-Ling Chuang, M. L., & Shaw, W. H. (2007). RFID: Integration Stages in Supply Chain Management. IEEE*Engineering Management Review, 35*(2), 80–87. doi:10.1109/EMR.2007.899757

Min, S., & Mentzer, J. T. (2004). Developing and measuring supply chain management concepts. *Journal of Business Logistics, 25*(1), 63–99. doi:10.1002/j.2158-1592.2004. tb00170.x

Miraz, G. M., Ruiz, I. L., & Gomez-Nieto, M. A. (2009). How NFC can be used for the compliance of European higher education area guidelines in European universities. In *Proceedings of First International Workshop on Near Field Communication* (pp. 3–8). Hagenberg. doi:10.1109/ NFC.2009.9

Mobitec. (2013). *Cuhk epcglobal RFID middleware.* Retrieved from http://mobitec.ie.cuhk.edu.hk/rfid/ middleware/

Mockapetris, P. (1987, November). *RFC1035 Domain Names, Implementation and Specification", Internet Engineering Taskforce - Network Working Group.* Retrieved September 2013, from http://tools.ietf.org/html/rfc1035

Monostori, L., Kemény, Z., Ilie-Zudor, E., Szathmári, M., & Karnok, D. (2009). Increased transparency within and beyond organizational borders by novel identifier-based services for enterprises of different size. *CIRP Annals – Manufacturing Technology, 58*(1), 417–420. DOI: 10.1016/j.cirp.2009.03.086

Moon, K. L., & Ngai, E. W. T. (2008). The adoption of RFID in fashion retailing: a business value-added framework. *Industrial Management + Data Systems, 108*(5), 596-612.

Moon, K. L., & Ngai, E. W. T. (2008). The adoption of RFID in fashion retailing: A business value-added framework. *Industrial Management & Data Systems, 108*(5), 596–612. doi:10.1108/02635570810876732

Morton, S. C., Dainty, A. R. J., Burns, N. D., Brookes, N. J., & Backhouse, C. J. (2006). Managing relationships to improve performance: a case study in the global aerospace industry. *International Journal of Production Research, 44*(16), 3227–3241. doi:10.1080/00207540600577809

Muller-Seitz, G., Dautzenberg, K., Creusen, U., & Stromereder, C. (2009). Customer acceptance of RFID technology: Evidence from the German electronic retail sector. *Journal of Retailing and Consumer Services, 16*(1), 31–39. doi:10.1016/j.jretconser.2008.08.002

Mulliner, C. (2009). Vulnerability analysis and attacks on NFC-enabled mobile phones. In *Proceedings of International Conference on Availability, Reliability and Security* (pp. 695–700). Fukuoka: Academic Press. doi:10.1109/ ARES.2009.46

Muñoz-Organero, M., Muñoz-Merino, P. J., & Kloos, C. D. (2012). Using Bluetooth to implement a pervasive indoor positioning system with minimal requirements at the application level. *Mobile Information Systems, 8*(1), 73–82. doi:10.3233/MIS-2012-0132

Myers, M. D., & Newman, M. (2007). The qualitative interview in IS research: Examining the craft. *Information and Organization, 17*(1), 2–26. doi:10.1016/j. infoandorg.2006.11.001

Nambiar, A. N. (2009). RFID technology: A review of its applications. In *Proceedings of the World Congress on Engineering and Computer Science* (Vol. 2, pp. 1253–1259). San Francisco, CA. Academic Press. Retrieved from http://www.iaeng.org/publication/WCECS2009/ WCECS2009_pp1253-1259.pdf

Naunchan, P., & Sutivong, D. (2007). *Adjustable cost estimation model for COTS-based development.* Paper presented at the 18th Australian Software Engineering Conference (ASWEC). Melbourne, Australia.

Ngai, E. W. T., Moon, K. K. L., Riggins, F. J., & Yi, C. Y. (2008). RFID research: An academic literature review (1995-2005) and future research directions. *International Journal of Production Economics, 112*(2), 510–520. doi:10.1016/j.ijpe.2007.05.004

Ngai, E., Cheng, T., Lai, K. H., Chai, P., Choi, Y., & Sin, R. (2007). Development of an RFID-based traceability system: Experiences and lessons learned from an aircraft engineering company. *Production and Operations Management, 16*(5), 554–568. doi:10.1111/j.1937-5956.2007.tb00280.x

Ngai, E., & Gunasekaran, A. (2009). RFID adoptions: Issues and challenges. *International Journal of Enterprise Information Systems, 5*(1), 1–8. doi:10.4018/jeis.2009010101

Ni, L. M., Liu, Y., Lau, Y. C., & Patil, A. P. (2003). LANDMARC: Indoor location sensing using active RFID. In *Proceedings of the First IEEE International Conference on Pervasive Computing and Communications* (pp. 407–415). Fort Worth, TX: IEEE. doi:10.1109/PERCOM.2003.1192765

O'Connor, M. C. (2004). Ending retail scams with RFID. *RFID Journal*. Retrieved January 27, 2014 from http://www.rfidjournal.com/article/articleview/1260/1/20/

Ondrus, J., & Pigneur, Y. (2005). *A Disruption Analysis in the Mobile Payment Market*. Paper presented at the 38th Annual Hawaii International Conference on System Sciences (HICSS). Wailea, HI.

Ondrus, J., & Pigneur, Y. (2007). *An Assessment of NFC for Future Mobile Payment Systems*. Paper presented at the International Conference on the Management of Mobile Business (ICMB). Toronto, Canada.

Oracle. (2014). *Java Management Extensions (JMX) Technology*. Retrieved from http://www.oracle.com/technetwork/java/javase/tech/javamanagement-140525.html

Ozdenizci, B., Ok, K., Coskun, V., & Aydin, M. N. (2011). Development of an indoor navigation system using NFC technology. In *Proceedings of Fourth International Conference on Information and Computing* (pp. 11 – 14). Phuket Island: Academic Press. doi:10.1109/ICIC.2011.53

Ozelkan, E., & Galambose, A. (2008). When does RFID make business sense for managing supply chains? *International Journal of Information Systems and Supply Chain Management, 1*(1), 15–47. doi:10.4018/jisscm.2008010102

Pacciarelli, D., D'Ariano, A., & Scotto, M. (2011). Applying RFID in warehouse operations of an Italian courier express company. *NETNOMICS: Economic Research and Electronic Networking, 12*(3), 209–222. doi:10.1007/s11066-011-9059-4

Pai, F. Y., & Huang, K. I. (2011). Applying the Technology Acceptance Model to the introduction of healthcare information systems. *Technological Forecasting and Social Change, 78*, 650–660. doi:10.1016/j.techfore.2010.11.007

Palazzi, C., Ceriali, A., & Dal Monte, M. (2009, August). RFID Emulation in Rifidi Environment. In *Proc. of the International Symposium on Ubiquitous Computing* (UCS'09). Beijing, China: UCS.

Pallant, J. (2010). *SPSS Survival Manual*. Open University Press, McGraw-Hill Education.

Palsson, H. (2008). *Using RFID technology captured data to control material flows*. La Jolla, CA: Academic Press.

Pampattiwar, S. (2012). Literature survey on NFC, applications and controller. *International Journal of Scientific and Engineering Research, 3*(2), 1–4. Retrieved from http://www.ijser.org/researchpaper/Literature-Survey-On-NFC-applications-and-controller.pdf

Paperno, E., Sasada, I., & Leonovich, E. (2001). A new method for magnetic position and orientation tracking. *IEEE Transactions on Magnetics, 37*(4), 1938–1940. doi:10.1109/20.951014

Park, B.-N., & Min, H. (2013). Global supply chain barriers of foreign subsidiaries: The case of Korean expatriate manufacturers in China. *International Journal of Services and Operations Management., 15*(1), 67–78. doi:10.1504/IJSOM.2013.050562

Park, N. (2011). Customized healthcare infrastructure using privacy weight level based on smart device. *Convergence and Hybrid Information Technology: Communications in Computer and Information Science, 206*, 467–474. doi:10.1007/978-3-642-24106-2_60

Pedroso, M. C., Zwicker, R., & de Souza, C. A. (2009). RFID adoption: Framework and survey in large Brazilian companies. *Industrial Management & Data Systems, 109*(7), 877–897. doi:10.1108/02635570910982256

Peffers, K., Tuunanen, T., Gengler, C. E., Rossi, M., Hui, W., Virtanen, V., et al. (2006). *The design science research process: A model for producing and presenting information systems research.* Paper presented at the 1st International Conference on Design Science Research in Information Systems and Technology (DERIST). Claremont, CA.

Piramuthu, S. (2012). Vulnerabilities of RFID protocols proposed in ISF. *Information Systems Frontiers, 14*(3), 647–651. doi:10.1007/s10796-010-9291-8

Prabhu, S., Su, X., Ramamurthy, H., Chu, C., & Gadh, R. (2006). *WinRFID –A Middleware for the enablement of Radio Frequency Identification (RFID) based Applications. In Mobile, Wireless and Sensor Networks: Technology, Applications and Future Directions.* John Wiley.

Pramatari, K., & Theotokis, A. (2009). Consumer acceptance of RFID-enabled services: A model of multiple attitudes, perceived system characteristics and individual traits. *European Journal of Information Systems, 18*(6), 541–552. doi:10.1057/ejis.2009.40

Priyantha, N. B. (2005). *The cricket indoor location system.* (Doctoral thesis). Massachusetts Institute of Technology. Retrieved from https://nms.csail.mit.edu/papers/bodhi-thesis.pdf

PRWeb. (2012). Retrieved on April 2014 from http://www.prweb.com/releases/RFID_radio_frequency/identification_technology/prweb9264497.htm

Ramanathan, R., Bentley, Y., & Ko, L. (2012). Investigation of the status of RFID applications in the UK logistics sector. *Logistics & Transport Focus, 14*(11), 45–49.

Ramanathan, R., Ko, L., Chen, H., & Ramanathan, U. (2014). Green characteristics of RFID technologies: An exploration in the UK logistics sector from innovation diffusion perspective. In I. Lee (Ed.), *RFID Technology Integration for Business Performance Improvement.* Academic Press.

Ramanathan, R., Ramanathan, U., & Ko, L. (2013). Adoption of RFID technologies in UK logistics: Moderating roles of size, barcode experience and government support. *Expert Systems with Applications, 41*(1), 230–236.

Rao, H., & Fu, W.-T. (2013). A general framework for a collaborative mobile indoor navigation assistance system. In *Proceedings of the 3rd International Workshop on Location Awareness for Mixed and Dual Reality* (pp. 21–24). Retrieved from http://www.dfki.de/LAMDa/2013/accepted/LAMDa13Proceedings.pdf#page=25

Reel, J. S. (1999). Critical success factors in software projects. *Software, 16*(3), 18–23. doi:10.1109/52.765782

Rekik, Y., Sahin, E., & Dallery, Y. (2008). Analysis of the impact of the RFID technology on reducing product misplacement errors at retail stores. *International Journal of Production Economics, 112*(1), 264–278. doi:10.1016/j.ijpe.2006.08.024

Renaudin, V., Yalak, O., Tome, P., & Merminod, B. (2007). Indoor navigation of emergency agents. *European Journal of Navigation, 5*(3), 36–45. Retrieved from http://infoscience.epfl.ch/record/109915/files/EJN July S-RenaudinLR-Reprint.pdf

Ren, Z., Anumba, C. J., & Tah, J. (2011). RFID-facilitated construction materials management (RFID-CMM) – A case study of water-supply project. *Advanced Engineering Informatics, 25*(2), 198–207. doi:10.1016/j.aei.2010.02.002

Retailers should brace for sharp increase in shoplifting. (2001). *Checkpoint Systems.* [Online]. Retrieved January 23, 2014 from http://retailindustry.about.com/library/bl/q4/bl_rf120401.htm

Retscher, G., Moser, E., Vredeveld, D., & Heberling, D. (2006). Performance and accuracy test of the WLAN indoor positioning system "ipos". In *Proceedings of the 3rd Workshop on Positioning, Navigation and Communication* (pp. 7–16). Retrieved from http://www.wpnc.net/fileadmin/WPNC06/Proceedings/6_Performance_and_Accuracy_Test_of_the_WLAN_Indoor_Positioning_System_IPOS.pdf

Reyes, P. M., & Jaska, P. (2007). Is RFID right for your organization or application? *Management Research News, 30*(8), 570–580. doi:10.1108/01409170710773706

RFID Aspire. (2013). *The AspireRFID project.* Retrieved from http://forge.ow2.org/projects/aspire/

Rhea Wessel. (2010). *Staff Jeans to Introduce RFID-Enabled Customer Services*. Retrieved September, 2013 from http://www.rfidjournal.com/articles/view?7899

Richardson, H. L. (2004). Bar codes are still getting the job done. *Logistics Today, 45*(12), 38–39.

Riedel, J., Pawar, K. S., Torroni, S., & Ferrari, E. (2008). A survey of Rfid awareness and use in the UK logistics industry. In *Dynamics in Logistics* (pp. 105–115). Springer Berlin Heidelberg. doi:10.1007/978-3-540-76862-3_9

Riemenschneider, C., Hardgrave, B., & Armstrong, D. (2007). *Is there a business case for RFID*. Fayetteville, AR: Information Technology Research Institute, Sam M. Walton College of Business, University of Arkansas.

Ringle, C. M., Sven, W., & Alexander, W. (2005). *SmartPLS 2.0*. Retrieved from http://www.smartpls.de

Rishabh, I., Kimber, D., & Adcock, J. (2012). Indoor localization using controlled ambient sounds. In *Proceedings of International Conference on Indoor Positioning and Indoor Navigation* (IPIN) (pp. 1–10). Sydney: IPIN. doi:10.1109/IPIN.2012.6418905

Roach, B. (2005). Origin of the economic order quantity formula: Transcription or transformation? *Management Decision, 43*(9), 1262–1268. doi:10.1108/00251740510626317

Roberti, M. (2005a). Retailers say RFID will take time. *RFID Journal*. Retrieved February 3, 2014 from http://www.rfidjournal.com/article/articleview/1344

Roberti, M. (2005b). Wal-Mart begins RFID process changes. *RFID Journal*. Retrieved February 3, 2014 from http://www.rfidjournal.com/article/articleview/1385/1/20)

Roberti, M. (2005c). Wal-Mart to expand RFID tagging requirement. *RFID Journal*. Retrieved February 3, 2014 from http://rfidjournal.com/article/articleview/1930/1/9/

Roberti, M. (2007). Greater security for RFID tags. *RFID Journal*. Retrieved February 3, 2014 from http://www.rfidjournal.com/blog/entry/2939

Roberti, M. (2010). Wal-Mart relaunches EPC RFID effort, starting with men's jeans and basics. *RFID Journal*. Retrieved September 1, 2013 from http://www.rfidjournal.com/articles/view?7753/

Roberts, C. M. (2006). Radio frequency identification (RFID). *Computers & Security, 25*, 18–26. doi:10.1016/j.cose.2005.12.003

Robinson, L. (2009). *A summary of Diffusion of Innovations*. Available at: htpp://www.enablingchange.com.au/Summary_Diffusion_Theory.pdf

Robles, J. J., Munoz, E. G., De la Cuesta, L., & Lehnert, R. (2012). Performance evaluation of an indoor localization protocol in a 802.15. 4 sensor network. In *Proceedings of International Conference on Indoor Positioning and Indoor Navigation* (IPIN) (pp. 1–10). Sydney: IPIN. doi:10.1109/IPIN.2012.6418936

Rogers, E. M. (1995). *Diffusion of innovations*. New York: Free Press.

Roh, J. J., Kunnathur, A., & Tarafdar, M. (2009). Classification of RFID adoption: An expected benefits approach. *Information & Management, 46*(6), 357–363. doi:10.1016/j.im.2009.07.001

Rong, S. (2004). *Radio Frequency Identification (RFID) and Its Application in the Library*. Hangzhou: The Library of Hangzhou Teacher's College.

Rosenblum, P. (2008). Managing shrink. *Chain Store Age, 84*(1), 72–78.

Rossi, M., Seiter, J., Amft, O., Buchmeier, S., & Trster, G. (2013). RoomSense: An indoor positioning system for smartphones using active sound probing. In *Proceedings of the 4th Augmented Human International Conference* (pp. 89–95). Stuttgart, Germany: Academic Press. doi:10.1145/2459236.2459252

Roussos, G. (2006). Enabling RFID in retail. *Computer, 39*(3), 25–30. doi:10.1109/MC.2006.88

Roussos, G., & Kostakos, V. (2009). RFID in pervasive computing: State-of-the-art and outlook. *Pervasive and Mobile Computing, 5*(1), 110–131. doi:10.1016/j.pmcj.2008.11.004

Rutner, S., Waller, M. A., & Mentzer, J. T. (2004). A Practical Look at RFID. *Supply Chain Management Review, 8*(1), 36–41.

Saab, S. S., & Nakad, Z. S. (2011). A standalone RFID indoor positioning system using passive tags. *IEEE Transactions on Industrial Electronics, 58*(5), 1961–1970. doi:10.1109/TIE.2010.2055774

Saito, W. H. (2011). Our naked data. *The Futurist, 45*(4), 42–25.

Sarac, A., Absi, N., & Dauzère-Pérès, S. (2010). A literature review on the impact of RFID technologies on supply chain management. *International Journal of Production Economics, 128*(1), 77–95.

Sarac, A., Absi, N., & Dauzère-Pérès, S. (2010). A literature review on the impact of RFID technologies on supply chain management. *International Journal of Production Economics, 128*(1), 77–95. doi:10.1016/j.ijpe.2010.07.039

Sarma, S. (2005). A history of the EPC. In S. Garfinkel, & B. Rosenberg (Eds.), *RFID* (pp. 37–55). Upper Saddle River, NJ: Addison-Wesley.

Sarma, S. E., Weis, S. A., & Engels, D. W. (2003). RFID systems and security and privacy implications. In C. Paar (Ed.), *B. S. Kaliski, çetin K. Koç* (pp. 454–469). Cryptographic Hardware and Embedded Systems. doi:10.1007/3-540-36400-5_33

Saxena, M., & Doctor, G. (2008). Radio Frequency Identification (RFID): Applications and Indian Scenario. *The IUP Journal of Information Technology, 4*(3), 72–78.

Sayraflan-Pour, K., & Perez, J. (2007). Robust indoor positioning based on received signal strength. In *Proceedings of 2nd International Conference on Pervasive Computing and Applications* (pp. 693–698). Birmingham, UK: Academic Press. doi:10.1109/ICPCA.2007.4365532

Scanlon, D. P., Swaminathan, S., Lee, W., & Chernew, M. (2008). Does competition improve health care quality? *Health Services Research, 43*(6), 1931–1944. doi:10.1111/j.1475-6773.2008.00899.x PMID:18793214

Scheerens, D. (2012). *Practical indoor localization using Bluetooth.* (Master's thesis). University of Twente. Retrieved from http://essay.utwente.nl/61496/

Scherrer-Rathje, M., Boyle, T. A., & Deflorin, P. (2009). Lean, take two! Reflections from the second attempt at lean implementation. *Business Horizons, 52*(1), 79–85. doi:10.1016/j.bushor.2008.08.004

Schmitt, P., Thiesse, F., & Fleisch, E. (2007). *Adoption and diffusion of RFID technology in the automotive industry.* St. Gallen, Switzerland: 15th European Conference on Information Systems.

Schreibfeder, J. (2008). *Cycle counting can eliminate your annual physical inventory.* Retrieved January 27, 2014 from http://www.effectiveinventory.com/article 9.html

Schuster, T. (2012). *Modellierung, Integration und Analyse von Ressourcen in Geschäftsprozessen* (Vol. 1). Karlsruhe: KIT Scientific Publishing.

Sciore. (1994). Using Semantic Values to Facilitate Interoperability Among Heterogeneous Information Systems. *ACM Transactions on Database Systems, 19*(2).

Seidman, S. J., Brockman, R., Lewis, B. M., Guag, J., Shein, M. J., & Clement, W. J. et al. (2010). In vitro tests reveal sample radio frequency identification readers inducing clinically significant electromagnetic interference to implantable pacemakers and implantable cardioverter-defibrillators. *Heart Rhythm: The Official Journal of the Heart Rhythm Society, 7*(1), 99–107. doi:10.1016/j.hrthm.2009.09.071 PMID:20129290

Sellitto, C., Burgess, S., & Hawking, P. (2007). Information quality attributes associated with RFID-derived benefits in the retail supply chain. *International Journal of Retail & Distribution Management, 35*(1), 69–87. doi:10.1108/09590550710722350

Senger, C., & Kaiser, T. (2006). Indoor positioning with UWB beamforming. In *Proceedings of the 3rd Workshop on Positioning, Navigation and Communication* (pp. 149–158). Retrieved from http://www.wpnc.net/fileadmin/WPNC06/Proceedings/26_Indoor_Positioning_with_UWB_Beamforming.pdf

Sharma, A., & Citurs, A. (2005). Radio Frequency Identification (RFID) Adoption Drivers: A Radical Innovation Adoption Perspective. In *Proceedings of Americas Conference on Information Systems (AMCIS)*, (pp. 1213-1218). AMCIS.

Sharma, A., Citurs, A., & Konsynski, B. (2007). Strategic and Institutional Perspectives in the Adoption and Early Integration of Radio Frequency Identification (RFID). In *Proceedings of 40th Annual Hawaii International Conference on System Sciences.* IEEE.

Shepard, S. (2005). *RFID Radio Frequency Identification.* McGraw-Hall, Inc.

Slettemeås, D. (2009). RFID - the 'next step' in consumer-product relations or Orwellian nightmare? Challenges for research and policy. *Journal of Consumer Policy, 32*(3), 219–244. doi:10.1007/s10603-009-9103-z

Smart, A. U., Bunduchi, R., & Gerst, M. (2010). The costs of adoption of RFID technologies in supply networks. *International Journal of Operations & Production Management, 30*(4), 423–447. doi:10.1108/01443571011029994

Smith, A. A., Smith, A. D., & Baker, D. J. (2011). Inventory management shrinkage and employee anti-theft approaches. *International Journal of Electronic Finance, 5*(3), 209–234. doi:10.1504/IJEF.2011.041337

Smith, A. D. (2005a). Reverse logistics and their affects on CRM and online behavior. *VINE: The Journal of Information and Knowledge Management, 35*(3), 166–181. doi:10.1108/03055720510634216

Smith, A. D. (2005b). Exploring the inherent benefits of RFID and automated self-serve Checkouts in a B2C environment. *International Journal of Business Information Systems, 1*(1-2), 149–183. doi:10.1504/IJBIS.2005.007405

Smith, A. D. (2008). Evolution and acceptability of medical applications of RFID implants among early users of technology. *Health Marketing Quarterly, 24*(1-2), 121–155. doi:10.1080/07359680802125980 PMID:19042524

Smith, A. D. (2009). Marketing and reputation aspects of neonatal safeguards and hospital-security systems. *Health Marketing Quarterly, 26*(2), 117–144. doi:10.1080/07359680802619818 PMID:19408180

Smith, A. D. (2011). Component part quality assurance concerns and standards: Comparison of world-class manufacturers. *Benchmarking: An International Journal, 18*(1), 128–148. doi:10.1108/14635771111109850

Smith, A. D., & Offodile, O. F. (2007). Exploring forecasting and project management characteristics of supply chain management. *International Journal of Logistics and Supply Management, 3*(2), 174–214.

Smith, A. D., & Offodile, O. F. (2008). Gauging web portals impact on supply chain management concepts. *International Journal of Logistics and Management, 4*(2), 184–206.

Smith, A. D., & Offodile, O. F. (2009). The perceived importance of major RFID-related technology initiatives among retail store managers. *International Journal of Services and Operations Management, 5*(4), 520–547. doi:10.1504/IJSOM.2009.024583

Smith, A. D., & Rupp, W. T. (2013a). Supply supplier integration, procurement, and outsourcing: Case study of SCM social capital benefits. *International Journal of Logistics Systems and Management, 14*(2), 221–241. doi:10.1504/IJLSM.2013.051340

Smith, A. D., & Rupp, W. T. (2013b). Data quality and knowledge/information management in service operations management: Regional supermarket case study. *International Journal of Knowledge-Based Organizations, 3*(3), 35–52. doi:10.4018/ijkbo.2013070103

Smithson, S., & Hirschheim, R. (1998). Analysing information systems evaluation: Another look at an old problem. *European Journal of Information Systems, 7*(3), 158–174. doi:10.1057/palgrave.ejis.3000304

Sneed, H. M. (2005). *Software-Projektkalkulation: Praxiserprobte Methoden der Aufwandsschätzung für verschiedene Projektarten.* Hanser.

Snyder, N. H., Broome, O. W., Kehoe, W. J., McIntyre, J. T., & Blair, K. E. (1991). *Reducing Employee Theft.* New York, NY: Quorum Books.

Song, B. (2013). Privacy issues in RFID. In A. Miri (Ed.), *Advanced Security and Privacy for RFID Technologies* (pp. 126–138). Hershey, PA: Information Science Reference. doi:10.4018/978-1-4666-3685-9.ch008

Soon, C.-B., & Gutiérrez, J. A. (2008). Effects of the RFID mandate on supply chain management. *The Journal of Theoretical and Applied Electronic Commerce Research, 3*(1), 81–91.

Sources: Target investigating data breach. (2013). *Krebs on Security.* Retrieved January 29, 2014 from http://krebsonsecurity.com/2013/12/sources-target-investigating-data-breach/

Sowa, J. (2000). *Knowledge representation*. Pacific Grove, CA: Brooks Cole Publishing Co.

Spekman, R., & Sweeney, P. (2006). RFID: From concept to implementation. *International Journal of Physical Distribution & Logistics Management, 36*(10), 736–754. doi:10.1108/09600030610714571

Storms, W. F. (2009). *Magnetic field aided indoor navigation*. (Master's thesis). Air Force Institute of Technology, Air University. Retrieved from http://www.dtic.mil/cgi-bin/GetTRDoc?Location=U2&doc=GetTRDoc.pdf&AD=ADA497156

Straube, F. (2009). *RFID in der Logistik - Empfehlungen für eine erfolgreiche Einführung*. TU Berlin, Univ.-Bibliothek.

Strueker, J., & Gille, D. (2008). *The SME Way of Adopting RFID Technology: Empirical Findings from a German Cross-Sectoral Study*. Paper presented at the 16th European Conference on Information Systems (ECIS). Galway, Ireland.

Subhan, F., Hasbullah, H., Rozyyev, A., & Bakhsh, S. T. (2011). Indoor positioning in bluetooth networks using fingerprinting and lateration approach. In *Proceedings of International Conference on Information Science and Applications* (pp. 1–9). Jeju Island: Academic Press. doi:10.1109/ICISA.2011.5772436

Summers, G. J., & Scherpereel, C. M. (2008). Decision making in product development: Are you outside-in or inside-out? *Management Decision, 46*(9), 1299–1314. doi:10.1108/00251740810911957

Sundmaeker, H., Guillemin, P., Friess, P., & Woelffl, S. (2010, March). *Vision and Challenges for Realizing the Internet of Things*. Academic Press. doi:10.2759/26127

Swaminathan, S., Chernew, M., & Scanlon, D. P. (2008). Persistence of HMO performance measures. *Health Services Research, 43*(6), 2033–2051. doi:10.1111/j.1475-6773.2008.00890.x PMID:18783460

Swedberg, C. (2009). Tennessee hospital tracks high-value items. *RFID Journal*. Retrieved February 20, 2014 from http://www.rfidjournal.com/articles/view?5106

Sweeney, P. J. (2005). *RFID for dummies*. Indianapolis, IN: Wiley Publishing.

Szmerekovsky, J. S., & Zhang, J. (2008). Coordination and adoption of item-level RFID with vendor managed inventory. *International Journal of Production Economics, 114*(1), 388–398. doi:10.1016/j.ijpe.2008.03.002

Tajima, M. (2007). Strategic value of RFID in supply chain management. *Journal of Purchasing & Supply Chain Management, 13*(4), 261–273. doi:10.1016/j.pursup.2007.11.001

Talluri, S., Chung, W., & Narasimhan, R. (2006). An optimization model for phased supplier integration into e-procurement systems. *IIE Transactions, 38*(5), 389–399. doi:10.1080/07408170500306554

Tang, L. L., & Tsai, W. C. (2009). *RFID adoption model for Taiwan's logistics service providers*. Taiwan: Graduate School of Management, Yuan Ze University.

Tari, J. J., & Sabater, V. (2004). Quality tools and techniques: Are they necessary for quality management? *International Journal of Production Economics, 92*(3), 267–280. doi:10.1016/j.ijpe.2003.10.018

Thiesse, F. (2005). *Architektur und Integration von RFID-Systemen*. Institut für Technologiemanagement, Universität St. Gallen.

Thiesse, F. (2007). RFID, privacy and the perception of risk: A strategic framework. *The Journal of Strategic Information Systems, 16*, 214–232. doi:10.1016/j.jsis.2007.05.006

Thiesse, F., Al-Kassab, J., & Fleisch, E. (2009). Understanding the value of integrated RFID systems: A case study from apparel retail. *European Journal of Information Systems, 18*(6), 592–614. doi:10.1057/ejis.2009.33

Thiesse, F., & Condea, C. (2009). RFID data sharing in supply chains: What is the value of the EPC network? *International Journal of Electronic Business, 7*(1), 21–43. doi:10.1504/IJEB.2009.023607

Thiesse, F., & Gross, S. (2006). Integration von RFID in die betriebliche IT-Landschaft. *Wirtschaftsinformatik, 48*(3), 178–187. doi:10.1007/s11576-006-0041-y

Thiesse, F., Staake, T., Schmitt, P., & Fleisch, E. (2011). The rise of the "next-generation bar code": an international RFID adoption study, *Supply Chain Management. International Journal (Toronto, Ont.), 16*(5), 328–345.

Tilch, S., & Mautz, R. (2011). CLIPS proceedings. In *Proceedings of International Conference on Indoor Positioning and Indoor Navigation* (IPIN) (pp. 1–6). IPIN. doi:10.1109/IPIN.2011.6071937

Ting, S. L., Kwok, S. K., Tsang, A. H. C., & Lee, W. B. (2011). Critical elements and lessons learnt from the implementation of an RFID-enabled healthcare management system in a medical organization. *Journal of Medical Systems*, *35*(4), 657–669. doi:10.1007/s10916-009-9403-5 PMID:20703523

Tiwari, A., Turner, C., & Sackett, P. (2007). A framework for implementing cost and quality practices within manufacturing. *Journal of Manufacturing Technology Management*, *18*(6), 731–760. doi:10.1108/17410380710763886

Toffaletti, S., & Soldatos, J. (2014). *RFID-ROI-SME Project Promises Big Help for Small Business*. Retrieved February, 2014 from http://www.rfidjournal.com/articles/view?7661

Tornatzky, L. G., & Klein, K. J. (1982). Innovation Characteristics and Innovation Adoption Implementation: A Meta-Analysis of Findings. *IEEE Transactions on Engineering Management*, *EM-29*(1), 28–45. doi:10.1109/TEM.1982.6447463

TraSer Project Consortium. (2006). *TraSer official project website*. Retrieved from http://www.traser-project.eu/

Trigony, N. (2012). *Challenges and approaches to improving the accuracy of indoor positioning systems*. Retrieved August 28, 2013, from http://talks.cam.ac.uk/talk/index/40689

Trunick, P. A. (2005). Where's the ROI for RFID? *Logistics Today*, *46*(1), 10–11.

Tsai, F.-M., & Huang, C.-M. (2012). *Cost-Benefit Analysis of Implementing RFID System in Port of Kaohsiung*. Paper presented at the International Conference on Asia Pacific Business Innovation and Technology Management (APBITM). Pattaya, Thailand.

Tsoulfas, G. T., & Pappis, C. P. (2006). Environmental principles applicable to supply chains design and operation. *Journal of Cleaner Production*, *14*(18), 1593–1602. doi:10.1016/j.jclepro.2005.05.021

Twist, D. C. (2005). The impact of radio frequency identification on supply chain facilities. *Journal of Facilities Management*, *3*(3), 226–239. doi:10.1108/14725960510808491

Tzeng, S.-F., Chen, W.-H., & Pai, F.-Y. (2008). Evaluating the business value of RFID: Evidence from five case studies. *International Journal of Production Economics*, *112*(2), 601–613. doi:10.1016/j.ijpe.2007.05.009

Uckelmann, D. (2012). Performance Measurement and Cost Benefit Analysis for RFID and Internet of Things Implementations in Logistics. In D. Uckelmann (Ed.), *Quantifying the Value of RFID and the EPCglobal Architecture Framework in Logistics* (pp. 71–100). Berlin, Germany: Springer. doi:10.1007/978-3-642-27991-1_4

Uckun, C., Karaesmen, F., & Savas, S. (2008). Investment in improved inventory accuracy in a decentralized supply chain. *International Journal of Production Economics*, *113*(2), 546–566. doi:10.1016/j.ijpe.2007.10.012

UN/ECE. (2003). *Core Component Technical Specification*. Retrieved from http://www.unece.org/fileadmin/DAM/cefact/codesfortrade/CCTS/CCTS_V2-01_Final.pdf, retrieved 2013-09-14

Ustundag, A. (2010). Evaluating RFID investment on a supply chain using tagging cost sharing factor. *International Journal of Production Research*, *48*(9), 2549–2562. doi:10.1080/00207540903564926

Ustundag, A., & Tanyas, M. (2009). The impacts of radio frequency identification (RFID) technology on supply chain costs. *Transportation Research Part E, Logistics and Transportation Review*, *45*(1), 29–38. doi:10.1016/j.tre.2008.09.001

van Blommestein, F. B. E. (2014). *Structured Communication for Dynamic Business*. (PhD thesis). University of Groningen. Retrieved from http://www.flowcanto.com/thesis.pdf

Vargas, M. (2000). *Theft: Retail's real Grinch*. Retrieved January 23, 2014 from http://retailindustry.about.com/od/statistics_loss_prevention/l/aa001122a.htm

Vargas, M. (2002). *Retail theft and inventory shrinkage*. Retrieved January 23, 2014 from http://retailindustry.about.com/od/statistics_loss_prevention/l/aa021126a.htm

Vazquez-Briseno, M., Hirata, F. I., Sanchez-Lopez, J. de D., Jimenez-Garcia, E., Navarro-Cota, C., & Nieto-Hipolito, J. I. (2012). Using RFID/NFC and QR-code in mobile phones to link the physical and the digital world. In I. Deliyannis (Ed.), *Interactive Multimedia* (pp. 219–242). InTech. doi:10.5772/37447

Veeramani, D., Tang, J., & Alfonso Gutierrez, A. (2008). A framework for assessing the value of RFID implementation by tier-one suppliers to major retailers. *The* Journal of Theoretical and Applied Electronic Commerce Research, *3*(1), 55–70.

Vicent, J. P. A. (2013). *WiFi indoor positioning for mobile devices, an application for the UJI smart campus.* (Master's thesis). Repositorio Universidade Nova. Retrieved from http://hdl.handle.net/10362/9193

Vigder, M. R., & Dean, J. (1997). *An architectural approach to building systems from COTS software components.* Paper presented at the Conference of the Centre for Advanced Studies on Collaborative Research (CASCON). Toronto, Canada.

Vijayaraman, B. S., & Osyk, B. A. (2006). An empirical study of RFID implementation in the warehousing industry. *International Journal of Logistics Management, 17*(1), 6–20. doi:10.1108/09574090610663400

Violino, B. (2013). Marks & Spencer rolls out RFID to all its stores. *RFID Journal.* Retrieved May 4, 2013, from http://www.rfidjournal.com/articles/view?10536

Visich, J. K., Li, S., & Khumawala, B. M. (2007). Enhancing product recovery value in closed-loop supply chains with RFID. *Journal of Managerial Issues, 19*(3), 436–452.

Visich, J. K., Li, S., Khumawala, B. M., & Reyes, P. M. (2009). Empirical evidence of RFID impacts on supply chain performance. *International Journal of Operations & Production Management, 29*(12), 1290–1315. doi:10.1108/01443570911006009

Vlachos, I. P. (2013). (Article in Press). A hierarchical model of the impact of RFID practices on retail supply chain performance. *Expert Systems with Applications.* doi:10.1016/j.eswa.2013.07.006

Vojdani, N., Spitznagel, J., & Resch, S. (2006). Konzeption einer systematischen Identifikation und Bewertung von RFID-Einsatzpotenzialen. *Zeitschrift für wirtschaftlichen Fabrikbetrieb, 3,* 102-108.

Vollmann, S. (1990). *Aufwandsschätzung im Software engineering: Neue Verfahren und Arbeitshilfen.* Vaterstetten bei München: IWT-Verl.

W3C. (2004). *XML Schema Part 2: Datatypes Second Edition, 2004.* Retrieved from http://www.w3.org/TR/xmlschema-2/

Waldmann, B., Weigel, R., Ebelt, R., & Vossiek, M. (2012). An ultra wideband local positioning system for highly complex indoor environments. In *Proceedings of International Conference on Localization and GNSS* (pp. 1–5). GNSS. doi:10.1109/ICL-GNSS.2012.6253125

Wamba, S. F. (2012). Achieving supply chain integration using RFID technology: The case of emerging intelligent B-to-B e-commerce processes in a living laboratory. *Business Process Management Journal, 18*(1), 58–81. doi:10.1108/14637151211215019

Wamba, S. F. (2012). RFID-enabled healthcare applications, issues and benefits: An archival analysis (1997-2011). *Journal of Medical Systems, 36*(6), 3393–3398. doi:10.1007/s10916-011-9807-x PMID:22109670

Wamba, S. F., Lefebvre, L. A., & Bendavid, Y., & Lefebvre, Él. (2008). Exploring the impact of RFID technology and the EPC network on mobile B2B eCommerce: A case study in the retail industry. *International Journal of Production Economics, 112*(2), 614–629. doi:10.1016/j.ijpe.2007.05.010

Wang, C., Wu, H., & Tzeng, N.-F. (2007). RFID-based 3-D positioning schemes. In *Proceedings of 26th IEEE International Conference on Computer Communications* (pp. 1235–1243). Anchorage, AK: IEEE. doi:10.1109/INFCOM.2007.147

Wang, C.-S., Huang, C.-H., Chen, Y.-S., & Zheng, L.-J. (2009). An implementation of positioning system in indoor environment based on active RFID. In Proceedings of 2009 Joint Conferences on Pervasive Computing (pp. 71–76). Academic Press. doi:10.1109/JCPC.2009.5420212

Wang, F., & Liu, P. (2005). Temporal management of RFID data. In *Proceeding of the Very Large Data Bases Conferences* (VLDB05), (pp. 1128-1139). VLDB.

Wang, H., & Jia, F. (2007). A hybrid modeling for WLAN positioning system. In *Proceedings of International Conference on Wireless Communications, Networking and Mobile Computing* (pp. 2152–2155). Shanghai: Academic Press. doi:10.1109/WICOM.2007.537

Wang, J. L., & Loui, M. C. (2009). Privacy and ethical issues in location-based tracking systems. In *Proceedings of the 2009 IEEE International Symposium on Technology and Society*. IEEE.

Wang, L. E. (2012). *iNavigation: An image based indoor navigation system*. (Master's thesis). Auckland University of Technology. Retrieved from http://hdl.handle.net/10292/4743

Wang, L.C. (2008). Enhancing construction quality inspection and management using RFID technology. *Automation in Construction, 17*(4), 467–479.

Wang, S., Liu, S., & Wang, W. (2008). The simulated impact of RFID-enabled supply chain on pull-based inventory replenishment in TFT-LCD industry. *International Journal of Production Economics, 112*(2), 570–586. doi:10.1016/j.ijpe.2007.05.002

Wang, Y. M., Wang, Y. S., & Yang, Y. F. (2010). Understanding the determinants of RFID adoption in the manufacturing industry. *Technological Forecasting and Social Change, 77*(5), 803–815. doi:10.1016/j.techfore.2010.03.006

Want, R. (2006). An introduction to RFID technology. *Pervasive Computing, 5*(1), 25–33. doi:10.1109/MPRV.2006.2

Want, R., Hopper, A., Falcão, V., & Gibbons, J. (1992). The active badge location system. *ACM Transactions on Information Systems, 10*(1), 91–102. doi:10.1145/128756.128759

Weinstein, R. (2005). RFID: A technical overview and its application to the enterprise. *IT Professional, 7*(3), 27–33. doi:10.1109/MITP.2005.69

Wharton, C., Bradford, J., Jeffries, R., & Franzke, M. (1992). *Applying cognitive walkthroughs to more complex user interfaces: Experiences, issues, and recommendations*. Paper presented at the SIGCHI Conference on Human Factors in Computing Systems. Monterey, CA.

Wharton, C. (1992). *Cognitive walkthroughs: Instructions, forms, and examples*. University of Colorado.

Wharton, C., Rieman, J., Lewis, C., & Polson, P. (1994). The cognitive walkthrough method: A practitioner's guide. In J. Nielsen, & R. Mack (Eds.), *Usability inspection methods* (pp. 105–140). New York: John Wiley & Sons.

Whitaker, J., Mithas, S., & Krishnan, M. S. (2007). A field study of RFID deployment and return expectations. *Production and Operations Management, 16*(5), 599–612. doi:10.1111/j.1937-5956.2007.tb00283.x

Wicks, A. M., Visich, J. K., & Li, S. H. (2006). Radio frequency identification applications in hospital environments. *Hospital Topics: Research and Perspectives on Healthcare, 84*(3), 3–8. doi:10.3200/HTPS.84.3.3-9 PMID:16913301

Wieczorrek, H. W., & Mertens, P. (2011). *Tipps und Tricks für Leiter von IT-Projekten Management von IT-Projekten* (pp. 297–306). Berlin, Germany: Springer.

Wierenga, J., & Komisarczuk, P. (2005). SIMPLE: Developing a LBS positioning solution. In *Proceedings of the 4th International Conference on Mobile and Ubiquitous Multimedia* (pp. 48–55). Academic Press. doi:10.1145/1149488.1149497

Wilson, J. M. (1995). Quality control methods in cycle counting for record accuracy management. *International Journal of Operations & Production Management, 15*(7), 27–38. doi:10.1108/01443579510090390

Wong, K. H. M., Hui, P. C. L., & Chan, A. C. K. (2006). Cryptography and authentication on RFID passive tags for apparel products. *Computers in Industry, 57*(4), 342–349. doi:10.1016/j.compind.2005.09.002

Wong, W. K., Zeng, X. H., Au, W. M. R., Mok, P. Y., & Leung, S. Y. S. (2009). A fashion mix-and-match expert system for fashion retailers using fuzzy screening approach. *Expert Systems with Applications, 36*(2), 1750–1764. doi:10.1016/j.eswa.2007.12.047

Woodman, O. J., & Harle, R. K. (2010). Concurrent scheduling in the active bat location system. In *Proceedings of 8th IEEE International Conference on Pervasive Computing and Communications Workshops* (pp. 431–437). Mannheim, Germany: IEEE. doi:10.1109/PERCOMW.2010.5470631

WS-i. (2006). *Webservice Interoperability Organisation Basic Profile Version 1.1 Final Material 2006-04-10.* Retrieved from http://www.ws-i.org/profiles/basicprofile-1.1.html

Wyld, D. C. (2006). RFID 101: The next big thing for management. *Management Research News, 29*(4), 154–173. doi:10.1108/01409170610665022

Xiao, J., Liu, Z., Yang, Y., Liu, D., & Han, X. (2011). Comparison and analysis of indoor wireless positioning techniques. In *Proceedings of International Conference on Computer Science and Service System* (pp. 293–296). Nanjing: Academic Press. doi:10.1109/CSSS.2011.5972088

Yang, Y., Boehm, B., & Wu, D. (2006). *COCOTS risk analyzer.* Paper presented at the 5th International Conference on Commercial-off-the-Shelf (COTS)-Based Software Systems. Orlando, FL.

Yao, A., & Carlson, J. (1999). The impact of real-time data communication on inventory management. *International Journal of Production Economics, 59*(1), 213–219. doi:10.1016/S0925-5273(98)00234-5

Yao, W., Chu, C.-H., & Li, Z. (2012). The adoption and implementation of RFID Technologies in healthcare: A literature review. *Journal of Medical Systems, 36*(6), 3507–3525. doi:10.1007/s10916-011-9789-8 PMID:22009254

Ye, R. (2012). *Ultra-wideband indoor localization systems.* (Doctoral thesis). Oregon State University. Retrieved from http://scholarsarchive.library.oregonstate.edu/xmlui/handle/1957/30349

Yick, J., Mukherjee, B., & Ghosal, D. (2008). Wireless sensor network survey. *Computer Networks, 52*(12), 2292–2330. doi:10.1016/j.comnet.2008.04.002

Yi, L., & Thomas, H. R. (2007). A review of research on the environmental impact of e-business and ICT. *Environment International, 33*(6), 841–849. doi:10.1016/j.envint.2007.03.015 PMID:17490745

Yin, R. K. (2009). *Case Study Research: Design and Methods* (4th ed.). Los Angeles, CA: Sage Publications Inc.

Yüksel, M. E., & Yüksel, A. S. (2011). RFID Technology in business systems and supply chain management. *Journal of Economic and Social Studies, 1*(1), 53–71. doi:10.14706/JECOSS11115

Yun, S., Lee, J., Chung, W., Kim, E., & Kim, S. (2009). A soft computing approach to localization in wireless sensor networks. *Expert Systems with Applications, 36*(4), 7552–7561. doi:10.1016/j.eswa.2008.09.064

Zafeiropoulos, A., Papaioannou, I., Solidakis, E., Konstantinou, N., Stathopoulos, P., & Mitrou, N. (2010). Exploiting Bluetooth for deploying indoor LBS over a localisation infrastructure independent architecture. *International Journal of Computer Aided Engineering and Technology, 2*(2), 145–163. doi:10.1504/IJCAET.2010.030542

Zang, C., & Fan, Y. (2007). Complex event processing in enterprise information systems based on RFID. *Enterprise Information Systems, 1*(1), 3–23. doi:10.1080/17517570601092127

Zare Mehrjerdi, Y. (2008). RFID-enabled systems: A brief review. *Assembly Automation, 28*(3), 235–245. doi:10.1108/01445150810889493

Zare Mehrjerdi, Y. (2011). RFID adoption: A systems thinking perspective through profitability engagement. *Assembly Automation, 31*(2), 182–187. doi:10.1108/01445151111117773

Zeilenga, K. (2006, June). *RFC4510 "Lightweight Directory Access Protocol (LDAP): Technical Specification Road-map".* Retrieved September 2013, from http://tools.ietf.org/html/rfc4510

Zhang, H. (2009). *An investigation of the relationships between lines of code and defects.* Paper presented at the 25th International Conference on Software Maintenance (ICSM). Edmonton, Canada.

Zhang, L., Wen, H., Li, D., Fu, Z., & Cui, S. (2010). E-learning adoption intention and its key influence factors based on innovation adoption theory. *Mathematical and Computer Modelling, 51*(11-12), 1428–1432. doi:10.1016/j.mcm.2009.11.013

Zhou, W., & Piramuthu, S. (2013). Technology regulation policy for business ethics: An example of RFID in supply chain management. *Journal of Business Ethics, 116*(2), 327–340. doi:10.1007/s10551-012-1474-4

Zinkiewicz, D. (2012). *Indoor navigation based on cloud computing*. Retrieved August 26, 2013, from http://ec.europa.eu/digital-agenda/events/cf/ictpd12/document.cfm?doc_id=23009

Zuo, Y. (2012). Survivability experiment and attack characterization of RFID. *IEEE Transactions on Dependable and Secure Computing, 9*(2), 289–302. doi:10.1109/TDSC.2011.30

About the Contributors

In Lee is a professor in the School of Computer Sciences at the College of Business and Technology at Western Illinois University (WIU) in the United States. He is the recipient of the 2013 Provost's Award for Academic Excellence in Scholarly Activities and a three-time winner of the Research Excellence Award in the College of Business and Technology at WIU. He is also a best paper winner and invited speaker at various conferences. He was a Keimyung Global Scholar during his sabbatical in 2009. He is the founding Editor-in-Chief of the International Journal of E-Business Research. He has published his research in such journals as *Journal of Small Business Management, Management Decision, Business Horizons, International Small Business Journal, Communications of the ACM, IEEE Transactions on Systems, Man and Cybernetics, IEEE Transactions on Engineering Management, International Journal of Production Research, Computers and Education, Decision Support Systems, Computers and Operations Research, International Journal of Production Economics, Knowledge and Process Management, Computers in Human Behavior, Business Process Management Journal, Computers and Industrial Engineering,* and others. Prior to his academic career, he worked for a number of multinational corporations, as well as served as a consultant for various government agencies and private organizations. His current research interests include social media, social enterprise, Web technology development and management, investment strategies for computing technologies, and mobile services. He received his BBA from Keimyung University in South Korea, MBA from the University of Texas at Austin, and PhD in Business Administration from the University of Illinois at Urbana-Champaign in the United States.

* * *

Michael Adeyeye is a Senior Research Fellow at the Cape Peninsula University of Technology, South Africa and a Research Associate at the University of Cape Town, South Africa, where he earned his second Masters and PhD degrees. His research interests include Web and multimedia service mobility technologies and context awareness, multimodal and multi-channel access, Web 2.0 and mobile applications, and Next Generation Network (NGN) applications and services. He is a member of the IEEE.

Edward T. Chen is a Professor of Management Information Systems of Operations in the Information Systems Department at the Manning School of Business at University of Massachusetts Lowell. Dr. Chen has published over sixty refereed research articles in scholarly journals such as *Information & Management, Journal of Computer Information Systems, Project Management, Comparative Technology Transfer and Society, Journal of International Technology and Information Management, International Journal of Innovation and Learning,* etc. Dr. Chen has served as vice-president, board director, track chair, and session chair of many professional associations and conferences. Professor Chen has also served as journal editor, editorial reviewer, and ad hoc reviewer for various academic journals. Dr. Chen has received the Irwin Distinguished Paper Award at the Southwestern Federation of Administrative Disciplines conference and the Best Paper Award at the International Conference on Accounting and Information Technology. His main research interests are in the areas of Project Management, Knowledge Management, Agile Software Development, and Green IT.

Hsin Chen is a lecturer in the Business Systems Department at Bedfordshire University, UK. She received her PhD from Brunel University in the UK. She has been involved in a number of UK funded research projects with an emphasis on entrepreneurship and Small and Medium Size Enterprises (SMEs). Her research interests include the adoption and impact of integration technologies, small business management, Social network, entrepreneurship, and e-commerce. She has published over twenty-five papers in refereed journals, books and international conference proceedings.

H. H. Cheung gained his BEng, MPhil, and PhD degrees from the IMSE Department at the University of Hong Kong. He is a member of the Hong Kong Computer Society, and has worked as a consultant in the RFID industry. Dr. Cheung has participated in a number of industrial RFID application projects in China and Hong Kong, including RFID-based systems for anti-counterfeiting of wine products, cattle meat processing management, logistics management of a global printing enterprise, government project asset management, and luggage management of a major international airport. Dr. Cheung has also substantial experience in development of IT software solutions. His research interests include Internet of Things technology, RFID applications, data mining, and virtual prototyping technology.

S. H. Choi is associate professor in the Department of Industrial and Manufacturing Systems Engineering at the University of Hong Kong. He gained both his BSc and PhD degrees in Mechanical Engineering at the University of Birmingham in the UK. Dr. Choi worked in the computer industry as CADCAM consultant before joining the University of Hong Kong. He has undertaken a number of industrial projects, and his current research interests focus mainly on computer applications in various areas, including e-commerce, CADCAM, advanced manufacturing systems, virtual prototyping, and RFID technology. Dr. Choi has extensive teaching experience at both the undergraduate and postgraduate levels, as well as a wide range of publications on his research work.

Tobias Engel is a PhD candidate at the chair for information systems since March 2011. He has over six years of industry experience with a focus in logistics management in the automotive industry. He graduated from the University of Applied Science Gießen-Friedberg as Dipl.-Logistiker (FH) in 2004 and has a MBA degree from the Technische Universität München. His research interest lies in the area of information visibility and its contribution towards value creation in supply chains. He has presented his work in international conferences such as the European Conference on Information Systems.

Andreas Englschalk is an undergraduate student of business administration at Ludwig-Maximilian-Universität München. His research interest lies in the area of information sharing in supply chains. As a student assistant at the Chair for Information Systems at Technische Universität München, he co-authored a publication at the Hawaii International Conference on System Sciences.

Suparna Goswami is a Research Fellow at the Technische Universität München, Germany. She holds a PhD in Information Systems from the National University of Singapore. Her research interests lie in the areas of Web 2.0 technologies and their implications, topics in human-computer interaction and digitally enabled inter-organizational networks. Her research has been published in premium journals such as the *Journal of Association of Information Systems, ACM Transactions on CHI, Journal of Database Management*, and *AIS Transactions on HCI*. She has presented her work in international conferences such as, International Conference on Information Systems, European Conference on Information Systems, the Academy of Management Annual Meeting, and the Pacific Asia Conference on Information Systems. She regularly serves in the program committees of conferences such as ICIS, ECIS, Pre-ICIS SIGHCI, WEB, and in the editorial board of AIS Transactions on HCI.

M. Hemalatha completed her MSc, MCA, MPhil, PhD (PhD, Mother Terasa women's University, Kodaikanal). She is a Professor and Head guiding PhD Scholars in the Department of Computer Science at Karpagam University, Coimbatore. She has twelve years of experience in teaching and published around one hundred and fifty papers in International Journals and also presented more than a hundred papers in various national and international conferences. She received the best researcher award in the year 2012, from Karpagam University. Her research areas include data mining, image processing, computer networks, cloud computing, software engineering, bioinformatics, and neural network. She is a reviewer in several national and international journals.

David Karnok is a research assistant, PhD student, and software developer/architect at the Engineering and Management Intelligence research laboratory at the Institute for Computer Science and Control at the Hungarian Academy of Sciences. He has a masters degree in mechanical engineering with the specialization in computer science and applications. David was involved in the EU funded project AD-VANCE and contributes to novel open-source projects such as RxJava. His present research focuses on ensuring the past- and future transparency of manufacturing process execution through data mining and the applicability of type-theory and lambda-calculus for process inference therein.

Nikolaos Kefalakis holds a Diploma in Electronic Computing Systems from the TEI of Piraeus, an MSc in Information Technology and Telecommunications from the AIT (Athens Information Technology) and is currently a PhD candidate at the Aalborg University of Denmark. Since February 2008, he has been working as a research scientist in the AGC Group of AIT where he has been involved in FP7 research projects. Specifically in the context of ASPIRE and OpenIoT FP7 projects, he is the manager, system architect, and developer lead of the AspireRFID OS project (http://wiki.aspire.objectweb.org/) and OpenIoT OS project (https://github.com/OpenIotOrg/openiot). Mr. Kefalakis' main area of technical expertise is Auto-ID Technologies (RFID, Barcodes...), Semantic Sensor Networks, Multitier architecture systems, RCP applications, Enterprise Systems, and Embedded and Electronics digital systems.

Zsolt Kemény received both his MSc in computer science and PhD in robot control at the Budapest University of Technology and Economics, in 1998 and 2004, respectively. In addition, to motion planning of mobile and redundant robots, his fields of interest include ontologies and topic maps, and recently, identity-based tracking and tracing. In 2003, he joined the Institute for Computer Science and Control of the Hungarian Academy of Sciences (MTA SZTAKI), and is, since 2004, senior researcher at the Laboratory of Engineering and Management Intelligence at the institute.

Lok Wan Lorraine Ko is currently a Far East Buyer, who is specialised in Supply Chain management at Staples Promotional Products Europe Ltd. She focuses on Far East projects collaborating with a large number of Chinese suppliers. Her role within the firm includes all aspects of the supply chain, sourcing, negotiating, project management, QC inspection and logistics. She was born in Hong Kong and lives in the UK. She holds an MSc in Operations Management from the University of Nottingham, and a BSc (Hon) in Logistics from Aston University, Birmingham. She is the author of two articles on the RFID adoption and application: "Adoption of RFID technologies in UK logistics: Investigation of the status of RFID applications in the UK logistics sector" (2013) and "Moderating roles of size, barcode experience and government support" (2014), in cooperation with Professor Ramakrishnan Ramanathan, Dr Usha Ramanathan, and Dr Yongmei Bentley. They are also the authors of many published articles on issues relating to Operations Management and Information Systems.

Helmut Kremar is a Full Professor of Information Systems and holds the Chair for Information Systems at the Department of Informatics, Technische Universität München, Germany, since 2002. He worked as a Postdoctoral Fellow at the IBM Los Angeles Scientific Center, as an Assistant Professor of Information Systems at the Leonard Stern School of Business, New York University, and at Baruch College, City University of New York. From 1987 to 2002, he was Chair for Information Systems, Hohenheim University, Stuttgart. His research interests include information and knowledge management, IT-enabled value webs, service management, computer-supported cooperative work, and information systems in health care and e-government.

A. Anny Leema earned her Bachelors of Computer science from Fatima College, Madurai in 1997. She received her Masters of Computer Applications from Bharathidasan University in 2002, and MPhil from Madurai Kamaraj University in 2004. In 2010, she joined the doctoral program in Computer Science at the Karpagam University, Coimbatore under the guidance of Dr. M. Hemalatha and awarded PhD in the year 2014. She is working as an Assistant Professor (Sr.Grade) in the Department of Computer Applications, B.S.Abdur Rahman University, Chennai. Currently she is guiding five PhD Scholars at B. S. Abdur Rahman University. She has sixteen years of experience in teaching and published eighteen papers in International Journals, two in National Journals, and a Chapter in a Book titled Computer Networks & Communications (NetCom). She also presented twenty three papers in National/ International conferences and attended several workshops/FDPs. Her research areas include Data Mining, Cloud Computing, RFID and Opinion Mining. She is a reviewer in national and international journals.

Konstantinos Mourtzoukos holds a Diploma in Electrical and Computer Engineering from the National Technical University of Athens and an MSc in Information Networking from the Carnegie Mellon University. Mr. Konstantinos Mourtzoukos currently is a Senior Software Developer at OpenBet. He is a software engineer with over 7 years of experience in all aspects of the development lifecycle. His focus has mainly been back-end systems / services, although he always likes to maintain a strong understanding of front-end systems and technologies. His passion is abstract system design, where he can put his excellent analytical and problem solving skill to better use.

Ram Ramanathan is the Director of Business at the Management Research Institute in the Business School of the University of Bedfordshire, Luton, UK. In the past, he has worked and taught in a number of countries, including the UK, Finland, the Netherlands, Oman, and India. His research interests include operations management, supply chains, environmental sustainability, economic and policy analysis of issues in the energy, environment, transport, and other infrastructure sectors. He has successfully completed a number of research projects across the world. He is on the editorial boards of many international journals. He has authored two books and edited one more. His research articles have appeared in many prestigious internationally refereed journals.

Usha Ramanathan is a Senior Lecturer in Business Systems at the University of Bedfordshire, UK. Her research interests include supply chain collaboration, Collaborative Planning Forecasting, Replenishment (CPFR), value of information sharing and forecasting, e-commerce, retail customer behaviour, and promotional sales. Usha uses case studies and quantitative approaches such as Structural equation modeling, simulation, AHP, and SERVQUAL for research and analysis. She has published in leading journals such as the *International Journal of Production Economics, Expert Systems with Applications,* and *Omega: The International Journal of Management Science.*

Wilson Sakpere is rounding off his Masters programme at the Cape Peninsula University of Technology, South Africa. He received his BEng (Honours) degree in Electrical Engineering from the University of Ilorin, Nigeria. He is a teaching assistant in the Information Technology Department at Cape Peninsula University of Technology. He is a registered member of the Nigerian Society of Engineers (NSE) and Institute of Information Technology Professionals, South Africa (IITPSA). His research interests include Near Field Communication, Positioning, and Mobile Navigation.

Alan D. Smith is presently a University Professor of Operations Management in the Department of Management and Marketing at Robert Morris University, located in Pittsburgh, PA. Previously, he was Chair of the Department of Quantitative and Natural Sciences and Coordinator of the Engineering Programs at the same institution, as well as the Associate Professor of Business Administration and Director of Coal Mining Administration at Eastern Kentucky University. He holds concurrent PhDs in Engineering Systems and Education from The University of Akron and in Business Administration (OM and MIS) from Kent State University, as well as an author of numerous articles and book chapters.

John Soldatos holds a BSc degree and a PhD degree (2000) both from the National University of Athens. Since 1996, he has had very active involvement in more than fifteen research projects in the areas of broadband networks, pervasive/cloud computing, and the internet-of-things. He is the initiator and co-founder of open source projects AspireRFID (http://wiki.aspire.ow2.org) and OpenIoT (https://github.com/OpenIotOrg/openiot). He has published more than 140 papers in international journals and conferences. Since 2003, he is with Athens Information Technology, where he is currently an Associate Professor. He has also been an Adjunct Professor at the Information Networking Institute (of the Carnegie Mellon University, 2007-2010) and a Honorary Research Fellow of the School of Computing of University of Glasgow (2014-2015).

Fred van Blommestein is a researcher at the faculty of Economics and Business at the University of Groningen. He also works as a consultant in the field of B2B and B2G communication. He has a PhD in Economics and Business, his thesis was titled "Structured Communication for Dynamic Business." Fred has been active in various international standardisation committees, among which UN/CEFACT and CEN/TC 225 (AIDC technologies). He was involved in the EU funded projects OpenXchange, TraSer, and ADVANCE. His present research focuses on methods to make interorganisational communication more dynamic.

B. Yang received the BEng degree in control technology and instrumentation from Beijing University of Posts and Telecommunications, Beijing, China in 2012. He is currently pursuing his MPhil degree in the Department of Industrial and Manufacturing Systems Engineering at the University of Hong Kong. He had participated in research projects on wireless sensor networks and ultra-low power RFID systems, before joining the Univerisity of Hong Kong. His current research interests include RFID technology, data mining and wireless sensor networks.

Y. X. Yang gained her BEng degree from the Department of Information Science and Engineering at the National Huaqiao University in China. She is currently pursuing her MPhil degree in the Department of Industrial and Manufacturing Systems Engineering at the University of Hong Kong. Miss Yang served in the project team of a monitoring system for filling assembly lines and wireless passive LED controllers at the National Huaqiao University from 2010 to 2012. She was the technical director of the entrepreneurship plan for Jingcheng Company Limited in Quanzhou, China in 2010. Miss Yang's current research interests focus on RFID applications, data mining, and marketing analytics for supply chain management and retail business improvement.

Index